AMERICA'S WARS

ALAN AXELROD

A Wiley Desk Reference

John Wiley & Sons, Inc.

For Anita
In love, peace

This book is printed on acid-free paper ⊗

Copyright © 2002 by Alan Axelrod. All rights reserved

Published by John Wiley & Sons, Inc., New York

Design and production by Navta Associates, Inc.

This publication is designed to provide accurate and authoritative information in regard to the subject matter covered. It is sold with the understanding that the publisher is not engaged in rendering professional services. If professional advice or other expert assistance is required, the services of a competent professional person should be sought.

Library of Congress Cataloging-in-Publication Data:

Axelrod, Alan, date.
  America's wars / Alan Axelrod.
    p. cm.
  Includes index.
  ISBN 0-471-32797-2 (cloth : alk. paper)
    1. United States—History, Military. I. Title.

E181 .A94 2002
355'.00973—dc21   2001046893

Printed in the United States of America

10 9 8 7 6 5 4 3 2 1

Contents

Introduction   1

CHAPTER 1 **Colonial and Native American Wars before 1754**   **7**

Conquest of the Hawikuh Pueblo, New Mexico, 1540   9

Acoma Revolt, 1599   10

Powhatan War, 1622–1644   11

Mohawk-Mahican War, 1624–1628   16

Pequot War, 1637   18

Iroquoian Beaver Wars, 1638–1684   22

Algonquian-Dutch War (Kieft's War), 1639–1645   27

Iroquois-French Wars, 1642–1696   30

Maryland's War with the Susquehannocks, 1643–1652   31

Maryland's Religious War, 1644–1654   32

Iroquois-Huron War, 1648–1650   33

Peach War, 1655–1657   34

Esopus Wars, 1659–1660 and 1663–1664   34

King Philip's War, 1675–1676   36

First Abnaki War, 1675–1678   43

Bacon's Rebellion, 1676   44

Popé's Rebellion, 1680   48

Leisler's Rebellion, 1689–1691   50

King William's War, 1689–1697   53

First Pima Revolt, 1695   56
Second Abnaki War, 1702–1712   56
Queen Anne's War, 1702–1713   56
Tuscarora War, 1711–1712   59
Fox Resistance, 1712–1733   61
Yamasee War, 1715–1716   63
Chickasaw Resistance, 1720–1724   63
Natchez Revolt, 1729   64
Dummer's War (Third Abnaki War), 1722–1727   64
King George's War, 1744–1748   65
Second Pima Revolt, 1751   68

CHAPTER 2 **The French and Indian War**   **69**
French and Indian War, 1754–1763   69
Cherokee Uprising of 1759–1762   94
Pontiac's Rebellion, 1763–1766   95

CHAPTER 3 **The American Revolution**   **101**
Regulators' Revolt, 1771   101
Lord Dunmore's War, 1774   102
American Revolution, 1775–1783   104

CHAPTER 4 **Conflicts of the Early Republic and the War of 1812** **162**
Shays's Rebellion, 1786–1787   162
Little Turtle's War, 1786–1795   164
Whiskey Rebellion, 1794   168
American-French Quasi-War, 1798–1800   169
Tripolitan War, 1801–1805   172
War of 1812, 1812–1814   174
Creek War, 1812–1814   186
Algerine War, 1815   188
First Seminole War, 1817–1818   189
Fredonian Rebellion, 1826–1827   191
Aroostook War, 1838–1839   192

CHAPTER 5 **Wars of the Indian Removal** **193**

Indian Removal Act of 1830 193
Second Seminole War, 1835–1842 196
Third Seminole War, 1855–1858 199
Black Hawk War, 1832 199

CHAPTER 6 **United States–Mexican War and Associated Conflicts** **205**

Texan War of Independence, 1835–1836 205
Bear Flag Rebellion, 1846 212
United States–Mexican War, 1846–1848 215

CHAPTER 7 **Early Indian Wars in the West** **229**

Mariposa War, 1850–1851 229
Yuma and Mojave Uprising, 1851–1852 230
Rogue River War, 1855–1856 231
Yakima War, 1855 233
Coeur d'Alene War (Spokane War), 1858 236
Paiute War (Pyramid Lake War), 1860 237
Apache and Navajo War, 1860–1868 238
Minnesota Santee Sioux Uprising, 1862 241

CHAPTER 8 **Civil War** **246**

"Bleeding Kansas" Guerrilla War, 1854–1861 247
Civil War, 1861–1865 249

CHAPTER 9 **Later Indian Wars in the West** **302**

Cheyenne and Arapaho War, 1864–1865 302
War for the Bozeman Trail, 1866–1868 304
Hancock's Campaign (Hancock's War), 1867 306
Snake War, 1866–1868 308
Sheridan's Campaign, 1868–1869 308
Modoc War, 1872–1873 310

Red River War (Kiowa War), 1874–1875 312

Apache War, 1876–1886 314

Sioux War for the Black Hills, 1876–1877 320

Nez Perce War, 1877 325

Bannock War, 1878 328

Sheepeater War, 1879 329

Ute War, 1879 331

Sioux War, 1890–1891 332

CHAPTER 10 **Spanish-American War and Other Imperialist Conflicts** 335

Walker's Invasion of Mexico, 1853–1854 336

Walker's Invasion of Nicaragua, 1855–1857 337

Philippine Insurrection, 1896–1898 338

Spanish-American War, 1898 339

Philippine Insurrection, 1899–1902 351

Boxer Rebellion, 1899–1901 352

Moro Wars, 1901–1913 357

Panamanian Revolution, 1903 359

Nicaraguan Civil War, 1909–1912 361

Villa's Raids (and the Pershing Punitive Expedition), 1916–1917 363

Nicaraguan Civil War, 1925–1933 366

CHAPTER 11 **World War I, 1914–1918** 368

CHAPTER 12 **World War II, 1939–1945** 383

CHAPTER 13 **Korean War, 1950–1953** 441

CHAPTER 14 **Vietnam War, 1954–1975** 459

CHAPTER 15 **Cold War Conflicts since 1958** **489**

Lebanese Civil War, 1958 490

Lebanese Civil War, 1975–1992 491

Nicaraguan Civil War, 1978–1979 494

Honduran Guerrilla War, 1981–1990 495

Nicaraguan Civil War, 1982–1990 496

Grenada Intervention, 1983 499

U.S. Invasion of Panama (Operation
Just Cause), 1989 501

Persian Gulf War, 1991 503

War in Bosnia, 1992–1995 508

Somalian Civil War, 1988– 511

Kosovo Crisis, 1996–1999 513

EPILOGUE **"The First War of the Twenty-First
Century"** **515**

Sources **525**

Index **531**

Introduction

During World War II, in the months preceding the Allied invasion of France, Lieutenant General George S. Patton repeatedly delivered variations of a single speech to formations of American troops preparing to embark from bases in England. The GIs who heard it never forgot it, and it is also familiar to the millions who have seen and heard the late George C. Scott deliver it in the opening scene of Franklin Schaffner's great screen biography of 1970, *Patton*. "Americans love to fight," Patton (and Scott) declared. "All real Americans love the sting of battle."

It is a sweeping assessment of the American character, which makes some nod in agreement, others grin in half embarrassment, and still others cringe. However we feel about it, the history presented in this book bears out the general's judgment. Apart from Norse voyages at the end of the Dark Ages, the first meaningful European contact with America came with the first voyage of Columbus in 1492. The first recorded armed conflict between the Spaniards and the people Columbus called Indians followed the very next year, and the first recorded conflict in territory now encompassed by the United States came in 1540, when the conquistador Coronado invaded and overran the Hawikuh Pueblo. How many wars were fought on the North American continent among native peoples, before European contact, is not recorded, but the warrior traditions and culture of many Native American groups suggests that American warfare was hardly a European import.

The Swiss historian Jean Jacques Babel once famously estimated that the approximately 5,500 years of recorded world history present a meager total of 292 years of peace. This statistic ratifies what we intuitively know: War is central to history—to world history in general and to American history specifically. During the era of European contact, principally the sixteenth, seventeenth, and early eighteenth centuries, wars in North America were wars of invasion, combat between colonists and Indians. Beginning in the late seventeenth century and extending well into the eighteenth, wars were increasingly fought between competing national colonial interests, especially the English and the French, and typically figured as the New World theaters of European wars. King William's War (1689–1697) was associated with Europe's War of the League of Augsburg; Queen Anne's War (1702–1713) with the War of the Spanish Succession; King George's War (1744–1748) with the War of the Austrian Succession; and the French and Indian War (1754–1763) with the ruinous Seven Years' War, sometimes characterized as the "first world war." In all of these European-American conflicts, Native Americans played a major role, both as targets of aggression and as allies aligned with one colonial interest against another, often demonstrating far more military skill and political savvy than generations of European-American historians have given them credit for.

The French and Indian War established English supremacy over French interests in North America and also brought to the fore many conflicts that had been developing between the English colonists and their mother country. In this sense it may be seen as a prelude to the American Revolution (1775–83), by which the colonists won independence from Britain. This war, treated at some length here, was highly complex, as much a civil war as a revolution, in that it did not simply pit colonists against Britons but also independence-seeking "patriots" against pro-British "loyalists" or "Tories." Indians played a major part in the conflict, too, many siding with the British (in the hope of stemming the westering tide of colonial settlement), a few with the Americans, and many more struggling to remain neutral. "Foreign" troops also figured in the Revolution—"Hessian" mercenaries hired by the British, and French naval and land forces allied with the Americans.

Once established, the young United States found itself fighting internal wars with various Indian tribes, two brief conflicts with dissident citizens (Shays's Rebellion [1786–1787] and the Whiskey Rebellion [1794]), and external wars in defense of its sovereignty: the American-French Quasi-War (1798–1800) and the Tripolitan War (1801–1805). Sovereignty was also an issue in the second major war with Britain, the War of 1812 (1812–1814), which jingoist historians quickly dubbed the "Second War of American Independence." However, the war—mostly disastrous for the young republic—was fought less over sovereignty issues than at the behest of frontier interests, who wanted always to expand the nation westward. Viewed in this light, the War of 1812 was the first of the United States' expansionist—or even imperialist—wars. It was followed by a series of wars with the Indians associated with a general campaign to "remove" the eastern tribes to remote locations west of the Mississippi River. The Creek War (1812–1814), the First Seminole War (1817–1818), the Second Seminole War (1835–1842), the Black Hawk War (1832), and the Third Seminole War (1855–1858), as well as military operations against the Cherokees directly pursuant to the Indian Removal Act of 1830, may be viewed collectively as the Wars of the Indian Removal.

During the War of 1812, U.S. forces invaded Canada with the ultimate object of annexing Canadian territory to the United States. The Wars of the Indian Removal also promoted U.S. expansion, albeit at the expense of the Indians. In 1835–1836, Texas, a Mexican state, won its independence and agitated for annexation to the United States. On March 1, 1845, Congress resolved to admit Texas into the Union, an action that prompted Mexico to sever diplomatic relations with the United States. Expansionists in the American government eagerly fanned this diplomatic crisis into the United States–Mexican War (1846–1848), by which the nation acquired much of the present Southwest and California. This acquisition opened up more of the West to settlement, which triggered a new series of wars with the Indians.

Another problem raised by western expansion was the creation of new territories and their eventual admission to the Union as states. The admission of each new state threatened to upset the tenuous congressional balance between slave-holding states and free states, so that, as the nation pushed westward, it also drifted closer to civil war. The prelude to that war occurred in Kansas during 1854–1861 as a bitter guerrilla conflict between slave interests and "free soilers," but the Civil War (1861–1865) itself, when it came, was even more savage, far bloodier, far longer, and far more terrible than anyone had imagined it could be. Politically, the Civil War not only settled the slavery issue forever but also decided whether the United States would or would not survive. Militarily, it was the greatest and costliest conflict the nation had and has ever fought. The North and the South were transformed into the closest thing to military states that has ever been seen in America, but the vast armies that were assembled during the war were swiftly disbanded upon its conclusion, and it was a very small U.S. Army—no more than twenty thousand men—that fought the so-called Indian Wars beginning at the end of the Civil War and culminating in the Wounded Knee massacre of December 1890 and the surrender of the Sioux Nation early the following year.

In 1893, the American historian Frederick Jackson Turner wrote a highly influential essay titled "The Significance of the Frontier in American History" in which he concluded that, historically, the United States had no need to pursue empires abroad as long as vast western spaces existed to be conquered within the continent. Once the frontier was settled, however, the free land divided and parceled out, the nation, Turner declared, would turn outward, in search of empires beyond the continent. Most historians today reject Turner's "frontier thesis"; yet, whether the thesis adequately accounts for it or not, the fact is that the United States did launch an unprecedented series of imperialist wars in the Caribbean, in Central America, in the Philippines, and even in China at the end of the nineteenth century and the beginning of the twentieth, shortly after the internal Indian Wars were concluded. The most important of these was the Spanish-American War (1898), which established the United States as the central power of the Western Hemisphere and, for the first time, as a major world power.

Not that the U.S. military, especially compared to the armies and navies of England, France, Germany, and Russia, was a formidable force when World War I broke out in Europe in 1914. The United States remained neutral until April 1917, but even as late as 1916, when U.S. entry into the war seemed increasingly inevitable, the regular army numbered only 133,000, a force so small that General Peyton C. March called it "scarcely enough to form a police force for emergencies within the territorial limits of the United States." Breakneck programs of recruitment, armament, and general expansion would bring U.S. forces to more than 4.5 million by Armistice Day in 1918.

Far more than the Spanish-American War, World War I thrust the United States into the arena of international politics and military performance. It was U.S. intervention that rescued the Allied cause—the cause of democracy. Yet again, however, as at the conclusion of the Civil War, the U.S. rushed to demobilize after the armistice of 1918, and the army of 4.5 million melted to a force of a few hundred thousand. On the eve of World War II, the United States had only the eighteenth-largest army in the world.

"Americans love to fight," George S. Patton told his troops. "All real Americans love the sting of battle." American history, not merely punctuated by war but propelled by it, bears him out—and yet Americans (save a minority of natural warriors such as Patton) have never truly reveled in this aspect of their character, certainly never to the extent of Japan or Germany, in which militarism became an aspect of national culture by the nineteenth century and destructively dominated it in the twentieth. If Americans love to fight, they nevertheless tend to disdain the military and have consistently resisted the creation and maintenance of large standing armies and navies. In the Civil War and in World War I, the nation demonstrated how quickly and massively it could mobilize men and industry for war. This was repeated in World War II, during which the American military swelled into the millions—more than 16 million U.S. troops served—and American war industries transformed the nation into the arsenal of democracy. To be sure, there was yet another mass demobilization after this war, but something had changed. Following World War I, the victorious Allies did their best to persuade themselves that they had fought a "war to end all wars." Following World War II, few harbored such illusions.

Almost immediately, the Soviet Union, a valuable ally against the Nazis, became the new totalitarian menace confronting the United States and other democracies. Of those democracies, only the United States, its infrastructure and civilian population untouched by the war just ended, was strong enough to mount credible opposition to Soviet expansion. The long Cold War era began, a period of armed peace, of limited military actions intended to "contain" communism wherever in the world it threatened to engulf a noncommunist nation, and a period of two major wars, the Korean War (1950–1953) and the Vietnam War (1954–1975). All of these conflicts—the "brushfire wars" as well as Korea (almost 6 million U.S. troops involved) and Vietnam (8.7 million U.S. troops)—were fought against a terrifyingly unique background.

World War II had come to a sudden end when the United States dropped two nuclear weapons on Japan, destroying Hiroshima on August 6, 1945, and Nagasaki on August 9. On August 15, Japanese emperor Hirohito made an unprecedented broadcast to the Japanese people, announcing surrender and citing as the reason for it the explosions of a "cruel new bomb." The postwar era saw the development of nuclear and even more destructive thermonuclear weapons by the United States, the Soviet Union (today the Commonwealth of Independent States), Britain, France, China, India, Pakistan, and almost certainly Israel. During the last half of the twentieth century, while fighting a series of limited wars with conventional weapons, the United States continually prepared for Armageddon—World War III.

The dual nature of American warfare in the postwar era raised the stakes of the limited wars, making it imperative to win these in ways that would not trigger a thermonuclear confrontation between the superpowers. At the same time, the U.S. focus on preparedness for strategic warfare (as global thermonuclear combat was called) often made the nation's military less capable of fighting limited, conventional conflicts. Paradoxically, combat in Korea, in Vietnam, and, more recently, in other theaters, including Central America, the Middle East, Africa, and the Balkans, often harked back to the earliest period of America's wars, resembling what were essentially ethnic and tribal guerrilla conflicts during the sixteenth, seventeenth, and eighteenth centuries. Despite horrific advances in weaponry, the Cold War and later conflicts have come close to closing a circle in the narrative of this nation's wars, taking us back to the beginning. This fact may be added to that other great paradox—of a warlike people who have traditionally disdained arms and armies—as characteristic of the military history of America, the subject of this book.

CHAPTER 1

Colonial and Native American Wars before 1754

On October 12, 1492, the *Santa Maria's* lookout sighted land, bringing to an end the first voyage of Christopher Columbus. The natives called their island Guanahani, but Columbus christened it San Salvador. Most modern historians believe this was present-day Watling Island, although, in 1986, a group of scholars suggested that the true landfall was another Bahamian island, Samana Cay, sixty-five miles south of Watling. Wherever they had landed, Columbus and his crew were greeted by friendly people of the Arawak tribe. Columbus, of course, believing that he had reached Asia—the "Indies"—called the native inhabitants Indians, and because he believed he was in the Indies, sailed on to Cuba, in search of the court of the emperor of China, with whom he hoped to negotiate an agreement for trade in spices and gold. When he was disappointed in this, Columbus sailed next to an island he called Hispaniola (today divided between the Dominican Republic and Haiti). Near Cap-Hatien, a Christmas Day storm wrecked the *Santa Maria*. Columbus ushered his crew to safety on shore, and installed a thirty-nine-man garrison among the friendly "Indians" of a place he decided to call La Navidad. Columbus and the rest of his crew left for Spain on January 16, 1493, sailing in the *Niña*.

The garrison Columbus left behind, among friendly natives, set about pillaging goods and ravaging women apparently as soon as their commander had departed. By night, the Indians retaliated, murdering ten Spaniards as they slept, then hunting down the rest of the garrison. When Columbus returned in November 1493, on his second New World voyage, not a single Spaniard was left alive. A cause for war was the very first of the Old World's exports to the New.

The four voyages of Columbus were followed by the invasion of the conquistadors—the Spanish "conquerors"—beginning with those led by Juan Ponce de Leon (c. 1460–1521) in the conquest of Puerto Rico during 1508–1509. Next, Jamaica and Cuba fell easily to the Spanish sword in 1510 and 1511. The war for Mexico was fought on a grander scale, by conquistadors led by Hernán Cortés, a minor nobleman who had cut short his university education to become an adventurer in the New World. On November 8, 1519, Cortés led his forces into Tenochtitlán, today's Mexico City, then, as now, a capital city. The Aztec emperor, Montezuma II, opened his city to the invaders, who marveled at its wealth and magnificence. Perhaps the conquest of Aztec Mexico would have been bloodless had not another conquistador intervened. Panfilo de Narvaez had been dispatched by Spanish authorities to arrest Cortés for having overstepped his authority in conquering Mexico. Hearing of his approach, Cortés set out to intercept him, leaving affairs in Tenochtitlán in the care of a subordinate, Pedro de Alvarado. In one of those sudden and inexplicable spasms of orgiastic cruelty that make up the "Black Legend" of the Spanish in the New World, Alvarado burst upon the celebrants of a feast in honor of the deity Huitzilopochtli and ordered their brutal slaughter. Men, women, and children were hacked and beaten to death.

Far from intimidating the Aztecs, this atrocity caused the people of Tenochtitlán to rebel against the men they had greeted so courteously. Cortés, returning to the city after having defeated Narvaez, arrived just in time to lead his men in a fighting flight out of the capital during what the Spanish dubbed the Noche Triste of June 30, 1520. Among the casualties of that "sad night" was Montezuma II himself. Cortés withdrew and regrouped. Ten months after the Noche Triste, he returned in force to lay siege against the city, cutting off all food and water to the inhabitants. For three months the people of the Aztec capital held out until, their numbers reduced by a smallpox epidemic (a disease apparently brought to Mexico by an African slave in the service of Narvaez), they surrendered to Cortés on August 13, 1521. Now the Aztec Mexican empire was his.

Conquest of the Hawikuh Pueblo, New Mexico, 1540

Cortés had gained what all the Spanish adventurers sought—personal wealth and a personal empire. His example stimulated more Spanish expeditions of conquest. These were directed northward, into the borderlands—that is, the area of the present United States. What animated these adventurers was the dream that another Aztec or Inca realm was waiting to be found and thrown open to conquest. As early as the first voyage of Columbus, Indians had told tales of villages bursting with vast treasuries of gold, the "Seven Cities of Cibola." The lust for gold required nothing more substantial than legend or hearsay to prompt Francisco Vazquez de Coronado (1510–1554) to set out in February 1540 to probe the unknown region north of the Rio Grande in search of the fabled Seven Cities. Coronado and his rapacious band of Spanish nobles, adventurers, slaves, and Mexican Indians wandered the Southwest for more than two years, during 1540–1542, traveling as far north as present-day Kansas. But early in the expedition, during July 1540, Coronado and his troops rode into the Zuni pueblo of Hawikuh in central New Mexico. One thing the experience of Cortés had taught all Spaniards who followed was to demand whatever one wanted. Coronado demanded the immediate surrender of the pueblo. By way of response, the peacefully inclined Zuni showered stones upon the conquistadors, knocking Coronado himself unconscious. After an hour of combat, however, Hawikuh fell, and Coronado, his head presumably throbbing, entered it—and, of course, found neither gold nor a golden city. Instead, he saw only more pueblos like Hawikuh, the humble mesa dwellings of the Piro, Kere, and southern and northern Tiwa, Tano, Towa, and Tewa peoples; to the west of these, he found more Zuni settlements; and farther westward, those of the Hopi. A few villages contained as many as two thousand inhabitants, though most hovered at about four hundred. The Pueblo peoples had learned to site their settlements atop tall mesas as a means of defending against chronic attacks from Utes, Navajos, and Apaches, tribes that, in contrast to the pueblo dwellers, were nomadic and warlike. After contact with Coronado, the Zuni realized that they now had acquired another enemy: the conquistadors. Coronado took Hawikuh pueblo and the surrounding Zuni territory as his headquarters. Then, during the winter of 1540–1541, he quartered most of his army in the territory of the southern Tewas, pillaging these people mercilessly, taking their food, their blankets, and whatever else seemed of value.

Acoma Revolt, 1599

After it became clear that the borderlands north of Aztec Mexico would yield no cities of gold, the Spanish lost interest in the region until 1595, when the Spanish crown commissioned Don Juan de Oñate (ca. 1550–ca. 1624) to establish a new colony north of the Rio Grande, in the region of present-day New Mexico. Oñate set off from Mexico City on April 30, 1598, leading four hundred soldiers, settlers, and Franciscan missionaries, together with some seven thousand head of cattle, north to the area of present-day El Paso, Texas, and then to the confluence of the Rio Grande and the Chama River. Claiming the region for Spain, he established his colonial capital at a pueblo he took over and called San Juan. In 1599 Oñate founded a new capital at the San Gabriel pueblo. From here he dispatched soldiers and friars to conquer and convert the Indians inhabiting the surrounding pueblos and to inform them that he, Don Juan de Oñate, was henceforward their new leader.

The Acoma Pueblo, scene of the 1599 revolt against the Spanish. The photograph dates from the 1930s. *Collection: National Archives and Records Administration*

In classic conquistador style, Oñate moved with speed and boldness, overawing the pueblos through a combination of martial display and acts of summary cruelty. Of all the pueblos, only one offered resistance. When the usual detachment of soldiers and priests arrived in December 1598 at Acoma, a pueblo perched high atop a steep-walled mesa in western New Mexico, the Keres Indians attacked and killed Oñate's emissaries. The governor responded by mounting a full-scale expedition against Acoma in January 1599. The troops fought their way up the mesa walls and stormed the pueblo. Some fifteen hundred Keres were killed in battle, including virtually all of the pueblo's warriors. As for the survivors, Oñate ordered public trials for the men. Those over the age of twenty-five—there were eighty of these—were sentenced to the amputation of one foot and were consigned to twenty years of penal servitude. (There is no record of just how useful the Spanish found their one-footed slaves.) Boys over age twelve but under twenty-five were not subjected to amputation, but were likewise condemned to twenty years of slavery. A pair of Hopis, who had the bad fortune to be visiting Acoma at this time, were sent back to their home pueblo—each minus a hand. Some five hundred women were not given trials, but were immediately consigned to penal servitude for twenty years. Children under twelve, whose souls, it was felt, were still ripe for salvation, were delivered into the care and instruction of the Franciscans. In this way the Acoma revolt was crushed, along with the Acoma pueblo.

Powhatan War, 1622–1644

The Powhatans were a collection of Indian tribes of eastern Virginia under the control or influence of the powerful chief (the "paramount chief," or *mamanatowick*) Wahunsonacock (ca. 1550–1618). The English knew him by his throne name, which was that of the people he led, Powhatan. Just when Powhatan inherited the six tribes near the falls of the James, Pamunkey, and Mattaponi Rivers is not known, but by 1608, he ruled at least thirty-two tribes.

In contrast to the Spanish, who had come to the New World in military force as economic and spiritual conquerors, the English came as traders, settlers, and (especially in the New England region) as religious dissidents in search of safe haven. If the English treated the Indians with less aggressive hostility than did the Spanish, this reflected a lack of military might rather than a purposeful plan of cordial contact. Following Sir Walter Raleigh's disastrous expedition to Roanoke (1584–1602)—the "lost colony," which, indeed, vanished with no trace, save for the legend "CROATOAN" carved into the bark of a tree—the first English arrivals in Jamestown, Virginia, in 1607 had come seeking gold, furs, sassafras (thought to be a sovereign cure for syphilis, then endemic in England), and (like Columbus and so many others) a shortcut passage to India. About 900 settlers arrived during the first three years of the colony, but by 1610, sickness and starvation had killed all but 150.

The earliest period of the Jamestown settlement was marked by few violent conflicts with the Powhatans. Perhaps they judged that the new-comers, sickly and inept, would soon perish and that therefore they were not worth fighting. As for the English, burdened as they were by disease and starvation, they were hardly in a position to take the offensive, even if

Reproduction of a seventeenth-century book illustration depicting Pocahontas pleading with her father, Powhatan, to spare the life of Captain John Smith.
Collection: ArtToday

they had wanted to, for the Powhatans in the region of Jamestown numbered perhaps ten thousand people distributed among approximately two hundred villages. Nevertheless, the most famous confrontation between the English and the Powhatans came very early, in December 1607. At that time, the soldier of fortune John Smith (ca. 1579–1631)—sent by the Virginia Company, financial backers of the Jamestown colony, as military adviser to the colonists—was captured by some of Powhatan's men while scouting out provisions along the Chickahominy River. Taken to the chief, he was (according to his own account) saved from execution through the intervention of the chief's thirteen-year-old daughter Pocahontas (a nickname meaning "frisky"; her real name was Matowaka). The story of Captain John Smith and Pocahontas is so thoroughly ingrained in American folklore that it is impossible to recover all of the historical facts of this incident; however, it is clear that Pocahontas subsequently facilitated Smith's initiation into her father's immediate circle, a most favored position Smith used to obtain corn from the Indians. Despite Pocahontas's intervention and Smith's apparently cordial relations with Powhatan himself, the colonists and the Indians did not form a truly friendly bond. While they traded with one another, they did so in a context of mutual distrust.

As colonial tobacco cultivation took hold, creating an ever greater need for land, relations between the English and the Powhatans deteriorated. By 1610, after the colonists appropriated for tobacco cultivation cleared Indian fields, the Powhatans alternately fought and traded with the English. In 1613 Samuel Argall, mariner and colonist, abducted not Powhatan but his daughter, Pocahontas, whom Governor Dale decided to hold hostage as a means of extorting good behavior from the Indians. A remarkable young woman, Pocahontas functioned more as an ambassador than she behaved as a hostage. She learned English, thoroughly ingratiated herself with the colonists, and ultimately married John Rolfe, one of the most prominent planters among them. Doubtless this marriage, combined with Powhatan's desire to continue profitable trading with the English, played a role in bringing about a truce in 1614. Despite the pressures created by the tobacco growers' increasing hunger for land, an uneasy peace endured between the settlers and the Powhatans until the death of Chief Powhatan in 1618. Opechancanough, Powhatan's half brother, succeeded the chief, and although he pledged continuing friendship with the English, he was never as committed to peaceful coexistence as Powhatan had been.

Reproduction of a seventeenth-century book illustration depicting John Rolfe's embassy to Powhatan. *Collection: ArtToday*

Early in 1622, a planter known to history only as Morgan ventured inland to trade with the Indians and was never heard from again. In March, Morgan's servants, seizing on flimsy evidence, determined that an Indian named Nemattanow (or Nematanou), prominent among the Powhatans, had ordered the death of their master. They quickly exacted revenge by murdering Nemattanow, for which Opechancanough, in turn, vowed vengeance. Hearing the chief's threats, the colonists grew bellicose and made threats of their own, which elicited from Opechancanough a renewed pledge of eternal friendship. As if to demonstrate his goodwill, on March 20, 1622, the chief personally served as guide to a group of planters traveling through the woods. Two days later, on Good Friday, came further gestures of apparent amity. To English settlements all along the James River, Captain John Smith later wrote, the Indians "as at other times . . . came unarmed into our houses with Deere, Turkies, Fish, Fruits, and other provisions to sell us, yea in some places sat downe at breakfast with our people, whom immediately with their owne tooles slew most barbarously, not sparing either age or sex, man woman or childe, so sudden in their execution, that few or none discerned the weapon or blow that brought them to destruction."

It was a brilliant and ruthless program of surprise attacks coordinated by Opechancanough. By the end of this Good Friday, 347 settlers had been killed—fully a third of the colony. Only the intervention of an Indian boy called Chanco, the Christianized servant of a colonist named Mr. Pace, saved Jamestown from total annihilation. When the boy's brother had ordered him to murder Pace, Chanco instead told his master of the plot. Pace alerted Governor Francis Wyatt, who proclaimed the English colony's new policy: "It is infinitely better to have no heathen among us, who were but as thornes in our sides, than to be at peace and league with them."

War between the Virginia settlers and the Powhatans now began in earnest and would span 1622–1632. In response to the initial surprise attacks, the colonists attempted to regain the initiative by going on the offensive. Despite the unflagging enmity between colonists and Indians, a grudging truce was concluded in 1632, far more the product of mutual exhaustion than any sense of having resolved differences. The new peace endured for a dozen years, until April 18, 1644, when the aged Opechancanough again launched a coordinated assault along the James. It was a devastating attack in which four hundred to five hundred colonists perished. But the Indians made little attempt to follow up on their victory. Perhaps they suddenly comprehended the futility of their action, for, although the attack was costly, the population of the Virginia colony now topped eight thousand.

In March 1646 the Virginia assembly at last decided that further struggle was fruitless and dispatched Captain Henry Fleet, the colony's interpreter, to find Opechancanough and negotiate a peace. Governor Berkeley, however, did not share the assembly's pacific sentiments and personally led a detachment of soldiers on a preemptive raid against the old chief's headquarters. Opechancanough, a spectacular hundred years old and nearly blind, was taken captive and transported to Jamestown, where a crowd of gawkers hurled insults at him. A melee resulted in which Opechancanough was shot and killed.

In October 1646 the assembly, this time with Berkeley's assent, finally concluded a peace with Opechancanough's successor, Necotowance. By treaty, the new chief acknowledged his people's dependence on the king of England and agreed that future chiefs would be appointed, or at least confirmed, by the governor. Boundaries were formally set, and neither side was permitted to enter the other's land without permission from the governor. Despite the officially sanctioned peace and the pledge to avoid encroachment on Indian lands, many settlers and planters refused to recognize any limit to settlement. In January 1652 a fleet was dispatched from England to compel obedience to Oliver Cromwell's government, including its desire to contain settlement. Not only did the fleet fail to intimidate the colonists of the frontier regions, it also incited a revolt, which ousted Berkeley from office. Virginia thereupon declared itself loyal to King Charles, and a series of interim governors refused to enforce the treaty with Necotowance, thereby spawning numberless skirmishes between colonists and Indians for many years.

By 1671, when Governor Berkeley returned to Virginia and was restored to office, disease, absence of trade, and the effects of what had amounted to a protracted war of attrition had drastically reduced the Indian population of Virginia's Tidewater. At Jamestown's founding, Powhatan led some 10,000 people. Now, sixty years later, perhaps 3,000 to 4,000 Powhatans remained. Of these, no more than 750 might be classed as warriors. War was no longer a viable option for these survivors.

Mohawk-Mahican War, 1624–1628

History primarily records "Indian warfare" as conflict between white settlers and Native Americans; however, the many and diverse Indian tribes and groups across the continent fought each other far more frequently and extensively than they engaged in combat with settlers and the various governments of the Americas. While few of these conflicts were chronicled, the Mohawk-Mahican War of 1624–1628 is a rare exception, although scant details of the war were recorded.

The Mahicans were an eastern tribe of the Algonquian linguistic group, occupying many villages along the upper Hudson River and hunting in the Hoosic and Housatonic Valleys and in southwestern Vermont. When Henry Hudson encountered them in 1609, they numbered (he estimated) about four thousand. Active traders before European contact, they became even more vigorous in commerce after the Dutch built trading posts, at Fort Nassau in 1614–1617 and at Fort Orange (modern Albany) in 1624. Indeed, they enjoyed a monopoly on trade with the Dutch, so that other tribes had to deal through them. To the Mohawks, western neighbors of the Mahicans, this situation was intolerable. One of five tribes confederated as the Iroquois League (see the discussion of the Iroquois Beaver Wars later in this chapter), the Mohawks had a strong warrior tradition and, through the seventeenth and eighteenth centuries, would earn a fearsome reputation for their skill at arms.

Like the later Beaver Wars, the Mohawk-Mahican War was fought for two trade objectives: first, to gain control of trapping territories, and second, to gain exclusive access to European traders and, consequently, European trade goods. While the catalyst for the war was trade with the Dutch, it is clear that enmity between the Mohawks and the Mahicans dates from long before European contact.

When the Dutch established Fort Nassau in 1614, its location in the heart of Mahican country automatically conferred privileged trading status on those Indians. Moreover, the trading post was so deeply within Mahican territory that the Mahicans readily resisted attempts at Mohawk incursion. In 1624, however, the Dutch West India Company opened a new trading post, at Fort Orange, with the intention of engaging in trade some of the northern Algonquian tribes allied with the Mahicans. Against this development, the Mohawks realized that action was called for. It was bad enough that the Mahicans were usurping trade, but to allow this to be extended to other tribes was intolerable. The Mohawks fully appreciated the politics of the situation. The northern Algonquian tribes were trading partners with the French of Canada. By building Fort Orange, the Dutch proposed to entice these Indians from trade with the French. Traditionally, the Mohawks, like the other Iroquoian tribes, had been hostile to the French. Now, in 1624, they negotiated a treaty with them, creating a Mohawk-French alliance to attack the Mahicans.

Very little is known about the progress of the ensuing war. Early in the seventeenth century, it is believed, the Mahicans could muster perhaps sixteen hundred warriors, whereas the Mohawks could field few more than eight hundred. Doubtless, alliance with the French helped to even these numbers; however, initially, the Dutch assisted their Mahican trading partners in defending against the Mohawk attacks. It is known that in 1626, seven Dutchman from Fort Orange were attached to a Mahican raid into Mohawk country. The Mohawks ambushed the raiding party, killing an unknown number of Indians and four of the Dutchmen. One of these unfortunates was killed and then eaten where he had fallen. The other three were bound and burned alive. This was quite sufficient to discourage the Dutch from further intervention in the war between the two tribes.

Whatever initial reverses the Mohawks may have suffered, it is clear that they soon regained the initiative, and by 1628 they had badly mauled the Mahicans, who fled from their lands west of the Hudson, abandoning this country forever. With the eviction of the Mahicans, the Mohawks now controlled the approaches to Fort Orange, and it was they who decided who could trade with the Dutch there. Never a strong military presence, and quite thoroughly impressed by Mohawk ferocity in combat, the Dutch acquiesced. Of all those involved in the war, only the Mahicans emerged as losers. The Mohawks had gained exclusive control of access to a highly profitable trading partner in the Dutch, and the Dutch, though they suffered coercion, nevertheless continued to enjoy brisk Indian trade. The French benefited from the victory of their Iroquoian ally in that the Mohawks barred the northern Algonquians from trading at Fort Orange; they therefore had no choice but to continue trading with the French, who were now free to charge higher prices than their Dutch competitors to the south.

Pequot War, 1637

Beginning in the 1630s, the growth of Dutch and English settlement in the Connecticut Valley was encroaching on the territory of the Pequots, an Algonquian tribe related to the Mohegans (not to be confused with the Mahicans) and, like them, originally settled along the Hudson River. In 1634 the ship of Captain John Stone, a disreputable "trader" and pirate, rode at anchor in the mouth of the Connecticut River. Indian raiders, most likely western Niantics, members of a satellite or "client" tribe of the Pequots, attacked and killed Stone. According to one Pequot version, Captain Stone had kidnapped a party of Indians, and Stone was killed by another group of Indians seeking to rescue the captives. Another Pequot variant held that the raid had been nothing more nor less than a case of mistaken identity. The killers, commissioned by the Pequots, thought that they were attacking Dutch traders who had killed a tribal sachem named Tatobam. On the English side, John Mason, who would emerge as an English hero of the war, neatly sidestepped the issue of kidnapping by saying that Stone, who had been trading with the Dutch, "procured" some Indians to guide two of his men and was then ambushed.

The conflicting stories notwithstanding, the Pequots, though they had not killed Stone, recognized that their tributary tribe had. Having no desire to provoke war with the English, they moved quickly to placate colonial authorities and, on November 7, signed the Massachusetts Bay–Pequot Treaty, whereby the Pequots agreed to hand over those guilty of Captain Stone's murder, to pay an exorbitant indemnity, to relinquish rights to any Connecticut land that the English might wish to settle, and to trade exclusively with the English. Although a portion of the promised indemnity was paid, the amount demanded, wampum worth £250, remained a sticking point, and the Pequot council failed to ratify the treaty. In addition, the Pequots never produced Stone's killers. For two years, the English forbore action upon what they claimed was a breach of the treaty. Then, on June 16, 1636, a Plymouth trader reported a warning he had received from Uncas, chief of the Mohegans. The Pequots, fearful that the colonists were about to move against them, apparently intended to make a preemptive strike. In July, acting on this information, Connecticut and Massachusetts Bay officials convened a conference with representatives of the Western Niantics and the Pequots at Fort Saybrook, on the Connecticut River. The colonists reasserted the demands of the 1634 treaty. The Indians apparently promised to comply, but a few days after the meeting, word reached colonial authorities that another trading captain, John Oldham, together with his crew, had been killed off Block Island. This time the perpetrators were Narragansetts or members of a tribe subject to them. The Narragansett sachems Canonchet (whom the English called Canonicus) and Miantonomo hastened not only to condemn the murder but also volunteered reparations and pledged to refrain from alliance with the Pequots in any dispute the English had with that tribe. Moreover, Miantonomo personally led two hundred warriors to Block Island to mete out vengeance on behalf of the Massachusetts Bay Colony.

The contrite gestures of the Narragansetts notwithstanding, the colonists decided it was time to act. On August 25, militiamen under Captains John Endecott, John Underhill, and William Turner were dispatched to Block Island to apprehend the killers of Stone and Oldham and to secure a "thousand fathoms" of wampum as reparation. Endecott landed on the island, made short work of the light resistance that met them, but then discovered that most of the populace had withdrawn to the forest. Disappointed, Endecott embarked his troops by boat to Fort Saybrook, intending to punish the Pequots, even though they had had nothing to do with the death of John Oldham. Endecott and his command fell upon the countryside, burning crops and destroying the Indians' shelters and stores of food, which provoked the Pequots to bloody war.

What had motivated Endecott's attack? Unthinking racism? Perhaps. But also at stake was a large part of the Connecticut Valley, control of which was disputed between the Bay Colony and a group of Connecticut settlers. Whoever successfully asserted dominance over the Pequots, whose country lay on either side of the Pequot River, squarely in the contested territory, would have a strong legal claim to the region. A Connecticut victory over the Pequots would also bring allied and associated tribes into line. For the moment, however, Endecott was in trouble. His actions at Fort Saybrook provoked Pequot warriors to besiege the fort and attack surrounding houses. The fighting continued intermittently in the vicinity of the fort for months.

By the spring of 1637, some thirty English colonists had fallen victim to the Pequots, and it was becoming clear that the war would develop into more than a local conflict. As word of Indian depredations and tortures spread throughout the colonies, Plymouth, Massachusetts, and

Connecticut authorities determined to unite in fighting the Pequots. While Massachusetts and Plymouth struggled to get a joint retaliatory expedition under way, Captain Mason set out from Hartford on May 10 with ninety colonists and sixty Mohegans under Uncas to attack the principal Pequot stronghold, the fort of Sassacus, on Pequot Harbor. The band reached Saybrook on May 15, and colonial authorities ordered Mason to make an immediate amphibious assault against Sassacus's fort. Mason decided instead to sail past that stronghold, enter Narragansett territory, and recruit additional Indian allies before attacking. After protracted negotiation, Mason, along with John Underhill, persuaded the Narragansetts to join forces against the Pequots. The English took on allies numbering five hundred troops, including a contingent of Narragansetts (under Miantonomo) and Eastern Niantics (under Ninigret). These were added to the force of sixty Mohegans already marching with the colonial troops.

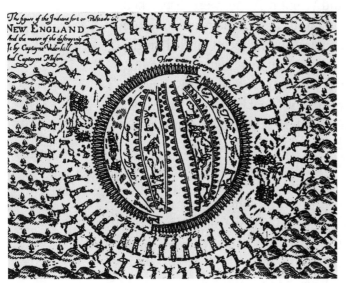

A highly stylized seventeenth-century diagram of a Pequot "fort."
Collection: ArtToday

Based on the incomplete records that survive, it is difficult to determine just what occurred, on May 25, as the colonial troops and their Indian allies approached Sassacus's fort. Either at this time or perhaps earlier, a renegade Pequot named Wequash revealed to the English the existence of another Pequot stronghold, on the Mystic River. It was closer than the original objective in Pequot Harbor, and Mason (according to his own account), aware that his men were "exceedingly spent in our March with extreme Heat and want of Necessaries," decided once again to act contrary to orders. He would attack at Mystic instead of the Pequot Harbor fort. The historian Francis Jennings theorizes that the decision to bypass Sassacus's fort to attack the Mystic stronghold was a deliberate choice to avoid a genuine battle and engage instead in the massacre of noncombatants. According to Jennings, Mason knew that the Mystic fort was peopled by women, children, and old men and was defended by only few warriors. Whatever the degree of deliberation that lay behind the assault, it was a slaughter. At first light on May 26, after firing a single volley, the Englishmen stormed the fort through entrances at opposite ends: Mason through the northeast, Underhill the southwest. Surprised by the attack, the greatly outnumbered Pequot warriors nevertheless fought with such fury that Mason quickly abandoned his plan to seize booty. Instead, he put the Indian camp to the torch, creating a conflagration so fierce that Underhill's men were forced to exit the fort as quickly as they had entered it. Eighty huts housing some eight hundred men, women, and children were set ablaze. Within an hour, six hundred to seven hundred Pequots perished, while English losses amounted to two dead and twenty to forty wounded. Mason records that only seven Pequots were taken captive, and another seven escaped.

Mason's victory was decisive, but the captain was well aware that he and his command were still deep in hostile territory. Moreover, they were exhausted by battle, short on provisions, and uncertain as to when their boats would arrive to retrieve them. As the commanders deliberated over their course of action, boats carrying Captain Daniel Patrick, forty fresh troops, and a store of ammunition were sighted. But simultaneously, so were some three hundred Pequot warriors, arrived from Sassacus's harbor stronghold. Captain Underhill, with a detachment of Narragansetts and English troops, skirmished with them. Perhaps this demonstration was sufficient to discourage an attack in force. In any case, the colonists were able to begin their march toward the harbor and their vessels, burning wigwams along the way and exchanging sporadic gunfire with a few Indian snipers.

It was late May or early June when Mason's and Underhill's forces united with the Massachusetts troops under Captain Patrick and then with a larger body of Massachusetts soldiers commanded by Israel Stoughton. Shortly thereafter, news reached them that a large number of Pequots had been discovered near the Connecticut River. Mason deployed the Narragansetts, who, pretending to offer the Pequots protection, surrounded the Pequot warriors. The colonial troops now moved in, capturing and then slaughtering hundreds of Indians. Those Pequots who managed to escape scattered, most of them finding their way to Manhattan Island. On July 13, English forces ran the Mystic survivors to ground in a swamp near New Haven and surrounded them. Some two hundred Pequots surrendered and concluded a treaty specifying that no Pequot might inhabit his former country and that the very name Pequot was to be expunged; those enslaved had to take the name of their "host" tribe.

Sassacus and other Pequot fugitives sought refuge among neighboring tribes, but the ruthlessness of the English had so intimidated the Indians of the region—few of whom were on friendly terms with the Pequots in any case—that no tribe gave the Pequot sachem sanctuary. Late in the summer, colonial authorities began to receive, as tribute from surrounding Indian groups, the severed heads of various Pequots. The Mohawks sent the head of the war chief Sassacus. The Treaty of Hartford, concluded on September 21, 1638, between the English and the Indian tribes allied with them, divided the survivors of the swamp siege as slaves among the allied tribes. For their part, the English colonists had achieved the objective of neutralizing what they saw as the Pequot menace, a menace they themselves had created.

Iroquoian Beaver Wars, 1638–1684

As with the *Mohawk-Mahican War, 1626–1628,* the Iroquoian Beaver Wars were fought among Native Americans and did not directly involve European settlers. Nevertheless, the Beaver Wars were an important episode in the complex development of white-Indian alliances and enmities, which would bear upon future colonial wars. Moreover, through these wars, the Iroquois League (or Iroquois Confederation) consolidated the military power and political-economic influence that would make it a pivotal force in the two largest conflicts of colonial North America, the French and Indian War and the American Revolution.

The Iroquois League consisted of the Mohawk, Oneida, Onondaga, Cayuga, and Seneca tribes, whose territory extended from the Hudson Valley in the east to the shores of Lake Ontario in the west—much of present-day western New York State. During the colonial era, the Iroquois League was more usually called the Five Nations. In the early seventeenth century, the Iroquois tribes aligned themselves with the Dutch as trading partners. When the English displaced the Dutch in New Amsterdam in 1664, the English traders inherited the alliance. To the west, the Hurons became trading partners of the French. (Several other western tribes, allied to the Hurons, also engaged in trade with the French—and became involved in the Beaver Wars. These tribes included the Tobaccos [also called the Petuns or Tionantati], Neutrals, Eries [or Cat People], Ottawas, Mahicans, Illinois, Miamis, Susquehannocks, Nipissings, Potawatomis,

Delawares, and Sokokis.) As the seventeenth century progressed, the western hunting grounds remained rich in beaver—the Indians' chief article of trade—and so the Huron-French commerce flourished. With overhunting, however, the number of peltries in the eastern hunting grounds rapidly diminished. As a consequence, Iroquois trade with the Dutch and, later, with the English suffered.

As early as 1638 and well into the 1640s, Huron and Iroquois war parties came to blows in frequent raids and counterraids. It was typical wilderness warfare—that is, the scale of violence ranged from apparently random scalpings to massed invasion of enemy villages, which were pillaged and burned. What little is known about the Iroquoian Beaver Wars comes from scattered reports by missionaries and traders, as well as from a body of traditional stories of the Iroquoian peoples. It is not possible to construct a detailed narrative of the wars, which were apparently battles related to one another by the common objective of acquiring control of western hunting and trapping territories. Among the notable battles were those that follow.

In the summer of 1645, the fortified and palisaded Huron trading town of St. Joseph, on Michigan's St. Clair River—the site of present-day Port Huron—was the target of an attack. The Iroquois approached in force, then waited nearby through the night. All through that night, the Huron defenders sang war songs to dishearten the attackers. This proved an ineffective tactic. By night, two Iroquois warriors crept up to the palisade and lay in wait until just before dawn. By first light, the Hurons, exhausted by having sung all night, had fallen asleep. One of the Iroquois climbed to the top of a Huron watchtower, sunk his hatchet into the slumbering head of one of the watchmen, and tossed another guard down to the other Iroquois outside of the palisade. He quickly scalped the hapless sentry. Yet no general attack followed this two-man sortie; the Iroquois simply turned their backs on Fort St. Joseph.

In general, the tribes of the Iroquois League rarely acted in perfect concert. The Mohawks were by far the most aggressive; among them the warrior tradition was strongest, and they had a compelling motive for aggression in that their hunting grounds were the most seriously depleted of any of the eastern tribes. The central tribes of the league increasingly resented the Mohawks' control over access to the Dutch trading post at Fort Orange. The westernmost Senecas, still enjoying amply stocked hunting grounds and having no quarrel with the Hurons, were disinclined to war. Ultimately it was the Europeans who forced a crisis. Although they would not become directly involved in the war, the directors of the Dutch West India Company, seeing an opportunity to usurp trade from the French, decided on April 7, 1648, to reverse their policy against trading arms to the Indians. To the Mohawks they traded about four hundred rifles. Without declaring war, the Dutch were arming their Indian allies against the French-backed Hurons.

Through most of the colonial period, alliances between the French and the Indians were based on both trade and on religion, through the work of Jesuit missionaries. The Indians received important benefits from the missionaries, including certain trade goods, food, and supplies. But life in what came to be called missionary towns also created dependence and dissension among the Indians. Worst of all, town life tended to breed epidemic disease, particularly smallpox.

St. Joseph, one of the most important of the Jesuit Huron missions, was at the southeastern frontier of Huron country and had been briefly attacked in 1645. It was fortified with wooden palisades and sheltered some two thousand Indians as well as Father Antoine Daniel's mission. On July 4, 1648, the Iroquois invaded the mission town, killing or capturing everyone and setting fire to the buildings.

Leaving St. Joseph ablaze, the Iroquois marched off with about seven hundred prisoners and attacked the nearby village of St. Ignace. For the most part, the town sheltered women, children, and old men, who suddenly found themselves trapped within their own palisaded fortifications when as many as a thousand Iroquois warriors burst through the stockade wall. The raid on St. Ignace was over in a few terrible minutes, and the attackers moved on to St. Louis, about three miles distant. But three Hurons who had escaped from St. Ignace warned the seven hundred inhabitants of St. Louis, most of whom fled. Some eighty warriors, together with those too old, too sick, or too infirm to move, remained, as did the town's two Jesuit missionaries, Fathers Brébeuf and Lalemant. Twice the small band of Huron warriors managed to turn back the Iroquois onslaught, killing perhaps thirty of the enemy. But there were just too many. At last, large numbers of warriors swarmed about the foot of the palisades, hacking through them with their hatchets. The surviving Huron defenders and the two Jesuits were captured and the town set ablaze. The prisoners were sent back to St. Ignace, where the Iroquois singled out the Jesuits for especially brutal torture.

Next, the Iroquois divided their number to launch further raids on smaller neighboring villages. Before them, the Huron fugitives fled toward the Tobacco Indians west of Lake Ontario. On March 17 the Iroquois unleashed an assault on Ste. Marie, palisaded and defended by forty well-armed Frenchmen augmented by perhaps three hundred Huron warriors. A detachment of these warriors ambushed the Iroquois advance guard outside of Ste. Marie but were suffering a severe beating until the main body of Hurons came to the rescue. This force succeeded in routing the Iroquois, who retreated in disorder to St. Ignace, then rejoined the main body of invaders at St. Louis and prepared for a renewed assault against Ste. Marie.

Reduced by half, the Huron defenders of Ste. Marie fought fiercely, killing as many as a hundred of the Iroquois while suffering the loss of all but twenty of their own number. In the end it was the Iroquois who were too badly shaken by the resistance they had met to capitalize on their victory. By the morning after the assault on Ste. Marie, fearing a Huron counterattack, they were in retreat. In a parting gesture, the Iroquois bound a number of their prisoners—men, women, and children—to stakes within St. Ignace, then put the town and these helpless souls to the torch.

During this time, a force of about seven hundred Hurons was assembling at St. Michel, not far from St. Joseph. They set off in pursuit of the retreating Iroquois but, no longer having the heart or stomach for a fight, allowed their quarry to slip away.

The Iroquois had not taken Ste. Marie, but the destruction they had visited upon the other Huron towns was sufficient to make refugees of the survivors. By the end of March, fifteen principal Huron towns had been abandoned. For all practical purposes the Huron nation had ceased to exist. As for the French Jesuit missions, without Indians to convert, many were abandoned, so that, as the Dutch had hoped, the French suffered defeat alongside their Huron allies.

Nor were the Iroquois finished with the Beaver Wars. In November and December 1649, Mohawks and Senecas turned on the Tobaccos. When word of an impending attack came to the mission town of St. Jean, the warriors there girded for combat with an enemy who, day after day, failed to appear. At length the Tobacco warriors decided to seize the initiative and ventured out in search of the Iroquois. It was a fatal step. At two o'clock on the afternoon of December 17, 1649, Iroquois warriors fell upon the now undefended town. Father Charles Garnier, one of the missionaries there, hastily performed the requisite baptisms and absolutions until he was cut down by three musket balls, then brained with a hatchet. Those who managed to survive the raid migrated westward. By the opening years of the eighteenth century they would mingle with surviving Hurons to become the Wyandots of Detroit and Sandusky, Ohio country.

By the early spring of 1650, a party of Hurons who had managed to escape to Île St. Joseph found itself confronting a new enemy: starvation. In March, with the lake still frozen, they began to abandon the island, making their way to shore across the softening ice. Some fell through and drowned, while others made it across and survived by fishing. This salvation proved to be no more than a respite. Iroquois war parties discovered them and pursued them, pathetic as they were, with a ferocity that stunned Jesuit observers.

From 1651 to 1653 the Iroquois waged continual war against the French and their Indian allies. There were apparently few battles of a magnitude approaching the assaults on the Tobaccos or the Neutrals, but the harassment was unremitting—at least until four of the five Iroquois tribes, clearly in an effort to end Mohawk domination of the Dutch trade, concluded a series of peace treaties at Montréal late in 1653.

But the ways of war proved difficult to leave. In 1654 the Senecas went to war with the Eries after an Erie man, member of a treaty delegation visiting a Seneca town, quarreled with a Seneca and killed him. The Senecas killed all thirty members of the delegation, unleashing a torrent of reprisals and counterreprisals, until the Eries captured an Onondaga chief. They were on the verge of burning him when he persuaded his captors that to do so would provoke a war with all of the Iroquois. Following tribal custom, the Eries offered the Onondaga to the sister of a member of the slain delegation, expecting that she would adopt him as a surrogate for her dead brother, thereby bringing honorable peace. Instead, the grief-stricken woman bitterly spurned him and, in the name of custom and honor, the chief was put to death after all. The execution did, indeed, trigger further war. As with the other Beaver Wars, little is known of this one, except that it was brief, fierce, and very costly to both sides. In the end, however, there was no doubt that the Iroquois had emerged victorious; for they indeed emerged, whereas the Eries ended the war no longer numerous enough to be called a nation or a tribe.

The destruction of the Eries in 1656 consolidated the power of the Five Nations, making them the dominant economic, military, and political force between the Ottawa River in the north and the Cumberland in the south. Their hegemony extended into Maine in the east, and as far as Lake Ontario in the west. Yet the Beaver Wars did not end with this achievement of dominion. During 1651–1652, the Mohawks attacked a people known as the Atrakwaeronons. Information recorded in Jesuit records suggests that this may have been another name for the Susquehannocks, although it is also possible that the Atrakwaeronons were a distinct tribe, albeit one closely allied to the Susquehannocks. In either case, the Mohawk raid yielded five hundred to six hundred captives and drew the Susquehannocks into a quarter century of sporadic warfare with the Iroquois.

In spite of years of victory, several defeats in 1663 prevented the Iroquois tribes from creating western monopolies on hunting and trade, although they did establish a strong presence in the West, as far as the Illinois and Mississippi Rivers. Yet such footholds were not sufficient to satisfy Iroquois ambition. In 1680 the Five Nations launched a major war against French-allied Indian bands living along the Illinois and Mississippi rivers. After initial victories, the Iroquois were defeated. Some years later, in what must be accounted the final phase of the Iroquoian Beaver Wars, they apparently fared no better against the Miamis, in the present states of Wisconsin and Michigan. (Also see *Iroquois-Huron War, 1648–1650.*)

Algonquian-Dutch War (Kieft's War), 1639–1645

Dutch-Indian relations were characterized by ambivalence. The Dutch typically vacillated between belligerence, often marked by gratuitous cruelty, and a timid defensiveness. In general, Dutch-Indian conflict was (in the earliest period of settlement) both less frequent and less violent than warfare between the English and the Indians and between the Spanish and the Indians. Nevertheless, over the years, relations decayed, a direct result of a developing desire, among Dutch settlers, for land. As the supply of the principal trade good, beaver, in the vicinity of Fort Orange dwindled under pressure of overtrapping, increasing numbers of Dutch colonists turned from trade to farming. The result was increased Dutch demand for land, at the expense of the Indians. By 1639, when Willem Kieft replaced Wouter Van Twiller as governor of New Netherland, acquisition of territory had at last become more important to the Dutch than maintaining friendly relations with the Indians. Kieft imposed heavy taxes on the Algonquian tribes in the vicinity of Manhattan and Long Island. In 1641 Dutch livestock, given free range to graze, destroyed cornfields belonging to Raritan Indians living on Staten Island. Obtaining no satisfaction from Kieft, the Indians retaliated by attacking some farmers, an action that, in turn, provoked retaliation from Kieft, who now offered a bounty on Raritan scalps. The following year, a wheelwright named Claes Rademaker was murdered by an Indian in revenge for the killing of the Indian's uncle, whom some settlers had assaulted for his beaver pelts. In response, Kieft marched a small army through the villages near New Amsterdam to intimidate the Indians. On its first foray, however, the army was anything but intimidating. Marching by cover of night, it managed to get itself lost.

Kieft decided to make up for the shortage of Dutch manpower by pressing the Mohawks into service. In February 1643, at Kieft's urging, a party of Mohawk warriors journeyed down the Hudson to extort, on behalf of themselves and the Dutch, tribute money from the Wappinger Indians. Terrified, the Wappingers fled to Pavonia (present-day environs of Jersey City, New Jersey) and to New Amsterdam, where they appealed to Kieft for protection. The governor responded by turning the Mohawks loose upon them. Mohawk warriors killed seventy Wappingers and enslaved others.

The worst was yet to come. During the night of February 25–26, Kieft dispatched Dutch soldiers to finish off refugees from the Mohawk assault. The night of horror in Pavonia would become infamous as the "Slaughter of the Innocents." The troops returned to New Amsterdam bearing the severed heads of eighty Indians, which soldiers and citizens used as footballs on the streets of New Amsterdam. Thirty prisoners also taken were tortured to death for the public amusement.

The "Slaughter of the Innocents" provoked a major Indian uprising. New Amsterdam and its outlying dependencies found themselves at war with eleven tribes. In March 1643, a panic-stricken Kieft attempted to negotiate with representatives of the Indians. An uneasy truce was concluded, but on October 1, 1643, nine Indians came to a fortification at Pavonia, where three or four soldiers were stationed to protect a local farmer. The Indians put on a show of friendliness, then turned on the soldiers and the farmer, sparing only the farmer's stepson, whom they took captive to Tappan. Next the war party put to the torch the farmer's house, together with all the houses of Pavonia. Emboldened by this act of vengeance, Indian tribes from the Delaware Bay to the Connecticut River soon embarked on the warpath. Terrorized settlers throughout New Netherland fled to New Amsterdam, which lay under siege for more than a year.

IN THEIR OWN Words

I remained that night at the governor's, sitting up. I went and sat in the kitchen, when, about midnight, I heard a great shrieking, and I ran to the ramparts of the fort, and looked over to Pavonia. Saw nothing but firing, and heard the shrieks of the Indians murdered in their sleep. . . . When it was day the soldiers returned to the fort, having massacred or murdered eighty Indians, and considering that they had done a deed of Roman valour, in murdering so many in their sleep; where infants were torn from their mother's breasts, and hacked to pieces in the presence of the parents, and the pieces thrown into the fire and in the water, and other sucklings were bound to small boards, and then cut, stuck, and pierced, and miserably massacred in a manner to move a heart of stone. Some were thrown into the river, and when the fathers and mothers endeavoured to save them, the soldiers would not let them come on land, but made both parents and children drown, children from five to six years of age, and also some decrepit persons. Many fled from this scene, and concealed themselves in the neighbouring sedge, and when it was morning, came out to beg a piece of bread, and to be permitted to warm themselves; but they were murdered in cold blood and tossed into the water. Some came by our lands in the country with their hands, some with their legs cut off, and some holding their entrails in their arms. . . .
—DAVID PIETERSZ DE VRIES, DESCRIBING THE PAVONIA MASSACRE, FEBRUARY 25–26, 1643, IN HIS *SHORT HISTORICAL AND JOURNAL NOTES OF SEVERAL VOYAGES*, 1655

Of the region's tribes, only the Mohawks, still bound in a profitable trading alliance with the Dutch, remained aloof from the war. The Dutch hired Captain John Underhill, who had distinguished himself in New England's *Pequot War, 1637,* to lead Dutch and English soldiers in a destructive sweep through the countryside, attacking Indians and burning their villages. Typically, Indian war strategy was based on quick, violent attacks in a brief war. The Dutch, hunkered down and having hired outside help, instead waged a war of attrition, to which the Indian attackers were ill equipped to respond. By 1644, the tribes lifted their siege of New Amsterdam and agreed to a peace, which generally prevailed for a decade, until the outbreak of the *Peach War* in 1655.

Iroquois-French Wars, 1642–1696

In 1609, the French explorer Samuel de Champlain accompanied a Huron Indian war party and killed some Iroquois Indians. This single incident became a source of enmity between the Iroquois and the French, and after Champlain died in 1635, Iroquois raiders set about terrorizing French settlements along the St. Lawrence and Ottawa Rivers, including the Jesuit missions. By 1650, the Iroquois established bases of operation at various strategic points, from which warriors waged combat against the French by both water and land. Repeatedly the French attempted to come to terms with the Iroquois, but peace never endured. The Iroquois were egged on by Dutch traders at Fort Orange, who kept their chief trading partners supplied with weapons and ammunition. The issue had expanded far beyond hatred of the French and was now a struggle for control of the beaver fur trade. The Iroquois objective was to monopolize the trade, diverting it from French outposts to Fort Orange. Viewed from this perspective, the war may be seen as an aspect of the *Iroquoian Beaver Wars, 1638–1684.*

By the early 1660s, the Iroquois had carried the war to the doorstep of Montréal, and it wasn't until 1666 that soldiers arrived from France to take the offensive. The Iroquois were not only pushed out of Canada, but were ultimately defeated in their homelands. It was now the Iroquois who sued for peace, and the resulting truce endured for nearly two decades. Relations deteriorated after the French began to move west, and antagonisms developed between the French and the English. A new French governor, the Marquis de Denonville, arrived in 1685 and decided that the time was ripe for an offensive move against the warring Senecas, westernmost of the Iroquois tribes. The governor led a large force into western New York and destroyed four Seneca villages in 1687. Far from subduing the Seneca, however, this action outraged the Indians, who nursed a scheme of vengeance, which reached fruition in 1689 when they swooped down the St. Lawrence River in large numbers to massacre the inhabitants of Lachine. From this settlement, war parties fanned out to terrorize the countryside as far as Montréal.

The Seneca made repeated attacks against Lachine and elsewhere, concentrating on French forts, towns, and small settlements. When the Comte de Frontenac (1620–1698) returned as governor of New France in 1689, he devoted himself to an organized campaign against the Iroquois generally and the Seneca in particular. Peace was restored in 1696; and in 1701 the Iroquois signed a treaty with France that permitted them to remain neutral during the ensuing colonial wars between the French and the English, culminating in the French and Indian War. But the intense combat of the closing years of the seventeenth century had irreparably damaged Iroquois unity, and although the Five Nations pledged to the French a policy of neutrality, individual Iroquois tribes would often violate these terms in the hope of regaining the military and economic dominance they had enjoyed in western New York and the Ohio country.

Maryland's War with the Susquehannocks, 1643–1652

The colony of Maryland declared war on the Susquehannock Indians on September 13, 1642. Its motives are obscure; perhaps it was to halt the incursion of Susquehannocks into territory occupied by what historians have called Maryland's client tribes—tribes semidependent on Maryland trade and government. These tribes included the Piscataways (also called Conoys), the Patuxents, and the Yoamacoes. Whatever the cause, militiamen did not mobilize until some time between July 1643 and June 1644. The first campaign seems to have involved few battles, as the Susquehannocks simply fled from the militia's guns. In a second confrontation, however, the colonists of Maryland's trading rival New Sweden aided the Indians, who prevailed against Maryland forces, capturing fifteen prisoners, two of whom they tortured to death. Although there is little record of this Susquehannock victory, it must have been something of a rout, since the Marylanders fled the field in such haste that they abandoned arms, including two "field pieces"—precious artillery hard to come by in the colonies. A relatively inactive state of war apparently continued from 1643 or 1644 to 1652, when the Susquehannocks, deeply embroiled in the *Iroquoian Beaver Wars, 1638–1684* with the Five Nations, decided to make peace on the Maryland front and negotiated a treaty. Within ten years the Maryland Assembly was calling the Susquehannocks a "Bullwarke and Security of the Northern parts of the Province" as the colony enlisted their aid in fighting the Iroquois.

Maryland's Religious War, 1644–1654

Maryland grew and prospered in the seventeenth century, with few troubles or altercations with local Indians. In fact, local Indians used the colonists for protection against incursions by hostile tribes such as the Susquehannocks, the Iroquois, and the Nanticokes on the Eastern Shore. Likewise, the colonists began to use the local Indians as a buffer against sporadic raids by those same hostiles. For several years, until settlement spread farther afield, the arrangement worked well for both colonists and local tribes. However, by the early 1640s this situation began to change when freemen of the colony demanded a greater voice in colonial affairs, and Susquehannocks and other Iroquoian tribes began raiding the livestock of outlying settlements.

Against this background of increasing tensions, Maryland began to feel the effects of the English Civil War. Governor Leonard Calvert returned to England and appointed Giles Brent as governor in his stead. Shortly thereafter, Richard Ingle, an ardent parliamentarian sea captain from London, arrived in Maryland. He led two years of anarchic raiding known as "the plundering time." Ingle was finally captured, tried four times by juries who reached no verdict, escaped, and continued to do business in Maryland waters.

In autumn 1644 Leonard Calvert returned to Maryland and traveled to Virginia, bearing letters of marque against parliamentary supporters. Ingle obtained similar letters of marque against royalists in 1645, and proceeded to raid in Maryland, attacking and plundering settlements and manors, capturing Jesuit missionaries and several important political leaders. These latter prisoners he carted off to England. Various lawsuits were instituted in England, but it was obvious that parliamentary forces were gaining the upper hand in England.

Maryland was in chaos. Calvert was still in Virginia, the temporary governor was in England, and a new government and governor were established by the council in an attempt to restore order. Calvert finally returned and restored order during spring 1647, but died suddenly in June. Before his death, Calvert appointed Thomas Greene, a staunch Catholic royalist, as governor. In mid-1648, however, Cecil Calvert, second Lord Baltimore (who had inherited Maryland from his father and who became first lord proprietor of the colony), shifted toward a pro-Parliament stance in an effort to preserve his colonial rights. Accordingly, although he himself was a Catholic, Baltimore demoted Greene to the council and replaced him with William Stone, a Protestant friendly to Parliament. By this time the council was heavily Protestant, contributing to a return of peace in Maryland. The second Lord Baltimore kept his colony until 1654, when tensions again increased, this time between Puritans and most others in Maryland. Internal and external Puritan hostilities caused proprietary forces under Stone to march north, where they engaged a smaller Puritan force near present-day Annapolis on the Severn River. Puritan forces were victorious in what became known as the Battle of the Severn on March 25, 1654. Baltimore did not regain full control of his colony again until the Restoration of Charles II in 1660.

Iroquois-Huron War, 1648–1650

The Huron Indians, who inhabited what is today Ontario, Canada, were longtime trading partners with the French and traditional enemies of the Iroquois. In 1648 the Dutch traders at Fort Orange, eager to usurp French trade, began supplying the Iroquois—chief trading partners of the Dutch—with guns and ammunition for a full-scale invasion of Huron territory. The invasion was brief and terrible. The Hurons were decimated, the survivors sent fleeing to various neighboring tribes in desperate search of refuge. Typically, Indian tactics called for short, sharp attacks, but in this case, the Iroquois relentlessly pressed their pursuit of the Huron refugees, also virtually destroying the Tobaccos, who had given shelter to many Hurons. The so-called Neutral Nation was wiped out next, in 1650.

Historians sometimes group this conflict together with the long Iroquois campaign to achieve a monopoly of trade known as the *Iroquoian Beaver Wars, 1638–1684.*

Peach War, 1655–1657

The Peach War, second of the major Dutch-Indian Wars (the first was the *Algonquian-Dutch War [Kieft's War], 1639–1645*), began when a Dutch farmer killed a Delaware Indian woman for picking peaches in his orchard. In retaliation, her family ambushed and killed the farmer. As word of the incident spread, other Delaware bands struck. Several settlers were killed at New Amsterdam, and 150 were taken captive. Governor Peter Stuyvesant called out the militia, which freed most of the captives and destroyed some of the Indians' villages. Following this, Dutch-Indian violence sporadically continued, debilitating Indians as well as settlers.

Esopus Wars, 1659–1660 and 1663–1664

The two Esopus Wars collectively constituted the third of the Dutch-Indian conflicts. By the 1650s, Dutch farmers were settling along the Rondout and Esopus Creeks, tributaries of the Hudson River. They purchased land from a group of Esopus Indians and, at first, relations were cordial, but deteriorated in the later 1650s, as local Esopus became increasingly dependent on alcohol, which they purchased from illicit traders operating in the vicinity of Fort Orange. In 1658, a drunken young warrior killed a settler and burned his farm, prompting Governor Stuyvesant to meet with Esopus leaders and demand reparations. He also pressured the Indians into selling more land to the colonists. Having secured these concessions, he persuaded the colonists to concentrate their far-flung settlement and cooperate with the militia in building a defensive fort, which Stuyvesant garrisoned with a small detachment of troops.

The new arrangement brought a measure of peace to the region until the Indians became impatient over the long delay in obtaining payment for the land they had ceded. For their part, the settlers became acutely aware of the Indians' ugly mood, and on September 21, 1659, a group of settlers decided to act preemptively. They ambushed a band of warriors who had been drinking brandy in the woods near the Dutch settlement. In the attack, one Esopus was killed, and the next day a number of young warriors exacted revenge by attacking some settlers. Some were killed, others captured. This success encouraged the Indians, some five hundred warriors, to lay siege to the fort, in which the local colonists now sought refuge. Traditional Indian battle tactics did not favor protracted siege, however, and by the time Stuyvesant arrived on the scene with reinforcements (October 10, 1659), the siege had been lifted. Nevertheless, the military strength of the Dutch was not sufficient to enable an offensive action against the Indians, and Stuyvesant's lieutenant, Johannes La Montagne, in command of Fort Orange, made overtures of peace.

The uneasy peace was broken by the Dutch in the spring of 1660, when Ensign Dirck Smith, commanding the garrison at Wiltwyck, New York, launched a number of assaults against the Indians. The Esopus, pressured by other tribes, finally agreed to a peace settlement, which was formalized on July 15, 1660.

Despite the treaty, hostilities sporadically continued. When a second Dutch settlement, Nieuwdorp (New Village), was founded near Wiltwyck, the Esopus sachems complained to Stuyvesant, pointing out that he had yet to deliver the promised payment for much of the Esopus land that had been ceded. At last, on June 7, the frustrated and desperate Esopus attacked Wiltwyck as well as Nieuwdorp. Historians deem this the start of the Second Esopus War.

The attackers waited until most of the men had left the villages to work the outlying fields. The Indians, arms concealed, then entered Wiltwyck and Nieuwdorp on pretext of trade. Once inside, they attacked, burning to the ground and killing or capturing virtually all of the inhabitants. Capitalizing on the element of surprise, the Indians immediately took control of the streets and put the buildings to the torch. They took numerous women and children hostage and sniped at the men as they returned to the village. At first the situation looked hopeless for the Dutch, but as more men returned from the fields, the tide turned in favor of the settlers. By the end of the day, the Battle of Wiltwyck was over. The town was still in Dutch hands, but some forty-five settlers had been captured, and twenty or more slain. A band of sixty-nine settlers, including a handful of refugees from Nieuwdorp, hunkered down in Wiltwyck and awaited a siege.

It did not come, but just outside the fort, skirmishing was sharp and frequent over the next several weeks. At length, Stuyvesant marched into

Wiltwyck and, by the end of June, reinforced the settlement with a contingent of sixty troops. The Dutch forbore to take the offensive, however, but attempted first to negotiate for the release of prisoners. Over the next several weeks a few captives were surrendered, but by the end of July the Dutch had resolved to counterattack. A force of 210 soldiers, settlers, slaves, and Indian allies mounted an attack on the Esopus stronghold. After a difficult trek over rough terrain, the party reached the Esopus "fort," only to find it deserted. The Dutch occupied the fort, using it as a base from which to dispatch a smaller force to give chase to the Indians. While these troops went about their work, others destroyed the Esopus's food caches.

Despite the pressure of these attacks, the Indians released only a few more hostages and quietly set about fortifying a new position. Deciding to act preemptively, the Dutch commander at Wiltwyck assembled a force of fifty men and assaulted the new Indian stockade on September 5. On their arrival at the fort, the Dutch discovered that the Indians were outside the stockade. The troops surrounded them and made a surprise attack, which sent the Esopus fleeing. The Dutch troops destroyed the guns and provisions the Indians had left behind in the fort. Thirty Esopus had been killed or captured, and twenty-three Dutch captives were recovered. Losses to the Dutch force were slight: six wounded and three killed. Three more Dutch expeditions were launched in the fall, but these resulted in few Indian casualties. Nevertheless, the Dutch military action, combined with the threat posed by alliances with the Mohawks, Nyacks, Hackensacks, and Wappingers, prompted the Esopus to sue for peace in May 1664. The Esopus ceded all their territory from the Hudson River up to the sites of the two destroyed forts.

King Philip's War, 1675–1676

King Philip's War was a catastrophe for New England's colonists and Indians alike. In the course of 1675–1676, half of the region's towns were badly damaged and twelve destroyed utterly, requiring the work of a generation to rebuild them. The fragile colonial economy suffered devastating blows, both as a result of the direct cost of the war—some £100,000—and because of the disruption of the fur trade with the Indians and the virtual cessation of coastal fishing and the West Indies trade. Not only did the war siphon off the manpower customarily devoted to these industries, but also many men never returned to their peacetime occupations; one in sixteen colonists of military age died. Many others—men, women, children—were also killed, captured, or starved. In proportion to New England's population of thirty thousand, King Philip's War was the costliest in American history. As for the Indians, at least three thousand perished, and many of those who did not die were deported and sold into slavery.

Causes

So far as colonial chroniclers were concerned, the cause of this terrible conflict was simple: King Philip, haughty chief of the Wampanoag Indians, betrayed the traditional friendship between his tribe and the English by waging war against New England's settlers, with the object of either annihilating them or driving them out of the country. In fact, the causes of King Philip's War, as with most white-Indian conflicts, were both more complex and more basic than this. Colonial land hunger and a rising population, combined with racism sanctioned by Puritan religious doctrine, met head-on with Philip's growing resentment of English insults to his sovereignty and encroachments on his power. Two major tribes, the Wampanoags and the Narragansetts, desired the benefits of trade with the English and vied with one another for colonial favor. At the same time, both tribes struggled to maintain some autonomy and retain land. As English pressure to sell more land increased, along with demands for greater and greater submission to colonial authority in matters of politics and religion, the rival tribes began to come together. Culturally, politically, and spiritually, the stage was set for conflict in New England.

Massasoit, chief of the Wampanoags and longtime friend of the English (it was through his aid that the Pilgrims survived their first terrible winter in the New World), died in 1661 at age eighty-one. His son Wamsutta, whom the English called Alexander, succeeded him as the tribe's principal sachem and continued the tradition of friendship with the English. However, under Wamsutta, the Wampanoags divided their loyalty between two competing English colonies, Rhode Island and Plymouth. The Plymouth Colony's Major (later Governor) Josiah Winslow seized Alexander at gunpoint and took him to Duxbury to answer conspiracy charges and—most important—to demonstrate his loyalty to Plymouth by selling land to that colony rather than to Rhode Island. During his captivity, Alexander contracted a fever and died. His twenty-four-year-old brother, Metacom or Metacomet, whom the English called King Philip, succeeded him as sachem and, like a number of other Wampanoags, suspected that Winslow had not merely brutalized Wamsutta but also had poisoned him. Relations between the colony and King Philip became increasingly strained. Early in 1671 Philip, outraged that the new Plymouth settlement of Swansea flagrantly encroached on his land, staged an armed display for the benefit of the town's citizens. On April 10, 1671, he was summoned to Taunton to acknowledge and apologize for such "plotting" and to agree to surrender his people's arms. By the end of September he was haled to Plymouth, where he stood trial for failure to abide by the Taunton agreement. Fined £100, the sachem was further humiliated by a requirement that he henceforth obtain colonial permission in all matters involving the purchase or sale of land; he was also forbidden to wage war against other Indians without authority from the colonial government.

For three years, Philip quietly forged anti-English alliances with the Nipmuck Indians and with his tribe's former rivals the Narragansetts. Then, in January 1675, came another revelation of Wampanoag designs against the English. John Sassamon (or Saussaman), a Christianized "Praying Indian" who had been Philip's private secretary, alerted the English to the sachem's plotting. On January 29, Sassamon's body was found on the ice of a frozen pond. Philip was accused of complicity in the murder and again haled into court, but won release for lack of evidence.

A nineteenth-century adaptation of a seventeenth-century engraved portrait of Metacomet, known to the New England colonists as King Philip. *Collection: ArtToday*

Outbreak

On June 11, just three days after other Indians were executed for the murder, word of Wampanoags arming near Swansea and Plymouth Town reached authorities. They also heard of scattered incidents of cattle killing and house looting in outlying settlements. Already, settlers were beginning to desert some towns: Swansea, adjacent to Wampanoag country, was the first to be partially abandoned, and Indians began appropriating property left behind. An outraged settler shot a looter—the first blood of the war.

In an uneasy and mistrustful alliance, Massachusetts, Plymouth, and Rhode Island joined forces to mobilize an army, which was mustered during June 21 through 23 at Miles's Garrison, opposite Philip's base of operations at Mount Hope Neck, Rhode Island—but not before Wampanoags had raided Swansea on the Sabbath, attacking townsfolk on their way to church. The town was attacked again—and half burned—a few days later, as worshipers returned from church. Four days later, Rhode Island militia captain Benjamin Church and his troops fell under attack near beleaguered Swansea. The hastily mustered colonial forces proved ineffectual again and again. Wampanoags staged lightning raids in the vicinity of Rehoboth and Taunton on June 29. Connecticut joined in the war effort on July 1 when it sent troops to aid Massachusetts, Plymouth, and Rhode Island, but Philip was negotiating an alliance of his own at this time, with the Pocasset squaw-sachem Weetamoo. In Rhode Island, Benjamin

IN THEIR OWN *Words* **The Taunton Agreement**

Whereas my Father, my Brother, and my self, have formally submitted ourselves and our People unto the Kings Majesty of England, and to the Colony of New Plimouth, by solemn Covenant under our Hand; but I having of late through my Indiscretion, and the Naughtiness of my Heart, violated and broken this my Covenant with my Friends, by taking up Arms, with evil intent against them, and that groundlessly; I being now deeply sensible of my Unfaithfulness and Folly, so desire at this Time solemnly to renew my Covenant with my ancient Friends, my Fathers Friends above mentioned, and do desire that this may testifie to the World against me if ever I shall again fail in my Faithfulness towards them (that I have now, and at all Times found so kind to me) or any other of the English Colonies; and as a real Pledge of my true Intentions for the Future to be Faithful and Friendly, I do freely engage to resign up unto the Government of New Plimouth, all my English Arms, to be kept by them for their Security, so long as they shall see Reason. For true Performance of the Premises, I have hereunto set my Hand, together with the Rest of my Council.

—CONCLUDED APRIL 10, 1671, AT TAUNTON, PLYMOUTH COLONY,
BETWEEN THE COLONY AND KING PHILIP

Church pursued Philip into a swamp near Tiverton. Nearby, in Captain Almy's "pease field," his twenty-man party was set upon by three hundred Indians for six hours, until they were rescued by an English river sloop.

Military and Diplomatic Failures

By mid-July much of New England was awash in blood, as Wampanoags were joined by Narragansetts and the Nipmucks of eastern and central Massachusetts. Discouraged by their army's performance against the Indians in close combat—and over Church's vigorous objections—colonial authorities soon broke off pursuit of Philip and instead built a fort to besiege him in the swamp, intending to starve him out. This strategic error only prolonged the war. With the English occupied in building forts, Philip was able to escape from Pocasset Swamp on July 29 and make for Nipmuck country to the northeast.

By the end of August, the theater of war had broadened into the upper Connecticut Valley, the Merrimac Valley, New Hampshire, and Maine. Having already endured months of bloodshed, the United Colonies officially declared war on September 9, levying an army of a thousand. But the litany of raid upon raid continued. Repeated attempts at negotiating peace or even a truce failed. A hopeful conference at Wickford, Rhode Island, between the English and the Narragansetts broke down on September 22. Worse, previously friendly Indians now turned on the colonists. Springfield, Massachusetts, having enjoyed cordial relations with the Indians for some forty years, maintained no garrisons. On October 4–5, it was raided, and thirty-two houses, about half the town, were destroyed. On October 18 or 19 some seven hundred Indians attacked Hatfield, Massachusetts, but were driven off.

The Great Swamp Fight

At this time the Narragansetts at last concluded a new treaty in Boston. Nevertheless, on November 2, Connecticut's colonial council resolved that the best way to prevent war with the Narragansetts was a peremptory strike against them. Plymouth and Massachusetts were in agreement on this, and the army of the United Colonies, called for in September, was at last mustering in November and into December. The army assembled at Wickford, Rhode Island, under the command of Plymouth governor Josiah Winslow. Winslow marched his thousand-man army, including a company under the redoubtable Benjamin Church, into a snowstorm on

December 18 to assault the stronghold of the Narragansett sachem Canonchet (whom the English called Canonicus) in a frozen swamp at Kingston, Rhode Island. They reached the Indian fort the following day, having suffered terribly in the intense cold. In fierce battle, eighty of Winslow's army perished, including fourteen company commanders; about six hundred Narragansetts—half of them women and children—died. Over the protests of the badly wounded Benjamin Church, who pointed out that the battered English would need the shelter of the Indians' wigwams for the bitter winter night, the colonials put the encampment to the torch, then retreated instead of pursuing the surviving Narragansetts, who escaped to Nipmuck country. The Great Swamp Fight inflicted heavy losses on the Narragansetts, but it also served to strengthen desperate anti-English alliances among the Wampanoags, Nipmucks, and Narragansetts.

With the new year, Philip attempted to extend his alliances beyond New England, taking many of his people to Mohawk country near Albany, New York, in search of ammunition and provisions in addition to friends. Unfortunately for Philip, New York governor Edmund Andros had reached the Mohawks first, persuading them not only to spurn the alliance but also to attack Philip, who was compelled to flee back to New England. The alliance Andros established effectively blocked the grand Indian confederacy all colonists feared, but New England forces were not prepared to take immediate advantage of Philip's predicament; despite the lopsided casualty figures from the Great Swamp Fight, Winslow's army, crippled by their losses (especially at the command level) and suffering from a lack of provisions, was immobilized for more than a month.

New England Bleeds

With the principal English force in disarray, the Indians rallied and renewed their offensive, raiding many settlements in Massachusetts, Rhode Island, and Connecticut. The early spring of 1676 marked the low point of the colonists' fortunes. Although Connecticut soldiers operating in western Rhode Island succeeded in capturing the important Narragansett sachem and war leader Canonchet, whom they subsequently executed, by the middle of the month the English area of settlement had greatly contracted. Despite emergency laws forbidding the evacuation of towns without official permission, the outlying settlements around Boston were largely abandoned.

By late spring of 1676, colonial forces at last began to take the offensive. Captain Daniel Henchman was sweeping through eastern Massachusetts at the end of April. On May 1, Indian hostiles finally agreed to negotiate ransom terms for English captives. Yet, as Henchman prevailed in eastern Massachusetts, Philip's warriors attacked the Plymouth town of Bridgewater on May 6 and launched a desperate general offensive against that colony, raiding Plymouth Town on May 11.

In western Massachusetts, Captain William Turner, leading a force of 150 mounted men, attacked an Indian encampment at the falls of the Connecticut above Deerfield, Massachusetts, on May 19. It was not so much a battle as it was a massacre: the soldiers poked their muskets into the wigwams and shot the Indians—including many women and children—as they slept. While the enemy was routed, the army failed to pursue, and the surviving Indians turned a retreat into a counterattack, killing about forty men, including Turner.

Turning Point

The colonists became more aggressive in attack and pursuit. Responding to reports of hostiles fishing in the Pawtucket River near Rehoboth, Captain Thomas Brattle led a combined force of colonists and Indian allies in attack, killing about a dozen of Philip's warriors, with the loss of one colonial soldier. On June 2 Connecticut major John Talcott launched a combined Indian-English assault against Philip in western Massachusetts. Early in the same month, Benjamin Church was authorized to build a new army on behalf of the United Colonies, using white and Indian soldiers. Still, Philip fought on, launching a massive but unsuccessful assault against Hadley, Massachusetts.

At Nipsachuck, Rhode Island, on July 2, John Talcott dealt the Narragansetts two crushing blows when he attacked a band consisting of 34 men and 137 women and children, killing all of the men and 92 of the women and children. On the next day, at Warwick, he slew 18 men and 22 women and children, taking 27 prisoners as well. At this time, too, war with the so-called North Indians—the Abnakis, the Sokokis, and the Pennacooks—came to an end when the Pennacook sachem Wannalancet signed a treaty with Major Richard Waldron, bringing peace to Maine.

While Benjamin Church prevailed in skirmishes at Middleborough and Monponsett on July 11 and, a week later, skirmished with Philip's men in and around Taunton, Major William Bradford was pursuing Philip himself, narrowly failing to run the Indian leader to ground on July 16.

The Hunt for Philip

Church received a second colonial commission on July 24, calling for a larger army of 200 men, of whom 140 were to be friendly Indians. The new army set out on July 30 in pursuit of the elusive Philip. Closing on their quarry, Church's troops killed Philip's uncle on July 31 and the next day captured the sachem's wife and son. Philip himself, however, managed to escape. Nevertheless, the demoralization of the Indians had become general. In August, a deserter from Philip's camp approached Church, offering to lead him and his men to Philip's camp. Church deployed his men around Philip's camp after midnight on August 12 and moved in at first light.

Philip took to his feet as an English soldier fired and missed. The marksmanship of an English-allied Indian called Alderman was better. Benjamin Church ordered the sachem's body butchered, awarding the head and one hand to Alderman. The remainder of the corpse was quartered and hung on four trees, customary practice in an execution for treason. With Philip's death, the war named for him had all but come to an end. On September 11 Church captured and executed Annawon, Philip's "chief captain." Sporadic skirmishes occurred through October, but the last sizable band of Indians surrendered on August 28.

In the aftermath of the war, many Indians were left demoralized and abject in their submission to the English. Others, however, had fled to Canada, New York, and the Delaware and Susquehanna Valleys, where they would meditate a revenge that exploded in a long series of raids and guerrilla actions culminating in the French and Indian War.

First Abnaki War, 1675–1678

The Abnaki (or Abenaki) Indians lived in the border region between New England and New France and were often staunch allies of the French against the English. The Abnakis were not a single tribe, but a loosely confederated collection of Algonquian tribes (including the Penobscot, Kennebecs, Wawenocks, and Androscoggins of New England's eastern frontier; the Pigwackets, Ossipees, and Winnipesaukes of the White Mountains; the Pennacooks of the Merrimack Valley; the Sokokis and Cowasucks in the upper Connecticut Valley; and the Missisquois and other groups in Vermont) broadcast throughout the region of present-day

Maine, New Hampshire, Vermont, and southern Québec. The English often referred to these tribes collectively as "the Eastern Indians."

The First Abnaki War may be viewed as a phase of *King Philip's War, 1675–1676,* or as a separate conflict. Increasingly threatened by English expansion, the Abnakis unleashed a guerrilla war against the English, hitting outlying frontier settlements in small-scale raids, often carrying off captives. These prisoners were either adopted into the tribe or sold to the French. Although the English defeated King Philip and his immediate allies, they did not fare as well against the Abnakis, to whom they promised, by a treaty of 1678, to pay an annual tribute.

The First Abnaki War was a prelude to other conflicts in which Abnaki warriors fought, both on their own and under the command of French officers. They participated in *King William's War, 1689–1697,* and in *Queen Anne's War, 1702–1713.* In the latter, the Abnaki role in the conflict is often called the *Second Abnaki War, 1702–1712.* Between 1722 and 1727, despite the long truce prevailing between England and France, the Abnakis fought sporadically against Massachusetts and New Hampshire in a series of engagements called *Dummer's War (Third Abnaki War), 1722–1727.* The outbreak of *King George's War (1744–1748)* once again saw the Abnakis and the French launch a joint effort, and Abnakis served with the French forces in almost every major campaign of the *French and Indian War, 1754–1763.*

Bacon's Rebellion, 1676

Traditionally, Bacon's Rebellion has been interpreted—or, rather, misinterpreted—as a kind of distant prelude to the *American Revolution, 1775–1783 (see chapter 3).* In fact, in and of itself, the short-lived "rebellion" was not terribly important, but its greater significance is in how it dovetailed into ongoing warfare between colonists and Indians.

In the 1670s, Maryland planters were hungering for more land, which prompted the colony to make accommodations with the Iroquois in violation of Maryland's alliance with the Susquehannocks. The colony's 1674 treaty with the Senecas (an Iroquois tribe) gave the Senecas license to campaign against the Susquehannocks and force them south, to the Potomac. The stage for a war between Maryland and its betrayed ally was thus set. The only requirement was an incident to serve as a curtain-raiser.

This came during July and August 1675, when a group of Maryland Nanticokes (also called Doegs) began a dispute with a wealthy Virginia planter, Thomas Mathew, who (they claimed) had failed to pay them for some goods traded. Unable to collect, the Indians appropriated some of Mathew's hogs, whereupon a party of the planter's men moved against the Indians, killing several and recovering the hogs. In turn, the Nanticokes took their revenge by killing three Virginians, including Mathew's herdsman. In response, the local militia killed a Nanticoke chief, which touched off a battle, which came to involve not only the Nanticokes but the more powerful Susquehannocks as well. As a result, Maryland and Virginia were swept by hit-and-run raids. Virginia's governor, William Berkeley, directed Colonel John Washington (great-grandfather of the future president) and Major Isaac Allerton to convene the officers of the militia regiments between the Rappahannock and the Potomac to conduct an inquisition into the raids and what had caused them. Berkeley was determined to act only if the investigation proved just cause. If it did, he would unleash the militia on a punitive campaign. Washington and Allerton, however, did not scruple to twist Berkeley's commission into an order to raise a militia immediately. Seven hundred fifty Virginians were duly organized, and the colonel and major wrote to Maryland authorities, who sent an additional 250 cavalry and dragoons under Major Thomas Trueman. Late in September 1675, this combined force of 1,000 surrounded the place that had been appointed by the Maryland Assembly as the home village of the Susquehannocks at the junction of Piscataway Creek and the Potomac, sheltering, at the time, about 100 warriors and their families. Despite an Indian flag of truce, the militia attacked. This treachery only served to escalate the war, increasing the frequency and ferocity of Indian raids. It was the Susquehannocks, however, who sought an end to the conflict. They sent a message to Governor Berkeley, declaring that with approximately ten common Englishmen killed for each of their chiefs slain, restitution had been made. They were now willing to conclude a peace. Berkeley, his back to the wall, rejected the offer, and the war continued. However, Berkeley's defensive strategy, which depended largely on construction of a chain of fortifications around the settled parts of the colony, leaving the frontier exposed, enraged Virginia's western settlers. The outlying regions were left to fend for themselves. Desperate, the frightened and angry frontier was ripe for rebellion.

The powder was packed in the keg, and one Nathaniel Bacon was on hand to strike a match. Cousin to Berkeley by marriage, Bacon had been expelled from Cambridge University for what the records specify only as "extravagances." In 1673 he left England for Virginia, possessing a new bride and £1,800 (given him by his father), money he used to buy two plantations on the James River. Governor Berkeley welcomed his in-law with an appointment to the House of Burgesses, but soon discovered that the young man was a fiery and unscrupulous demagogue. While drinking with friends, Bacon heard about a group of frontiersmen who had had enough of Berkeley's cautious policies and who were preparing to take Indian matters into their own hands. Bacon quickly insinuated himself among them as their leader, and in a first campaign, early in May 1676, Bacon took his band to pay a call on the Occaneechi Indians, who lived along the Roanoke River, near the present Virginia–North Carolina state line. When Bacon announced that he was going off to fight the Susquehannocks, the Occaneechis offered to do the fighting for him, as proof of their friendship with the English. Bacon eagerly accepted the offer, and sent the Occaneechi warriors on their way.

When the war party returned in triumph, bearing Susquehannock prisoners and a captured cache of fur, Bacon attempted to appropriate the pelts for himself and his men. Even more outrageously, he proposed to seize as slaves a group of Manikin Indians who, operating as insurgents within the Susquehannock camp, had been instrumental allies in achieving victory. The Occaneechis, shocked, refused to relinquish either the fur or their allies. Bacon responded by ordering an attack, then ran off with as many of the pelts as possible.

On their return to the English settlements, Bacon and his "boys" were generally welcomed as heroes. Berkeley, however, posted Bacon as a traitor on May 26, 1676, and had him arrested when he entered Jamestown to take his seat in the House of Burgesses. An apparently much abashed Nathaniel Bacon contritely acknowledged his transgression and was duly pardoned by Berkeley, who released him on June 5. In the meantime, seeing that Berkeley was distracted by the actions of his in-law, Sir Edmund Andros, governor of the duke of York's patent territories (which encompassed New York), took steps to forestall the kind of disaster that had befallen New England in *King Philip's War, 1675–1676.* Andros offered the Susquehannocks refuge within his colony, provided that they stop raiding Maryland and Virginia. Some accepted the offer and took refuge peacefully; others continued to raid Maryland settlers, periodically fleeing to the protection of the Iroquois within New York. Maryland responded angrily to Andros's intervention, which, to the likes of Bacon and his followers, seemed yet another example of tyranny from the indifferent seats of power. Thus the young demagogue's atonement was short-lived. Bacon returned to Henrico County in Virginia and raised an army of five hundred men, which he led into Jamestown on June 23, demanding that the Burgesses commission him commander of all forces fighting the Indians.

IN THEIR OWN *Words*

. . . Now my friends I have lived 34 yeares amongst you, as uncorrupt and dilligent as ever Governor was, Bacon is a man of two yeares amongst you, his person and qualities unknowne to most of you, and to all men else, by any vertuous action that ever I heard of, And that very action which he boasts of, was sickly and fooleishly, and as I am informed treacherously carried to the dishonnor of the English Nation, yett in itt, he lost more men then I did in three yeares Warr, and by the grace of God will putt myselfe to the same daingers and troubles againe when I have brought Bacon to acknowledge the Laws are above him, and I doubt not but by God's

assistance to have better success then Bacon hath had, the reason of my hopes are, that I will take Councell of wiser men then my selfe, but Mr. Bacon hath none about him, but the lowest of the people. . . .

To conclude, I have don what was possible both to friend and enimy, have granted Mr. Bacon three pardons, which he hath scornefully rejected, suppoaseing himselfe stronger to subvert then I and you to maineteyne the Laws, by which onely and Gods assisting grace and mercy, all men must hope for peace and safety. I will add noe more though much more is still remaineing to Justifie me and condemne Mr. Bacon, but to desier that this declaration may be read in every County Court in the Country . . .

—FROM VIRGINIA GOVERNOR WILLIAM BERKELEY'S
PUBLIC CONDEMNATION OF NATHANIEL BACON, MAY 19, 1676

Bacon's men aimed their guns at the burgesses, who were watching the proceedings from the windows of the State House. It was reported that Bacon swore repeated oaths as he again demanded a commission: "Dam my Bloud, I'le Kill Governor Councill Assembly and all." At this, one of the burgesses waved his handkerchief from the window: "You shall have it, You shall have it." With that, the burgesses summarily commissioned him.

Thus legitimated, Bacon set out on another campaign, and again his objective was a band of Indians friendly to his own colony: the Pamunkeys of eastern Virginia. In the meantime, back in Jamestown, on July 29, Governor Berkeley succeeded in effecting the repeal of Bacon's commission and once again proclaimed him a traitor. But such was Bacon's popularity and such were the burgesses' fear of him that the governor could not recruit an army to oppose the rebel. Indeed, within a week of Berkeley's declaration, a group of Virginia's most substantial planters took an oath to support Bacon, who, for his part, continued indiscriminately to kill Indians.

At last, on the Virginia frontier, Bacon received word of Berkeley's latest edict against him. Angrily, he broke off Indian fighting long enough to return to Jamestown on September 13. His first act was to seize the wives of burgesses loyal to the governor. Taking them hostage, he used them as human shields to protect his men as they constructed siege lines before the town. This quickly completed, Bacon forced Berkeley and his meager band of supporters out of the capital and into exile on the Eastern Shore. Then, on September 18, the rebels burned Jamestown, hated center of Tidewater power.

At this point, Bacon's Rebellion was at its height, with Bacon master of all but the Eastern Shore of Virginia. But his ascendancy would prove short-lived. From his place of exile, the determined governor managed to rally a substantial force against Bacon. Berkeley quickly retook Jamestown and pursued Bacon and his diehard followers to a stand at Yorktown. There, in October, Nathaniel Bacon died, cut down not by Berkeley's musket balls but by disease. His death brought an instant end to his rebellion as well as to the unauthorized war against the Indians of Virginia.

Popé's Rebellion, 1680

By the middle of the seventeenth century, after fifty years of Spanish tyranny in the American Southwest, the Pueblo Indians were moved to form a desperate alliance with their hereditary enemies the Apaches—a tribe whose very name is derived from the Zuni word for enemy—who were renowned and feared as great warriors. Following some two years of Apache and Pueblo guerrilla raids, during which colonial authorities were forced to stop sending supply caravans to their frontier outposts, Governor Antonio de Oterrmín, in 1672, arrested forty-seven Pueblo "medicine men" (essentially lesser chiefs), hanged three, and imprisoned the rest in Santa Fe, the territorial capital. Among these prisoners was Popé, a medicine man from the important Tewa Pueblo.

Popé languished in captivity for several years, nurturing dreams of vengeance against the Spanish. Eventually released, he went into hiding in Taos. From this place he covertly organized a major rebellion, coordinating armed action among the far-flung pueblos by means of a sophisticated system of couriers to ensure a simultaneous uprising on August 13, 1680. Popé was ruthless in his effort to preserve secrecy; he ordered his own brother-in-law killed on mere suspicion of treachery. But despite his precautions, word of the rebellion leaked, and Popé decided to launch the operation early, on August 10.

Premature though it was, Popé's Rebellion was devastating. The major missions at Taos, Pecos, and Acoma were burned and the priests murdered, their bodies piled on the hated altars. Lesser missions throughout the frontier province also fell, and the outlying haciendas—the major ranches—were destroyed along with their inhabitants. On August 15, Popé and his army of five hundred advanced on Santa Fe itself, killing no fewer than four hundred settlers and twenty-one of the thirty-nine missionaries domiciled there. The garrison assigned to the defense of Santa Fe consisted of only fifty men, who, nevertheless, were armed with a brass cannon. They used this artillery to keep Popé's forces at bay for four days before the city finally fell. Entering Santa Fe on August 21, Popé installed himself in the palace Governor Oterrmín had hastily evacuated. Some twenty-five hundred survivors of the invasion fled downriver, some refusing to stop until they reached present-day El Paso, Texas. Behind them they left all they had owned.

Popé's Rebellion might be counted as one of very few contests between European-Americans and Native Americans in which the latter triumphed. However, unfortunately for the long-suffering Pueblos, Popé no sooner drove the Spanish out than he set himself up as a tyrant whose capacity for cruelty and oppression was at least as great as that of the Spanish. For eight years he plundered and taxed his people. By the time of Popé's death in 1688, the pueblos were in a chronic state of civil war. The year after the tyrant's death, the Spanish reclaimed Zia Pueblo, and in 1692 Governor Don Diego de Vargas exploited the confusion prevailing throughout the pueblos to retake Santa Fe by siege. Within another four years, all of the pueblos had once again submitted to Spanish rule, with the sole exception of the serene Hopis, whom the Spanish, it seems, simply overlooked.

Leisler's Rebellion, 1689–1691

In 1688, after King James II consolidated what had been the Dutch West India Company colony of New Netherland (acquired from the Dutch in 1664) into the Dominion of New England, religious and political unrest shook what was now called New York. Regarded as a kind of subcolony or district of the Dominion of New England, New York was administered by a military lieutenant governor, Francis Nicholson, and a board of councilors, all of whom were subordinate to the dominion governor, Edmund Andros. Into this climate of discontent came news of warfare between England and Holland. On January 10, 1689, Governor Andros issued orders that New York and the rest of the Dominion of New England were to be held for King James II. Shortly after this, word reached colonial officials that the Netherlandish prince, the Protestant William of Orange, had successfully invaded England in the Glorious Revolution and that James II, England's Catholic king, had attempted to flee. Seeking to preserve dominion control of New York, Lieutenant Governor Nicholson attempted to keep news of the flight of James II secret. It leaked rapidly, however, and an uprising was soon organized in New York.

In Boston, the uprising was already well under way. On April 18, Bostonians arrested and imprisoned Andros, together with his council. With this, Nicholson's New York government was shaken to its foundation. Days later, on May 3, 1689, Suffolk County, on eastern Long Island, ousted the officials of James II's government. The Suffolk Militia then advanced on New York City, gathering the support of militia forces from Jamaica and Queens, Long Island, as well as Westchester County, all of which had successfully overthrown the Catholic king's officials.

Preparing to mount his defense of New York City, Nicholson reinforced his regular troops and New York City militiamen, garrisoning Fort James with a contingent of Irish Catholic soldiers who had fled the rebellion in Boston. As would repeatedly prove to be the case, intense friction developed between the regular British troops and the provincial militiamen.

When the Irish Catholic forces were added to the mix, the situation became explosive—even before the arrival of the Suffolk troops. On May 30, when Nicholson reprimanded a militia captain, Hendrick Cuyler, for stationing a sentry without his permission, tempers flared, and Nicholson loudly proclaimed that he would rather "sett the town in fyre" than endure the likes of this insubordination. At these words, the New York militia mutinied and, on May 31, seized Fort James. The militiamen attempted to turn over command of the fort to Nicholas Bayard, one of Nicholson's councillors. When he refused, they turned to the next official in line, Jacob Leisler.

On June 2, Leisler entered Fort James with forty-nine men, vowing to hold it until all of the rebellious forces had joined him there. On June 3, the New York militia captains issued a declaration of their intention to hold Fort James until they had received instructions from William of Orange. They did not have long to wait. On June 4 a ship arrived with official papers declaring the abdication of James II in favor of the Protestant monarchs William and Mary. Nicholson and his council refused to make a public declaration in favor of the new rulers, however, and Nicholson set sail for London on June 11 to present his version of the state of government in New York. Ten days later, a Connecticut militia contingent arrived in New York bearing a printed proclamation of the authority of William and Mary. Leisler made this proclamation on behalf of the New York militia, then tried to persuade New York mayor Stephen Van Cortlandt to make a civil proclamation. When he refused, Leisler assumed responsibility for making the civil proclamation. This served to inflame the passions of New Yorkers, who rioted and attempted to seize Bayard and Van Cortlandt. That pair fled to Albany to organize opposition to Leisler.

Leisler, until now a humble German merchant and mere captain of militia, found himself spearheading a revolution. Under his direction, Fort James became a heavily fortified strongpoint. On June 28, 1689, a revolutionary committee of representatives from all over New Jersey and New York named Leisler "captain of the fort," then, on August 16, elevated him to the post of provincial military commander. On August 20, the revolutionary committee dispatched one Joost Stol to the court of William and Mary to present the rebels' case for wholly revising the government of the colonies. In the meantime, although King William had ordered that all Protestant (but not Catholic) colonial officials appointed by James II would retain their posts, the committee began calling for local elections to bring entirely new officials to office.

The promise of resolution seemed to come in December 1689, when a ship bearing William's letter of instructions arrived; however, this document was ambiguously addressed to Nicholson "or in his absence, to such as for the time being takes care for preserving the peace and administering the laws in His Majesties province of New York." When a conflict developed as to just who should take possession of the letters, Leisler acquired them, summarily assumed Nicholson's title of lieutenant governor, formed a new council, and dissolved the revolutionary committee. For good measure, he arrested and jailed any who might oppose him, including Nicholson's councillors.

All of this was played out against a background of increasing fears of a Catholic backlash in the province of New York. Protestant supporters of William and Mary feared a plot from Catholic partisans of the deposed James II, and, on February 8, 1690, the worst fears suddenly seemed justified when a force of French and Indians descended on the frontier outpost of Schenectady in a fierce lightning raid. Such swift and terrible outbreaks always sent shock waves of alarm through the colonies, but now panic was universal. The hitherto stubborn settlers of Albany immediately capitulated to Leisler, asking for the protection of his government. For his part, Leisler assumed dictatorial powers, immediately ordering the arrest of all Catholics and Catholic sympathizers throughout the province. He convened an assembly to raise money for the defense of the frontier, and he sent appeals to the other colonies to join with his government in a congress aimed at dealing with the French-Catholic threat. This occasioned, in May 1690, the first intercolonial congress held in British North America, attended by delegates from Massachusetts, Connecticut, Plymouth Plantation, and New York. An amphibious offensive against French Canada was planned at the Congress, and Leisler's power, prestige, and authority reached its height.

Yet all was not well for the Leisler government. His man in London, Joost Stol, returned to New York to report that his mission on behalf of the revolutionary committee had not gone well and that Nicholson had been sent back to America, thoroughly vindicated, as governor of Virginia. In June, New Yorkers rioted against Leisler to protest taxation and the imprisonment of his opponents without hearing or trial. Suffolk County, the Long Islanders who had been instrumental in the early days of the insurrection, now deserted Leisler, and the failure of the offensive against Canada humiliated his government. Not only had anticipated Indian allies failed to materialize, but also smallpox had decimated the colonial troops.

Troops under Captain Richard Ingoldsby arrived from England on January 25, 1691, but when the captain demanded that Leisler surrender Fort James, he refused, protesting that he would relinquish the fort only to Henry Sloughter, who had been appointed royal governor of the province. Sloughter, however, had yet to arrive in New York, and the standoff between Ingoldsby and Leisler spread into riotous violence on March 17 as pro-Leisler and anti-Leisler forces vied for control of New York City. Just two days later, however, the belated Sloughter arrived and put an end to the violence by arresting Leisler and his council. They were tried for treason, found guilty, and sentenced to death. Leisler and Jacob Milborne were hanged on May 16, 1691, but the other sentences were commuted, pending the "king's pleasure" in the matter.

In truth, Sloughter now realized that, in executing Leisler, he had created a martyr, and although the fighting had ceased, New York seethed with rebellion and was precariously balanced on the brink of civil war. But it was the moderation of William that staved off outright warfare. In 1692, his court directed that all proceedings against the Leislerians be halted, and in 1695 the king personally reversed the New York court's convictions of Leisler and Milborne, returning to their heirs the properties seized by the colony. All of the others convicted were released. While these actions cooled passions, they did not extinguish them, and Leisler's Rebellion, in and of itself brief and relatively bloodless, remained a source of bitter dispute in New York for the next twenty years.

King William's War, 1689–1697

Shortly after he came to power, England's King William III joined the League of Augsburg and the Netherlands on May 12, 1689, to form the Grand Alliance in opposition to France's Louis XIV, who had invaded the Rhenish Palatinate on September 24, 1688. The resulting war, in Europe, was an eight-year conflict known as the War of the League of Augsburg. Chronic hostilities in the North American colonies were also exacerbated by war between the European mother countries. On this continent, the war was dubbed King William's War, and it pitted the French and the Abnaki Indians *(see First Abnaki War, 1675-1678)* against the English and their Iroquois allies.

Louis de Buade, comte de Frontenac, governor of New France, wanted to invade New York, but lacked the troop strength to do so. Instead, he proposed to fight what he called *la petite guerre,* a little war, using a phrase that would eventually metamorphose into guerrilla war. It was a style of combat that exploited the available military resources: small, stealthy bands of woodsmen and skilled Indian warriors, all "soldiers" who were ready and willing to fight a war consisting not so much of battles as of ruthless murders, committed without warning or mercy, and without distinguishing between combatants and civilians. The French made use, first and foremost, of their Abnaki allies, encouraging them to terrorize the English settlements throughout Maine and New Hampshire. Through the summer of 1689, raiding intensified to such an extent that the English were forced to abandon their posts east of Falmouth, Maine. Boston authorities mustered and dispatched an army of six hundred, but such a conventional military force had little effect against Indian guerrilla fighters, and whereas conventional armies traditionally suspended combat in the winter, Frontenac used the onset of the season to assemble a combined force of 160 Canadians and about 100 Indian allies to exploit the weakness of the English position. His plan was to mount a three-pronged assault from Montréal into New York, New Hampshire, and Maine. After reaching the Hudson via a miserable, frozen trek down Lake Champlain to the southern tip of Lake George, the commanders of the assault force decided to attack Schenectady, which was closer than Albany. On the afternoon of February 8, 1690, after marching across bitterly cold, frozen swampland, they reached the vicinity of the settlement. Attacking after nightfall, they met with no resistance from a village that was "guarded" by nothing more formidable than a pair of snowmen. In the span of two hours, the French and the Indians ravaged Schenectady, killing sixty men, women, and children, most of them in their beds. On March 27, another segment of Frontenac's forces attacked Salmon Falls, New Hampshire, where they killed thirty-four settlers, and in May, Fort Loyal (Falmouth, Maine) was attacked by a combined force of Canadians and Abnakis; almost a hundred English colonists were killed.

On May 1, 1690, delegates from Massachusetts, Plymouth, Connecticut, and New York convened at Albany, where they determined to take the offensive by invading Canada with two land forces from New York and New England, joined by a naval force that would sail up the St.

Lawrence River. The combined assault was led by Sir William Phips. On May 11, 1690, with fourteen vessels, he took Port Royal, Acadia (present-day Annapolis Royal, Nova Scotia), but fared poorly overland. By November, Phips's army, decimated by smallpox, was compelled to withdraw.

In the course of 1690, French forces evicted the English from their Hudson Bay outpost at the mouth of the Severn River, and in 1691 the French retook Port Royal. Nevertheless, Frontenac's "little war" produced nothing but little victories. To be sure, the guerrilla actions spawned much terror, but they accomplished nothing of enduring strategic value. Most significantly, the Iroquois remained loyal to the English, though they paid dearly for that loyalty. Of all the combatants, they suffered the greatest losses in the war.

In September 1691, the superannuated hero of *King Philip's War, 1675–1676,* Benjamin Church, was called out of retirement to lead three hundred militiamen to Saco, Maine, an English outpost that had been the target of repeated attacks. Like the French, Church won no single decisive engagement; however, he did make headway, sufficiently wearing down the Abnakis to bring several sachems to peace talks in October. The result was a formal treaty on November 29, 1691, in which the Abnakis agreed to release captives, to inform the English of any French designs against them, and to refrain from hostilities until May 1, 1692.

Treaty formalities notwithstanding, the dreary pattern of raid and counterraid continued. No sooner had they signed a peace than the Abnakis violated their pledge, joining with Canadians to attack York, Maine, on February 5, 1692. In June it was Wells, Maine, that fell under the hatchet. On June 6 Deerfield, Massachusetts, destined to suffer in war after frontier war, was raided. In January 1693 a French expedition against Mohawk villages in New York was exceptional only in size and strategic effect. Three hundred Mohawks, most of them women, children, and old men, were captured. Many others fled to the Caughnawaga Mission in Canada. This was particularly significant in that the Caughnawagas, although Iroquois, were Catholic converts allied not with the English but the French. The colonial wars between European-Americans were beginning to tear apart ancient Indian alliances and solidarities.

In September 1697 the Treaty of Ryswick ended the War of the League of Augsburg. With this treaty, the conflict officially ended in America as well, although violence continued spasmodically on the frontier.

First Pima Revolt, 1695

In 1695 the Pima Indians of lower Pimeria Alta—encompassing present-day Sonora, Mexico, and southern Arizona—staged a short-lived revolt, which included widespread looting and burning of Spanish property, as well as a campaign of terror against missionaries. Little is known of the uprising other than that it was very quickly put down. Descendants of these rebels carried off the *Second Pima Revolt, 1751,* half a century later.

Second Abnaki War, 1702–1712

The Second Abnaki War (1702–1712) may be considered a phase of *Queen Anne's War, 1702–1713,* or may be considered separately from that conflict. Whereas Queen Anne's War was a widespread conflict, the Second Abnaki War was confined to Abnaki-French attacks on the English settlements of Maine's frontier. In the course of a decade, about three hundred English settlers were killed in towns from Wells to Casco. Abnaki raiding ceased when the English and the French brought the War of the Spanish Succession to an end with the Treaty of Utrecht. Once French support had been withdrawn, the Abnakis found themselves unable to defeat the English and were compelled to sue for peace in 1712.

Queen Anne's War, 1702–1713

Like *King William's War, 1689–1697,* Queen Anne's War was the American theater of a larger European conflict. England, Holland, and Austria, fearful of an alliance between France and Spain, formed a new anti-French Grand Alliance in 1701 after King Charles II of Spain, a Hapsburg, died in 1700, having chosen a Bourbon as his successor. The French supported Charles II's own nominee, Philip of Anjou, a grandson of Louis XIV, as his successor; England, Holland, and Austria gave their support to the second son of Hapsburg emperor Leopold I, the obscure Bavarian archduke Charles. So the War of the Spanish Succession was declared in Europe on May 4, 1702, and, under the name of Queen Anne's War, it spread to the colonies on September 10, 1702, when the South Carolina legislature authorized an expedition to seize the Spanish-held fort and town of St. Augustine, Florida. First a British naval expedition plundered the town;

then, in December, a mixed force of five hundred colonists and Chickasaws assaulted the fort. Failing to breach it, they turned to further pillaging before putting the old settlement to the torch.

South Carolina's actions brought a series of Indian raids in retaliation, to which James Moore, former South Carolina governor, responded
by leading a force of militia and Chickasaws through the territory of the
Appalachees of western Florida during most of July 1704. Moore and his
men killed or captured the inhabitants of seven villages, virtually wiping
out the tribe. They also destroyed thirteen of fourteen Spanish missions in
the country. In contrast to the typical pattern of raid and reprisal in white-
Indian warfare, Moore's vigorous action had profound strategic effect,
opening a path directly into the heart of French Louisiana territory and
the settlements along the Gulf of Mexico.

For their part, the French had been active in recruiting alliances
among the southern tribes. By means of cajolery and bribery, French colonial officials courted the Choctaws, Cherokees, Creeks, and Chickasaws.
The last-mentioned tribe adhered to their English alliance, and the Cherokees managed to maintain a neutral stance. Some bands of Creek Indians
sided with the French, but, by far, France's most powerful ally would prove
to be the Choctaws, who marched to intercept Moore's relentless advance
and successfully blocked him, preventing his passage into Louisiana.

Up north, the French had Indian alliances that were both more
extensive and of longer standing. In the north particularly, English colonial authorities typically treated the Indians with contempt, provoking
and angering them even as French authorities courted and recruited them.
It was the Abnakis who, in the north, proved the English colonists' fiercest
opponents. On August 10, 1703, a party of settlers broke into and plundered the Maine house belonging to the son of Jean Vincent de l'Abadie,
baron de St. Castin. Because his mother was the daughter of an Abnaki
chief, St. Castin was likewise a chief, and the attack on his house touched
off raids along 200 miles of northern New England frontier.

Farther north, in Nova Scotia, Benjamin Church, hero of *King Philip's
War, 1675–1676,* and now so old that he had to be helped over fallen logs in
his path, marched 550 men into Acadian French territory, visiting terror
upon two settlements, Minas and Beaubassin, in July 1704. Above Nova Scotia, in Newfoundland, between August 18 and 29, a mixed force of French
and Indians operating out of Placentia destroyed the English settlement at
Bonavista in a series of raids in retaliation for Minas and Beaubassin.

IN THEIR OWN
Words

They came to my house in the beginning of the onset, and by their violent endeavors to break open doors and windows, with axes and hatchets, awaked me out of sleep; on which I leaped out of bed, and, running towards the door, perceived the enemy making their entrance into the house. I called to awaken two soldiers in the chamber, and returning toward my bedside for my arms, the enemy immediately broke into the room, I judge to the number of twenty, with painted faces, and hideous acclamations. I reached up my hands to the bedtester for my pistol, uttering a short petition to God. . . . Taking down my pistol, I cocked it, and put it to the breast of the first Indian that came up; but my pistol missing fire, I was seized by three Indians, who disarmed me, and bound me naked, as I was in my [night]shirt, and so I stood for near the space of an hour. Binding me, they told me they would carry me to Quebeck. . . .

I cannot related the distressing care I had for my dear wife, who had lain in but a few weeks before; and for my poor children, family, and Christian neighbors. The enemy fell to rifling the house, and entered in great numbers into every room. . . . The enemies . . . insulted over me awhile, holding up hatchets over my head, threatening to burn all I had; but yet God, beyond expectation, made us in a great measure to be pitied; for though some were so cruel and barbarous as to take and carry to the door two of my children and murder them, as also a negro woman; yet they gave me liberty to put on my clothes, keeping me bound with a cord on one arm, till I put on my clothes top the other; and then changing my cord, they let me dress myself, and then pinioned me again. Gave liberty to my dear wife to dress herself and our remaining children. . . .

[Along the three hundred-mile march to Quebec, Williams and his wife became separated. Williams attempted to discover her whereabouts.] I asked each of the prisoners (as they passed by me) after her, and heard that, passing through [a river], she fell down, and was plunged over head and ears in the water; after which she travelled not far, for at the foot of that mountain, the cruel and bloodthirsty savage who took her slew her with his hatchet at one stroke, the tidings of which were very awful.

—FROM *THE REDEEMED CAPTIVE RETURNING TO ZION*, WRITTEN BY DEERFIELD, MASSACHUSETTS, MINISTER JOHN WILLIAMS IN 1706–1707

In the north as well as the south, the war dragged on in a succession of murders, raids, and counterraids. In an effort to achieve decisive victory and break the ruinous cycle of give-and-take, in 1710 the colonies sent a contingent of English-allied Mohawk chiefs to England and the court of Queen Anne. The visit was carefully orchestrated to win sympathy and substantial support for the plight of the colonies. The Indians were carefully arrayed in "savage" attire—by no less than a London theatrical costumer—and they made a court sensation. Queen Anne immediately authorized a contingent of English troops to be sent to the colonies, the land forces under the command of Colonel Francis Nicholson and the naval transports and warships under Sir Francis Hobby. Acting in concert, the land and sea forces reduced Port Royal, Nova Scotia, by October 16, 1710. The following summer, all of French Acadia fell to the British. Flushed with victory, Hobby's subordinate, Sir Hovendon Walker, led another naval expedition, this one aimed at Québec, only to be shipwrecked at the mouth of the St. Lawrence River with the staggering loss of sixteen hundred men. The next year, another move against the French Canadian capital was badly mismanaged and had to be aborted. Yet, by this time, King Louis XIV was war weary and burdened by debt. He was ready to end the war, both in the New World and the Old. Besides, the original source of the conflict, the issue of who would succeed to the Spanish throne, had become moot. In the course of the eleven-year struggle, Archduke Charles, the Bavarian candidate supported by the Grand Alliance, had died, and Louis's grandson Philip of Anjou ascended the throne by default. Fate and nature having taken his side in the matter of Spain, Louis XIV signed the Treaty of Utrecht on July 13, 1713, ceding to the English Hudson Bay and Acadia, but retaining Cape Breton Island and other small islands in the St. Lawrence. The Canadian boundaries, however, remained unsettled and, of course, would prove a source of ongoing contention. As for the Abnakis and other French-allied Indians, they signed a treaty with the New Englanders, pledging to become loyal subjects of Queen Anne.

Tuscarora War, 1711–1712

During the period of early contact, the Tuscaroras, who lived along the coastal rivers of North Carolina, were inclined to be friendly to their colonist neighbors. By the second decade of the eighteenth century, however, their peaceful ways had been rewarded with nothing but abuse, especially at the hands of local white traders. The Tuscaroras were also preyed upon by the Indian allies of the English, the Iroquois, whose raiding parties, descending from the north, ambushed isolated groups of Tuscarora hunters. With seemingly limitless patience, the Tuscaroras endured, always acting to avoid out-and-out war. They saw their best hope in leaving North Carolina for Pennsylvania, but North Carolina's colonial government refused to provide them the required permission to leave. At last, in 1710, came a new provocation. A band of Swiss immigrant colonists organized by an entrepreneur named Baron Cristoph von Graffenried settled on a tract of North Carolina land at the confluence of the Neuse and Trent Rivers. They christened the settlement New Bern. That the land was already occupied by a Tuscarora village disturbed Graffenried not at all, and instead of even making a show of negotiation with the Indians, the baron instead lodged a complaint with North Carolina's surveyor general, eliciting from him an affirmation that, as far as the government of North Carolina was concerned, the Graffenried settlers held clear title to the land. Graffenried drove the Tuscaroras off. In response, on September 22, 1711, a Tuscarora raiding party attacked New Bern and other settlements in the area, killing two hundred settlers, including eighty children. Graffenried himself was captured, but he secured his release, along with the Indians' pledge not to attack New Bern again, by promising to live in peaceful harmony with the Tuscaroras. As was often the case with those who concluded peace agreements with neighboring Indians, however, Graffenried, whether or not he negotiated in good faith, exercised little effective control over his settlers. One of them, William Brice, thirsting for revenge, ignored Graffenried's promise and moved against the local Coree tribe, allies of the Tuscaroras, capturing a chief, whom he roasted alive. The Tuscaroras, as well as the Corees and other, smaller tribes, were provoked to renewed raiding.

Officials of the North Carolina government called on South Carolina for aid. From this colony, Colonel John Barnwell, an Irish immigrant, led thirty militiamen and five hundred Indian auxiliaries, mostly of the Yamasee tribe, in a sweep of the Tuscarora settlements as well as those of their allies. The destruction was extensive and, heartened by victory, Barnwell further augmented his forces with a contingent of North Carolinians, then went on, in March 1712, to attack the stronghold of the Tuscarora "king" known to the English as Hancock. The North Carolina men proved to be unreliable assets, however. When they met fiercer opposition than they had anticipated, they broke ranks in a panic, thereby ruining the assault. Barnwell fell back, and the Tuscaroras offered peace talks. A frustrated Barnwell refused, however, and the Tuscaroras began to torture their captives to death—in full view of Barnwell's men. Faced with this spectacle, his ranks losing their collective nerve, Barnwell agreed to withdraw from the area in exchange for the release of the captives. The Tuscaroras agreed, released the surviving prisoners, and Barnwell returned to New Bern.

On his return, the North Carolina colonial assembly deemed his expedition an abortive failure, and ordered Barnwell and his men back to the front. Barnwell secured a larger force, marched back to Hancock's stronghold, and intimidated the chief sufficiently to extort his signature on a treaty. On his way back to New Bern, Barnwell violated his own treaty by seizing a party of Tuscaroras and selling them as slaves. Thus war was renewed in the summer of 1712, and North Carolina again appealed to South Carolina for help. This time the neighboring colony sent Colonel James Moore with a force of thirty-three militiamen and a thousand Indians. They arrived in November 1712, took on the North Carolina troops as reinforcements, and in March 1713 struck at the principal concentration of Tuscarora warriors. Hundreds of Tuscaroras died in this battle and perhaps four hundred were captured. The proceeds from their sale into slavery, at £10 each, helped defray the cost of the campaign. Many Tuscaroras who escaped death or enslavement fled northward, eventually as far as New York, where they were given asylum among the Iroquois and, in 1722, were admitted into the Iroquois League as its "sixth nation." A smaller faction, led by a chief the English called Tom Blount, remained in North Carolina, signing a peace treaty on February 11, 1715.

Fox Resistance, 1712–1733

In 1722, New York's governor William Burnet vigorously vied with the French for the profitable trade with the Senecas and other Iroquois tribes. Except for the Mohawks, the easternmost Iroquois tribe, which was steadfastly allied with the English, the tribes of the Iroquois confederation generally struggled to remain neutral in the contest between France and

England. By the 1720s, however, they were moving more actively to play one side against the other to achieve a balance of power they perceived as beneficial to them. But in 1729, when a combination of French and Indians, chiefly Ojibwa, attacked the Foxes, whose territory was the western shore of Lake Michigan in the present states of Illinois and Wisconsin, the Iroquois as a whole moved closer to an alliance with the English.

The Fox Indians were far western allies of the Iroquois, who, in their now disintegrating effort to monopolize inland trade *(see Iroquoian Beaver Wars, 1638–1684),* needed all the western allies they could get. Since at least the late seventeenth century, the Foxes had been sporadically at war with the Ojibwa tribe, also called Chippewa, who were concentrated in present-day northwestern Wisconsin. The French, who established profitable trading relations with the Ojibwa, aided that tribe in its ongoing contest with the Foxes. In response, the Foxes repeatedly harassed French traders and raided their frontier outposts. In 1712, the Foxes planned an attack on the French fort at Detroit—an assault that proved destructive but not definitive. Detroit held.

The attack on Detroit marked the beginning of what historians call the Fox Resistance, which lasted from 1712 until approximately 1733. By the 1720s, Fox raiding had become so intense, however, that not only was trade between New France and the Ojibwa disrupted, but also the very lifeline connecting New France in the north with Louisiana in the south—Lake Michigan, the upper Mississippi, and the portages connecting them—was menaced. Realizing that the colony was seriously threatened by Fox hostility, the French met among themselves and with their Ojibwa allies in a series of councils to determine an overall strategy. The most ambitious solution suggested was outright extermination of the Fox tribe. Appealing as this was to many, French authorities thought it impractical and decided instead to round up the Foxes and "relocate" them to Detroit, where the well-armed garrison of the fort could monitor and control their activities. Several French-Ojibwa campaigns were mounted with little success, but by 1729 and especially 1730, the attacks against the Foxes became fiercer. The next year, French-Ojibwa policy turned from the idea of concentration to the original objective of extermination. The Foxes were forced to flee east to territory controlled by the English-allied Iroquois in the hope of finding refuge. Getting to this safe haven was difficult, however, and most who attempted to escape the relentless slaughter were caught and killed.

The great Fox massacre of 1729–1730 ended the Fox Resistance. In one respect, the loss of this tribe was a blow to the English, yet it also served to strengthen the English alliance with the Iroquois.

Yamasee War, 1715–1716

Shortly after Chief Tom Blount signed the treaty of February 11, 1715, formally ending the *Tuscarora War, 1711–1712,* the Yamasee War erupted in South Carolina. Like the Tuscaroras of North Carolina, the Yamasees of South Carolina had freely associated with their white neighbors. Like the Tuscaroras as well, they had suffered many wrongs at the hands of traders and squatters, including land fraud and enslavement. On Good Friday, April 15, 1715, the Yamasees, Catawbas, and other smaller tribes, probably at the instigation of the French, suddenly attacked English settlements north of present-day Savannah, Georgia, which was then under the jurisdiction of South Carolina. Settler cabins were burned, and more than a hundred persons killed. The survivors fled to Charleston, where South Carolina's governor, Charles Craven, quickly mustered his militia. By June he had managed to drive the Yamasees from their villages. In the fall of 1715, Craven pressed the pursuit of the Yamasees, chasing them into Spanish Florida. His militia, merciless, harried the tribe to the point of extinction.

In 1716, Craven employed his Cherokee allies to drive out the small remainder of Yamasees from Georgia, as well as members of the Lower Creek tribe. Although resistance was surprisingly stiff, the Cherokee-English alliance carried the day in this, the final battle of the brief and bloody Yamasee War.

Chickasaw Resistance, 1720–1724

Along with the Cherokee, the English found allies among the Chickasaw, who, like the Cherokee, warred against the French and the French-allied Creeks and Choctaws. The Chickasaw Resistance began in 1720, when the tribe chose to defy French authority by maintaining trade relations with the English and by allowing English traders to "invade" territory claimed by France along the Mississippi River. In an attempt to reassert control, the French incited their Choctaw allies to raid Chickasaw settlements. In turn, the Chickasaw retaliated with raids of their own, not only against Choctaw villages but also against French shipping on the Mississippi, operating vigorously enough to create a trade blockade. For the next four years, the Chickasaw and Choctaw engaged in an ongoing exchange of raids, which were suspended by an armistice concluded in 1724.

Natchez Revolt, 1729

On November 28, 1729, the Natchez Indians, centered a little east of the present Mississippi city that bears their name, rose up against Fort Rosalie, a French settlement and military outpost, killing about two hundred French colonists and carrying out scattered raids throughout the lower Mississippi Valley. Relations between the French and the Natchez had been marked by violence in the past, but open warfare had been averted largely through the efforts of Tattooed Serpent, brother of the Natchez principal chief known as the Great Sun. After Tattooed Serpent died, however, the governor of Louisiana, Sieur Chepart, foolishly ordered the removal of the Natchez from their sacred Great Village, opposite Fort Rosalie on the bluffs of the Mississippi. Despite the pacific counsel of the tribal "queen mother," Tattooed Arm, the Natchez took up the hatchet. Among those taken captive in the attack on Fort Rosalie was the governor, who was clubbed to death.

The French retaliated against the Natchez by dispatching several invasion forces out of New Orleans. The Natchez and the Yazoo Indians, who had joined in the uprising, were decisively defeated in battle. Those captured were sold into West Indian slavery. Survivors sought refuge among the Chickasaws.

Dummer's War (Third Abnaki War), 1722–1727

Dummer's War is known variously as the Third Abnaki War, Grey Lock's War, Father Rasles's War, and Lovewell's War. In theory, warfare between the English and the Abnakis had been ended by the Treaty of Portsmouth, which followed the Treaty of Utrecht, ending *Queen Anne's War, 1702–1713*. Yet neither of these treaties resolved the fundamental land issues that had incited conflict between the Abnakis and the English in the first place. With an ever-expanding English colonial population, these issues were hardly on a course to resolve themselves. Despite new treaties concluded in 1717 and 1719, the Abnakis were enraged by territorial encroachment, the presence of well-garrisoned English forts on their lands, and the abusive and crooked practices of English traders. The friction became so intense that Governor Samuel Shute of Massachusetts at last declared war on the Abnakis, calling them "Robbers, Traitors and Enemies to his Majesty King George."

In contrast to *King William's War, 1689–1697, Queen Anne's War, 1702–1713,* and *King George's War, 1744–48,* Dummer's War remained local, with troops of Massachusetts and New Hampshire pitted against the Abnakis as the New York colony and the Iroquois League looked on without actively participating. Although much of the war consisted of the usual guerrilla routine of raid and counterraid, the English particularly targeted the French Jesuit missionary Sebastian Rasles, who was seen as having incited the Abnaki to continual warfare. Rasles was assassinated by Captain Jeremiah Moulton, who also destroyed Rasles's missionary village at Norridgewock. The death of Father Rasles greatly dispirited the Abnakis, who were further demoralized the following spring when Captain John Lovewell defeated the Pigwackets (Abnaki allies) in the White Mountains and then burned the Indian town at Penobscot. At this, many of the Abnakis fled to Canada, seeking refuge among the French missionaries there.

To the west of this action, in the Green Mountains of present-day Vermont, the English did not enjoy similar success. The war chief Grey Lock led his Missisquoi Abnakis from the Champlain Valley in a number of highly destructive raids along the Massachusetts frontier. In an effort to contain the attacks, the English built Fort Dummer near present-day Brattleboro, Vermont, but the installation did little to abate the attacks. Indeed, Grey Lock continued to harass the frontier even after the eastern Abnakis signed Dummer's Treaty of 1727, which officially ended Dummer's War.

King George's War, 1744–1748

After *Queen Anne's War, 1702–1713,* England and Spain concluded an *asiento,* a contract permitting the English to trade with the Spanish colonies in goods and slaves. When British traders almost immediately abused the privileges granted by the *asiento,* Spanish officials responded energetically. One British captain, Robert Jenkins, claimed that Spanish coast guards cut off his ear during an interrogation. Historians doubt his tale (he probably lost his ear in a barroom brawl), but his countrymen were more than willing to believe him, and in 1739 they declared war on Spain, the "War of Jenkins's Ear."

Within a year, the War of Jenkins's Ear had melted into a much larger conflict. In Europe it was called the War of the Austrian Succession (1740–1748). The death of Holy Roman Emperor Charles VI in 1740 brought several challenges to the succession of his daughter Maria Theresa as monarch of the Hapsburg (Austrian) lands. Eager to lay claim to the Hapsburg territories, King Frederick the Great of Prussia invaded Silesia. France, Spain, Bavaria, and Saxony aligned themselves with Frederick's Prussia, while Britain came to the aid of Maria Theresa. Combat spread to the colonies, where the conflict was called King George's War, after King George II of England.

Reflecting the European hostilities, James Oglethorpe, principal founder of Georgia, invaded Spanish-held Florida in January 1740. Aided in the west by the Creeks, Cherokees, and Chickasaws, none of whom had any love for the Spanish, Oglethorpe captured Fort San Francisco de Pupo and Fort Picolata, both on the San Juan River. He besieged St. Augustine from May through July but was compelled to break off when Spanish forces threatened him from behind. His troops successfully repulsed a Spanish counterattack on St. Simon's Island, Georgia, in the Battle of Bloody Marsh, June 9, 1742, but after Oglethorpe's second attempt to capture St. Augustine failed, in 1743, the Georgia governor withdrew from Florida.

In the north, neither side vigorously prosecuted the American phase of the war until the French made an unsuccessful assault on Annapolis Royal (Port Royal, Nova Scotia) late in 1744. This was followed by the war's only major "set" (i.e., European-style) battle, the British siege of Louisbourg on Cape Breton Island, Nova Scotia. On June 16, 1745, after a siege of forty-nine days, the fort at Louisbourg fell to William Pepperell, who commanded forty-two hundred Massachusetts militiamen. Boasting the greatest concentration of cannon in North America and guarding the approach to the vital St. Lawrence River, Louisbourg was indeed a great prize. But, for the most part, King George's War, like the other colonial wars, consisted not of sieges and formal battles but of guerrilla warfare, much of it using Indian "auxiliaries" to do the fighting. William Johnson, a brilliant guerrilla tactician who enjoyed excellent relations with the Indians, personally financed a series of smaller Mohawk raids against French supply lines and similar targets throughout the balance of the war. Collectively these had a significantly disruptive impact in what amounted to a wilderness war of attrition. For their part, the French-allied Indians made lightning raids on a number of New England settlements. The war intensified by the end of 1745; on November 28–29, the French, with Indian allies, captured and burned Fort Saratoga, New York. Throughout the next year, Indians, again mostly Abnakis, attacked many New England towns. Fort Massachusetts, at the western foot of Hoosac Mountain, fell to an attack by a combination of French and Indians on August 20, 1746. Bereft of the fort's protection, Deerfield, frequent target of Indian raids, was once again exposed to attack, and on August 25 the so-called Barrs Fight occurred in the southwestern part of Deerfield Meadows.

Although the majority of Indians involved in King George's War allied themselves with the French, the English could rely on the Mohawks in the Northeast. Officially the other Iroquois tribes struggled to maintain neutrality, but they, too, inclined generally toward the English. Iroquois neutrality nominally extended to Iroquois-dependent tribes in the Ohio country, preeminent among which were the Shawnees. Nevertheless, a delegation of Ohio warriors came to Philadelphia in November 1747 asking for arms to fight the French. They had been won over not by official agents of any government, but by traders such as the wily, rapacious, and resourceful George Croghan. Toward the end of King George's War, during August and September 1748, Pennsylvania and Virginia officially commissioned another trader, Conrad Weiser, to treat with the Ohio tribes. As a result of his efforts, the Wyandots, whose territory lay just above that of the Shawnees, joined Pennsylvania's celebrated Chain of Friendship, a unique alliance between the Pennsylvania colony and a number of Indian tribes. A few months earlier, on July 20, 1748, the Miamis (also called Twightwees, a name derived from the cry of the crane), from present-day Indiana and western Ohio, had joined the chain. Indeed, King George's War accomplished little for the colonial powers except to establish or to solidify various alliances with Indian tribes and factions. Broadly speaking, in the course of the war, the Iroquois tribes (especially the Mohawks) grew closer to the English, while many of the Algonquian tribes attached themselves—usually with considerable enthusiasm—to the French. Otherwise, no great territories were definitively won or lost, and the peace brought by the Treaty of Aix-la-Chapelle (which ended both the War of the Austrian Succession and King George's War) on October 18, 1748, was little more than an armistice in prelude to the *French and Indian War, 1754–1763 (see chapter 2).*

Second Pima Revolt, 1751

In 1751, the Pimas of upper Pimeria Alta, present-day northern Arizona and New Mexico, many of them descendants of survivors of the *First Pima Revolt, 1695,* fifty-six years earlier, insurgents who had fled north, staged a more successful uprising than their forebears. The leader of the 1751 campaign was a Pima the Spanish called Luis Oacpicagigua, who had earlier served the Spanish masters as captain-general of the western Pimas. He had now come to believe that the incursion of ever-greater numbers of Spanish settlers would force his people into abject slavery on ranches and in mines. Like Popé *(see Popé's Rebellion, 1680),* Luís had a genius for coordinating action, and he managed secretly to unite many Pimas, Papagos, Sobaipuris, and Apaches.

On the night of November 20, 1751, Luís and some of his men killed eighteen Spaniards whom he had been entertaining at his home in Saric. One, however, a Padre Nentvig, escaped to Tubutama and spread the alarm. Nevertheless, during the following weeks, rebels attacked missions and ranches in Caborca, Sonoita, Bac, and Guevavi. While destructive, the raids failed to coalesce into the general uprising Luís had planned. Before long the Sobaipuris and the Apaches backed out of the alliance, and many Papagos and Pimas failed to push the rebellion forward as well. Despite these setbacks, it required the action of a large Spanish colonial force and several months of combat to put down the rebellion. After Luís surrendered, the Spanish exercised wise restraint. Rather than give the Pima cause a martyr by executing Luís, they sought to co-opt him by securing his pledge to see to the reconstruction of the churches that had been ruined during the uprising. In fact, this promise was never kept, and the Pimas never again wholly submitted to Spanish rule. For the next century and a half they waged low-level guerrilla warfare, first against the Spanish, then the Mexicans, and finally the Americans. This contributed to a tradition of virtually institutionalized guerrilla warfare among the Indians of the Southwest, including the Apaches, the Navajos, and the Comanches. The fighting would not definitively end until final defeat of Geronimo in 1886.

CHAPTER 2

The French and Indian War

French and Indian War, 1754–1763

The treaty of Aix-la-Chapelle, which ended *King George's War, 1744–1748,* on October 18, 1748, brought fleeting peace to the American frontier but no enduring stability. On March 16, 1749, King George II granted vast western tracts to the Ohio Company, a powerful syndicate of British traders and speculators, conditioning the grant on the stipulation that within seven years, the company had to plant a settlement of a hundred families and build a fort for their protection. The grant and its stipulation immediately renewed enmity with the French and the Indians, who believed that the new charter would bring an invasion into their lands.

Alliances Old and New

The fears of the French and their Indian allies were entirely justified, for, throughout 1749, an influx of British traders did "invade" territories that had been the exclusive trading province of the French. The traders set about recruiting Indian support against the French in the region. In response to the English activity in French territory, Jacques-Pierre de

Jonquière, marquis de La Jonquière and governor of New France, built Fort Rouillé (at the location of present-day Toronto) to cut off trade between the northern Great Lakes and Oswego, the British stronghold on the southern shore of Lake Ontario in New York. Jonquière also strengthened the fortifications at Detroit and launched a raid against the Shawnees, most powerful among the tribes who traded with the English in the Ohio country. This action, insufficient to do decisive damage to the Shawnees, served only to drive them more deeply into the English fold. For their part, British colonial authorities actively encouraged the aggressiveness of English traders. British negotiators acquired more western land from the Indians. From May to July 1752 the British negotiated a

CHRONOLOGY   French and Indian War

1754: *War begins in May, when George Washington leads a small group of American colonists to victory over the French, then builds Fort Necessity in the Ohio territory. In July, Washington surrenders the fort and retreats.*

1755: *General Edward Braddock arrives in Virginia with two regiments of English troops in February. In July, a French and Indian force defeats Braddock at the Battle of the Wilderness. Braddock is mortally wounded.*

1756: *In Europe, the Seven Years' War begins.*

1757: *In June, William Pitt becomes England's secretary of state and establishes a policy of unlimited warfare.*

1758: *In July, the English are badly defeated at Lake George, New York; nearly two thousand are lost in an attack against French forces* at Fort Ticonderoga. In November, the French abandon Fort Duquesne (Fort Pitt). Settlers rush into the territory vacated by the French.

1759: *French Fort Niagara falls to the English. In the South, the Cherokees ally with the French against the English.*

1760: *In September, Québec falls to the English.*

1762: *England declares war on Spain and successfully attacks Spanish outposts in the West Indies and Cuba.*

1763: *The French and Indian War and the Seven Years' War end with the Treaty of Paris. France yields to England all French territory east of the Mississippi River except New Orleans. The Spanish cede eastern and western Florida to the English in return for Cuba.*

treaty at Logstown (Ambridge, Pennsylvania) between the Iroquois Six Nations, the Delawares, the Shawnees, and the Wyandots on the one side, and Virginia and the Ohio Company on the other, securing from the Indians a quitclaim to the entire Ohio country.

While Miami delegates were engaging in preliminary negotiations at Logstown, news reached them that Pickawillany (present-day Piqua, Ohio), their "capital" and the center of English trade in the Ohio country, had been raided and largely destroyed by French-led Indian forces on June 21, 1752. In response to the raid, Tanaghrisson, chief of the Senecas, westernmost of the Iroquois tribes, requested of the Virginia Logstown delegates that their government build a fort at the forks of the Ohio, the site of present-day Pittsburgh, for the Senecas' defense against the French and their Indian allies. Virginia authorities did not build the fort, nor did they respond to the attack on Pickawillany. The lack of action sent the Miamis back into the French fold, a move that would undo the Logstown Treaty and drive English trade out of the Ohio Valley.

This was a golden moment for the French, and Ange Duquesne de Menneville, Marquis Duquesne, who had replaced La Jonquière as governor of New France on July 1, 1752, lost no time in seizing it. He ordered the construction of new forts to secure the Ohio country and to protect the thin French lifeline extending from Montréal down to New Orleans. This succeeded in thoroughly intimidating the Iroquois, thereby neutralizing a key English ally. English-allied tribes throughout the Ohio country were similarly intimidated. Those tribes that appealed to the English for help in resisting the French were generally turned away. Thus, on the eve of a major war, the English lost most of their Indian allies.

The March toward War

In August 1753, even as England's few precious Indian alliances were falling apart, in far-off London, Lord Halifax, a principal booster of Britain's North American empire, was prodding the cabinet toward a declaration of war against France. Using as his basis the 1713 Treaty of Utrecht, which stipulated an acknowledgment that the Iroquois were British subjects, and bolstering his claims by allusions to Iroquois land deeds from 1701 and 1726, Halifax asserted English rights to Iroquois lands, including those the Iroquois claimed by conquest—that is, the Ohio country. Halifax argued before the cabinet that the French, in trading throughout the Ohio Valley, had committed an act of war by invading

Virginia. Cabinet and crown authorized Virginia governor Robert Din-widdie to take measures to evict the French from territory under his juris-diction. The governor lost no time in commissioning twenty-one-year-old George Washington to carry an ultimatum to Captain Jacques Legardeur de Saint-Pierre, commandant of Fort LeBoeuf (present-day Waterford, Pennsylvania).

Washington set out from Williamsburg on October 31, 1753, with a small delegation. At Fort LeBoeuf, on December 12, 1753, Captain Legardeur politely rebuffed Washington and rejected Virginia's order to vacate. On hearing this, Governor Dinwiddie ordered Captain William Trent to build a fort at the forks of the Ohio. Construction began in January 1754 and proceeded without any interference from the French. Once completed, the fort was garrisoned with a party of troops far smaller than the facility's strategic position warranted.

The War Begins

As spring brought English pressure against French-speaking Acadians in Nova Scotia, the season also saw the French move against the new British fort at the forks of the Ohio. Captain Claude-Pierre Pécaudy de Contre-coeur, latest commandant of Fort LeBoeuf, sent six hundred men against the fort's garrison of forty-one. On April 17, 1754, the garrison prudently surrendered, and Contrecoeur renamed the stronghold Fort Duquesne.

In the meantime, Governor Dinwiddie, on April 17, the very day that the Ohio fort fell, sent George Washington—now promoted to lieu-tenant colonel—with 150 militiamen to reinforce a position that, unknown either to Dinwiddie or to young Washington, the British no longer held.

On May 28 Washington led forty of his provincials and a dozen Indian warriors in a surprise assault on a thirty-three-man French recon-naissance party. In the ensuing combat, ten of the Frenchmen were killed, and the remaining twenty-three surrendered. Washington claimed the first victory of his military career in an encounter that may be considered the first real battle of the French and Indian War.

Aware that the French would likely retaliate in strength, Washington attempted to recruit more Delaware Indian warriors, but could muster no more than forty men. It was apparent to Washington that his force would not stand a chance against the main body of the French, and he organized a full retreat. But it was already too late: The French were too close, and his own troops were exhausted. Therefore, at Great Meadows, in northwestern Pennsylvania, not far from Fort Duquesne, Washington ordered the hasty erection of a makeshift stockade, which, with grim appositeness, he dubbed Fort Necessity.

On July 3, Major Coulon de Villiers led a mixed force of nine hundred—including French regulars as well as Delawares, Ottawas, Wyandots, Algonquins, Nipissings, Abnakis, and so-called "mission" (French-allied) Iroquois—to Great Meadows. Vastly outnumbered, inadequately fortified, and fighting in driving rains that dissolved earthen entrenchments and rendered swivel guns useless, Washington surrendered Fort Necessity on July 4, 1754, after half of his command had been killed. The survivors were permitted to leave, save for two who were taken back to Fort Duquesne as hostages. There the easygoing French, elated with their victory, treated the prisoners as guests rather than captives. Given free run of the fort, Captain Robert Stobo made careful observations of its defenses and even meticulously paced off the fort's interior dimensions. Using friendly Delaware visitors, Stobo managed to smuggle detailed plans of Fort Duquesne to Philadelphia, along with a suggestion that Indian allies be used to attack the fort immediately. Stobo's suggestion went unheeded. Throughout the first four years of this long and costly war, the English showed a dogged contempt for Indians as allies, even as they were dealt one devastating lesson after another from French-allied Indians. The British attitude of contempt extended even further. Not only did regular British officers disdain Indian alliance, they were also thoroughly contemptuous of colonial—"provincial"—troops and their officers. Friction between the mother country and the colonies was political as well. Some of the colonies resisted participation in the war. In New York, for example, powerful mercantile interests, which had long engaged in a profitable smuggling trade with Montréal, refused to cooperate with attempts to meet the French threat. Through a combination of political and strategic inflexibility and shortsightedness and a failure of unifying leadership that squandered solidarity and alliance among Indians and provincials alike, the British crown had put itself at a profound disadvantage during the early years of the French and Indian War.

With the fall of the Ohio fort and the defeat of Washington it was the English, not the French, who suffered expulsion from the Ohio country. In the aftershock of this defeat, the Iroquois, the only Indian allies remaining to the English, wavered. To bring colonial factions into line and to bolster the Iroquois alliance, a panicky congress was convened at Albany from June 19 to July 10, 1754. The Albany Congress not only failed to produce an acceptable plan for unified colonial action but also concluded a poorly thought-out treaty with the Iroquois, which succeeded only in sending the Delaware and other tribes into the arms of the French.

The Indian Alliances Crystallize

Many Indian leaders were well aware that, French or English, the white men intended to take their lands. But they could not ignore the struggle in their midst. The Iroquois, for the most part, with the exception of the staunchly pro-English Mohawks, struggled to remain neutral, whereas most of the other tribes sided in varying degrees with the French. The Delawares and other eastern tribes, having good reason to fear dispossession from their lands at the hands of the English, were fairly reliable French allies. Later in the war, however, when the English deigned to negotiate with them, they did show a willingness to stop raiding. The Delawares were generally supported in the West by the Shawnees. In the Northeast, the Abnakis proved to be extremely loyal to the French. Also reliable were the Ojibwas, Ottawas, and Potawatomis, Ohio country tribes known collectively among themselves as the Three Fires. Their links to French interests included a long tradition of trade and intermarriage. In contrast to the arrogant and parsimonious attitude of the English in Indian affairs, the French were more respectful of Indian culture, more liberal with presents, and showed a high degree of willingness to intermarry. Strictly in terms of trade, however, the French were often at a disadvantage, possessing goods of less variety, less desirability, and greater cost than what English traders generally had to offer. Not that the French approach was entirely kindhearted and openhanded. When gifts and cultural rapport failed, the French pitted one tribe against another, characteristically employing their western allies to menace recalcitrant eastern tribes and bring them into line.

The French used the vast Ohio country as a staging area for raids into the East. Many raids on Pennsylvania, Maryland, and Virginia involving Shawnees, Delawares, and some French-allied Iroquois were staged from Fort Duquesne. In these cases, one or two French officers typically led a group of Indians. Sometimes, however, raids were motivated solely by Indian concerns and were, therefore, led by Indians. This was the case when the Delawares devastated the German settlers of Pennsylvania's

Tulpehocken Valley in revenge for their having driven out the tribe's "royal family."

The Iroquois, as always, were a special case, and alliances with either the English or the French were quite tenuous.

The Regulars Enter the Fray

In December 1754 the crown authorized Massachusetts governor William Shirley to reactivate for service two colonial regiments, about two thousand men. These regiments were to be joined by two of the British army's least reputable regiments, which set out for America in January 1755 from Cork, Ireland, under Major General Edward Braddock, a tough, blustering, courageous, but ultimately dull commander. When the French responded the next month by dispatching to Canada seventy-eight companies of the king's regulars, British authorities expanded the American-bound contingent to seven regiments, some ten thousand men. It was now clear that what had started as a brushfire war in the immediate vicinity of Fort Duquesne was rapidly escalating and would soon be a continental conflict.

Indeed, the French and Indian War was about to become part of an even greater struggle. In 1756, the war that had started in North America began to creep around world. Prussia invaded Saxony; then, in 1757, the Holy Roman Empire declared war on Prussia, which responded by invading Bohemia. Bound by a web of alliances and secret agreements, the French, the British, the Spanish, and the Russians joined what would be known to history as the Seven Years' War. More than thirty major battles were fought in Europe, India, Cuba, the Philippines—and in North America.

Recognizing that France's position as a world power was at stake, the French government in North America embraced escalation by openly authorizing Indian hostility against the British colonies on February 17, 1755. A few days after this, on February

An early twentieth-century depiction of British Brigadier General Edward Braddock's conference with militia colonel George Washington prior to the disastrous Battle of the Wilderness. *Collection: ArtToday*

23, Braddock arrived in Williamsburg, Virginia, and on April 14, in Alexandria, he convened a council of war at which he laid out his plan of attack. He directed that Brigadier General Robert Monckton would campaign against Nova Scotia, while he himself would take Forts Duquesne and Niagara. Governor Shirley, leading provincial forces, would strengthen and reinforce Fort Oswego and then proceed to Fort Niagara—in the unlikely event that Braddock was detained at Fort Duquesne. William Johnson, who enjoyed a high degree of rapport with the Mohawk allies, was slated to take Fort St. Frédéric at Crown Point.

In the meantime, on April 23, 1755, Admiral Edward Boscawen set sail from England for the colonies to intercept an anticipated French troop-transport fleet. That fleet sailed from Brest on May 3, later than the British anticipated, and bad weather hindered Boscawen's operations. On June 8, 1755, he managed to seize only two ships, the *Lys* and the *Alcide*, which, between them, carried about one-tenth of the French expeditionary force. The majority of the French army, then, did land, although Boscawen was effective in delaying the arrival of reinforcements at Fort Beauséjour, the Nova Scotian center of guerrilla resistance against the English.

By May 19, 1755, when Massachusetts rangers set sail from Boston to attack the French forts of Nova Scotia, Fort Beauséjour had already been compromised by a British agent provocateur, Thomas Pichon, who had insinuated himself among the fort garrison and had counseled the men to surrender. Two thousand Massachusetts provincials under John Winslow, together with a handful of British regulars commanded by General Monckton, easily took the fort on June 16, after what was termed a "velvet siege" of four days. Fort Gaspereau, across Cape Chignecto, surrendered the next day without a shot. By the end of the month the British held Nova Scotia except for Louisbourg, the ideally positioned naval base at Cape Breton, which guarded the St. Lawrence River. This formidable fortress was still firmly in French hands.

In July, Acadian representatives refused to submit to the loyalty oath the victorious British demanded. Therefore, on July 28, 1755, Governor Charles Lawrence ordered the deportation of all of Nova Scotia's Acadians. Over the succeeding weeks and months, six thousand to seven thousand in all were sent into exile throughout the colonies, especially in Louisiana, where, after the passage of years, their name would be contracted to the familiar "Cajuns." Following the expulsion of the Acadians, the Micmac Indians, their neighbors, fought a war of resistance against the British, although some did attempt to remain neutral. Neutral or combatant, the Micmacs, like the Acadians, were ultimately dispossessed of their lands.

Battle of the Wilderness

While General Monckton and the Massachusetts provincial forces were achieving success in Nova Scotia, General Braddock was struggling to get his centerpiece expedition to Fort Duquesne under way. He faced two major problems. First, his battle plan called for the recruitment of Indian allies, but, understandably enough, they failed to materialize. Second, like most British regular officers, Braddock was contemptuous of the provincials, and he did not deign to consult the governors on his plan of attack. The result was that the colonies generally resisted war levies and even refused to render the most rudimentary cooperation except for Pennsylvania, which, at the urging of Benjamin Franklin (who was postmaster general of the colony at this time), obtained wagons for Braddock's army and built him a road.

Preparations at long last completed, Braddock finally led two regiments of British regulars and a provincial detachment (under Washington) out of Fort Cumberland, Maryland. It was an unwieldy force of twenty-five hundred men, laden with heavy equipment, which made a wilderness passage all that more difficult. Along the way, French-allied Indians harried English settlements and sniped at the advancing army. After weeks of toiling through virgin forest, Braddock acted on the advice of Washington to detach a lightly equipped "flying column" of fifteen hundred men to make the initial attack on Fort Duquesne, which Braddock believed was defended by no more than eight hundred French and Indians. By July 7 the flying column set up a camp ten miles from their objective.

Fort Duquesne's commandant, Claude-Pierre Pécaudy de Contrecoeur, had been using Potawatomi and Ottawa scouts to observe Braddock's clumsy advance. What he saw discouraged him. Although lumbering, the British force was huge, and it certainly outnumbered Duquesne's defenders. Contrecoeur contemplated surrender, but Captain Liénard de Beaujeu prevailed upon him instead to take the initiative. Beaujeu convinced Contrecoeur to send him at the head of his available force—72 regulars of the French *Marines* (naval forces), 146 Canadian militiamen, and 637 assorted Indians—in a preemptive attack on

Braddock as he approached the fort. On the morning of July 9, 1755, Beaujeu deployed his forces in ravines on either side of Braddock's line of march.

The attack fell swiftly and with total surprise upon the van of the British army. At first, however, Braddock's men reacted well. The grenadiers, his elite troops, effectively returned French fire. After one shot neatly dispatched Beaujeu, his second-in-command, Jean-Daniel Dumas, rallied the French forces and set them about new tactics. Rather than continue to confront the British in the open, he regrouped and deployed his Indians in the trees on either side of the road and on a height overlooking

IN THEIR OWN Words

July 18, 1755

Honored Madam:

As I doubt not but you have heard of our defeat, and, perhaps, had it represented in a worse light, if possible, than it deserves, I have taken this earliest opportunity to give you some account of the engagement as it happened, within ten miles of the French fort, on Wednesday the 9th instant.

We marched to that place, without any considerable loss, having only now and then a straggler picked up by the French and scouting Indians. When we came there, we were attacked by a party of French and Indians, whose number, I am persuaded, did not exceed three hundred men; while ours consisted of about one thousand three hundred well-armed troops, chiefly regular soldiers, who were struck with such a panic that they behaved with more cowardice than it is possible to conceive. The officers behaved gallantly, in order to encourage their men, for which they suffered greatly, there being near sixty killed and wounded; a large proportion of the number we had.

The Virginia troops showed a good deal of bravery, and were nearly all killed; for I believe, out of three companies that were there, scarcely thirty men are left alive. . . . [T]he dastardly behavior of those they call regulars exposed all others, that were inclined to do their duty, to almost certain death; and, at last, in despite of all the efforts of the officers to the contrary, they ran, as sheep pursued by dogs, and it was impossible to rally them.

The General [Braddock] was wounded, of which he died three days after. Sir Peter Halket was killed in the field, where died many other brave officers. I luckily escaped without a wound, though I had four bullets through my coat, and two horses shot under me. . . .

—LETTER FROM GEORGE WASHINGTON, AGE TWENTY-THREE, TO HIS MOTHER, MARY WASHINGTON, DESCRIBING BRADDOCK'S DEFEAT AT THE BATTLE OF THE WILDERNESS the road. The result was complete confusion among the British ranks. Now they could not see the enemy, but knew only that his fire was devastating. The British began firing wildly, often hitting each other. Braddock conducted himself with great courage, combined with his customary incomprehension. He had five horses shot from under him as he set about rallying his troops. But it was to no avail. That the general was learning nothing is attested to by his orders to Washington's Virginians to form up in ranks. Of all the troops, they had been holding their own by fighting like the Indians, from cover. Those who now mustered into European-style platoons were quickly mowed down. At last, Braddock himself was mortally wounded and had to be carried off the field by two provincial soldiers. Of 1,459 British regular and provincial officers and men engaged, only 462 would return from the battle. Washington, though unhurt, had had two horses shot from under him, and his coat had been pierced by four bullets. French casualties were no more than 60 men.

In their panic, the British troops flung away a fortune in arms and ammunition and abandoned their artillery. They also left behind Braddock's well-stocked money chest and, worst of all, his personal papers, which detailed the proceedings of the council of war, including the campaigns proposed against Forts Niagara and St. Frédéric. Hearing of the battle, many Indians, hitherto neutral or even inclined to side with the English, took up with the French and attacked English settlements along the length of the frontier.

Acting on the information found in Braddock's abandoned papers, a jubilant Governor Vaudreuil altered his war plans. He had intended to move against Fort Oswego, on the southern shore of Lake Ontario. Now, learning that Forts Niagara and St. Frédéric would be the objects of English attack, he reinforced these positions, using the cannon the English had left behind in their flight from the Battle of the Wilderness.

Battle of Lake George

While the Pennsylvania, Maryland, and Virginia frontiers were convulsed by Indian raids in the aftermath of the Battle of the Wilderness, William Johnson was encamped at the southern tip of Lake George, preparing, as Braddock had ordered, to move against Fort St. Frédéric. Vaudreuil had sent Jean Armand, baron de Dieskau, with a mixed force of three thousand French and Indians (many of them "mission" Iroquois) to reinforce the fort. Johnson had received erroneous intelligence placing the French numbers as high as eight thousand. In reality, Johnson's forces were about equal to Dieskau's, but he thought he would be fighting a desperate defensive battle rather than the offensive assault originally planned.

But Dieskau decided to act against Governor Vaudreuil's instructions, which were simply to reinforce Fort St. Frédéric against the anticipated English attack. Instead, he now detached about fourteen hundred of his regular and Indian troops, moved out of the fort, and launched a preemptive strike on Johnson's camp. News of his approach reached Johnson late on the night of September 7, 1755. Instead of consolidating his forces in camp, Johnson ordered a thousand militiamen and two hundred Mohawks to reconnoiter the approach. Hendrick (Theyanoguin), chief of Johnson's Mohawk allies, understood that this was a mistake. "If they are to be killed, they are too many," he observed. "If they are to fight, they are too few." Nevertheless, the party left camp at sunrise, as ordered, while the balance of the troops remained behind to fortify the camp as best they could from behind a breastwork built of logs.

Chief Hendrick (Theyanoguin), a Mohawk ally of the British, who was killed in the Battle of Lake George. *Collection: ArtToday*

The reconnaissance column marched into an ambush. Its commander, Colonel Ephraim Williams, was shot dead, as was Chief Hendrick. The party, under withering fire, retreated toward the camp and was met by reinforcements, which managed to check Dieskau's pursuit. Meeting this resistance, the baron retreated to regroup for a final assault on the camp itself.

Fortunately for Johnson's forces, now all collected in the rudely fortified camp, Dieskau was insufficiently daring to make a final, overwhelming thrust. Instead he set up a static line of fire, which had minimal effect. Johnson's return fire, from his fortification, was devastating, especially from his two cannon, which sent balls crashing through the thick forest. The battle went on for more than four hours, until the French lines finally wavered, then broke. At this the English emerged from cover and charged the retreating Frenchmen. Dieskau, wounded, was taken captive.

Instead of adhering to Braddock's plan by advancing to Fort St.

Frédéric after Dieskau's defeat, Johnson began construction of an English fort, Fort William Henry, on the southern end of Lake George. George Washington, returned from the debacle at the Battle of the Wilderness, persuaded authorities to build even more forts between the Potomac and James and Roanoke Rivers, down into South Carolina. The British, who had started the war with the intention of evicting the French from their western lands, now adopted a broad defensive strategy, hoping to prevent the French from pushing them any farther east.

For his part, Governor Vaudreuil also decided to change his war plans. He rejected Dieskau's criticism of his Indian allies. Instead, the Battle of Lake George persuaded him of the strategic necessity of fighting a guerrilla war, making extensive use of Indians and targeting civilians.

Fort Bull and the Supply of Fort Oswego

An abstract of French military dispatches from Canada for the winter of 1755–1756 reported that "the French and Indians have, since Admiral [sic] Braddock's defeat, disposed of more than 700 people in the Provinces of Pennsylvania, Virginia and Carolina, including those killed and those taken prisoner." New York was similarly ravaged, while New England, perhaps more accustomed to Indian warfare, seems to have suffered less. Meanwhile, early in 1756, having failed to take Forts Frontenac and Niagara as prescribed in Braddock's battle plan, Massachusetts governor Shirley retreated to Albany to regroup and, on March 17, dispatched Lieutenant Colonel John Bradstreet to reinforce Fort Oswego, on the southeastern shore of Lake Ontario, which was one of the most important English bases.

It was too late, for the French were already well on their way to cutting the supply line to Oswego. On March 27, 1756, a total of 360 Indians, Canadians, and French regulars under the command of Lieutenant Gaspard-Joseph Chaussegros de Léry attacked Fort Bull, at the western end of the portage between the Mohawk River and Wood Creek, which feeds into Lake Oneida. Great quantities of munitions and stores, all intended for Fort Oswego, were destroyed, and the massacre at Fort Bull was terrible.

Bradstreet responded to this disaster with a swiftness and resolve that astounded the French. In Albany he built 100 new *bateaux* (riverboats) and, with 1,000 men and a total of 350 bateaux, he delivered food and supplies over 160 miles from Albany to Oswego by the end of May, thereby averting collapse of the fort due to starvation. On July 3, as Bradstreet and his men were returning from Oswego, a combined force of about 700

Canadians and Indians ambushed his advance group of about 300. Bradstreet rallied his badly outnumbered troops and charged the attackers, using Indian hatchets as well as European firearms. Stunned by the ferocity of this response, the larger force retreated to the banks of the Oswego River. It was a poor choice of refuge; for, cornered, they could either fight or swim. There was no third alternative. They chose to swim the river, which made them easy targets for Bradstreet's men.

But such British triumphs were rare during the first three years of the war. By June 1756, British settlers in Virginia had withdrawn 150 miles from the prewar frontier, and George Washington moaned to Governor Dinwiddie that "the Bleu-Ridge is now our Frontier."

More British Disasters

On May 11, 1756, Louis Joseph, marquis de Montcalm, arrived in Canada to take charge of French and provincial forces. Less than a week later, on May 17, England officially declared war on France in the start of the Seven Years' War. After successfully supplying Oswego and defeating the ambush, Bradstreet, on July 12, warned his commanders that the vital fort was in grave danger. But Governor Shirley, who respected Bradstreet, had been relieved of command of the provincial forces by Major General James Abercromby, a British regular. Rather than heed the words of a provincial officer, Abercromby excluded Bradstreet from a council of war held on July 16. Furthermore, impatient with the lack of conventional military discipline shown by the "bateaumen" (riverborne frontiersmen) who had fought so brilliantly under Bradstreet, he summarily discharged four hundred of them. They were probably the best fighting men the English had.

Abercromby next ordered Major General Daniel Webb, another regular officer, to prepare his regiment for departure to Oswego. But neither Abercromby nor Webb perceived any need for haste. On July 23, 1756, John Campbell, fourth earl of Loudoun, arrived in the colonies to take overall charge of all British forces, regular and provincial. He reached Albany on July 28 and managed to get Webb moving, at least as far as Schenectady, just fifteen miles away. There Webb spent more than two weeks arguing about contracts for provisions. By August 14, his regiment had reached German Flats (Herkimer, New York), still a hundred miles from Oswego. On that very date, Fort Oswego fell to the French.

Montcalm, with three thousand French and Indian troops, had

invested the fort on August 11. The demoralized garrison put up a feeble resistance, and when its commander was killed by a random cannon shot, the troops surrendered on August 14. The fall of Oswego meant that the British had yielded Lake Ontario to the French, thereby strengthening French communication with Fort Duquesne and the West. It was now out of the question to attack Fort Niagara, and the Iroquois, still officially neutral, inclined more sharply to the French victors. It was a blow even more severe than the defeat of Braddock.

Despite the awful lessons of Oswego, which should have taught the British commanders the value of Indian allies and of provincial troops, Loudoun continued the British military practice of alienating both groups. The highest provincial commanders were to be outranked by any captain of regulars. General Edward Winslow, a commander of provincials, tried to explain to Loudoun that enlisting his men into the regular forces would violate the resolutions of colonial assemblies. Weary of wasting time in argument, he moved his troops to Lake George to attack Fort Ticonderoga, only to have Loudoun recall his forces to protect Albany, even though that settlement was in no immediate danger. On their arrival in the capital, Loudoun decried the "mutiny" among the provincials, discharged and disbanded them, and relieved Winslow of command.

In the meantime, on August 20, having received word of Oswego's fall, General Webb advanced to the portage known as the "Great Carrying Place." There Major Charles Craven was rebuilding some forts, but Webb, noting that Craven's troops were undisciplined and the forts far from completed, panicked. Fearing the advance of the French, he ordered the forts burned (lest they fall into enemy hands), and he withdrew to German Flats without even having sighted the enemy.

Thus 1756 went very badly for the British: Oswego fell, and Webb ran from its defense; Winslow was forced by his own commander to relinquish Lake George; Loudoun spent more time and energy arguing with provincials than he did fighting the French; and the Iroquois neutrals, once inclined toward the English, turned increasingly to the French.

The Ascendancy of Pitt

In December 1756, William Pitt became British secretary of state for the Southern Department, which put him in direct charge of American colonial affairs. Despite halfhearted support from the king and outright opposition from the powerful duke of Cumberland, within three weeks of taking office Pitt ordered two thousand additional troops to Halifax, Nova Scotia, intending to bring the war into Canada through the St. Lawrence Valley and against Québec. The first objective was the always troublesome French naval base at Louisbourg. With its defeat, Acadia would fall, cutting off New France from communication with Europe. While this plan was sound, its execution suffered from massive logistical bottlenecks, which delayed it until August 1757, when the British commanders concluded that the season was too late and the enemy now too strong to attempt an assault on Louisbourg. They withdrew to New York.

In the meantime, in New York, General Webb was camped with four thousand troops near Fort William Henry. Since April he had been receiving intelligence of a massing of French troops at Fort Ticonderoga, but he did nothing about it. July brought further information, making it clear that Montcalm was preparing for an assault on Fort William Henry. Still, Webb failed to act.

Montcalm began his advance against Fort William Henry on July 29. By taking the fort, he hoped to gain control of the so-called Warpath of Nations, the link connecting the ocean, the Hudson River, Lake George, Lake Champlain, and the Richelieu River, which leads into the St. Lawrence. The link between Lake George and Lake Champlain was a vital part of this system. In an effort to gain control of it, the French had built Forts Ticonderoga and St. Frédéric on Lake Champlain, at the northern end of Lake George, and the British had built Fort William Henry at the southern end of Lake George and, south of that, Fort Edward, on the headwaters of the Hudson. For much of the war, armies fighting in the eastern theater faced one another between these sets of forts.

Marquis Montcalm, the brilliant young French commander whose uncharacteristic errors of judgment at the Battle of Québec led to the fall of that city and, ultimately, French defeat in the French and Indian War.
Collection: ArtToday

Even with the information he had been receiving, Webb, according to a contemporary historian of the war, was "struck . . . with such panic, that he resolved to retire to Fort Edward that same night; but with much persuasion was prevailed upon to stay till next morning: when he marched off early, with a strong artillery, leaving the defence of the fort to [Lieutenant] Colonel [George] Monro and Colonel Young with 2,300 men." To be more precise, Webb decamped on August 4, refusing to reinforce the fort and leaving Monro with the advice "to make the best [surrender] terms left in your power." Of Monro's 2,372 men, only 1,100 were fit for duty at the time; the remainder were down with disease and injury. Opposing him, Montcalm commanded 7,626 men, including 1,600 Indian allies.

Webb's surrender advice notwithstanding, Monro and his small band fought valiantly, holding out for a full week before capitulating on August 9, 1757. As he had at Fort Oswego, Montcalm promised the defeated commandant safe conduct for his garrison. As at Oswego, too, the Indians ambushed and slaughtered the departing garrison. Perhaps as many as 1,500 soldiers, women, and children were massacred or taken prisoner after the surrender of Fort William Henry.

The fall of Fort William Henry and the subsequent massacre represented the nadir of British fortunes in the French and Indian War. As William Pitt's military reform policies began to take effect, however, the tide slowly turned. Pitt reversed crown policy by cooperating with the colonists rather than dictating to them, and he ensured that colonial assemblies would have a voice in managing funds used to prosecute the war. In response, Massachusetts, which Loudoun had accused of mutiny, raised a large and effective army. On December 30, 1757, Pitt recalled Loudoun and appointed General James Abercromby as commander in chief of American operations. Abercromby was certainly not a great general, but he was an improvement on Loudoun, and, besides, Pitt reduced the scope of his office so that abler commanders, nominally serving under him, were given more freedom of movement and power of decision. Perhaps most important of all, Pitt sought, rather than shunned, Indian allies, promising them that after the war, Great Britain would enforce a boundary line to restrict white encroachment into their lands.

Pitt personally selected Brigadier General John Forbes, one of his best commanders, to assault—for the third time—Fort Duquesne. In contrast to the thickheaded Braddock, Forbes willingly worked with the Pennsylvania governor and colonial assembly to obtain the supplies and recruit the men he needed for the campaign. Initially, he was also more successful in recruiting Indian allies. However, problems with supply and disputes among commanders delayed Forbes's expedition and made his new Indian allies restless, many of whom abandoned the enterprise. In September an army of five thousand provincials, fourteen hundred elite

Scottish Highlanders, and dwindling numbers of Indians, at last slowly advancing toward Fort Duquesne, bogged down in the rain-soaked quagmire of Loyalhanna (present-day Ligonier, Pennsylvania). As a result of this setback, even more Indians deserted the expedition.

The Indians were not the only impatient warriors. One of Forbes's subordinate commanders, Colonel Henry Bouquet, could stand the waiting at Loyalhanna no longer. On September 11 he ordered eight hundred Highlanders under Major James Grant to reconnoiter in the vicinity of Fort Duquesne. The troops arrived near the fort on September 14 in the dead of night. At dawn on September 15, Major Grant ordered the drums to beat, thinking to inspire and inspirit his men. Whatever effect they had on the Highlanders, they certainly alerted the French to Grant's presence. Suddenly a sortie of French and Indians poured from the fort and overran the Highlanders, killing a third of them, including Grant.

To Forbes, literally stuck in the mud, his Indian allies deserting him, his provincial forces soon to leave as well when their enlistments expired, Grant's defeat came as a terrible blow. Yet this disaster was not an unalloyed triumph for the French. Losses among their Indian auxiliaries were heavy, prompting many Indians to reconsider their alliance with the French. Seizing their plunder, most deserted the fort. When the so-called Far Indians (Potawatomis, Ojibwas, and Ottawas) left the French fold, only the Ohio allies were left. Unknown to the French, these were about to be neutralized by a treaty concluded at Easton, Pennsylvania. In October 1758, the Treaty of Easton returned to the Iroquois western lands the Six Nations had earlier ceded to Pennsylvania. It further stipulated that the Iroquois would freely grant the Delawares—hitherto, for the most part, French allies—the right to hunt and live on these lands. The Iroquois thus became landlords to the Delawares, a position of power that pleased them while providing the Delawares with land west of the Appalachians and Alleghenies. Insofar as the Iroquois were allies of the English, the new relationship also meant peace between the English and the Delawares. This was enforced by a provision that European settlement would not encroach on the returned territory. The Treaty of Easton was the single most important diplomatic move of the war.

The British Fail at Fort Ticonderoga

While French-Indian alliances were crumbling, General Abercromby assembled sixteen thousand troops at Lake George for a march against

Fort Ticonderoga, which the French had renamed Fort Carillon. Abercromby dispatched Bradstreet in advance, and he and his provincials readily overcame the fort's outer defenses. Bradstreet asked Abercromby for leave to attack the fort itself, before Montcalm could call up reinforcements, but Abercromby demanded that Bradstreet await the arrival of the main body of English troops.

It was a fatal decision, for it gave Montcalm ample time not only to bring up reinforcements from Fort St. Frédéric, but also to construct highly effective entrenchments and fascines, using fallen trees and branches much as later armies would employ barbed wire. Even with reinforcements, Montcalm had only three thousand men to defend Fort Ticonderoga, but he had transformed it into a formidable position.

The British, nevertheless, also occupied a key position. They held the high ground, called Mount Defiance, which made Fort Ticonderoga vulnerable to artillery—had Abercromby chosen to put artillery there. Instead, however, he stationed William Johnson and four hundred Mohawks atop Mount Defiance—a position from which they could never even be committed to battle.

Johnson's lofty perch did give him a fine view of the debacle that unfolded when Abercromby attacked on July 8. If Abercromby had fatally delayed while waiting for his forces to assemble, he now blundered into action prematurely. Instead of waiting for the main body of his artillery to arrive—for, even poorly placed, cannons could have blasted away at the French lines—he sent his regulars against Montcalm's defenses in a series of bayonet charges. Montcalm, who had been prepared to retreat, now found that his greatly outnumbered forces could simply mow down the charging Highlanders. In a series of bayonet charges, 464 British regulars fell dead and 1,117 were wounded, while provincial losses numbered 87 dead and 239 wounded. The French, outnumbered more than five to one, lost 112 officers and men, with 275 wounded. Abercromby could do no more than retreat to Albany with his stunned and demoralized army.

Louisbourg and Fort Frontenac
Fall to the English

Ticonderoga was to be the last major French triumph of the war, however. On July 26, 1758, Major General James Wolfe and Brigadier General Jeffrey Amherst, transporting a force of 9,000 regulars and 500 provincials in a fleet of 40 ships, at long last took Louisbourg, Nova Scotia.

At the end of the next month, Bradstreet assembled a provincial task force—1,112 men from New York, 675 from Massachusetts, 412 from New Jersey, and 318 from Rhode Island, supplemented by 300 bateaumen, 135 British regulars, and 70 Iroquois—to seize Fort Frontenac, near present-day Kingston, Ontario. The objective seemed so formidable that when they learned of it, the Iroquois contingent promptly deserted.

Actually, Fort Frontenac was nearly defenseless. Governor Vaudreuil and General Montcalm had withdrawn most of its garrison to Fort Ticonderoga in anticipation of a renewed assault there. Although he did not know it, Bradstreet and his 3,000 men surrounded a mere 110 inmates of the fort, including men, women, and children. Fort Frontenac fell on August 27, after a token resistance of two days. Bradstreet captured 60 precious cannon and 800,000 livres' worth of provisions. With the loss of Frontenac, the French lifeline to Forts Niagara and Duquesne was severed. The French now relinquished control of Lake Ontario to the English, and Bradstreet took possession of a nine-vessel French fleet, loading two ships with booty and burning the rest.

British general James Wolfe, who fell at the Battle of Québec, but lived long enough to learn that he had succeeded in taking the city.
Collection: ArtToday

The Fall of Fort Duquesne

Fort Duquesne, to which General Forbes was slowly drawing closer, was now without a source of artillery and supplies. François-Marie Le Marchand de Lignery, the fort's commandant, aware that he would soon be forced to release his militiamen from Illinois and Louisiana, as well as his dwindling Indian allies, launched a desperation raid on Forbes's position at Loyalhanna on October 12, 1758. Repulsed, Lignery retreated to the fort, his few remaining Indian allies now badly shaken. One month later he launched another raid. While chasing this force off, Forbes captured three prisoners, who revealed just how weakly Fort Duquesne was held. On November 24, as Forbes's army was preparing to move out of Loyalhanna, they heard a distant explosion. Sending what remained of his garrison downriver to Illinois country, Lignery had blown up Fort Duquesne and retired to Fort Machault (present-day Franklin, Pennsylvania) to plan a counterattack. When Forbes's army at last marched into Fort Duquesne, they found it gutted and deserted. The heads of Highlanders captured earlier had been skewered atop stakes, the soldiers' kilts tied below.

Ruined or not, Fort Duquesne was a great prize, for the nation that controlled the "forks of the Ohio" controlled the gateway to the West. Forbes renamed Duquesne Fort Pitt and, having taken it, he now had to garrison and hold it. Massive troop desertion soon left Fort Pitt with a garrison of only two hundred men, far too few to withstand a determined counterattack. Indian allies, who traditionally disliked the static warfare a fort represented, were also certain to melt away, unless they could be plied with presents. Through the good offices of Israel Pemberton, a Philadelphia merchant and Quaker pacifist, Forbes received £1,400 worth of gifts, and another £3,000 soon followed. They came just in time to steady the Indians' resolve.

The "Year of French Disaster"

The year 1759 would prove disastrous for the French. Pitt proposed a rationally conceived three-pronged campaign against the French, which included the capture of Fort Niagara and the reinforcement of Fort Oswego to sever the West from the St. Lawrence River. Second, the plan called for a strike through the Lake Champlain waterway into the St. Lawrence Valley. Third would be an amphibious assault on Québec itself.

Early in the year the Fort Pitt garrison was expanded to 350 as Brigadier General John Stanwix prepared to use the fort as a base for a 3,500-man force to operate throughout the Ohio country. In February, William Johnson proposed an expedition against Fort Niagara via the country of the Six Nations. Indian allies could be acquired along the way. In April, the Seneca, the Iroquois tribe most inclined toward the French, at last became discouraged by the failure of the French to provide satisfactory trade goods. Accordingly, in April they proposed to assist the English in an attack on Fort Niagara. That same month, the Oneida chief Conochquieson told William Johnson that all the Six Nations were "ready to join and revenge both Your Blood and ours upon the French."

While Johnson set about gathering more allies for the assault on Niagara, General Wolfe prepared to take Québec. On May 28, 1759, Rear Admiral Philip Durrell landed a detachment on the Ile-aux-Coudres, in the St. Lawrence River northeast of Québec. His troops advanced downriver to Île d'Orleans, nearer to Québec, to await the main amphibious force under Wolfe and Vice Admiral Charles Saunders, which landed on June 27. By July, Wolfe's army of nine thousand men was in possession of the northern shore of the St. Lawrence above Québec. Montcalm attempted to burn the British fleet at anchor by chaining rafts together, setting them ablaze, and sending them downriver, but British seamen in small boats managed to repel these assaults.

For the next two and a half months, Wolfe probed Québec's defenses without success. Failing to penetrate, the British commander turned to terrorism against the civilian population, bombarding the city day and night with his artillery, purposely concentrating his fire on residential rather than military targets. For his part, Montcalm was no less ruthless. When, after weeks of siege and bombardment, the citizens of Québec expressed their desire to surrender, the general threatened to turn his Indians loose upon them.

While the siege of Québec ground on, General Amherst decided to put the Niagara command in the hands of a regular army officer, Brigadier General John Prideaux, with William Johnson as his second-in-command. On July 8, Prideaux presented Niagara's commandant, Captain Pierre Pouchot, with a demand for his surrender. Pouchot pretended not to understand English, and the siege commenced.

Pouchot appealed to Lignery, now at Fort Machault, for reinforcements. Lignery had been assembling a force of a thousand for a counterattack on Fort Pitt, but he now abandoned his assault in order to relieve Niagara. In the meantime, at Fort Niagara, as the British forces prepared for the assault, an accidental shot from one of his own guns killed Prideaux on July 19. Over the protest of Lieutenant Colonel Eyre Massey, a regular army officer, William Johnson assumed command. At this point, news of Lignery's approach reached Johnson. Whether by Johnson's order or of his own volition, Massey took charge of a position held by New York captain James De Lancey, who had erected barricades against Lignery's approach. While Indian allies—six hundred Mohawks under the command of nineteen-year-old Joseph Brant and apparently operating independently of Johnson and Massey—attacked from the sides of the road, De Lancey led a bayonet charge against Lignery as Massey ordered a volley of fire. "We killed 200 and took 100 prisoners," De Lancey reported. Among the prisoners were five senior officers. Pouchot capitulated, and Niagara fell to the British on July 23. On July 26 the French, outnumbered by Jeffrey Amherst, unceremoniously abandoned and blew up Fort Ticonderoga. Amherst moved against Fort St. Frédéric next, taking it on July 31.

The French retreated down the Richelieu River. Québec, however, remained unbreached.

During the summer of 1759, Wolfe made several unsuccessful and costly attempts to storm Québec. But it wasn't until September 12 that Wolfe managed a stealthy approach to the Plains of Abraham, the high ground above the city. General Montcalm did not anticipate an attack from this direction and fortified another position, at Beaumont. At daybreak on September 14, Montcalm, his troops, and the citizens of Québec were astonished to see an army forming battle lines on the Plains of Abraham. The French commander could have attacked while Wolfe's mustering forces were still relatively small, but he waited until he had brought up his men up from their position at Beaumont. Yet he did not wait for additional reinforcements from Cap Rouge. The result was that Montcalm ended up ordering a charge against the advancing British that was simultaneously too late and premature. He committed forty-five hundred troops, mostly colonials, to battle. The British held their fire until the last possible moment. Then they delivered it into the poorly organized French ranks with devastating effect.

After months of failed assaults, the climactic battle was over in a quarter of an hour, leaving two hundred French troops dead and another twelve hundred wounded. British losses were sixty dead and another six hundred wounded. Among the fatalities on either side were the two commanders, Montcalm and Wolfe.

By the time the comte de Bougainville arrived with reinforcements, the British forces were securely ensconced on the high ground, and the fresh French troops were compelled to withdraw. Québec formally surrendered on September 18, 1759, effectively bringing to an end French power in North America.

Thayendanegea, known to the English as Joseph Brant, was a Mohawk warrior allied to the British in the French and Indian War. He would emerge as a major British ally in the American Revolution as well. This image was engraved from the portrait George Romney made in 1774, after Brant visited England. *Collection: National Archives and Records Administration*

War Ends, Fighting Continues

The fall of Québec had decided the war, but the fighting did not end. The French still held Montréal and the Richelieu River as far as Île-aux-

Noix, at the bottom of Lake Champlain. Britain's commander in chief, Jeffrey Amherst, could have pushed his advantages, but, always cautious, he chose instead to consolidate his positions, and the winter passed without event.

In the meantime, all was not well in Québec. While fewer than 250 English soldiers died during the siege of the city, 1,000 succumbed to disease while garrisoning it, and another 2,000 became unfit for service. After the long siege and the effects of Wolfe's policy of laying waste the countryside, there was little left in Québec to sustain an occupying force. Hauling parties sent to gather precious firewood were subject to attack from Indians still faithful to the French. General James Murray, commanding the garrison, made attempts to foil the mounting French effort to retake the capital, but in May 1760 he was badly beaten in a battle before the city. One thousand of his men—a third of his troops fit for service—were killed before he finally retreated into Québec, where he and his men now endured a French siege until the arrival of the British fleet relieved them.

Final Phases

From this point on, the British steadily gained ground, as William Haviland, marching from Crown Point (the former French Fort St. Frédéric), captured Chambly on September 1, 1760, and Amherst and Murray joined forces in an assault on Montréal. On September 8, 1760, Governor Vaudreuil surrendered the province of Canada. Nevertheless, the French fought on, in hopes of salvaging something they could bring to the peace table; however, much of the action throughout the remainder of the war was less between the English and the French, aided by their Indian allies, than between the English and various groups of Indians.

During 1760, having promised the Delawares and the Shawnees that the English had no intention of occupying their lands, Amherst nevertheless built more forts in the West. The Senecas had come over to the English side to rid themselves of the French. Now Amherst began granting land—Seneca land—to his officers as a reward for faithful service. The Ottawas, Potawatomis, and Ojibwas also had reason for alarm, first over the ever-growing presence of the English at Fort Pitt and then at Detroit. On September 12, 1760, Amherst ordered Major Robert Rogers, celebrated as the heroic guerrilla leader of his famous Rangers, to take actual possession of Detroit, Fort Michilimackinac (on Michigan's Upper

Peninsula), and other western outposts formally ceded to the English after the fall of Montréal.

As the British took over Detroit, the local Indians ostensibly renounced their loyalty to the French. The Senecas, however, were wary and resentful of the continued and increasing British presence at Niagara. At last the Senecas consulted with other Iroquois League chiefs at Onondaga to plan a coordinated uprising. On July 3, encouraged by local Frenchmen, two Seneca chiefs bore a war belt to Indians in the vicinity of Detroit, inviting the western tribes to join them in resisting the English. The Detroit Indians rejected the belt and disclosed the planned rebellion to the commandant of Fort Detroit. At this point William Johnson, long a supporter of the Iroquois Six Nations, decided that with the French defeated, the Indians had become a threat rather than an asset. Accordingly, he set about stirring up intertribal discord.

In the meantime, in the Northeast, the British had concluded a treaty with the pro-French Micmac Indians in Nova Scotia. The crown craved peace with the Indians, for fighting them was an expensive undertaking. Royal policy notwithstanding, Nova Scotia's governor, Jonathan Belcher Jr., feigned compliance with the crown's directive while simultaneously usurping the land of the local Micmacs. Resentment seethed among the Indians.

Spain's Last-Minute Entry and the Treaty of Paris

Spain belatedly joined the Seven Years' War in Europe on the side of France, and England declared war on the new combatant on January 2, 1762. British sea power rapidly prevailed against Spain. On February 15, 1762, the French island of Martinique fell to the English, followed by St. Lucia and Grenada. On August 12, 1762, Havana yielded to a two-month siege, and Manila fell on October 5. On November 3 France concluded the secret Treaty of San Ildefonso with Spain, in which France ceded to Spain all of its territory west of the Mississippi as well as the isle of Orleans in Louisiana. These cessions were by way of compensation for the loss of Spain's Caribbean holdings. With the Treaty of Paris, concluded on February 10, 1763, France ceded all of Louisiana to Spain and the rest of its North American holdings to Great Britain. Spain recovered Cuba (in compensation for the loss of territories in Florida and in the Caribbean), and France retained the Caribbean islands of Guadeloupe, Martinique, and St. Lucia. The treaty at last ended both the American and the

European phases of the Seven Years' War; however, discontent among the Indians of the frontier regions ensured that while the French and Indian War was over, warfare would continue sporadically and chronically.

Cherokee Uprising of 1759–1762

The Indians of the northern Great Lakes were not the only formerly French-allied faction spoiling for continued war; at about the time that Québec was taken, trouble began to erupt in the South. The Cherokees had been English allies since South Carolina governor Charles Craven had concluded a treaty with them, by which they supplied warriors in exchange for a commitment from the colonials to defend, in their absence, their families against the Creeks and the Choctaws. With this commitment came several frontier forts and outposts, so that the promise of defense was now perceived as a threat of encroachment. The Indians knew the apparently inevitable sequence of events all too well: Forts were built, settlers followed, the Indians were pushed away.

In 1758 a group of Cherokee warriors, slowly making their way home after abandoning General Forbes's long campaign against Fort Duquesne, seized some wild horses. A group of Virginia frontiersmen encountered the Indians, claimed the horses were theirs, and attacked the party. Twelve Cherokees were killed. The frontiersmen then not only sold the horses but also collected bounties on the Cherokee scalps, claiming that they had been taken from hostile Indians. The Cherokees retaliated, killing twenty to thirty settlers. Soon the southern frontier was swept by a full-scale uprising that would require two armies and two years to put down.

Colonel Archibald Montgomery and his Scottish Highlanders conducted the first campaign, which met with heavy and highly effective guerrilla resistance led by the Cherokee war chief Oconostota. A larger army, consisting of Carolina Rangers, British light infantry units, Royal Scots, and Indian allies, next swept through Cherokee country, bringing total war to warriors as well as their families. After a relentless round of crop and village burning, the Cherokees finally capitulated in the winter of 1762, ceding much of their eastern land and agreeing to a boundary separating them from the English settlers. The boundary would not endure for long.

Pontiac's Rebellion, 1763–1766

Within a few days of the Treaty of Paris formally ending the *French and Indian War, 1754–1763,* the Ottawa tribe, led by Chief Pontiac, together with leaders from other tribes, most notably the Delawares, the Iroquois (principally the Senecas), and the Shawnees, began a series of attacks on the western outposts the French had just officially relinquished to the English. This was a general Indian uprising in the Old Northwest, but the influence of the enormously popular, if often unreliable, nineteenth-century historian Francis Parkman affixed the label "Pontiac's Rebellion" to the entire violent episode. Pontiac, while important, was actually only one among several Indian leaders who cooperated in an attempt to resist English encroachment on their land. The so-called rebellion, spanning 1763 to late 1764, included Delawares, the Iroquois (principally the Senecas), and the Shawnees in addition to the Ottawas.

The source of the conflict can be traced to the fall of Detroit to the British on November 29, 1760, and General Jeffrey Amherst's decision to abolish the custom of giving gifts to the Indians. He was particular about cutting off their supply of ammunition, which made hunting difficult or even impossible. In contrast to the English, the French had always been liberal with gifts, and the sudden loss of arms and ammunition would likely mean starvation and death.

In the wake of Amherst's edict ending the flow of gifts, a prophet arose among the Delawares, counseling the Indians to reject all the ways of the white man and return to a pure Indian life, the way of the ancestors. Although the prophet charged his listeners to keep the peace, traders and agents in the vicinity of Detroit were worried. The so-called Delaware Prophet was one more instance of Indian discontent and "conspiracy." In 1763, however, as soon as France had capitulated in the *French and Indian War, 1754–1763,* ceding virtually all of its territory to Britain—without consulting any Indian allies concerning these cessions—the Indians in the vicinity of

A late nineteenth-century depiction of Pontiac, an Ottawa chief who was among the leaders of a costly Indian "uprising" immediately after the close of the French and Indian War.
Collection: ArtToday

95

Detroit were roused to "rebellion" again. Pontiac called a grand council on April 27, 1763, urging the Potowatomis and the Hurons to join his Ottawas in a joint attack upon Detroit. Four days later, Pontiac visited the fort with a group of his warriors, ostensibly to entertain the garrison with a ceremonial dance. His real purpose was to size up the outpost's defenses. On May 5 Pontiac outlined his plan of assault: The Indians would conceal muskets, tomahawks, and knives under their blankets. Once they were inside the fort, the attack would begin. The operation was scheduled for May 7, but was thwarted by an informant whose identity is unknown. Fort Detroit's garrison of 120 Royal Americans and Queen's Rangers was prepared for Pontiac's entrance on the appointed day. The chief came with 300 warriors, each with a blanket thrown over his shoulder, but he quickly realized that he had lost the element of surprise. Though he outnumbered the garrison two to one, Pontiac aborted his plan and withdrew from the fort.

Yielding to pressure from some of the warriors, who accused him of cowardice, Pontiac tried to enter the fort again on May 8, but garrison commander Henry Gladwin told him that he would admit only the chiefs, no warriors. Wishing to create an aura of innocence, the chief organized an intertribal game of lacrosse just outside the fort. At the game's conclusion, Pontiac told Gladwin that he and his warriors would be back the next day for counsel, whereupon the commandant announced again that he would admit only the chiefs.

Frustrated again, and again pressured by his warriors, Pontiac began raiding the settlers in the vicinity of the fort. Next, Pontiac's Ottawas, joined by Wyandots, Potowatomis, and Ojibwas, began firing into the fort. After some six hours the attackers, exhausted, backed off. Five of Gladwin's men had been wounded; few of the Indians had been hurt. Following this battle, on May 10, Pontiac conferred with other Indians and local Frenchmen. The French counseled a truce, and Pontiac allowed that he, too, desired peace. Pontiac dispatched some of the Frenchmen and four Indian chiefs to the fort with a request that Captain Donald Campbell be sent out to negotiate. Gladwin did not trust Pontiac and refused to order Campbell to go; the captain, however, volunteered, reassured by the French that he would be treated as an ambassador. No sooner was Campbell outside the fort, however, than he was seized by the Indians and held hostage. On May 11, Pontiac ordered Gladwin and his garrison out of Fort Detroit, telling him that it would be stormed by fifteen hundred warriors within an hour. Gladwin refused, and about six hundred Indians opened fire on the fort, maintaining the assault until after seven in the evening. Again Pontiac demanded surrender; again Gladwin refused, declaring that he would discuss no terms of settlement until Campbell was released. In the meantime, Indian parties continued to ambush and raid settlers in the vicinity of the fort, and Pontiac sent war belts to the Miamis and to the French in Illinois country, inviting their support.

The French, however, were no longer confident of Pontiac's ability to control his warriors. Reports were being received from French farmers, who complained of harassment at the hands of Indians allied to Pontiac. In an eloquent speech to a delegation of French settlers, the chief apologized for the actions of some of his followers and pledged his undying loyalty to France. He managed to win enough support to make war in earnest. Events proceeded rapidly—and violently.

During early June, after the fall of Michilimackinac and a number of other forts, attacks began farther east. Forts Pitt, Ligonier, and Bedford in Pennsylvania were all besieged, but they managed to hold out. About

IN THEIR OWN *Words*

From a letter from Col. Henry Bouquet to Gen. Jeffrey Amherst:

P.S. I will try to inocculate the Indians by means of [smallpox-contaminated] Blankets that may fall in their hands, taking care however not to get the disease myself.

As it is pity to oppose good men against them, I wish we could make use of the Spaniard's Method, and hunt them with English Dogs. Supported by Rangers, and some Light Horse, who would I think effectively extirpate or remove that Vermine.

H.B.
13 July 1763

Amherst's reply to Bouquet, July 16, 1763:

P.S. You will Do well to try to Innoculate the Indians by means of Blankets, as well as to try Every other method that can serve to Extirpate this Execrable Race. I should be very glad your Scheme for Hunting them Down by Dogs could take Effect, but England is at too great a Distance to think of that at present.

June 16, 1763, Senecas killed the entire fifteen- or sixteen-man garrison at Fort Venango (Franklin, Pennsylvania), except for the commandant, a Lieutenant Gordon, whom they forced to write (from dictation) a list of grievances addressed to the king of England. Following this, after three days of torture, Gordon likewise died. On June 18, the Senecas moved on to Fort LeBoeuf (present-day Waterford, Pennsylvania) and burned it, killing six or seven of the thirteen-man garrison. Joined by Ottawas, Hurons, and Ojibwas, the Senecas attacked Fort Presque Isle (Erie, Pennsylvania) on June 20. The Indians put the fort to the torch, and thirty soldiers surrendered on a pledge that they would be given safe conduct to Fort Pitt. Despite their promise, the Indians divided up the defeated men among the four tribes as prisoners.

When a group of Delawares demanded the surrender of Fort Pitt on June 24, Simon Ecuyer, commanding in the absence of Colonel Henry Bouquet, refused. General Amherst ordered Bouquet to commit an act of germ warfare by disseminating smallpox among the Indians. Bouquet, in turn, ordered Ecuyer to summon Delaware chiefs to the fort for a conference. There Ecuyer presented them with a handkerchief and two blankets from the fort's smallpox-ridden hospital. Not only did the attackers soon retreat, but also a rescued white captive of the Delawares later reported that the disease was epidemic in the tribe.

Fort Niagara endured a Seneca siege and was never taken. Detroit also survived siege—five months of it, from May to September—at the hands of the Ottawas, Ojibwas, Potawatomis, Hurons, Shawnees, Delawares, and Eries.

In the meantime, Colonel Bouquet was leading Fort Pitt's relief column, about 460 men, including Highlanders of the famous Black Watch regiment. On August 5, when they were within thirty miles of Pittsburgh, at a spot called Edge Hill, a party of Delawares, Shawnees, Mingos, and Hurons ambushed the column's advance guard. Bouquet's forces held the high ground throughout the long afternoon of battle, but they were surrounded. Bouquet, however, had a plan. He planted a thin line of men along the crest of Edge Hill, so that when the sun came up on August 6, the Indians would be tempted by the sight of a weakly held position. The gambit worked. Seeing the soldiers, the Indians made a radical departure from their accustomed fighting style. Abandoning the stealthy tactics of forest warfare, they rushed into the open to charge the English position, breaching the line with little trouble. Then they discovered that Bouquet had hidden in reserve two full companies, which now smashed into the attackers. Losses were probably equal in number—for Bouquet it was fifty men killed and sixty wounded—but the Delawares also lost two chiefs and, having failed to stop the relief column from reaching Fort Pitt, gave

IN THEIR OWN *Words*

King George III's Proclamation of 1763

. . . *A*nd whereas it is just and reasonable, and essential to our Interest, and the Security of our Colonies, that the several Nations or Tribes of Indians with whom We are connected, and who live under our Protection, should not be molested or disturbed in the Possession of such Parts of Our Dominions and Territories as, not having been ceded to or purchased by Us, are reserved to them or any of them, as their Hunting Grounds—We do therefore, with the Advice of our Privy Council, declare it to be our Royal Will and Pleasure that no Governor or Commander in Chief in any of our Colonies of Québec, East Florida or West Florida, do presume, upon any Pretence whatever, to grant Warrants of Survey, or pass any Patents for Lands beyond the Bounds of their respective Governments as described in their Commissions: as also that no Governor or Commander in Chief in any of our other Colonies or Plantations in America do presume for the present, and until our further Pleasure be known, to grant Warrants of

Survey, or pass Patents for any Lands beyond the Heads or Sources of any of the Rivers which fall into the Atlantic Ocean from the West and North West, or upon any Lands whatever, which, not having been ceded to or purchased by Us as aforesaid, are reserved to the said Indians, or any of them. . . . And whereas great Frauds and Abuses have been committed in purchasing Lands of the Indians, to the great Prejudice of our Interests, and to the great Dissatisfaction of the said Indians: In order, therefore, to prevent such Irregularities for the future, and to the end that the Indians may be convinced of our Justice and determined Resolution to remove all reasonable Cause of Discontent, We do with the Advice of our Privy Council strictly enjoin and require that no private Person do presume to make any purchase from the said Indians of any Lands reserved to the said Indians, within those parts of our Colonies where We have thought proper to allow Settlement. . . .

Given at our Court at St. James's the 7th Day of October 1763, in the Third Year of our Reign.

God Save The King

99

up a decisive battle. History would record it as the Battle of Bushy Run, named for the stream beside which Bouquet was camped.

The siege of Detroit was lifted in September, and on October 3, 1763, Pontiac at last agreed to a peace in return for a pledge (embodied in King George III's Proclamation of 1763) that English settlement would stop at the Allegheny Mountains. This limit became known as the Proclamation Line. While he was a key participant in the rebellion, Pontiac was not the "supreme commander" of a centrally controlled movement. So, while he signed a treaty, other Indians involved in the uprising sporadically continued hostilities for another year.

Pontiac's Rebellion was an intensely violent coda to the *French and Indian War, 1754–1763.* According to a contemporary estimate, two thousand English civilians and more than 400 soldiers were killed. No one knows how many Indians died, especially when the ravages of smallpox are taken into consideration.

CHAPTER 3

The American Revolution

Regulators' Revolt, 1771

After the English victory in the *French and Indian War, 1754–1763 (see chapter 2),* many Americans felt great pride in being part of the mighty British Empire. For many, however, the good feelings were soon vanquished by the series of taxes and duties the crown imposed on the colonies in an attempt to recoup some of the expense of the long wilderness war. The towns of New England, especially Boston, harbored the strongest streak of radicalism and ultimately agitated for and organized the Revolution. In the frontier regions, much of the population was Tory in sympathy, loyal to the crown; however, much of the frontier was chronically disaffected, feeling that the East Coast centers of government—and, by extension, the mother country across the Atlantic—cared little about the inland settlements. The alienation of the frontier was intensified by the Proclamation of 1763 *(see Pontiac's Rebellion, 1763–1766 [chapter 2]),* which sought to limit the westward expansion of settlement. The dirt-poor farmers of the western counties of North Carolina were among those with grievances against the Tidewater aristocrats who held the reins of colonial government. In 1768 they formed an association to protest what they saw as unjust taxation and the thoroughly corrupt justices of the peace, who had been sent from the East to administer law for the frontier. In 1769 the association turned militant, as a group of farmers and settlers formed the Regulators, a political and paramilitary vigilante band. The Regulators won control of the provincial assembly, which sufficiently alarmed the British colonial governor, William Tryon (1729–1788), to dissolve the assembly before it could take any action. After this, the Regulators increasingly turned to vigilante violence. In response, the colonial government passed the Bloody Act (1771), which proclaimed the rioters guilty of treason. Amid escalating tension later in 1771, Governor Tryon dispatched twelve hundred militiamen into the area. They confronted some two thousand Regulators on May 16, 1771, at the Battle of Alamance Creek. Although outnumbered, the militiamen were much better armed and disciplined. They soundly defeated the Regulators, making prisoners of those identified as ringleaders. Six Regulator leaders were subsequently hanged, and the others were compelled to swear allegiance to the eastern Tidewater government.

Lord Dunmore's War, 1774

During the early 1770s, Lord Dunmore, the royal governor of Virginia, announced that he would issue patents for land on both sides of the Ohio River in the vast western territory claimed by his colony. In April 1773 he commissioned a party under Michael Cresap and John Floyd to survey the territory. In May militia captain Thomas Bullitt arrived in the camp of the Shawnee chief Black Fish to tell him that Lord Dunmore intended to settle land explicitly reserved for the Shawnees by the Treaty of Fort Stanwix of 1768. Black Fish responded that he would attack anyone who crossed the river into Kentucky, and, menacingly, he sent braves to observe the surveying party. When some of the party did cross the river on May 29, 1773, a Shawnee named Peshewa—Wild Cat—went down to them, unarmed, to warn them back. He was shot and killed. By way of retaliation, Shawnees killed some of the surveyors, then captured another, but sent him back to Wheeling (in present-day West Virginia) to warn all others that any Virginian who attempted to cross the Ohio would be killed. The Shawnees added that they had an ally in the fur trader George Croghan.

The message duly delivered, Dr. John Connolly, Dunmore's magistrate of western Pennsylvania, concluded that a conspiracy existed among the Shawnees, fur traders, and Pennsylvanians—who disputed Virginia's claim to the Ohio country and would (Connolly believed) stop at nothing to evict Virginians from the region. With Dunmore's blessing, Connolly effectively declared war against the Shawnees.

Like Black Fish, Chief Cornstalk, principal leader of the Ohio Shawnees, wanted to prevent a white invasion, but he also realized the futility of warfare with the whites. At the invitation of George Croghan, Cornstalk journeyed to Fort Pitt (recently renamed Fort Dunmore) to negotiate a peaceful resolution to the conflict. As they returned from the fort, Cornstalk, his brother Silverheels, and another Shawnee, Non-hel-e-ma, were attacked by a party of frontiersmen. Silverheels was fatally wounded in the skirmish, and all hope of peace was thereby shattered. Resolved now to fight, Cornstalk sought aid from the Miamis, Wyandots, Ottawas, and Delawares, all of whom declined to offer alliance or assistance. Those Mingos, Senecas, and Cayugas who had removed to southern Ohio also expressed a desire to remain neutral, but they were driven to fight by a slaughter instigated by Michael Cresap's men. Fearing a general Indian uprising, Lord Dunmore officially declared war on June 10, 1774, and raised a militia. On September 8, leading fifteen hundred militiamen, Dunmore got under way. His plan was to journey to Fort Pitt, then descend the Ohio River to its juncture with the Kanawha, where he would rendezvous with Andrew Lewis. Lewis had been assigned to recruit an additional fifteen hundred militiamen. The combined forces of Dunmore and Lewis were then to cross the Ohio and destroy the Shawnee villages there.

John Muir, first earl of Dunmore, known as Lord Dunmore, British royal governor of Virginia at the outbreak of the Revolution. The portrait is by W. L. Shepherd. *Collection: ArtToday*

Dunmore was a blustery commander when plans were drawn up, but he proved timid in action. Fearful that his boats would be ambushed, he abandoned his plan to rendezvous with Lewis on the Ohio and instead proceeded slowly overland to the Scioto River in central Ohio. In the meantime, Lewis, as yet unapprised of Dunmore's change in plan, had reached Point Pleasant, the appointed rendezvous, on October 6 with about a thousand men—all that he could muster. On October 9, the trader Simon Girty arrived at Lewis's camp to tell him of the revised plan; he conveyed Dunmore's new order that Lewis cross the Ohio and meet Dunmore near the Scioto River.

The movements of both Dunmore and Lewis had been observed by Shawnee scouts. Cornstalk gathered about seven hundred warriors—Shawnees and Mingos, as well as some Wyandots and Delawares. Cornstalk resolved to attack Lewis on the morning he was to leave Point Pleasant to unite with Dunmore. Unfortunately for Cornstalk, an unauthorized hunting party from Lewis's camp discovered the Indians lying in wait and alerted Lewis, who sent out two companies to attempt a preemptive ambush. This failed, but the action did buy Lewis time to erect some crude defenses out of fallen trees. The battle on October 10 was pitched and brutal. Lewis prevailed, pushing the Indians back, but the cost to him was high: 222 of his men (including his brother, Charles) were killed or badly wounded. About half as many Indians died. All commanders, Indian and white, emerged from the battle enraged and disgusted. Cornstalk was appalled by the halfhearted performance of his Mingo, Delaware, and Wyandot allies. Among his own people, even those who had sought war now urged Cornstalk to make peace. The chief, who had not wanted war in the first place, now reasoned that hostilities having commenced, it was foolhardy and disgraceful to seek quarter. But since his warriors lacked the stomach to continue fighting, he had no choice. On the English side, Lord Dunmore's army was near mutiny. The men were restless, eager to press on with the punitive campaign their leader, Dunmore, lacked the resolve to undertake. At last Lewis boldly defied Dunmore's order to halt his march against the Shawnee towns. His advance was stopped by Dunmore himself, at the point of a sword, only a half mile from the villages. Hotheads on both sides clamored for vengeance, but Cornstalk and Dunmore concluded a truce on October 26, 1774.

American Revolution, 1775–1783

King George III (r. 1760–1820) was the inheritor of a line of German-born (Hanoverian) British monarchs who, collectively, demonstrated little regard for effective government and even less regard for their English subjects. Among his early actions was a decision to enforce a series of

Navigation Acts, the first of which had been on the books since the mid-seventeenth century. These acts had been founded on a policy historians call the mercantile system, a form of economic nationalism calling for strict government regulation of trade and commerce. Under mercantilism, the sole function of colonies was to enrich the mother country by furnishing raw materials (on the production side), which the mother country used to create manufactured goods that the colonies would (on the consumption side) purchase. The terms of production as well as consumption would be dictated by the mother country rather than a free market. Following from this policy, the Navigation Acts restricted some colonial trade (both imports and exports) to dealing exclusively with the mother country and, in all other cases, ensured that the mother country would get a disproportionate share of the profits. Until the ascendance of George III, enforcement of the Navigation Acts depended not on central authority but on local customs officials in American ports, many of whom were ready to accept bribes or favor friends and neighbors. Crown officials, in the days before George III, typically ignored much of the corruption and laxity in enforcement. The pro-American British politician Edmund Burke approvingly labeled this tolerant attitude "salutary neglect." In 1760, however, George III ordered strict enforcement of the Navigation Acts, reviving a 1755 law that had been enacted (but little used) by George II, authorizing royal customs officers to issue writs of assistance to local provincial officers, compelling them to cooperate in identifying contraband and arresting anyone evading the acts. The writs also gave royal officials the right to search not only warehouses but also private homes—entirely at will and without court order.

Even after the Treaty of Paris ended the *French and Indian War, 1754–1763 (see chapter 2),* humiliating France and effectively neutralizing Spain's New World power, England groaned under massive debt. To make the colonies pay for some of the continued expense of defending them, George III decided to use the acts not so much for their original purpose, which had been to regulate trade, but as the basis of a whole series of new taxation measures. Many colonists objected that George was now doing what no British monarch had done before: taxing Americans, even though they were not represented in Parliament.

Next, during the premiership of Lord Grenville, the first of a series of colonial taxation acts, the Grenville Acts, were pushed through Parliament. These heavy import and export duties outraged the colonists, not

Lexington and Concord, Massachusetts, April 19, 1775: *Patriots successfully harass the British retreat to Boston.*

Capture of Fort Ticonderoga, New York, May 10, 1775: *Triumph of patriot commanders Ethan Allen and Benedict Arnold.*

American Retreat from Canada, December 31, 1775: *Culmination of a disastrous American invasion attempt.*

Long Island, New York, August 27, 1776: *Washington, defeated, retreats to Manhattan.*

New York City falls to the British, September 15, 1776: *Washington retreats across New Jersey and into Pennsylvania.*

Trenton, New Jersey, December 26, 1776: *Washington crosses the Delaware, reenters New Jersey, counterattacks, and defeats Howe.*

Princeton, New Jersey, January 3, 1777: *A second important patriot victory.*

Brandywine, Pennsylvania, September 11, 1777: *Washington's defense of Philadelphia collapses; British general Howe captures Philadelphia on September 22.*

Germantown, Pennsylvania, October 4, 1777: *Washington's counterattack against Howe is defeated, but is sufficiently gallant to persuade France to make a formal alliance with the United States.*

Saratoga, New York (Freeman's Farm, September 19, 1777; Bemis Heights, October 7, 1777): *Burgoyne surrenders his army to American forces (October 17) in this major patriot triumph.*

Monmouth, New Jersey, June 28, 1778: *A hard-fought draw that proves especially costly to the British.*

Cherry Valley (New York) Massacre, November 11, 1778: *Major raid by British-allied Indians, which triggers a large-scale response from the Continental Army.*

Savannah, Georgia, falls to the British, December 29, 1778: *A major blow to the patriot cause in the South.*

Stony Point, New York, August 19, 1779: *Brilliant victory for the Continental Army's "Mad Anthony" Wayne.*

Bonhomme Richard defeats *Serapis*, September 23, 1779: *John Paul Jones's most famous naval victory.*

Charleston, South Carolina, falls to the British, May 12, 1780: *This gives the British control of all major American ports except Boston.*

Camden, South Carolina, June 13, 1780: *A humiliating defeat at the hands of the British.*

King's Mountain, North Carolina, October 7, 1780: *Turns the tide of war in the South in favor of the Americans.*

Cowpens, South Carolina, January 17, 1781: *American frontiersman Daniel Morgan defeats the despised British leader of Tory forces, Banastre Tarleton.*

The Major Battles (continued)

Guilford Court House, North Carolina, March 15, 1781: *A tactical draw that nevertheless inflicts heavy losses on the British.*

Siege of Yorktown, Virginia, October 9–October 18, 1781: *Franco-American*

amphibious victory forces Cornwallis to surrender his army and, for all practical purposes, ends the Revolution.

Treaty of Paris ratified, September 23, 1783: *The United States wins independence.*

only because of the burden they created during the business recession that followed the *French and Indian War, 1754–1763 (see chapter 2),* but also because they seemed inherently tyrannical. Among the Grenville Acts was the Sugar Act of 1764, which taxed imports of molasses from the French and Dutch West Indies. By way of enforcement, the Sugar Act abrogated trial by jury, thereby imposing tyranny upon tyranny.

The first colonial protest in response to the Grenville Acts was the Non-Importation Agreement of 1764, a boycott of a wide variety of English goods. Instead of yielding to the boycott, Grenville ushered the Stamp Act through Parliament, which was put into force on March 22, 1765. The Stamp Act taxed all kinds of printed matter, including newspapers, legal documents, and even dice and playing cards. All such items required a government stamp, as proof that the tax on them had been paid.

Response to the Stamp Act was swift. Samuel Adams, a Boston brewer, bankrupt businessman, and brilliant political agitator, organized one of the first of many secret societies that sprung up in the colonies specifically to oppose the Stamp Act. Adams's group, like the others that would quickly follow, called itself the Sons of Liberty, and members made it their business to intimidate the stamp agents, who, under threat, resigned. In the meantime, in Virginia, passage of the Stamp Act motivated Patrick Henry, member of that colony's House of Burgesses, to introduce the Virginia Resolves of 1765. The most important of the resolves asserted that Virginia's colonial legislature had the sole right to tax Virginians, and to legislate on purely Virginian issues. At the same time the Stamp Act was legislated, Parliament passed the Mutiny Act of 1765, which included a provision for quartering troops in private houses. Soon after, Parliament passed the Quartering Act, which eliminated the provision requiring private homeowners to billet soldiers, but also required colonial authorities to furnish barracks and supplies for British troops—at the colony's expense. Colonial legislatures resisted the new acts by refusing to allocate funds for the support of troops. Most importantly, each protest brought the colonies another step closer to union, culminating in the Stamp Act Congress, convened at New York City during October 7–25, 1765, and including delegates from South Carolina, Rhode Island, Connecticut, Pennsylvania, Maryland, New Jersey, Delaware, and New York. Virginia, New Hampshire, North Carolina, and Georgia declined to participate. The congress issued a fourteen-point Declaration of Rights and Grievances, declaring (among other things) that Parliament had no right to tax the colonies and that the crown's vice-admiralty courts had no right of jurisdiction in the colonies. Parliament repealed the Stamp Act (March 18, 1766), but simultaneously passed the Declaratory Act, which asserted Parliament's authority to make laws binding on the American colonies "in all cases whatsoever."

In August 1766, Charles Townshend accepted the post of chancellor of the exchequer (the British secretary of the treasury) under Prime Minister William Pitt. When Pitt suffered a mental breakdown, Townshend took control of the cabinet and pushed through a series of acts named for him. The Townshend Acts included the Townshend Revenue Act, an act establishing a new system of customs commissioners, and an act suspending the New York Assembly. The Revenue Act imposed duties on lead, glass, paint, tea, and paper imported into the colonies, specifying that revenues generated would be used for military expenses in the colonies and to pay the salaries of royal colonial officials. The latter provision took away from colonial legislatures the power of the purse, at least as far as compensating royal colonial officials was concerned. Now these administrators would answer exclusively to the crown. Had Charles Townshend purposely set out to provoke the colonies into rebellion, he could not have devised a more effective means of doing so than the Revenue Act and the customs commissioners deployed pursuant to it. The colonies instituted a boycott of British goods so effective that the Townshend duties were repealed on April 12, 1770—save for the duty on tea.

Protest Turns Militant

The first truly militant protest against the new revenue policies occurred in the frontier, especially among the Regulators of North Carolina (see

Regulators' Revolt, 1771), but various clashes occurred in colonial cities as well. The most infamous of these was the Boston Massacre of March 5, 1770.

With economic times hard on colonists as well as British troops quartered in Boston, an off-duty soldier sought part-time work at Grey's ropewalk, a maker of ship's rope. Among underemployed and unemployed colonists, the idea of a British "lobsterback" taking even one precious job from them was sufficient to spark a riot, which, by nightfall, grew to major proportions. A club flew out from the mob, finding its mark on Private Hugh Montgomery and knocking him off his feet. Rising, he cocked his musket and fired into the crowd. The shot went wild, hitting no one, but it provoked another club attack, which was answered by a lunge of a soldier's bayonet and then another musket blast. This shot mortally wounded one Samuel Gray. Another shot hit Crispus Attucks, a forty-year-old runaway slave from Framingham, Massachusetts. Attucks was the first man killed outright in the Boston Massacre. As some historians see it, he was the first fatality of the American Revolution. Before the Boston Massacre was over, two more citizens were killed, and another fell with a wound that would prove mortal. In the aftermath of the incident, a colonial court indicted Captain Thomas Preston and six of his men on charges of murder. Two prominent colonial attorneys, Josiah Quincy and John Adams (the same John Adams who would figure as one of the nation's most important revolutionaries and founding fathers), volunteered to defend the accused. Mob rule, Adams believed, would be fatal to people aspiring to liberty. Preston and four of his men were acquitted. Two others were found guilty, not of murder, but manslaughter, and were discharged from military service with a brand on the thumb. Despite the efforts of revolutionary agitator Samuel Adams to use the Boston Massacre to stir Americans to revolution, the trial and the repeal of the Townshend Acts in April 1770 actually improved relations between America and the mother country—for a short time.

The Boston Tea Party

After the Boston Massacre and other incidents of colonial anger and defiance, even the conservative government of King George III was beginning to sense the danger of full-scale rebellion, and by 1773 it had repealed most of the taxes on import commodities. The king stubbornly insisted, however, on retaining a tax on tea, less with the purpose of raising revenue

Contemporary
engraving by John
Bufford depicting
the Boston
Massacre. *Collection:*
National Archives
and Records
Administration

than to assert and preserve Parliament's authority to tax the colonies. This notwithstanding, it was easy to evade the tea tax simply by purchasing smuggled tea from Dutch sources. Insofar as the tea tax encouraged colonists to buy from the Dutch, the British East India Company, not the colonials, suffered most from the tax. George's prime minister, Lord North, realized that it was in the crown's interest to aid the East India Company, which, in return for an officially sanctioned monopoly on the tea trade, bore the expenses of the civil and military government of British India. He therefore engineered the Tea Act of May 10, 1773, whereby the taxes levied on British East India Company tea were greatly reduced, making the East India tea cheaper than the smuggled tea. North believed this would deprive colonial radicals of one of their prize causes. However, to make the tea as cheap as possible for consumers, the Tea Act allowed the East India Company to sell its tea directly to designated consignees, thereby cutting out many American merchants. This moved colonial radicals to action. They intimidated tea consignees in Philadelphia, New York, and Charleston into resigning. American captains and harbor pilots refused to handle the East India Company cargo. The tea ships were turned back to London from Philadelphia and New York. A ship was permitted to land in Charleston, but the tea was impounded in a warehouse. In Boston, matters took a more dramatic turn. When three tea ships landed at Boston Harbor, the Sons of Liberty prevented their being unloaded. But Massachusetts' royal governor, Thomas Hutchinson, refused to issue permits to allow the ships to leave the harbor and return to London. A standoff developed, and when Hutchinson would not yield, three well-organized troops of colonists, fifty men in each troop, their faces painted to resemble Mohawks, raced to Griffin's Wharf. They climbed into boats, rowed out to the three tea ships, boarded the vessels, then jettisoned into Boston Harbor 342 tea chests valued at $90,000—a great fortune in eighteenth-century America.

George III and Parliament reacted to the Boston Tea Party with unprecedented harshness. Parliament passed a series of Coercive Acts, which colonial activists dubbed the Intolerable Acts. The acts closed the port of Boston, greatly curtailed the Massachusetts colonial government, and extended the hated Quartering Act, making it possible that British troops would be permanently quartered in Boston. General Thomas Gage, a veteran of the *French and Indian War, 1754–1763 (see chapter 2),* was named both commander in chief of British forces in America and royal governor of Massachusetts in April 1774. On June 1 Gage swiftly implemented the most odious of the Intolerable Acts, the Port Act, which closed Boston to overseas traffic as well as to seaborne shipments from other colonies. When the Massachusetts General Assembly defiantly convened in Salem, having been banished from Boston, Gage dissolved this body, but the delegates barred the doors against Gage's messenger. During this period, the exiled and outlawed assembly voted a proposal to convene a Continental Congress, with delegates from all the colonies.

Engraving of Thomas Gage, commander in chief of British forces in America and military governor of Massachusetts at the outbreak of the Revolution. *Collection: National Archives and Records Administration*

The Continental Congress Convenes

Fifty-six delegates from twelve colonies (Georgia abstained) heeded the call of the exiled Massachusetts Assembly for a Continental Congress, which convened at Carpenter's Hall, Philadelphia, on September 5, 1774.

The congress endorsed the Suffolk Resolves, which pronounced the Intolerable Acts unconstitutional, urged Massachusetts to form an independent government and to withhold taxes from the crown until the acts were repealed, advised citizens to arm themselves, and recommended a general boycott of English goods. In all, the Continental Congress declared thirteen acts of Parliament (passed since 1763) unconstitutional, and each of the delegates pledged their colony's support of economic sanctions against Britain until all the acts were repealed.

First Victory

Even as the Continental Congress was forging a union among historically disparate colonies, General Gage gathered and consolidated his forces. On September 1, 1774, one of his Boston-based detachments seized cannon and powder from arsenals in nearby Cambridge and Charles Town. Defiantly, the Salem-based Provincial Congress appropriated £15,627 to buy new military supplies and authorized John Hancock to head a Committee of Safety and call out the militia, whose members were dubbed "minutemen" because these citizen-soldiers pledged themselves to be armed, assembled, and prepared for battle on a minute's notice.

On December 14, 1774, Paul Revere, a silversmith who served as courier to the Boston Sons of Liberty, rode out to warn the local commander, John Sullivan, of Gage's plan to seize munitions stored at Fort William and Mary guarding Portsmouth Harbor, New Hampshire. Sullivan led a band of volunteers to the fort and so stunned the British guards that they surrendered without a fight. Sullivan carried off the guns and powder that had been stored at the fort. This incident might be counted the first patriot victory in a war that had yet to be declared.

Escalation

After the Provincial Congress had appropriated funds to purchase military supplies, called for the organization of the minutemen, and set up a Committee of Safety, events began to unfold with a speed that all but overwhelmed Gage. He deployed and quartered his troops but was beset by patriot saboteurs, who sunk supply barges, burned the straw intended for the soldiers' beds, and wrecked provision wagons. In the meantime, acts of disorder and rebellion were breaking out all over New England. At midnight of February 25, 1775, Gage sent Colonel Alexander Leslie with the 240 men of the 64th Foot Regiment from Castle William, Boston Harbor, to Salem, Massachusetts, where, he had heard, the rebels were storing stolen cannon and munitions. However, the colonial communications network was so well developed by this time that a rider warned the Patriots at Salem, who swiftly moved the nineteen cannon stored there. At Salem, a confrontation took place between Leslie's redcoats and forty minutemen under Colonel Timothy Pickering, but a battle was avoided.

In the meantime, King George III and Parliament proposed the Plan of Reconciliation, whereby Parliament would refrain from taxing the colonies if their assemblies would voluntarily contribute toward some of the costs of imperial defense. Yet, even while offering this concession, the crown continued to punish New England, this time by passing the Fishery Act, which restricted the trade of New England to Britain, Ireland, and the West Indies, and banned the colony from fishing in Newfoundland's rich waters. After passage of this act, Massachusetts revived the Provincial Congress, which promptly set about transforming the colony into an armed camp. Gage responded to these developments, on April 12, by imposing martial law and summarily declaring all of the residents of Massachusetts to be "in treason." He did, however, offer full pardons to everyone except the chief troublemakers, John Adams and John Hancock. On April 16, Paul Revere was dispatched to ride to Lexington, Massachusetts, to warn Adams and Hancock to flee. Immediately after this mission, Revere commenced his most celebrated action, commemorated in the verse of Henry Wadsworth Longfellow, in which he arranged the signal that would alert the Charlestown countryside to the movement of Gage's troops.

During the day, on April 18, Gage dispatched mounted officers out along the Concord road to clear it of rebel couriers. That night, six hundred to eight hundred of Gage's best troops quietly assembled on Boston Common and were put under command of Lieutenant Colonel Francis Smith, assisted by Major John Pitcairn of the Royal Marines. When they marched out at ten-thirty that night, Revere's confederate set two lanterns aglow in the North Church steeple, signaling the courier that the British were indeed bound for Concord.

Battle of Lexington

In the predawn hours of April 19, the British regulars disembarked from the whaleboats that had taken them from Boston to Lechmere Point on the northern side of Boston Harbor, in modern-day Charlestown. From there they marched northwest to the village of Lexington, which lay between Boston and Concord. There, on Lexington's green, they came upon seventy or so minutemen. Outnumbered by the redcoats, militia captain Jonas Parker ordered his men neither to surrender nor to attack, but to disband—taking their weapons with them. At this, Major Pitcairn repeated his demand that the rebels lay down their weapons. In response, shots rang out, and a British soldier was hit in the leg. The redcoats returned fire, the minutemen replied, then the redcoats commenced a bayonet charge. The militiamen scattered. Eight minutemen, including Parker, lay dead on Lexington green. Ten more were wounded. A single British soldier was slightly hurt. The Battle of Lexington, which most historians consider the true opening battle of the American Revolution, was over.

IN THEIR OWN *Words*

I am satisfied that one active campaign, a smart action, and burning two or three of their towns, will set everything to rights.

—MAJOR JOHN PITCAIRN, ROYAL MARINES, APRIL 1775, SHORTLY BEFORE THE BATTLES OF LEXINGTON AND CONCORD

Battle of Concord

From Lexington, the British continued their march to Concord. Into this town militia companies came from the surrounding communities. The most reliable estimate of American strength at Concord is that 3,763 Americans were engaged, but probably no more than half this number were involved in the battle at any one time. At the moment of the British arrival, there were about 400 minutemen, under the command of local resident Colonel James Barrett, assembled on a ridge overlooking Concord. The minutemen descended on the British and exchanged fire with the redcoats, letting loose a volley Ralph Waldo Emerson ("Hymn Sung at the Completion of the Concord Monument, April 19, 1836") would dub "the shot heard 'round the world." Three British regular soldiers died in the volley and nine more lay wounded. The redcoats retreated into the center of town.

In the meantime, from Boston, some 1,400 redcoats, including 460 Royal Marines, drawing two six-pound cannons and led by thirty-three-year-old Lord Hugh Percy, were just beginning their march to Concord. All along the way, the column was sniped at by militiamen crouched behind stone walls, trees, and even in houses. As Percy's column approached, Lieutenant Colonel Smith withdrew toward Lexington, his light infantry mounting several successful counterattacks against poorly organized groups of colonial militia. Yet more and more militiamen poured into the Concord area, taking up sniper positions on either side of the road, peppering Smith's retreating column with continual fire. After almost twenty hours of fighting and retreating, Smith's force entered Lexington and there joined with Percy's column of reinforcements from Boston. Percy trained his six-pounders against the Americans, which kept them at bay for a time. But more militiamen were continually arriving. Fortunately for the British, despite the American numbers, the militia groups were ill-disciplined and their actions uncoordinated. Still, the militiamen persisted in harassing the column all the way back to Charlestown, where Smith and Percy at last found refuge within range of the big guns of their warships riding at anchor in the harbor. Seventy-three redcoats were confirmed dead, and another twenty-six, missing, were presumed dead. One hundred seventy-four British soldiers were wounded. On the American side, forty-nine had died, five were reported missing, and forty-one lay wounded.

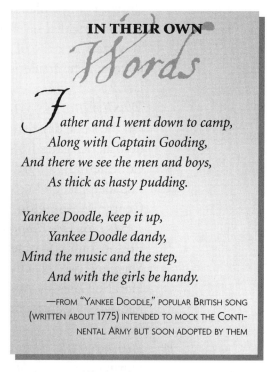

IN THEIR OWN Words

*Father and I went down to camp,
Along with Captain Gooding,
And there we see the men and boys,
As thick as hasty pudding.*

*Yankee Doodle, keep it up,
Yankee Doodle dandy,
Mind the music and the step,
And with the girls be handy.*

—FROM "YANKEE DOODLE," POPULAR BRITISH SONG (WRITTEN ABOUT 1775) INTENDED TO MOCK THE CONTINENTAL ARMY BUT SOON ADOPTED BY THEM

When the Second Continental Congress convened in Philadelphia, a month after the Battles of Lexington and Concord, finding that a revolution had been started by local action, Congress moved to take charge of the fight. It voted to mobilize 13,600 troops, and it called on local militia forces throughout New England to march to Boston, with the intention of laying under siege the British forces headquartered there.

Fort Ticonderoga Falls

Connecticut authorities responded to the news of Lexington and Concord by sending Benedict Arnold, a prosperous New Haven merchant and now captain of militia, to Massachusetts. He quickly persuaded the Massachusetts authorities to appoint him colonel of militia and put him in charge of a mission to capture Fort Ticonderoga, strategically located at the point where Lake George drains into Lake Champlain. But the Connecticut assembly had already approved a plan to take Fort Ticonderoga, and they had given the assignment to Ethan Allen. In the end, Arnold agreed to a joint command with Allen.

The fort fell to a surprise assault by a small force of eighty-three men on May 10. Now the patriots had gained a gateway to Canada and a base from which Allen launched an expedition against the nearby post of Crown Point, which, weakly garrisoned, fell without resistance. Together, the forts yielded seventy-eight precious artillery pieces, six mortars, three howitzers, a cache of cannonballs, flints for flintlock muskets, and other materiel. The artillery would be put to effective use in the siege of Boston.

Washington Is Given Command

On the same day that Ethan Allen and Benedict Arnold took Fort Ticonderoga, delegates from all the colonies except Georgia met in the Second Continental Congress at the State House (later Independence Hall), Philadelphia, and created the Continental Army under the command of George Washington, provincial hero of the *French and Indian War, 1754–1763 (see chapter 2),* with Artemas Ward (already commanding the Boston militia), Israel Putnam of Connecticut, Philip Schuyler of New York, and two recently retired officers of the British army, Charles Lee and Horatio Gates, as Washington's lieutenants. By the end of 1775, Congress had 27,500 Continental soldiers on its payroll, from all the colonies.

Bunker Hill

During the spring of 1775, New Englanders poured into Cambridge and adjacent towns to lay siege against Boston. By the end of May some ten thousand colonial troops surrounded the city. In the meantime, on May 25, HMS *Cerberus* sailed into Boston Harbor, bearing three major generals to assist Thomas Gage in crushing the rebellion: William Howe, the senior officer; John Burgoyne; and Henry Clinton. Gage lost no time in assigning Howe to crush the American army in a single blow. Howe decided on an amphibious attack to secure the high ground at Charlestown, a place called Bunker's Hill or Bunker Hill. Covering these operations would be the big guns of the men-of-war riding at anchor in Boston Harbor, which the British firmly controlled. Once Bunker Hill was secured, the forces of Howe and Clinton could crush the American flanks in a pincers movement converging on Cambridge.

It was a good plan, but it depended on secrecy and surprise. The local

Committee of Safety, however, had such a well-developed network of spies that General Artemas Ward, in command of the so-called Boston Army, quickly learned of it. The local Committee of Safety wanted Ward's army to seize, occupy, and fortify Bunker Hill before Gage could attain it. Putnam decided to concentrate his forces not on Bunker Hill, as directed, but on Breed's Hill, which was closer to Boston. He would put some men in a fortified position on Bunker Hill to cover any retreat. Putnam's decision was a serious tactical error. Higher, steeper, and farther from the ships of the Royal Navy, Bunker Hill could have been made virtually impregnable, whereas Breed's Hill, lower and less steep, was more exposed and vulnerable.

While 1,200 Americans dug furiously into Breed's Hill, Gage and Howe prepared to attack with 2,500 men supported by land-based artillery as well as by ship-mounted cannon. At dawn on June 17, the British fleet opened fire on the American position. Gage and Howe were as surprised by the naval action as were the

IN THEIR OWN *Words*

I found a mixed multitude of People here, under very little discipline, order, or Government. I found the enemy in possession of a place called Bunker's Hill, on Charles Town Neck, strongly Intrenched, and Fortifying themselves; I found part of our Army on two Hills, (called Winter and Prospect Hills) about a Mile and a quarter from the enemy on Bunker's Hill, in a very insecure state; I found another part of the Army at this Village; and a third part at Roxbury, guarding the Entrance in and out of Boston.

. . . [The British] Force, including Marines, Tories, &c., are computed, from the best accounts I can get, at about 12,000 Men; ours, including Sick absent, &c., at about 16,000; but then we have a Cemi Circle of Eight or Nine Miles, to guard to every part of which we are obliged to be equally attentive; whilst they, situated as it were in the Center of the Cemicircle, can bend their whole Force (having the entire command of the Water), against any one part of it with equal facility. . . .

—LETTER FROM GEORGE WASHINGTON TO HIS BROTHER JOHN AUGUSTINE WASHINGTON, JULY 27, 1775

Americans and hastily decided to disembark from the Mystic River side of the peninsula and march around to the American rear. This required waiting for a favorable tide, which gave the Americans an additional six hours to continue digging in and reinforce their positions. At 1:00 P.M., twenty-three hundred redcoats disembarked at Moulton's Point, at the tip of Charlestown Peninsula, but soon found themselves under heavy attack. Following accepted British military doctrine, Howe ordered a concentrated artillery bombardment to precede the attack. After a few shots rang out, the guns fell silent. Howe, it seems, had marched into battle with six-pounder cannons supplied with twelve-pound balls. Most of the ammunition was useless. In the meantime, the navy bombarded Charlestown with carcasses (incendiary cannonballs), which set all the village ablaze. As the town burned in the background, Howe ordered a bayonet charge into the Yankee position fronting the Mystic. It was in response to this charge that Colonel William Prescott issued perhaps the most memorable battle command in American military history: "Don't fire until you see the whites of their eyes!"

The British assault, courageous and dashing, was foolhardy. Under withering close-range fire from the men of Israel Putnam and Stark, 96 of the 350 redcoats committed to the charge were killed in three American volleys. Every member of Howe's personal staff was either killed or wounded. Howe, although he remained in the forefront, was unhurt—though badly shaken.

Although stunned, Howe prepared a second wave of assault within a quarter of an hour. Again the redcoats were cut down and withdrew. Yet the attack had taken its toll on the American defenders as well, who were beginning to buckle. In a third assault, the redcoats broke through to the Yankee positions on Breed's Hill, and the patriots conducted a fighting retreat. Although the British won the day, they had taken the heavier losses. Of 2,400 men actually engaged in combat, 1,054 had been shot, of whom 226 died. Henry Clinton confided to his diary: "A dear-bought victory; another such would have ruined us."

The Canadian Campaign

Canada rebuffed American invitations to join in rebellion against the mother country, whereupon Congress, on June 27, 1775, ordered an invasion of Canada to be led by Major General Philip Schuyler. Schuyler, however, delayed until September, by which time George Washington had authorized the eager Benedict Arnold to lead a simultaneous operation. The plan was for Arnold to take Québec while Schuyler attacked Montréal. In the meantime, Richard Montgomery, Schyler's second-in-command, learned that a British expedition was preparing to recapture Fort Ticonderoga and Crown Point and announced that he was not going to wait to begin the march to Canada. On September 4, General Schuyler caught up with Montgomery, and the two led the assault on St. Johns, a British fort and barracks. A siege was called for during which Schuyler, in ill health to begin with, was taken sick and had to be invalided home. Montgomery, now in command of the American forces, sent Ethan Allen and a militia officer named John Brown to recruit a handful of rebellious Canadians to aid in maintaining the siege. Instead, Allen and Brown decided to attack Montréal without delay. The poorly planned attack failed, and British general Guy Carleton took Allen and twenty of his men captive. (Clapped into irons and shipped to England, Allen narrowly avoided trial for treason. In June 1776 he was paroled in New York City.) Ethan Allen's reckless attempt on Montréal had not merely failed but also had seriously compromised the American cause among Canadians by solidifying popular Canadian sentiment against participation in the Revolution. Worse, the botched raid on Montréal moved many vacillating Indians, both in Canada and the lower colonies, to side with the victorious British.

Allen's failure was a prelude of larger disaster to come. Montgomery managed to take and occupy Montréal, but as winter set in, his men were cold and hungry. In the meantime, Arnold struggled to march his eleven hundred volunteers from Cambridge, Massachusetts, to assault Québec. Starvation and desertion had reduced his command to six hundred men by the time he reached the southern bank of the St. Lawrence River on November 9. With his pitiful "army," Arnold crossed the St. Lawrence on two nights, November 13 and 14, marched over the Plains of Abraham, and defeated the militia stationed there to defend Québec. Suddenly eight hundred British regulars menaced the invaders, who hastily withdrew to Pointe aux Trembles. On December 2 Montgomery came to the rescue, bringing the combined American forces to about a thousand men. Together they marched back to Québec, then halted. They now realized that they lacked the artillery needed for a speedy siege, and yet could not expect to survive a Canadian winter camped outside the town. Moreover, the terms of enlistment for all of Arnold's New Englanders would expire at the end of the year, and they would be free to go home. Montgomery and Arnold decided to go for broke and attack at once. On December 31, with a blizzard in full force, they made their assault. The result was a costly defeat, with more than half of the remaining American invasion force ending up as casualties: 48 dead, 34 wounded, 372 made captive. Although painfully wounded, Arnold refused to give up. For five months, from January to May 1776, he and his command lingered on the outskirts of Québec while Congress and George Washington scraped together a force to send to his relief. By April 2, 1776, sufficient reinforcements had arrived to bring American strength outside of Québec to two thousand, although disease, desertion, and expiration of enlistment reduced this number to about six hundred men fit for duty. It was too small a number to attempt to storm the fortified town. British reinforcements approached and, even worse, an epidemic of smallpox broke out among the American army. Congress sent General John Sullivan with reinforcements to try to salvage something of the Canadian operation. Sullivan, in turn, directed General William Thompson to take two thousand of his best troops to Trois-Rivières, on the northern bank of the St. Lawrence, halfway between Montréal and Québec. There they were overwhelmed by superior British forces. British general Guy Carleton could easily have cut off the retreat of the American forces, but he didn't know what he would do with perhaps as many as two thousand prisoners, so he left the invaders to fend for themselves in the swamps, where they were ambushed by Indians and Canadian militiamen. At least four hundred American troops were wounded, killed, or captured, while British losses numbered eight killed and nine wounded.

Canada: The Final Phase

Once it was clear to them that the invasion of Canada had collapsed, the British began preparing a counteroffensive invasion from Canada. It was critical to gain control of the waterway straddling Canada and America, Lake Champlain, and both sides scrambled to cobble together shallow-draft fleets. Employing local materials and improvised tools, Benedict Arnold supervised construction of four large galleys and eight or nine smaller gundalows. For their part, the British dismantled an oceangoing vessel and rebuilt it at St. Johns. They did the same for two smaller schooners and a large gundalow. The British also had numerous smaller vessels, including longboats and gunboats.

Arnold left Crown Point with ten craft on August 24, 1776, and anchored the boats off rocky Valcour Island. By October 11 he was in command of fifteen vessels. When he saw the size of the approaching British fleet—twenty gunboats, thirty longboats, and several larger vessels—he hurriedly pulled back all of his boats. But it was too late, and over the next three days the two makeshift fleets slugged it out, with the outnumbered and outgunned American vessels getting the worse of it. By the morning of the October 13 Arnold had two large vessels left, in which he made his escape, keeping up a running fight with the pursuing British fleet all the way to Buttonmould Bay on the Vermont shore of Lake Champlain. There he beached and burned the wrecks of his two ships and traveled overland to Crown Point. Realizing that he could not hold this position, he burned the buildings of Crown Point and retreated to Fort Ticonderoga, back to the point from which the Canadian venture had begun two years earlier. Yet this defeat gained something for the Americans and cost something for the British. By keeping Carleton occupied, Arnold took the momentum out of the British advance, and the approaching winter put an end to plans for Carleton's forces to invade the lower colonies and link up with William Howe. Such a move would have cut the colonies in two, severing the north from the south, and quite possibly have crushed the Revolution. By enduring a tactical defeat, Arnold had effectively achieved a strategic victory.

The Siege of Boston

The Battle of Bunker Hill left General Thomas Gage dazed, demoralized, and intimidated. By June 1775, some fifteen thousand provincial troops were positioned just outside Boston, placed under the command of General Artemas Ward. Gage's army, now bottled up in the city, numbered sixty-five hundred; with naval personnel, the total came to eleven thousand.

With Boston under siege, American general Henry Knox marched to Fort Ticonderoga, more than three hundred miles from Cambridge, to fetch the artillery captured there so it could be used to bombard Boston in preparation for an attack on the British garrison. Knox left Cambridge on November 16, 1775, and returned with the artillery on January 24, 1776. In a spectacular feat of military engineering, Washington's forces quietly fortified Dorchester Heights, then placed there the guns Knox had brought. Wishing to extend their control of the high ground, the Americans stealthily moved to occupy nearby Nock's Hill during the night of March 9 but were quickly driven off with a few casualties. It made no difference. Surrounded and outnumbered, General Howe decided to abandon Boston, and he did not contest the American occupation of Dorchester Heights. From March 7 to March 17 the British ships were loaded. Redcoats blew up their headquarters at Castle William to keep it from falling into rebel hands. The American forces stood by silently as some eleven thousand redcoats, together with about a thousand Tories (loyalists), boarded the ships for evacuation. By secret agreement, the Americans had promised the British that they would not attempt to prevent the evacuation; in return, the British pledged not to put Boston to the torch. Washington believed the troops would evacuate to New York; instead, they did not disembark until they had reached Halifax, Nova Scotia. The siege of Boston had consumed eight months, during which only twenty patriot soldiers had been killed. In a face-off with perhaps the finest army in the world, the patriots had prevailed.

Common Sense

Although the war was under way in 1775, the colonial tide was not entirely turned toward independence. Then, on January 9, 1776, Thomas Paine, an English immigrant (he settled in Philadelphia in November 1774), published *Common Sense,* a forty-seven-page pamphlet that made the argument for independence more simply, thoroughly, and persuasively than any document that had come before it. Paine developed two central themes: that republican government was

Engraving of Gilbert Stuart's portrait of General Henry Knox, the artillery master of the Continental Army. *Collection: National Archives and Records Administration*

inherently and inescapably superior to government by hereditary monarchy, and that equality of rights was the chief birthright of humanity, which no just government could fail to support and defend. Swept by a wave of popular support for independence largely engendered by *Common Sense,* the Continental Congress, on February 18, 1776, authorized privateers: merchant ships given permission to raid and capture British vessels. On February 26 it embargoed exports to Britain and the British West Indies. On March 3 Congress sent Silas Deane to France to negotiate for aid. On March 14 Congress moved against the Tories, ordering that they be disarmed. On April 6 it opened all American ports to the trade of all nations save Britain. Now, one after the other, in some cases after intense but compact debate, all of the colonies voted for independence.

While the colonies voted, Congress appointed a committee to draft a declaration of independence, naming to it John Adams, Benjamin Franklin, Robert Livingston, Roger Sherman, and Thomas Jefferson. Jefferson took primary responsibility for drafting the document, drawing on the ideas of the seventeenth-century British philosopher John Locke to create a manifesto that justified and explained, to Americans, to the

English, and to the world, the reasons behind the American Revolution. After revision and approval, the Declaration of Independence was signed on July 4, 1776.

Shift in British Strategy

In the years and then months that preceded the Revolution, British troops were concentrated in Boston precisely because this town was the heart and source of the rebellion. But with defeat in Boston, they decided to shift the focus of operations from Massachusetts, the hotbed of rebellion, to those places where the spirit of revolution was weakest, where Tories outnumbered patriots. After evacuating Boston and removing to headquarters in Halifax, the British command now turned its attention to two places where Tories abounded: South Carolina and New York. At this point, the actions in the North and the South became quite distinct.

Washington's Strategic Error

New York City was strategically critical. Whoever controlled the city and its harbor also controlled the Hudson River, principal avenue into the American interior. The new British plan called for General Howe, currently in Halifax, to sail southward with a large army to take and occupy New York City. From this base he would spread his control of the Hudson River north to Albany, thereby isolating New England from the other colonies. From Canada, a British force led by General Guy Carleton would join Howe at Albany. Together the two could operate at will and defeat in detail the remnants of rebellion.

In January 1776 Washington detached from Boston siege duty General Charles Lee to set up the defense of New York. Lee proposed placing 4,000 to 5,000 troops on Long Island, taking care to fortify Brooklyn Heights, which overlooked lower Manhattan. Uptown on the island of Manhattan, he would place troops for the defense of Kings Bridge, which connected Manhattan with the Bronx on the mainland. Lee reasoned that given the naval superiority of the British, he could not hope to hold Manhattan as a fortress, but from the surrounding high ground, he could effectively attack a British invasion force.

By the last week of August, General Howe had mustered 31,625 troops, of whom 24,464 were fit for duty. In addition to the vast array of troop transports, Admiral Richard Howe was prepared to support the land forces with 30 combat ships, including 10 ships of the line and 20

frigates, together representing a total of perhaps 1,200 guns. It may well
have been the largest expeditionary force England had, to that time, ever
sent overseas. Against these enormous forces, Washington had 20,000
troops deployed on Long Island, Governor's Island in New York Harbor,
off the lower tip of Manhattan, and elsewhere in and around New York
City. This was the bulk of America's military strength. If they were lost, the
Revolution would be over.

Washington was a great leader of men, but his grasp of military tactics and strategy was in many respects flawed. By splitting his forces
between Manhattan and Long Island, with the East River and Long Island
Sound between them, Washington had exposed his army to the British
fleet, whose warships could attack—and whose transports could deliver
soldiers—anywhere along Manhattan and Long Island.

Battle of Long Island

On the night of August 26, most of the British began to land in an area of
southeastern Brooklyn called then, as it is today, the Flatlands. Ten thousand troops were deployed in a broad movement to the northeast,
through Bedford (today's Brooklyn neighborhood of Bedford-Suyvesant),
so that the main thrust of the attack, when it came on the morning of
August 27, rushed in on General John Sullivan's left flank, precisely the
opposite direction from which it had been expected. While Generals Clinton, Cornwallis, and Hugh Percy attacked from the northeast, five thousand Hessians (German mercenary troops in the British service) pressed
in due north from the Flatlands, and seven thousand Highlanders
attacked from the west (from New York Bay, the only direction the Americans had anticipated). The effect of an attack from three sides with a total
of twenty-two thousand men overwhelmed the thirty-one hundred
Americans positioned before the Brooklyn Heights fortifications. Despite
the overwhelming numbers, patriot general William Alexander (popularly
called Lord Stirling in deference to an inherited Scottish title) held out
long enough to exact a heavy toll on the Highlanders. But by noon it was
over, and those who had survived the attack were falling back on the
works at Brooklyn Heights.

Considering their overwhelmingly superior numbers, Howe's commanders had accomplished remarkably little. The American army on
Long Island was still intact, and now it was ensconced behind the heavily
fortified works of Brooklyn Heights. Moreover, the winds were against the

British fleet, so General Howe's admiral brother was unable to offer support from the water. Howe decided to dig in, so that he could take his time in the assault on the Brooklyn Heights fortress. Washington remained confident at first that Brooklyn could be held, and so he brought some of his Manhattan units into the fortifications at Brooklyn Heights. By the twenty-eighth, however, he realized that his position on Brooklyn was untenable and ordered a stealthy evacuation back to Manhattan, entirely undetected by the British, during the stormy and foggy night of August 29–30. He had saved his army.

Battle of New York

Washington's army, now deployed exclusively in Manhattan, was poorly supplied and subject to the impending expiration of militia enlistments. General Nathanael Greene advised Washington to burn and abandon New York, but Congress barred this. Washington resolved to make the best of it, but again erred tactically. On September 7 he deployed his troops thinly over sixteen miles of ground, leaving the weakest position in the middle of Manhattan Island. On September 15, calm weather and favorable winds allowed the British fleet to sail up the Hudson and East Rivers, flanking Manhattan. British guns were now trained on Manhattan all along its length. Transport barges landed at Kip's Bay, where 34th Street today ends at FDR Drive. At 11:00 A.M. a brief naval barrage was ordered, and then troops were landed, unopposed, in eighty-five flatboats. The handful of militiamen in the area fled before them, spreading panic to other units in what is now midtown. Washington personally attempted to rally the troops, but without success. All rushed northward to the protection afforded by Harlem Heights and Fort Washington. But instead of pursuing, the British set up headquarters in the Murray house (owned by a prominent Tory) in the neighborhood known today as Murray Hill. From here they would slowly advance northward. Washington had presented the British with an opportunity to annihilate his army, but the overly cautious and conventional Howe failed to take advantage of it.

Many decades of building have flattened most of Manhattan's naturally undulating topography, but in the eighteenth century it was an island of hill and dale. The most commanding heights (unflattened even today) lay above the present location of 125th Street. From this location, Harlem Heights, the American defenders could see, on September 15, a line of British soldiers advancing northward along the eastern road. At the same time, along the western road, Aaron Burr, a young New Jersey man who was among Washington's handful of staff officers, led the columns of Knox and Putnam up from the Battery, at the southern tip of Manhattan. Such was the rugged landscape of eighteenth-century Manhattan that while the observers on the heights saw the parallel advance of the two columns, neither of those columns could see or hear the other.

A notch called McGowan's (or McGown's) Pass pierced the hilly, wooded tract running down the center of Manhattan. If any of the British troops happened to scout the pass, the advancing Americans would be cut off and lost. This time, however, fortune favored the patriots, and the men of Putnam and Knox, unseen by the British, reached and scaled Harlem Heights, where they were welcomed into the ranks of the defenders.

By nightfall on September 15, Howe had established forward posts from McGowan's Pass (at the northeast corner of Central Park today) southwest to the Hudson River (at about the location of 105th Street). Before dawn of the sixteenth, Lieutenant Colonel Thomas Knowlton led a hundred elite Connecticut Rangers down the so-called Hollow Way, a steep descent from Harlem Heights to the Hudson. He ran into elements of the famed Black Watch Highland troops and engaged them fiercely, but was forced to retreat as more Highlanders arrived. The British misinterpreted the retreat as the beginning of a general flight, and the advance elements of Howe's invading force now attacked in anticipation of triggering a rout. Instead, they got a full-scale fight that sent the Highlanders running in full retreat across a buckwheat field that fronted the Hudson (on the site of today's Barnard College). To the American defenders, this small victory was greatly heartening. To Howe, it was discouraging out of all proportion. With thousands of well-equipped troops and a mighty naval fleet at his disposal, he could have struck Washington's position from the flanks or the rear. Instead, he did nothing.

By the middle of October, Howe had still not moved against Fort Washington and Harlem Heights.

Battle of White Plains

Yet Howe was not entirely idle. Washington observed that Howe's barges were probing for Hudson landings in Westchester, above his own position. Obviously the British commander was preparing an encirclement. In view of this, on October 16, Washington decided that the time had come to evacuate Manhattan. Slowly his troops crept northward to White Plains, in Westchester County, where he placed his troops on three hills. As before, he deployed his troops poorly, neglecting to fortify Chatterton Hill—the highest and, therefore, most important of the three hills. When he arrived, Howe focused his attack against this weak position and took Chatterton Hill. Yet, once again, the main chance had eluded him. Had he pressed the advantages gained, he might have destroyed Washington's army. Instead, he merely sent the Americans into withdrawal farther north. Taking a position at North Castle, Washington now had free access to supplies from New England. Fed and in possession of some new equipment, his troops felt so refreshed that they interpreted White Plains as a victory. In fact, White Plains had been lost—yet the Americans had suffered perhaps 150 killed and wounded, whereas the British suffered 214 casualties and the Hessians 99.

The Loss of Fort Washington

When he evacuated Manhattan, Washington left a garrison of 2,000 men to hold Fort Washington, at the northern tip of the island. Reinforcements had raised this number to nearly 3,000. When the defenders refused to yield, Howe attacked from three directions on November 16. At three o'clock that afternoon, Fort Washington was surrendered to the British; with it, 2,818 American officers and men became prisoners of war. Fifty-three Americans had fallen in battle; the number of wounded is unknown. British and Hessian losses were much heavier: 458 killed or wounded. The loss of Fort Washington, the capture of so many men, and the loss of arms and ammunition were grave blows, and four days later, Fort Lee also fell. These losses were added to the fact that all of Manhattan and a substantial swath along the New Jersey bank of the Hudson were now in British hands. The American army was split into three branches: Charles Lee was up in North Castle, Westchester County; General William Heath was at Peekskill, up the Hudson from Manhattan; and Washington took the main body of troops on a long retreat through New Jersey.

Washington's Retreat

Washington understood that he did not have to defeat the British army; indeed, he accepted the reality that he could not. What he did have to do was keep the American army intact and fighting. Washington understood that he might lose cities and he might lose battles, but he could still win independence—or, at least, a favorable settlement from the crown—if he could outlast the British will to continue prosecuting a distant and costly war. But keeping the American army intact was no easy task. Casualties, the expiration of enlistments, and capture had reduced Washington's command to about 16,400 troops. The commander's first object was to consolidate this number for operations in New Jersey. During this process of consolidation, the patriot forces were especially vulnerable, but fortunately for Washington, Howe chose not to attack, but to bed down for the season. General Charles Cornwallis was sent to harass Washington and chase him beyond New Brunswick, just to give the British elbow room for their winter hibernation.

Cornwallis decided to interpret his assignment more broadly. Boasting that he would bag Washington as a hunter bags a fox, he drove his troops swiftly and unsparingly. He was closing in on Newark by November 29, which sent Washington and his headquarters force of four thousand running to New Brunswick just steps ahead of Hessian advance guards. Leaving Alexander at Princeton to delay the British advance, Washington reached Trenton with his main force on December 3. His best hope was that Charles Lee would meet him there, but Lee was days distant. Washington, who had already prepared for an evacuation across the Delaware River into Pennsylvania, sent his troops across on December 7, and deployed them along some twenty-five miles of Pennsylvania riverfront. As a precaution, he sent troops to find and destroy every boat of any size for seventy-five miles up and down the lower Delaware. He meant to make it very difficult for the British to give chase. Cornwallis gave up. He secured permission from Howe to halt at the Delaware, to wait for spring, when he and Howe might finish off the American army.

Delaware Crossing

By Christmastime, Washington found that he had no more than six thousand troops fit for duty. If he waited for more troops, current enlistments would expire, which might reduce the forces on the Delaware to a mere fourteen hundred. Moreover, as winter wore on, a hard freeze of the river would make it possible for the boatless British to cross and to attack. What to do with the six thousand men of an apparently defeated army? Washington boldly decided on a counteroffensive.

On Christmas Night, Washington loaded twenty-four hundred veteran troops and eighteen cannons into the stout Durham boats he had hoarded to keep out of British hands. While Washington crossed in a

Engraving of
Emanuel Leutze's
*Washington
Crossing the
Delaware. Collection:
National Archives
and Records
Administration*

vicious winter storm at McKonkey's Ferry (modern Washington Crossing), nine miles above Trenton, another thousand militiamen, commanded by General James Ewing, were to cross at Trenton Ferry to block any retreat of Hessians who occupied Trenton. Colonel John Cadwalader was to cross the Delaware at Bordentown in a diversionary move. But Ewing never made it across, and Cadwalader was so delayed that he was of no real help. Another aspect of Washington's plan was for his men to disembark at midnight, but the weather caused so many delays that the men were not all across before three o' clock on the morning of the twenty-sixth. It took another hour before they were all ready to march, which meant that the attack, which depended entirely on surprise, would not occur in the darkness before daybreak, but in broad daylight. The objective of this ragtag army was an encampment of Hessians, the crown's hired guns, among the best-trained and hardest-fighting soldiers of Europe.

Battle of Trenton

Despite the need to attack in daylight, Washington could still count on the element of surprise—and the fact that the Hessians would be groggy from their Christmas celebrations. The Americans descended on Trenton at seven-thirty on the morning of December 26. Washington's units closed in from the northwest, the north, the northeast, the south, and the southeast. Roused from his stupor, Colonel Johann Rall tried to rally his panicked men, but was himself cut down and mortally wounded. Even

Copy of an 1850 lithograph depicting the surrender of the Hessian troops to George
Washington after the Battle of Trenton. *Collection: National Archives and Records Administration*

without Ewing and Cadwalader, the attack went remarkably well. Trenton—and 918 Hessian prisoners, as well as a wealth of equipment and stores—now belonged to the Americans. Washington's forces had suffered no more than 4 wounded. Of the approximately 1,224 Hessians engaged, 106 were killed or wounded, the remainder captured.

In the absence of Ewing and Cadwalader, Washington could not press the offensive on to Princeton and New Brunswick, as he had planned. He withdrew across the Delaware, back into Pennsylvania. Nevertheless, the triumph at Trenton had an immediate salutary effect on the Continental Army. Generals Henry Knox and Thomas Mifflin successfully pleaded with their men to extend their enlistments, set to end on December 31, six more weeks. With six more fighting weeks to use, Washington crossed his army into New Jersey once again, taking up a position at hard-won Trenton. Cornwallis rushed almost eight thousand fresh troops from Princeton to Trenton. Washington sent a covering force under General Edward Hand, who, with help from some miserable weather, managed to delay Cornwallis' advance.

Battle of Princeton

Washington hurriedly erected defensive works along the Assumpink Creek just south of Trenton and left a small force of four hundred there with orders to make noise and keep the fires lighted to decoy Cornwallis. The ruse worked. Cornwallis delayed his attack, and the main body of Washington's army slipped silently toward Princeton and New Brunswick.

The Battle of Princeton began on the morning of January 3, and was concentrated at the orchard of William Clark, near a Quaker meetinghouse. At first the American militiamen panicked, unable to load faster than the British could thrust with bayonets. Assuming personal command, Washington rallied the troops long enough to allow General Knox to position and fire his artillery into the British attackers—and for Daniel Hitchcock's brigade of Rhode Islanders and Massachusetts men, along with Pennsylvanians under Edward Hand, to come pounding to the aid of General Hugh Mercer's beleaguered troops. The British were sent running back in panic along the Trenton road. Washington resisted the impulse to pursue the fleeing attackers, because he knew they would lead him straight to the superior numbers of Cornwallis's main army. Instead, Washington advanced into Princeton and engaged the few British soldiers remaining there. He quickly took Princeton but could not afford to occupy it, knowing that Cornwallis would counterattack soon. Worse, Washington realized that he had to abandon his plan to capture New Brunswick, where, he knew, the British stored massive quantities of supplies, together with a war chest of some £70,000. Capturing New Brunswick, Washington believed, might bring about a favorable peace, but he saw that after Trenton and Princeton, his threadbare army had no more left to give. Washington rode west to Morristown to make winter camp. For now, the Revolution was saved, but the Continental Army dwindled as enlistments expired. Moreover, Howe, Cornwallis, and Baron Wilhelm von Knyphausen, commander in chief of the Hessians, stunned by their collective failures, idled their troops in the small corner of New Jersey left to them. The war was sullenly deadlocked until spring.

Fresh Troops, New Allies

Early spring 1777 brought the American cause an influx of fresh troops and a willingness among many veterans to extend their enlistments. In Paris, Benjamin Franklin and Silas Deane, congressional emissaries, were gradually persuading the French government to conclude a formal alliance with the United States. Although King Louis XVI continued to hang back from such an outright arrangement, his government authorized French merchants to begin to ship war materiel to America in quantity. In June, Marie Joseph Paul Yves Roch

Engraving of George E. Perrine's portrait of the Marquis de Lafayette. *Collection: National Archives and Records Administration*

Gilbert du Motier, marquis de Lafayette, arrived with a party of other idealistic adventurers (including Baron de Kalb), all eager to impart European military expertise to the officers and men of the Continental Army.

Burgoyne's Plan

If spring brought new hope to Washington, it also seemed to stiffen the British resolve. General John Burgoyne now proposed a three-pronged attack on New York: A principal force would advance south from Canada, down Lake Champlain and the upper Hudson; simultaneously, a smaller force would operate through the New York frontier country, from Oswego through the Mohawk Valley. These two operations would be coordinated with Howe, who would send another major force up the Hudson, meeting Burgoyne's principal force at Albany, thereby effecting a pincers movement that would amputate New England from the rest of the colonies.

It was a good plan, but, foolishly, Lord Germain, the British minister in charge of the conduct of the war, approved both it and General Howe's plan to capture Philadelphia. This made it impossible for Howe to coordinate with Burgoyne and thereby doomed the entire plan.

An engraving of a portrait of General John Burgoyne by S. Hollyer.
Collection: National Archives and Records Administration

Fort Ticonderoga Recaptured

Burgoyne began his move south from St. John's, Newfoundland, to Lake Champlain on June 17, 1777. He commanded a force of seven thousand infantrymen, British regulars as well as German mercenaries, in addition to a small force of English and German artillerists, four hundred Indian auxiliaries, and a few Canadian and Tory adventurers. On July 1, Burgoyne divided his forces at Lake Champlain. The British contingent went down the western side of the lake, while the Brunswick mercenaries, under Baron Friedrich von Riedesel, took the eastern side. By the time Burgoyne arrived at Fort Ticonderoga, he discovered that the Americans, under General Arthur St. Clair, had abandoned it. On July 7 a British unit under General Simon Fraser encountered a New Hampshire regiment in retreat from Fort Ticonderoga. The New Hampshiremen surrendered, but the rear guard of St. Clair's main force, commanded by Colonel Seth Warner, rallied and struck at Fraser. Fraser, on the verge of defeat, was about to withdraw when Baron von Riedesel, long delayed over rugged terrain, arrived with his mercenaries. Von Riedesel's men flanked the American position, then charged in on it with a devastating bayonet attack. Hearing the sounds of battle, St. Clair ordered a militia unit to the rescue—but the militiamen refused to budge. Warner ordered his troops to scatter and save themselves. The survivors—about six hundred of a thousand troops engaged (three hundred men were captured, about fifty killed)—straggled to rejoin St. Clair's main column, which was camped at Fort Edward, on the Hudson.

After taking Fort Ticonderoga, Burgoyne completed construction of a wilderness road approaching Albany, intending to meet up with General Barry St. Leger from the Mohawk Valley and Howe from the south, to deliver the crushing blow to the rebels and return to England in triumph. But on August 3, while camped near Fort Edward, waiting for his full forces to assemble, he received word from Howe that he would attack Philadelphia and be unable to join Burgoyne's operation.

Battle of Oriskany

Falsely informed by POWs that the American stronghold at Fort Stanwix was formidably garrisoned, St. Leger delayed his planned attack on the fort, giving time for the patriot militia general Nicholas Herkimer to coordinate an attack on him and his mixed force of British regulars, Tory units, and Indians at the Indian town of Oriskany, ten miles southwest of Fort Stanwix. One of St. Leger's Indian scouts brought the British commander word of the militia's advance. St. Leger dispatched four hundred Indians and an equal number of loyalist troops to ambush Herkimer's force. The Indians and loyalists struck at 10:00 A.M. on August 6. Most of the American officers were killed in the opening minutes of the battle. Herkimer himself was severely wounded, his leg shattered by a musket ball. Nevertheless, propped up against a saddle, he continued to direct the fight. Although one entire American regiment broke and ran, most of the patriots fought fiercely, suffering and inflicting heavy casualties. A sudden thunderstorm

Baron Friedrich von Riedesel, commander of Brunswick mercenary forces. *Collection: National Archives and Records Administration*

brought a temporary halt to the battle, providing time for the forces to regroup on higher ground. The British-allied Indians, disheartened by their heavy losses, suddenly retreated. With their desertion, the loyalist troops had no choice but to withdraw as well. The American forces were in no condition to give chase. Indeed, the Battle of Oriskany was a grim disaster for all concerned. Half of the American forces were killed, wounded, or captured. The British lost thirty-three killed, with forty-one wounded, and the Indians' losses were the heaviest of all: seventeen Senecas killed, including their chief warriors, and sixteen wounded; sixty to eighty Indians from other tribes were also killed or wounded, as were twenty-three war chiefs. Neither side could claim victory, but St. Leger again demanded surrender of Fort Stanwix. The commandant, Colonel Marianus Willet, refused to yield. In the meantime, General Philip Schuyler, encamped fifty miles away, dispatched a Massachusetts brigade to the relief of the fort; a short time after this, he also sent the First New York Regiment under General Benedict Arnold. Arnold managed to deceive St. Leger into believing that he commanded a vast number of troops, and the British general hastily lifted the siege on August 22, leaving behind a large store of equipment and artillery. This act of panic persuaded a number of Indian leaders to withdraw their support from the British. While the Battle of Oriskany, then, was a bloody draw, its aftermath put the British forces at a distinct disadvantage.

Battle of Bennington

In addition to British regulars, Tory militia forces, and Indian auxiliaries, the British crown employed some thirty thousand mercenary troops against the Americans. They were men from various German states, misleadingly lumped together under the name Hessians, probably because their principal commanders, a succession of three men, all came from Hesse-Cassel and Hesse-Hanau. Burgoyne detailed Hessian troops under Lieutenant Colonel Frederick Baum to take Bennington, Vermont. Opposing Baum were two hundred militiamen under General John Stark and four hundred men, led by Seth Warner, of the Vermont militia. On August 16, Stark and Warner moved in for a preemptive attack, with an enveloping movement from the front, rear, and flanks. In the shock of the initial assault, the Indians, Tories, and Canadians panicked and fled. The Germans and the British, dug in on a hilltop, held their ground and were joined by some of their fleeing comrades. For two hours, Stark and

Warner kept up the pressure. With ammunition dwindling, Baum's troops finally began to flee, except for his faithful dragoons. Baum, determined to save the day, ordered his men to draw sabers and charge into the Americans. It was a gesture both futile and fatal. When Baum fell, mortally wounded, his dispirited men surrendered. In the meantime, however, more German mercenaries arrived, led by Lieutenant Colonel Heinrich von Breymann. They were met at the outskirts of Bennington by Stark's troops, and by additional arrivals from the contingent of Vermont militiamen. Together these troops counterattacked von Breymann's forces. In the end, of the combined British and German forces, 207 lay dead and another 700 were taken prisoner. Thirty Americans fell in battle, and perhaps 40 more were wounded. It was, by any measure, a great patriot victory, which not only raised American morale but also deprived Burgoyne of supplies he badly needed, ending any possibility of his executing his grand strategy of splitting the American colonies in two.

Target: Philadelphia

William Howe left Burgoyne high and dry in upstate New York because he was lured by the prize Philadelphia appeared to be. As the home of the Continental Congress, it was effectively the capital of the rebellion and, moreover, it was the leading metropolis of the American continent, center of colonial wealth and culture. The capture of Philadelphia might well deal a decapitating blow to the Revolution. The attack was also a gambit to entrap Washington, who did, indeed, make the strategically obvious and faulty move of throwing everything he had into the defense of the city. What Howe hadn't counted on was how costly to the British the American defense of Philadelphia would be. Nor had he guessed that the colonials in New York and Vermont would beat Burgoyne even without the help of George Washington's army.

Battle of the Brandywine

After many delays, Howe transported fifteen thousand troops from New York to Philadelphia via Cape Charles and thence up the Chesapeake. He disembarked at Head of Elk, Maryland, fifty-five to sixty miles from Philadelphia, his troops sickly and weak from having been cooped up in ships during the summer. Howe's long delays gave Washington plenty of time to assemble and move his army. On August 24, 1777, the commander in chief and his Continental Army—at this point numbering about eleven thousand men—paraded through Philadelphia, marching southward to meet Howe, Cornwallis, and Baron Wilhelm von Knyphausen, the new commander in chief of the German mercenaries. On September 11, early in the morning, British troops were sighted near Kennett Square, Pennsylvania. Washington dispatched his main forces to meet them, only to discover, too late, that they were merely a diversionary force. Washington had left many of the upstream fords across Brandywine Creek undefended, and this is where Howe's main force now attacked the Americans from the right rear. All along the placid Brandywine, the thin American line began to give way. Howe threw von Knyphausen's Germans squarely against the American center at Chadd's Ford, while he and Cornwallis crossed the Brandywine at two other unguarded fords, outflanking Washington's army. Von Knyphausen broke through the American center and captured the Continental artillery, turning the guns on the retreating Americans. In great disarray by nightfall, Washington's army withdrew to Chester, Pennsylvania, where it regrouped and was still interposed between Howe and Philadelphia. Of some 11,000 American troops engaged at Brandywine, 1,200 to 1,300 were casualties, perhaps 400 of this number taken as prisoners. Eleven precious artillery pieces were captured. Howe, in overall command of 12,500 men, lost 577 killed and wounded, all but 40 of whom were British regulars.

The Paoli Massacre

From Chester, after resting the night, Washington fell back closer to Philadelphia. The British Army was now fifteen miles outside the revolutionary capital. On September 18, the Continental Congress evacuated to Lancaster, Pennsylvania, and then to York. In the meantime, on September 16, at White Horse Tavern and at Malvern Hill—both west of Philadelphia—Washington briefly engaged Howe's Hessians, using his small cavalry, which had just been organized and trained by the Polish patriot Casimir Pulaski. Washington then dispatched General Anthony (best known later as "Mad Anthony") Wayne with 1,500 men and four cannon to Warren's Tavern, near the town of Paoli, to harass the British rear guard. Wayne's camp was surprised during the night of September 20–21 by an attack so brutal that local residents dubbed the encounter the Paoli Massacre. Wayne estimated his losses at 150; Howe claimed his men had killed 500. Nevertheless, Wayne did manage to save his cannons and most of his men.

Philadelphia Falls

After the Paoli Massacre, Washington moved his troops to Pott's Grove (present-day Pottstown), Pennsylvania, whereupon Howe, changing direction, started his main body of troops across the Schuylkill River. On September 23, General Charles Cornwallis marched four British and two Hessian units into Philadelphia, unopposed. After taking possession of the city, he bedded down his forces in Germantown, just to the north of the city.

Washington was all too familiar with defeat and had learned that the best response to it was to attack. Audaciously, he resolved to attack precisely the position at which the British were strongest, Germantown, today a Philadelphia neighborhood, but in the eighteenth century, a village just north of the city. He hit Howe's advance units at dawn of October 4 with a force of 8,000 Continentals and 3,000 militiamen against 9,000 British troops. The British advance troops, the Fortieth Regiment, retreated to the large stone house of Benjamin Chew, which provided formidable protection from which the British poured fire on Continental general John Sullivan's troops. This delayed the American advance and created much confusion, which ultimately spoiled the attack. Washington had no choice but to order all forces to withdraw. From a military point of view, Germantown was a fiasco—150 American soldiers died, 521 were wounded, and 400 were captured. (Howe's casual-

"Mad Anthony" Wayne, painted by Edward Savage. *Collection: National Archives and Records Administration*

ties were 535 killed or wounded.) Yet, from a political and a psychological point of view, Germantown was something of a success. French observers were impressed by the fact that Washington, having lost Philadelphia, nevertheless made bold to attack. What they saw moved their government a step closer to outright alliance with the patriots. Nor did the officers and men of the American forces see Germantown as a defeat, but, rather, as a narrowly missed victory.

Burgoyne Resolves to Continue His Advance

If Washington was being battered in Pennsylvania, Burgoyne likewise reeled from one blow after another. The Hessians had been beaten at

Bennington, Barry St. Leger had failed to take Fort Stanwix, and General Howe was too busy in Philadelphia to join him in Albany. Yet Burgoyne continued to advance toward Albany, his original objective. Along the way, local patriots wrecked many small bridges spanning countless streams, slowing Burgoyne's progress to a mile per day—and often less. Advance parties, foraging for food, were continually sniped at. On September 16, Burgoyne still saw nothing, but he heard the distant rat-a-tat of reveille drums. Somewhere to the south, then, the main strength of the enemy must lay, and Burgoyne dispatched a party to reconnoiter. They found tracks leading to an abandoned farm.

Battle of Saratoga: First Phase, Freeman's Farm

Freeman's Farm was little more than an unharvested wheat field, but Burgoyne was anxious to draw the Americans out into battle in the open. He was so anxious that he made the basic tactical blunder of dividing his forces in the face of the enemy. The divided army, three columns, were out of sight of one another, which made it impossible to coordinate their movements. Seeing the vulnerable position of the British, American general Horatio Gates did nothing but wait. Frustrated, his subordinate, the dashing and impetuous Benedict Arnold, urged Gates to action. At last the commander ordered riflemen under the wily frontiersman Daniel Morgan and light infantry led by Henry Dearborn to make contact. Acting from ambush, Morgan's riflemen killed every British officer in the advance line, then charged into the line, causing it to stampede in panic. Suddenly, however, Morgan's men collided with the main body of the British center column. Now the pursuers became the pursued, retreating to the woods in complete disarray. Morgan, however, kept his head and rapidly re-formed his troops. As for the British, the encounter had so shaken and stunned them that as the advance-line survivors ran back toward the main body, many in the main body opened fire indiscriminately, wounding and killing their own men. Seeing the frenzied action, Burgoyne decided not to wait for a signal from Fraser's column, but fired his own signal gun and moved the main body of his troops onto Freeman's Farm, forming battle lines along its northern edge. As for the American response, the evidence is that Benedict Arnold, not Horatio Gates, effectively assumed command of the next phase of the battle. With Burgoyne's ranks neatly formed, European-style, in the clearing, Morgan and Dearborn took positions along the southern edge of the clearing, and seven more American regiments were sent down from Bemis Heights, just south of the farm. For the next three or four hours, a firefight pitted American wilderness tactics against the formal tactics of European soldiers. Firing from cover, the Americans cut through the ranks of the three British regiments standing shoulder to shoulder. The British suffered severe losses, but they retained their discipline and were able to return effective fire, augmented by artillery. Burgoyne's objective was to hold out until von Riedesel and Fraser arrived with reinforcements. The Americans wanted to destroy the British forces in detail before the arrival of those fresh troops. At last, however, von Riedesel broke through from the east and opened up on the Americans with cannon. Arnold had returned to Bemis Heights to get more troops, so was absent from the field when the Germans arrived. Essentially leaderless, therefore, the Americans held their ground for a time, but fell back as darkness settled over Freeman's Farm. By day's end, Burgoyne had lost some 600 men. American losses totaled 309, including 65 killed, 208 wounded, and 36 missing. Gates had more than enough men at Bemis Heights—4,000—to swoop down on the 900 men von Riedesel had left to guard Burgoyne's supplies. With his supplies gone, Burgoyne would have been faced with the choice of surrender or starvation. But Gates did not seize the initiative. When Arnold protested the lack of action, Gates relieved him of command. Only after a number of Gates's other officers protested was Arnold persuaded to stay on.

Battle of Saratoga: Second Phase, Bemis Heights

The next phase of the Battle of Saratoga moved from Freeman's Farm to Bemis Heights. Between the two fights was a lull of some days as Gates refused to press the action and Burgoyne awaited the arrival of reinforcements while also constructing elaborate entrenchments and redoubts on Bemis Heights. By now, however, Gates had been reinforced by the arrival of troops under General Benjamin Lincoln. Burgoyne was now outnumbered, 11,000 to 5,000. On October 7, feeling that he could no longer wait for Clinton's reinforcements or destruction at the hands of Gates, Burgoyne decided to send a reconnaissance in force of 1,650 men to determine just what he was facing. Gates dispatched Daniel Morgan to attack the right flank of the reconnaissance force and General Enoch Poor to attack the left. Morgan's men rushed wide around Burgoyne's troops to take up positions in the woods, from which they could fire on both flank and rear. Officially barred from headquarters, Benedict Arnold had nevertheless allowed brother officers to persuade him to stay in camp after Freeman's Farm. Now, with neither orders nor authorization, he gathered up a detachment to attack the breastworks behind which some of Burgoyne's men had taken shelter. Next, seeing Continental troops marching toward the British right, Arnold galloped directly across the line of fire to lead them away from the right and instead into a frontal assault against "Breymann's redoubt," a position held by Hessians. Arnold did not escape this attack unscathed. His horse was shot from under him, and then he took a bullet in the leg. Unable to continue, he had to be carried from the field.

Without Arnold to lead it, the American charge quickly petered out. But the damage to Burgoyne's army had already been done. The British suffered 600 killed or wounded, whereas American casualties were fewer than 150. Burgoyne fell back on Saratoga with his survivors as Gates continually harassed him in pursuit. On October 12 Gates maneuvered around Burgoyne, cutting off all access to the Hudson and, therefore, any hope of withdrawal north to safety. The next day, Burgoyne surrendered.

Gates was in a position to dictate harsh terms, but instead treated Burgoyne with great liberality. On October 16, the two commanders drew up the Saratoga Convention, by which the British and Hessian troops were permitted not only to avoid becoming prisoners of war, but also to return to England "on condition of not serving again in North America during the present contest."

That an American force had defeated an entire British army, driving it from the country, validated the Revolution not only in America but also in much of the international community—most significantly in France, which was at last moved to declare a full and open alliance with a nation that now called itself the United States of America.

The Valley Forge Winter

The end of 1777 was a critical time for Washington and his army. Washington, threatened by the so-called Conway Cabal, a movement among a handful of his officers to unseat him as commander in chief, successfully retained his position but, as usual, was faced with the problem of holding his army together during the long winter. Soldiers were ill clothed, and starvation was a real possibility; although it never came to that for the men, many of the army's horses did die for want of food. The troops' spirits were somewhat warmed by the news that, on December 17, 1777, the government of Louis XVI had declared its decision to recognize, openly and officially, American independence. Treaties of alliance were concluded, which were ratified by the Continental Congress on May 4, 1778. Nevertheless, about twenty-five hundred men died during the six months in camp. If the Valley Forge experience had a positive aspect, it was that the men who survived emerged a far more effective army for having been trained and drilled through the winter to European military standards by Baron Friedrich von Steuben (a Prussian general in volunteer service to the patriot cause), Lafayette, and other foreign officers.

IN THEIR OWN

Words

ith regard to military discipline, I may safely say no such thing existed [in the Continental Army]. The formation of the regiments was as varied as their mode of drill, which consisted only of the manual exercise.

—BARON VON STEUBEN, 1778

Effect of the Franco-American Alliance on the British

The effect of the Franco-American alliance on British forces was swift and dramatic, resulting in the transfer of many troops to the French West Indies, thereby relieving some of the pressure on patriot forces. The British garrison holding Philadelphia was transferred to New York City in March 1778, and Philadelphia was thus relinquished to the rebels.

Battle of Monmouth Courthouse

Before dawn on June 16, 1778, Clinton began removing artillery from the redoubts around Philadelphia. Noting this, Washington concluded that the British were preparing for some operation in New Jersey. By June 18, ten thousand British regulars and three thousand local Tories had left Philadelphia and were moving toward Haddonfield, New Jersey. Washington ordered Charles Lee to intercept. On June 28, an advance unit of New Jersey militiamen engaged some of Clinton's best regiments and was in desperate need of assistance. When Lee failed to respond, Washington ordered him to attack at once. But Lee made the tactical mistake of scattering his troops, and the attack failed. Lee ordered a retreat, temporarily stranding the small command of Anthony Wayne, who narrowly averted disaster. Washington rode into the mass of Lee's retreating men. Relieving Lee, he assumed personal command and, as Lafayette later remarked, he "stopped the retreat" by his physical presence and "calm courage." But Lee's failures had caused the Americans to lose the initiative, and the two sides fought near Monmouth Courthouse, in severe midsummer heat, until both the Americans and the British withdrew, exhausted. The battle was a draw: 356 Americans were killed, wounded, or missing, and 358 British were killed or wounded (some historians believe that British losses were much higher). While the Americans held the field, the British kept their army intact and were able to complete the evacuation from Philadelphia. Court-martialed, Charles Lee was removed from service.

Indian Warfare

The American Revolution is not easy to treat in brief, chronological compass. While it spanned nearly eight years, its major battles were few. Between major engagements, fighting continued as wilderness warfare between European Americans and Indians. During the Revolution, most Indian tribes that did not manage to remain neutral sided with the British. British-allied tribes included the powerful Mohawks, as well as other members of the Iroquois confederation, the Senecas, Cayugas, and Onondagas. Only the Oneidas and the Tuscaroras from the Iroquois confederation allied themselves with the Americans. They were joined in their support for the American cause by the Mahicans (also called the Stockbridge Indians). Indian warriors were active from the beginning of the war, and by September 1776, the entire American frontier throughout Virginia, Pennsylvania, and New York was in a state of panic created by sporadic Indian raids.

The Cherry Valley Massacre

Cherry Valley, about forty miles west of Schenectady, New York, had been subject to raids since 1776, but its settlers did little to defend themselves. Colonel Samuel Campbell weakly augmented his small militia force there by outfitting twenty-six boys with wooden rifles and pointed hats made of paper. The ruse fooled even Joseph Brant—at first—prompting him to attack nearby Cobleskill instead of Cherry Valley. Thirty-one Americans were killed and six wounded; Cobleskill itself was burned to the ground. Next, Pennsylvania's Wyoming Valley took the full brunt of Indian warfare. Back in New York, Joseph Brant again turned his attention to Cherry Valley, raiding Andrustown, seven miles west of Cherry Valley, on July 18. With 50 warriors and a few Tories, he captured fourteen settlers and killed eleven before burning the town. Next, on September 12, Brant attacked German Flats (present-day Herkimer) on the Mohawk River, destroying the evacuated village. Brant returned to Cherry Valley on November 10, 1778, and destroyed the settlement.

Washington Counterattacks

Cherry Valley was typical of the fighting in the wilderness, in which the Revolution took on the aspect of a bitter civil war conducted outside the rules of "civilized" combat. The Cherry Valley Massacre moved George Washington to authorize an ambitious campaign of retaliation against the Iroquois confederation, committing forces that might well have been used to greater advantage elsewhere. To an increasing degree, Indians became military objectives and fell victim to the conflict between the colonies and the mother country.

On June 18, 1779, General John Sullivan began marching a force of twenty-five hundred men from Easton, Pennsylvania, to the Susquehanna. Washington's overall strategy was three-pronged: Sullivan would cut a swath through the valley of the Susquehanna, up to the southern border of New York; General James Clinton (no relation to British general Henry Clinton), commanding fifteen hundred troops, would move through the Mohawk Valley to Lake Otsego and then proceed down the Susquehanna; and Colonel Daniel Brodhead would lead six hundred men from Fort Pitt up the Allegheny. At Tioga, Pennsylvania, Sullivan and Clinton would join forces, move north to Niagara, and meet Brodhead at Genesee. As they progressed, they were to sweep all that lay before them.

IN THEIR OWN
Words

I flatter myself that the orders with which I was entrusted are fully executed, as we have not left a single settlement or field of corn in the country of the [Iroquois], nor is there even the appearance of an Indian on this side of the Niagara.
—GENERAL JOHN SULLIVAN, REPORT TO THE CONTINENTAL CONGRESS, SEPTEMBER 1779

The Old Northwest and Kentucky

In the eighteenth and early nineteenth centuries, the "Northwest" was the frontier area lying north of the Ohio River and east of the Mississippi; historians call this the Old Northwest. By fall 1775, Shawnees began raiding the new Kentucky settlements. On or about July 4, 1776, at a grand Indian council among the Shawnees, Iroquois, Delawares, Ottawas, Cherokees, Wyandots, and Mingos, Chief Cornstalk formally abandoned neutrality and allied his followers with the British. By the end of January 1777, raids had driven most settlers from Kentucky, until only Harrodsburg and

Boonesboro could muster a body of men—just 103—to oppose the Shawnee chief Black Fish. On April 24, he turned against Boonesboro. During a four-day siege, 1 settler was killed and 7 wounded, including Daniel Boone, founder of the settlement, among the wounded. Yet Boonesboro survived, and Black Fish withdrew, periodically returning to attack this and other settlements. By this time, George Rogers Clark had persuaded Virginia authorities to make Kentucky a county of that state, and he was commissioned to raise and command a Kentucky militia. He decided to begin by attacking the British western forts at Kaskaskia, Cahokia, and Vincennes (in today's Illinois and Indiana), then to march to Detroit and capture that important stronghold, from which the British supplied their Indian auxiliaries. It was futile, Clark reasoned, to fight Indian raiders. Permanent victory required the destruction of Indian sources of supply. Early in June 1777, Clark discovered that the British garrison at Kaskaskia had been withdrawn to Detroit and that the surrounding settlements up to Cahokia were virtually defenseless. While Clark formulated his plan of attack and assembled the necessary forces, Shawnees, in concert with Wyandots, Mingos, and Cherokees, raided the area of Wheeling (in present-day West Virginia) during midsummer 1777. This moved Congress to dispatch General Edward Hand to recruit Pennsylvanians, Virginians, and Kentuckians for an attack on a British Indian supply depot on the Cuyahoga River, near present-day Cleveland, Ohio.

On February 8, 1778, the Shawnee chief Blue Jacket, with 102 warriors, captured a salt-making party of 27 at Blue Licks, Kentucky. Among the captives was Daniel Boone. He pretended to turn traitor, accepted adoption into the Shawnee tribe, and offered to cooperate with Henry Hamilton, England's ruthless liaison with the Indians, known to them as "Hair Buyer" because he paid bounties for patriot scalps. By feigning cooperation, Boone managed to delay an attack on Fort Pitt (at present-day Pittsburgh) and to gather information on an attack planned against Boonesboro. Armed with this information, Boone escaped just in time to mount a successful resistance at the settlement named for him. His brilliant and courageous undercover work helped save the frontier during the American Revolution.

Clark's Campaign

While Black Fish and other Indians terrorized the frontier, George Rogers Clark struggled to recruit troops. By the end of May 1778 he had managed to muster only 175 men to march against Kaskaskia and Cahokia, the first leg in a planned assault on British-held Detroit. On June 26, 1778, he embarked from Corn Island in flatboats, shot the rapids, and reached the mouth of the Tennessee River in four days. At Fort Massac, he and his men proceeded overland to Kaskaskia (in what is now southwestern Illinois), which, lightly defended, surrendered without a shot. From this new base, Clark took Cahokia and Vincennes. The fall of key forts in the Old Northwest certainly made life harder for the raiding Indians, but it also served to make them more desperate. Raiding became so severe in 1780 that Clark was forced to turn his attention from taking Detroit to raising a militia force to oppose the raiders. With about a thousand men, he managed to disperse the Shawnees, but his plans to take Detroit were spoiled by the need to oppose other raids mounted by Indians and Tories—many directed by the indefatigable Joseph Brant.

Late-Phase Combat in Upstate New York

General Sullivan's campaign of destruction, warmly greeted by the settlers of upstate New York, had not only failed to provide relief, but had actually inflamed the Indians. In the spring of 1780, Colonel Daniel Brodhead led five hundred to six hundred men in a month-long campaign along the Allegheny River and deep into Indian territory, destroying ten Mingo, Wyandot, and Seneca towns as well as some five hundred acres of corn in retaliation for raids. But on May 21, 1780, Sir John Johnson organized a massive assault on the forts and strong houses of the Mohawk Valley. With four hundred Tories and two hundred Indians, he burned Johnstown on May 23. During the summer, Joseph Brant hit the settlements of Caughnawaga and Canajoharie, then started down the Ohio, where he intercepted and ambushed a Pennsylvania militia force under Archibald Lochry. Out of a force of a hundred, five officers and thirty-five men were killed and forty-eight men and twelve officers were captured. The victorious Brant and his men turned back to New York, where they rejoined Johnson's Tories and a Seneca chief named Cornplanter. With a combined force of eighteen hundred, they descended upon the Scoharie Valley on October 15 and then progressed up the Mohawk River, burning everything they encountered. In a five-day raid, Johnson and his Indian allies had destroyed as much as General Sullivan had in a month-long campaign.

Joseph Brant had been wounded during Johnson's raid, and was out of action until early 1781, when he returned to harry the Mohawk Valley and Cherry Valley. With patriot fortunes in crisis, Colonel Marianus Willett was assigned command of the region. He had only 130 Continental troops and a handful of militiamen, but his vigorous and skillful action put an end to raiding for the rest of the summer of 1781. When attacks resumed in October, Willett engaged in desperate combat with Tories and Indians led by Walter Butler, who was fatally wounded. With his death, the raiders dispersed.

In the meantime, Joseph Brant met with Abraham, chief of the so-called Moravian Indians, members of the Delaware tribe who had been Christianized by Moravian missionaries. When Brant failed to recruit Abraham and his followers to fight the Americans, British authorities ordered these Indians' removal from Pennsylvania to the Ohio country. They set out for the Sandusky River, but by early 1782 a harsh winter famine compelled them to seek permission to move back temporarily to their western Pennsylvania mission towns on the Tuscarawas River. The Moravians arrived just after the Mohawks and the Delawares conducted a series of particularly brutal raids in the area. In February, Colonel Brodhead, now commander of the Continental army's Western Department, dispatched Colonel David Williamson to "punish" the hostiles. At Gnaddenhutten, Ohio, Williamson told Abraham and the forty-eight men, women, and boys gathered in the settlement that he had been sent to take them back to Fort Pitt, where they would be protected from all harm. At Williamson's request, Abraham sent runners to a neighboring missionary-Indian town, Salem, to fetch the Indians there and bring them back to Gnaddenhutten. No sooner was this done than Williamson had the wrists of each Indian bound behind him; when the fifty or so people from Salem arrived, he had them likewise bound. In the morning, Williamson announced that they would be put to death as punishment for what the Delawares had done. That night, each of the captives—ninety men, women, and children—was killed by a mallet blow to the back of the head. Two youths somehow escaped to tell the tale, and the Gnaddenhutten Massacre was subsequently condemned, but Williamson was not punished. The massacre, of course, provoked large-scale Indian retaliation, which pushed into Kentucky and nearly led to the abandonment of the Kentucky frontier.

The Southern Theater: Early Phases
During the early years of the Revolution, fighting in the South constituted virtually a separate war from the struggle in the North. At first there was

very little attempt, on either side, to coordinate the two theaters. As the British saw it, the South, in contrast to New England, harbored a large Tory population, and after the fall of Boston to the patriots, British military strategists turned to parts of the South where loyalism ran high.

The First Assault on Charleston

On June 4, 1776, ten British warships and thirty troop transports dropped anchor off Charleston Bar. British commander Henry Clinton's plan was to close in on Sullivan's Island and bombard the fort there. During this bombardment, the troop transports would unload onto Long Island, a short distance from Sullivan's Island. The infantry would then march onto Sullivan's Island and take the fort. Once that was done, invading Charleston itself would be a simple matter. The fort resisted stoutly, however, and Clinton's landing was badly botched. Sixty-four Royal Navy sailors died and 131 were wounded, while American losses in the fort numbered 17 dead and 20 wounded. The invasion was canceled, and years would pass before Charleston was attacked again.

The Fall of Savannah

The disappointment at Charleston prompted the British largely to neglect the South for the next two years, but after the Franco-American alliance was concluded in 1778, British strategy once again changed. From the end of 1778, the South became a principal focus of the British war effort. Savannah was the first target in the renewed southern campaign. On November 27, 1778, Lieutenant Colonel Archibald Campbell was dispatched from Sandy Hook, New Jersey, with 3,500 troops and a naval escort. On December 23, Campbell's command anchored off Tybee Island, at the mouth of the Savannah River. Defending Savannah were 900 Continental soldiers and a militia force of perhaps 150, all commanded by Gen. Robert Howe (no relation to the British Howe brothers). On December 29, 1778, Campbell fought the American defenders into retreat, and he marched into Savannah.

The Attempt to Retake Savannah

In the early autumn of 1779, French admiral D'Estaing, having failed in the first Franco-American amphibious operation against Newport, Rhode Island, and having withdrawn to the French West Indies, now decided to assist the Americans in the South, even though Washington wanted his fleet to coordinate operations with Continental troops in the North. Thirty-three French warships, mounting two thousand guns and escorting transports carrying more than four thousand French soldiers, surprised the British off the Georgia coast. D'Estaing quickly captured two British warships and two store ships, one of which carried a large payroll intended for the British garrison at Savannah. D'Estaing's fleet then briefly withdrew, returning on September 9 to land troops on Tybee Island. On September 16, with American units having joined him, D'Estaing demanded the surrender of Savannah "to the arms of the king of France." British general Prevost asked for a twenty-four-hour truce to consider his response. D'Estaing foolishly obliged, and Prevost used the time to mount a defense with more than three thousand troops. With the expiration of his twenty-four hours, he informed the admiral that he would fight. The battle did not commence until October 9. Combined French and American attack forces numbered fewer than 5,000, but Prevost enjoyed the advantage of defending from a fortified position. Prevost's men not only held, they also counterattacked, killing or wounding 800 of the allies (650 French). Among those killed was the dashing Polish officer who had virtually created the Continental cavalry, Casimir Pulaski. British losses were perhaps 100 killed or wounded. General Benjamin Lincoln, in overall command of the American forces, wanted to give the attack a second try, but D'Estaing feared bad weather and the fleet of the enemy. He withdrew to Martinique in the Indies, and the British occupation of Savannah would last through July 1782.

The Second Assault on Charleston

Charleston was still in patriot hands, but in the spring of 1779, General Prevost drove Gen. William Moultrie's American forces back upon the town. Learning that General Lincoln was approaching with a large American relief force, Prevost withdrew to Savannah for the moment, looting and pillaging the countryside on his way. It was not until year's end that Henry Clinton assembled a new force to strike at Charleston. A force of more than 11,000 set sail from New York on December 26, 1779. Bad weather delayed its arrival in the South until February 11, 1780, when troops were landed on Johns Island, thirty miles below Charleston. Defenses had been neglected since the early months of the war, and General Clinton slowly built up a siege force around Charleston. On April 1, Clinton's engineers began to dig a series of trenches from which siege operations would be conducted.

Although a force of 750 Virginia Continentals, having slipped past the British troops, arrived on April 6 to reinforce the garrison, the situation was becoming hopeless. The garrison could do no more than watch as Clinton engineered his painstaking siege. By April 10, with a major part of his siege works in place, Clinton demanded surrender from General Lincoln. When Lincoln refused, the British began bombarding on April 13, using mainly incendiary shot, which set part of the city ablaze. Still, Lincoln held out. His hope was that General Isaac Huger, encamped with a number of militiamen and 300 to 500 Continentals at Monck's Corner, South Carolina, would somehow provide a means of resistance or, at least, escape. On April 14, however, Banastre Tarleton and Patrick Ferguson led British and Tory forces in a surprise attack on Huger's encampment. American losses, of men, supplies, and badly needed cavalry mounts, were high, and Huger barely escaped with his life. With the defeat at Monck's Corner, Lincoln's garrison was left with no means of withdrawal from Charleston. On April 21, Lincoln offered terms to Clinton. The British commander responded with a demand for unconditional surrender. Two nights later a group of Americans sortied out against the British, but were quickly repulsed. It was a futile gesture. On May 8 Clinton issued another demand for uncondi-

Joshua Reynolds's portrait of Banastre Tarleton, Britain's most highly skilled—and ruthless—commander in the South. *Collection: National Archives and Records Administration*

tional surrender, which Lincoln rejected, holding out for better terms. Clinton's response the next night was a massive artillery barrage. Now it was the citizens of Charleston who petitioned Lincoln to yield. The American commander turned over Charleston to Henry Clinton on May 12, 1780. Five thousand American soldiers instantly became prisoners of war, and 400 precious artillery pieces and some 6,000 muskets also fell to the enemy. It was the single greatest patriot defeat of the Revolution—and threw open all of South Carolina to the British.

The Naval War

Britain possessed the most powerful navy in the world. In 1775 it included 131 ships of the line, each mounting at least 64 guns, some more than 100, and 139 major craft of other classes, many of them highly maneuverable frigates. By the end of the Revolution, in 1783, the total number of vessels had swelled to 468. Against this, at the start of the war, the United States had no navy at all. The first vessels acquired were a fleet of small craft brought together from various private sources during the siege of Boston. Congress authorized construction of 13 frigates, and by the end of the war, the U.S. Navy had 53 ships. The "official" fleet was variously augmented by state navies and by privateers, armed commercial vessels authorized to prey upon enemy shipping.

The Nassau Campaign

During March 3–4, 1776, the newly created Continental Navy carried out its first—and only—*planned* major naval operation in the war. Esek Hopkins, a Rhode Island farm boy turned sailor, was put in command of the first squadron of the new navy. He surprised British forces on Nassau (then called Providence or New Providence), Bahamas, by landing a force of U.S. Marines in their first action of the war, an assault on Fort Montagu. The raid not only took the fort but also netted a hundred cannon, a mortar, and the governor of the island, Monfort Browne, who was taken captive.

John Paul Jones

Among the junior officers serving in Esek Hopkins's small fleet (eight vessels, the largest of which were two merchant ships converted into small frigates of twenty-four and twenty-eight guns), was a young Scots immigrant named John Paul Jones. On April 6, 1776, just a little over a month after his triumph at Nassau, Esek Hopkins was leading five Continental ships back from the West Indies when the twenty-gun British frigate *Glasgow* attacked the flotilla about midnight off Block Island, part of the state of Rhode Island. *Glasgow* inflicted twenty-four casualties among the American sailors and severely disabled one of the ships. After the encounter with *Glasgow,* the American fleet began to fall apart. Officers and crew took up privateering or simply left the service altogether. Hopkins, whose action in Nassau had shown him to be an able seafarer, was nevertheless no great leader, and as the newborn Continental Navy struggled to survive, Hopkins was censured by Congress. When the inactive fleet was blockaded by the British in December 1776, his subordinates complained to Congress of his incompetence, and Hopkins was relieved of command. Another consequence of the *Glasgow* encounter was the court-martial of the captain of *Providence* for cowardice, and his replacement by Jones. While in command of *Providence* and a small flotilla, Jones captured or sunk twenty-one British warships, transports, and commercial vessels, as well as a Tory privateer by, the end of 1776.

On June 14, 1777, Jones was given command of the sloop *Ranger* and was ordered to France to take command of the frigate *Indien,* which was being built in Amsterdam for the Continental Navy. When he arrived in December, he found that the ship had been given to France by the American treaty commissioners, so he continued to sail in *Ranger,* leaving Brest on April 10, 1778, with a crew of 140. During April 27–28, 1778, Jones raided Whitehaven on Solway Firth in Scotland, spiking the guns of two forts and burning three British ships. Jones next crossed the Irish Sea to Carrickfergus, where he captured the British sloop *Drake* in a short, sharp action. He lost 8 men killed or wounded, but inflicted 40 casualties on the British. By the time he returned to Brest, on May 8, he had seven prizes and a good many prisoners.

In the summer of 1779, the French, having now entered the war, prepared five naval vessels and two privateers for Jones to lead, using a refitted East Indiaman called *Duras,* which Jones renamed *Bonhomme Richard.* With this vessel, sailing clockwise around the British Isles, Jones captured seventeen British ships. On September 23, 1779, off Flamborough Head, along the York coast, in the North Sea, Jones sighted two warships convoying forty British merchant vessels. The warships were the forty-four-gun *Serapis* and the twenty-gun *Countess of Scarborough.* Jones pursued *Serapis* while his three other vessels, *Vengeance, Pallas,* and *Alliance,* chased *Countess.* In the opening moments of this moonlit battle, two of Jones's largest cannon exploded, so that he was critically outgunned. But Jones nevertheless outmaneuvered *Serapis,* and rammed her stern. This put *Bonhomme Richard* in a position from which none of her guns could be brought to bear, and the captain of *Serapis,* seeing this, called out: "Has your ship struck?" —meaning "struck colors," or surrendered. Jones replied with perhaps the single most famous utterance in American naval history: "I have not yet begun to fight."

At this, the vessels separated, and *Serapis* now collided with *Bonhomme Richard.* Jones lashed on, tying the British vessel to his, then pounded it at point-blank range with his cannons that were still functioning. After two hours of this beating, it was *Serapis* that struck her colors.

The Southern Backcountry

As mentioned, during the earlier part of the war, the southern and northern theaters constituted virtually separate conflicts. In the South, the British concentrated mainly on the port cities of Charleston and Savannah, taking Savannah on the first attempt and Charleston, after a long hiatus, on a second attempt. Following the Battle of Monmouth Courthouse (New Jersey), on June 28, 1778, much of the major action of the war moved south—and no longer just to the principal towns, but to the backcountry as well.

The Waxhaws Massacre

While the British forces in America were notably lacking in aggressive leaders, Banastre Tarleton was an exception. After the British captured Charleston, Tarleton was assigned to mop up patriot forces in the Carolina countryside. His first victory—already mentioned—came at Monck's Corner (April 14, 1780). This was followed by the Battle of Lenud's Ferry, South Carolina, on May 6, an action against survivors of the Monck's Corner battle and fresh troops under Colonel Anthony White, resulting in the death or wounding of forty-one American troops and the capture of sixty-seven.

If Tarleton proved himself a brilliant wilderness fighter at Monck's Corner and Lenud's Ferry, he would be accused of utter ruthlessness at Waxhaws, South Carolina. Colonel Abraham Buford's Third Virginia Continentals, about three hundred men, were marching to reinforce Charleston during Henry Clinton's siege of the city. Charleston fell before Buford reached it, and this American commander now found himself leading the only substantial body of organized American troops remaining in South Carolina. Cornwallis ordered Tarleton (and others) to pursue Buford. By the early afternoon of May 29, Tarleton reached the tail end of Buford's column at Waxhaws, having ridden 105 steamy wilderness miles in 54 hours. Tarleton attacked savagely and overran the Americans. Buford hoisted a white flag but, according to legend, Tarleton failed to honor it and ordered a massacre. The fact is that Buford's losses had been so severe that they resembled a massacre. There is no evidence that Tarleton ordered an atrocity.

Battle of Camden

Against George Washington's recommendation, the Continental Congress put in command of the South the man who had been given credit for the victory at Saratoga, General Horatio Gates. Gates marched against Camden, South Carolina, held by 2,200 troops under Cornwallis. Along the way, Gates acquired militia reinforcements to augment his Continentals, amassing a force of more than 4,000. Gates's camp was swept by an epidemic of dysentery, however, that reduced the number of troops fit for combat. Despite this, during the night of August 15–16, 1780, Gates ordered a march to Camden. At about two-thirty on the morning of August 16, his column encountered that of Cornwallis. The fight degenerated into an American rout after two principal officers, Ortho Williams and Baron De Kalb, were wounded (De Kalb fatally). As many as 1,900 Americans died, and nearly 1,000 were taken prisoner. British losses were 68 killed and 350 wounded. As for Gates, the general fled the field before the conclusion of the battle.

Battle of King's Mountain

Cornwallis left Camden on September 8, 1780, having driven the American army from South Carolina. His next objective was North Carolina, and he moved toward it in three columns. While he led the main force, Tarleton headed up the British Legion and the regular light infantry, and Major Patrick Ferguson led the Tories. Once they reached North Carolina, the British met stiff resistance from diehard patriots. The British took Charlotte on September 26, 1780, but, in doing so, incurred substantial losses at the hands of patriot militia under Colonel William Davie. Cornwallis now found it difficult to maintain communication with his base in Camden, and the war in the Carolinas, like the war in New Jersey, New York, and other northern states, was dissolving into a series of local feuds between patriot and Tory neighbors. In an effort to recruit into the regular British army some of the many Tories who were undertaking guerrilla activities against their patriot neighbors, Cornwallis assigned Ferguson to lead the Tories along the foothills. Observing this, a group of patriot militia leaders attacked Ferguson, who retreated to the Catawba River and then up King's Mountain, on the border between North and South Carolina. Here Ferguson took his stand on October and was completely surrounded by the patriot forces. Ferguson himself was killed in the very act of killing an American officer. After the death of their leader, the Tory force surrendered, having lost four hundred killed or wounded. Seven hundred Tories became prisoners, a dozen of whom were summarily hanged in reprisal for British executions of Tory deserters who had taken up arms against their former comrades. The patriots suffered eighty-eight casualties. For the Americans, King's Mountain was a welcome triumph after so many defeats in the South. Cornwallis's advance was not only stopped dead in its tracks, but also the British general was forced to pull his troops back into South Carolina. King's Mountain put an end to significant Tory influence in North Carolina.

Battle of Cowpens

After the failures of Lincoln and Gates, Washington succeeded in appointing General Nathanael Greene to overall command of the region. Greene did not reach the field until December 1780, however, and in the interim, South Carolina partisans continually harried the British forces. When Greene arrived on the scene, he saw how effectively the American guerrillas worked, and assigned the most effective guerrilla leader, Daniel Morgan, to harass British positions in the western wilderness of South Carolina while Greene himself supported the operation of partisans in the north-central portion of the state. For his part, Cornwallis realized that Greene had divided his forces, and he dispatched Tarleton to take care of Morgan while he personally led an attack on Greene. On January 16, 1781, Morgan, commanding a thousand men, learned that Tarleton was nearby with eleven hundred Tories and regulars. Morgan decided to make a stand at Cowpens, little more than a backwoods South Carolina cattle pasturage. He proceeded, quite purposely, to violate

A portrait, engraved from a painting by Alonzo Chappel, of the militia commander Daniel Morgan. *Collection: National Archives and Records Administration*

every tenet of military common sense. To begin with, he positioned his men so that the Broad River cut off any avenue of retreat. Morgan was determined that for his militia, it would be do or die. Second, he put his rawest militiamen in the front line, backing them up with the Continentals and seasoned men from Virginia. Farthest to the rear, he held his cavalry—the very troops that are conventionally employed in the frontmost line.

Tarleton resolved to use a bayonet charge against Morgan, since bayonets had thoroughly terrified the provincial troops at Camden. Morgan, however, was prepared for a bayonet charge. "Look for the epaulets!" he had commanded his riflemen, describing just when to fire on an advancing line.

"Pick off the epaulets!" After firing in this manner, the American front line, the green recruits, sheared off to the left and around to the rear. Now the British moved against the second line, the seasoned men. Tarleton's troops were overconfident and attacked in very poor order. This, Morgan saw, was a blunder, and in a brilliant action, he ordered his green troops, who had returned to the American rear, to swing out and behind Tarleton's left while he put his cavalry into motion around to the rear of Tarleton's right. It was a double envelopment. Morgan had emulated the tactics the great Carthaginian general Hannibal had used to defeat the Romans at Cannae (in southeastern Italy) in 216 B.C. Cowpens not only preserved half of Greene's army, but also cost Cornwallis 100 killed, 229 wounded (and captured), and 600 captured (unwounded). Of 66 British officers engaged, 39 died. American losses were 12 killed and 60 wounded. Morgan's victory at Cowpens marked the turning of the tide in the South.

Swamp Warfare

Daniel Morgan was not the only effective guerrilla leader among the southern patriots. Francis Marion, grandson of fiercely independent Huguenots who had settled in South Carolina as early as 1690, was long active in the local militia, fighting Indians. On August 20, 1780, following the terrible American defeat at Camden, a mixed detachment of Tories and British regulars, escorting a large number of American prisoners, was hit fast and hard by men who suddenly materialized from out of a swamp. The attack came so swiftly that the Tory and British soldiers released their prisoners and ran, assuming they were about to fall prey to a major force. In truth, it was Marion at the head of no more than seventeen men. By this time, Tories and patriots alike were calling him the Swamp Fox.

Battle of Guilford Courthouse

After Cowpens, Cornwallis stripped his remaining troops of all the baggage that had for so long encumbered British armies in the American wilderness, and with his streamlined force pursued Greene's army northward, all the way to the Dan River, near the Virginia border. Once across that river, Greene took all the boats with him. Cornwallis found himself on the near shore of the Dan, desperately low on supplies (having sacrificed them to gain speed), and had to return to Hillsboro for resupply. In the meantime, Greene took the initiative. He recrossed the Dan into North Carolina to attack Cornwallis's lines of communication. Greene was careful, however, to avoid an all-out action until he had assembled enough men to outnumber Cornwallis. In the meantime, operations against local Tories—including a massacre of four hundred of them by Gen. Andrew Pickens—largely deprived the British general of his base of loyalist support.

At last, on March 14, 1781, Greene chose his battlefield: Guilford Courthouse, North Carolina. Aiming to duplicate the success of Daniel Morgan at Cowpens, he put his greenest troops up front, with the more seasoned veterans backing them up. The battle commenced the next day, with Greene ordering the front-line militia to fire two volleys before withdrawing to the rear. After discharging its volleys, however, the militia failed to retire in an orderly fashion, but instead rushed back chaotically, so that they were unable to get into position to effect a double envelopment. Greene also failed to deploy his cavalry for a decisive blow. The result was that Cornwallis had enough time to retaliate by firing grapeshot—in the process killing some of his own men in addition to the patriots. While

Cornwallis had not been driven from the field, he had lost a quarter of his army, and this was sufficient to prompt his evacuating the interior of North Carolina. Cornwallis led his men to Wilmington, on the Carolina coast.

Virginia

After the British withdrawal from the interior of North Carolina, the focus of the southern theater shifted north, to Virginia. Benedict Arnold, who had turned traitor in May 1779, offering to the British a scheme to surrender West Point, led a raid into Virginia beginning in December 1780, destroying, among other sites, a foundry and gunpowder factory at Westham and much of Virginia's new capital city, Richmond.

An engraving of John Trumbull's portrait of Benedict Arnold, a skilled and courageous Continental Army general who became the most infamous turncoat of the Revolution. *Collection: National Archives and Records Administration*

General Friedrich Wilhelm von Steuben, who now commanded patriot forces in Virginia, attempted to ambush Arnold en route to Westover, seat of the prominent Byrd family, but was deftly outmaneuvered. Arnold turned on Steuben's forces and neatly routed them. Arnold then encamped at Portsmouth for the winter.

Washington had dispatched Lafayette early in 1781 to fight Arnold in

Virginia. Lafayette took three light infantry regiments from the ranks of New England and New Jersey Continental troops to rendezvous with a French fleet. Because of a British blockade of Newport, Rhode Island, however, the French fleet was delayed and overtaken by a British fleet under Admiral Marriot Arbuthnot. The Battle of Chesapeake Bay, March 16, 1781, was a narrow French victory, but it nevertheless prompted French admiral Charles-René-Dominique Destouches, commander of the French squadron based at Newport, Rhode Island, to abandon the plan to join the Virginia expedition. In the meantime, the British commander in chief, Henry Clinton, was able to ship two thousand reinforcements to Benedict Arnold—along with Arnold's command replacement, William Phillips.

The abortive failure of yet another Franco-American amphibious operation put the patriot cause in grave peril. Steuben had only a handful of Continentals and a miscellany of militia troops to defend Virginia against the onslaught of three thousand British regulars and Tory auxiliaries. Lafayette was at Head of Elk, on the Chesapeake, 150 miles from Richmond. As for Washington, he was facing the very real prospect of watching his main army disband for want of food. In the meantime, General William Phillips and Benedict Arnold, on April 30, reached the James River and were poised to take Richmond. What stopped them was the arrival of Lafayette and twelve hundred Continentals.

Cornwallis was determined to destroy Lafayette and his small army. He consolidated a force of seventy-two hundred men by late spring of 1781 and intended to throw all of these against whatever Continentals and militia troops Lafayette could muster—about three thousand in all. At this time, in Petersburg, General William Phillips suddenly succumbed to typhoid fever, and Cornwallis assumed direct command of all British and Tory forces in Virginia. Recognizing that he greatly outnumbered Lafayette, Cornwallis ordered an advance out of Petersburg and pursued Lafayette northward. The Frenchman repeatedly eluded the British commander, who finally gave up the chase. He would content himself with turning John G. Simcoe and Banastre Tarleton loose on the Virginia countryside. Safe for the moment from Cornwallis, Lafayette received reinforcements—three Pennsylvania regiments under no less a commander than Anthony Wayne. With a total now of forty-five hundred men—and officers of Wayne's caliber with them—Lafayette felt ready to make a decisive move. He turned upon Cornwallis's army, which was traveling down

Virginia's York Peninsula. Lafayette sent his own force southward by a variety of roads to give the illusion of greater numbers. On June 26, 1781, elements of Pennsylvania and Virginia regiments caught up with Simcoe's Tories—the highly disciplined Queen's Rangers—at a tavern called Spencer's Ordinary. A short, sharp fight developed in which neither side could claim victory, and the Rangers broke free, leaving their wounded behind in the tavern.

General Charles Cornwallis, whose surrender at Yorktown heralded the end of the American Revolution. The engraving is from a painting by Sir William Beechey.
Collection: National Archives and Records Administration

Cornwallis Marches to Yorktown

Cornwallis engaged American forces under Lafayette and Anthony Wayne at Jamestown Ford (July 6, 1781) and narrowly defeated them, but chose not to pursue them. Instead he pressed on to Portsmouth, apparently intending to follow General Clinton's orders that he send troops to New York. In the interim, however, Clinton changed Cornwallis's orders: He was to occupy and hold a position in Virginia. Cornwallis decided to take and hold Yorktown, a sleepy tobacco port on the York River. To secure a means of supply and escape, Gloucester Point, on the opposite bank of the river, also had to be occupied, so Cornwallis committed forces there as well. Yorktown gave Cornwallis access to support from the Royal Navy, but it also made him vulnerable to being cut off by an enemy naval force.

Turning from New York to Virginia

Early in July 1781, the French army joined the Americans above New York. Initial contact with the enemy, however, persuaded Washington that the British were prepared to defend the city fiercely. Worse, Admiral François Joseph Paul, comte de Grasse, a senior French admiral commanding a large fleet and given broad discretionary orders, decided that the Chesapeake Bay offered the best approach to the mainland from the West Indies. He would not come as far north as New York. With a New York campaign now out of the question, Washington turned instead to Virginia. With French general Jean Baptiste Rochambeau, Washington would reinforce Lafayette and Wayne against Cornwallis while de Grasse would cut off the British commander's seaborne sources of reinforcement, communication, and supply. De Grasse would also land three West Indian regiments for use in the campaign against Cornwallis. By August 21, then, the march to Virginia was on.

Battle of the Capes

On September 1, Henry Clinton realized that Washington and Rochambeau were headed not for New York, as they tried to make him believe, but for Virginia. British admirals Samuel Graves and Samuel Hood set out from New York to intercept de Grasse's West Indian fleet and a French supporting fleet under Admiral Jacques-Melchior Saint-Laurent, comte de Barras, which had left Newport, Rhode Island. For the first time in its North American campaigns, the French fleet operated with brilliant efficiency. De Grasse beat the British to the Chesapeake, and French cruisers assumed positions in the James River to block Cornwallis, preventing his escape to the south. More French vessels blockaded the mouth of the York River, while the rest of de Grasse's fleet waited for the approach of the Royal Navy at the mouth of the Chesapeake.

For the present, Cornwallis was bottled up at Yorktown and could only await the onslaught of Washington and Rochambeau. However, if Admiral Graves acted boldly, he could still smash the French fleet and free Cornwallis. The two navies made contact on September 5, 1781, in Chesapeake Bay, at the Battle of the Capes. Admiral de Grasse enjoyed the advantages of numbers and firepower. The Battle of the Capes began at 4:00 P.M. and was over by six. Graves and Hood withdrew from the Chesapeake and returned to New York, leaving Cornwallis stranded at Yorktown.

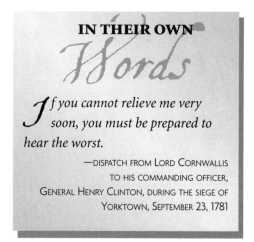

IN THEIR OWN *Words*

If you cannot relieve me very soon, you must be prepared to hear the worst.

—DISPATCH FROM LORD CORNWALLIS
TO HIS COMMANDING OFFICER,
GENERAL HENRY CLINTON, DURING THE SIEGE OF
YORKTOWN, SEPTEMBER 23, 1781

The Siege of Yorktown

By September 9, De Barras's fleet arrived to join de Grasse in Chesapeake Bay. With complete control of the bay now secured, de Grasse was able to land additional troops, so that when the allied forces were all assembled at Williamsburg, Virginia, they numbered sixteen thousand men. Cornwallis had some six thousand troops: Tarleton's Legion was posted at Gloucester, just across the York River from Yorktown, while the main force was bottled up within the fortifications of Yorktown itself.

On September 17, Washington and Rochambeau met aboard the *Ville de Paris* to plan the investment of Yorktown. The plan was simple: While de Grasse maintained control of the sea, the allies would encircle Yorktown and bombard it, using guns landed by de Grasse's ships. While this went on, allied engineers would dig trenches by which to approach the fortifications. With such an advantage of numbers, it was almost certain that the siege of Yorktown would succeed, if the allies made no gross blunders.

Beginning on October 1, 1781, American batteries started pounding Yorktown, and on October 6, Washington, with an uncharacteristically ceremonial flourish, personally broke ground for the first approach trench. On October 14, Alexander Hamilton and a French officer led a furious nighttime bayonet attack against defenders of two redoubts near the York River. These objectives secured, the approach trenches were now extended all the way to the river, completely cutting Cornwallis off. In desperation, on October 16, Cornwallis sent out a sortie of 350 men against a line of allied trenches. The defenders of these positions fell back, but the attackers were soon repulsed by French grenadiers. Cornwallis seized on a last hope: a nighttime breakout across the York River, to Gloucester Point, and then a forced march northward, all the way to New York. The first troops, the Guards and units of light infantry, were sent out in boats. The plan was for them to reach Gloucester Point, then send the boats back for more troops. A sudden storm, however, stranded the boats at Gloucester. There would be no escape. Cornwallis agreed to unconditional surrender on October 17, 1781. The formal surrender took place on October 19; seven thousand British prisoners of war now marched off to prison camps. Cornwallis and his principal officers were spared the indignity of captivity and were paroled to New York.

IN THEIR OWN *Words*

With an heart full of love and gratitude I now take leave of you. I most devoutly wish that your latter days may be as prosperous and happy as your former ones have been glorious and honorable.

—WASHINGTON'S PARTING WORDS
TO HIS OFFICERS AT FRAUNCES TAVERN,
NEW YORK, DECEMBER 13, 1783

Yorktown certainly did not wipe out the British presence in the United States, but it did end the British will to continue resisting the revolution. Facing possible action from the combined fleets of Spain and France, the British Parliament, on December 20, concluded that it was no longer possible to continue to fight to hold America. Fighting continued sporadically in the South, but peace negotiations commenced in Paris on April 12, with Benjamin Franklin acting as lead treaty commissioner for the United States. Franklin and the other commissioners pushed for and achieved three objectives: recognition of independence, adequate continental territory, and access to international waterways and to the rich fisheries of Newfoundland. By October 5, an agreement had been hammered out specifying U.S. boundaries, a program for the evacuation of British troops, access to the Newfoundland fisheries, and free trade on and navigation of the Mississippi. On November 30, 1782, a provisional treaty awaited ratification of the governments, and on September 3, 1783, the Treaty of Paris, having been duly ratified, was definitively signed.

CHAPTER 4

Conflicts of the Early Republic and the War of 1812

Shays's Rebellion, 1786–1787

Under the Articles of Confederation, the federal government of the United States had no authority to raise revenue by direct taxation and, as a consequence, found itself unable to compensate adequately the veterans of the *American Revolution, 1775–1783 (see chapter 3)* who had created the new nation. Demobilized troops of the Continental Army received little, if any, of the back pay due them. What payment they did collect was typically made in so-called "Continental notes," which were of such little value that the phrase "not worth a Continental" entered popular speech as a synonym for worthless. Even the states that had approved the issue of these notes now refused to accept them in payment of taxes. The lot of former officers improved when they were compensated mainly with land in the Ohio country, but enlisted veterans were left in the lurch. In rural Massachusetts, the veterans were especially hard pressed. They had not been paid, their crops brought dismal prices in a postwar depression economy, and they were subject to heavy taxation endorsed by the state's conservative governor, James Bowdoin. The situation was most acute in western Massachusetts, whose citizens felt themselves cheated of equitable representation by the provisions of the state constitution of 1780. Finding no relief from the government, these westerners began banding together in a paramilitary movement called "the Regulation." "Regulators" were groups of five hundred to two thousand men who, armed with clubs and muskets, marched on circuit court sessions with the object of intimidating the magistrates and postponing pending property seizures until the next gubernatorial election, which, they hoped, would see the conservative Bowdoin replaced by a more liberal governor.

For some five months, Regulators were active in Northampton, Springfield, and Worcester as well as in smaller towns. Strictly by means of intimidation, they succeeded in keeping the courts closed; no shots were fired, and there were no casualties. However, those members of the new national government who favored a strong concentration of federal authority saw the "rebellion" in western Massachusetts as an opportunity to demonstrate the urgent validity of their position. George Washington's future secretary of war, Henry Knox, personally investigated conditions at Springfield, where, he believed, the Continental Arsenal was vulnerable. Knox reported to Congress that the Regulation was indeed a full-scale rebellion led by one Daniel Shays (ca. 1745–1825), a former captain in the Continental Army. Knox, who advocated not only a strong central government but also a strong standing army, portrayed "Shays's Rebellion" as the work of radicals and anarchists who wanted to abolish private property, erase all debts, and generally incite a civil war. Knox knew that neither Massachusetts nor the federal government were in a position to finance an army to oppose the Shaysites, so he collaborated with Governor Bowdoin in appealing to Boston merchants to finance a force of forty-four hundred volunteers under Revolutionary veteran General Benjamin Lincoln.

Lincoln led his force to the Springfield Arsenal and there, during January 24–25, 1787, confronted fifteen hundred Regulators under Shays, Luke Day, and Eli Parsons. Lincoln fired a cannon into the assembled Regulators, killing three and sending the others into flight. Lincoln pursued and captured a number of "ringleaders." Several were tried for treason, two were hanged, and the Regulator movement came to an end. As for the namesake of the "rebellion," Daniel Shays fled to Vermont and later was granted a pardon.

Except for the final encounter, Shays's Rebellion consisted of a series of intimidating but bloodless demonstrations against a catastrophic taxation policy during a postwar depression. Knox and other Federalists, however, stirred fears that Shays's Rebellion was a civil war in the making and would soon spread to all thirteen states. This fear provided a large portion of the impetus to convene, in Philadelphia in May 1787, a Constitutional Convention, which scrapped the weak Articles of Confederation and drew up a Constitution mandating a strong central government to which the states were ultimately subordinate.

Little Turtle's War, 1786–1795

After the *American Revolution, 1775–1783,* a large number of settlers poured into Kentucky and the Ohio country. Victorious in the Revolution, the United States regarded the Indians of the Northwest, who had allied themselves with the British, as a conquered people who had forfeited their civil rights. Nevertheless, the federal government did attempt to regulate white settlement, and it did offer to buy—albeit cheaply—Indian territory rather than simply appropriate it. The Shawnees, however, resisted all negotiations and, in January 1786, a Shawnee chief named Kekewepellethe, known to the Americans as Tame Hawk, declared that the land desired by the settlers was Shawnee and always would be Shawnee. U.S. treaty commissioner William Butler replied to Tame Hawk that, on the contrary, the land was the sovereign territory of the United States. Under threat of war, and with his people suffering the effects of a hard winter and the ravages of the recently concluded Revolution, Kekewepellethe agreed to relinquish the entire Miami Valley. Immediately, however, other Shawnee bands, together with the Miamis, repudiated the agreement and, led principally by the war chiefs Blue Jacket (Shawnee) and Little Turtle (Miami), the Shawnees and the Miamis intensified a campaign of hit-and-run raids that had begun during the Revolution.

During the fall of 1786, Revolutionary War hero George Rogers Clark raised a 2,000-man militia in Kentucky and marched toward the Wabash Valley, where Shawnees, Miamis, and Ottawas were known to be meeting with British agents, who, in violation of the Treaty of Paris, had failed to clear out of U.S. territory. Clark, now an aged and infirm alcoholic, failed to encounter the enemy, and his militia returned home. Another 800 militiamen, under Colonel Benjamin Logan, attacked Shawnee villages on the

Miami River soon after this, but to little effect. In the summer of 1787, Logan conducted a more intensive raid, destroying large stocks of Shawnee provisions. This outrage served to unite the Shawnees more closely with the Miamis and with other tribes in the region, including Ottawas, Ojibwas (Chippewas), Kickapoos, and Potawatomis. Together, these tribes—sometimes also joined by Chickamaugas and Cherokees—raided white settlements along the Cumberland River during 1788.

By 1790, weary of chronic Indian trouble, settlers appealed for a federal campaign against the Indians throughout the entire Ohio Valley. A combined force of 1,216 federal troops—dubbed the First American Regiment—and 1,133 militiamen, all under the command of Josiah Harmar, marched against Little Turtle and Blue Jacket during the autumn of 1790.

The Indian leaders were well informed of Harmar's plan of attack. Secretary of War Henry Knox, fearful that the British in the area would interpret the movements of the army as an attack on them, directed territorial governor Arthur St. Clair to tell Major Patrick Murray, the British commandant at Detroit, that an attack was being launched against the Indians, not His Majesty's subjects. Murray thanked St. Clair for the information—then promptly informed the Indians.

On October 19, Harmar dispatched 150 mounted militiamen under John Hardin in hopes of locating a few Indians to fight. Little Turtle and his Miami warriors ambushed Hardin's company, which withdrew in panic, collided with infantrymen sent as reinforcements, and sent them into retreat as well. Only 30 regulars and 9 militiamen stood their ground against the attack. Harmar had no choice but to withdraw, and on October 21 he sent a small body of regulars and 400 militiamen back to Kekionga as a rear guard, which, again, encountered an ambush. This time it was Blue Jacket and his Shawnees who attacked. As before, the militia fled—but not before 108 of them had been killed; 75 regulars also were slain. Indians losses were heavy as well, perhaps 100 warriors killed. The only thing that saved Harmar's force from complete annihilation was a total lunar eclipse that took place the night following the battle, which the Ottawa warriors took as an evil omen, so, against the protests of Blue Jacket, they refused to press on with the fight.

After Harmar's defeat, the Shawnees and allied tribes staged a series of winter raids—highly daring and unusual, since Indians typically avoided fighting in the winter. Early in January 1791, Blue Jacket and 200

Shawnees laid siege to Dunlap's Station, a settlement near Cincinnati. Other outposts also were attacked, and even flatboat traffic on the Ohio River was routinely ambushed.

At the height of the violence in 1791, the British in the area suddenly volunteered to intercede. They had begun to fear that the incessant raiding would unleash a massive American force, which would drive out not only the Indians, but the British as well. These negotiations broke down, however, and the federal government assembled a force of 2,300 men under the command of Governor St. Clair.

The expedition advanced to the Great Miami River and built Fort Hamilton. St. Clair made painfully slow progress toward the Indian settlements. Eventually St. Clair led a detachment of 1,400 men on what he hoped would be a swifter march toward their objective. On November 3, 1791, this force made camp on a plateau above the upper Wabash River— a badly chosen, very vulnerable position. At dawn on November 4, Little Turtle and Blue Jacket led 1,000 warriors against the camp from three directions. Once again, the American troops panicked. Many soldiers dropped their weapons, ran about wildly, or cowered in prayer. After three hours of battle, about 500 men fled. Six hundred twenty-three officers and enlisted men died, along with 24 civilian teamsters; 271 soldiers were wounded. The Indians lost 21 warriors and had 40 wounded. In proportion to the number of men fielded that day, St. Clair's defeat stands as the worst loss the U.S. Army has ever suffered.

St. Clair resigned as commander of the First American Regiment and was replaced by the very able Revolutionary general "Mad Anthony" Wayne. In April 1792—after the Shawnees responded contemptuously to an offer of peace—Wayne recruited and carefully trained a force of 1,000 men, which he grandiosely dubbed the Legion of the United States. He marched westward, recruiting more troops as new peace talks began, faltered, and broke down.

During the long process of the talks, Wayne built a strong fort at Greenville, Ohio, and then, farther west, erected an advance position, Fort Recovery, on the very site of St. Clair's defeat. While Wayne consolidated his position, many of the allies of the Shawnees and the Miamis, restive under idleness, began to desert the cause. Fearing they would lose more warriors, Little Turtle and Blue Jacket decided to attack. On June 30, 1794, they hit a supply pack train, routing some 140 Legionnaires. Thus victorious, Blue Jacket and the youthful Tecumseh—a brilliant warrior who would earn his greatest fame in the *War of 1812, 1812–1814,* attempted to recall their men, but the Ottawas and other allies insisted on pressing the fight on to Fort Recovery itself. There Wayne's artillery turned them back, inflicting heavy losses.

As the Indian alliance continued to disintegrate, the bulk of the American forces—2,200 regulars and 1,500 Kentucky militiamen—arrived at Fort Recovery. Wayne ordered a more advanced stockade, Fort Adams, to be built, which was followed by another post, Fort Defiance. Just downstream from this newest fort, Little Turtle was counseling the leaders of his 1,500 remaining warriors that victory over Wayne was impossible. He called for peace negotiations. However, both Blue Jacket and Tecumseh refused to yield, and overall command of the Indian forces passed to Blue Jacket. Little Turtle was assigned to command only his 250 Miamis.

Blue Jacket decided to attack the Legion of the United States at a point opposite the rapids of the Maumee River. Pocked with deep ravines and strewn with the trunks of trees that had been blown down by a long-past tornado, the site was known as Fallen Timbers. The rugged terrain would provide the Indians ample cover and concealment. Wayne, whose scouts had informed him of the Indians' position, halted on August 17 a few miles short of Fallen Timbers. He rapidly built Fort Deposit, caching there all that was unnecessary for combat. On August 20, he advanced against Blue Jacket.

Perhaps Wayne's delay had been a brilliant stroke of strategy; perhaps it was just dumb luck. In any case, it exploited the warriors' custom of fasting before battle in order to put an edge on reflexes and ferocity. The Indians had expected an encounter on the eighteenth, so they had advanced to Fallen Timbers without rations on the seventeenth. By the twentieth, they had gone hungry for three days. Some warriors left to look for food; many of the others were feeling weak. An excellent tactician, Blue Jacket planed to encircle Wayne in a vast, half-moon-shaped line. Unfortunately for his plan, an Ottawa commander acted prematurely, leading his men in a charge against the advance guard of 150 mounted Kentucky militia. This induced a panic, but Wayne was no Arthur St. Clair, and he quickly rallied the main body of his troops. Turning defeat into victory, he routed Blue Jacket. Retreating to Fort Miami, a British outpost, Blue Jacket and his warriors were stunned when the commandant, Captain William Campbell, under orders to remain neutral, refused to admit the Indians to the fort.

The Battle of Fallen Timbers broke the back of Indian resistance in the Ohio Valley. After the battle, Wayne set about destroying all of the now-abandoned Indian towns he could find, and in January 1795 Blue Jacket came to Fort Greenville, in western Ohio near the present Indiana state line, to negotiate a treaty with Anthony Wayne. The Treaty of Greenville secured white occupancy of lands northwest of the Ohio River, established yet another "permanent" boundary of white settlements west of the present state of Ohio, and instituted a program of compensation for territory lost ($20,000 as a lump sum and an annual payment of $9,500). For their part, the British agreed at last to vacate the Old Northwest, the U.S. government successfully asserted control over this important frontier territory, and the peace of the Ohio country endured until the outbreak of the *War of 1812, 1812–1814.*

Whiskey Rebellion, 1794

For many proindependence Americans, the principal object of the *American Revolution, 1775–1783 (see chapter 3)* had been to achieve freedom from direct taxation by a remote government; however, George Washington's secretary of the treasury, Alexander Hamilton, structured a direct taxation plan aimed at financing the national debt and supporting a substantial central government, a government that would, in fact, take precedence over state and other local governments. In this way, Hamilton believed, the United States would not only gain financial viability but also would be forged into a genuine nation rather than a collection of confederated states. At Hamilton's urging, Congress, on March 3, 1791, enacted a federal excise tax on spirits distilled in the United States. Opposition to this federal tax was both rapid in coming and intense in feeling. The focal point of protest was western Pennsylvania, where federal tax collectors were harassed, threatened, intimidated, and even assaulted. A number were tarred and feathered, as were certain distillers who chose to cooperate with the revenue officials.

Violence reached a flash point during the summer of 1794 when, on July 16, a band of about five hundred attacked the home of General John Neville, Allegheny County's inspector of the excise. Neville did not meekly submit to the attack, but defended his home with the aid of a small detachment of U.S. Army regulars. Two of the attackers were killed and six wounded. Outnumbered, however, Neville and his men made their escape, leaving the house to the mercy of the mob, which looted and then burned it.

The attack on Neville briefly emboldened the Whiskey Rebellion insurgents, who assembled at Braddock's Field, near Pittsburgh, on August 1, 1794, almost 6,000 strong. Yet a full-scale rebellion failed to gel. By August 3, the 6,000-man "army" had dissolved and dispersed. But this did not satisfy President George Washington, who announced on August 7 that he was calling out the militia to restore order and to enforce the excise tax. Simultaneously with this show of force, Washington dispatched to western Pennsylvania a team of commissioners to offer amnesty to all those who agreed to swear an oath of submission to the United States. Although organized violence was at an end, few came forth to swear the oath. At last, therefore, on September 25, Washington ordered 12,950 militiamen and volunteers from Pennsylvania, New Jersey, and Maryland to march to Pittsburgh. This large force managed to apprehend and arrest a small number of participants in the Whiskey Rebellion, but the majority of the prominent insurgents fled and hid. All those arrested were subsequently granted presidential pardons.

The suppression of the Whiskey Rebellion was of negligible military significance, but it was politically very important. It demonstrated the willingness—and the capacity—of the federal government to enforce national laws. It asserted the authority of a central government, even in the western reaches of the new nation. Yet even as it enforced national law, the national government heeded a key lesson of the Whiskey Rebellion, which revealed the depth and intensity of popular resentment of federal taxation. In 1800, during the administration of President Thomas Jefferson, Congress repealed the federal excise tax on whiskey.

American-French Quasi-War, 1798–1800

Friction between France and the United States, close allies during the *American Revolution, 1775–1783 (see chapter 3),* began in the course of the peace negotiations that ended the Revolution, as it became clear that France was more interested in opposing Britain and furthering the territorial ambitions of its ally Spain than in truly upholding the cause of U.S. independence. Deviating from the terms of the Franco-American alliance, the U.S. treaty commissioners made what was in effect a separate peace with Britain. This created outrage and a feeling of betrayal in the French court. Not that the French court was destined to endure. The fall of the Bourbon monarchy in the French Revolution brought renewed warfare between France and Britain in 1793, and Franco-American relations deteriorated yet further because the revolutionary French government interpreted U.S. policy as deliberately favoring British interests over those of France. The French Girondist government sent Edmond Charles Édouard Genêt—by the etiquette of the Revolution known as Citizen Genêt—to the United States to secure U.S. aid to France in its expanding war with England. After President Washington rebuffed Genêt's overtures, the French emissary directly approached American privateers with proposals that they prey on British shipping in U.S. coastal waters. When Washington warned Genêt that the federal government would not tolerate his violating national sovereignty with such proposals, Genêt responded with a threat to appeal directly to the American people. At this, Washington requested that the French government recall Genêt. In fact, at this point, the Jacobins had ousted the Girondists in France, and the new government demanded that the United States now extradite Genêt as a traitor to France. The president who had asked for Genêt's recall now refused to extradite him to certain death on the guillotine, and "Citizen" Genêt ultimately became a naturalized U.S. citizen. The Genêt affair exacerbated tensions between France and the United States.

A year after the episode, in 1794, President Washington sent Supreme Court chief justice John Jay to negotiate a boundary and trade treaty with Great Britain. A key condition of the Treaty of Paris that had ended the *American Revolution, 1775–1783 (see chapter 3)* was the British evacuation of outposts on the western frontier. Not only did the British government fail to enforce this provision, but also American settlers in the region believed that British interests were inducing the Indians to raid. Additionally, the boundaries between British North America and U.S. territory were also hotly disputed. For their part, the British also had grievances, chief among which was a claim that Americans were repudiating prerevolutionary debts owed British creditors and that the federal government had not compensated loyalists for property confiscated during the Revolution. When Britain began routinely intercepting American merchant ships on the high seas and "impressing"—abducting—certain American sailors (deemed to be British navy deserters or simply British subjects) into service in the Royal Navy, the Anglo-American crisis reached a critical point. President George Washington appointed Jay to negotiate a "Treaty of Amity, Commerce, and Navigation," which laid a firm foundation for amicable Anglo-American trade, secured the British evacuation of the frontier forts, and secured the limited right of American ships to trade in the British West Indies.

As Anglo-American relations improved, Franco-American affairs became increasingly heated. Concerned, President John Adams authorized the U.S. minister to France, Charles Cotesworthy Pinckney, to call on the French Directory in an effort to patch up relations. That legislative body indignantly refused to receive the American minister, whereupon Adams dispatched a commission consisting of Pinckney, John Marshall, and Elbridge Gerry to Paris in 1797 with the object of negotiating a new treaty of commerce and amity with France. French prime minister Charles Maurice de Talleyrand-Périgord sent three agents to greet the commissioners and conveyed the message that before a treaty could even be discussed the United States would have to "loan" France $12 million and pay Talleyrand a personal bribe of $250,000. On April 3, 1798, an outraged Adams presented to Congress the correspondence of the commission, which designated the French agents not by name but by the letters X, Y, and Z. Congress published the correspondence, and thus the American public learned of the "XYZ Affair." The affront moved the nation to mobilize for war against its former ally.

Indeed, by the time the XYZ Affair came to light, French naval operations against the British in the West Indies were already beginning to interfere with U.S. shipping, and Congress authorized the rapid completion of three great frigates—*United States, Constellation,* and *Constitution*—as well as the arming and training of some eighty thousand militiamen. Congress also commissioned a thousand privateers to capture or repel French vessels, and no less a figure than George Washington was recalled to command the army. On May 3, 1798, the undeclared war became the occasion for the formal creation of the U.S. Department of the Navy.

In July 1798, Stephen Decatur, commanding the sloop *Delaware*, captured the French schooner *Croyable* off the New Jersey coast. Renamed the *Retaliation*, the vessel was retaken by the French in November 1798 off Guadaloupe. On February 9, 1799, the freshly commissioned USS *Constellation* captured the French frigate *Insurgente*. Additional exchanges took place sporadically through 1800, mainly in the Caribbean. Of ten important engagements, the French recapture of *Croyable/Retaliation* was the only American loss.

Despite the aggressiveness of the fledgling U.S. Navy and American support for the Haitian independence movement led by former slave Toussaint Louverture, war between France and the United States was never formally declared. When Napoleon assumed the leadership of the French government by his coup d'état of November 9, 1799, he sent unofficial word to American authorities that France sought reconciliation with the United States. For Napoleon, the problem was that he needed the support of neutral Denmark and Sweden to lend legitimacy to his new government, and he was therefore eager to be seen as a supporter of the rights of neutrals such as the United States. The result of the change in French attitude was the *Convention between the French Republic and the United States of America,* of 1800, which officially brought an end to what had been an unofficial war. The treaty embodied a list of contraband goods—war materiel subject to confiscation by either side—but specified that except for this contraband, "it shall be lawful for the Citizens of either Country to sail with their ships and Merchandize . . . from any port whatever, to any port of the enemy of the other, and to sail, and trade with their ships, and Merchandize, with perfect security, and liberty, from the countries ports, and places, of those who are enemies of both, or of either party, without any opposition, or disturbance whatsoever and to pass not only directly from the places and ports of the enemy aforementioned to neutral ports, and places, but also from one place belonging to an enemy, to another place belonging to an enemy, whether they be under the jurisdiction of the same power, or under several, unless such ports, or places shall be actually blockaded, besieged, or invested." This clause, the heart of the treaty, directly addressed the source of the quasi-war conflict and reinstated amicable relations. Equally important, it ended any implied *military* alliance between France and the United States.

Tripolitan War, 1801–1805

After the successful conclusion of the *American Revolution, 1775–1783 (see chapter 3),* the new republic faced a number of serious military crises. The most critical was the unremitting guerrilla warfare between the Indians and settlers of the frontier regions, especially in the Ohio country.

But the United States was also threatened from abroad by the "Barbary pirates," Muslim seafarers who had been operating from the so-called Barbary states (present-day Morocco, Algeria, Tunisia, and Libya) off the coast of North Africa since the seventeenth century. These pirates were not simply criminals; rather, they enjoyed the financial and political backing of wealthy merchants and even political leaders. It is accurate to describe the "piracy" as an organized government activity.

To avoid harassment, capture, and confiscation of cargoes, "Christian" nations plying North African waters routinely paid extortionary tribute money to the Barbary (Berber) states. Initially the United States, like other nations, paid the tributes demanded, but U.S. officials saw this as both an insult and a threat to American sovereignty. Accordingly, the United States successfully fought a series of limited naval wars to win the right of free navigation of the North African waters. These "Barbary Wars" spanned 1801 to 1815, with the most concentrated action occurring in the Tripolitan War of 1801–1805. The background of the wars goes back even further—for the United States, at least to 1785, when Great Britain encouraged Algiers to capture two U.S. vessels. Thomas Jefferson, at the time American minister plenipotentiary to France, attempted to recruit the aid of Portugal, Naples, Sardinia, and Russia, as well as France, in an anti-Algerian alliance. When France declined to cooperate, the alliance collapsed, and Britain encouraged further Algerian action in which twelve American ships were captured and more than a hundred American sailors imprisoned. This prompted the United States to negotiate a treaty with the bey of Algiers in 1795, pledging tribute to secure release of the captives and to ensure freedom of navigation. Additional treaties were concluded with Tunis and Tripoli.

Despite the treaties, the idea of tribute never sat well with the U.S. government or with the American people, and there was a long delay in sending the tribute money. Shortly after the inauguration of President Thomas Jefferson in 1801, Pasha Yusuf Qaramanli, Tripoli's ruler, unofficially declared war against the United States. Jefferson concluded a coalition with Sweden, Sicily, Malta, Portugal, and Morocco against Tripoli, which forced Qaramanli to back down. For the next two years, one U.S. frigate and several smaller U.S. Navy vessels patrolled the Tripolitan coast. This mission proceeded successfully until the frigate USS *Philadelphia* ran aground in October 1803 and was boarded by Tripolitan sailors, who captured three hundred U.S. sailors, took the ship as a prize, and prepared to use it against the Americans. In February 1804, however, Lieutenant

Stephen Decatur, with daring and stealth, entered Tripoli Harbor and burned *Philadelphia.* After this, Commodore Edward Preble stepped up the ongoing bombardment of Tripoli, and Decatur was hailed as a great American naval hero.

Against the background of the ongoing bombardment, William Eaton, U.S. consul at Tunis, proposed an alliance with Ahmed Qaramanli, the brother Yusuf had deposed in 1795. Eaton also recruited an army of Arabs and Greeks and joined these to a contingent of U.S. Marines to support the restoration of Ahmed as ruler of Tripoli. Eaton's force captured the city of Derne in 1805 just as the Jefferson government, which had neither opposed nor supported the Eaton plan, concluded a treaty of peace with Yusuf on June 4, 1805. The treaty ransomed the prisoners for $60,000 and, although it made no explicit mention of the subject of tribute, it put a de facto end to the practice of tribute payment by establishing free and unhindered commerce between the United States and Tripoli. At home, the treaty was celebrated as a great triumph for the fledgling U.S. Navy. See also *Algerine War, 1815,* later in this chapter.

"Decatur's Conflict with the Algerine at Tripoli. Reuben James Interposing His Head to Save the Life of His Commander." Copy (1804) of an engraving after a painting by Alonzo Chappel. *Collection: National Archives and Records Administration*

War of 1812, 1812–1814

The War of 1812 has been called America's "second war of independence" and has been justified as a fight to protect and enforce U.S. sovereignty, which was being violated by the British in three major ways. First, despite the Treaty of Paris, ending the *American Revolution, 1775–1783 (see chapter 3),* and Jay's Treaty, resolving certain territorial disputes, British commercial interests, mostly fur trappers and traders, repeatedly "invaded" U.S. territory on the western frontier. Second, British interests incited anti-American Indian hostility in the West in an effort to evict U.S. commercial interests from the frontier region. Third, the Royal Navy routinely "impressed"—abducted for service in the Royal Navy—American merchant sailors unilaterally deemed to be deserters from the British navy or, at the very least, British subjects liable for service.

It is this third point that traditionally has been cited as the principal cause of the War of 1812. It is true that Britain was at war with Napoleonic France during this period and therefore had an urgent need of sailors to man its warships, and it is also true that Royal Navy vessels frequently intercepted and boarded the ships of neutrals, including merchant vessels of the United States, to impress into the British service men arbitrarily deemed to be British subjects. Yet it is also true that the United States declared war on Great Britain on June 18, 1812, even though, on June 16, Great Britain had agreed to end impressment on the high seas, effective June 23. That impressment was thus rendered a nonissue is evident from the silence of the Treaty of Ghent (which ended the war on December 24, 1814) on the subject. It was, in fact, the first two issues mentioned, relating to the sovereignty and peace of U.S. western territories, that more nearly describe the true causes of the war. Viewed more cynically, however, the *single* most pressing origin of the conflict was the republic's insatiable hunger for new territory. The most attractive parcel of new land was so-called Spanish Florida, which in 1812 extended as far west as the Mississippi River. Because Spain was an ally of Great Britain against Napoleon, American "War Hawks" (congressmen and others who favored war) reasoned that victory in a war against Britain would ultimately result in the acquisition of its ally's territory, which would be joined to the vast western territories acquired by the Louisiana Purchase. Thus the War Hawks, led by Henry Clay of Kentucky, persuaded President James Madison to declare war. It was soon bitterly clear, however, that contemplating the fruits of victory was much easier than actually achieving victory.

Much of the action in the War of 1812 was along the U.S.-Canadian frontier region between Detroit and Lake Champlain. Ostensibly the United States was fighting to defend its sovereignty; however, the initial American strategy was hardly defensive. Many American politicians and military leaders saw as their objective an invasion of Canada, which would add new, economically productive territory to the United States. For their part, the British sought to fight the war in U.S., not Canadian, territory. Forces shipped from England expanded the theater of operations to include the mid-Atlantic coast and the U.S. territories around the Gulf of Mexico. Thus the War of 1812 came to encompass a far-flung portion of North America, from Canada to New Orleans.

As in the *American Revolution, 1775–1783 (see chapter 3),* the ambi-

CHRONOLOGY   Principal Events of the War of 1812

1812

June 1: *President James Madison recommends a declaration of war*

June 4: *House of Representatives passes a war bill*

June 18: *Senate passes the House bill, and Madison signs*

July 17: *Michilimackinac falls to the British*

August 15: *Fort Dearborn Massacre*

August 16: *Detroit falls to the British*

October 13: *Battle of Queenston*

November 23: *U.S. invasion of Canada collapses*

November 27: *United States attacks Fort Erie*

December 26: *Britain begins blockade of Chesapeake and Delaware Bays*

1813

January 23: *Raisin River Massacre*

April 15: *United States occupies West Florida*

April 27: *Battle of York*

May 26: *British blockade expands*

May 27: *Battle of Fort George*

August 30: *Battle of Fort Mims*

September 10: *Battle of Lake Erie*

October 5: *Battle of the Thames; Tecumseh slain*

November 9: *Battle of Talladega*

December 18: *Fort Niagara falls to the British*

1814

January 22: *Battle of Emuckfau*

January 24: *Battle of Enotachopco*

March 27: *Battle of Horseshoe Bend*

July 3: *United States captures Fort Erie*

July 5: *Battle of Chippewa*

July 25: *Battle of Lundy's Lane*

August: *U.S. financial crisis—public credit collapses and U.S. banks suspend specie payments*

August 8: *Peace talks begin in Ghent, Belgium*

August 9: *United States and Creek Nation sign Treaty of Fort Jackson*

August 24: *United States badly defeated at Battle of Bladensburg, Maryland*

August 24: *British general Ross burns Washington*

September 11: *Battles of Plattsburgh and Lake Champlain*

September 12: *Battle of Mobile Bay*

September 13: *Battle of Baltimore*

September 14: *Francis Scott Key writes "The Star-Spangled Banner"*

December 23: *Prelude to Battle of New Orleans*

December 24: *Treaty of Ghent is signed*

1815

January 8: *Battle of New Orleans*

February 11: *Treaty of Ghent reaches the United States*

February 16: *Senate ratifies the Treaty of Ghent; the war ends*

tion to invade Canada proved grandiose and impractical. The Revolution had been fought, in part, against the evils of maintaining a standing army—the British "Quartering Act"—and thus, from the very period of the nation's origin, the people and government of the United States resisted the idea of maintaining a large standing army. But now that the United States had declared war against a great European power, it was forced to confront the fact that it had a standing army of only twelve thousand regular troops to fight the war. Moreover, these forces were broadcast across a vast territory and were led by generals of very uneven ability, most having attained their rank through political connections rather than military prowess. As to the U.S. Navy, its officers were of a higher caliber than those of the army, but it was nevertheless a puny force compared to the mighty Royal Navy. These facts notwithstanding, American strategists devised plans for a three-pronged invasion of Canada: a penetration from Lake Champlain to Montréal; another across the Niagara frontier; and a third into Upper Canada (Ontario) from Detroit. Undermanned, poorly led, and thoroughly uncoordinated, all three prongs would fail.

IN THEIR OWN *Words*

An Act Declaring War Between the United Kingdom of Great Britain and Ireland and the Dependencies Thereof and the United States of America and Their Territories.

Be it enacted by the Senate and House of Representatives of the United States of America in Congress assembled, That war be and the same is hereby declared to exist between the United Kingdom of Great Britain and Ireland and the dependencies thereof, and the United States of America and their territories; and that the President of the United States is hereby authorized to use the whole land and naval force of the United States to carry the same into effect, and to issue to private armed vessels of the United States commissions or letters of marque and general reprisal, in such form as he shall think proper, and under the seal of the United States, against the vessels, goods, and effects of the government of the said United Kingdom of Great Britain and Ireland, and the subjects thereof.

APPROVED, June 18, 1812

Chosen to command American forces north of the Ohio River—three hundred regulars and twelve hundred Kentucky and Ohio militiamen (who soon deserted and had to be replaced by Michigan volunteers)—was the governor of Michigan Territory, William Hull (1753–1825). Hull had been a minor hero of the Revolution, but he was nearly sixty years old when he led his forces across the Detroit River into Canada on July 12, 1812. His objective was to take Fort Malden, which guarded the entrance to Lake Erie, but as he approached, he believed himself outnumbered, so he repeatedly delayed his assault. The delays afforded the highly capable British commander, Major General Isaac Brock, sufficient time to bring his regulars into position. While Brock maneuvered, the American garrison at Fort Michilimackinac, guarding the Mackinac Straits between Lake Huron and Lake Michigan, was overrun and surrendered without a fight on July 17, 1812.

On August 2, the brilliant Shawnee political and war leader Tecumseh began harassing and ambushing Hull's columns. Terrified, the American commander, still believing himself vastly outnumbered (at this time, Tecumseh actually led only about seven hundred warriors), hurriedly withdrew from Canada and headed back to Fort Detroit. Now Brock united his six hundred men with Tecumseh's warriors, marched on Fort Detroit, and intimidated Hull into surrendering without a shot, on August 16. (Hull was later convicted of cowardice and sentenced to death by firing squad, but he was pardoned by President James Madison.)

The day before Hull surrendered Detroit, Fort Dearborn (at the site of present-day Chicago) also surrendered to a mixed force of British and Indians. As troops and settlers evacuated the fort, Potawatomi Indians attacked, killing 35 men, women, and children, mainly by torture.

In the Northeast, New York militia general Stephen Van Rensselaer led 2,270 militiamen and 900 regulars in an assault on Queenston Heights, Canada, just across the Niagara River. Part of this force, mostly the regulars, got across the river before General Brock, having rushed to Queenston from Detroit, pinned them down on October 13. At this the rest of the militia refused to cross the international boundary and stood by as 600 British regulars and 400 Canadian militiamen overwhelmed their comrades. The result was a terrible and humiliating American defeat: 250 U.S. soldiers died, and 700 became prisoners of war. The British lost a mere 14 men killed and 96 wounded. However, the British suffered one staggering loss: Isaac Brock fell in battle.

Despite the defeat of Hull and Van Rensselaer, the principal U.S. force had yet to attack. Major General Henry Dearborn led 5,000, mostly militiamen, down Lake Champlain, and, on November 19, was about to cross into Canada. Suddenly the militia contingent asserted its "constitutional rights" and flatly refused to fight in a foreign country. Faced with

IN THEIR OWN
Words

Maj James Miller 4th Us Inf
Upper Canada, August 27th 1812

My Dearest Ruth,
When I last wrote you my feelings were very different from what they now are. I then thought that things appeared prosperous and flattering. I considered we had a sufficient force to bear down all opposition and I still think had we done as we ought we could carried conquest to a very considerable extent, but alas times are now altered we are all Prisoners of War. Sunday on the 9th, I was on a march from Detroit to the river Reason with the 4th Regt. and a Detachment of Ohio Militia consisting of six hundred in the whole in order to guard some provisions which was coming on for our Army. About sixteen miles from Detroit at a place called Maguago near an Indian town or rather betwixt two Indian towns, I was attacked in a thick wood by a superior number of British and Indians. They made the first attack a very heavy fire upon us then the most hideous yell by the Indians. The woods

appeared to be full of them. I had all my men formed to the best advantage the moment we saw their fire. I ordered a general charge which was instantly obeyed by every officer and soldier. We visited closer on them then made a general fire upon them and put them to flight. We drove them through the woods firing and charging them without a halt for more than two miles completely defeated them and drove them every devil across Detroit River home to their own Fort except those who we took prisoners and killed, which was a considerable part of them. My killed and wounded amounted to seventy five, Sixteen of whom were killed dead on the ground. They took no prisoners from me. I secured the body of every man I had killed or wounded. We took five prisoners, but made no Indian prisoners. We gave them no quarters. They carried off their wounded generally from the number of the enemy found dead. Their loss of killed and wounded must have been nearly double to ours. We wounded the famous Tecumseh in the neck, but not sufficiently to kill him. Lieut. Larrabee has lost his left arm in consequence of a wound in the action. No officer was killed, but five wounded. Lieut. Larrabee the worst.

mutiny, Dearborn withdrew without significantly engaging the enemy, and thus ended the project to invade Canada.

The rapid collapse of Detroit and Fort Dearborn, coupled with the total failure of the Canadian campaign, laid the Midwest open to Indian assault and British invasion. The British had been highly successful in recruiting Indian allies, especially among the Shawnee and associated tribes in the Midwest, because the Indians believed that a British victory would push the aggressive American invaders out of their territory. Although guerrilla warfare thus became intense along the frontier, neither the British nor their Indian allies were able to capitalize decisively on the advantages they gained. U.S. commander Zachary Taylor drove off a Potawatomie assault on Fort Wayne, Indiana Territory, on September 5, 1812, and although most of the so-called Old Northwest (corresponding to much of the present-day Midwest) did fall under Indian control, a coordinated British assault on the region, which might have brought the War of 1812 to a quick and devastating end, never materialized. The Indians' British allies were insufficiently aggressive. While Tecumseh was eager to push the fight, Colonel Henry Proctor, the British commander who had taken over from the slain Brock, was as dull and hesitant as his predecessor had been brilliant and aggressive. He declined to support Tecumseh. This bought U.S. general William Henry Harrison enough time to mount effective counterattacks. As 1812 drew to a close, Harrison destroyed villages of the Miami Indians near Fort Wayne (this despite the fact that Miamis were noncombatants), and he raided what amounted to Indian refugee camps near present-day Peru, Indiana.

William Henry Harrison, victor at the Battle of Tippecanoe, as depicted in a copy of a popular print published in the mid-nineteenth century. *Collection: National Archives and Records Administration*

In January 1813, Harrison moved against Fort Malden, advancing across frozen Lake Erie, only to suffer a major defeat on January 21 at the hands of Proctor and a contingent of Red Stick Creeks led by a skilled chief named Little Warrior. The origin of the disaster was the premature action of one of Harrison's subordinate commanders, James Winchester. Moving out ahead of schedule, he was attacked by Little Warrior at Frenchtown (present-day Monroe, Michigan), on the Raisin River. Of 960 American troops engaged, 400 were killed and about 500 made prisoner. Only 33 evaded death or capture. Yet, once again, Proctor failed to capitalize on what he had achieved. Between July 21 and 23, 1813, even though he commanded some 3,000 combined British and Indian troops, Proctor did not even attempt to capture a crucial U.S. supply depot, Fort Stephenson on the Sandusky River, which was defended by a mere 150 men under the heroic Major George Croghan.

Recognizing Proctor's inept lack of aggression, his Indian allies began to desert him, thereby giving the Americans a reprieve. This did nothing to alter the fact that the Americans of the Old Northwest had suffered a stunning defeat during 1812–1813. By the fall of 1813, 4,000 had been killed or captured, compared to combined British and Indian losses of no more than 500.

While American land forces achieved no major victories in 1812— and, indeed, suffered a number of serious reverses—the tiny U.S. Navy achieved some remarkable results. The British blockaded U.S. naval and commercial shipping with 1,048 Royal Navy vessels, against which the U.S. Navy could bring to bear only 14 seaworthy craft in addition to a motley fleet of privateers. Nevertheless, U.S. frigates emerged victorious in a series of single-ship engagements, the most famous of which were the battles between the USS *Constitution* ("Old Ironsides") and the British frigate *Guerrière,* off the coast of Massachusetts on August 19, 1812, and between *Constitution* and *Java,* off the Brazilian coast on December 29, 1812. Impressive as they were, these triumphs were hardly sufficient to break the blockade, which tightened into a stranglehold that destroyed American trade and brought the U.S. economy to the brink of collapse.

In 1813, as mentioned, renewed American attempts to invade Canada failed, and the Niagara frontier was stalemated. At the end of 1813, the attempt to attack Montréal in a combined assault, with one force advancing along Lake Champlain and another sailing down the St. Lawrence River from Lake Ontario, also collapsed. In the West, however, the American situation became somewhat brighter. After the January disaster at Fort Malden, William Henry Harrison set about rebuilding and even enlarging his army, which grew into a force of eight thousand by the late summer of 1813. While Harrison resurrected U.S. land forces, a dashing young naval officer named Oliver Hazard Perry hastily cobbled together an inland navy. Beginning in March 1813, he directed construction of an armed flotilla at Presque Isle (present-day Erie), Pennsylvania, while he trained his sailors in artillery techniques. By August he was ready to move his vessels onto Lake Erie. On September 10 he engaged the British fleet in a battle so fierce that he had to transfer his flag from the severely damaged brig *Lawrence* to *Niagara,* from which he commanded nothing less than the destruction of the entire British squadron. He sent to General Harrison a message that instantly entered into American history: "We have met the enemy and they are ours."

Perry's great victory cut off British supply lines and forced, at long last, the abandonment of Fort Malden—as well as a general British evac-

IN THEIR OWN *Words*

From *Cartel for the Exchange of Prisoners of War Between Great Britain and the United States of America,* concluded November 28, 1812

Article I

The Prisoners taken at sea or on land on both sides shall be treated with humanity conformable to the usage and practice of the most civilized nations during war; and such prisoners shall without delay, and as speedily as circumstances will admit, be exchanged. . . .

Article VII

No prisoner shall be struck with the hand, whip, stick or any other weapon whatever, the complaints of the prisoners shall be attended to, and real grievances redressed; and if they behave disorderly, they may be closely confined, and kept on two thirds allowance for a reasonable time not exceeding ten days. They are to be furnished by the government in whose possession they may be, with a subsistence of sound and wholesome provisions, consisting of, one pound of beef, or twelve ounces of pork; one pound of wheaten bread, and a quarter of a pint of pease, or six ounces of rice, or a pound of potatoes, per day to each man; and of salt and vinegar in the proportion of two quarts of salt and four quarts of vinegar to every hundred days subsistence. Or the ration shall consist of such other meats and vegetables (not changing the proportion of meat to the vegetables, and the quantity of bread salt and vinegar always remaining the same) as may from time to time be agreed on, at the several stations, by the respective agents of the two governments, as of equal nutriment with the ration first described. Both Governments shall be at liberty, by means of their respective agents to supply their prisoners with clothing, and such other small allowances, as may be deemed reasonable, and to inspect at all times the quality and quantity of subsistence provided for the prisoners of their nations respectively as stipulated in this article.

uation from the Detroit region and a retreat east. On October 5, 1813, Harrison overtook the retreating British columns and their Indian allies at the Battle of the Thames. The great Indian leader Tecumseh fell in this battle, and although no one knows who killed him, it is certain that with his death, the Indians' last real hope of halting the northwestward rush of white settlement likewise died.

The victories of Perry and Harrison turned 1813 from another year of disaster into one of at least potential triumph. Although American forces achieved no other major victories during this year, the Battle of Lake Erie and the Battle of the Thames were sufficient to suggest that the tide of war might be turning. But then, in Europe, Paris fell (March 30, 1814), Napoleon's marshals mutinied (April 1), and the emperor abdicated (April 4, 1814). Napoleon was exiled to the island of Elba, and, it seemed, the long series of Napoleonic Wars were at an end. The British could now turn their fuller attention to the war in North America.

Supplied with more ships and more troops, including veterans of the campaigns against Napoleon, British command drew up plans to attack in three principal areas: in New York, along Lake Champlain and the Hudson River, which would sever New England from the rest of the union; at New Orleans, which would block the vital Mississippi artery; and in Chesapeake Bay, to threaten Washington and to create a diversion that would draw off and pin down U.S. manpower. The objective was to beat down the United States and thereby extort major territorial concessions in return for peace. The victories of 1813 notwithstanding, by the fall of 1814, the American situation looked black. Strangled by blockade, threatened on three fronts, the United States was hurtling toward economic ruin. In New England, some opponents of the war had begun talking about leaving the Union. From December 15, 1814, to January 5, 1815, twenty-six delegates from five New England states gathered at the Hartford Convention (Hartford, Connecticut) to protest the disastrous Democratic-Republican conduct of the war. Formal consideration of secession never got very far, but the closed-door meetings raised alarms nationwide that the delegates were plotting ways to take their states out of the Union. To many citizens, the country seemed to be falling apart.

Militarily, the situation grew increasingly grim. Late in the summer of 1814, American resistance to the attack in Chesapeake Bay folded, and the British, under Major General Robert Ross, triumphed in Maryland at the Battle of Bladensburg (August 24). Green Maryland militiamen commanded by the inept General William H. Winder broke and ran under fire. Ross then easily invaded Washington, D.C., where he burned most of the public buildings, including the Capitol and the White House. President Madison and most of the government fled into the countryside. From Washington, Ross advanced north on Baltimore. His amphibious forces bombarded Fort McHenry, in Baltimore Harbor, during September 13–14, 1814. The event was witnessed by a young Baltimore lawyer, Francis Scott Key (1779–1843), who was being detained on a British warship. Key kept vigil through the night of shot and shell and, at "dawn's early light," saw that the "Star-Spangled Banner" yet waved over the fort. That bastion had not fallen to the British, who, meeting much stiffer resistance here than they had in Washington, ultimately withdrew. Key, of course, was moved to memorialize the experience of that night in verse, which eventually (March 3, 1931) became the lyrics to our national anthem.

The salvation of Baltimore was a hopeful sign, but, nevertheless, while Washington burned and Baltimore fell under attack, ten thousand British veterans of the Napoleonic Wars advanced into the United States from Montréal. Opposing them on land was an inferior American force, but on September 11, 1814, American naval captain Thomas MacDonough engaged the British squadron on Lake Champlain. The result of this critical battle was the destruction of the squadron. Thus deprived of a vital link in communication and supply, the British army retreated, and the offensive along Lake Champlain collapsed.

Throughout much of the war, both sides made continual efforts to reach a peaceful conclusion, even as they continued battle. As early as March 1813, President Madison accepted Russia's offer to mediate. The British rejected the mediation in July 1813 but made separate peace overtures, which Madison accepted in January 1814. Talks were delayed until July, then convened at Ghent, Belgium. Britain's initial demands were unacceptable, calling for the establishment of an Indian buffer state in the U.S. Northwest and territorial cessions along the Canadian border. The American victory at the Battle of Lake Champlain greatly strengthened the U.S. negotiating position, especially after Britain's own duke of Wellington—victor over Napoleon—refused to take command in Canada. At last, the war-weary British decided to forgo territorial demands, and the United States, on its part, withdrew its demand that Britain recognize American neutral rights—in effect renouncing a major reason for having gone to war in the first place. The Treaty of Ghent, signed on December 24, 1814, officially restored the *status quo antebellum,* and the document was unanimously ratified by the U.S. Senate on February 17, 1815. Beyond ending the war, little was definitively resolved by the Treaty of Ghent, although it did establish a joint U.S.-British commission to set a definitive boundary between the United States and Canada. (Thorny boundary issues were not satisfactorily resolved until the Webster-Ashburton Treaty of August 9, 1842.) The signatories also agreed to "engage to put an end . . . to hostilities with all the Tribes or Nations of Indians with whom they may be at war . . . and forthwith to restore to such

Tribes or Nations respectively all the possessions, rights, and privileges which they may have enjoyed or been entitled to in one thousand eight hundred and eleven previous to [the War of 1812]." The treaty's Article X included a clause concerning the slave trade: "Whereas the traffic in slaves is irreconcilable with the principles of humanity and justice, and whereas both His Majesty and the United States are desirous of continuing their efforts to promote its entire abolition, it is hereby agreed that both the contracting parties shall use their best endeavors to accomplish so desirable an object."

In theory, the Treaty of Ghent may have restored the *status quo antebellum,* but in actuality the United States was not the same after the war as it had been before. It languished under a crippling economic depression, but it also benefited from withdrawal of British support for "hostile" Indians; this made the West that much riper for white expansion. Nor did the treaty bring an immediate

"General Andrew Jackson. The Hero of New Orleans, 1815." Lithograph by James Baillie, made during the 1840s. *Collection: National Archives and Records Administration*

end to the war. Word of the Treaty of Ghent did not reach General Andrew Jackson, who was marching on New Orleans, having defeated the Red Stick Creeks in the *Creek War, 1812–1814* (discussed later in this chapter).

Jackson's objective was to engage the fifty-three hundred British regulars under Gen. Edward Pakenham, who, supported by naval forces under Vice Admiral Sir Alexander Cochrane, were en route to the city from Jamaica. Jackson's forces consisted of thirty-one hundred Tennessee and Kentucky volunteers, in addition to New Orleans militiamen and a collection of locals (including "free colored" volunteers), bringing his total force to about forty-seven hundred men.

On December 23, 1814, Jackson first engaged the British forces and unsuccessfully attempted to drive them off. On December 28 and again on January 1, 1815, Pakenham jabbed at Jackson's defenses with a reconnaissance in force and with an artillery bombardment. At last, on January 8, Pakenham launched his principal attack, against Jackson's line on the eastern bank of the Mississippi. Simultaneously he made a smaller attack against positions on the western bank of the river. The secondary attack succeeded, but the main assault failed disastrously, as the advancing British ranks withered under volleys of Jackson's grapeshot and canister shot. British casualties were twenty-four hundred killed and wounded. Among the slain were Pakenham and his two senior subordinates. Jackson lost about seventy men and had forced the British to withdraw.

To most Americans, it mattered little that the Battle of New Orleans had been fought *after* the Treaty of Ghent had officially concluded the war. It mattered even less that the War of 1812 had been overwhelmingly a losing proposition for the young republic. Jackson's triumph made the war seem like an American victory. While the Treaty of Ghent resolved little, the effect of the war was to strengthen the bonds of nationhood.

Creek War, 1812–1814

The British made much use of Indian allies during the *War of 1812, 1812–1814,* especially in the Old Northwest. In the Deep South, particularly along the Gulf Coast, white-Indian warfare amounted to a separate war fought simultaneously with the War of 1812. In Georgia, Tennessee, and the Mississippi Territory, the Creek confederacy was plagued by violent dissension between those who advocated cooperation with whites and those determined to expel white settlers from Creek lands. The former were generally the Lower Creeks, also called the White Sticks, who lived mainly in Georgia, and the latter were the Upper Creeks, or Red Sticks, who lived to the west of the White Sticks and somewhat farther from white settlement. Little Warrior, of the Red Sticks, fought against the Americans in the War of 1812, taking part in the massacre of James Winchester's command on the Raisin River (near present-day Monroe, Michigan) on January 21, 1813, and raiding settlers along the Ohio on his way home from that battle. As Little Warrior journeyed homeward, the White Stick chief, Big Warrior, ambushed him, took him captive, and executed him. This greatly widened the gulf between the White Stick and Red Stick factions and intensified the violence of their ongoing conflict.

Equipped by the Spanish in Pensacola, Florida, Red Sticks led by a half-breed known as Peter McQueen attacked a party of settlers at Burnt Corn Creek in present-day Alabama. But the worst catastrophe for the settlers came on August 30, 1813, when William Weatherford (Red Eagle), a half-breed partisan of Tecumseh, attacked Fort Mims, north of Mobile, Alabama, on the lower Alabama River. Major Daniel Beasley, commanding the fort's garrison of Louisiana militia, ignored the warnings of black slaves who reported seeing Indians in the tall grass outside the stockade. At noon 1,000 Red Sticks attacked, using, among other weapons, flaming arrows. When it was all over, more than 400 settlers had been killed, 36 escaped, and most of the black slaves were spared. It was to be the last Indian attack on a settlement east of the Mississippi, and it brought down a terrible vengeance. The Tennessee legislature authorized $300,000 to outfit a large army under Major General Andrew Jackson, who advanced into Red Stick country with 5,000 Tennessee militiamen, 19 companies of Cherokee warriors, and 200 White Sticks. Early in November 1813, a detachment under Colonel John Coffee (including Davy Crockett) ambushed a large contingent of Red Sticks at Tallashatchee, in Calhoun County, Alabama. Red Stick losses were 186 killed; Coffee lost 5 killed and 41 wounded. Later in the month, Jackson marched a few miles south of Tallashatchee to the relief of Talladega, a White Stick fort that had been held under siege. It was reported that 290 Red Sticks died in this engagement. Jackson's losses were 15 killed and 85 wounded. Following this engagement, Jackson and General William Claiborne fruitlessly pursued Red Eagle for two months, during which time Jackson's forces were diminished by desertions and the expiration of short-term enlistments. Jackson was unable to resume offensive operations until January 1814, when he received 800 new troops. During the month, he engaged the Red Sticks at Emuckfau and at Enotachopco Creek. Jackson was ruthless in the destruction of Red Stick towns.

By March, Jackson's militia had been augmented by the addition of 600 regulars from the U.S. Thirty-ninth Infantry. With this force he attacked Horseshoe Bend, a peninsula on the Tallapoosa River. After a day-long battle on March 27, 1814, in which Jackson's army besieged and bombarded the Red Sticks' desperately defended position, about 750 of the 900 Red Stick warriors engaged lay dead. Losses among Jackson's white troops were 32 killed and 99 wounded. Jackson's Cherokee auxiliaries lost 18 killed and 36 wounded, while White Stick Creek allies counted 5 dead and 11 wounded. Red Eagle appeared in Jackson's camp a few days after the battle and formally surrendered. Jackson allowed him to depart in peace, but he was not nearly so generous to the other Indians—Red Stick foe and White Stick and Cherokee allies alike. The Treaty of Horseshoe Bend, which formally ended the Creek War, extorted twenty-three million acres from the Red Sticks as well as the White Sticks—a total of two-thirds of *all* Creek tribal lands. White American settlement was thus extended from the Tennessee River to the Gulf of Mexico. As to the Cherokees, Tennessee militiamen stole their horses, vandalized their property, took their food, and generally abused women, children, and old men.

Algerine War, 1815

Like the *Tripolitan War, 1801–1805,* the conflict with Algiers—the so-called Algerine War—was one of the Barbary Wars, fought by the United States to end state-sanctioned piracy by the Barbary States. During the *War of 1812, 1812–1814,* the U.S. warships that had been keeping the Barbary pirates in check were withdrawn from the Mediterranean. This encouraged the dey of Algiers to resume preying on American commerce in the region. The dey expelled the U.S. consul, imprisoned or enslaved U.S. nationals, and then declared war on the United States for having violated a 1795 treaty by which the United States had pledged payment of extortionary tribute in return for safe passage of commerce vessels. In response to the declaration of war and with the pressures of the War of 1812 having ended, Commodore Stephen Decatur led a ten-ship squadron into the Mediterranean and, between March 3 and June 30, 1815, captured two Algerian warships, then sailed into the harbor of Algiers. With his artillery trained on the city, Decatur demanded cancellation of tribute and the release of all U.S. prisoners without ransom. The June 30 Treaty of Peace with Algiers also incorporated the dey's pledge to end state-sanctioned piracy.

From Algiers, Decatur proceeded to Tunis and Tripoli, where, at cannon's mouth, he compelled similar treaties and also secured compensation for American vessels that had been seized at the behest of the British during the War of 1812. Thus the brief Algerine War ended U.S. participation in the Barbary Wars and represented a triumph of sovereignty for the young American republic. Despite the treaty of 1815 and another concluded in 1816, Algerian piracy remained a diminished threat to the shipping of the United States and other non-Muslim nations until France captured Algiers in 1830.

First Seminole War, 1817–1818

As the *War of 1812, 1812–1814* drew to a close, the British built a fort in Florida—which was a Spanish colony at the time—at Prospect Bluff on the Apalachicola River. During the summer of 1815, after the war, the British abandoned the fort to a group of Seminoles and a band of fugitive slaves. Known locally now as "Negro Fort," it posed a threat to navigation on the Apalachicola, the Flint, and the Chattahoochee Rivers and, as a refuge for escaped slaves, also affronted all Southern slaveholders. In spring 1816, the U.S. Army built Fort Scott on the Flint River fork of the Apalachicola in Georgia, and, in July, an attack against Negro Fort was launched from Fort Scott. Land forces were supported by two gunboats on July 27. The skipper of one of the gunboats decided to heat a cannonball red hot before firing it. The result of a direct hit on Negro Fort's powder magazine was an explosion said to have been the biggest bang on the American continent to that date. About three hundred African Americans, including men, women, and children, died, along with about thirty Seminoles. This incident pushed the Seminoles to the brink of war. When Lieutenant Colonel Duncan Lamont Clinch rushed in after the explosion to seize twenty-five hundred muskets, a thousand pistols, five hundred swords, and a quantity of powder belonging to the Seminoles, war became a certainty.

Yet the Seminoles, aware that Clinch had used the captured weapons to arm the rival Coweta tribe, delayed action until November 1817, when a Seminole chief named Neamathia, who occupied a village called Fowl Town, fourteen miles east of Fort Scott, issued a stern message to Brigadier General Edmund Gaines, overall commander of the area, warning all whites to stay out of his village. In response, Gaines dispatched a force of 250 men under Major David E. Twiggs to arrest Neamathia at Fowl Town. Twiggs attacked, and although Neamathia escaped, his soldiers killed four warriors and a woman, then burned the town. This brought retaliation from the villagers and the Red Stick Creek leader Peter McQueen nine days later. (The Red Stick Creeks were closely allied with the Seminoles.) Of 40 soldiers, 7 soldiers' wives, and 4 children attacked, all but 4 men (who escaped) and 1 woman (taken captive) were killed.

General Andrew Jackson was now sent to Fort Scott, where he organized a force of 800 regulars, 900 Georgia volunteers, and a large number of friendly White Stick Creeks, led by William McIntosh and Major Thomas Woodward. In March 1818 they rebuilt Negro Fort as Fort Gadsden and used it as a base from which to launch a ruthless attack against the Seminoles. Jackson drove through the Mikasuki Seminole villages in the vicinity of present-day Tallahassee and pursued the Indians to St. Marks, a Spanish fort and town in which they sought refuge. By the time Jackson reached St. Marks, the Indians had fled, but, disregarding Spanish sovereignty, Jackson claimed possession of the town on April 7, 1818.

On April 9 Jackson set off for Suwannee Town, 107 miles to the east, to attack Indians led by Chief Boleck (a name the whites corrupted to Billy Bowlegs). On the way to Suwannee Town, Jackson's scouts reported that McQueen was hiding in a swamp near the Econfina River with 150 Seminole and Red Stick warriors and 100 women and children. Jackson attacked McQueen's camp on April 12, killing 37 of McQueen's warriors and capturing others, including the women and children (among them was future Creek and Seminole leader Osceola, age fourteen). McQueen and at least 100 warriors escaped. Jackson induced McQueen's sister to betray McQueen in exchange for the release of the women and children. The woman deceived Jackson, however, and fled with the released prisoners into Okefenokee Swamp without revealing her brother's whereabouts.

Jackson pressed on to Suwannee Town, only to find it deserted. He went on to take Pensacola—again, without respecting Spanish sovereignty—on May 26, 1818. Jackson's rash action created a minor diplomatic crisis, which ended almost immediately when Spain decided to abandon Florida and cede its territory to the United States. This brought about a rush of white settlement, which effectively sent the remaining Seminoles and Red Sticks into hiding and brought an end to the First Seminole War. Peter McQueen was never captured, and he lived out his remaining years quietly near Tampa Bay.

Fredonian Rebellion, 1826–1827

In 1820 Moses Austin, an American entrepreneur, secured a grant from the Spanish government to establish a colony of American settlers in Texas (in the five present-day counties of Bastrop, Fayette, Grimes, Montgomery, and Washington), which, at the time, was a territorial possession of the Spanish Empire. Austin fell ill and died in 1821, before he could begin the project of settlement. His son, Stephen F. Austin, pledged to carry out his father's plans. In the interim, however, Mexico achieved independence from Spain by the Revolution of 1821, and in 1824 the new Mexican government enacted special legislation to enable twelve hundred American families to settle in the Mexican territory of Texas. Additional agreements negotiated in 1825, 1827, and 1828 brought even more settlers.

Although Austin was by far the most famous and important of the Texas colonial entrepreneurs, another American, Virginia-born Hayden (also spelled Haden) Edwards, also secured a charter (*emprasario*) from the fledgling Mexican government in 1825 to establish a colony of some two hundred families in eastern Texas, near Nacogdoches. Mexican nationals had laid prior claim to the land but could not produce legal title to it. A rancorous dispute developed as Edwards demanded that the current occupants of the land produce legal titles to the land or pay him for the value of the acreage claimed. Stephen Austin attempted to avert a crisis with a series of letters warning Edwards that he was stirring up trouble for all American colonists. But this was to no avail. Edwards persisted in his demands, provoking the occupants of the disputed region to petition the Mexican government for aid.

In May 1826, leaving his brother Benjamin in charge of the colony, Edwards set off for Louisiana to recruit more settlers. In June the Mexican government revoked Edwards's charter and ordered him and his colonists out of the country. Benjamin Edwards responded defiantly: With a force of thirty volunteers, he occupied a building known as the Old Stone Fort.

A flag bearing the legend "Independence, Liberty, and Justice" was raised, and Edwards proclaimed the independent republic of Fredonia. On December 21, 1826, Benjamin Edwards and a handful of followers even adopted a constitution. But as Mexican troops closed in on Nacogdoches, Benjamin Edwards and his volunteers fled to join Hayden Edwards in Louisiana. The Fredonian Rebellion had lasted six weeks.

Aroostook War, 1838–1839

Neither the Treaty of Paris, which ended the *American Revolution, 1775–1783,* nor Jay's Treaty of 1794 resolved all of the vexing questions of precisely where the Canadian-U.S. border lay. In 1838 the demarcation between Maine and New Brunswick became a particularly hot issue as Maine farmers sought to cultivate land in the Aroostook River Valley, which Canadian lumber interests deemed Canadian territory. The bickering began in 1838, and in February of the next year, a group of Maine land agents were arrested by Canadian officials for attempting to remove lumbermen from the disputed area. In response to the arrest, Maine officials called out the militia, and New Brunswick responded in kind. With the two sides about to face off, President Martin Van Buren dispatched a small force of army regulars under General Winfield Scott to the Aroostook River Valley. Scott exercised great restraint and skillfully managed to negotiate an agreement between Maine and New Brunswick officials that headed off armed conflict and sent the opposing militia forces home. Although Scott's agreement included the establishment of a boundary commission, the underlying dispute was not definitively put on the course to settlement until the 1842 Webster-Ashburton Treaty. That treaty triggered a heated "Battle of the Maps," which, like the Aroostook War, was bloodless.

CHAPTER 5

Wars of the Indian Removal

Indian Removal Act of 1830

Every president prior to Andrew Jackson voiced the belief that the separation of Indian from white settlement would be beneficial to whites as well as Indians, but it was during the Jackson administration that the Indian Removal Act of 1830 was legislated by Congress. On the face of it, the Indian Removal Act was nothing more than a program of land exchange, by which federal subsidy, protection, and new western land would be given in exchange for Indian lands east of the Mississippi River. Yet while the letter of the law provided for at least some degree of equitable treatment, the execution of the law was typically both ruthless and devious. The tribes primarily targeted by the Indian Removal Act of 1830 were the Choctaws, Chickasaws, Cherokees, Creeks, and Seminoles living in Georgia, Alabama, Mississippi, and the territory of Florida (ceded to the United States by Spain in 1819). They were to be "removed" to a more or less vaguely defined "Indian Territory" in the present state of Oklahoma, as well as in portions of Kansas and Nebraska. Many of the Creek Indians had already been dispossessed by the Treaty of Horseshoe Bend, which ended the *Creek War, 1812–1814 (see chapter 4).*

IN THEIR OWN
Words

**Indian Removal Act,
May 28, 1830**

*B*e it enacted ... That it shall and may be lawful for the President
of the United States to cause so much of any territory belonging
to the United States, west of the river Mississippi, not included in any state or
organized territory, and to which the Indian title has been extinguished, as
he may judge necessary, to be divided into a suitable number of districts, for
the reception of such tribes or nations of Indians as may choose to exchange
the lands where they now reside, and remove there. . . .

SEC. 5. And be it further enacted, *That upon the making of any such
exchange as is contemplated by this act, it shall and may be lawful for the
President to cause such aid and assistance to be furnished to the emigrants as
may be necessary and proper to enable them to remove to, and settle in, the
country for which they may have exchanged; and also, to give them such aid
and assistance as may be necessary for their support and subsistence for the
first year after their removal. . . .*

In 1831, pursuant to the Indian Removal Act, the Choctaws left Mississippi and western Alabama for Indian Territory. The Chickasaws signed removal treaties in 1832 and 1834. The fate of the Cherokees is well documented. Tribal officials sued Georgia for redress of tribal grievances against that state and won a decision from the U.S. Supreme Court in the 1832 case of *Worcester v. Georgia*. Georgia's persecution and abuse of the Cherokees was found to be unconstitutional; but the Supreme Court decision proved a hollow victory, since President Jackson refused to take steps to enforce the decision. Under pressure, the Cherokees split into the so-called National Party, by far the majority, who advocated resistance to removal, and the so-called Treaty Party, a minority who favored acquiescence to removal. The federal government chose to deal only with the Treaty Party, and on December 29, 1835, concluded with that faction a treaty calling for the complete removal of the Cherokees by 1838. By the 1838 deadline only two thousand Cherokees had been removed, and

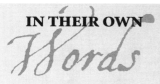
Major General Winfield Scott's address to the Cherokees remaining in northern Georgia, May 10, 1838

Cherokees! The President of the United States has sent me with a powerful army, to cause you, in obedience to the treaty of 1835, to join that part of your people who have already established in prosperity on the other side of the Mississippi. Unhappily, the two years which were allowed for the purpose, you have suffered to pass away without following, and without making any preparation to follow; and now, or by the time that this solemn address shall reach your distant settlements, the emigration must be commenced in haste, but I hope without disorder. I have no power, by granting a farther delay, to correct the error that you have committed. The full moon of May is already on the wane; and before another shall have passed away, every Cherokee man, woman and child in those states must be in motion to join their brethren in the far West.

My friends! This is no sudden determination on the part of the President, whom you and I must now obey. By the treaty, the emigration was to have been completed on or before the 23rd of this month; and the President has constantly kept you warned, during the two years

allowed, through all his officers and agents in this country, that the treaty would be enforced.

I am come to carry out that determination. My troops already occupy many positions in the country that you are to abandon, and thousands and thousands are approaching from every quarter, to render resistance and escape alike hopeless. All those troops, regular and militia, are your friends. Receive them and confide in them as such. Obey them when they tell you that you can remain no longer in this country. Soldiers are as kind-hearted as brave, and the desire of every one of us is to execute our painful duty in mercy. We are commanded by the President to act towards you in that spirit, and much is also the wish of the whole people of America.

Chiefs, head-men and warriors! Will you then, by resistance, compel us to resort to arms? God forbid! Or will you, by flight, seek to hide yourselves in mountains and forests, and thus oblige us to hunt you down? Remember that, in pursuit, it may be impossible to avoid conflicts. The blood of the white man or the blood of the red man may be spilt, and, if spilt, however accidentally, it may be impossible for the discreet and humane among you, or among us, to prevent a general war and carnage. Think of this, my Cherokee brethren! I am an old warrior, and have been present at many a scene of slaughter, but spare me, I beseech you, the horror of witnessing the destruction of the Cherokees. . . .

President Martin Van Buren, who succeeded Andrew Jackson, assigned General Winfield Scott to round up and remove the recalcitrant Cherokees. Except for small numbers who successfully hid in the mountains, the Cherokees of the Southeast were confined to camps during the summer of 1838 and, during the fall and winter of 1838–1839, were marched off to Indian Territory along the twelve-hundred-mile route that came to be called the Trail of Tears. Of fifteen thousand forcibly marched, four thousand died before reaching Indian Territory.

General Winfield Scott, hero of the War of 1812, was assigned the grim task of "removing" the Cherokees to Indian Territory pursuant to the Indian Removal Act of 1830.
Collection: ArtToday

Second Seminole War, 1835–1842

Of all the southeastern tribes removed pursuant to the act of 1830, only the Seminoles—and factions of the Creeks, who were very closely associated with the Seminoles—offered sustained armed resistance. The *First Seminole War, 1817–1818,* which predates the Indian Removal Act of 1830, is discussed in chapter 4; the *Second Seminole War, 1835–1842,* erupted after the 1835 removal treaty had been concluded with the Cherokee minority. Like the Cherokees and other tribes, the Seminoles were persecuted in Georgia and in Florida territory with the object of forcing them to accept removal. In 1831, the tribe's suffering was compounded by a severe drought, which prompted a group of Seminole leaders to sign a provisional removal treaty on May 9, 1832. A key provision of the treaty was the tribe's right to approve, prior to removal, the site selected for their resettlement. Seven Seminole representatives were dispatched to Indian Territory to examine the site, but before they could return with their report, a U.S. Indian agent coerced tribal authorities into signing a final treaty, binding the Seminoles to leave the Southeast by 1837. Organized Seminole resistance to removal began to take shape under a leader known to local whites as Billy Powell and whose Seminole name was Osceola (he may actually have been a Red Stick Creek; the Creeks and Seminoles were closely related politically and by intermarriage). Early in the winter of 1835, Osceola recognized that the government was preparing to remove the Seminoles by force. He decided to act proactively by negotiating with the local Indian agent, Wiley Thompson, to put off removal until January 15, 1836. His object was to buy time for his people to prepare for war. Indian agent Thompson suspected that Osceola was up to something and ordered the suspension of the sale of gunpowder to the Indians. This led to a series of confrontations between Osceola and Thompson, and in October 1835, Osceola led a secret council of war. By this time only six chiefs remained in favor of removal. Osceola announced to these holdouts that anyone who wanted to go West would be killed. Late in November, Osceola and twelve other warriors ambushed and assassinated the most important holdout, Charley Emathla.

With this assassination, the Second Seminole War began. The Seminoles named Osceola their war chief, with the warriors Jumper and Alligator as his lieutenants. Osceola coordinated with King Philip, leader of the Seminoles living east of St. John's River, to attack plantations in that region. Osceola deployed his own men in the thick swamps near the Withlacoochee River, just southwest of Fort King. From here, beginning in December, Osceola launched a series of raids on farms and settlements. He targeted in particular roads and bridges he knew were essential to moving troops, supplies, and especially artillery.

The first full-scale battle in the Second Seminole War was the Battle of Black Point, December 18, 1835, west of the village of Micanopy. With eighty Seminoles, Osceola raided and plundered a wagon train. When thirty mounted militiamen happened on the scene, their commander, Captain John McLemore, ordered a charge. Only a dozen of his men obeyed, however, and they were quickly forced to retreat. Eight men of McLemore's command died and six were wounded.

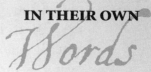

IN THEIR OWN

Words

Osceola's response to Indian agent Wiley Thompson, after Thompson decreed an end to gunpowder sales to Indians, 1835

Am I a Negro? Am I a slave? My skin is dark, but not black! I am an Indian—a Seminole! The white man shall not make me black! I will make the white man red with blood, and then blacken him in the sun and rain, where the wolf shall smell of his bones, and the buzzard live upon his flesh!

Osceola was an able strategist and a brilliant tactician who made especially effective use of reconnaissance, so that he seemed to be aware of every movement of the white forces. While King Philip drew off army strength by raiding plantations along the Atlantic coast, Osceola turned his attention to Fort King.

Next, having learned that Brigadier General Clinch intended to attack Seminole villages near the Withlacoochee River, Osceola and Alligator set out with 250 warriors to intercept him. This was a daring move, since Osceola understood that Clinch's contingent numbered 550 mounted Florida militiamen and 200 federal regulars. He also understood, however, that this force was encumbered by heavy wagons and unwieldy equipment, which made moving through the swamp slow and noisy, rendering the expedition ripe for ambush.

Osceola, leader of the Seminole resistance to "removal." *Collection: ArtToday*

Osceola watched and waited. When he discovered that the column was marching south of the expected ford across the Withlacoochee River, he ascertained an ideal position from which to mount an ambush, and there he planted an old canoe. General Clinch saw the canoe and used it to cross the river a few men at a time while a makeshift bridge was under construction. On the far side of the river, troops were instructed to stand down and stack arms. They were off their guard. At noon on December 31, 1835, Osceola and Alligator attacked the far side of the river, killing four men and wounding fifty-two (one mortally) before withdrawing. Although he was outnumbered almost three to one, Osceola succeeded in driving off Clinch's force, causing him to abort his offensive campaign.

These few violent clashes, at the outset of the war, proved to be the only action even approaching formal battles during the next seven years of the Second Seminole War. A series of white commanders were sent to bring the war to a decisive close, and, successively, each failed: Edmund Gaines, Duncan Clinch, Winfield Scott, Robert Call, Thomas Jesup, Zachary Taylor, Alexander McComb, Walker Armistead, and William Worth. General Jesup did succeed in capturing Osceola on October 21, 1837, not through military skill, but by treacherously violating a truce. The war chief was imprisoned at Fort Moultrie, South Carolina, where he fell ill and died on January 30, 1838.

After Osceola's death (he was buried at Fort Moultrie with full military honors), Alligator and Chief Boleck (known to whites as Billy Bowlegs) continued to lead the Seminole resistance. Nevertheless, between 1835 and 1842, some three thousand Seminoles submitted to removal and were marched to Indian Territory. The cost to the federal forces was exorbitant: For every two Seminoles sent West, one soldier died, a total of fifteen hundred. In monetary terms, the Second Seminole War cost the federal government $20 million. It ended in 1842 not as a result of any decisive victory on either side but because the government ceased operations.

Third Seminole War, 1855–1858

Thirteen years after the *Second Seminole War, 1835–1842* ended, a party of surveyors working in the Great Cypress Swamp stole or vandalized some crops belonging to followers of Billy Bowlegs. Bowlegs and a band of followers approached the surveyors, demanding compensation and an apology. When they were given neither, a pattern of raiding was reinstated. Most of the sporadic fighting was between volunteers, not regular army troops, and the Indians. At last, on March 5, 1857, Billy Bowlegs consented to leave Florida for Indian Territory. He negotiated a cash settlement of several thousand dollars, and took with him 165 followers. This left at least 120 Seminoles behind, whose descendants remain in Florida today. The United States declared the Third Seminole War concluded on May 8, 1858.

Black Hawk War, 1832

Although the Indian Removal Act of 1830 was directed primarily at Indians in the Southeast, a program of removal was also pressed in the Midwest.

In the first decade of the nineteenth century, Black Hawk was a chief of the separate but intimately allied Sac and Fox tribes, who lived, for the most part, in Illinois and Wisconsin, on the eastern bank of the Mississippi. Although he was a skilled military commander, Black Hawk was not a sophisticated diplomat, and he was duped into affirming a treaty of 1804 by which the Sacs and Foxes had ceded some fifty million acres to the federal government. Enraged at having been tricked, Black Hawk turned hostile and, in the *War of 1812, 1812–1814 (see chapter 4),* fought alongside Tecumseh against U.S. settlers. After the war, Black Hawk found himself repeatedly engaged in disputes with new waves of settlers, who pillaged Sac and Fox villages, fenced cornfields, and even plowed up Indian burial grounds. When Black Hawk protested to the U.S. Indian agents at Rock Island, Illinois, he was told to move West, across the Mississippi. Indeed, Black Hawk did range across the river, mainly to hunt, and in 1829, when he returned from a hunt, he found that a white family had settled in his lodge. The U.S. General Land Office now declared that the entire region, including Black Hawk's land, was subject to public sale. At first Black Hawk lived with the intruders, spending summers on his usurped land, and winters west of the Mississippi. Then, in April 1832, he crossed the river and marched eastward with two thousand men, women, and children—the "British Band," so called because of their former alliance with the British in the *War of 1812, 1812–1814 (see chapter 4).* These followers were dedicated not only to Black Hawk but also to a supporter of his, a charismatic figure known as the Winnebago Prophet.

Black Hawk, leader of the "British Band" of the Sac and Fox. *Collection: ArtToday*

By no means did the British Band represent all of the Sacs and Foxes. Chief Keokuk led a large faction that opposed Black Hawk and favored accommodation with the federal government. Keokuk alerted Indian agent Felix St. Vrain to the approach of the British Band. Keokuk also complied with General Henry Atkinson's request that he attempt to persuade Black Hawk and the British Band to return to the western bank of the Mississippi. Black Hawk angrily refused, and Atkinson appealed to Illinois governor John Reynolds for militiamen to supplement his small contingent of 220 U.S. regulars in the region. Among the 1,700 militia arrivals was a lanky young Abraham Lincoln.

On April 28 Atkinson marched his militia force to Yellow Banks on the Mississippi, where he expected to find Black Hawk and his British Band.

Even as he expressed his contempt for Atkinson's delegation, however, Black Hawk must have been disturbed by the presence of Winnebago chiefs among the emissaries, for the Winnebagos had promised to support him.

In the meantime, on May 1, 1832, Atkinson mustered into federal service 1,500 mounted militiamen and 200 infantry volunteers, who joined 340 infantry regulars under Colonel Zachary Taylor. On May 9 Atkinson ordered the mounted militia, under General Samuel Whiteside, to march up the Rock River via the village of the Winnebago Prophet. In the meantime, Atkinson himself would transport the volunteer and regular infantry by boat and join Whiteside as fast as he could. Two additional battalion-strength militia units also were patrolling the area. Major Isaac Stillman's command was ranging east from the Mississippi, and Major David Bailey's men were combing the territory between the Rock River and settlements along the Illinois. With an advance scouting party of 275 men, Stillman camped just north of the mouth of the Kyte River on May 14. The militia, eager for a fight but wholly undisciplined, shared out its whiskey ration. At this time Black Hawk, encamped with about 40 warriors in advance of his British Band, learned of the presence of the troopers and was now convinced that he would get no help from the Winnebagos. Worse, Potawatomi envoys announced to him that their tribe would not supply the corn so urgently needed by the British Band. The bad news persuaded Black Hawk that further resistance would be futile, and he accordingly sent three warriors under a white flag to Stillman's camp. As a precaution, Black Hawk sent an additional five warriors to follow the first three as observers.

The three representatives entered the camp and announced that Black Hawk wanted a conference. Unfortunately, at this point one of the militiamen sighted the five Indian observers out on the prairie. Alarm spread throughout the whiskey-charged battalion, and with neither orders nor order, the militiamen charged after the five Indians. Shots were fired, and two of the five warriors were killed. Back at the camp, two of the three emissaries managed to escape. The surviving Indian scouts ran back to Black Hawk's camp and told him of the treacherous violation of the truce. Although overwhelmingly outnumbered, Black Hawk ambushed the militia, which broke and ran, spreading alarm to those who remained at Stillman's camp on the Kyte. In this way 40 Sac and Fox braves defeated 275 well-armed Illinois militiamen in a "battle" that quickly became known as "Stillman's Run."

Emboldened by what they took to be the opposing army's incompetence and cowardice, Black Hawk and his warriors terrorized the frontier with raids of great violence, including a raid on Indian Creek in which fifteen settlers were murdered and mutilated and two girls abducted. Stillman's Run and the Indian Creek Massacre greatly disrupted the Illinois frontier. In response to the crisis, Atkinson mustered additional militia forces, together with Indian auxiliaries drawn from the Sioux and Menominee tribes. The mixed force pursued Black Hawk and the British Band toward the headwaters of the Rock River. At the Kishwaukee River, Black Hawk encountered a band of Winnebagos who, now that the British Band had tasted triumph, offered themselves as guides to find refuge near the Four Lakes in present-day Dane County, Wisconsin. To cover his escape, Black Hawk dispatched more war parties into the settlements.

Meanwhile, Black Hawk and the British Band continued to evade the soldiers, as militiamen, almost always acquitting themselves disgracefully, skirmished with scattered war parties.

Late in June, white-allied Potawatomis and Winnebagos reported that Black Hawk was lodged above Lake Koshkonong. By this time, Atkinson had managed to muster into the federal service three brigades of militia, together with a battalion of regulars and a company of spies. But even with three thousand militiamen and four hundred regulars, the general remained so hesitant to press an offensive that President Andrew Jackson and the War Department called in Major General Winfield Scott with another eight hundred regulars, six companies of rangers, and assorted militia to coordinate with Atkinson in a definitive strike against Black Hawk. While this force was gathering at Chicago, Black Hawk and two hundred warriors attacked a fort on the Apple River, about fourteen miles from Galena, Illinois. For twelve hours, a twenty-five-man garrison held off the Indians, who finally withdrew, plundering livestock and property on the way.

By the end of June, Atkinson's forces were at last on the move in pursuit of Black Hawk, but by the second week in July, Atkinson's command had still failed to encounter the British Band, and the troops were running low on supplies. Militiamen whose enlistments were coming to an end began dropping out of the campaign (among this number was Abraham Lincoln). Scott's army, still in Chicago, was likewise beginning to fall apart, the victims of a deadly cholera epidemic.

As hard as conditions were for the troops, Black Hawk and his people were also in dire straits, subsisting on a starvation diet of bark and roots, and they were now hiding too far from the white settlements to raid them. Black Hawk, who had begun the war because he refused to move west of the Mississippi, now sought to escape across the river. He decided to head for the Wisconsin River and then to the Mississippi, which he would cross to the safety of the Great Plains. But on July 11, Colonel Henry Dodge encountered a party of Winnebagos who reported that Black Hawk was camped on the rapids of the Rock River. Dodge pulled together six hundred militiamen and set out. When they reached the rapids on July 18, however, Black Hawk was nowhere to be found. The Winnebagos living nearby revealed that the British Band was now camped just twenty miles north. Sending word to Atkinson, Dodge followed a clear trail and was soon skirmishing with the rear guard of the British Band. By July 22 Dodge had killed some seventy of Black Hawk's followers, and that day, Neapope, Black Hawk's chief lieutenant, appeared at Dodge's camp with what amounted to an offer of surrender. In the absence of interpreters, however, Dodge could not comprehend the proposal, and he continued to pursue Black Hawk.

On July 24 Atkinson, in command of some regulars and part of a militia brigade, met up with Dodge's forces and handpicked thirteen hundred men to press on after Black Hawk through country previously untraveled by whites. On August 1, 1832, when Black Hawk convened a council at the junction of the Bad Ax and Mississippi Rivers, the British Band had been reduced by desertion, starvation, and battle deaths to only five hundred people. The chief advised continuing up the Mississippi to seek refuge among the Winnebagos. His people resisted this, however, having lost all faith in these supposed allies. Most set about hastily constructing canoes or rafts to cross the Mississippi. Some made it across, but the majority were still on the eastern bank as the steamboat *Warrior* hove into view, loaded with soldiers and a six-pounder gun. After abortive attempts at negotiation, *Warrior* opened fire, bombarding the British Band for two hours before breaking off to replenish its fuel supply. Twenty-three of the British Band were killed, others were delayed crossing the river, and only a few of Black Hawk's closest followers went with him northward.

On August 3 Atkinson's and Dodge's thirteen-hundred-man command arrived. The Indians who had remained on the eastern bank of the Mississippi attempted to surrender, but the troops, frustrated by weeks of fruitless pursuit and months of general panic, stormed their position in eight hours of frenzied slaughter. During the mayhem *Warrior* returned, after taking on firewood, to train her six-pounder on what remained of the British Band. Although about two hundred Sacs and Foxes did make it to the west bank, white-allied Sioux intercepted most of them there, capturing or killing them. As for Black Hawk, who had fled north, the Winnebagos among whom he had sought refuge proved yet again treacherous. In exchange for a $100 reward and twenty horses, they betrayed the chief to white authorities. He was arrested and imprisoned, and was in prison when General Scott concluded a treaty on September 19, 1832, with the surviving Sacs and Foxes who had failed to escape. The treaty required the cession of a strip of land fifty miles wide, running virtually the entire length of Iowa's Mississippi River frontage—about six million acres, in addition to the many more millions of acres ceded in the 1804 treaty. The treaty further stipulated the total removal of the Indians by June 1, 1833, and extorted a pledge that the Sacs and Foxes would never come back. In return, the United States paid the Sacs and Foxes $660,000. Black Hawk remained in prison for a year before he was permitted to return to what was left of his people, in exchange for his pledge never to act again as their chief.

CHAPTER 6

United States–Mexican War and Associated Conflicts

War with Mexico was the major American conflict between the *War of 1812, 1812–1814 (see chapter 4)* and the *Civil War, 1861–1865 (see chapter 8).* The *Texan War of Independence, 1835–1836,* was a critically significant prelude to the United States–Mexican War, while the *Bear Flag Rebellion, 1846* was little more than a sideshow conflict attendant upon the main event.

Texan War of Independence, 1835–1836

As briefly discussed in the entry on the *Fredonian Rebellion, 1826–1827 (see chapter 4),* a number of U.S. entrepreneurs, known by the Spanish term *empresarios,* sought to establish colonies of American settlers in what is now the state of Texas. Moses Austin was the most significant of the first *empresarios;* he negotiated a land grant in Texas from the Spanish government, but died before he could begin the actual process of settlement. Austin's son, Stephen F. Austin, took up the project and, when Mexico won its independence from Spain in the Revolution of 1821, it was he who renegotiated the grants with the new Mexican government. Thus, by the mid-1820s, Austin and others established growing colonies of Americans in what was now the Mexican state of Coahuila y Texas. Beginning during this same period, the U.S. government made overtures to Mexico for the purchase of Texas. President John Quincy Adams offered $1 million for the territory, and his successor, Andrew Jackson, offered $5 million. Both were turned down; Jackson, however, was not above pursuing highly questionable diplomatic and financial tactics to push the sale, and he even broached the subject of war. Congress, however, was reluctant both to provoke war with Mexico and to annex a territory populated mainly by Southerners and that would certainly, therefore, seek admission to the union as a slave state, thereby upsetting the delicate balance between slave and free states.

If the United States' attitude toward Texas annexation was ambivalent, the attitude of the growing Texas population toward Mexico was increasingly certain in its hostility. Historians have suggested several reasons for this hostility. Some believe that the predominantly Southern Protestant colonists resented having to answer to predominantly Catholic Mexico and feared that they would lose their freedom of religion. Perhaps this was a factor in the growing discontent among Texans, but the fact is that in 1834, the Mexican government issued a guarantee of religious freedom (as well as the freedom to express "political opinions"). Other historians have pointed to a conflict between Mexican laws prohibiting slavery and the manifest desire of many Texas settlers to maintain ownership of slaves. While it is true that Mexico had abolished slavery and proposed abolition in Texas, the government compromised with a presidential exemption in 1829: Texas, of all Mexican states, would be permitted to retain slavery. Still other historians have pointed to issues of trade and taxation as the causes of colonial discontent, or to the inefficiency of the Mexican government. All of these likely contributed to the growing desire among Texans to become independent from Mexico, but the overwhelming motive for independence was cultural. By 1836, the American population of Texas was fifty thousand, while Mexicans in Texas numbered a mere thirty-five hundred. The territory had become de facto American, and American Texans felt racially, morally, and politically superior to Mexicans.

Within Texas, factionalism developed between the early settlers and the steady stream of newcomers. The latter tended to agitate for independence, while the more established settlers typically sought a *modus vivendi* with the Mexican government. Mexican politics were also unsettled at the time, as Antonio López de Santa Anna sought to overthrow the government of Anastasia Bustamente. In this, Stephen Austin and the more established Texans saw an opportunity for achieving greater autonomy without open rebellion. Santa Anna voiced a policy of accommodation with the Texans. Austin negotiated peace with him and pledged the support of Texas in his bid for control of the Mexican government. With the victory of Santa Anna, Austin went a step further and presented a petition for the separate statehood of Texas within the Mexican Republic. In the meantime, with the blessing and support of Andrew Jackson, Sam Houston, veteran of Jackson's command in the *War of 1812, 1812–1814 (see chapter 4)* and a former congressman from and governor of Tennessee, arrived in Texas and soon assumed leadership of a Texas volunteer army. In 1833 Houston drafted a state constitution, which Austin took to Mexico City. After waiting five months for an audience with Santa Anna, Austin finally saw the president, who pledged to remedy all Texas grievances—short of allowing its creation as a separate state. Austin left, feeling that, while he had not achieved all that he hoped for, he had accomplished a great deal. At Saltillo, however, he was suddenly arrested, sent back to Mexico City, and imprisoned there on a charge of having written a letter urging Texas statehood.

Released in 1835, Austin was embittered and broken in health. In his absence, the independence faction among the Texans—the "War Dogs"—had increased in number and influence, and now even Austin threw his support behind rebellion.

The first armed uprising occurred in June 1835, when thirty Texans forced the surrender of the small garrison and customs house at Anáhuac. Other Texas communities disavowed this action, but they also refused to surrender the rebels to Mexican authorities. Provoked, Santa Anna repudiated his liberal policies and declared himself absolute dictator of Mexico. As for Texas, he now threatened to extend the antislavery ban to this region. When, at the end of

Antonio López de Santa Anna, the nemesis of Texas independence and commander of Mexican forces during the United States–Mexican War. *Collection: ArtToday*

1835, Santa Anna dispatched additional troops to Texas, Austin's support for revolution became vehement. He invited Americans to pour into

Texas—"each man with his rifle." "War," he declared, "is our only recourse."

On October 2, 1835, Mexican cavalry crossed the Rio Grande and demanded the surrender of a cannon in Gonzales. In response, locals put together a small army that forced the Mexicans, under General Martín Perfecto de Cós, to retreat to San Antonio. Austin personally led a five-hundred-man force in a siege of San Antonio during November. Simultaneously, representatives of the dozen American communities in Texas met to decide just what they were fighting for: independence, or a return to Mexico under the provisions of the liberal 1824 constitution. It was decided to create a provisional government, which would appeal to Mexican liberals for statehood within a constitutionally governed Mexico. Considering all options, however, Austin and other Texans also traveled to Washington, where they sounded out President Jackson on the potential for annexation to the United States. As for the troops who still besieged Cós in San Antonio, the privations of winter were taking a toll. When the temporary commander of the force decided to withdraw to winter quarters at Gonzales, the fiery frontiersman Ben Milam roused the volunteers for an assault on San Antonio. "Who will go with old Ben Milam?" became the first rallying cry of the Texas revolution.

On December 5, 1835, an army now swollen to fifty-three hundred volunteers stormed the city and fought the outnumbered Cós in the streets. With about eleven hundred troops, the Mexican general withdrew to barracks in a tumbledown fortress that had been converted from the town's old namesake mission. Officially called San Antonio de Valero, the compound was popularly known as the Alamo, for its proximity to a stand of cottonwoods (*alamos* in Spanish). When the Texans trained their artillery against the Alamo's walls, Cós surrendered, and the Texans occupied and repaired the fort.

With the revolution thus auspiciously launched, Houston and Texas governor Henry Smith urged a concerted commitment to independence. Certain land speculators, however, who had amassed their holdings by bribing Mexican legislators, feared that independence would bring nullification of their claims. For this reason they backed sending a force to Matamoros, a Mexican town at the mouth of the Rio Grande known to harbor large numbers of anti–Santa Anna liberals. The speculators hoped that by seizing Matamoros, they could unite with the Mexican liberals, depose Santa Anna, and restore the liberal federalism of the 1824 Mexican constitution—in the process retaining a government friendly to their real-estate claims. Led by James W. Fannin Jr., the mission to Matamoros was rife with dissension and never reached its destination. Instead, Fannin and his men established themselves in a fort at Goliad.

By this time, January 1836, Santa Anna was on the march with an army of some five thousand to punish the Texas rebels. From the Alamo came news that the Texas garrison there was tired, unpaid, and hungry. There was much talk of giving up and returning to the United States. Houston, in fact, had little interest in defending the Alamo, a remote outpost. He believed that the garrison should withdraw, and that the stand be made closer to San Felipe de Austin (modern Austin, Texas), country easier to defend and more difficult to attack. Even worse than expending forces to defend the Alamo was Fannin's proposal from Goliad. He wanted to abandon this position to make the attack on Matamoros. To do this, Houston understood, would allow Santa Anna clear passage into the interior of Texas. Under pressure, then, Houston decided to concentrate his main forces sixty miles east of San Antonio, at Gonzales. He sent Jim Bowie to San Antonio to supervise the evacuation and destruction of

Sam Houston, leader of Texas independence and president of the Republic of Texas. *From Harper's Pictorial History of the Civil War, 1866*

the Alamo and the removal and transportation of its artillery. In the meantime, Houston successfully negotiated a treaty with the Cherokees of Eastern Texas to secure their neutrality.

Arriving at the Alamo, Jim Bowie decided to ignore Houston's orders. With Colonel James C. Neill, the garrison commander there, Bowie concluded that the fortress was actually a formidable obstacle to Santa Anna's advance and that its defenders would not be "driven from the post of honor." By the time Santa Anna reached the vicinity of San Antonio, he had about 2,000 troops fit for duty. Neill and Bowie had little more than 100 men. They appealed to Fannin for reinforcements, but he refused, reasserting his intention to leave Goliad for an assault on Matamoros. Colonel William B. Travis, a longtime leader of the Texas war faction, did bring a handful of reinforcements, as did David (Davy) Crockett, who led a dozen volunteers from Tennessee. By February 11, 1836, Neill had left the Alamo, and command of about 150 men was now with Bowie and Travis. They knew Santa Anna was on his way with a vastly superior force, but they believed he would wait until spring before marching through the barren and forbidding country south of San Antonio. That should give ample time for reinforcements to arrive from all over the United States—for Travis's pleas for aid were continual.

In fact, Santa Anna entered San Antonio on February 25. A number of noncombatants, mostly women and children, now took refuge with the Alamo garrison. To make matters worse, Travis had fallen ill after having been injured while placing a cannon. He was confined to a cot. At the last minute, 25 new reinforcements arrived—against Houston's orders—from the Gonzales militia. The defenders of the Alamo now numbered 187. Santa Anna unleashed a continual artillery bombardment, which, after a full week, had failed to kill a single Texan, even as the defenders' grapeshot and rifle fire took a heavy toll among the attackers. At last, on March 6, with the walls of the fortress crumbling, Santa Anna deployed 1,800 men to storm the Alamo. It was not a skillful attack, and it cost the Mexicans about 600 killed, but sheer numbers prevailed. After ninety minutes of fighting, almost all of the Alamo's defenders had fallen, and the old mission fortress was now in Mexican hands. Davy Crockett and the few

The Alamo. This illustration was made at the outbreak of the Civil War. *From* Harper's Pictorial History of the Civil War, *1866*

other prisoners Santa Anna had taken were summarily executed. The women and children who had sought refuge in the Alamo were released, however, and Santa Anna charged one of their number, Susannah Dickerson, to tell all of Texas what had happened at the Alamo. Santa Anna believed her tale would discourage all further rebellion.

Santa Anna was, of course, mistaken. The fall of the Alamo provided the Texas revolution with a pantheon of martyrs to avenge and a stirring battle cry to spur such vengeance: "Remember the Alamo!"

After the fall of the Alamo, Houston ordered Fannin to destroy the fortress at Goliad and retreat. This he did on March 18, but the 400 men of his command were delayed by having to offload, then reload overburdened pack animals to ford the San Antonio River. This delay allowed a 1,400-man force under Mexican general José Urrea to envelop Fannin's troops out in the open. After a desperate two-day defense, Fannin, on March 20, surrendered. Less than a week later, the ruthless Santa Anna ordered Urrea to execute his prisoners. This, the Mexican leader was convinced, added to the massacre at the Alamo, would end the rebellion in Texas. Indeed, in what became known as the "Runaway Scrape," thousands of panic-stricken Texans fled eastward to the U.S. border, with the main body of Mexican troops close behind. The Texas provisional government likewise decamped, but Sam Houston, unshakable, penetrated to the opportunity within the disaster. He turned flight into what he called strategic retreat, and by April he had raised and trained an army of 740 determined men.

Santa Anna was now camped with about 700 troops on an open plain west of the San Jacinto River, near Galveston Bay. Houston put his troops in position to attack. At the eleventh hour, Santa Anna received reinforcements, which gave him substantial superiority of numbers, at about 1,600 men. Houston understood that the time was now or never, and, outnumbered though he was, he ordered an assault. The Battle of San Jacinto, April 21, 1836, consumed eighteen minutes and resulted in complete and overwhelming victory for the Texans. Santa Anna and his soldiers were routed utterly, and Houston's troops gave chase, unleashing upon the Mexicans all the brutality Santa Anna had earlier directed against the Alamo defenders and Fannin's command. When the slaughter was over, 630 Mexicans lay dead, far more than all of the Texans who had fallen in the entire brief war. Texas losses were very light; Houston had been severely wounded in the leg.

As for Santa Anna, he was captured, having ignominiously disguised himself as a private soldier. He was brought before the wounded Houston, fully expecting to be executed. Instead, the Texas leader compelled Santa Anna to sign the Treaty of Velasco in exchange for his life. By this document, Santa Anna agreed to evacuate all Mexican soldiers from Texas and to recognize the former province as an independent and sovereign republic.

Santa Anna was imprisoned in Texas for two months, then was sent to Washington, where President Andrew Jackson received him and, regarding him as a head of state, subsequently released him (under escort) to Vera Cruz, Mexico. In the meantime, the new government of Mexico repudiated the Treaty of Velasco. Signed under duress, it might well have failed generally to gain international recognition, but nevertheless, most nations, including the United States, acknowledged it, and Texas now stood as an independent republic.

Bear Flag Rebellion, 1846

After Texas won its independence from Mexico in 1836, many in that fledgling republic lobbied for annexation to the United States and eventual statehood. Congress was slow to respond to the annexation bid, however, in part over issues involving the assumption of the Texas republic's debts and in part over fear of inciting war with Mexico, but mainly because annexation would inevitably lead to the admission of Texas to the union as a slave state. The always delicate congressional balance between slave and free states would thus be upset. What finally moved lame duck President John Tyler to urge Congress to adopt an annexation resolution in 1844–1845 were overtures from France and England, both of which seemed to be eyeing Texas either as an intimate ally or as a possible colonial possession. The resolution was enacted, and Tyler's successor, James K. Polk, admitted Texas to the Union on December 29, 1845. Meanwhile, however, England and France had turned their attention to California. In 1839 the Mexican Congress and a swarm of the nation's British creditors agreed on a plan to settle half the nation's debt by land grants of some 125 million California acres. The scheme failed to move forward, but in that same year a British official posted in Mexico published a widely read history and promotional tract depicting California as an ideal place for "receiving and cherishing the superfluous population of Great Britain." Two years later, Sir Richard Pakenham, Britain's minister in Mexico City, went so far as to urge the planting of a British colony in California. Private colonization schemes were also proposed, one by an Englishman and another by an Irish priest. The French presence in California consisted of a diplomatic agent, Duflot de Mofras, who was stationed there after some Frenchmen had been killed during Mexican revolutionary activity in 1840. Mofras openly urged the French government to take steps to acquire the country. Once again, in the face of imminent foreign designs, President Polk was moved to act. He sent an emissary, John Slidell of Louisiana, to Mexico City to negotiate the purchase of California for the sum of $40 million. Slidell did not even get his foot in the door; Mexican president Herrera refused to see him. Willing neither to brook a diplomatic sleight nor to give up California, Polk commissioned the U.S. consul at Monterey, California, Thomas O. Larkin, to organize, covertly, California's small but prosperous and influential American community into a separatist movement sympathetic to annexation. Larkin might have succeeded in this mission had Polk given him sufficient time, but the president had been made nervous by rumors that the English vice consul in San Francisco was successfully wooing southern California's governor, Pio Pico, to the notion of accepting a British protectorate.

Polk's rapidly growing impatience coincided with the activities in California of John Charles Frémont, an intrepid western explorer who was surveying prospective transcontinental railroad routes for the U.S. Bureau of Topographical Engineers. Frémont was camped with sixty armed men near the fort John A. Sutter had built in northern California. The presence of these troops sufficiently disturbed José Castro, Mexico's governor of northern California, that he ordered them to leave California. Frémont responded by moving his men to a hilltop, Hawk's Peak, over which he raised the Stars and Stripes. Before Castro could dispatch a military force to counter this act of defiance, Larkin intervened to defuse the situation. Frémont and his band retired to the lower Sacramento Valley and then started for Oregon, but on the way, they were met by a messenger, Lieutenant Archibald Gillespie, who brought letters from Frémont's father-in-law, Missouri senator Thomas Hart Benton, as well as news that war between the United States and

President James K. Polk. *Collection: ArtToday*

Mexico was imminent; that the U.S. warship *Portsmouth* was anchored in San Francisco Bay; that the rest of the Pacific fleet was anchored off Mazatlán; Mexico, primed for attack; and that U.S. and Mexican troops faced each other across the Texas border. According to Frémont's later account, Gillespie delivered one additional item: secret orders from President Polk authorizing him to take action to bring about rebellion in California. Most historians, however, do not believe Frémont. Most conclude that he turned back to California entirely on his own initiative, and, on his own initiative, assumed command of what would soon be called the Bear Flag Rebellion.

The Bear Flag Rebellion was enacted by a handful of men and on a small scale, but its consequences were far-reaching. Frémont set up his camp close to the American settlements near Sutter's Fort. Many of the settlers, fired up by rumors of impending Mexican attack, gathered at the camp for protection and to formulate a plan of action. Among this group was a motley band of hunters, trappers, and sailors who had jumped ship, all under the loose leadership of one Ezekiel Merritt. Merritt informed Frémont that he had been told that a herd of horses was being driven to the Mexican militia for use in a campaign against the settlers. With Frémont's approval, Merritt and his crew intercepted the horses and diverted them to the American camp. Having committed this act, Merritt anticipated Mexican reprisals and therefore determined to continue the offensive. In company with another Anglo-Californian leader, William B. Ide, Merritt took thirty followers to Sonoma on June 14, 1846, intent on capturing this, the chief settlement in the area. The party surrounded the home of Mariano G. Vallejo, a retired Mexican army colonel and the town's leading citizen, and informed him that he was a prisoner of war. The colonel was, in fact, a liberal-minded supporter of California annexation to the United States. He eagerly entertained his "captors" over a breakfast of a freshly killed bull so that they could negotiate "surrender" terms. After a considerable time, none of the three negotiators emerged from the Vallejo house. Ide sent another man in, and when he, too, disappeared, Ide himself entered the house—where he found everyone in a collective drunken stupor, the unfinished instrument of surrender lying on the table. Ide completed the surrender document, and Vallejo signed it.

John Charles Frémont, intrepid western explorer, inept military commander, and leader of the Bear Flag Rebellion. *Collection: ArtToday*

Twenty-five men remained in Sonoma as a garrison, Ide's followers named him president of the California Republic, and a flag emblazoned with the image of a grizzly bear was raised over the town plaza on June 15. Vallejo was shipped off to Frémont.

On June 24, in a brief exchange dubbed the Battle of Olompali, Ide drove off the small force Governor Castro had mounted against the Bear Flaggers. Two American lives were lost. Meanwhile, by having consented to receive Vallejo as a prisoner, Frémont had dropped any pretense to neutrality in the Bear Flag Rebellion. On June 25 he marched his small force into Sonoma, summarily took over command from Ide, and set out with 134 men to avenge the 2 deaths suffered at Olompali. He did this by killing 3 Mexicans encountered along his march south. The main body of Castro's force fled before Frémont's approach. On July 1, Frémont took the Presidio at San Francisco. It was an easy victory, inasmuch as the fortress had been without garrison for many years. Nevertheless, Frémont took the precaution of spiking a Spanish cannon there, even though that antique hadn't been fired for at least half a century.

The Texas Republic lasted a decade before it was annexed to the United States. In contrast, the Republic of California endured less than a month. On July 7, 1846, Commodore John D. Sloat, U.S.N., landed at Monterey, took the harbor and the town without firing a shot, raised the Stars and Stripes, and claimed possession of California in the name of the United States. Frémont was named commander of the California Battalion and would now fight in the *United States–Mexican War, 1846–1848,* with which the Bear Flag Rebellion, for all practical purposes, now merged.

United States–Mexican War, 1846–1848

For the background of the war, see the previous entries in this chapter.

Initial Deployment and First Action

On March 1, 1845, Congress resolved to admit Texas into the Union. This prompted the Mexican government, which had repudiated the Treaty of Velasco by which a defeated General Santa Anna had recognized Texas independence, to sever diplomatic relations with the United States. President Polk had no desire to enter into an immediate war with Mexico, and he continued to pursue efforts to negotiate claims to Texas as well as to

Upper California. In the meantime, however, with the Texas government's acceptance of annexation anticipated on July 4, Polk ordered Brigadier General Zachary Taylor to take up positions on or near the Rio Grande to repel any invasion. Beginning on July 23, 1845, Taylor transported most of his fifteen-hundred-man force by steamboat from New Orleans to the plain at the mouth of the Nueces River near Corpus Christi. Throughout the rest of the summer and into the fall, more troops arrived, creating a force of about four thousand. The men drilled, watched, and waited, until negotiations with Mexican government irretrievably broke down in

CHRONOLOGY   Principal Events of the United States–Mexican War

1846

April 25: *Mexican troops cross the Rio Grande to attack U.S. dragoons*

May 8: *Battle of Palo Alto*

May 9: *Battle of Resaca de la Palma*

May 13: *U.S. declares war on Mexico*

May 18: *U.S. troops occupy Matamoros*

July 7: *U.S. naval forces occupy Monterey, California*

July 14: *U.S. forces occupy Camargo*

August 16: *Santa Anna returns to Mexico from Cuban exile*

August 18: *General Stephen W. Kearny occupies Santa Fe, New Mexico*

September 21–23: *Battle of Monterrey, Mexico*

November 14: *U.S. Navy seizes Tampico*

November 16: *U.S. forces occupy Saltillo*

1847

February 3–4: *Battle of Pueblo de Taos, New Mexico*

February 22–23: *Battle of Buena Vista*

March 9: *Ten thousand U.S. troops land at Vera Cruz*

March 9–29: *Siege of Vera Cruz, culminating in Mexican surrender of Vera Cruz*

April 18: *Battle of Cerro Gordo*

August 19–20: *Battles of Contreras and Churubusco*

September 8: *Battle of Molino del Rey*

September 13: *Battle of Chapultepec*

September 13–14: *Battle for Mexico City*

September 14–October 12: *Siege of Puebla*

September 15: *Occupation of Mexico City*

1848

February 2: *Treaty of Guadalupe Hidalgo signed, ending the war*

March 10: *U.S. Senate ratifies Treaty of Guadalupe Hidalgo*

May 25: *Mexican Congress ratifies Treaty of Guadalupe Hidalgo*

February 1846. Taylor was ordered to advance a hundred miles down the coast to the Rio Grande. He established a supply camp at the coastal town of Point Isabel, where ships could keep his army fed and furnished, and he deployed most of his troops eighteen miles southwest of Point Isabel, on the Rio Grande, just opposite the Mexican border town of Matamoros. Here he erected Fort Texas, equipped with stout siege guns. Even as he established his position, Taylor sent conciliatory messages to his Mexican counterpart across the river. The replies were consistently hostile. At last, on April 25, 1846, General Mariano Arista led a substantial Mexican force across the river and into Texas, where he attacked an advance detachment of sixty dragoons under Capt. Seth B. Thornton. Eleven Americans were killed, and the other troops, including Thornton, were captured; many had been wounded. Taylor dutifully reported to President Polk that hostilities had commenced. He appealed to Texas and Louisiana for five thousand militia volunteers. To prevent capture of his Point Isabel supply base, Taylor left Major Jacob Brown to command a small artillery garrison at Fort Texas while he took the main body of troops back to Point Isabel. Here Taylor quickly and efficiently strengthened his fortifications; resupplied his army; and, on May 7, with twenty-three hundred troops, began his return to Fort Texas.

Battle of Palo Alto

On the march to Fort Texas on May 8, Taylor sighted Arista's advancing Mexican army at a place called Palo Alto. Some four thousand troops blocked the road to Fort Texas along a mile-long front. Taylor was not only outnumbered two to one (part of his twenty-three-hundred-man force was far to the rear, guarding the supply wagons), he was traversing terrain favorable to cavalry—and Arista had far more cavalry

General Zachary Taylor, early in the war. *Collection: ArtToday*

than Taylor, the bulk of whose force consisted of dragoons, mounted infantry. The advantages Taylor enjoyed, however, included superior artillery and excellent young officers, among them two junior lieutenants named Ulysses S. Grant and George G. Meade, both graduates of West Point. Acting in consultation with officers such as these, Taylor skillfully deployed two eighteen-pounder siege guns in the center of his line and the rest of his lighter field artillery where they could be brought to bear rapidly and mercilessly. He used the siege guns to fire canister shot, deadly antipersonnel rounds, while his lighter guns rapidly fired solid shells. The effect was devastating, and the Mexicans, despite their superior numbers, could return fire with nothing more than obsolete bronze four- and eight-pounders. These lacked sufficient range to do more than lob cannonballs so feebly that the Americans could actually dodge the bouncing and rolling incoming rounds.

The American artillery barrage had been so fierce that the dry grass of Palo Alto was set ablaze, bringing a halt to the battle. When action resumed, the Mexicans were in retreat, having lost 320 killed and 380 wounded. Taylor's losses were 9 killed and 47 wounded. At nightfall Taylor bivouacked, and, at first light, saw the entire Mexican force continue its retreat. Had he been a more aggressive officer, Taylor would have given immediate chase. Instead, he strengthened defenses around his supply train, then set off after Arista's army.

Battle of Resaca de la Palma

Taylor reached a dry riverbed called Resaca de Palma, five miles from Palo Alto, at 2:00 P.M. on May 9. His scouts reported that the Mexican forces were well entrenched in a nearby ravine called Resaca de la Guerra, and that ponds and chaparral protected their flanks. To dislodge the Mexicans, Taylor dispatched his "flying artillery"—a highly mobile artillery detachment—under Lieutenant Randolph Ridgely to attack. Ridgely came under heavy fire from a Mexican artillery battery, which was subsequently overrun by U.S. dragoons commanded by Captain Charles A. May. Unfortunately, however, the dragoons were caught in the infantry crossfire as they returned to the American lines, and the Mexicans retook their artillery position. Later, U.S. infantry would again capture the artillery.

The rugged landscape made Taylor's artillery less effective than it had been on the open plain at Palo Alto. For this reason the battle soon became an infantry engagement, with much hand-to-hand combat. Mexican forces, still reeling from the defeat at Palo Alto, had little stomach for close fighting and soon fell back on Matamoros. At least 547 Mexican troops were killed or wounded at Resaca de la Palma, and most historians believe the casualty count was probably even higher. (Taylor's losses were 33 killed and 89 wounded.) In the aftermath of battle, even more Mexican soldiers died, either drowned in the Rio Grande or victims of the guns of Fort Texas. That installation had been besieged for two days during the Palo Alto and Resaca de la Palma battles, but withstood the onslaught with the loss of two men, including Major Jacob Brown, the commanding officer. The fort was renamed for him.

Taylor once again failed to capitalize fully on his victory. Had he effected a crossing of the Rio Grande, he almost certainly would have captured Arista's entire force. As it is, his crossing was delayed until May 18, by which time Arista's army had retreated well into the interior.

IN THEIR OWN *Words*

Lieutenant Daniel Harvey Hill, U.S. Fourth Artillery, on Camp Life, 1846

It becomes our painful task to allude to the sickness, suffering and death, from criminal negligence. Two-thirds of the tents furnished the army on taking the field were worn out and rotten, and had been condemned by boards of survey appointed by the proper authorities in accordance with the provisions of the army regulations on that subject. Transparent as gauze, they afforded little or no protection against the intense heat of summer, or the drenching rains and severe cold of winter. Even the dews penetrated the thin covering almost without obstruction.

Such were the tents, provided for campaigning in a country almost deluged three months in the year, and more variable in its climate than any other region in the world, passing from the extreme of heat to the extreme of cold within a few hours. During the whole of November and December, either the rains were pouring down with violence, or the furious "northers" were shivering the frail tentpoles, and rending the rotten canvass [sic]. For days and weeks, every article in hundreds of tents was thoroughly soaked. During those terrible months, the sufferings of the sick in the crowded hospital tents were horrible beyond conception. The torrents drenched and the fierce blasts shook the miserable couches of the dying. Their last groans mingled in fearful concert with the howlings of the pitiless storm.

Every day added to the frightfulness of the mortality. The volley over one grave would scarce have died on the air when the ear would again be pained by the same melancholy sound. . . . At one time, one-sixth of the entire encampment were on the sick report, unfit for duty, and at least one half were unwell. Dysentery and catarrhal fevers raged like a pestilence. . . .

Formal Declaration of War and Overall Strategy

With war already under way, Congress enacted a declaration of war, and President Polk signed it on May 13. An appropriation of $10,000,000 was made, and the authorized strength of the regular army increased from about 8,500 men to 15,540. In addition, a call-up of 50,000 one-year volunteers also was authorized. Polk had one major objective in fighting the war: to obtain all Mexican territory north of the Rio Grande and Gila River, all the way west to the Pacific Ocean. To achieve this objective, the army's senior commander, General Winfield Scott, a hero of the *War of 1812, 1812–1814 (see chapter 4),* drew up a three-pronged plan. Taylor would march west from Matamoros to Monterrey, Mexico; once Monterrey was taken, all of northern Mexico was vulnerable. At the same time, Brigadier General John E. Wool would march from San Antonio to Chihuahua, Mexico; from there, he could advance farther south, to Saltillo, near Taylor's force at Monterrey. Finally, Colonel Stephen Watts Kearney would advance out of Fort Leavenworth, Kansas, to take Santa Fe and, from here, continue all the way to San Diego, California. This third prong would later be modified, as part of Kearny's force, under Colonel Alexander W. Doniphan, would make a remarkable advance deep into Mexico, via Chihuahua to Parras. The initial war plan did not contemplate a deeper invasion, to include the capture of the Mexican capital, Mexico City. Polk and Scott hoped that achieving the objectives of the three-pronged strategy would quickly force Mexico to capitulate and yield the territory the United States coveted. In July, however, Polk discussed with Secretary of War William L. Marcy a plan to invade Mexico City by means of an amphibious landing at Vera Cruz. Logically, at this point, Polk would have put Scott in command of the entire war. But he felt that Scott was overly cautious, and after Palo Alto and Resaca de la Palma, he decided to promote Taylor to brevet major general and put him in charge of all operations. For now, the three-pronged plan would be the strategy of choice.

A typical U.S. Army officer of the period, Bezaleel W. Armstrong, West Point graduate, 1845, second lieutenant, Second Dragoons, served at Vera Cruz and Mexico City. *Daguerreotype from National Archives and Records Administration*

The Advance on Monterrey

The major problems Taylor faced were logistical, mainly dealing with transportation. He wanted to move 6,000 men to Monterrey via Camargo, a town on the San Juan River at which he would establish a supply base. From here, a road led to Monterrey in the Sierra Madre foothills—125 miles away. As he struggled to cobble together means of transportation, Taylor was joined by short-term militiamen, so that, by August 1846, 15,000 troops were massed at Camargo. Here they sweltered in triple-digit temperatures, and many sickened. When, at the end of August, Taylor was finally ready to begin his overland advance from Camargo to Monterrey, he did so with fewer than half of the troops available to him: 3,080 regulars and 3,150 militiamen. The rest languished, sick, at Camargo. About a quarter of Taylor's force was mounted; the remainder consisted mainly of infantry, with a small detachment of artillery. (Perhaps the ablest mounted troops were those of the First Mississippi Rifle Regiment, led by Colonel Jefferson Davis, a West Pointer who would later serve as U.S. secretary of war and, later still, as the first and last president of the Confederate States of America.)

Taylor's force reached Monterrey on September 19 and found it defended by 7,000 Mexican troops in strong positions and equipped with more modern, heavier British-made artillery than they had had at Palo Alto. After dispatching engineers to assess the formidable Mexican fortifications, Taylor commenced his attack on September 20 by sending one division of regulars with 400 Texas Rangers to cut off the road to Saltillo. This mission was accomplished by September 21, but at the high cost of 395 killed or wounded. At the same time, Taylor began an artillery bombardment, then closed in with his main forces from the east. On September 22, Taylor's troops were fighting in the streets of Monterrey. By September 23, the Mexican defenders had been pushed into the town's central plaza. Taylor ordered his ten-inch mortar to lob shells onto this area, which soon elicited an offer of surrender. The Mexican commander did not capitulate abjectly, but asked Taylor for permission to withdraw and to institute an eight-week armistice. As usual, Taylor demonstrated a minimum of aggressiveness. He granted the terms requested, reasoning that he, too, had taken heavy casualties (many to disease), was low on provisions and ammunition, and was distant from his base at Camargo. Moreover, he felt that granting magnanimous terms might be conducive to negotiations, for Polk had agreed to a proposal from, of all people, Santa Anna, who had been living as an exile in Cuba since a rebellion had ended his dictatorship in Mexico. The wily leader promised to help the United States negotiate a favorable peace, including a Rio Grande boundary for Texas and the possession of California, in return for $30 million and safe conduct to Mexico. Polk balked at the money, but he did allow Santa Anna to return to Mexico. Unknown to Polk, once restored to his homeland, Santa Anna had no intention of negotiating peace, but

IN THEIR OWN *Words*

A U.S. Officer's Account of the Battle of Monterrey, September 22, 1846

Our battalion was immediately formed in line of battle under this fire, and we were ordered to charge. . . . Judge of my astonishment, when I beheld the four companies of regulars marching by a flank to the right. I saw Col. Watson shouting, but as to hearing a command, that was an impossibility, owing to the deafening roar of the cannon and musketry. I saw the head of our line changing its direction, and I knew at once that the point of attack was changed, and ran to the head of my company to intercept the head of the column. I reached it just as Col. Watson was dismounting from his horse, which the next moment fell from a shot. The colonel cried out to the men, "Shelter yourselves, men, the best way you can." At this time, the battalion was scattered over a space of about an acre, and the men were lying down, the shot in most instances flying over our heads; but the guns were soon depressed, and the shot began to take effect.

I was lying close to Col. Watson, alongside of a hedge, when he jumped up and cried out, "Now's the time, boys, follow me." We were now in a street or lane, with a few houses on either side, and within a hundred yards of three batteries which completely raked it, in addition to which, two twelve-pound guns were planted in the castle on the right, and completely enfiladed the whole distance we had to make. Add to this, the thousand musketeers on the house-tops, and in the barricades at the head of the street up which we advanced, and at every cross street, and you may form some idea of the deluge of balls poured upon us. . . . Onward we went, men and horses falling at every step. Cheers, shrieks, groans and words of command added to the din, whilst the roar of the guns was absolutely deafening.

We had advanced up the street under this awful and fatal fire, nearly two hundred yards, when we reached a cross street, at the corner of which all who had succeeded in getting this far alive, halted, as if by mutual consent. I was shaking Col. Watson by the hand, while he was complimenting me, when a shower of grape, round and canister shot came from the corner above, and five officers fell, and I do not know how many privates. . . .

instead set about raising an army to defeat Zachary Taylor. In the meantime, however, Polk, on October 11, condemned Taylor for having allowed the Mexican army to escape. He ordered an immediate end to the armistice, and, on November 13, Taylor dispatched 1,000 men to Saltillo to seize control of the only road to Mexico City from the north and the road to Chihuahua. Saltillo fell to the Americans on November 16. Next, on November 14, naval forces took the town of Tampico, and in December General Wool arrived from San Antonio with 2,500 men. Headed for Chihuahua, he learned that the Mexicans had abandoned the town, so he united with Taylor's main force at Monterrey.

Conflict of Command

Taylor wanted to deploy a defensive line connecting Parras, Saltillo, Monterrey, and Victoria, but was then informed that President Polk had authorized General Scott to make an amphibious assault on Vera Cruz. Eight thousand of Taylor's troops were to be detached to join Scott's force. Left with 7,000 men, mostly volunteers, Taylor was ordered to evacuate Saltillo and go on the defensive at Monterrey. Taylor deemed these orders mere "advice," and instead of following them, he left small garrisons at Monterrey and Saltillo, then sent 4,650 men eighteen miles south of Saltillo to Agua Nueva. Unknown to him, Santa Anna was only thirty-five miles from Agua Nueva.

Photograph of Thomas Jackson. Immortalized in the Civil War as "Stonewall" Jackson, he served with distinction in the U.S. Army during the United States–Mexican War. *Collection: ArtToday*

Battle of Buena Vista

Taylor's scouts spotted Santa Anna's army on February 21, 1847. Taylor withdrew to Buena Vista, just south of Saltillo, a position that was more easily defended. He was outnumbered three to one. On February 22, Santa Anna demanded his surrender. When Taylor refused, Santa Anna fired a few artillery shells, then the two armies jockeyed for position. The battle began in earnest on February 23 and at first the Mexicans pushed the Americans back, but Jefferson Davis's Mississippi Rifles boldly attacked the Mexican cavalry as it tried to outflank Taylor's main body. Now the Mexicans began to fall back, until they were reinforced by a fresh division of reserves. Once again the tide of battle seemed certain to turn in favor of Santa Anna, but two batteries, plus Davis's Mississippians and an Indiana regiment, fell upon the attackers. Surprise was total, and Santa Anna, having lost perhaps as many as 2,000 men killed or wounded, retreated toward San Luís Potosi. American losses were 264 men killed and 450 wounded. Superior American artillery and the boldness of Jefferson Davis, as well as the fearless leadership of Zachary Taylor, had made up for inferior numbers. Buena Vista revealed Taylor's weaknesses as a military strategist and tactician, but the battle also demonstrated his great personal courage and ability to inspire absolute loyalty. With victory at Buena Vista, the Mexican army was no longer a threat to the lower Rio Grande.

Stephen Watts Kearny, who led an army of the United States from Missouri to California via Santa Fe. *Collection: Library of Congress*

Kearny's March

While Taylor won his victories in Mexico, Colonel Stephen Watts Kearny led a spectacular march from Fort Leavenworth, Kansas, to Santa Fe, New Mexico. There the provincial governor, Manuel Armijo, set up an ambush at steep-walled Apache Canyon, only to see his ill-disciplined troops flee in panic before Kearny's approach. Santa Fe fell to Kearny without a shot. From here, Kearny pressed on to California, reaching San Diego in December 1846. He found that a U.S. naval squadron had already secured the California ports.

Doniphan's March

In November 1846, Colonel Alexander Doniphan detached 856 Missouri volunteers from Kearny's main force in Santa Fe and marched south to pacify the upper Rio Grande region. He crossed the river at El Paso, where he defeated a force of 1,200 Mexicans. On February 27, 1847, his volunteers approached Chihuahua and discovered that it was defended by 2,700 Mexican regulars and perhaps 1,000 civilian volunteers. Doniphan deployed his vastly outnumbered troops with great skill, succeeding in outflanking the defenders. The so-called Battle of Sacramento was over in two hours. Eight hundred Missourians had defeated almost 4,000 Mexicans, inflicting at least 300 fatal casualties while suffering no more than 1 dead and 5 wounded.

Amphibious Operation at Vera Cruz

By March 2, 1847, when General Winfield Scott commenced operations leading to the landing at Vera Cruz—the first amphibious landing in U.S.

Army history—the Americans were in control of northern Mexico, thanks to the victories of Taylor and Doniphan. Scott landed 10,000 men at Vera Cruz during the night of March 9. He met with little opposition from the outnumbered Mexican force of 4,300 within the city walls. Storms beginning on March 12 greatly imperiled the landing of American artillery, but by March 22, all was in place. On that day, Scott commenced bombardment of Vera Cruz. When his mortars failed to bring about surrender, Scott called on Commodore Matthew C. Perry to open up with his naval guns. Vera Cruz surrendered on March 29.

Battle of Cerro Gordo

From Vera Cruz, Scott advanced on Jalapa, seventy-four miles along the national highway leading to Mexico City. His troops hauled heavy artillery and newly designed rockets for the assault on Jalapa as well as Mexico City. Major General Dwight E. Twiggs was in the lead with 2,600 men and a full complement of artillery. On April 11, after he had progressed about thirty miles, Twiggs's scouts informed him that Mexican artillery covered a key pass near the village of Cerro Gordo.

IN THEIR OWN
Words

George B. McClellan on U.S. Volunteer Troops, Letter of December 5, 1846

I was perfectly disgusted coming down the river. I found that every confounded Voluntario in the "Continental Army" ranked me—to be ranked and put aside for a soldier of yesterday, a miserable thing with buttons on it, that knows nothing whatever, is indeed too hard a case. I have pretty much made up my mind that if I cannot increase my rank in this war, I shall resign shortly after the close of it. I cannot stand the idea of being a Second Lieutenant all my life. . . .

I have seen more suffering since I came out here than I could have imagined to exist. It is really awful. I allude to the sufferings of the Volunteers. They literally die like dogs. Were it all known in the States, there would be no more hue and cry against the Army, all would be willing to have so large a regular army that we could dispense entirely with the volunteer system. The suffering among the Regulars is comparatively trifling, for their officers know their duty and take good care of the men. . . .

In fact, near Cerro Gordo, Santa Anna had 12,000 men and artillery deployed throughout the rocky defile through which the Mexico City highway passed. He was prepared to attack the only means by which he believed Scott could transport his artillery. As for Twiggs, advancing on the morning of April 12, he was spared from a surprise attack by the premature firing of the Mexican batteries. Twiggs pulled his troops back and, on April 14, was reinforced to a strength of 8,500 by the arrival of General Scott. Among the officers under Scott's command was a young captain named Robert E. Lee. He scouted out the principal Mexican artillery emplacement on a high hill called El Telegrafo and discovered a rugged, undefended pass by which Scott could bring his artillery to bear on the Mexican rear—without traversing the national highway. Scott and his force made their way through thick forest and brush, hoisting heavy siege artillery with ropes. On April 17, Scott installed a rocket battery on a hill to the right of El Telegrafo. On the next morning, the Americans began the attack. Santa Anna had not been taken entirely by surprise, but he had lacked sufficient time to protect his flank adequately. His huge army, poised for the kill, now broke and ran. More than 1,000 Mexicans died or were wounded, while Scott had 417 casualties, including 64 killed.

Advance Toward Mexico City

From the great victory at Cerro Gordo, Scott moved on to Jalapa and then to Puebla, the second-largest city in Mexico. Its citizens, who hated Santa Anna, surrendered to Scott without resistance on May 15, 1847. At the moment, Scott's greatest enemy was not the Mexican army but the expiration of volunteers' enlistments and the ravages of disease, especially yellow fever. With the onset of summer, his force had been reduced to 5,820 men fit for duty. In July, at Puebla, he was reinforced from Vera Cruz to a total strength of about 10,000.

While Scott prepared to march out of Puebla and on to Mexico City, a State Department official, Nicholas P. Trist, opened negotiations with Santa Anna. President Polk was anxious that Scott advance to the capital to keep up the pressure on the Mexicans. This prompted Scott to take a bold gamble. He decided to commit all of his troops to the advance, which meant leaving his line of communication, from Vera Cruz to Puebla, entirely undefended. He moved out on August 7. Reaching Ayolta on August 10, fourteen miles from the city, Scott saw that the direct road was heavily defended by fortified positions. Undaunted, he moved southward and approached the city from the west, by way of a fifteen-mile-wide lavabed called Pedregal. Considered impassable, it had been left undefended, but Robert E. Lee found a mule path to the village of Contreras. A force under Brevet Major General Gideon J. Pillow was beaten back from Contreras on August 19, but the arrival of reinforcements enabled a new attack at dawn on August 20. The Mexican defenders, taken wholly by surprise, were routed. Seven hundred Mexicans died in the battle and 800 were captured, among them 4 generals. Scott lost 60 killed or wounded.

Unlike Taylor, Scott was an aggressive commander who ordered an immediate pursuit of the retreating Mexicans. Despite his losses, Santa Anna managed to keep his army intact and took a defensive position at Churubusco. The Mexican general had converted a stone-walled church and convent into twin fortresses. From behind this position, the Mexicans fought fiercely with cannon and muskets, fully aware that they were in a desperate defense of their capital city. It was by far the most vigorous Mexican defense of the war, and Scott's troops made slow progress against it. By late afternoon, however, the Mexicans' ammunition was running low, and Scott made his move.

The Battle of Churubusco cost almost 4,000 Mexican casualties, killed or wounded. Scott also took heavy losses: 155 killed, 876 wounded. But Scott's victory brought a request from Santa Anna to reopen peace negotiations. The American commander proposed a brief cease-fire, and for two weeks, the U.S. State Department's Nicholas Trist and the Mexicans talked. It soon became clear to Scott that Santa Anna had sought the armistice as nothing more than a respite. On September 6, the American called a halt to discussions and commenced his final approach to Mexico City.

Battle of Chapultepec

Scott now commanded about 8,000 effectives, whereas Santa Anna, even after multiple defeats, had 15,000 men to defend Mexico City and had used the two-week armistice to strengthen the defenses in and around the city. Outnumbered though he was, Scott methodically set about taking the capital. On September 8 he stormed and seized El Molino del Rey, a cannon foundry just west of Chapultepec Castle. On September 13 he began an assault on Chapultepec with an artillery barrage, then sent three columns over the approaches to the hilltop fortress. Despite heavy fire from the fortress, the Americans overran Chapultepec by nine-thirty in the morning.

Fall of Mexico City

The Battle of Chapultepec resulted in an estimated 1,800 Mexican casualties and 130 U.S. dead, with 703 wounded. Exhausted, the Mexicans defended the capital city, fighting in the streets and house to house as best they could. But the spirit had gone out of the defenders, and the city surrendered on September 14, 1847.

Peace Negotiations

With the city occupied and even as Puebla fell under siege by Mexican forces (the siege lasted from September 14 to October 12, when American reinforcements from Vera Cruz drove off the attackers), peace negotiations began. Polk wanted Scott to continue fighting, to force the most extreme terms upon the Mexicans. But both the general and Nicholas Trist believed that the situation of the Mexican government was extremely delicate. If negotiations were delayed, it was likely that there would be no unambiguous authority to negotiate with; moreover, it was clear that right now, the Mexicans were very eager to end the war. Ignoring word from Washington, Trist and Scott continued to negotiate, producing the Treaty of Guadalupe Hidalgo, which was signed on February 2, 1848, and ratified by the U.S. Senate on March 10. After considerable rancor, Mexico exchanged final ratifications with the United States on May 30.

It is not surprising that President Polk was somewhat dubious in his evaluation of the treaty, for, in view of the extent of the American victory in the war, its terms were perhaps more generous than they absolutely needed to be. In return for the cession to the United States of "New Mexico"—the present state of New Mexico and portions of the present states of Utah, Nevada, Arizona, and Colorado—and California, as well as the renunciation of claims to Texas above the Rio Grande, Mexico was to be paid $15 million. Moreover, the United States agreed to assume all claims of U.S. citizens against Mexico, which (as subsequently determined by a specially appointed commission) amounted to an additional $3 million. Further, the United States made restitution to Mexico for customs duties it had been unable to collect because of the war. The treaty delineated a boundary line separating Mexico and the United States, and both sides subscribed to pledges of "peace and friendship." In 1853 the Treaty of Guadalupe Hidalgo was modified by the Gadsden Treaty, which formalized the U.S. acquisition by purchase of additional territory from Mexico.

CHAPTER 7

Early Indian Wars in the West

The Indian Removal Act was passed in 1830 (see Chapter 5), but by the mid-1830s, white settlement was already pushing far beyond the Mississippi River as the Oregon Territory was opened. Warfare between whites and Indians moved with the tide of settlement.

Mariposa War, 1850–1851

The Indian tribes whites called "Diggers," bare-subsistence people who lived in California's gold country, were brutally swept aside by prospectors during the 1848–1849 Gold Rush. Those Indians who did not succumb to violence died from disease, either contracted as a direct result of contact with whites or, indirectly, due to the hardships of dispossession and disruption. By the end of the Gold Rush era, the Digger population had been reduced by two-thirds, but in 1850, the Miwoks and the Yokuts, two "Digger" tribes who lived in the foothills of the Sierra Nevada and the San Joaquin Valley, rose up against the miners who had invaded their country. Led by Chief Tenaya, warriors attacked prospectors and burned trading posts belonging to James D. Savage. In retaliation, Savage led a militia force, called the Mariposa Battalion (after Mariposa County), against them in 1851. Tenaya and approximately 350 warriors evaded Savage's first campaign. A second campaign resulted in the capture of the chief and many warriors, and the brief Mariposa War came to an end.

Yuma and Mojave Uprising, 1851–1852

More formidable than the uprising of Miwoks and the Yokuts in the Mariposa War was resistance from the Yumas and the Mojaves, who lived in southwestern Arizona and southeastern California. The Yumas controlled the Yuma Crossing, a ford across the Colorado River near the mouth of the Gila. Partly in protest against the abuses they had suffered at the hands of invading whites, Antonio Garra, leader of a Yuma tribe called the Cupanga-kitoms, notified San Diego County authorities that his people would not pay the taxes levied on them. By November 1851, Garra and other Yuma leaders planned a revolution that would unite their tribes with the Mojaves and the Yokuts of the San Joaquin Valley, as well as various tribes in Baja California.

On November 10, 1851, a party of sheep drovers with some fifteen hundred animals reached the Colorado. The next day the party divided, five men continuing on with the sheep, the remainder making camp with a veteran of the Mexican War, Lieutenant Thomas "Fighting Tom" Sweeny and his small command. Presently, about five hundred Yumas surrounded the camp, but then retired when Sweeny threatened them with a twelve-pounder howitzer. Another party of Indians attacked the drovers who had remained with the sheep, killing four of the five. On November 12, Sweeny's troops were augmented by the arrival of reinforcements. However, Camp Independence (as Sweeny's garrison was called) was continually besieged throughout November and into early December. Sweeny and a garrison now numbering about a hundred men withdrew from the camp on December 6.

Elsewhere in California, the most serious Indian attack occurred on November 23 at Warner's Ranch. This raid prompted California settlers to organize militia forces. Antonio Garra, however, was captured not by militiamen but by a band of Cahuilla Indians, who refused to take part in the rebellion. Garra and other rebels were tried and executed. Next, army major H. P. Heintzelman mobilized eighty troopers and, on Christmas

Day 1851, attacked and defeated a rebel Indian band near the Cahuilla villages in Coyote Canyon. Treaties were summarily concluded. Along the Colorado, however, the Yumas maintained control until March and April 1852, when a mixed force of U.S. Army regulars and California volunteers under Heintzelman raided Yuma villages during March and April. After unsatisfactory negotiation attempts, Heintzelman surprised a band of Yumas near present-day Blythe, California, on September 29. They fled without offering battle. Then, on October 2, 1852, the Yumas held a grand council with the army in which they asked for forgiveness and permanent peace terms. This marked the end of the Yuma and Mojave Uprising of 1851–1852.

Rogue River War, 1855–1856

The early Indian wars in "Oregon Country"—the region encompassed by the present states of Oregon and Washington—were more violent than the California wars. The "Whitman massacre" of November 29, 1847, in which two Cayuse Indians killed the frontier missionary-physician Marcus Whitman, his wife, and perhaps another dozen while settlers in the belief that the whites had brought a deadly plague of measles among them, prompted U.S. president James K. Polk to set into motion the organization of the Oregon Territory on August 14, 1848. This allowed him to use federal troops to suppress any Indian violence. Even before the territory was organized, however, the Whitman Massacre prompted a local zealot, Cornelius Gilliam, to recruit 550 Oregon militiamen for a punitive expedition against the Cayuses. That the Whitman Massacre had been perpetrated by a few Indians and had not been endorsed by the Cayuses at large did not matter to Gilliam, who merely attacked the first Indian camp he and his men encountered, killing about 20 Indians and suffering 5 casualties among his own force.

Memorial sculpture of Marcus Whitman, whose death at the hands of Cayuse Indians contributed to the incitement of the Rogue River War. *Collection: ArtToday*

During September 1855, the local violence was intensified by rumors of a developing war between Yakimas and settlers east of the Cascades. As whites began to menace all Indians, hostile or not, Captain Andrew Jackson Smith, commanding Fort Lane, just north of the present California-Oregon state line, found it necessary to offer Indian men, women, and children the protection of the fort. Before Smith could admit all of the endangered Indians into this refuge, however, a band of settlers raided a nearby camp, killing twenty-three Rogue Indians, including old men, women, and children. The next day, October 17, Indian war parties took revenge, killing twenty-seven settlers in the Rogue Valley and burning the hamlet of Gallice Creek. With the bulk of the regular army forces off fighting the Yakimas, Walla Wallas, Umatillas, and Cayuses in what was now being called the *Yakima War, 1855,* Captain Smith could do little with his small garrison except try to keep it from being overrun. Conducting siege warfare was alien and distasteful to most Indian war cultures. Typically, sieges, even against inferior numbers, sooner or later broke down. By the spring of 1856, the Takelma and Tutuni chiefs known to the whites as Limpy, Old John, and George, weary of fighting, agreed to surrender to Captain Smith at a place called Big Meadows. However, apparently on the spur of the moment, the chiefs reconsidered and, instead of surrendering, mustered some two hundred warriors in an attack on Smith's fifty dragoons and thirty infantry troopers. Fortunately for Smith, a pair of Indian women had tipped him off to the attack, and Smith, outnumbered as he was, skillfully deployed men on a hilltop offering a good defensive position. The attack, on May 27, 1856, was fierce and determined, but Smith held out through the next afternoon,

IN THEIR OWN *Words*

Defendant's Request, Whitman Massacre Trial, 1851

United States v. Telokite et al.

Telokite one of the defendants makes oath that a certain Indian named Quishem now in the Cayuse country he thinks will be a material witness for the defendants in this case. That the materiality of said witness was not known in time to have him in attendance at this term of the court. He expects & believes that said witness will prove that the late Dr Whitman administered medicines to many of the Cayuse Indians and that afterwards a large number of them died, including amongst them the wives and children of some of these defendants. He expects further to prove by said witness that a certain Joseph Lewis, who resided at Waiilatpu informed these defendants a few days before the 29 November 1847 that the Cayuse Indians were dying in consequence of poison being administered to them by the late Marcus Whitman and he had heard Dr Whitman say that he would kill off all of the Cayuse Indians by the coming of the ensuing spring—that he would then have their horses and lands. Witness will also prove it is the law of the Cayuse Indians to kill bad medicine men.

when reinforcements under Captain Christopher C. Augur arrived. With Augur, Smith counterattacked, routing the Rogue Indians, who subsequently surrendered and accepted consignment to a reservation.

Yakima War, 1855

In May 1855, Isaac Stevens, governor of Washington Territory, hastily concluded treaties binding the tribes east of the Cascade Mountains—including the Nez Percés, Cayuses, Umatillas, Walla Wallas, and Yakimas—to retire to reservations in exchange for government subsidies. Stevens pledged that removal to the reservation would be delayed for two or three years. Most of the tribal representatives believed that resistance was futile and that Stevens's offer and pledge, though distasteful, were the best treatment they could hope for. Nevertheless, a stubborn minority, including the revered Yakima chief Kamiakin, refused to sign. When Stevens broke his pledge and opened the treaty territory to immediate settlement, Kamiakin responded by forging an alliance among the Walla Wallas, Umatillas, and Cayuses, as well as his own Yakima faction. Kamiakin prudently counseled patience as he organized and planned an assault against superior forces, but eager young warriors acted independently—and rashly. A group of five braves led by Kamiakin's nephew, Qualchin, attacked and killed six prospectors

IN THEIR OWN Words

Request to Open Indian Lands, 1857

In the document excerpted here, the Oregon territorial legislature petitions the U.S. General Land Office to survey the Table Rock Reservation for purchase. Such pressure to settle lands occupied by Indians was unceasing and a continual source of conflict in Indian-white relations.

To the Commissioner of the General Land Office

Your memorialists the Legislative Assembly of the Territory of Oregon most respectfully represent:

That by the treaty of the tenth of September 1853, made with the Rogue River tribe of Indians in southern Oregon, a Reservation was established on the North side of Upper Rogue River in said Territory . . . [Y]our memorialists respectfully urge your Department to direct the completion of the survey of said Reserve; and that the efforts and influence of the same be used to have said reservation vacated and opened for preemption and purchase.

> *And as in duty bound will ever pray,*
> *Adopted December 18 1857*
> *L. F. Grover*
> *Speaker of the House of Representatives*
> *James K. Kelly*
> *President of the Council*

Isaac Ingalls Stevens, the zealous governor of Washington Territory, whose eagerness to acquire land triggered the Yakima War. *Collection of the author*

in mid-September 1855. The local Indian agent sent to investigate the incident also was killed. Although Kamiakin did not approve of this premature act, he issued a warning that a similar fate would befall all whites who ventured east of the Cascades. In October, a small force of regulars, eighty-four men and a howitzer under Major Granville O. Haller out of Fort Dalles (on the southern bank of the Columbia River), reconnoitered the eastern face of the mountains with the intention of coordinating a pincers attack against the Indians with fifty men from Fort Steilacoom (far to the north, just below Seattle) under Lieutenant W. A. Slaughter. Five hundred of Kamiakin's warriors ambushed Haller's column, killing five of their number, forcing them to abandon their howitzer, and driving the remainder back to the fort. Fortunately for Slaughter's command, the lieutenant had been warned of the action and escaped the area by making a night march back to Puget Sound.

Now that few troops were in the area, local Indians raided a settlement along the White River above Seattle, killing nine people. The survivors of the attack fled in panic to Seattle, where they hastily erected a stockade in anticipation of a siege. At this point Lieutenant Slaughter reappeared and engaged the Indians repeatedly until they gradually broke off the attack on Seattle. Slaughter was killed in this action.

At about this time, Colonel James Kelley led a unit of militiamen into the Walla Walla homelands along the Walla Walla and Touchet Rivers. Encountering the Walla Walla chief Peo-Peo-Mox-Mox, who had just burned Fort Walla Walla (an abandoned Hudson's Bay Company facility), Kelley agreed to a peace parley with him. Kelley stated his terms, and Peo-Peo-Mox-Mox sent one of his men back to the village, ostensibly to communicate the terms to the people there. As a precaution, Kelley held Peo-Peo-Mox-Mox and six other chiefs as voluntary hostages. Apparently the message Peo-Peo-Mox-Mox had sent was an order to attack, for Kelley and his men soon found themselves charged by what was described as "hordes" of Indians. While fending off the attack, Kelley's men killed Peo-Peo-Mox-Mox in a scuffle. After a four-day battle, the attacking Indians at last withdrew, and the triumphant Oregon volunteers brazenly displayed to fellow settlers the chief's ears and scalp. This outrage moved the Umatillas and the Cayuses to vengeance. On February 23, raids along the lower Rogue River destroyed more than sixty homes and left thirty-one settlers dead. One hundred thirty survivors of the raids took refuge near Gold Beach, where they were besieged for almost a month. Seaborne rescue efforts were repeatedly foiled by a heavy surf that prevented landing. Eventually, however, the Indians withdrew. General John Ellis Wool

IN THEIR OWN *Words*

Settler and militia attacks on peaceful Indians often touched off major wars. The following is a report from the time of the Yakima War.

Headquarters Northern District.
Department of the Pacific.
Camp at Fort Dalles O. T. [Oregon Territory] Apl 27, 1856.

Governor,

I have the honor to inclose herewith, a copy of a communication this day received from Mr R. R. Thompson, Indian Agent at this place.

As I march into the Yakima country to-morrow morning, with all my disposable force, I am much embarrassed by these wanton attacks of the Oregon Volunteers, on the friendly Indians. Were I to accede to the request of the Agent, to furnish a force to protect these Indians, during the fishing season, it would diminish my force, to such an extent, as to render nugatory my campaign in the Yakima country. Under these circumstances, and presuming that you still retain authority over the Oregon Territorial jurisdiction, I have to request that they may be withdrawn from the country on the north side of the Columbia river. Very Respectfully
I have the honor to be,
Your most Obt Servt,
G. Wright
Col. 9 Inft
Comndg

Governor Curry
Salem
O. T.

dispatched 500 regulars under George H. Wright to track down Kamiakin and the other hostiles. By this time, however, the fight seemed to have gone out of the Yakimas, and General Wool declared the Yakima War ended.

But Kamiakin was not quite finished. He continued to raid east of the Columbia River, and during 1857–1858 he stirred the Coeur d'Alene and Spokane Indians to join the uprising, the *Coeur d'Alene War (Spokane War), 1858,* which is treated in the following section.

Coeur d'Alene War (Spokane War), 1858

Late in 1857, a group of Colville, Washington, prospectors, victims of sporadic Indian raids, petitioned for protection by U.S. troops. In May 1858, 158 regulars out of Fort Walla Walla and under the command of Lieutenant Colonel Edward J. Steptoe marched to the gold camp of Colville to impress the Palouse, Spokane, and Coeur d'Alene Indians with the prowess of the U.S. Army. Steptoe was unaware that Kamiakin had stirred passions over the proposed Missouri-to-Columbia road, which would cut through Indian land. He believed his mission was merely to placate a handful of panicky miners. More than 1,000 warriors intercepted the column about twenty miles south of the present-day city of Spokane. The warriors told Steptoe to turn back and go home. Steptoe complied, but all through the rest of the day and into the next, the warriors followed his retreating column, taunting the men with jeers. On May 17 the Indians suddenly attacked the column, killing 2 officers. Steptoe made for a defensive hilltop position, then managed to escape by night to the safety of Fort Walla Walla. Outraged by Steptoe's humiliation, the regional commander ordered Colonel George Wright to conduct a vigorous punitive campaign against the hostiles.

On September 1, 1858, about 600 warriors met Wright's superior force (which was augmented by friendly Nez Percés) in the open on Spokane Plain. On September 5, they fought on another open field, at Four Lakes. After winning both battles, Wright sent a detachment to various Indian camps to demand the surrender of those who had led the attack on Steptoe and his men. Fifteen braves were hanged, and others were made prisoner.

Chief Kamiakin had been injured by artillery fire in the Battle of Spokane Plain, but he made his escape to British Canada. His brother-in-law, Owhi, approached Wright to make peace, only to be seized and forced to summon his son, the war leader Qualchin. Before Owhi's eyes, Wright summarily hanged the young man. In a subsequent escape attempt, Owhi himself was shot and killed. Wright's cruelty did not enrage the tribes of the Columbia Basin, but dispirited them. They laid down weapons and marched off to the reservations specified in Govenor Stevens's treaties—treaties the Senate rushed to ratify on March 8, 1859.

Paiute War (Pyramid Lake War), 1860

Williams Station was one of a pair of trading posts in Carson Valley along the important California Trail, serving the Central Overland Mail and the Pony Express. Early in May 1860, 2 miners abducted and raped 2 girls of the Southern Paiute tribe. The incident provoked the Southern Paiutes not only to rescue the girls but also, by way of vengeance, to torch the station and to kill those occupying it—5 men. On May 8, word of the "Williams Station Massacre" reached the Wells, Fargo office in Virginia City, Nevada. Fearing a major uprising, perhaps as many as 2,000 miners, a mob rather than a disciplined force of volunteers, assembled long enough to telegraph the governor to request arms. No sooner was the message sent than the mob dispersed, but a miner, Henry Meredith, organized a new force drawn from the Nevada mining towns. At Dayton, Nevada, Meredith's men were

Paiute Indians, documented by a Smithsonian Institution photographer early in the twentieth century. *Collection: ArtToday*

joined by Major William M. Ormsby and volunteers from Carson City. Ormsby assumed command of a force that now numbered no more than 105 men and led them to Pyramid Lake, in the heart of Paiute country.

The Paiute chief Numaga laid an ambush at Big Bend in the Truckee River Valley. In this narrow pass, at 4:00 P.M. on May 12, 1860, Paiute warriors fell on Ormsby's column. Poison-dipped arrows—the Paiute weapon of choice—killed 46 of the volunteers, almost half of Ormsby's force. The rest fled in a panic that soon spread throughout the Comstock region. California's governor sent troops to the area under the command of a former

Texas Ranger, Colonel Jack Hays (Hayes), whose force was augmented by a small detachment of U.S. Infantry regulars out of San Francisco. Together with a few local volunteers, Hays's force numbered close to 800 men, who headed for the Truckee River late in May. The force encountered a handful of Paiutes near the site of the ambush, skirmished with them, then pursued them to Pinnacle Mountain, where they encountered more Indians. In the battle that took place here, 25 warriors died. With that, the short-lived Paiute War ended.

Apache and Navajo War, 1860–1868

For the most part, the *Civil War, 1861–1865 (see chapter 8)* affected the military situation in the American West indirectly, by drawing off a great deal of manpower from the western outposts. This encouraged so-called uprisings among the Apaches and the Navajos.

The Apaches had a long history of aggression not only against Anglo and Mexican settlers in Arizona but also against other tribes. In contrast to many others, Cochise, a chief of the Chiricahua Apaches, was inclined to like Americans and, indeed, had concluded a profitable contract with the Butterfield Overland Mail to supply wood to the station at Apache Pass. The unwarranted accusations of John Ward, a disreputable Arizona rancher, prompted the arrest of Cochise and five others on February 4, 1861, for having raided Ward's ranch and kidnapped his son. When Cochise protested his innocence, Second Lieutenant George N. Bascom announced that he and his party would be held captive until the boy and Ward's stolen cattle were returned. Cochise drew his knife, slit the canvas of the conference tent, and escaped. The five other hostages remained behind. In retaliation for his arrest, Cochise gathered his warriors and raided the Butterfield station, killing one employee and taking another, James F. Wallace, prisoner. When a small wagon train passed by the station, Cochise captured it, along with eight Mexicans and two Americans who had been riding with it. The Mexicans he ordered bound to the wagon wheels and burned alive. The Americans—the two from the wagon train and the station employee—he offered to exchange for the captives Bascom still held. Bascom refused and summoned reinforcements from Fort Buchanan. Seventy dragoons under Lt. Isaiah N. Moore arrived on February 14, only to find that Cochise and his braves had vanished. The soldiers scouted the area and found the bodies of the three American hostages, pierced by lances and mutilated. By way of reprisal, Bascom hanged his prisoners. This elicited a vow from Cochise to exterminate all Americans in Arizona Territory.

Shortly after the "Bascom Affair," the *Civil War, 1861–1865 (see chapter 8)* broke out, and the federal garrisons in the region were reduced. Confederate Lieutenant Colonel John Robert Baylor took advantage of the Union's weakened position to sweep through the southern New Mexico Territory, from the Rio Grande to California. Baylor's efforts were followed during the winter of 1861–1862 by a larger Confederate invasion led by General Henry Hopkins Sibley, whose mission was the capture of all of New Mexico. Sibley moved up the Rio Grande, intent on taking Fort Union, headquarters of Colonel Edward R. S. Canby, commander of the Department of New Mexico. Learning that the majority of New Mexicans were loyal to the Union, Canby hastily sought to organize them as the First and Second Regiments of New Mexican Volunteers. This gesture, however, failed to bring the volunteers under Canby's control. Lieutenant Colonel Manuel Chaves, second-in-command of the Second Regiment, was placed in charge of Fort Fauntleroy (soon renamed Fort Lyon because Colonel Fauntleroy defected to the Confederacy) at Ojo del Oso on August 9, 1861, with a detachment of 210 officers and men. As the Canby treaty of February 1861 promised, Chaves's men began distributing rations to the Navajos in August and September. In addition to food, they provided alcohol and set up gambling. A series of horse races were run, during which accusations of cheating led to a riot in which Chaves's soldiers killed as many as 40 Navajos, including women and children. Survivors fled and began to raid the countryside.

Canby responded by arresting Chaves and ordered John Ward, the local Indian agent, to attempt to persuade the Indians to gather at Cubero, where they could be given the "protection" of the government. Canby's aim was to concentrate the Indians where they could be watched and kept from making alliances with Confederate forces. Canby also dispatched the celebrated Kit Carson, commander of the First New Mexico Volunteer Cavalry, to move vigorously against any Navajos who persisted in raiding.

Since the "Bascom Affair," the settlements and trade routes between El Paso and Tucson had been exposed to the wrath not only of Cochise's band of Chiricahua Apaches but also the Mimbreño Apaches, under Chief Mangas Coloradas. The federal abandonment of Forts Buchanan, Breckinridge, Stanton, and Fillmore in the face of the Confederate invasion of New Mexico was interpreted by the Apaches as a sign that the "bluecoats" feared *them,* and beginning in July 1861, the Mescalero Apaches vigorously raided the subsistence herds of local settlers. The Mescaleros were not intimidated, in July 1862, when they saw more bluecoats approaching from the west. This was the van of Colonel James Henry Carleton's California Column. On July 15, Carleton's troops marched into Apache Pass and were promptly ambushed by seven hundred warriors under Cochise. The troops used howitzers to drive off the attackers. On January 17, 1863, Mangas Coloradas agreed to meet with Captain E. D. Shirland. Despite his flag of truce, the chief was seized and delivered to headquarters camp, where he was treacherously executed. This action provoked new vengeance raids.

On September 18, 1862, Canby, who had been promoted to brigadier general, was temporarily transferred to an eastern command. He was replaced by Carleton, who now assumed command of the Department of New Mexico. Carleton proposed to round up all Navajos and Apaches and send them to a forty-mile-square reservation at the Bosque Redondo on the Pecos River in New Mexico. In response, many Mescaleros fled to Mexico, while others did march to Bosque Redondo.

Kit Carson, famed New Mexico Indian-fighter in the Apache and Navajo War. *Collection: ArtToday*

While Kit Carson continually pursued the Mescaleros to force them onto the reservation, four companies of his First New Mexico Volunteer Cavalry, commanded by Lieutenant Colonel J. Francisco Chavez, established Fort Wingate near Mount Taylor, on the border of Navajo country. Ever since the ill-fated horse race at Fort Fauntleroy/Lyon, Navajos had been raiding Rio Grande settlements. The new fort, together with the campaign against the Mescaleros, prompted eighteen important Navajo chiefs, including the renowned Delgadito and Barboncito (but not Manuelito), to come to Santa Fe seeking terms of peace. Carleton told them that the only alternative to war was to take their people to the Bosque Redondo reservation. He set a deadline of July 20, 1863, after which "every Navajo that is seen will be considered as hostile and treated accordingly." When Barboncito refused to go to the reservation, Carleton, on June 15, concentrated Kit Carson's regiment at Fort Wingate. After the July 20 deadline came and went, Carson was ordered out with 736 men and officers to make full-scale war on the Navajos. While Lieutenant Colonel Chavez remained at Fort Wingate with two companies, Carson's men established Fort Canby at Pueblo, Colorado, and campaigned against the Indians, doing the most damage by destroying Navajo fields and orchards. Over the succeeding months, desperate Navajos offered themselves in surrender, and were marched off to the Bosque Redondo.

By late 1864, three-quarters of the Navajo tribe had accepted concentration on the reservation. Eventually eight thousand Navajos crowded the reservation, but with an inefficiency and inhumanity that had become routine in administering federal reservations, the government failed to supply sufficient rations to feed this population. A treaty was finally concluded on June 1, 1868, returning the Indians to their homeland and declaring it their new reservation. By this gesture of humanity and common sense, the grim Navajo war was ended.

Minnesota Santee Sioux Uprising, 1862

The Civil War *(see Civil War, 1861–1865 [chapter 8])* shortage of military manpower affected all parts of the transmississippi West, including the upper Midwest. In Minnesota, the Santee Sioux (a division of the Sioux often called the Dakota, consisting of the Mdewakantons, Wahpekutes, Sissetons, and Wahpetons) at first accepted the wartime policy of "concentration" that the Apaches and Navajos had so vigorously resisted. But, confined to a narrow strip of land along the upper Minnesota River, they soon suffered the effects of a crop failure and found themselves hemmed in by growing numbers of Scandinavian and German immigrants. Santee resentment grew, and it boiled over into rage when funds and supplies guaranteed them by an 1851 treaty failed to materialize. In a climate of desperation and anger, on Sunday, August 17, four young Mdewakanton men robbed and killed five local settlers. The influential Mdewakanton chief Little Crow believed the youths' rash act would bring ruin down upon them all. Nevertheless, he decided that the die had been cast, and, on August 18, led a band of warriors in an attack on a local trader's store. Simultaneously with this raid—in which Andrew J. Myrick, the trader, was killed—additional war parties swept across the Minnesota countryside. Settlers fled, and refugees began arriving at Fort Ridgely by ten o'clock in the morning. Captain John S. Marsh commanded a garrison of only seventy-six men and two officers. He dispatched a messenger to Lieutenant Timothy J. Sheehan, who was taking fifty men to Fort Ripley on the Mississippi River. In the meantime, Marsh left Fort Ridgely with a detachment of forty-six men, headed for the Lower Agency. Along the way, they saw the smoldering ruins of settlers' houses and mutilated corpses. At the Redwood Ferry, which crossed the Minnesota River to the Lower Agency, Marsh and his men were ambushed. Twenty-five of forty-six men—including Marsh—died, and another five were wounded. The survivors reached Fort Ridgely, now commanded by Lieutenant Thomas P. Gere, who could muster only twenty-two able-bodied men. The rest of the garrison, including himself, were sick with the mumps.

Gere sent a messenger to Fort Snelling (modern Minneapolis), asking for reinforcements; the messenger also managed to overtake Thomas J. Galbraith, commanding the volunteer Renville Rangers, who rode back to Fort Ridgely. Even augmented by Galbraith's men, the fort was in a poor position to withstand an Indian attack. An unstockaded collection of wooden buildings, its only real defense consisted of two twelve-pounder mountain howitzers, a twenty-four-pounder of the same type, and a six-pounder field gun.

The first onslaught came on August 19, led by Little Crow, Mankato, and Big Eagle. The attackers halted just before reaching the fort and, in full view of the soldiers, held a lengthy council. Surprisingly, the Indians

IN THEIR OWN *Words*

On August 15, 1862, Santee Sioux chief Little Crow went to the Indian Agency at the Minnesota River to ask government agent Thomas J. Galbraith to distribute government-stockpiled provisions to his hungry people.

"*We have no food, but here are these stores filled with food,*" he demanded of Galbraith.

With Galbraith was trading post operator Andrew J. Myrick.

"*So far as I'm concerned,*" *Myrick contemptuously remarked,* "*if they are hungry, let them eat grass or their own dung.*"

In the massacre that followed, Myrick would be among the first to fall. The Indians stuffed the dead man's mouth with grass.

turned away from Fort Ridgely and made for the nearby settlement of New Ulm. It was a reprieve for the fort, which was soon reinforced not only by Galbraith but also by 50 men under Lieutenant Sheehan, making a total of 180 defenders. At three in the afternoon of August 20, however, a war party of about 100 began firing into New Ulm. Militia and towns-people staged a desperate defense. Little Crow turned the attack against Fort Ridgely again, and then, on August 23, renewed the assault on New Ulm. By the time the Indians withdrew, most of the town lay a smoldering ruin, and 2,000 citizens evacuated to Mankato.

At dawn on September 2, a large party of warriors under Big Eagle, Mankato, and Gray Bird attacked Captain Hiram P. Grant's camp at the head of a deep gulch called Birch Coulee. In the initial onslaught, twenty-two troopers were killed and sixty wounded; nevertheless, the remainder managed to stave off utter annihilation long enough for a relief column under Colonel Samuel McPhail to reach them. The rescuers, however, soon found themselves surrounded as well. A howitzer was brought to bear, which drove off the Indians and enabled McPhail's command to reach a defensible position, which they held until September 3, when the

The town of New Ulm, Minnesota, continues to commemorate the resistance of New Ulm to the siege of the Santee Sioux with annual reenactments of the battle. The uniforms worn by these reenactors are copied from that of a Civil War officer, Second Lieutenant Richard Fischer, who returned to his home in time to defend against the Indian attack. *Collection: National Archives and Records Administration*

main body of militia colonel Henry Hastings Sibley's force arrived. Grant had withstood a thirty-one-hour siege.

The Battle of Birch Coulee provoked harsh criticism of Sibley's lack of aggressiveness in the face of an emergency that now reached beyond the borders of Minnesota into Wisconsin and Dakota Territory, as Indians raided throughout the region. Sibley resisted the temptation to cave into criticism and act rashly; he knew that he needed more troops and that the militiamen he presently commanded were raw and required further training. It was not until September 19, with the addition of officers and men from Minnesota infantry regiments and a mounted company of Renville Rangers, that Sibley, now commanding 1,619 soldiers, felt ready to move. But the Indians decided to move first. At dawn on September 23, about 700 warriors took up positions in ambush along the road that Sibley's column would take out of its camp near Wood Lake. The Indians attacked prematurely, and the Battle of Wood Lake resulted in the deaths of 7 troopers and about 30 Indians. Little Crow's army rapidly dissolved, and beginning on September 26, Sibley accepted the surrender of about 2,000 hostiles and the release of about 370 captives.

While the Battle of Wood Lake was a severe blow to the uprising, it did not end hostilities on the Plains. Indeed, the battle marked the beginning of years of warfare with the Sioux. The theater of war shifted now from Minnesota to Dakota Territory after Santee Sioux refugees and Teton Sioux, as well as the Cheyenne, were provoked to war. In the spring of 1863, General John Pope ordered Sibley to travel up the Minnesota River, crossing into Dakota Territory to Devil's Lake, while Sully went up the Missouri and turned northeast to meet him. It was intended as a show of force that would discourage Santee and Yanktonai Sioux from massing for another uprising.

The Indians who were gathered near Devil's Lake were Sisseton Sioux led by Standing Buffalo, who considered himself at peace. Not far from them were Indians of the same tribe who were followers of Inkpaduta, a hostile chief, as well as Teton Sioux (including Hunkpapas and Blackfeet), who were potentially hostile. Sibley and Sully commanded a total of about 4,200 troopers. On July 24, 1863, Sibley at last made contact with Standing Buffalo and Inkpaduta's followers and arranged a parley near Big Mound, northeast of present-day Bismarck, North Dakota. Clearly, Standing Buffalo wanted no war, but at the start of the parley, a young partisan of Inkpaduta shot and killed the surgeon of the Minnesota Rangers. At this, Sibley's artillery opened on the Indians, the cavalry routing them from one defensive position to the next until nightfall. On July 26, Sibley pressed the pursuit, burning villages and using his artillery to counter Sioux attacks. Sibley continued the pursuit until July 29, when he decided that 150 Indians killed (at a cost of 12 Minnesota casualties) was sufficient vengeance.

Inkpaduta was found on September 3 near Whitestone Hill (northwest of present-day Ellendale, North Dakota) by four companies of the Sixth Iowa Cavalry under Major Albert E. House. Badly outnumbered, House seemed destined for certain destruction and would have been annihilated had he not managed to get a message to Sully, who brought the rest of the brigade to his rescue. A savage battle ensued in which 22 soldiers fell, 50 were wounded, and some 300 warriors died. Two hundred fifty women and children were taken captive.

What had begun as certain triumph for Inkpaduta ended in disaster for the Sioux. Yet it prompted few Indians to seek peace. When the spring of 1864 brought rumors of Sioux resistance along the Missouri and the routes of Montana-bound prospectors, General Pope ordered Sibley to establish forts on Devil's Lake and the James River. Sully was also to increase the military presence in the Dakotas and was directed to hunt for Sioux assiduously and aggressively.

On July 28, 1864, 3,000 troops under Sully's command reached Killdeer Mountain, where—according to Sully's account—they faced some 6,000 warriors (Indian accounts number the warriors at no more than 1,600). A cavalry attack was out of the question in the hilly and heavily wooded terrain, so Sully dismounted his men and formed them in a hollow square, in which formation they advanced on the hostile camp. Gunfire was exchanged, and then Sully opened up with his howitzers. In the end, Sully's losses were light at the Battle of Killdeer Mountain: 5 killed, 10 wounded. He estimated that he had killed 150 warriors (the Indians said it was 31 dead), and, even worse, the Sioux were forced to flee, leaving behind precious stores of food and other supplies.

Following the battle, Sully resumed the hunt for more Sioux, engaging in a few sharp exchanges, including the rescue of a group of settlers under attack at Fort Rice (in present-day North Dakota), before the war dissolved into other conflicts with the Plains tribes in the later phases of the Indian Wars (see chapter 9).

CHAPTER 8

Civil War

The issue of slavery poisoned the American republic from its inception. Beginning with the Constitution's Three-fifths Compromise, a series of uneasy compromises between the interests of southern slave states and northern free states were cobbled together over the years as the addition of each new state to the Union brought bitter debate over whether the state would be admitted with or without slavery. The Missouri Compromise of 1820 and the Compromise of 1850 postponed but did not prevent armed conflict, which was precipitated by the election to the presidency, in 1860, of Abraham Lincoln. By no means a radical abolitionist (he believed the Constitution protected slavery where it already existed), Lincoln was a candidate who nevertheless had made clear his intention to stop the extension of slavery to new states and territories. During the months preceding the outbreak of war, most of the slaveholding states seceded from the Union. Deeming this a violation of the Constitution and federal sovereignty, the Lincoln administration prepared to wage war. The seceded states, in the meantime, called themselves the Confederate States of America and likewise girded for battle.

Although the Civil War commenced with an attack on Fort Sumter, in Charleston Harbor, at four-thirty on the morning of April 12, 1861, the West had experienced at least two preludes to the major conflict.

"Bleeding Kansas" Guerrilla War, 1854–1861

In 1818, the U.S. Senate consisted of twenty-two senators from northern states and twenty-two from southern states. Now the territory of Missouri, part of the Louisiana Purchase, petitioned Congress for admission to the Union as a slaveholding state. The balance threatened suddenly to shift. Representative James Tallmadge of New York responded to Missouri's petition by introducing an amendment to the statehood bill calling for a ban on the further introduction of slavery into the state (but persons who were slaves in the present territory would remain slaves after the transition to statehood) and for the emancipation of all slaves born in the state when they reached twenty-five years of age. Thus, by attrition, slavery would be eliminated from Missouri. The House passed the Tallmadge amendment, but the Senate rejected it, adjourning afterward without reaching a decision on Missouri statehood. When the Senate reconvened, a long, rancorous, and tortured debate began. Northern senators held that Congress had the right to ban slavery in new states. Southerners asserted that new states had the same right as the original thirteen: to determine whether or not they would allow slavery. At last, in March 1820, a compromise was hammered out. By the Missouri Compromise, it was agreed that Missouri would enter the Union as a slave state, but, simultaneously, that Maine (hitherto a part of Massachusetts) would be admitted as a free state. Thus—for the moment—the slave state/free state balance was maintained. But the Missouri Compromise also looked toward the future and specified that a line be drawn across the Louisiana Territory at a latitude of 36°, 30', north of which slavery would be permanently banned—except in the case of Missouri.

The Missouri Compromise staved off civil war, but no one was truly happy with it, and the *United States–Mexican War, 1846–1848 (see chapter 6),* jolted the compromise into crisis. During the first year of the war, Congress sought a means of bringing the conflict to a quick end by appropriating $2 million to compensate Mexico for what the lawmakers euphemistically termed "territorial adjustments." Seizing opportunity,

Pennsylvania congressman David Wilmot introduced an amendment to the bill, called the Wilmot Proviso, that would have barred the introduction of slavery into any land acquired by the United States as a result of the *United States-Mexican War, 1846–1848 (see chapter 6).* In response to the Wilmot Proviso, South Carolina's John C. Calhoun offered four resolutions, including one stating that the enactment of any national law regarding slavery violates the Constitution and the doctrine of states' rights, and another holding that the people have the right to form their state governments as they wish, provided that such government is republican in principle. Calhoun then demanded action on his resolutions, declaring that the failure to maintain a strict balance between the demands of the North and the South would surely mean "civil war."

Now a long debate began on ways to bolster the Missouri Compromise. When it was clear that the debate was stalemated, Senator Lewis Cass of Michigan advanced the doctrine of "popular sovereignty," which provided for the organization of new territories without mention of slavery one way or the other. Only when the territory wrote its own constitution and applied for admission as a state would the people of the territory itself vote the proposed state slave or free. However, it was proposed that California, made independent by the *United States–Mexican War, 1846–1848 (see chapter 6),* would be admitted to statehood directly, without passing through an interim of territorial status. At this, Southerners recoiled, assuming that California would vote itself free, as would, later, New Mexico. So Senators Henry Clay of Kentucky and Daniel Webster of Massachusetts worked out a new compromise. California would be admitted as a free state, but the other territories acquired as a result of the United States–Mexican War would be subject to popular sovereignty. Moreover, the slave trade in the District of Columbia would be discontinued. However, to appease the South, a strong fugitive slave law was passed, explicitly forbidding Northerners to grant refuge to escaped slaves. The Compromise of 1850 offended as many interests as it placated. The 1850 compromise augmented the 1820 Missouri Compromise, but, four years after it was enacted, when the territories of Nebraska and Kansas applied for statehood, Congress responded by repealing the Missouri Compromise altogether and passing the Kansas-Nebraska Act. This extended the doctrine of popular sovereignty beyond territory acquired as a result of the United States–Mexican War, totally eliminating the 1820 slave-free line.

If the situation of 1850 had been explosive, the Kansas-Nebraska Act of 1854 applied the match to the fuse, for while there was never any doubt that Nebraskans would vote themselves a free state, Kansas, to the south of Nebraska, was very much divided on the issue. Following passage of the Kansas-Nebraska Act, proslavery Missourians and antislavery Iowans ("Free Soilers") streamed across the territory's eastern border, each side striving to achieve a majority for the purpose of creating a state constitution either mandating slavery or prohibiting it. Many of the Missourians, after electing a proslavery territorial legislature, retreated to Missouri, but the Iowans remained, and soon a chronic state of civil warfare developed between pro- and antislavery factions in what came to be called "Bleeding Kansas."

Typical of the violence was the 1856 raid against the Free Soil stronghold of Lawrence, Kansas. Proslavery "border ruffians" raided in 1856, set fire to a hotel and a number of houses, destroyed a printing press, and killed several townspeople. During the night of May 24, John Brown, a radical abolitionist who had taken command of the territory's so-called Free Soil Militia, led four of his sons and two other followers in an assault on proslavery settlers along the Pottawatomie River. Brown and his militia killed five unarmed settlers. The raid on Lawrence and Brown's retaliation following it are the only events of Bleeding Kansas that can be likened to battles. Guerrilla violence—widespread mayhem—continued with sporadic intensity through 1858, by the end of which two hundred people were dead and some $2 million in prop-

Militant abolitionist John Brown.
Collection of the author

erty had been destroyed. The violence was greatly reduced after 1858, but continued sporadically even after Kansas was admitted to the Union as a free state in 1861. The state saw guerrilla action throughout the Civil War.

Civil War, 1861–1865

The chaos of Bleeding Kansas was but one prelude to the great conflict to come. At the height of the violence on the Plains, in 1857, the U.S. Supreme Court denied the appeal of one Dred Scott, a fugitive slave. Essentially the Court held that as long as slavery was legal, the United

1861

April 13: *Fort Sumter surrenders*

July 21: *First Battle of Bull Run ends in a Union defeat*

November 1: *George B. McClellan becomes Union general in chief*

1862

February 16: *Fort Donelson falls to Ulysses S. Grant*

March 8: *Confederates defeated at Pea Ridge, Arkansas*

March 9: *Battle of* Monitor *vs.* Merrimac *inaugurates a new era in naval warfare*

March 28: *Union forces halt the Confederate invasion of New Mexico at the Battle of La Glorieta Pass*

April 6: *Grant absorbs heavy casualties at Shiloh, Tennessee*

April 25: *Flag Officer David Farragut, USN, captures New Orleans*

May 23–25: *Thomas J. "Stonewall" Jackson bests Union forces in Shenandoah Valley*

June 25–July 1: *The Seven Days battles*

August 29–30: *Jackson and James Longstreet triumph at the Second Battle of Bull Run*

September 5: *Robert E. Lee invades Maryland*

September 17: *The Union gains a narrow victory at Antietam, Maryland*

September 22: *Abraham Lincoln issues the Preliminary Emancipation Proclamation; the Final Emancipation Proclamation is issued on January 1, 1863*

October 8: *The Battle of Perryville ends Confederate invasion of Kentucky*

December 13: *Union general Ambrose Burnside suffers a crushing defeat at Fredericksburg, Virginia*

1863

January 26: *Burnside is replaced as Army of the Potomac commander by "Fighting Joe" Hooker*

May 2: *"Stonewall" Jackson routs Hooker at Chancellorsville, but is mortally wounded by friendly fire*

July 1–3: *Union victory at Gettysburg, Pennsylvania, marks the turning point of the war*

July 4: *Vicksburg, Mississippi, falls to U. S. Grant*

September 19–20: *Federal forces are defeated at Chickamauga, Georgia*

November 24–25: *Major Union victories at the Battles of Chattanooga and Lookout Mountain*

1864

March 12: *U. S. Grant is named general in chief of the Union armies*

May 5: *After taking heavy casualties at the Battle of the Wilderness (Virginia), Grant advances toward Richmond*

May 5: *William T. Sherman commences the Atlanta Campaign*

May 8–19: *Battle of Spotsylvania*

June 3: *Grant suffers heavy casualties at the Battle of Cold Harbor, but continues his advance on Richmond*

June 15: *Grant commences a nine-month siege of Petersburg, Virginia*

Principal Events of the Civil War (continued)

July 11–12: *Confederate Lieutenant General Jubal Early harasses Washington, D.C.*

July 20–August 2: *The Battle of Peachtree Creek opens Sherman's Atlanta Campaign; Sherman occupies Atlanta on September 1*

November 8: *Lincoln is reelected, with Andrew Johnson as vice president*

November 15: *Leaving Atlanta in flames, Sherman begins his destructive March to the Sea*

November 30–December 16: *After the Battles of Franklin and Nashville, Tennessee falls to the Union*

December 21: *Savannah, Georgia, falls to Sherman*

1865

January 31: *Congress sends the Thirteenth Amendment, abolishing slavery, to the states*

February 17: *Sherman takes Columbia, South Carolina*

April 1–2: *Philip Sheridan defeats Confederate Major General George Pickett at Five Forks, Virginia, thereby turning Lee's flank at Petersburg and enabling Grant to break through the Confederate lines after a nine-month siege*

April 2–4: *The Confederate government flees Richmond, and the Union army marches into the city*

April 9: *Lee surrenders the Army of Northern Virginia to Grant at Appomattox Court House, Virginia*

April 14: *John Wilkes Booth shoots President Lincoln, who dies the next morning.*

May 13: *The last skirmish of the war takes place at Palmito Ranch, outside of Brownsville, Texas. It is a Confederate victory.*

May 26: *General Edmund Kirby Smith surrenders Confederate troops west of the Mississippi, thereby ending the war.*

States was obliged to protect the rights of slaveowners. The decision put slavery beyond compromise. The only way to overcome the rights of slaveholders was to abolish slavery, and the only way to abolish slavery was by civil war.

The Dred Scott decision energized abolitionists, including those who were highly militant. In 1857 John Brown, the man who had led the terrible vengeance against the proslave faction in Bleeding Kansas, moved from that state to Boston, a hotbed of abolitionism. There Brown raised cash to finance a raid he was planning on the federal arsenal at Harpers Ferry, Virginia (in present-day West Virginia). He intended to use the guns and ammunition to arm the slaves of the South for a massive rebellion.

Raid on Harpers Ferry

On the night of October 16, 1859, Brown led sixteen white men and five black men to the federal arsenal at Harpers Ferry, at the confluence of the Shenandoah and Potomac Rivers. He and his band quickly took the armory and Hall's Rifle Works nearby, then hunkered down to defend the prize, holding hostage some sixty residents of Harpers Ferry, including the great-grandnephew of George Washington. Brown dispatched two of his black "soldiers" to alert local slaves, confident that they would rise in revolt and join him at Harpers Ferry. Nothing of the kind happened, and the fighting began when citizens of Harpers Ferry surrounded Brown's position, opened fire, and killed two of the abolitionist's sons. Gunfire continued sporadically throughout the morning and afternoon, when Lieutenant Colonel Robert E. Lee, U.S. Army, arrived at the head of a company of marines. On the morning of October 18, Lee sent a demand for Brown's surrender. When Brown refused, Lee ordered the marines to storm Brown's position. The battle lasted three minutes. Brown sustained a saber wound, and all but four of the raiders holed up in the firehouse were killed. Four hostages, including the town's mayor, died, as did one marine. Brown and his surviving followers were tried by the state of Virginia for treason, conspiracy to foment servile insurrection, and murder. Ten days after the raid, all were sentenced to hang. At his execution, on December 2, 1859, Brown spoke forcefully and calmly. The abolitionist cause now had a martyr, and the Harpers Ferry raid drove the North and the South farther apart than they had ever been.

> **IN THEIR OWN**
> *Words*
>
> *I*, John Brown, am now quite certain *that the crimes of this* guilty land *will never be purged* away *but with Blood. I had* as I now think vainly *flattered myself that without* very much *bloodshed, it might be done.*
>
> —JOHN BROWN, NOTE INTENDED TO BE READ AFTER HIS EXECUTION

Election of 1860 and the Final Failure of Peace

In the aftermath of Harpers Ferry, the Republican Party, created in 1854 from a host of small abolitionist parties, nominated Abraham Lincoln of Illinois as its candidate for president. Lincoln was no abolitionist, but he and his party were sufficiently opposed to slavery to provoke radical Democrats in the South to threaten secession. Following Lincoln's election, seven Southern states immediately made good on their threat to secede: South Carolina, Mississippi, Florida, Alabama, Louisiana,

Tennessee, and Texas. Several attempts at reconciliation were made, but all failed. On December 26, 1860, six days after South Carolina seceded, Major Robert Anderson moved his small garrison from the highly vulnerable Fort Moultrie, on Sullivan's Island, South Carolina, to the stronger and more readily defended Fort Sumter. As if it were a sovereign nation, South Carolina protested this action to outgoing president James Buchanan. Instead of surrendering the fort, Buchanan sent supplies and reinforcements to Fort Sumter by way of an unarmed civilian merchant steamer, *Star of the West.* As the vessel passed Charleston, South Carolina volunteers fired warning shots, which turned it back. Fort Sumter would neither be reinforced nor surrendered, and Buchanan put off any further action, leaving matters entirely to the new president.

Fall of Fort Sumter

Little more than a month after Lincoln's inauguration, at 4:30 on the morning of April 12, 1861, Pierre Gustave Toutant Beauregard, formerly of the U.S. Army and now a general in the provisional army of the Confederate States of America, ordered his artillery to open fire on Fort Sumter, in Charleston Harbor. Major Anderson, who had been

Fort Sumter, South Carolina, after it was occupied by the Confederate Army.
Collection: U.S. Army Military History Institute

Beauregard's artillery instructor at West Point, held the fort through Saturday, April 13, then finally surrendered—without having suffered any casualties. The Civil War had begun.

The Anaconda Plan

Appointed to lead the Union Army was the aged and rotund hero of both the *War of 1812, 1812–1814 (see chapter 4)* and the *United States–Mexican War, 1846–1848 (see chapter 6),* Winfield Scott. Scott understood that it would take time to organize an effective army to combat the rebellion and decided to buy that time by means of a two-pronged blockade of the Confederacy. He would cut off southern Atlantic and Gulf ports while simultaneously sending some sixty thousand troops and a flotilla of naval gunboats down the Mississippi to take New Orleans. By these two means, Scott proposed to cut off the South economically—it would be unable to import or export goods—and to cut it in two geographically, East from West. The grandiose blockade was derisively dubbed Scott's Anaconda, but as the Union rushed to construct more ships, it became increasingly effective.

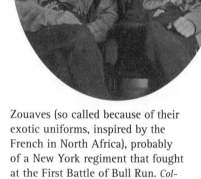

Zouaves (so called because of their exotic uniforms, inspired by the French in North Africa), probably of a New York regiment that fought at the First Battle of Bull Run. *Collection: Library of Congress*

The Border States

The so-called border states—Delaware, Kentucky, Missouri, West Virginia, and Maryland—were slave states, but had not voted to secede. If the Union lost them, the war would likely be lost. Most critical was Missouri. While its legislature favored the Union, its governor was a secessionist. Shortly after the fall of Fort Sumter, he had attempted to seize the federal arsenal at St. Louis. A confrontation between the governor's pro-Confederate militia and a detachment of the Union army on May 10, 1861, sparked an anti-Union riot that resulted in the deaths of twenty civilians.

The state, however, did not secede, but would be the scene of brutal guerrilla warfare throughout the war.

First Battle of Bull Run

After the fall of Fort Sumter, Virginia seceded on April 17, Arkansas on May 6, North Carolina on May 20, and Tennessee (though deeply divided) on June 8.

In July, with an army of some thirty-five thousand men massed in Alexandria, Virginia, General Irvin McDowell was directed to make a major offensive move. His mission was to attack a Confederate force of some twenty thousand men under P. G. T. Beauregard at Manassas Junction, on Bull Run Creek, a position controlling the best route direct to Richmond, which was now the Confederate capital. McDowell's poorly disciplined troops first made contact with the enemy on July 18. The Confederates drove back one Union division, which bought time for reinforcement of the Confederate forces at Bull Run Creek. General Joseph E. Johnston eluded Federal forces in the Shenandoah Valley to bring his ten thousand men to the Manassas battlefield. When the First Battle of Bull Run took place, on July 21, it pitted thirty-five thousand Union troops against almost thirty-thousand Confederates.

At first McDowell's forces succeeded in driving the Confederates from their defensive positions and turned the Confederate left flank. But as Confederate troops broke and ran, Brigadier General Thomas J. Jackson and his Virginians stood their ground and fought back fiercely. General Barnard Bee (who would die in battle the next day) pointed to Jackson and his stalwarts: "There's Jackson standing like a stone wall!" Bee shouted. "Rally behind the Virginians!" (From that day forward, Jackson was known as "Stonewall.") For the rest of that afternoon, the battle seesawed until, late in the day, the Confederates delivered a massive counterthrust, with Stonewall Jackson in the lead. Now it was the Union lines that broke, and panic-stricken soldiers fell back toward Washington. Union losses at the First Battle of Bull Run were 2,896 killed, wounded, or missing. Confederate casualties amounted to 1,982.

The Bull Run battlefield, after the first battle. *Collection: U.S. Army Military History Institute*

McClellan Assumes Command

In the aftermath of Bull Run, President Lincoln replaced McDowell as commander of the Army of the Potomac with George Brinton McClellan. In western Virginia, McClellan had scored two modest victories (Philippi, June 3, and Rich Mountain, July 11), securing for the Union the region that would, in 1863, become West Virginia, a new Union state severed from the Confederate Old Dominion. McClellan quickly proved himself a brilliant administrator who created a viable army out of an undisciplined rabble. His first engagement as commander of the Army of the Potomac, however, resulted in defeat at the Battle of Ball's Bluff (October 21), fought on a steep wooded hill some thirty miles up the Potomac from Washington.

The "Young Napoleon," George B. McClellan, with his wife, Ellen Marcy McClellan.
Collection: National Archives and Records Administration

River War

Appointed to top command, McClellan delayed major action and devoted much time to organizing and training his troops. In the meantime, west of the war's principal coastal theater, Union general John Charles Frémont built a gunboat fleet to operate on the Mississippi, Tennessee, and Cumberland Rivers. He also appointed Brigadier General Ulysses S. Grant to command the key position of Cairo, Illinois, where the Ohio joins the Mississippi River.

In September, Kentucky ended its neutral stance and declared itself for the Union. This prompted Confederate general Leonidas Polk to invade. He took and occupied Columbus, on commanding bluffs above the Mississippi. Grant responded by taking Paducah, which controlled the mouths of the Tennessee and Cumberland Rivers. Confederate general Albert Sidney Johnston (no relation to Joseph E. Johnston, the ranking officer at First Bull Run) now secured the Mississippi by reinforcing Columbus, and he also fortified the Cumberland and Tennessee rivers, arteries by which the North might be invaded. Johnston built Fort Henry on the Tennessee and Fort Donelson on the Cumberland.

In November 1861, the Union's Major General Henry Wager Halleck was given command of the area west of the Cumberland, and Brig. Gen. Don Carlos Buell was given command east of that river. Union general George H. Thomas defeated Confederates at Mill Springs, Kentucky, on January 19, 1862. After this, Halleck dispatched Grant with fifteen thousand men and a squadron of ironclad gunboats under naval flag officer Andrew Foote against Fort Henry on the Tennessee. That bastion fell to Grant and Foote on February 6.

From Fort Henry, Grant turned sharply to the east and marched to the Cumberland for an attack against Fort Donelson, again in concert with Foote's gunboats. Johnston reinforced the Cumberland River position with some fifteen thousand troops pulled out of Bowling Green, Kentucky, and Fort Donelson held out against the Union onslaught for three days before it fell to Grant on February 16, 1862. With the fall of the river forts, Johnston was forced to evacuate Nashville, leaving behind supplies the Confederacy could ill afford to lose, and the strongly fortified and strategically critical position at Columbus also was abandoned.

Battle of Shiloh

The Union forces in the area failed to coordinate sufficiently to attack the Confederates with superior numbers. Confederate generals P. G. T. Beauregard and Albert Sidney Johnston were able to regroup at Corinth, Mississippi. Grant, in the meantime, established his camp with some forty-two thousand men at Pittsburg Landing, Tennessee, on the western bank of the Tennessee River, just northeast of the Confederate position at Corinth. Grant set up his headquarters tent next to a log-built Methodist meetinghouse called Shiloh Chapel. Believing the Confederates would stay in Corinth for the present, Grant failed to defend his camp adequately, and on April 6, Albert Sidney Johnston and P. G. T. Beauregard attacked it. The Battle of Shiloh began with Union panic. For its opening twelve hours, the fighting was one-sided: the Confederates captured Shiloh Chapel and pushed the Union lines almost into the river. Union defeat seemed certain, but one of Grant's subordinate commanders, William Tecumseh Sherman, rallied his troops and thereby averted a rout. Others also fought heroically to save the day for the Union. General Benjamin M. Prentiss made an extraordinary stand on a wooded elevation in the heart of the Union's position. The Confederate attackers called it the Hornets' Nest, because of its stubborn resistance. The stand was made at a terrible cost, but it bought time until the arrival of reinforcements. As the reinforced Union army rallied, Confederate general Albert Sidney Johnston suffered a fatal wound, and the South lost one of its ablest commanders. On Monday, after fighting another ten hours, Confederate general Beauregard withdrew his army to Corinth.

Shiloh began as a Union disaster but ended as a narrow Union victory, which set into motion the defeat of the Confederacy in the war's western theater. The cost was unprecedented: Of 62,682 Union soldiers

IN THEIR OWN

Words

Later famed as the journalist and explorer who found the long-lost African missionary, physician and explorer Dr. David Livingstone, Henry Morton Stanley, as a youth, fought with the Dixie Grays at Shiloh:

[I saw] a young Lieutenant, who, judging by the new gloss on his uniform, must have been some father's darling. A clean bullet-hole through the centre of his forehead had instantly ended his career. A little further were some twenty bodies, lying in various postures, each by its own pool of viscous blood, which emitted a peculiar scent, which was new to me, but which I have since learned is inseparable from a battlefield. Beyond these, a still larger group lay, body overlying body, knees crooked, arms erect, or wide-stretched and rigid according as the last spasm overtook them. The company opposed to them must have shot straight.

It was the first Field of Glory I had seen in my May of life, and the first time that Glory sickened me with its repulsive aspect, and made me suspect it was all a glittering lie. . . .

engaged at Shiloh, 1,754 were killed, 8,408 wounded, and 2,885 missing. Confederate losses were 1,723 killed, 8,012 wounded, and 959 missing out of 40,335 men engaged.

Action in Missouri

As already mentioned, Missouri was torn between its pro-Confederate governor and its mostly pro-Union legislature, and Union forces were defeated at the Battle of Wilson's Creek on August 10, 1861. The inept but well-meaning John Charles Frémont, given command of a newly created Western Department, ignored this defeat and, on August 30, not only declared martial law in Missouri but also, without Lincoln's authorization, proclaimed the emancipation of Missouri's slaves. Frémont also began confiscating property of known Confederate sympathizers. Frémont's impetuous actions served only to further enrage Missouri secessionists and, worse, drove many undecided Missourians into the Confederate camp. Guerrilla warfare, general throughout Missouri, now intensified. Confederate general Sterling Price won another victory at Lexington,

Missouri, on September 13, 1861, and Frémont, relieved of command, was transferred to West Virginia.

Inspired by the Confederate victories at Wilson's Creek and Lexington, and fired up by Frémont's emancipations and confiscations, a pro-South rump minority of the Missouri legislature convened in October 1861 at Neosho and voted to secede. Although the Neosho group was not the legally constituted legislature, Confederate president Jefferson Davis quickly welcomed the state into the Confederacy.

Battle of Pea Ridge

Faced with reinforced Union troops under Brigadier General Samuel R. Curtis, Confederate general Sterling Price, lacking support, withdrew into Arkansas with the intention of joining forces there with a unit under General Ben McCulloch. Unexpectedly, General Earl Van Dorn intercepted both Price and McCulloch and reinforced the units of both commanders. These reinforcements included several thousand Indians led by Cherokee general Stand Watie. In Arkansas the Confederates now had an army of about 14,000 men to oppose the 11,250 troops under General Curtis.

Curtis decided to take up a strong defensive position at Pea

> **IN THEIR OWN Words**
>
> *Our Presidents, Governors, Generals and Secretaries are calling, with almost frantic vehemence, for men.—"Men! men! send us men!" they scream, or the cause of the Union is gone; and yet these very officers, representing the people and Government, steadily and persistently refuse to receive the very class of men which have a deeper interest in the defeat and humiliation of the rebels, than all others. . . . What a spectacle of blind, unreasoning prejudice and pusillanimity is this! The national edifice is on fire. Every man who can carry a bucket of water, or remove a brick, is wanted; but those who have the care of the building, having a profound respect for the feeling of the national burglars who set the building on fire, are determined that the flames shall only be extinguished by Indo-Caucasian hands. . . .*
>
> —FREDERICK DOUGLASS MAKES THE CASE FOR UNION ARMY ENLISTMENT OF AFRICAN AMERICAN TROOPS, AUGUST 1861

Ridge, on high ground overlooking Little Sugar Creek. He formed his line of battle by March 6, and at dawn on March 7, skirmishing began near Elkhorn Tavern. Before long, a pitched battle developed. The Federal troops held their ground against Van Dorn throughout the first day of battle, but on March 8, the Confederate attack was renewed and redoubled. Curtis seized the initiative and drove Van Dorn's forces from the field. Ordered now by higher command to assist in the defense of the Mississippi River forts, under attack by Grant, Van Dorn left Arkansas.

Inasmuch as the Confederates left the field, Pea Ridge must be accounted a Union victory. Yet Curtis had incurred more casualties than Van Dorn. Of the 11,250 Federal troops engaged at Pea Ridge, 1,384 were killed, wounded, or missing. Of some 14,000 Confederates, 800 became casualties.

Jayhawkers vs. Bushwhackers

The Union's costly victory at Pea Ridge drove the Neosho legislature out of the state, but it also created a chaotic climate of bitter guerrilla warfare between pro-Union raiders called Jayhawkers and pro-Confederate irregulars called Bushwhackers. Most notorious among the Bushwhackers was William Clarke Quantrill (1837–1865), who held a captain's commission in the Confederate army. With William C. "Bloody Bill" Anderson, Quantrill wreaked havoc on Kansas border patrols and Missouri's Union militia. Counting all of the guerrilla actions and skirmishes, 1,162 engagements took place in Missouri during the course of the Civil War— 11 percent of all the engagements in this conflict.

Arizona Proclaimed a Confederate Territory

The section *Apache and Navajo War, 1860–1868 (see chapter 7)* touches on Confederate lieutenant colonel John Robert Baylor's sweep through the southern New Mexico Territory, all the way from the Rio Grande to California. After the capture of several installations, Baylor proclaimed the Confederate Territory of Arizona, which encompassed all of present-day Arizona and New Mexico south of the thirty-fourth parallel. He also named himself territorial governor. Baylor's almost unopposed advance was followed during the winter of 1861–1862 by a larger Confederate invasion led by General Henry Hopkins Sibley. Sibley's mission was to take the rest of New Mexico and to seize the silver mines of Colorado, which would greatly enrich the Southern war chest.

Sibley advanced up the Rio Grande with the objective of capturing Fort Union, headquarters of Union commander E. R. S. Canby, and occupying a critical position on the Santa Fe Trail. As discussed in chapter 7, Sibley engaged Canby at Valverde, New Mexico, on February 21, 1862, emerged victorious, and went on to take Santa Fe. From there, he advanced to capture Fort Union.

Battle of La Glorietta Pass

To reach Fort Union, Sibley had to traverse La Glorieta Pass through the Sangre de Cristo Mountains. There, on March 26, 1862, Union troops under Colonel John Slough, reinforced by Colorado volunteers commanded by Major John M. Chivington, met Sibley's Texans in a two-day battle. On March 28 both sides, exhausted, declared victory. However, the North had clearly won the day. The Confederates lost 121 men killed to the Union's 31, and Sibley was forced to retreat to Texas. Some historians have called this battle the "Gettysburg of the West," because it turned the tide against the Confederates in the Southwest.

During the action at La Glorietta, Colonel James H. Carleton led the First California Regiment of Infantry into New Mexico Territory and set about evicting the Confederates from the present-day state of Arizona. The culminating battle of Carleton's sweep was fought on April 15, 1862, at Picacho Peak, New Mexico. The westernmost action of the Civil War, it all but ended the brief existence of the Confederate Territory of Arizona.

War in Texas

At the outbreak of the Civil War, Governor Sam Houston, hero of Texas independence, defied his fellow Texans by supporting the Union and resisting secession. In February 1861, however, his state seceded, and Houston had no choice but to resign his office.

In October 1862, a U.S. naval assault captured the port city of Galveston, which was occupied by Union troops in December. The Confederates retook Galveston on January 1, 1863. The Union maintained a naval blockade of the port. By late 1863, with the Mississippi River firmly in Union hands, Texas was cut off from the rest of the South.

McClellan's Inaction

Compared to the early battles in the East and along the Mississippi, the action in the farther West was fought on a small scale. But at least it *was* action. To the consternation of President Lincoln and the Northern public, George B. McClellan declined to make aggressive use of his army. Lincoln issued an imperative order to him on March 8, 1862. A few days later, on March 11, 1862, Lincoln formally relieved McClellan as general in chief of the armies, returning him to command of the Army of the Potomac only and then urging him to lead that army from Washington to Richmond. McClellan responded with a much more roundabout plan: to transport his army in ships to a position below General Joseph E. Johnston's lines, outflanking him, as it were, by sea—and thereby avoiding a major battle in the process. When it became apparent that during the long interval of McClellan's inaction, Johnston had left his position at Manassas (site of the First Bull Run battle) and moved south to the Rappahannock River, closer to Richmond, McClellan decided to ferry his troops down to Fort Monroe, near Newport News and Hampton Roads, in the southeastern corner of Virginia, well below the rebel capital. His plan was to land, then proceed north toward Richmond via the peninsula separating the York and the James Rivers. That geographical feature gave the operation its name: the Peninsula (or Peninsular) Campaign.

Operations on the North Carolina Coast

While the main body of the Union army idled, other troops under Ambrose E. Burnside, landed at Roanoke Island, North Carolina, on February 7. In a small-scale engagement, Burnside defeated the Confederate garrison there (February 8), then led his forces onto the mainland, where he took New Bern on March 14 and Beaufort on April 26.

Battle of Hampton Roads:
Monitor *vs.* Virginia (Merrimack)

McClellan, about to commence his Peninsula Campaign, worried that the Confederate ironclad *Virginia* (modified from the captured U.S.

The deck of USS *Monitor*. The innovative revolving turret is clearly visible behind the men. Note the African American deckhand in the front and to the right. The U.S. Navy was partially integrated during the Civil War.
Collection: Library of Congress

steamship *Merrimack*) posed a threat to his water route. To oppose *Virginia*, the Union navy had built the *Monitor*, a low-profile, raftlike vessel equipped with a unique revolving turret mounting two eleven-inch guns. Monitor was launched on March 6, 1862, and set out for Hampton Roads two days later. On that day, March 8, conventional wooden-hulled Union vessels blockading the harbor, in concert with Union shore batteries, opened fire on *Virginia*, but the cannonballs bounced off her sides. *Virginia* sank USS *Cumberland* and severely damaged four other Union vessels.

The next day, March 9, USS *Monitor* arrived at Hampton Roads and took up a position athwart one of the disabled ships, USS *Minnesota*. *Virginia* opened fire on *Monitor*, and the two vessels pounded one another for the next three hours. Unwieldy though it was, *Monitor* readily outmaneuvered the slower and even clumsier *Virginia*. The Battle of Hampton Roads was a draw—though *Monitor* had saved *Minnesota*, had prevented the Confederates from breaking the blockade of Richmond, and had averted yet another Union military disaster.

Peninsula Campaign Begins

Ninety thousand men of the Army of the Potomac landed in Virginia on April 4 and advanced on Yorktown the next day. Instead of attacking the town, they settled in for a siege, which provoked another angry directive from Lincoln. McClellan based his caution on erroneous estimates of enemy numbers calculated by his spymaster, private investigator Allan J. Pinkerton. In fact, Confederate general Joseph E. Johnston had only fifteen thousand men at Yorktown, about a sixth of McClellan's force. By delaying, McClellan gave Johnston ample time to reinforce and to construct stout defensive works around Richmond.

Jackson's Shenandoah Campaign: Battle of Kernstown

Robert E. Lee and the other principal Confederate military commanders counted on Lincoln's anxiety to defend Washington at all costs. This vulnerability, they believed, gave them an opportunity to leverage their inferior numbers against the superior Union forces. Thomas J. "Stonewall" Jackson was ordered to sweep through Virginia's Shenandoah Valley to persuade the North that an invasion of the capital, from the west, was imminent. Jackson's Shenandoah Valley campaign was intended to compel the Union to divide its comparatively numerous forces, which could then be attacked and defeated in detail.

Union private George A. Stryker, a New York volunteer. *Collection: Library of Congress*

The first battle of the campaign was fought on March 23, 1862, at Kernstown, near Winchester, Virginia. Jackson believed he was attacking the four-regiment rear guard of Union general Nathaniel Banks's army, but found himself up against an entire 9,000-man division. After suffering a sharp defeat, Jackson retreated. But this tactical defeat was also a strategic triumph, for the Battle of Kernstown persuaded Northern leaders that an invasion of Washington was indeed in the works, and 35,000 men, under General Irvin McDowell, were detached from McClellan's peninsular command and dispatched to reinforce the defense of Washington. For that reason, McClellan had "only" 90,000 men at Yorktown. On May 8, Jackson repulsed Federal forces at McDowell, Virginia, but suffered almost twice the casualties—498 vs. 256—of his attackers.

Jackson's Shenandoah Valley campaign was perhaps the most spectacular and brilliant military maneuvering of the entire war. The Confederate commander used about 17,000 men to tie down more than 50,000 Union soldiers, which denied McClellan the overwhelming numbers he felt necessary to attack Richmond. The Shenandoah Campaign saved the Confederate capital.

Battle of New Orleans

David Farragut, commander of the Union fleet that took New Orleans. *From Harper's Pictorial History of the Civil War, 1866*

In mid-April 1862, at the direction of David Dixon Porter, one of the Union navy's senior commanders, David Glasgow Farragut sailed a Mississippi River fleet in an assault on New Orleans. By April 24 Farragut had reduced the defensive forts, and General Ben Butler advanced to take possession of the fallen forts as well as the now undefended city of New Orleans. With its capture, the gulf port was in Union hands again, and a crucial lifeline was denied to the Confederates.

Yorktown and Williamsburg

In May, McClellan finally attacked Yorktown, only to discover that Confederate forces had withdrawn from that town to move closer to Richmond. Cavalry under General James Ewell Brown ("Jeb") Stuart covered their withdrawal, and on May 4–5, Union generals George Stoneman and Joseph Hooker engaged the rear guard inconclusively at Williamsburg. McClellan claimed victory at both Yorktown and Williamsburg, which were, in fact, inconsequential battles.

Battle of Fair Oaks and Seven Pines

At the end of May 1862, most of McClellan's army was north of the Chickahominy, except for a corps commanded by General Erasmus Darwin Keyes. Perceiving the vulnerability of Keyes's isolated position, Confederate general Joseph E. Johnston attacked him at Fair Oaks and Seven Pines on May 31, 1862. The result was an inconclusive and bloody battle between almost equally matched forces: Of 41,797 Union troops engaged, 5,031 were casualties; of 41,816 Confederates, 6,134 became casualties. Johnston was so severely wounded that he withdrew from action for a time and was replaced by Robert E. Lee, hitherto a fairly undistinguished commander. Lee would emerge as the Confederates' de facto general in chief and one of the great commanders in all military history.

Stuart's Ride

On June 12–15, 1862, Jeb Stuart led twelve hundred Confederate cavalrymen in a spectacular reconnaissance that completely circled the Union positions in Virginia. "Stuart's Ride" made the young brigadier a legend, even as it humiliated McClellan. Realizing that he had put his army in a vulnerable position, McClellan began to move it—except for a single corps—south of the Chickahominy. From there he decided to begin his drive to Richmond in earnest. McClellan ran into stout resistance on June 25, at Oak Grove, near Mechanicsville, along the Chickahominy River. His forces fell back, but timely reinforcement drove back the Confederate pickets. The Union forces then moved up to occupy positions around Oak Grove.

The Seven Days

Lee's plan was to bring the bulk of his army—sixty-five thousand troops—to the northern bank of the Chickahominy to overwhelm the twenty-five thousand Union troops under General Fitz-John Porter, isolated on that side of the river. It was a high-risk strategy, since it would leave only the thinnest of lines to defend Richmond, south of the river. The payoff, however, would be the destruction of Porter's corps. Unfortunately for Lee, Stonewall Jackson, whose performance had been superb in the Shenandoah Valley, bivouacked on June 26 instead of joining the attack against Porter. Impatient and impetuous, General A. P. Hill attacked on his own initiative, without Jackson and without Lee's orders. The Battle of Mechanicsville was not, therefore, the decisive Confederate victory it might have been, but, instead, was as bloody as it was indecisive. As usual, McClellan fell prey to inflated estimates of the size of the Confederate army. Over the protests of subordinates, he ordered the withdrawal of his entire army to the James River, below and *away from* Richmond.

Lee was not about to let McClellan withdraw unscathed. Over the next week, Lee seized the initiative and used every opportunity that presented itself to attack the Army of the Potomac. McClellan's corps commanders conducted highly effective rearguard actions punctuated by counterjabs that made McClellan's strategic blunder costly for Lee as well. At Gaines's Mill, 34,214 Union troops were engaged, of whom 893 died, 3,107 were wounded, and 2,836 were reported missing. While the

Confederates forced a Union retreat, their casualties were even heavier, numbering 8,751 killed or wounded.

After his retreat from Gaines's Mill, McClellan ordered a withdrawal to the James River. Lee restrained himself until he was certain of McClellan's direction. Then Lee laid out a highly complex plan of attack. Its complexity ensured its failure. Although the Battle of Savage's Station began with a vigorous Confederate assault on June 29, it lacked coordination. As in earlier encounters, the Federal rear guard was punishing to Lee, and the day was saved for the Union by severe thunderstorms, which forced an end to battle. Losses in the engagement at Savage's Station were 1,590 killed or wounded on the Union side, and 626 on the Confederate side.

After his withdrawal from Savage's Station, McClellan concentrated his forces at Frayser's Farm, behind White Oak Swamp. He was deployed also in a line to Malvern Hill to protect the Union supply trains on their way to Harrison's Landing on the James River. In response, Lee again made a plan for a coordinated attack, but once again, the necessary coordination failed. Still, Lee pushed McClellan back, though at heavy cost. Whereas Union casualties at Frayser's Farm were 2,853 killed or wounded, Confederate losses totaled 3,615 killed and wounded.

After Frayser's Farm, McClellan withdrew to Malvern Hill, a low, two-mile-wide rise alongside the James River. This withdrawal incontrovertibly signaled the failure of the Peninsula Campaign, which also meant failure to take Richmond. Malvern Hill was farther from the Confederate capital than McClellan had been at the start of the Seven Days. Nevertheless, at Malvern Hill McClellan had found high ground, which could not be flanked and which put Lee at a great disadvantage. Recognizing nevertheless that this was his last opportunity to destroy the Army of the Potomac, Lee attacked Malvern Hill on July 1. As before, Lee's subordinate commanders failed to coordinate with one another. This, combined with the difficult terrain, made it impossible to do anything other than attack piecemeal. Lee was repulsed. At this, two of McClellan's field officers, Porter and Colonel Henry J. Hunt, urged a Union counterattack, but McClellan, whose fear of Robert E. Lee was great, ordered withdrawal to Harrison's Landing. McClellan would remain there until mid-August.

Seven Days Assessment

Without doubt, the Seven Days battles were a costly strategic failure for the Union army. From a tactical point of view, however, they might be seen as a Union victory, though hardly a glorious one. Commanding the larger army, McClellan had sustained about sixteen thousand casualties, killed or wounded, whereas Lee's smaller force suffered nearly twenty thousand casualties, but had saved Richmond. Among the Union casualties of the Seven Days was George Brinton McClellan. He had not been wounded, but he had been discredited, and Lincoln removed him from command of the Army of the Potomac, replacing him with the unpopular and irascible John Pope.

Battle of Cedar Mountain

Jackson attacked part of Pope's army at Cedar Mountain, near Culpepper, Virginia, on August 9. The battle forced Pope into retreat north of the Rappahannock River. Now Lee executed another high-stakes gamble by violating one of the unbreakable roles of military tactics: He divided his army in the presence of the enemy. Separated from Pope by only the shallow Rappahannock, Lee put half his forces under the command of Major General James Longstreet, to occupy Pope's front, while he sent the other half under Stonewall Jackson on a roundabout march to the northwest— to make a surprise attack on the rear of Pope's army.

Raid on Catlett's Station

While this maneuvering was under way, a detachment of Pope's troops made a lightning raid in which they captured not only Jeb Stuart's adjutant but also snatched Stuart's ornate plumed hat and scarlet-lined cloak. Eager to redress these outrages, Stuart raided the railroad behind Pope's lines. On August 22 he overran Pope's headquarters camp at Catlett's Station and made off with $35,000 in payroll greenbacks, Pope's personal baggage (including his dress uniform coat), three hundred prisoners, and papers that gave Lee critical information about Pope's battle plans. On August 26 Jackson also hit Pope, destroying his supply depot at Manassas Junction, Virginia—site of the first Bull Run battle—cutting off Pope's rail and telegraph communications.

Pope turned to pursue Jackson, but was unable to find him until Jackson engaged Brigadier General Rufus King at Groveton on August 28. In this fierce skirmish, both Confederate division commanders were wounded, and the Union's "Black Hat Brigade" (or "Iron Brigade," as it was later called) demonstrated great heroism, incurring a terrible 33 percent casualty rate. Alerted now to Jackson's position, Pope ordered his forces to form up near Groveton.

Second Battle of Bull Run

Positioned near the site of the first Battle of Bull Run, Pope confidently launched an attack on August 29, 1862, badly battering Jackson's Confederates, who withdrew only after repulsing a number of Union advances. Pope prematurely declared victory and resolved to pursue Jackson on the next day. Pope was unaware that the second half of Lee's divided army, under General Longstreet, had yet to join the battle. On August 30, five divisions under Longstreet rushed the Union flank along a two-mile front, inflicting a costly tactical defeat on Pope. However, Longstreet's failure to attack on the first day of battle cost Lee what should have been a decisive strategic victory. Although defeated, Pope's army was at least able to retreat intact. At the Second Battle of Bull Run, Pope commanded 75,696 Union troops against the Confederates' 48,527. He lost 1,724 killed, 8,372 wounded, and 5,958 missing. Confederate losses numbered 1,481 killed, 7,627 wounded, and 89 missing. The defeat at Second Bull Run earned Pope dismissal as commander of the Army of the Potomac. McClellan, who had never been officially relieved of command of the Army of the Potomac, was once again put in charge of it.

Lee Invades the North

Pope's defeat at the Second Battle of Bull Run was a hard blow to the Union. Lee decided to exploit what he judged the low ebb of the North's fortunes by invading. On September 5, 1862, Lee led his 55,000-man Army of Northern Virginia across the Potomac into Maryland. Lee drew up Special Order No. 191, which detailed his plan for opening the invasion of the North. The general distributed copies of the order to his chief subordinates. One of these copies was carelessly discarded and fell into McClellan's hands. The order revealed Lee's plan to divide his forces: Jackson would lead men toward Harpers Ferry, and Longstreet would head up a column toward Hagerstown, Maryland. Even armed with this information, McClellan grossly overestimated the size of Lee's army and declined to take decisive action.

Battle of Antietam

Instead of moving decisively, McClellan temporized by sending General Alfred Pleasanton to engage Hill at South Mountain on September 14. The battle went well but cost the Union more precious time—time Lee used to set up a defensive line at the western Maryland town of Sharpsburg, behind Antietam Creek.

McClellan's plan was to strike at both of Lee's flanks, then attack the center with his reserves. But, like Lee at the Seven Days, McClellan was

unable to achieve the proper level of coordination to execute his plan effectively. The initial assault on April 17 was uncoordinated and piecemeal. Union general Joseph "Fighting Joe" Hooker drove back Stonewall Jackson's brigade so far and so quickly that Lee was forced to order up reserves. By midday the fighting focused on a sunken farm road soon to be christened "Bloody Lane," after the five hours of slaughter that took place here. By midafternoon a Yankee division under Gen. Ambrose Burnside forced a crossing of the stone bridge that still bears the Burnside name. The division broke through the Confederate line, only to be crushed by a surprise counterattack from A. P. Hill, whose troops had just arrived from Harpers Ferry. Although Lee's left absorbed a violent blow, the Confederate general's personal leadership was sufficient to rally a countercharge that drove back the Federals in confusion.

Ambrose Burnside (seated in front of the tree), popular, earnest, and tragically unsuited to high command.
Collection: Library of Congress

The dead in "Bloody Lane" on the Antietam battlefield.
Collection: Library of Congress

Despite poor execution, McClellan did substantially outnumber the Confederates. By dint of superior numbers, the Union troops drove Lee's forces back to the outskirts of Sharpsburg. Nevertheless, McClellan persisted in his belief that he did not enjoy an advantage, and he therefore declined to pursue the withdrawing Confederates, allowing them to escape back across the Potomac and into Virginia. Antietam may be counted a Union victory, inasmuch as it ended the first Confederate invasion of the North; yet, by letting Lee slip through his fingers, McClellan ensured the survival of the Army of Northern Virginia. The cost of what historians call the "single bloodiest day of the war" was

2,108 Union troops killed, 9,549 wounded, and 753 missing out of 75,316 engaged. The Confederates fielded 51,844 men and lost some 2,700 killed, 9,024 wounded, and approximately 2,000 missing.

Preliminary Emancipation Proclamation

President Lincoln focused on what McClellan had achieved rather than on what he had failed to accomplish, and he deemed Antietam a sufficient victory to warrant his issuing the Preliminary Emancipation Proclamation on September 22, 1862. The "final" Emancipation Proclamation, which liberated slaves in the parts of the Confederacy that were not under the control of the Union army, was published on January 1, 1863. It gave the war a new moral force as a campaign to free the slaves.

Chambersburg Raid and the End of McClellan

Following Antietam, McClellan did nothing. Lee, in the meantime, sent Stuart on a daring raid into Pennsylvania—no slaveholding border state, like Maryland, but a free Union state. During October 9–12, on his way to raid the town of Chambersburg, Jeb Stuart rode around McClellan for the second time. Although the raid was of little military significance, it shocked, outraged, and humiliated Northern military and political leaders alike. Nevertheless, it was October 26 before McClellan finally began to march, getting under way so slowly that Lee was able to interpose his army between the Federal forces and Richmond. On November 7, 1862, McClellan was officially relieved of command of the Army of the Potomac. He was replaced by the modest, affable, and marginally competent Ambrose Burnside.

IN THEIR OWN Words

In March 1862, journalist George H. Boker published satirical verses about George B. McClellan, which became a popular song, "Tardy George".

What are you waiting for, George, I pray?—
To scour your cross-belts with fresh pipe-clay?
To burnish your buttons, to brighten your guns;
Or wait you for May-day and warm spring suns?
Are you blowing your fingers because they are cold,
Or catching your breath ere you take a hold?
Is the mud knee-deep in valley and gorge?
What are you waiting for, tardy George?

. . . .

Are you waiting for your hair to turn,
Your heart to soften, your bowels to yearn
A little more towards "our Southern friends,"
As at home and abroad they work their ends?

. . . .

Battle of Fredericksburg

Burnside deployed his forces north of the Rappahannock River at Warrenton, Virginia, thirty miles from Lee's army, which consisted of only two corps, commanded by Stonewall Jackson and James Longstreet. Burnside's best chance would have been to attack between the separated wings of Lee's army, defeating each wing in detail. He chose instead to continue to advance on Richmond and attack south of Warrenton, at Fredericksburg.

General Sumner's division arrived at a position across the Rappahannock from Fredericksburg on November 17. Confederate general Longstreet would not reach the town until the next day. Here was another opportunity: Burnside should have ordered Sumner to cross the river immediately. He did no such thing, but instead waited for the arrival of five pontoon bridges and ordered Sumner's troops to make camp on the river's northern bank. Longstreet had ample time to entrench defensively in the hills south of Fredericksburg, especially as Burnside's delay stretched into days. By December 11 a total of 78,000 Confederates were securely dug in on the southern bank of the Rappahannock. On this same day Burnside's bridges were in place, and the Union crossing began.

Burnside ordered an artillery barrage before he commenced the crossing. Perhaps the barrage was intended to wipe out Confederate snipers, who were taking a toll of Union troops. All the barrage succeeded in doing, however, was level the town. This served not only to enrage the Confederates but also provided open fields of fire for the Confederates entrenched in the hills around the town.

The Battle of Fredericksburg commenced in earnest on December 13, 1862, when Burnside made a series of hopeless assaults on the Confederates' impregnable hilltop positions. Even as the Federal dead piled up before a stone wall in front of a sunken road below the Confederates' chief position at Marye's Heights, Burnside continued to order one assault after another—fourteen charges in all, each of them a suicide mission—before withdrawing back across the Rappahannock. The Battle of Fredericksburg still stands

Confederate major identified as John Roberts. His unit and fate are unknown. *Collection: Library of Congress*

as the worst defeat in the history of the U.S. Army. Of the 106,000 Union soldiers engaged, 12,700 were killed or wounded. Confederate losses were 5,300 killed or wounded out of some 72,500 engaged.

Burnside's Mud March

After the disaster of Fredericksburg, Burnside was determined to attempt a second crossing of the Rappahannock. Lincoln personally vetoed this movement, and the Army of the Potomac settled into winter quarters until January 20, 1863, when Burnside embarked on a plan to envelop Lee's army via a river crossing called Banks's Ford. A two-day torrent of icy rain transformed the scarred landscape into a quagmire, and the attempt to cross Banks's Ford was dubbed the "Mud March." The spectacle of an entire defeated and demoralized army bogged down in mud prompted Abraham Lincoln to replace Burnside on January 26, 1863. The new commander of the Army of the Potomac would be Joseph "Fighting Joe" Hooker.

Battle of Chancellorsville

Hooker's Army of the Potomac had been reinforced to a strength of 130,000 men—versus the 60,000 men of Lee's Army of Northern Virginia. Hooker's plan was to deploy about one-third of his forces under General John Sedgwick in a diversionary attack across the Rappahannock above Lee's Fredericksburg entrenchments. Simultaneously, Hooker himself would lead another third of the army in a long swing up the Rappahannock to come around to attack Lee on his vulnerable left flank and rear. Except for about 10,000 cavalry troopers, who would be used to disrupt Lee's lines of communication to Richmond, the remainder of the Army of the Potomac would be held in reserve at Chancellorsville, ready to reinforce either Sedgwick's or Hooker's wings, as needed. The first part of Hooker's plan unfolded flawlessly. By April 30, 1863, Hooker had estab-

Company E, Fourth U.S. Colored Troops, musters in Baltimore in the summer of 1863.
Collection: U.S. Army Military History Institute

lished about 70,000 men in Chancellorsville and had set up headquarters in Chancellor House, a plantation home outside of the town. Hooker then dispatched his cavalry to cut the Richmond, Fredericksburg, and Potomac Railroad.

As good as Hooker's plan was, Lee grasped it immediately and sent his own cavalry, under Jeb Stuart, to control the roads into and out of Chancellorsville. Unable to send patrols out, Hooker was effectively blinded. Suddenly confused, he deployed his men defensively in hastily erected breastworks close to Chancellorsville instead of advancing on to his chosen battlefield, about twelve miles east of town. In the meantime, having concluded from Stuart's reconnaissance that Hooker intended to attack him from the flank and rear through a thicket known as "the Wilderness," Lee sent ten thousand men under Jubal Early to divert the Union troops at Fredericksburg, while he led the remainder of his army against Hooker at Chancellorsville. Then General Lee devised an even more daring plan. As he had done against Pope at the Second Battle of Bull Run, Lee divided his army in the presence of the enemy. On the night of May 1, he found a scout who could lead Stonewall Jackson's corps through the confusion of "the Wilderness" and put him in a position to strike at Hooker's exposed flank. Lee proposed to divide his army yet again, giving twenty-six thousand men to Jackson for the surprise attack against Hooker's flank, while he retained seventeen thousand to hold attacks against Hooker's front. Early's men would continue to hold the Union troops at Fredericksburg. In broad daylight, Lee had to move his twenty-six thousand men across the Federal front. Union troops under Gen. O. O. Howard saw Jackson's movement, but were unable to persuade either Howard or Hooker that this movement represented any danger.

Two hours before dusk on May 2, Jackson attacked Howard, in command of Hooker's right flank. The results were devastating. One entire Federal corps panicked and was routed; then Hooker's entire army was knocked out of its prepared positions. This raised the curtain on a battle that would continue through May 4 and that would send Hooker out of Chancellorsville in full retreat, until he had withdrawn north of the Rappahannock. The cost to Hooker was staggering. Facing at Chancellorsville an army less than half the size of his, he lost seventeen thousand casualties—about 17 percent of the numbers directly engaged. Lee's thirteen thousand casualties accounted for an even greater percentage of his much smaller force: about 25 percent. Perhaps the greatest loss of all to Lee was the death of Thomas "Stonewall" Jackson, a victim of friendly fire.

IN THEIR OWN *Words*

Stonewall Jackson's physician, Dr. Hunter McGuire, recalled the general's death:

His mind . . . began to . . . wander, and he frequently talked as if in command upon the field. . . .

About half-past one he was told that he had but two hours to live, and he answered . . . feebly but firmly, "Very good; it is all right."

A few moments before he died he cried out in his delirium, "Order A. P. Hill to prepare for action! Pass the infantry to the front rapidly. Tell Major Hawks—" then stopped, leaving the sentence unfinished.

Presently a smile . . . spread itself over his pale face, and he said quietly, and with an expression as if of relief, "Let us cross over the river and rest under the shade of the trees."

Invasion of Pennsylvania

For the South, Chancellorsville was a Pyrrhic victory, involving large losses and the paramount loss of Jackson. Lee resolved to carry out a swift, massive, and punishing raid into Northern territory in the hope that it would demolish the Union's will to continue the fight and thereby force a favorably negotiated peace. The price of failure of the invasion was high: possibly the destruction of an army.

Beginning on June 3, 1863, Lee moved north, dividing his army into three corps. Leading the movement was a corps commanded by James Longstreet. He paused at Culpepper Court House, Virginia, while another corps, under Richard S. Ewell, advanced against fragmentary Union detachments still in the lower Shenandoah Valley. The third corps, commanded by A. P. Hill, remained at Fredericksburg, confronting the Yankees there. Hooker's plan for responding to these movements was simply this: Ignore them and advance against Richmond. Lincoln would not accept what he deemed a dangerous strategy and ordered Hooker to pursue a defensive course only and follow Lee.

Battle of Brandy Station

Hooker followed Lee doggedly. After a skirmish at Franklin's Crossing, Virginia, Hooker ordered a full-scale cavalry reconnaissance under Alfred Pleasanton to ascertain the extent and significance of Lee's movements. The result of this, on June 9, was the Battle of Brandy Station. It was the first real cavalry engagement of the Civil War and the largest cavalry engagement ever fought in North America. In all, some 20,000 horsemen were engaged at Brandy Station, charging and countercharging for a full twelve hours of battle. Union casualties numbered 936 killed, wounded, or captured; Confederate casualties were 523. Confederate general Jeb Stuart remained in possession of the field, so Brandy Station must be counted a Union defeat, yet for the first time in the war, the Federal cavalry had held its own against the legendary Jeb Stuart and had performed valuable reconnaissance. Hooker now knew Lee was leaving Fredericksburg and was heading north.

Battle of Winchester

The Battle of Brandy Station also yielded information for Lee, who now was aware that Hooker knew of his movements. Outguessing his opponent, Lee concluded that Hooker might now turn to advance on Richmond—the very plan Hooker had, in fact, proposed, but that had been overruled. On June 10 Lee dispatched Ewell to attack the remaining Union garrisons in the Shenandoah Valley, which would (Lee hoped) force Washington to recall the Army of the Potomac for its own defense.

Ewell clashed with Union troops at Berryville (June 13) and Martinsburg (June 14). The Federals evaded capture in these two engagements, but Ewell's attack on Winchester, Virginia (June 13–15) was a Union disaster. The Confederates bottled up the Union garrison in the forts just west of the town. A total of 4,443 Yankees became casualties, of whom 3,538 were taken prisoner. Ewell's losses were a mere 269.

Stuart's Raid

The first units of the Army of Northern Virginia crossed the Potomac into Maryland on June 15. Stuart skillfully used his cavalry to create a counterreconnaissance screen to prevent Pleasanton's Union cavalry from discovering Lee's objective: Washington or Pennsylvania? This action produced cavalry duels at Aldie, Virginia (June 17), Middleburg, Virginia (June 19), and Upperville, Virginia (June 21). Following these engagements, Stuart wheeled toward the east, riding around Hooker's rear and flank. Stuart's "Gettysburg Raid" disrupted Hooker's supply lines and captured 125 U.S. Army wagons at Rockville, Maryland, as well as took some 400 prisoners in skirmishes at Fairfax Court House, Virginia (June 27), Westminster, Maryland (June 29), Hanover, Pennsylvania (June 30), and Carlisle, Pennsylvania (July 1). But the Union forces proved to be much more spread out and active than Stuart had expected, so that the great ride around the army took much longer than he had anticipated. For ten days Stuart was out of touch with Lee, who, therefore, was rendered blind even as he advanced into Pennsylvania. Lee could only assume that Hooker had not yet followed him across the Potomac, so he deployed his forces in a long line, with their rear at Chambersburg, Pennsylvania, and their front at York, about 50 miles to the east. Unknown to Lee, Hooker *had* crossed the Potomac (during June 25–26), and it was not until June 28 that Lee learned the entire Army of the Potomac was concentrated around Frederick, Maryland, directly south of the fifty-mile-long and highly vulnerable flank of the Army of Northern Virginia. Lee also learned that Joseph Hooker had been replaced as commander of the Army of the Potomac by Major General George Gordon Meade. The armies of Meade and Lee were about to meet at a Pennsylvania village called Gettysburg.

Battle of Munfordville

During the period in which McClellan was entrenching on Virginia's James River after the failure of his Peninsula Campaign, and after Grant had won his victories over the Confederate forts on the Mississippi, Confederate major general Edmund Kirby Smith left Knoxville, Tennessee, to invade central Kentucky on August 14, 1862. Two weeks later, Confederate general Braxton Bragg left Chattanooga to join Kirby Smith in Kentucky. On August 30 Union general Don Carlos Buell ordered the pursuit of these invaders.

On September 14, 1862, Munfordville, Kentucky, was attacked by Confederate troops, who suffered serious losses. The Federals reinforced Munfordville, only to be attacked by General Bragg, who led a larger force on September 16. Confederate general Simon Bolivar Buckner demanded the surrender of the 4,133-man Union garrison, which surrendered without firing a shot. The loss of Munfordville temporarily cut Buell's communications with Louisville. Had Bragg pressed his advantage, he might have done Buell serious damage. Instead, he decided to avoid further battle until he could unite with Kirby Smith. Bragg's purpose was to occupy Kentucky and recruit troops there before he engaged in large-scale combat.

Battle of Iuka

But Bragg didn't have the luxury of time. On September 19 General William S. Rosecrans, under Grant, defeated seventeen thousand Confederate troops commanded by General Sterling Price at Iuka, Mississippi.

Price withdrew southward, and Confederate general Earl Van Dorn moved to join him.

Battle of Corinth

Van Dorn believed that Corinth, Mississippi, was held lightly by a handful of Union troops. Accordingly, he paused to attack Corinth on October 3, only to discover that the town was actually held by twenty-three thousand of Rosecrans's troops—versus Van Dorn's twenty-two thousand—and Grant moved quickly to reinforce the position. Fighting was heaviest on October 4 and resulted in Van Dorn's hasty withdrawal to Holly Springs.

Battle of Perryville

Van Dorn's defeat isolated Bragg in Kentucky, cutting him off from reinforcement. On October 8, Union general Don Carlos Buell maneuvered Bragg, now highly vulnerable, into battle at Perryville, Kentucky. Buell's combined forces amounted to 36,940 men versus Bragg's 16,000 at Perryville. Despite Buell's advantage, however, his victory was modest. Although he pushed Bragg and Kirby Smith out of Kentucky and into eastern Tennessee, he did not pursue them—and, yet again, an opportunity for a decisive triumph was lost. General Rosecrans was tapped to replace Buell as commander of the Department of the Ohio.

Vicksburg Campaign

Buell's lukewarm victory was all too typical of Union military practice. Nevertheless, by the middle of October the Union had at least beaten back the Confederate invasion of Kentucky, and Grant could turn his attention once again to the drive down the Mississippi.

Grant understood that complete control of the river—and, with it, the final isolation of the western from the eastern Confederate states—called for the capture of Vicksburg, a fortress town heavily defended by artillery and occupying a high bluff overlooking the river.

A massive Union siege gun known as "Whistling Dick," used to bombard Vicksburg during the long siege of that city. *Collection: Library of Congress*

Battles of Holly Springs and Chickasaw Bluffs

In December Grant established an advance base at Holly Springs, Mississippi, preparatory to a planned movement of about forty-thousand troops down the Mississippi Central Railroad to link up with thirty-two thousand riverborne troops led by William Tecumseh Sherman. Van Dorn's Confederate cavalry raided Holly Springs on December 20, catching Colonel R. C. Murphy's Eighth Wisconsin Regiment sleeping. After destroying $1 million worth of supplies at Holly Springs, Van Dorn raided one Union outpost after another. In the meantime, the remarkable Confederate general Nathan Bedford Forrest led his cavalry against the railroad, destroying sixty miles of it. These actions stopped Grant's advance cold, and Sherman, without Grant's support at Chickasaw Bluffs (just a few miles north of Vicksburg), failed as well during December 27–29, 1862.

One of the canals General Ulysses S. Grant ordered dug as a means of avoiding the Confederate guns defending the river approach to Vicksburg. *From* Harper's Pictorial History of the Civil War, *1866*

Battles of Jackson and Champion Hill

Grant had been ordered to move south once he crossed the Mississippi to link up with forces under General Nathaniel Banks for a joint assault on Port Hudson, Louisiana. Learning that Banks was bogged down in his fruitless Red River Campaign, however, Grant decided to move immediately against Jackson, Mississippi, where Confederate reinforcements were being assembled. On May 14, 1863, Grant used corps under McPherson and Sherman to take Jackson. After the fall of that town, the Union engaged Confederate forces at Champion's Hill on May 16. The position fell to the Union after heavy losses on both sides: of 29,373 Union troops engaged, 410 were killed, 1,844 wounded, and 187 were missing; of an estimated 20,000 Confederates, 381 died, about 1,800 were wounded, and 1,670 were missing.

Vicksburg: Initial Assaults

Grant's victories at Jackson and Champion's Hill finally put him in position for a frontal attack on Vicksburg. He ordered an assault on May 19 but was repulsed. He tried again on May 22 and again was repulsed, with some thirty-two hundred casualties. It became clear to Grant that Vicksburg would yield only to a prolonged siege. From late May through the beginning of July, two hundred heavy Union artillery pieces and siege mortars continuously pounded Vicksburg, visiting great destruction and hardship on the civilian as well as military population of the town. Surrender came on July 4, 1863. With Gettysburg, the taking of Vicksburg should be judged the turning point of the Civil War. Vicksburg's fall put the Mississippi River wholly in Union hands.

Gettysburg: June 30

As mentioned earlier, Jeb Stuart's raid put him out of touch with Lee and thereby deprived the Confederate general of critical intelligence as he invaded Pennsylvania. General George Meade, who had taken over command of the Army of the Potomac on June 28, cautiously tried to provoke combat south of the Susquehanna River. On June 30, a Confederate infantry brigade unexpectedly encountered a Union cavalry brigade on a reconnaissance foray near the town of Gettysburg, Pennsylvania. This chance encounter became the basis of what most historians regard as the most momentous battle of the Civil War.

Gettysburg: First Day

General John Buford was an outstanding Union cavalry commander, who, on his arrival at Gettysburg, immediately grasped the importance of holding the high ground called McPherson's Ridge, just west of town. Although he knew that he would be badly outnumbered in the coming engagement, he also knew that he would have a great advantage fighting from the high ground and that his men would also be fighting with brand-new breach-loading Spencer carbines, which would allow them to load and fire much faster than the Confederates, who used obsolescent muzzle-loading muskets. He decided, therefore, to fight it out rather than withdraw.

The battle began at nine on the morning of July 1. Buford's dismounted cavalry held off the first waves of General Henry Heth's and General William Pender's Confederate infantry divisions while General John Reynolds's I Corps and General O. O. Howard's XI Corps rushed to

IN THEIR OWN

Words

May 28. . . . We are utterly cut off from the world, surrounded by a circle of fire. Would it be wise like the scorpion to sting ourselves to death? The fiery shower of shells goes on day and night. . . . People do nothing but eat what they can get, sleep when they can, and dodge the shells. . . . I watched the soldiers cooking on the green opposite. The half-spent balls . . . were flying so thick that they were obliged to dodge at every turn. At all the caves I could see . . . people . . . sitting, eating their poor suppers at the cave doors, ready to plunge in again. As the first shell again flew they dived, and not a human being was visible. The sharp crackle of the musketry-firing was a strong contrast to the scream of the bombs. I think all the dogs and rats must be killed or starved: we don't see any more pitiful animals prowling around. . . .

—ANONYMOUS DIARIST, VICKSBURG, MISSISSIPPI

George Gordon Meade, Union commander at Gettysburg. *From* Harper's Pictorial History of the Civil War, *1866*

reinforce Buford. Reynolds's troops began to arrive by ten-thirty in the morning, but by this time the Confederates had mustered most of their superior strength. Union I Corps commander Reynolds took personal command of the celebrated eighteen-hundred-man "Iron Brigade" in McPherson's Woods, to the west of the ridge, but within minutes he fell to a Confederate sniper. By the time O. O. Howard and his XI Corps arrived, shortly before noon, the situation had become confused. Union forces were repeatedly pushed back, only to rally and counterattack, but when Howard, who assumed overall command in the field following the death of Reynolds, tried to join a division commanded by Major General Carl Schurz to the beleaguered brigades of I Corps, the units failed to meet, and the combined strength of Confederate units under Generals Robert Rodes, Jubal Early, and A. P. Hill at last drove the Federals off McPherson's Ridge and their other positions west and north of Gettysburg. Union forces now retreated into the town, fighting hand-to-hand near Pennsylvania College before withdrawing southeast of town down the Baltimore Pike.

Day one of the Gettysburg battle ended with a Confederate victory. Lee directed Ewell to press his initial gains—"if practicable"—but Ewell demurred. Thus, although the high ground of McPherson's Ridge had been forfeited, the Union army was given a reprieve and found new high ground: East Cemetery Hill, Cemetery Ridge, and Culp's Hill, running from due south to southeast of town. For their part, the Confederates had also taken up high-ground positions: Oak Hill, northwest of town, and Seminary Ridge, due west of Gettysburg.

Gettysburg: Day Two

At dawn of the second day of battle, July 2, Robert E. Lee, though ill and exhausted, was optimistic. With Stuart still absent, Lee was not aware of how many more Union troops were massing at Gettysburg—but he knew they *were* massing, and this knowledge made him eager to finish what had been started the day before. General Longstreet dissented, offering his opinion that most of the Army of the Potomac would be massing against the Confederates on this day. He feared that the Army of Northern Virginia would be overrun and overwhelmed. His advice was to practice "strategic offense—tactical defense": to manipulate the Union army into attacking the Confederate army where and when it was strategically advantageous to the Confederacy and, when attacked, to defend, inflicting great losses on the Federals. This defensive posture had worked brilliantly at the two Bull Runs, at Antietam, and at Fredericksburg. Longstreet proposed a withdrawal to the south and a move against Meade from the rear. Lee, however, was determined to attack. He would not withdraw his army after it had won a victory.

On day two of battle, the Union line was deployed in a giant fishhook pattern. The hook's barb was just south of Culp's Hill, its turn was at Cemetery Hill, and the end of its shaft—its tie end—was at two hills south of town, called Little Round Top and Big Round Top. Lee directed Longstreet to attack the Union left, the shaft of the fishhook running along Cemetery Ridge and terminating at the Little and Big Round Tops. Lee was northwest of the fishhook, where the curve met the shaft. Ewell, to the north and the northeast, above the curve of the fishhook, was to be prepared to swing down to smash into the Union's right.

George Gordon Meade, the Union commander, saw that he was surrounded on three sides, but he also appreciated that the Federal position occupied the high ground and therefore commanded clear fields of observation and clear fields of fire. Moreover, Meade now had almost ninety thousand men at Gettysburg, opposing seventy-five thousand Confederates. It was a dangerous position, but it was also a powerful one.

The southernmost Union corps, the tie end of the fishhook terminating at the Round Tops, was commanded by Major General Daniel Sickles. Without orders from Meade, Sickles impulsively advanced his III Corps to Houck's Ridge and the Peach Orchard northwest of the Round Tops, thereby exposing the Union's left flank to Longstreet's offensive. Fortunately, Longstreet was as reluctant as Sickles was impulsive. It was four in the afternoon before the Confederate commander commenced his attack. One of his subordinates, Major General John Bell Hood, hit Sickles through an area called the Devil's Den. Hood's division pushed Sickles back to Little Round Top. Just before Hood's men attacked Sickles, Brigadier General Gouverneur K. Warren, Meade's chief engineer, noticed that Little Round Top was undefended, save for a few signalmen. He realized in an instant that Hood's division would seize that high ground and thereby find itself in a position to crush the Union's flank. Warren rounded up a brigade led by Colonel Strong Vincent and sent it to occupy Little Round Top. Vincent was soon killed in the action. A brigade under Brigadier General Stephen Weed also fought Hood. Among Weed's regiments, occupying the extreme south end of the Federal flank, was the Twentieth Maine, a battle-battered regiment commanded by Colonel Joshua Lawrence Chamberlain. No professional soldier, Chamberlain was a professor of rhetoric at Bowdoin College, who had volunteered to serve. The regiment he led was at less than half strength—fewer than five hundred men, including some deserters who had been put under his guard. With these men, the rhetoric professor not only held off a superior force of Alabama troops but also defeated them, by means of a fierce downhill bayonet charge (he used bayonets because he had run out of ammunition). Sickles had put the Union line in harm's way. Chamberlain had saved it.

The Confederates still held Devil's Den, below Little Round Top, and fired on the reinforced defenders of that hill from behind boulders. The action was fierce as well in the Peach Orchard and Wheat Field, to the northwest of Little Round Top. Meade and Major General Winfield Scott Hancock—now leading II Corps—quickly redressed Sickles's blunder by redeploying forces to check each major Confederate attempt at a breakthrough. At sundown the Confederates attacked Cemetery, East Cemetery, and Culp's Hills. The Federals held on to all their positions except at Culp's Hill, but then counterattacked there at four-thirty on the morning of July 3 and, after seven hours of fighting, turned back the Confederates.

Gettysburg: Day Three

As July 3 dawned, the Union army still possessed the high ground. Lee, however, believed that he had sufficiently worn down the army to destroy it by an all-out attack. Over Longstreet's protest, Lee ordered an offensive that would become perhaps the most celebrated action of the war. Pickett's Charge (Pickett commanded three of the nine brigades—a total of fifteen thousand men—massed for the attack) began at one-thirty in the afternoon. The Confederates advanced in close order. Ten thousand of the fifteen thousand engaged in the charge were cut down, and with the defeat of Pickett's Charge, the Battle of Gettysburg effectively ended.

The Union fielded 88,289 men at Gettysburg, of whom 3,155 were killed; another 14,529 were wounded, mortally wounded, or captured; and 5,365 were missing. Of 75,000 Confederates engaged, 3,903 were killed; 18,735 were wounded, mortally wounded, or captured; and 5,425 were reported missing in action. The crucial objectives the Union had achieved were to avoid defeat and to drive the Confederates out of Northern territory. But had Meade pursued Lee's badly battered army, the North would have scored a victory that probably would have hastened the end of the Confederacy. As it was, the victory at Gettysburg did much to hearten the war-weary North, and it absolutely ended any vestige of hope the South had for securing foreign support for the Confederate cause.

The Action Shifts

Although both Vicksburg and Gettysburg heartened the Union, these victories produced no great initiatives. If anything, the pace of the war slowed, reflecting the exhaustion of both sides. Following Gettysburg, Lee entrenched his troops at Williamsport, Maryland. Meade refrained from attacking, and by July 14, the Army of Northern Virginia was back in Virginia, Major General Harry Heth having fought a brilliant rearguard action against Union forces at Falling Waters, Maryland. From this point, the principal action shifted from Mississippi and Pennsylvania to central Tennessee and northern Georgia.

Fall of Chattanooga

Union general William Starke Rosecrans, commanding the Army of the Cumberland, had been sparring with Braxton Bragg, general in command of the Confederate Army of Tennessee, since the end of October 1862. Rosecrans had avoided disaster at the Battle of Stones River, Tennessee, during December 30, 1862–January 3, 1863, but had yielded ground to Bragg. Lincoln wanted Rosecrans to seize the initiative, take Chattanooga, then Knoxville, and thereby gain control of eastern Tennessee. Through a skillful series of feints and deceptions, Rosecrans moved his troops behind Bragg's right flank near Tullahoma. By July 4, after another flanking move-

IN THEIR OWN *Words*

My brave boys were so full of hope and confident of victory as I led them forth! Over on Cemetery Ridge the Federals beheld a scene which has never previously been enacted—an army forming in line of battle in full view, under their very eyes—charging across a space nearly a mile in length, pride and glory soon to be crushed by an overwhelming heartbreak.

Well, it is all over now. The awful rain of shot and shell was a sob—a gasp.

I can still hear them cheering as I gave the order, "Forward!" the thrill of their joyous voices as they called out, "We'll follow you, Marse George, we'll follow you!" On, how faithfully they followed me on—on—to their death, and I led them on—on—on—Oh God!

I can't write you a love letter today, my Sally. But for you, my darling, I would rather, a million times rather, sleep in an unknown grave.

Your sorrowing

soldier

—LETTER OF GENERAL GEORGE PICKETT TO HIS FIANCÉE, JULY 3, 1863, THE NIGHT AFTER "PICKETT'S CHARGE" AT THE BATTLE OF GETTYSBURG ment, he forced Bragg, outnumbered, to retreat from Tullahoma and withdraw to Chattanooga.

Now Rosecrans begged for reinforcements to take Chattanooga. When none were forthcoming, Rosecrans resolved to keep maneuvering. He executed a surprise crossing of the Tennessee River thirty miles west of Chattanooga. Rosecrans marched through a series of gaps in Lookout Mountain, the long ridge running south-southwest of Chattanooga, and targeted the Western and Atlantic Railroad, Bragg's supply and communications line to Atlanta. Once Rosecrans had severed this link, Bragg evacuated Chattanooga.

Major (later Lieutenant Colonel) James T. Weaver, commander of the Sixtieth North Carolina at the Battle of Chattanooga. *Collection: Library of Congress*

Battle of Chickamauga

Remarkably, Rosecrans had taken Chattanooga at almost no cost. The logical thing would have been to concentrate his forces in Chattanooga, resupply them, then resume the offensive against Bragg. Instead Rosecrans, without pausing for resupply, pushed his three fatigued corps, which became separated in the mountain passes. In the meantime Bragg halted at La Fayette, Georgia, twenty-five miles south of Chattanooga. Here he was reinforced and, on September 19, turned on Rosecrans. The place of the counterattack was Chickamauga Creek, in Georgia, twelve miles south of Chattanooga.

During the night preceding the battle, both sides shifted and moved troops. In the thick woods, neither side knew the other's position, nor were the commanders fully aware of the disposition of their own troops. At daybreak Union general George Henry Thomas ordered a reconnaissance near Lee and Gordon's Mill, a local landmark on Chickamauga Creek. These troops, led by Brigadier General John Milton Brannon, encountered and drove back the dismounted cavalry of Nathan Bedford Forrest. But Forrest called on nearby infantry units for help, and a full-scale battle suddenly exploded. Soon every division of the three Union corps was engaged, the Confederates held two divisions in reserve, and the fighting was some of the bloodiest in the western theater. At the end of the day, neither side had gained any advantage. During the night, both sides hastily dug in as best they could in the thickly wooded terrain. At nine o'clock the next morning, September 20, the Confederates attacked, and for the next two hours the Federals held them off.

The terrain of Chickamauga was so confusing that Rosecrans, although a competent commander, could not obtain an accurate picture of how his own units were deployed. By midmorning of the second day of battle, his aim was to fill what he thought was a gap in his right flank. To do this he ordered troops from what he believed was the left to plug the gap in the right. However, not only was there no gap, Rosecrans actually ended up moving troops out of the right flank, thereby *creating* the gap he had meant to plug. At eleven-thirty, Longstreet attacked this weak point, mauling divisions commanded by Major General Philip Sheridan and by Brigadier General Jefferson Columbus Davis. The Union's right was driven onto its left. At this point the Battle of Chickamauga threatened to become a Union disaster perhaps even greater than Fredericksburg. In many places the army was simply crumbling away. Rosecrans and two of his corps commanders, Thomas Leonidas Crittenden and Alexander McDowell McCook, fled to Chattanooga. But Major General George Henry Thomas did not run. Instead, he rallied units to block Longstreet on the south. Because Bragg was no longer holding any men in reserve, he could not exploit Longstreet's initial breakthrough. In the meantime, Union general Gordon Granger violated his orders to remain in place to protect the army's flank and decided, instead, to reinforce Thomas with two brigades. Thomas—later hailed as the "Rock of Chickamauga"—was able to hold the field until nightfall. He had saved the Army of the Cumberland from destruction, though the casualty rolls were terrible enough: Of 58,222 Union troops engaged, 1,657 were killed, 9,756 wounded, and 4,757 were missing. Confederate losses were 2,312 killed, 14,674 wounded, and 1,468 missing out of 66,326 engaged.

Philip Sheridan, General Sherman's right hand and the most famous Union cavalry commander of the war. *From* Harper's Pictorial History of the Civil War, *1866*

The Battle of Chickamauga was a tactical victory for Braxton Bragg, but his losses were greater than Rosecrans's, and he could not exploit his tactical gains to create a strategically decisive victory. However, because Rosecrans personally fled the field, he was relieved of command. Bragg also would be relieved, as commander of the Army of Tennessee, at the end of December 1863.

Siege of Chattanooga

The Union's Army of the Cumberland was in Chattanooga, and now Bragg's Confederates laid siege to them there. Two army corps were detached from Meade and dispatched under the command of Joseph Hooker. They arrived on October 2, while Sherman led part of the Army of the Tennessee east from Memphis, and Ulysses S. Grant was given command of all military operations west of the Alleghenies. Grant efficiently punched through a Confederate outpost on the Tennessee River west of Lookout Mountain and opened up a supply route to beleaguered Chattanooga.

Battle of Lookout Mountain (Battle above the Clouds)

Sherman arrived at the Union rallying point—Bridgeport, Alabama—on November 15. On November 24 Grant ordered Major General Joseph Hooker to take Lookout Mountain, the eleven-hundred-foot prominence looming over the Tennessee River just outside Chattanooga. Hooker commenced an uphill battle from eight in the morning until after midnight. Early on the morning of November 25, soldiers from the Eighth Kentucky Regiment scrambled up to the summit and planted the Stars and Stripes. The sun had broken through the fog, creating a spectacle that war correspondents dubbed the "Battle above the Clouds."

Assault on Missionary Ridge

On the afternoon of November 25, Grant ordered Thomas to lead the Army of the Cumberland forward to take the Confederate rifle pits at the base of Missionary Ridge south of Chattanooga and just to the east of Lookout Mountain. Thomas's men, having been trapped so long in Chattanooga, were eager to advance. They not only took the rifle pits but also, on their own initiative, kept going, charging up the steep slope of Missionary Ridge to sweep all Confederate forces before them, breaking Bragg's line where it was strongest. Missionary Ridge capped the defeat of the Confederacy in the West.

Grant Takes Command

After Vicksburg, it became clear to Abraham Lincoln that he had finally found a general to lead the Union armies. On March 12, 1864, Ulysses S. Grant was appointed supreme commander of all the Union armies. Grant saw that the taking of cities and the occupation of Southern territory meant little as long as the Confederate armies remained in the field.

Victory would come not with the occupation of land, but by the destruction of armies. The two main armies to kill were Robert E. Lee's Army of Northern Virginia, and the Army of Tennessee, now under the command of Joseph E. Johnston, who had replaced Bragg. Grant took on the task of fighting Lee and assigned Johnston to his trusted colleague William Tecumseh Sherman, who became commander of the Military Division of the Mississippi. Sherman was to move down the route of the Western and Atlantic Railroad, advancing inexorably against Atlanta, in the process eating up the Army of Tennessee. As Sherman advanced on Atlanta, forcing Johnston to fight him to defend the city, Grant would advance on Richmond, less with the object of taking the Confederate capital than to fight the Army of Northern Virginia, which would rush to the capital's defense. In addition to the main body of the Army of the Potomac, Grant aimed two other armies at Richmond: the Army of the James, thirty-three thousand men under Ben Butler, and a force in the Shenandoah Valley, led by Franz Sigel. The grand operation began on May 4, 1864.

Lee's Strategy

His defeat at Gettysburg persuaded Lee that the South would not win the Civil War; however, the will of the North to prolong the fighting was by no means certain. Abraham Lincoln was up for reelection in November 1864, and his principal opponent, none other than George B. McClellan, wanted a quick end to the fighting—an armistice and a negotiated peace. Much of the South was in ruins, but if Lee could keep up the pressure, making each battle costly for the Union, he might not only force the defeat of Lincoln at the polls but also bring about a favorable peace.

The Wilderness Campaign

On May 4, 1864, Grant led the 120,000-man Army of the Potomac across the Rapidan River toward open country south of the river. His target was Lee's badly outnumbered 66,000-man Army of Northern Virginia. Lee, however, seized the initiative by attacking the Federal columns as they passed through the tangled and densely forested area known as the Wilderness, the same Wilderness that had brought such disastrous confusion to "Fighting Joe" Hooker at Chancellorsville almost a year to the day earlier. Without an open field for deployment, Grant could not bring his overwhelming strength to bear at any particular point, nor could he make effective use of his artillery.

The main fighting spanned May 5–6, with intense gunfire igniting many brushfires; indeed, 200 soldiers suffocated or burned to death during the night of May 7–8. The first day of battle was bloody and indecisive. On the second day, Confederate general James Longstreet took command and drove in the two flanks of the Union army, forcing Grant to withdraw. Grant's losses were 17,666 (2,246 killed, 12,073 wounded, and 3,347 missing) out of 101,895 engaged. Two Union generals were killed, two wounded, and another two captured. Confederate records indicate that of 61,025 engaged, 7,500 were killed, wounded, or missing. Two Confederate generals were killed, another was mortally wounded, and four more were wounded but recovered, including James Longstreet, hit by friendly fire.

Battle of Spotsylvania

Defeat at the Wilderness was difficult, but Grant kept hold of one grim fact: He could afford to lose men. Lee could not. The North had a far greater population than the South and a much more vigorous economy. So instead of withdrawing in defeat, Grant advanced southward, to Spotsylvania Court House, at a crossroads on the way to Richmond. Grant would force Lee to fight and fight again. Even if Lee won this day and the next, he would lose men with each fight. With each fight, even in victory, the Army of Northern Virginia would waste away.

A Confederate rifle pit at Spotsylvania. The Civil War saw the beginning of trench warfare.
Collection: U.S. Army Military History Institute

Surmising Grant's next move, Lee beat him to the Spotsylvania crossroads. A skirmish was fought on May 8, then a major, prolonged battle developed, lasting through May 19—eleven days of fierce combat. Through it all, Grant kept shifting his troops to the left, always probing for Lee's flank, the most vulnerable aspect of any army. Brilliantly, Lee continually covered his flank.

Battle of Yellow Tavern

The two armies held one another in a death grip. Philip Sheridan, commander of the Army of the Potomac's ten-thousand-man cavalry, proposed a cavalry breakout toward Richmond to draw Jeb Stuart and the Confederate cavalry, about forty-five hundred troopers, into a fight. This, he hoped, would give Grant the edge he needed to resolve the current struggle. Seeing Sheridan's advance, however, Stuart placed his cavalrymen squarely between the Union column and Richmond, at an abandoned wayside inn called Yellow Tavern—just six miles north of the Confederate capital. The two cavalries engaged on May 11. Although Sheridan enjoyed a two-to-one advantage, Stuart had secured a formidable defensive position. After three hours, Sheridan withdrew—but not before one of his troopers shot an ostentatiously uniformed officer. It was Jeb Stuart, who died the following day. For Lee, his loss was second only to that of Stonewall Jackson at Chancellorsville.

Battle of Mule Shoe

On May 11 Grant ordered Major General Winfield Scott Hancock to attack, with twenty thousand men, Richard Ewell's corps. Ewell had deployed his men in entrenchments shaped like an inverted "U," which gave the resulting battle the name of Mule Shoe. Hancock commenced the attack at four-thirty on the morning of May 12. After a quarter hour, his men had punched through the Confederate lines. Over the next forty-five minutes, they captured at least two thousand prisoners (some sources say four thousand), including two generals, and twenty artillery pieces. But then the advance was stopped, and for the rest of the day and well into the night, combat was hand-to-hand. "Mule Shoe" thus became "Bloody Angle," which one of Grant's aides described as "probably the most desperate engagement in the history of modern warfare."

Battle of North Anna River

Mule Shoe was the last battle near Spotsylvania. From here, Grant moved south to the North Anna River (May 24). Lee's defensive positions were too strong to overrun. But battle cost him men. And still Grant pressed closer to Richmond. At Totopotomoy Creek (May 26–30), once again, the Confederate defenses held.

Battles of New Market and Bermuda Hundred

While Grant and Lee battered one another in northeastern Virginia, Major General Franz Sigel lost a desperate battle against Confederate general John C. Breckenridge at New Market, in the Shenandoah Valley, on May 15.

Benjamin Butler's Army of the James advanced up the river for which it was named, only to be defeated at Bermuda Hundred late in May. Butler had encamped his forces on the Bermuda Hundred peninsula, thereby allowing himself to be cut off and bottled up. With the Army of the James neutralized, Lee was able to draw badly needed reinforcements from that front to use against Grant.

IN THEIR OWN Words

Tuesday, June 7th —Cold Harbor . . . At daylight this morning all was quiet. The enemy advanced a white Flag, asking permission to bury their dead, which was granted. We had an armistice of two hours. The quietness was really oppressive, It positively made us feel lonesome, after a continual racket day and night for so long. We sit on the works and let our legs dangle over on the front and watch the Johnnies carry off their dead comrades in silence, but in a great hurry. Some of them lay dead within twenty feet of our works—the live Rebel looks bad enough in his old torn, ragged Butternut suit, but a dead Rebel looks horrible all swelled up and black in the face. After they were through there was nothing left but stains of Blood, broken and twisted guns, old hats, canteens, every one of them reminders of the death and carnage that reigned a few short hours before. When the 2 hours was up we got back in our holes and they did the same. . . .

—DANIEL CHISHOLM, COMPANY K, 116TH PENNSYLVANIA REGIMENT, DIARY ENTRY

Battle of Cold Harbor

On the night of June 1, Grant and Lee raced toward a crossroads called Cold Harbor, six miles northeast of Richmond. As usual, Lee arrived first and was therefore able to dig into defensive positions. During June 1–2, Grant lost five thousand men beating against the entrenchments. On June 3 he charged the positions with sixty thousand Federal troops, which were cut to ribbons by Confederate cavalry. Some seven thousand fell in a single hour at Cold Harbor—and most of these within the opening eight minutes of battle.

Siege of Petersburg

Grant slipped his army out of Cold Harbor under cover of darkness and crossed the Chickahominy. Lee could only assume that he was heading for Richmond and so dispatched most of his troops to the outskirts of the city. But Grant had decided on a new objective: Petersburg, a rail junction vital to the supply of Richmond. The Union commander reasoned that by taking Petersburg, Richmond would be cut off from the rest of the Confederacy and would fall. Lee found himself the victim of surprise. When sixteen thousand Federals arrived at Petersburg on June 15, only three thousand Confederates, under P. G. T. Beauregard, were there to defend it. For the Union, Petersburg would prove yet another heartbreaking missed opportunity. The Federal troops under Major General William Farrar "Baldy" Smith were exhausted and slow to attack. Smith also mishandled his assaults against Petersburg during June 15–18, and Beauregard was able to reinforce his position. Instead of a quick victory, Grant settled in for a long siege.

Battle of the Crater

Colonel Henry Pleasants, a mining engineer now in command of a Pennsylvania regiment made up of coal miners, proposed to break through the Confederate fortifications around Petersburg by tunneling under them and blowing them up. The tunnel was completed on July 27 and was packed with four tons of black powder. The charges were ignited on July 30, and 175 feet of Confederate entrenchments suddenly exploded, sending men and debris hundreds of feet into the air, burying an entire regiment, and creating a breach in the Confederate line ripe for exploitation. Pleasants's commanding officer, Ambrose Burnside, had planned to use a "colored" division to make the initial attack through the gap, but his commander, Major General George Meade, substituted at the last minute a totally unprepared white division. The resulting advance was a disaster, as the untrained soldiers charged directly into the 34-foot-deep blast crater rather than around it. Here they were trapped, helpless targets for Confederate riflemen. Union casualties in the assault topped four thousand. Once again, the Union had lost an opportunity to achieve a decisive breakthrough. The Petersburg Siege would drag on for nine months.

Lieutenant General Ulysses S. Grant at Cold Harbor, Virginia, 1864. *Collection: National Archives and Records Administration*

The Atlanta Campaign Begins

As Grant settled into the siege of Petersburg, Sherman began his advance to the key railroad terminus of Atlanta. His army marched out of Chattanooga and into Georgia on May 5, 1864. Sherman commanded a hundred thousand men against Joseph Johnston's sixty-two thousand, and as Sherman pressed on toward Atlanta, Johnston pulled back, but built up reinforcements as he did so.

Unidentified sergeant of the Twenty-Third Massachusetts Volunteers, a unit that fought at Cold Harbor. *Collection: Library of Congress*

Battle of Peachtree Creek

Johnston's retreats were tactically sound. He knew he could not beat Sherman, but he *could* keep his own army intact and delay the taking of Atlanta long enough to cost Lincoln reelection, thereby bringing in a Democratic administration willing to negotiate a favorable peace. But the Confederate government was not in agreement with this strategy. Seeing a Yankee army on Atlanta's doorstep, Jefferson Davis, on July 17, replaced the prudent and able Johnston with the dashing and impetuous John Bell Hood.

Atlanta was strongly defended by earthworks. Sherman decided not to assault these directly, but to cut the four rail lines into the city, which would force the Confederates to come out for a fight or to retreat. The one flaw in executing this plan, however, was a gap left between McPherson's Army of the Tennessee and Schofield's Army of the Ohio on the one hand and Thomas's Army of the Cumberland on the other. While Schofield and McPherson approached the city from the east, Thomas crossed Peachtree Creek, north of the city. It was at this gap that Hood chose to attack in the July 20 Battle of Peachtree Creek. Thomas successfully defended against Hood's onslaught, thereby preserving his army so that he could join up with McPherson and Schofield.

Major General William Tecumseh Sherman. *Collection: National Archives and Records Administration*

Battle of Atlanta

On July 22, Hood attacked McPherson's Army of the Tennessee, very nearly flanking it by swinging around it to the east. McPherson was killed in the battle, and his army was attacked simultaneously from the front and the rear. Despite this, the Union rallied and, with superior numbers, forced Hood back into his defensive works.

Battle of Ezra Church

Now that he had cut the rail lines north and east, Sherman brought his army down around to the southwest, to seize the Macon and Western Railroad. On July 28 Hood emerged again and attacked the Army of the Tennessee, now commanded by O. O. Howard, at Ezra Church, west of the city. In a hard fight, Howard repulsed Hood, inflicting heavy losses on the Confederates.

Although Atlanta was within his grasp, Sherman was well aware that Hood's army was still intact. If Hood managed to hold him off long enough, the remarkable and ruthless Nathan Bedford Forrest might attack from the rear. Sherman understood that he was vulnerable. On August 25, therefore, Sherman suddenly ceased bombardment of Hood's entrenchments. On August 26 most of Sherman's army disappeared, leading Hood to conclude that Sherman had retreated.

In fact, he had swung far to the south, cutting the Macon and Western Railroad, the last rail connection into the city. Forrest was still too far to the northwest to come to Hood's aid, and, on September 1, Hood now grasped what Sherman had done. To avoid being trapped in Atlanta, the Confederate commander evacuated the city. On September 1 the Union army was in possession of Atlanta. Sherman ordered the city evacuated of noncombatants, and he transformed it into a fortress.

IN THEIR OWN Words

General Sherman's reply to the mayor of Atlanta's plea that he rescind his order of evacuation:

. . . *I assert that our military plans make it necessary for the inhabitants to go away. . . .*

You cannot qualify war in harsher terms than I will. War is cruelty, and you cannot refine it. And those who brought war into our country deserve all the curses and maledictions a people can pour out. I know I had no hand in making this war, and I know I will make more sacrifices today than any of you to secure peace. But you cannot have peace and a division of our country. . . .

You might as well appeal against the thunderstorm as against the terrible hardships of war. They are inevitable, and the only way the people of Atlanta can hope once more to live in peace and quiet at home is to stop the war. . . .

I want peace, and I believe it can only be reached through union and war; and I will ever conduct war purely with a view to perfect an early success. But, my dear sirs, when peace does come, you may call on me for anything. Then will I share with you the last cracker, and watch with you to shield your homes and families against danger from every quarter.

Now you must go, and take with you the old and feeble, feed and nurse them, and build for them in more quiet places proper habitations to shield them against the weather until the mad passions of men cool down and allow the Union and peace once more to settle over your old homes at Atlanta.

Battle of Allatoona Pass

Early in October 1864, leaving a corps in Atlanta to hold the city, Sherman gave chase to Hood, who attempted to disrupt the Federals' dangerously overextended lines of supply even as Sherman was trying to pin him down for a fight to the finish. At Allatoona Pass, on October 5, Hood menaced a Federal supply depot commanded by Brigadier General John M. Corse. Hood demanded Corse's surrender, but he refused as Sherman signaled to him "Hold the fort." That phrase immediately entered the English language as a common figure of speech. Corse held, and Hood withdrew.

Sherman's victory in Atlanta had deprived the Confederacy of a major rail hub and industrial city, and it ensured the reelection of President Lincoln. The victory in Atlanta revealed to Sherman that the Confederacy was falling apart. Instead of going after Hood's army, Sherman proposed ignoring that army to advance instead with sixty thousand of his troops southeast to Savannah in a "March to the Sea." This would accomplish two immediate objectives: It would cut the Confederacy in two, north and south, just as the victories along the Mississippi River had severed it east from west. It would also allow Sherman to come at Lee's Army of Northern Virginia from the south even as Grant continued to bear down on it from the north—a pincers movement. Grant agreed.

By the middle of November, Sherman and Hood turned away from each other, Sherman marching to the sea, and Hood toward Nashville. Hood's plan now was to coordinate with Nathan Bedford Forrest to overwhelm the thirty thousand men under Major General George Thomas, who had been sent to clear the Confederates out of Tennessee. This, Hood hoped, would draw Sherman out of Atlanta to rescue Thomas. At the very least, it would halt Sherman's raid of the Deep South. In the meantime, on November 11, Sherman ordered everything of military significance in Atlanta destroyed. The result, by November 16, was a blaze that consumed virtually all of Atlanta.

Sherman's March to the Sea

Sherman marched southeast from Atlanta, toward Savannah, Georgia, cutting a swath of destruction as he went, doing whatever he could to devastate the lives of Southern civilians. His idea was to deprive the Confederacy of popular support and destroy its will to fight. On December 21, 1864, Sherman reached Savannah, which surrendered without a fight. On February 16, 1865, Sherman's army reached the South Carolina capital of Columbia. The city surrendered on February 17, a day on which fires destroyed half the town. On February 18, the day after Columbia was occupied, the Confederates abandoned Fort Sumter as Union troops closed in on Charleston. Without ceremony, the Stars and Stripes were raised above Fort Sumter for the first time since April 13, 1861.

Battles of Spring Hill and Franklin

While Sherman marched to the sea, Major General George Thomas strengthened and augmented his forces to fifty thousand men in Nashville during early November. He was girding for the attack he anticipated from Hood and Forrest. Hood had been advancing against Union general John M. Schofield, maneuvering him into a vulnerable position at Spring Hill, Tennessee, on November 29, which could have cut off his retreat from Columbia, Tennessee, to Franklin, just south of Nashville. But Schofield managed to continue his withdrawal.

At Franklin, Tennessee, on November 30, Hood, frustrated and impetuous as usual, ordered a frontal assault on Schofield's well-defended position. Of the eighteen thousand men Hood fielded, more than six thousand were killed or wounded, and Schofield continued his withdrawal to Nashville to unite with Thomas's force. Hood had fewer men than Thomas to begin with. Now, with fewer still, he was outnumbered two to one. Thomas attacked on December 15–16, decisively defeating Hood. Forrest's extraordinary rearguard action staved off the outright destruction of the Army of Tennessee, but it did not prevent a rout. That army was effectively neutralized as a fighting force.

Closing in on Richmond

While Sherman was taking Atlanta, then marching to the sea, and while the Union forces in Tennessee were neutralizing both Hood and Forrest, Grant was still fighting the long siege of Petersburg, tightening the noose around Richmond.

For the Confederates, the question was how to counter the threat to Richmond. On June 27, 1864, Jubal Early set off from Staunton, chief town of Virginia's Shenandoah Valley, with an army of 14,000. He boldly invaded Maryland. Suddenly, on July 5, it occurred to Union commanders that Washington was in jeopardy, and they scrambled to reinforce the capital's defenses.

On July 9, Early's subordinate commanders attacked Federal troops under Major General Lew Wallace at Monocacy, Maryland, near Frederick, just forty miles northwest of Washington. The Federals were routed. Early did not give chase, because he could not afford to be bogged down with Union POWs. Of 6,050 Federal troops engaged at Monocacy, 1,880 were wounded, killed, or missing. Early suffered fewer than 700 casualties among the 14,000 troops he had in action.

After Monocacy, Early menaced Baltimore with a cavalry brigade while he marched the main body of his army on Washington. Grant rushed men from Petersburg to defend the capital, which also called on administrative troops and civilians to pitch in. On July 11 Early reached the outer forts defending the capital. The War Department summoned all available forces, including old soldiers from the Soldiers' Home and disabled veterans from the Invalid Corps. At the last minute, the Twenty-fifth New York Cavalry appeared, and Early withdrew. When the Army of the Potomac's VI Corps arrived on July 12, the Confederate commander began a general retreat during the night of July 12–13, backtracking all the way to the Shenandoah Valley.

Robert E. Lee, commanding general, Army of Northern Virginia.
Collection: National Archives and Records Administration

Through the first week of August, Early harassed small Union units in the Shenandoah Valley until Grant finally dispatched Phil Sheridan with about forty-eight thousand men to "pacify" the Valley. It was important to neutralize this region, because it was an open backdoor to Washington, as well as an avenue to Baltimore and Philadelphia, and, a region of great fertility, it served as the breadbasket of the Confederate armies. Sheridan pursued Early relentlessly, burning barns, burning crops, and destroying cattle all along the way.

On October 19 Early surprised the Federal position at Cedar Creek, Virginia, sending Union troops into a disordered retreat. Sheridan rallied them and, by four in the afternoon, made a counterattack that transformed the Federal rout into the victory that brought Sheridan's Shenandoah Valley Campaign to a successful conclusion. At Cedar Creek, Sheridan had lost 5,665 men, killed, wounded, or missing, of 30,829 engaged; Early lost 2,910, killed, wounded, or missing, of 18,410.

Lee's Proposal

Slowly but inevitably, the Confederate defenders of Petersburg were starving. Lee persuaded Jefferson Davis that the only chance of averting total defeat and unconditional surrender lay in a breakout from

Petersburg and a retreat southeast, so that he could unite his forces with the ragged remnants of the Army of Tennessee. Although this would mean the fall of Richmond, the army would remain intact, and if it inflicted sufficient damage on Sherman, a favorably negotiated peace still might be possible.

Petersburg Breakout: The Battle of Fort Stedman

Lee assigned Major General John Brown Gordon to attack with twelve thousand men a hardened Union position called Fort Stedman, which was a mere 150 yards from the Confederate lines. If Grant could be forced to contract his lines, a breach would be created through which Lee could push a portion of his army and begin his march into North Carolina. Confederate sappers began cutting down obstructions in front of the fort in the predawn hours of March 25. The attack followed at 4:00 A.M. and was sharp and stunning. Fort Stedman fell, and a thousand Union soldiers—plus a Union general—were made prisoners of war. Gordon tried next to capture smaller forts behind Fort Stedman, but failed. By seven-thirty in the morning Union reinforcements poured in, forcing the Confederates back into the confines of Fort Stedman. At eight Lee, watching from his lines, ordered a retreat. But the Federals had begun raking the line of retreat with artillery fire. Of twelve thousand men engaged, the Confederates lost four thousand killed, wounded, or captured. There would be no Petersburg breakout.

Battle of Five Forks

Grant had never been idle at Petersburg. All during the nine-month siege, he had been extending his lines westward to force Lee to stretch his much thinner lines until they broke. The Battle of Fort Stedman made it clear to Grant that Lee's lines were now stretched beyond the breaking point. He therefore attempted a drive around Lee's right but was repulsed. Then General Sheridan returned from the Shenandoah Valley with twelve thousand cavalry troopers, and on March 31 headed for Five Forks, a junction not only crucial to the Confederates' contemplated move into North Carolina but also vital to their army's line of supply. Lee dispatched nineteen thousand (some estimates put this figure at a mere ten thousand) men under George Pickett to hold Five Forks, but Sheridan was reinforced by an infantry corps. Outnumbered, Pickett also was outgeneraled. Sheridan routed him at Five Forks, taking five thousand prisoners.

Petersburg Siege Ends

Grant broke through Lee's Petersburg lines on April 2 in a lightning attack that resulted in the death of Confederate general Ambrose Powell Hill. Lee fell back on the town of Petersburg, evacuated it, and retreated west toward Amelia Court House. On this day, too, Jefferson Davis gave the order for the Confederate government to evacuate Richmond. Danville, Virginia, would become the new Confederate capital.

Lee's Final Moves

Somewhat fewer than fifty thousand men were all that remained of the Army of Northern Virginia. Still hoping to give the South some basis from which to negotiate as favorable a peace as possible, Lee marched west with the object of reaching Amelia Court House, where he expected to find supplies and gain access to the Richmond and Danville Railroad, which would take his army to that of Johnston.

Battle of Amelia Springs

By April 5 the bulk of Lee's army was concentrated at Amelia Court House, thirty miles west of Petersburg. He was blocked by Sheridan and others from making a break down the Richmond and Danville Railroad. Worse, in the confusion of Richmond's fall, no one had sent out the rations to the town. The army would continue to go hungry.

Battle of Little Sayler's Creek

Lee turned to the southwest, bound for Rice Station, where he could get supplies by rail before pushing south to link up with Johnston. Grant ordered attacks to intercept Lee. Pursuing Federal forces hit the Confederate wagon train, and at Little Sayler's Creek, Confederate general Richard S. Ewell counterpunched, driving back the Union center. Federal reinforcements not only checked this penetration but also surrounded Ewell's badly outnumbered command. Three Confederate commanders—Richard H. Anderson, Bushrod Johnson, and George Pickett—were able to escape, but Ewell remained to fight to the bitter end. He was captured, along with five other Confederate commanders and a third of the remaining Army of Northern Virginia.

Battle of High Bridge

Although Confederate general John Brown Gordon suffered heavy losses at Little Sayler's Creek, he was able to rally his troops and lead them west to

High Bridge, a structure built on sixty-foot piers across the Appomattox River at Farmville. There he joined Longstreet in retreating across the bridge, leaving Fitzhugh Lee to fight a rearguard action. The Confederates should have burned High Bridge once all of the units had crossed it, but they left it intact, and the Federals quickly closed on the rear of Lee's army.

Appomattox Station and Appomattox Court House

On April 8, Lee's army was concentrated between Appomattox Station, on the rail line, and Appomattox Court House, a few miles to the northeast. Major General George A. Custer's division moved swiftly against Appomattox Station, drove off two Confederate divisions, and captured their supply train as well as thirty guns. Custer then pressed on toward Appomattox Court House, where he discovered the Confederate defenses just to the southwest of the town. Sheridan, with the main body of troops, caught up with Custer and prepared to launch an attack the next day. But on April 9, 1865, it was two of Lee's generals, John Brown Gordon and Fitzhugh Lee, who attacked first. Union cavalry and infantry came in from the northeast and the southwest. The Army of Northern Virginia numbered now perhaps thirty thousand soldiers, of whom only half were armed. Trapped, Lee sent word to Grant that he was prepared to surrender. On April 9, 1865, Lee met Grant in the McLean farmhouse and readily negotiated the terms of the surrender of the Army of Northern Virginia.

The War Ends

Although Lee surrendered only what he commanded, the Army of Northern Virginia, the event, for all practical purposes, ended the Civil War. Montgomery, Alabama, fell on April 12, and Federal troops entered Mobile the same day. On April 13, Sherman occupied Raleigh, North Carolina, where, during April 17–18, he hammered out a broad armistice. Abraham Lincoln had been assassinated by fanatical Southern sympathizer John Wilkes Booth on April 14, so it was the new president, Andrew Johnson, who repudiated the agreement Sherman and Johnston had concluded. On April 26, Johnston accepted a narrower armistice, identical to what Grant had offered Lee, and on that date as well, the Confederate cabinet met to dissolve itself.

Early in May, Richard Taylor surrendered the Department of East Louisiana, Mississippi, and Alabama. On May 10, President Johnson declared that armed resistance was "virtually at an end," but three days later, at Palmito Ranch, near Brownsville, Texas, Confederate troops under Edmund Kirby Smith skirmished with Federals. This small engagement was the last fighting of the war. Smith surrendered to Canby on May 26. The very last Confederate commander to surrender was Stand Watie, son of a full-blooded Cherokee father and a half-blooded Cherokee mother, a brigadier general from Indian Territory. He laid down arms on June 23, 1865, at Doakville, Indian Territory.

Because the United States refused to recognize the sovereignty of the Confederacy, no treaty formally ended the war. Instead, President Johnson issued a Proclamation of Amnesty and Pardon for the Confederate States (May 29, 1865) and a pair of proclamations declaring the rebellion to be ended (April 2 and April 20, 1866).

IN THEIR OWN *Words*

General Order No. 9   April 10, 1865

After four years of arduous service marked by unsurpassed courage and fortitude, the Army of Northern Virginia has been compelled to yield to overwhelming numbers and resources. I need not tell the brave survivors of so many hard fought battles, who have remained steadfast to the last, that I have consented to this result from no distrust of them; but, feeling that valor and devotion could accomplish nothing that could compensate for the loss that must have attended the continuance of the contest, I have determined to avoid the useless sacrifice of those whose past services have endeared them to their countrymen.

By the terms of the agreement, officers and men can return to their homes and remain there until exchanged. You will take with you the satisfaction that proceeds from the consciousness of duty faithfully performed; and I earnestly pray that a Merciful God will extend to you his blessing and protection.

With an unceasing admiration of your constancy and devotion to your Country, and a grateful remembrance of your kind and generous consideration of myself, I bid you all an affectionate farewell.

(Sgd.) R. E. Lee
Genl.

—LEE'S FINAL ORDER TO THE ARMY OF NORTHERN VIRGINIA

Significance and Consequences

Of the 1,556,000 soldiers who served in the Union army during the Civil War, 359,528 were killed and 275,175 were wounded. Of the approximately 850,000 men of the Confederate forces, at least 258,000 died and some 225,000 were wounded. This means that 41 percent of the Union soldiers and 57 percent of the Confederate soldiers who fought were either killed or wounded, making the Civil War by far the costliest conflict in American history.

It is easy to understand why losses were so great. Advances in technology and industrialization produced weapons of unprecedented destructiveness, which outran military battle doctrine and defensive tactics. The result, often, was slaughter rather than combat.

What did the sacrifice of so many human lives purchase? First, the Northern victory achieved nothing less than the salvation of the United States as a federal republic and nation rather than as a mere voluntary confederation of separate states. Second, the war resolved the single greatest issue left unresolved by the *American Revolution, 1775–1783 (see chapter 3):* the fate of slavery. While it is an oversimplification and distortion to say that the Civil War was fought over the slavery issue, it is a fact that without slavery, there would have been no Civil War. With the end of slavery came a radical change in Southern life and culture—the end of the Southern plantation aristocracy. This change also brought some beginnings, including institutionalized racism in the South, which was only exacerbated by the North's imposition of a harsh Reconstruction policy on the Southern states. Reconstruction also contributed to the chronic impoverishment of the South and ensured that the regional resentment of the South against the North would not begin to fade until far into the twentieth century. Yet, remarkably, the Civil War, unlike civil conflicts in many other nations before and since, *did* end. No chronic guerrilla action persisted after Appomattox, and the Confederate states and people were, finally, wholly reintegrated into the Union. In this important sense, the Civil War was a definitive conflict that, for all the social and economic problems it left in its wake, did produce an overwhelmingly positive result.

CHAPTER 9

Later Indian Wars in the West

The period from 1866 to 1891 is typically identified with what the U.S. military referred to as the "Indian Wars." For purposes of historical understanding, we might push the first date back two years, to the Cheyenne and Arapaho War, 1864–1865. For the historical context of the later Indian Wars see *Chapter 5: Wars of the Indian Removal* and *Chapter 7: Early Indian Wars in the West.*

Cheyenne and Arapaho War, 1864–1865

During the mid-1860s, Governor John Evans of Colorado tried and failed to secure mineral-rich Cheyenne and Arapaho hunting grounds in exchange for consignment to reservations and government subsidy. When peaceful negotiation had been exhausted, the governor called on Colonel John M. Chivington, military commander of the territory, to sweep the Indians out, notwithstanding that of all the Plains tribes, the Cheyennes and the Arapahos had given the white settlers very little excuse for a fight. Chivington was rabid and vocal in his hatred of Indians. In an 1864 speech in Denver, he called for the extermination of all Indians, including infants.

Although most Cheyennes were inclined toward maintaining peaceful relations with their white neighbors, a militant faction, a group of young warriors known as the Hotamitainio (Dog Soldier Society), provided sufficient provocation for Chivington to declare all the Cheyennes to be at war. Based on this, he launched a number of attacks in 1864, which provoked Indian counterraids in response. To meet the crisis they had themselves created, Governor Evans and Colonel Chivington formed the Third Colorado Cavalry, composed of short-term, hundred-day enlistees drawn mainly from the territory's rough mining camps. When winter came, however, a large number of Indians, led by Black Kettle, an older chief opposed to the Dog Soldiers, sued for peace. Evans and Chivington met with the Cheyennes and Arapahos. As a gesture of submission to military authority, the Indians left the meeting and marched to Sand Creek, about forty miles northeast of Fort Lyon. Presumably acting on Chivington's instructions, Major Scott J. Anthony cut the Indians' government-mandated rations and demanded the surrender of their weapons. When a group of unarmed Arapahos approached the fort to trade buffalo hides for rations, Anthony responded by firing on them. As Major Anthony continued to promote the deterioration of relations with the Indians, the Third Colorado Cavalry slowly gathered at Fort Lyon. On November 28 Chivington deployed his seven-hundred-man force, which included four howitzers, around the Sand Creek camp of Black Kettle's people, then, unprovoked, charged into the camp and committed a catalog of atrocities. In all two hundred Cheyennes, two-thirds of them women and children, were killed. Nine chiefs also perished, although Black Kettle escaped.

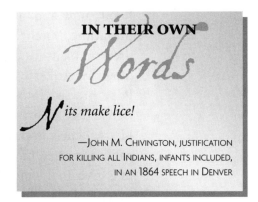

IN THEIR OWN *Words*

N its make lice!

—JOHN M. CHIVINGTON, JUSTIFICATION FOR KILLING ALL INDIANS, INFANTS INCLUDED, IN AN 1864 SPEECH IN DENVER

The Sand Creek Massacre served to unite the Southern Sioux, Northern Arapaho, and Cheyenne in a series of retaliatory raids during late 1864 and early 1865, which the U.S. Army labeled the Cheyenne-Arapaho War.

On January 7, 1865, a thousand Sioux and Cheyenne warriors raided and looted the tiny settlement of Julesburg, Colorado, which was guarded by an outpost called Fort Rankin. Raiding continued as the Indians worked their way north. On February 4, 5, 6, and 8, large numbers of Indians skirmished indecisively with much smaller army units near Forts

Mitchell and Laramie. The raids in these areas were costly: fifty settlers killed, fifteen hundred head of cattle taken, buildings burned, large quantities of stores stolen or destroyed. Brigadier General Robert B. Mitchell scrambled to organize an effective military response but was foiled by flood, snow, and bitter cold, which made it impossible to maneuver. In the meantime, Mitchell's commanding officer, Major General John C. Pope, drew up plans for a grand offensive, which called for cavalry to carry out offensive strikes while infantry guarded the mail and emigration trails. Pope pressed into infantry service "Galvanized Yankees," Confederate POWs paroled on condition that they serve the Union armies in the West. Like Mitchell, Pope fell afoul of the bad weather, and his outspoken arrogance alienated members of Congress, who cut off funding for his grand offensive. In the meantime, negotiators were dispatched to hammer out a peace with the Cheyennes, Arapahos, Kiowas, and Comanches, even as the pattern of Indian raid and fitful military response continued.

On July 26, 1865, between 1,000 and 3,000 warriors massed to attack a cavalry unit guarding the North Platte River crossing of the Oregon–California Trail. Major Martin Anderson, commanding the eleventh Kansas Cavalry and elements of two Ohio units at Upper Platte Bridge, 130 miles north of Fort Laramie, dispatched Lieutenant Caspar W. Collins and twenty cavalry troopers to escort a wagon train. The detachment was ambushed by hundreds of warriors. Fighting with great skill, the troopers made it back to the stockade with the loss of five of their number, including Lieutenant Collins. Indian losses were high, at 60 killed and 130 wounded. Brigadier General Patrick E. Connor responded by sending 3,000 troopers into Powder River country, where they destroyed one Arapaho village and engaged the Sioux. Once again, the weather brought an end to the campaigning. Indeed, the onslaught of premature winter storms brought an end to the entire Cheyenne and Arapaho War.

War for the Bozeman Trail, 1866–1868

Chief Red Cloud of the Oglala Sioux refused to yield to demands that he sell to the government the land traversed by the Bozeman Trail—beginning at Julesburg, Colorado, and forming the shortest route to the gold fields of Virginia City, Montana—and he further warned that he would not permit whites even to use the trail. In response, Colonel Henry B.

Carrington marched out of Fort Laramie, Wyoming, on June 17, 1866, and began garrisoning three forts along the Bozeman Trail: Fort Reno at the forks of the Powder River; Fort Phil Kearny (his headquarters) at the forks of Piney Creek; and Fort C. F. Smith near the Bighorn River, in Montana. Red Cloud, however, struck the forts before they were completed, forcing the troops into a desperate defensive posture. Carrington refused to act aggressively, deciding to begin no offensive operations until the forts were completed. Fed up with repeated Indian harassment, one of Carrington's officers, Captain William J. Fetterman, boasted that with eighty men he could "ride through the entire Sioux nation." On December 6, 1866, Indians attacked a wagon train hauling wood to the fort. Carrington chose his boastful captain and another officer, Lieutenant Horatio S. Bingham, to lead thirty cavalrymen to drive the marauding Sioux west while he personally led a detachment of twenty-five mounted infantry to cut the Indians off from behind. Unfortunately, Fetterman and Bingham's inexperienced troops panicked under attack and allowed their mounts to stampede out of control. Lieutenant Bingham was killed, and Carrington, tied down in battle with another band of Indians, failed to rendezvous with Fetterman's troops. All of the soldiers hastily withdrew to Fort Phil Kearny, leaving the Indians free to mount their attack on the wood train. On December 21 they massed between fifteen hundred and two thousand warriors, who hid in ravines and along a ridge near the trail. Again, Carrington dispatched Fetterman to relieve the besieged train, taking care to warn him not to pursue the Indians beyond Lodge Trail Ridge, between Big Piney Creek and the Bozeman Trail, but to remain on the wood road, drive the Indians off, and then retire. This time, however, Fetterman did not rely on raw recruits, but handpicked a force of experienced infantrymen and cavalrymen. Leading men he trusted, Fetterman had no intention of following Carrington's order to keep to the wood road and to do nothing more than relieve the wood train. He intended to move offensively against the Sioux and marched his men away from the wood road and toward the Bozeman Trail, disappearing behind the Sullivant Hills.

When Carrington heard distant gunfire, he sent forty infantry and dismounted cavalrymen under Captain Tenodor Ten Eyck to assist Fetterman. Reaching the summit of the ridge, the men saw hundreds of warriors and soon discovered the naked and mutilated bodies of Fetterman and his command: eighty dead, precisely the number of soldiers Fetterman had said he needed to "ride through the entire Sioux nation." Apparently

Fetterman had been lured into an ambush laid by the brilliant Oglala warrior Crazy Horse.

For the army, the Fetterman Massacre was a stunning defeat and a bitter humiliation, but the Sioux did not repeat their triumph. In the Hayfield Fight, on August 1, they attacked a group of haycutters near Fort C. F. Smith. On August 2 they again struck out, at woodcutters near Fort Phil Kearny, in the Wagon Box Fight (called this because the soldiers took refuge behind a makeshift corral of wagon bodies, or "boxes"). By the time of these skirmishes, the army had replaced the cumbersome muzzle-loaded weapons Fetterman had carried with much more efficient modern breech-loaders. The Indians, stunned by the rapidity of the soldiers' fire, suffered substantial casualties and withdrew.

Yet they refused to make peace, and this led to *Hancock's Campaign (Hancock's War), 1867.*

Hancock's Campaign (Hancock's War), 1867

General William Tecumseh Sherman sent General Winfield Scott Hancock to campaign against the Southern Cheyennes, the Southern Arapahos, the Kiowas, the Oglalas, and the Southern Brulé Sioux. On April 8, 1867, Hancock marched a column of soldiers to a combined Cheyenne and Sioux village to impress the Indians with the might of the army. Doubtless recalling the treachery of Sand Creek, the women and the children of the village scattered for the hills as they saw the soldiers approaching. Although Hancock instructed his principal field officer, Lieutenant Colonel George Armstrong Custer (whose rank had been reduced from major general in a U.S. Army reorganization following the Civil War) commanding the Seventh Cavalry, to surround the village to prevent the men from escaping as well, by morning all the lodges were deserted. From this Hancock concluded that war had commenced and ordered Custer to hunt down the fleeing Cheyennes and Sioux.

From April through July, Custer and the Seventh Cavalry chased the Indians, who now terrorized Kansas. At length, exhausted, Custer and his command withdrew. What had begun as an offensive campaign quickly degenerated into a series of mostly futile attempts to defend civilian settlements. The effort was doomed, since four thousand officers and men spread over fifteen hundred miles of major trails could never patrol the region effectively. Thus "Hancock's Campaign" ended as another costly army failure, which now spurred the federal government to negotiate peace terms with the tribes of the southern and central plains.

Two sets of treaties were concluded, one at Medicine Lodge Creek, Kansas, in 1867, and the other at Fort Laramie, Wyoming, the next year. The Medicine Lodge treaties established Cheyenne, Arapaho, Kiowa, Comanche, and Kiowa-Apache reservations in Indian Territory (present-day Oklahoma). The 1868 Fort Laramie treaties gave to Red Cloud most of what he had fought for, including white abandonment of the Bozeman Trail forts. This last concession would appear to be an abject confession of defeat; however, by 1868, technology had intervened to make the Bozeman Trail all but obsolete. The transcontinental railroad was rapidly pushing west and would soon supplant the great trail.

Although the treaties pledged all sides to perpetual peace, the reality was that the Cheyennes remained sharply divided into a peace faction versus the militant Dog Soldiers, who would not yield to confinement on a reservation. Together with elements of the Brulé and the Oglala Sioux, as well as Cheyennes and Arapahos, the Dog Soldiers raided throughout 1868 in western Kansas and eastern Colorado, killing a total of seventy-seven settlers, wounding nine, and stealing a great deal of stock. As for the Kiowas and the Comanches, in February 1868, Indian agent Jesse Leavenworth arrived at their new reservation in Indian Territory, only to find himself without the promised rations to distribute to the winter-hungry Indians. Outraged and desperate, several thousand Kiowas and Comanches set out in raids on Texas. When Kiowa and Comanche raiders burned Leavenworth's headquarters at the Wichita Agency, the agent summarily resigned. With that the last vestige of federal authority standing between the Indians and the citizens of Texas had vanished.

While the Kiowas and the Comanches were raiding the southern plains, the Cheyennes began agitating for the guns and ammunition that the Medicine Lodge treaty had promised them. Tall Bull, a Dog Soldier chief, had led a raid on a neighboring Indian village, and the Indian Bureau was now fearful of issuing the promised weapons. Repeated threats of war finally outweighed these fears, and the bureau yielded, commencing distribution. Unfortunately, a band of about two hundred Cheyennes had not heard about the bureau's decision and commenced raids on settlements along the Saline and Solomon Rivers, destroying much property, killing fifteen men, and allegedly raping five women. The terror moved the federal government to reverse its pacific policy, and Sherman authorized *Sheridan's Campaign, 1868–1869*, which followed the *Snake War, 1866–1868.*

Snake War, 1866–1868

In the Northwest at this time, violence erupted among the Yahuskin and Walpapi bands of the Northern Paiutes, popularly known as the Snakes, who inhabited southeastern Oregon and southwestern Idaho. The so-called Snake War was not a series of formal battles but a virtually continuous pursuit punctuated by numerous guerrilla actions. During the two-year period, Brevet Major General George Crook and his Twenty-third Infantry engaged the Snakes at least forty-nine times and, more important, kept them on the run in what amounted to a war of attrition. By the middle of 1868 the Snakes had lost 329 killed, 20 wounded, and 225 captured. When their most revered war chief, Pauline (or Paulina), was slain, the Snakes sued for peace. A minority of the Snakes remained at large and later joined the Bannocks and the Cayuses in the *Bannock War, 1878.*

Sheridan's Campaign, 1868–1869

Following the Cheyenne attacks on the Saline and Solomon Rivers in 1868, William Tecumseh Sherman and his immediate subordinate, Philip Sheridan, decided to embark on a campaign of total war against the Plains Sioux, beginning with an aggressive winter campaign. In the early autumn of 1868 Sheridan dispatched Major George A. Forsyth with fifty hand-picked plainsmen to patrol settlements and travel routes. On September 17 the small company encountered six hundred to seven hundred Dog Soldiers and Oglala Sioux in western Kansas. Forsyth's greatly outnumbered party took refuge on an island in the nearly dry Arikara Fork of the Republican River. Their sole advantage was their modern repeating carbines. Rapid fire twice turned back the Indians' headlong charges. As was true of many Plains warrior societies, the Dog Soldiers believed that peaceful contact with whites would contaminate and attenuate their fighting spirit. In the attack on Forsyth, one of the Cheyennes' most capable war chiefs, Roman Nose, was forced to restrain himself from joining the first two charges because he had broken his "protective medicine" by inadvertently eating bread that had been touched by a metal fork—an "unclean" eating utensil of the white man. By the time of the third charge, however, Roman Nose could no longer resist. He joined the fray in the full belief that, contaminated as he was, this meant certain death. Roman Nose did fall in battle, and the shock of his death prompted the attackers to break off the third charge. Falling back, they laid siege to the island. With half of Forsyth's company now dead or wounded, two messengers managed to slip through the Indian lines and travel ninety miles to Fort Wallace. A relief column arrived on the eighth day of the siege and drove off the Indians.

Sheridan's winter campaign was three-pronged: One column was to approach from Fort Bascom, New Mexico; another from Fort Lyon, Colorado; and the third, under Custer, from Fort Dodge, Kansas. They would converge on the Indians' winter camps on the Canadian and Washita Rivers, in Indian Territory.

Custer led his Seventh Cavalry to a Cheyenne camp on the Washita, surrounded it, and, on November 27, 1868, attacked the sleeping village. The impetuous Custer had attacked fifty Cheyenne lodges belonging to Black Kettle, survivor of Sand Creek and an ardent advocate of peace. Joined by warriors from other camps, Black Kettle's people counterattacked. Custer held his position and also managed to destroy 900 Indian ponies and set tepees ablaze. At dusk he marched his men toward the Indian camps downstream, as if he intended to attack them next. Seeing this, the Indians broke off their counterstrike and prepared to defend the other camps. The feigned attack did not materialize, and at nightfall, Custer and the Seventh Cavalry quietly slipped out of the Washita Valley. The Battle of Washita resulted in the deaths of 5 soldiers and the wounding of 14. Fifteen troopers were missing, their bodies discovered later. Indian casualties numbered 103 dead, including 93 women, old men, and children—as well as Chief Black Kettle, who had been cut down alongside his wife. The brutality of Washita succeeded in persuading a substantial number of Indians to retire to the reservation.

Following the battle, Major Eugene Carr and Major Andrew Evans patrolled the plains north and west of the Washita, looking for parties of holdouts. On Christmas Day 1868, Evans discovered a Comanche village consisting of sixty lodges at Soldier Spring, on the north fork of the Red River, and a Kiowa camp a short distance downstream. Evans opened the attack with howitzers, forcing the Comanches to clear out of the village. With three hundred troopers of the Third Cavalry, Evans entered the village, destroying it and its stores of dried buffalo meat and other provisions. Two hundred Comanches and Kiowas returned to counterattack, but withdrew after a day-long battle. His own men exhausted and his horses spent, Evans could not pursue the retreating Indians, but he had done them great harm by destroying their winter provisions. Some of the Kiowas sought refuge among the Kwahadi Comanches, but most surrendered to Forts Cobb and Bascom.

Winter storms prevented Custer from launching a new offensive against the Cheyennes until March 1869. By this time the hostiles had moved west into the Texas Panhandle. On March 15, 1869, at Sweetwater Creek, Custer discovered the villages of Medicine Arrow and Little Robe. Aware that the Indians held two white women hostage, Custer restrained his customary recklessness. Instead of attacking, he called for a parley—and during the talks seized three chiefs. He sent one back with surrender terms, demanding that the hostages be released or he would hang the other two. The Cheyennes complied, and promised to follow Custer to Camp Supply (and thence to their assigned reservation) as soon as their ponies were strong enough to make the trip. Custer, whose own horses were dying for want of food and whose troops were exhausted, had little choice but to take them at their word; he and his command could not delay in returning to Camp Supply. For good measure, though, he kept the two remaining hostages.

The Indians, however, did not report as they had promised. Worse, the Dog Soldiers, led by Tall Bull, refused to stop fighting and decided instead to join forces with the Northern Cheyenne in the Powder River country. On July 11, 1869, the Fifth Cavalry, commanded by Major Carr and numbering in its rank a scout named William F. Cody—Buffalo Bill—came upon the Dog Soldiers' camp at Summit Springs, Colorado. With 250 troopers and about 50 Pawnee allies, Carr descended on the village. Surprise was complete, Tall Bull was killed, and the cavalry's victory was total. It proved a decisive victory because it spelled the end of the power and influence of the Dog Soldiers in western Kansas.

Modoc War, 1872–1873

The Modocs were a small tribe, numbering no more than four hundred to five hundred individuals, living in the rugged Lost River Valley of northern California and southern Oregon. During the 1860s the Modoc chief Captain Jack (Kintpuash) and his followers settled on the Lost River, near Tule Lake, getting their living for about seven years by trade with the neighboring white settlers. As the pace of white settlement increased during the late 1860s, pressure mounted for the Modocs' removal to their assigned reservation. After only three months of confinement, however, Captain Jack and sixty to seventy Modoc families returned to the Lost River. Thomas B. Odeneal, superintendent of Indian Affairs, recommended that the Modocs be removed by force to the Klamath reservation. Accordingly, on November 29, 1872, Captain James Jackson and Troop B, First Cavalry—three officers and forty men—entered Captain Jack's camp and began to disarm the Indians. A scuffle between a trooper and an Indian resulted in an exchange of gunfire. Jackson claimed that sixteen Modocs had been killed; actually, only one had been killed and another wounded, while the troopers suffered one killed and seven wounded (one mortally). The army designated the scuffle the Battle of Lost River.

While Jackson was dealing ineffectually with Captain Jack and his followers, a vigilante group of ranchers attacked a smaller group of Modocs, followers of a man known to local whites as Hooker Jim. In the attack, two whites were killed and a third wounded. As Hooker Jim and his people rushed to join forces with Captain Jack, fourteen more settlers were killed along the way. United, Captain Jack and Hooker Jim mustered about sixty warriors, who took up hiding in the lavabeds south of Tule Lake, the place the Indians called the Land of Burnt-Out Fires. Local whites would soon refer to the area as Captain Jack's Stronghold.

On the night of January 16, 1873, Lieutenant Colonel Frank Wheaton deployed a force of 225 regular army troops and about 100 militiamen around Captain Jack's Stronghold. Wheaton ordered a howitzer barrage, then attacked at dawn. But Captain Jack's warriors were invisible among the lava flows. From ambush they easily picked off troopers. Nine of Wheaton's men were killed and 28 wounded at the Battle of the Stronghold. When the

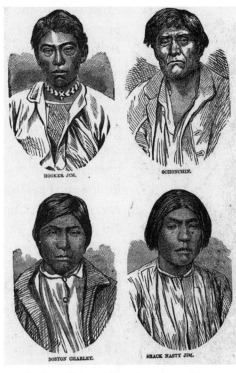

The leaders of the Modoc War, pictured in a book illustration of the period: Hooker Jim (top left), Schonchin (top right), Boston Charley (lower left), and Shack Nasty Jim (lower right). *Collection: Library of Congress*

army proved unable to dislodge the Modocs by force, President Ulysses S. Grant appointed a peace commission to treat with the Modocs. For part of March 1873 and well into April, the commissioners ineffectually negotiated. On Good Friday, April 11, 1873, Captain Jack, pressured by other warriors, assassinated General E. R. S. Canby and another negotiator and wounded a third, then fled with his warriors to the lava beds. The murder of E. R. S. Canby outraged General Sherman and the entire military community. Colonel Alvin C. Gillem led two infantry formations through the lavabeds in search of the Modocs. He began by pounding Modoc positions with howitzers and mortars during April 15–17. The barrage had little effect, and on April 26, Modoc warriors sighted a reconnoitering party of 5 officers, 59 enlisted men, and 12 Indian scouts under Captain Evan Thomas. With 22 braves, a Modoc named Scarfaced Charley attacked, killing all 5 officers and 20 men, and wounding another 16.

The Modoc victories were taking their toll on army resources as well as morale. Despite their triumphs, however, most of the Modoc warriors were coming to believe that continued resistance was futile. By the middle of May, with food and water scarce, the Modocs dispersed. On May 28, assisted by Hooker Jim, who had been captured earlier, a cavalry detachment found Captain Jack, his family, and a number of followers. Captain Jack evaded his pursuers briefly, but he and his family were cornered in a cave on June 3. Captain Jack and others identified as ringleaders—Boston Charley, Black Jim, and Schonchin John—were tried, convicted, and hanged.

Red River War (Kiowa War), 1874–1875

The assassination of General E. R. S. Canby by the Modoc chief Captain Jack (Kintpuash) on April 11, 1873, had repercussions beyond the fate of the small Modoc tribe. The government and the military abandoned President Grant's conciliatory "peace policy" and launched an offensive against the Indians of the southern Plains. This is sometimes called the Kiowa War but is more accurately termed the Red River War, since it involved the Comanches and the Cheyennes as well as the Kiowa tribe.

In the spring of 1874, pressured by the ongoing extermination of buffalo by white hunters and at the instigation of war leaders Satanta and Big Tree, Comanche, Cheyenne, and Kiowa warriors launched a series of major raids: On June 27, Comanches and Cheyennes hit a white hunter village at Adobe Walls in the Texas Panhandle; on July 12, the Kiowa chief Lone Wolf ambushed Texas Rangers at Lost Valley. Throughout this period, warriors struck at ranchers and wayfarers in Kansas and Texas. Based on these depredations and on the disintegration of the peace policy following the *Modoc War, 1872–1873,* Sherman secured federal approval to invade the Comanche and Cheyenne reservations. Generals John C. Pope (in command of forces in Kansas, New Mexico, parts of Colorado, and Indian Territory) and Christopher C. Augur (commanding Texas and parts of Indian Territory) were ordered to converge on the Staked Plains region of the Texas Panhandle. Columns were to approach from Fort Sill, Indian Territory, and from Texas, New Mexico, and Kansas.

Colonel Nelson A. Miles, one of Pope's best field commanders, led eight troops of the Sixth Cavalry and four companies of the Fifth Infantry south from the Canadian River into Indian Territory. As this force of 774 troopers approached the Staked Plains escarpment on August 30, it encountered some 600 Cheyennes. The running battle was fought across twelve miles of the Staked Plains during five hours and culminated in a Cheyenne stand at Tule Canyon. The Indians were exhausted as well as demoralized, but Miles, by this point, also realized that he had insufficient supplies to press the attack further. Reluctantly, he withdrew to resupply his force, destroying abandoned Indian villages as he did so.

Nelson A. Miles in the uniform of a lieutenant general. Miles was one of the army's most effective Indian-fighters. *Collection: National Archives and Records Administration*

As was often the case in Plains warfare, the elements presented the most formidable enemy to either side. Drought plagued the region and left Miles without supply. On September 7 the drought gave way to torrential rain. Miles rendezvoused with a force of 225 troopers of the Eighth Cavalry under Major William R. Price, and thus reinforced, slogged northward through the mud in search of supply. On September 9, about 250 Comanche and Kiowa warriors, including the war chiefs Lone Wolf, Satanta, and Big Tree, attacked an army supply train, holding it under siege for three days until Price's column approached. Miles's main force, still short on provisions, was unable to pursue the fleeing attackers. General Augur's most capable field officer, Colonel Ranald S. Mackenzie, commanding the Fourth Cavalry, approached from the southwest. During the night of September 26, a total of 250 Comanches attacked the Fourth Cavalry's camp near Tule Canyon. Mackenzie held his ground, then struck back in the morning with all eight cavalry troops, mustering 21 officers and 450 men. This force readily drove the Indians off. Next, acting on information from Tonkawa scouts, Mackenzie pressed on to Palo Duro Canyon, where he surprised a combined Kiowa-Comanche-Cheyenne village, routing the warriors there. Though he killed only 3 Indians, Mackenzie destroyed the village and all its provisions. He appropriated 1,424 Indian ponies, selected about 400 of the best mounts for his own men, then slaughtered the remainder.

Into October, soldiers under the command of Colonel George P. Buell burned more villages, while Miles and Price pursued a chief known as Gray Beard and his band of Cheyennes. What the troopers failed to destroy, the storms of winter did. During the late fall and winter, with their villages in ruins and their people cold and hungry, Kiowas and Cheyennes began to straggle into Forts Sill and Darlington, resigned to accepting reservation life. Satanta, together with Woman's Heart and other Kiowa war chiefs, surrendered at the Darlington Agency on October 7, 1874. Increasing numbers of Indians turned themselves in as the brutal winter wore on.

Apache War, 1876–1886

In 1875, federal officials decided to abolish the four separate Apache reservations that had been established in Arizona and New Mexico and remove all of the Apaches to one large Arizona reservation, at San Carlos. Ordered to the reservation in 1876, about half of the Chiricahua Apaches went, and the remainder scattered into Mexico. The Warm Springs (Ojo Caliente) Apaches were ordered to the reservation the following year. Again, some dispersed, some marched to San Carlos. San Carlos was barren, hot, and disease-ridden. In this place of misery, two militant leaders rose up, Victorio (a Warm Springs Apache chief) and Geronimo (a Chiricahua). Victorio made the first break from San Carlos on September 2, 1877, leading more than 300 Warm Springs Apaches and a few Chiricahuas out of the reservation. For a month, Victorio and his people resisted the pursuing soldiers, but they were finally compelled to surrender at Fort Wingate, New Mexico. After the surrender they were permitted to return to their homeland at Ojo Caliente, there to dwell while the government debated their fate. Within a year they were ordered to return to San Carlos. Most did, but Victorio, together with 80 warriors, made an unsuccessful break for Ojo Caliente. In 1879 he even attempted to settle with the Mescalero Apaches on their reservation, but on September 4 of that year, believing he was about to be arrested, Victorio led 60 warriors in a raid on the camp of Troop E, Ninth Cavalry, at Ojo Caliente. In the engagement, 8 troopers were killed and 46 ponies appropriated. Following this raid, an influx of Mescalero Apaches brought Victorio's strength to some 150 men, who set about terrorizing the Mexican state of Chihuahua, much of western Texas, southern New Mexico, and Arizona. In response, Mexican and U.S. forces cooperated in pursuit of Victorio, who managed to elude them for more than a year. By the fall of 1880, however, Victorio's warriors began to wear out. Colonel George P. Buell united his regular infantry and cavalry with Mexican irregulars commanded by Colonel Joaquin Terrazas to run Victorio to ground in Chihuahua. As it became clear that they were about to make contact with the Indians, Terrazas summarily ordered Buell and his troops out of the country. The honor of destroying Victorio would belong to a *Mexican* officer.

Geronimo, Chiricahua Apache leader of Indian resistance in the Southwest. *Collection: National Archives and Records Administration*

During October 15–16, 1880, Terrazas engaged Victorio at the Battle of Tres Castillos, which resulted in the deaths of seventy-eight Indians, including Victorio and sixteen women and children. It was the end of the period known as "Victorio's Resistance"; however, those who evaded Terrazas made their way back to New Mexico and eventually united with Geronimo in a last-ditch effort to escape confinement at the San Carlos Reservation.

Goyahkla—known to the whites as Geronimo—was one of a number of Apache leaders who frequently gathered at the Ojo Caliente Reservation in New Mexico to organize raids. When authorities realized that the reservation was functioning as a headquarters of resistance, it was ordered closed. Indian agent John P. Clum arrested Geronimo, along with sixteen other leaders, on April 20, 1877.

After a year at San Carlos, Geronimo escaped to Mexico, but again returned to the reservation in 1880, following a long pursuit by Mexican troops. During this second period of his residence on the reservation, a prophet arose among the Apaches, Nakaidoklini, who preached the resurrection of the dead and a return to the halcyon days when the Apaches held sway across the Southwest. Federal officials regarded the prophet and his new Indian religion as dangerous, and on August 30, 1881, Col. Eugene A. Carr, commanding Fort Apache, led 79 regulars, 23 White Mountain Apache scouts, and 9 civilians to seek out Nakaidoklini at his village on Cibicu Creek. After the prophet was arrested, Carr's troops set up camp outside the village. About a hundred followers of Nakaidoklini attacked the encampment. The White Mountain scouts mutinied, killing their captain, a sergeant shot and killed Nakaidoklini, and Carr's command barely escaped the swarm of attackers. No sooner did the soldiers retire to Fort Apache than the Indians attacked them there. The nation's newspapers carried panic headlines announcing that Carr's entire command had been butchered, and army regulars rushed into the San Carlos area from all over the Southwest. Since the Apaches had cut the telegraph lines, Carr was unable to communicate with the outside world until September 4. Sherman was relieved to learn that Carr's command was intact, but the entire incident made Sherman that much more determined to end "this annual Apache stampede."

By the end of September, Naiche—son of the great leader Cochise—the Nednhi chief Juh, the Chiricahua leader Chato, and Geronimo, with seventy-four braves, were again heading for Mexico. On October 2 they fought off pursuing troops under the command of Major General Orlando B. Willcox and then stole across the border, where they united with the survivors of the Battle of Tres Castillos, and fought against Terrazas on October 15–16, 1880. Word reached Willcox that the war leaders planned to enter the United States again in January 1882, to force the Warm Springs Apaches, led by Chief Loco, into an alliance. Willcox alerted all of his border patrols. No incursion was detected, however, until suddenly, on April 19, 1882, an Apache war party, having evaded all patrols, stormed back to San Carlos, killed the reservation police chief, Albert D. Sterling, and compelled Loco, along with several hundred Indians, to return to Mexico with them. On the way back to Mexico, Apache raids killed thirty to fifty whites. Lieutenant Colonel George A. Forsyth, with five troops of the Fourth Cavalry and a unit of scouts, gave chase—without result until April 23, when a patrol found the hostiles holed up in Horseshoe Canyon of the Peloncibbos. Forsyth engaged the warriors, who managed to evade him, killing five troopers and wounding seven. After this, two troops of the Sixth Cavalry under Captain Tullius C. Tupper took up the chase, all the way into the Mexican state of Chihuahua, where, on April 28, they attacked. But the Apaches had dug into defensive positions that were so strong, Tupper exhausted his men as well as his ammunition without doing much damage. Joined by the main body of Forsyth's command, Tupper continued south in pursuit of the enemy. On April 30, Forsyth and Tupper encountered a unit of Mexican infantry commanded by Colonel Lorenzo García. The colonel boasted that his men had succeeded in surprising the Apaches, who were distracted by having to defend against Tupper's pursuit. Garcia claimed to have killed seventy-eight warriors and to have captured thirty-three women and children. With this, the Mexican colonel ordered the American military out of his country.

The next Apache blow was delivered on July 6, 1882, by a White Mountain Apache warrior named Natiotish, a militant partisan of the slain Nakaidoklini. He led a small force back to the San Carlos Reservation, where he killed the new police chief, J. L. "Cibicu Charlie" Colvig, along with three of his deputies. Following this, Natiotish led about sixty White Mountain Apaches in raids throughout the Tonto Basin. No fewer than fourteen troops of cavalry fanned out in search of the renegade. Near General Springs, between Fort Apache and Fort Verde, the White Mountain chief set an ambush, concealing his warriors at the edge of a narrow canyon. His plan was to annihilate a Sixth Cavalry column led by Captain Adna R. Chaffee as it rode through the canyon. On July 17, however, Chaffee's scout, Al Sieber, discovered the ambush. Chaffee's column was then reinforced by two troops from the Third Cavalry and another two from the Sixth, the captain deploying them so they flanked the would-be ambushers. In the resulting Battle of Big Dry Wash, Natiotish suffered losses estimated at sixteen to twenty-seven dead, with many more wounded. The survivors limped back to the reservation, and the White Mountain Apaches' days of raiding were thus ended.

Now the army faced only the Chiricahuas and the Warm Springs Apaches. Led principally by Geronimo, these were, however, formidable adversaries. By this time Sherman had relieved Orlando B. Willcox as commander of the Department of Arizona and replaced him with Brigadier General George Crook (who had commanded the Department of Arizona from 1871 to 1875). Beginning in September 1882, Crook set about his task methodically. He recruited Indian scouts and informants, thereby infiltrating reservation cabals before they developed. Next, armed with a reciprocal treaty signed with Mexico on July 29, 1882, Crook organized an expedition authorized to penetrate far below the border, into the Mexican state of Chihuahua, in pursuit of Geronimo. Crook held off his principal offensive until Apache intermediaries negotiated with the hostiles south of the border. In response to these peace feelers, in March 1883, a pair of Apache raiding parties hit Mexican and American targets.

Geronimo and another warrior, Chihuahua, led a band through Sonora, Mexico, stealing stock, while Chato and the warrior Benito led another band into the United States. On March 21, a total of 25 warriors rampaged through Arizona and New Mexico, killing 11 whites. There would be no more negotiations. Gen. Sherman ordered Crook to move into Mexico immediately. Crook quickly recruited 193 scouts from among the White Mountain Apaches and put them under the command of Captain Emmet Crawford and Lieutenant Charles B. Gatewood. Crook added to these a troop of the Sixth Cavalry under Chaffee and a supply train sufficient to sustain a protracted campaign. These units now pursued Apache raiders into the most remote reaches of Mexico's Sierra Madre. On May 15, 1883, the scouts attacked the encampment of Chato and Benito, killing 9 warriors and destroying 30 lodges. It was a highly significant action, since the Apaches had assumed that their wilderness position was undiscoverable as well as invulnerable. The attack prompted Apache leaders, including Geronimo himself, to negotiate with Crook. Geronimo and the others agreed to return to San Carlos. Geronimo and the other Chiricahuas did not arrive until March 1884, and then they brought great unrest to San Carlos. In May 1885 Geronimo, Naiche, Chihuahua, and old chief Nana, with 134 others, bolted from the reservation and headed again for Mexico. Crook sent two forces into Mexico, one under Captain Crawford and Lieutenant Britton Davis (a troop of men of the Sixth Cavalry and 92 scouts) and another led by Captain Wirt Davis and Lieutenant Matthias W. Day (a troop of Fourth Cavalry and 100 scouts). These units crossed the Mexican border on June 11 and July 13, respectively. Crook also deployed about 3,000 troopers to patrol the border country to keep the Apaches from reentering the United States.

The campaign soon stretched into a long, frustrating pursuit as Geronimo repeatedly eluded Crawford and Davis in Mexico and even managed to slip through Crook's broad 3,000-man net to cross into Arizona and New Mexico, where he terrorized the citizenry. In October 1885 Crook recalled Crawford and Davis to his Fort Bowie headquarters in Apache Pass. There he reequipped them for another foray into Mexico.

Crook boldly sent Crawford at the head of two companies of scouts, not only White Mountain Apaches but also Chiricahuas—members of the very band they were pursuing. Except for two lieutenants, Crawford's command included no regular army personnel at all. Wirt Davis commanded his own scouts, San Carlos–resident Apaches, and a troop of cavalry.

It was Crawford's command that discovered the Apache camp on January 9, 1886, two hundred miles south of the border, in Sonora. But Geronimo and the others fled, and Crawford was left to destroy an abandoned camp. Yet, after running so long, the renegades were tired and sent a squaw to Crawford's camp, with a message that Geronimo was prepared to talk about surrender. A conference was set for January 11. On the morning of that day, however, Captain Crawford was killed by Mexican militiamen. The peace conference was postponed and took place two days later at Canyon de los Embudos, on March 25, 1886. Crook attended personally and offered only two choices: death or two years of exile in the East. After a conference among themselves, the Apaches accepted the latter.

On the way to Fort Bowie, Arizona, the place agreed upon for the formal surrender, Geronimo encountered a whiskey peddler. He imbibed and, thus fortified, bolted, taking twenty men and thirteen women with him. At this point Crook also received a telegram from General Sheridan ordering him to retract the surrender conditions and accept only unconditional surrender. The exhausted and disheartened Crook summarily resigned his command and was replaced by Nelson A. Miles, veteran of the Sioux Wars and a brigadier general as of 1880. Miles sent a strike force under Captain Henry W. Lawton to run Geronimo to ground once and for all. Starting into Mexico on May 5, Lawton's men chased the Apaches through the entire summer of 1886, penetrating Mexico as far as two hundred miles south of the border and traveling a total distance of two thousand miles without once actually engaging the enemy. The pursuit took its toll on Lawton's command, but it was even harder on the Indians. By the end of August, Geronimo was again ready to talk. Geronimo's formal surrender took place at Fort Bowie, and the Apache leaders were sent on their way to imprisonment in Florida. Eventually they were allowed to return to the West, but only as far as a reservation in Indian Territory. Geronimo died at age eighty at Fort Sill, Oklahoma, in 1909.

Sioux War for the Black Hills, 1876–1877

Provoked by continued incursions into their lands, the Sioux of the northern Plains routinely raided settlements in Montana, Wyoming, and Nebraska during the 1870s. In 1874 George Armstrong Custer led a military expedition into the Black Hills and discovered gold. Within a year, in violation of the Treaty of Fort Laramie (April 29, 1868), thousands of prospectors swarmed the Black Hills. The government attempted to purchase or lease the Black Hills, but the Sioux, considering the land sacred, refused to make a deal. At the end of 1875, the federal government stopped negotiating and ordered the Indians to report to an agency and reservation by January 31, 1876, or be hunted and killed as hostiles. When the deadline elapsed, General Sheridan attempted to launch a winter campaign of the kind that had been successful on the southern Plains. The attempt proved abortive. General George Crook did manage to lead 900 men out of Fort Fetterman, on the North Platte River in Wyoming, on March 1, 1876, and, while battling winter storms, searched the Powder

John Gibbon, one of the key commanders in the Indian Wars of the West. *Collection: Library of Congress*

River country for Indians. After three discouraging weeks, he found a trail and dispatched Colonel Joseph J. Reynolds with about 300 cavalry troopers to attack a village of 105 lodges beside the Powder River. Although taken by surprise, the Oglalas, under He Dog, and the Cheyennes, led by Old Bear, counterattacked so effectively that Reynolds was forced to withdraw to Crook and the main column. Crook's truncated winter campaign succeeded only in galvanizing the Sioux into a large and unified fighting force under the inspired leadership of Crazy Horse and Sitting Bull.

Late in the spring of 1876, Sheridan initiated another campaign, intending that General Alfred Terry would lead a force from the east (including Custer and his Seventh Cavalry), Colonel John Gibbon would approach from the west, and Crook was to march out of Fort Fetterman. The plan was to converge on the Yellowstone River, even as the Indians were traveling that way. On the morning of June 17, Crook, with more than a thousand men, halted for a rest at the head of the Rosebud. Crow and Shoshoni scouts attached to

Crook's column sighted Sitting Bull's Sioux and Cheyennes as they descended upon Crook's position. The scouts gave sufficient warning to avert disaster, but even so, the Indians withdrew only after a sharp six-hour fight in which Crook's column took a severe beating before it, too, retreated. After the Battle of the Rosebud, the Sioux established a camp. In the meantime, Terry's column united with that of Colonel Gibbon at the mouth of the Rosebud, both commanders unaware of Crook's retreat. The officers of both commands, including Custer, convened in the cabin of the Yellowstone steamer *Far West* to lay out a campaign strategy.

They believed they would find the Sioux encampment on the stream that the Indians called the Greasy Grass and that white men called the Little Bighorn. What they had no notion of was the size of the camp. Augmented by the arrival of agency Indians, who left the reservation for the spring and summer, the Sioux village now consisted of about seven thousand people. The *Far West* plan called for Custer to lead his Seventh up the Rosebud, cross to the Little Bighorn, then proceed down its valley from the south as Terry and Gibbon marched up the Yellowstone and the Bighorn to block the Indians from the north. In that way Sitting Bull would be caught between the pincers of a two-column flanking operation.

The operation stepped off on the morning of June 22. It was assumed that Custer's highly mobile Seventh Cavalry would be the first to make contact and would therefore begin the fight, driving the Indians against the other column so that the Sioux would be caught between Custer and the forces of Gibbon and Terry. Custer departed from the plan of crossing to the Little Bighorn Valley south of the Indians' position, however, when he determined that the trail was much fresher than anticipated. Indeed, on June 25, Custer's scouts not only discovered a Sioux camp but also warriors nearby. Custer made no attempt to ascertain the number of Indians in and around the camp. His sole focus was to attack before the always elusive enemy could elude him. Custer accordingly led his men across the

George Armstrong Custer, "boy general" of the Civil War, controversial Indian-fighter, and "martyr" at the Battle of the Little Bighorn. *Collection: National Archives and Records Administration*

divide between the Rosebud and the Little Bighorn, dispatching Captain Frederick W. Benteen with three troops, 125 men, to the south to make sure the Sioux had not moved into the upper valley of the Little Bighorn. As Custer approached the Little Bighorn River, he spotted about 40 warriors and sent Major Marcus A. Reno, with another three troops, after them. Neither Custer nor his superiors had any idea of just how many warriors they were going up against. Later estimates put the number at 1,500 to 6,000. Whatever the precise number, Custer's combined strength of 600 was greatly outmatched. Moreover, his force had been divided.

Reno's squadron of 112 men, in pursuit of the 40 warriors seen earlier, was soon engulfed by masses of Sioux. Custer and his command joined the fight, still unaware of how badly outnumbered they were. Warriors led by the Hunkpapa chief Gall surged across the Little Bighorn, pushing the troopers back. As Gall pressed from the south, Crazy Horse pushed in from the north. Within an hour, Custer and his men had been killed. Benteen united with a remnant of Reno's command as it withdrew from the Bighorn Valley. The combined forces of Reno and Benteen—368 officers and men—dug in along the bluffs and fought off a day-long siege. On the next day, June 26, the siege was renewed, but was lifted as Terry and Gibbon approached. Casualties among the commands of Reno and Benteen were heavy, but the fate of Custer had been disastrous: 200 mutilated corpses were strewn over the Little Bighorn battlefield.

In the wake of Custer's defeat, Congress authorized an increase in the army's strength and gave to the military control of the Sioux agencies. But the Custer disaster seemed to dispirit the army, and except for the Battle of Slim Buttes, September 9, there was little attempt to engage the Indians until November, when the Fourth Cavalry's Ranald Mackenzie won a significant victory in the Bighorn Mountains against a Cheyenne band led by Dull Knife and Little Wolf. With eleven hundred troopers and Indian scouts out of Fort Fetterman, Mackenzie surprised a village of two hundred lodges in a canyon of the Powder River's Red Fork on November 25. About four hundred warriors defended the village in fierce combat, but by the afternoon Mackenzie took the village, destroyed provisions, and appropriated seven hundred fine ponies. He also recovered scalps, uniforms, and equipment—the grim souvenirs of Custer's defeat at the Little Bighorn. Mackenzie lost one officer and five enlisted men, and sustained twenty-six wounded. Forty Cheyenne were killed in the Battle of Red Fork, but far more suffered and died, provisionless and without shelter, in the below-zero cold that followed combat. Casualties among the scouts are unrecorded, but doubtless they paid a heavy toll.

Indian scouts were essential to the success of military operations in the West, but they also easily fell out of military control. After the November 25 battle, a delegation of Cheyenne, Miniconjou, and Sans Arc chiefs came to talk peace with Colonel Nelson A. Miles. They approached his Tongue River cantonment on December 16, only to be attacked by Crow scouts, who killed five. Miles sent the Sioux the Crows' ponies as atonement and apology, but the incident had been enough to discredit the peace faction among the assembled Sioux, and the Indians harried the Tongue River cantonment throughout the balance of the month. In response to this action, Miles took five companies of the Fifth Infantry and two of the Twenty-second—about 350 men and two artillery pieces—up the Tongue Valley in search of the hostiles. The Indians made it easy for Miles to find them, for they were lying in ambush. As often happened, however, the young warriors could not be restrained from acting prematurely, and on January 7, 1877, Miles's scouts captured a party of Cheyenne women and children. About 200 warriors attempted to recover them; they not only failed in this, they also alerted Miles to the presence of the much larger party of warriors who waited in ambush. Miles was thus prepared for the 500 Sioux and Cheyenne, led by Crazy Horse, who attacked his camp the next day. The Battle of Wolf Mountain was fought in a severe snowstorm, which hampered the attackers more than the soldiers, and when it was over, Miles was able to boast that he had "taught the destroyers of Custer that there was one small command that could whip them as long as they dared face it."

Following Wolf Mountain, Sitting Bull decided to take his Hunkpapa Sioux north into Canada. The Miniconjous, Oglalas, Sans Arcs, and Cheyennes dispersed widely. In early April, however, large groups of Cheyennes surrendered to officials at the Indian agencies. Crazy Horse brought the Oglalas to the Red Cloud Agency and surrendered.

The Sioux War for the Black Hills was by no means over. Fifty-one lodges of Miniconjous under Lame Deer, having vowed never to surrender, made for the Rosebud to hunt buffalo. Miles gathered a squadron of Second Cavalry together with six companies of infantry and, on May 1, marched up the Tongue River in search of Lame Deer. Leaving behind the slow-moving infantry, Miles took four cavalry troops west and, on May 7, acting on information from his scouts, surprised Lame Deer's camp on a

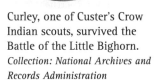

Curley, one of Custer's Crow Indian scouts, survived the Battle of the Little Bighorn. *Collection: National Archives and Records Administration*

Rosebud tributary called Muddy Creek. One of Miles's scouts, the Mini-conjou Hump, until recently an adversary of the army, persuaded Lame Deer and his head warrior, Iron Star, to give up. Shaken by the presence of Hump, the two Indians laid their rifles down and approached Miles and his adjutant, George W. Baird. The tension, however, was great, and when a scout rode up, drawing his rifle on Lame Deer and Iron Star, apparently intending nothing more than to keep them covered, the two Indians went for their own weapons. Lame Deer fired at Miles, who dodged the shot (which killed an unfortunate cavalryman behind him), and the soldiers then opened fire, killing Lame Deer. Iron Star fell next. And so the brief Battle of Muddy Creek ended with fourteen Sioux dead, including the chief and the head warrior. Among the troopers, four enlisted died, and another seven were wounded. The general pursued the fleeing Sioux to the Rosebud before returning to burn the village and appropriate the ponies.

Gall, one of the Sioux battle leaders at the Little Bighorn. *Collection: National Archives and Records Administration*

Throughout the summer, a series of skirmishes followed, but the greatest threat to the uneasy peace was Crazy Horse, who proved on the reservation to be an "incorrigible wild man, silent, sullen, lordly, and dictatorial," as the Indian agent described him. Fearing that he would stir a general revolt, Crook ordered his arrest and confinement. Taken into custody on September 5, 1877, he was stabbed to death in a scuffle involving soldiers and Indians.

The Northern Cheyennes reported to the Cheyenne and Arapaho Agency in Indian Territory during August 1877, but they hated the reservation and fared poorly on it during the winter of 1877–1878. On September 7, 1878, Dull Knife and Little Wolf led three hundred Northern Cheyennes in a break for the north. A combination of regular army troops and citizen volunteers pursued the fugitives in a campaign that came to be called the Pursuit of the Northern Cheyennes. As they fled with their people, the two chiefs fell to quarreling, and the fugitive band was divided between them, Dull Knife's faction surrendering to soldiers at Camp Robinson on October 23, 1878, and Little Wolf's continuing northward. Dull Knife's group, held in the barracks at Camp Robinson, in the northwestern corner of Nebraska, refused to return to Indian Territory. The camp commandant, Captain

Henry W. Wessells Jr., cut off all food and water in an attempt to force their departure south. After a week of thirst and starvation, the Indians made a break for it on the night of January 9, 1879. About half of Dull Knife's people were shot down before the government, bowing to public pressure, granted the remainder their wish to live with the Sioux at the Pine Ridge Reservation in southwestern Dakota Territory.

As for Little Wolf, he and his faction kept ahead of the army throughout the long winter. Exhausted, they finally surrendered on March 29, 1879, at the Little Missouri River. Five years later, in 1884, the Tongue River Reservation was established in southeastern Montana, which gave the Northern Cheyenne a homeland they found livable.

Sitting Bull remained in Canada with approximately four thousand Hunkpapa, Oglala, Miniconjou, Sans Arc, and Blackfoot Sioux as well as a handful of Nez Percés. In October 1877, General Terry, with the cooperation of the Canadian Northwest Mounted Police, located Sitting Bull in Canada and attempted to persuade him to come back to a reservation in the United States. Sitting Bull rebuffed Terry, but on July 19, 1881, he traveled with them to Fort Buford, in northwestern Dakota Territory, where he at last surrendered.

Sitting Bull (Tatonka-I-Yatanka), Hunkpapa Sioux, was perhaps the most universally revered Indian leader at the close of the Indian Wars. *Collection: National Archives and Records Administration*

Nez Perce War, 1877

The Nez Perce tribe lived in and about the Wallowa Valley of Washington. The tribe became sharply divided into "treaty" and "nontreaty" factions after an 1863 gold rush prompted the revision of an existing treaty that excluded the mineral-rich lands from the reservation. Those Indians whose homes remained within the revised boundaries—about a hundred warriors and fifty women led by White Bird—signed the revised document and agreed to sell the excluded lands; those who were dispossessed by the revision refused to sign. Most prominent among the latter was the venerable Chief Joseph, who repudiated the treaty and lived with his people in the Wallowa Valley, now deemed to be outside of the reservation. Despite this, few whites were interested in the Wallowa Valley, and Joseph was left in peace. Indeed, in 1873, two years after Joseph's death, President Grant even set aside part of the Wallowa Valley as a legitimate reservation. At about this time, however, Oregon settlers began to pressure the Grant administration into reopening the tract to white settlement. When Young Joseph, who had become chief after the death of his father, refused to vacate the disputed land, General Oliver O. Howard warned the Indians that they had one month to move to the reservation or be driven off by force. Young Joseph and the other chiefs knew that war would be fruitless, and so, with their people, they marched off to the reservation. However, a group of young warriors killed four whites notorious for their abuse of Indians. Joseph and his brother Ollikut tried to persuade their people that the best course now was to explain to authorities that the killings had not been sanctioned by the tribal council, but the diehard nontreaty Indians decided instead to flee south toward the Salmon River, killing fifteen more settlers.

Chief Joseph the Younger, leader of the Nez Perce resistance. *Collection: National Archives and Records Administration*

Howard dispatched a hundred cavalrymen under Captain David Perry out of Fort Lapwai. Locals persuaded Perry to make a forced night march to intercept the Nez Perces before they reached the mountains beyond the Salmon River. At dawn on June 17, Perry's exhausted command arrived at White Bird Canyon. Chief Joseph now sent a delegation of Nez Perces to Perry under a flag of truce, intending to talk peace. Perry had picked up a handful of civilian volunteers, and these undisciplined men were the first to encounter the truce party. Ignoring the white flag, they opened fire. The Indians responded by firing against Perry's front and both flanks, routing Perry's command and killing thirty-three men and one officer.

On June 22, Howard mustered about four hundred men to bottle up the Indians in White Bird Canyon. Settlers convinced Howard that Chief Looking Glass, whose village was near the forks of the Clearwater, was planning to join the hostiles. Howard sent Captain Stephen G. Whipple with two troops of cavalry and a pair of Gatling guns, together with a band of local volunteers, to surprise the village. Whipple discovered, however, that Looking Glass advocated neutrality, and the captain decided to open talks with him. The civilian volunteers provoked a fight, however, and on July 1, the regulars had to use the Gatling guns against the village, sending forty warriors and their families fleeing for their lives—and instantly converting Looking Glass into a militant. Ten days of pursuit and attack followed the July 1 Gatling gun onslaught, through which the Indians gained the advantage. On July 9–10 they held a force of volunteers under siege at a place the would-be pursuers dubbed Mount Misery. The siege, while hard on the civilian volunteers, also occupied the Indians long enough for Howard to bring his main force undetected to the rear of the Nez Perces.

On July 11, the Battle of Clearwater began. After a bloody two-day combat, the Indians were driven from the field, but, exhausted by the desperate battle, Howard failed to pursue the scattering bands and, as a result, lost an opportunity to bring the war with the Nez Perces to an immediate conclusion. It was not until August 9 that the army again made contact with the Nez Perces, when Colonel John Gibbon, leading 15 officers, 146 enlisted regulars, and 45 volunteers, surprised a camp on the Big Hole River, Montana. Under the leadership of Looking Glass, the Indians quickly rallied and counterattacked, killing two of Gibbon's officers, 22 regulars, and 6 civilians, and wounding 5 more officers, 30 enlisted men, and 4 civilians. Indian losses were also heavy—at least 89 dead—but Gibbon was sent limping back to his station as the Nez Perces fled about 100 miles, killing 9 whites, seizing 250 horses, and raiding a wagon train before they entered the newly established Yellowstone National Park. Here they produced great panic among the tourists.

O. O. Howard, who lost his right arm in the Civil War, led the pursuit of the Nez Perce. *From* Harper's Pictorial History of the Civil War, *1866*

Howard, along with the Seventh Cavalry under Colonel Samuel D. Sturgis, gave chase, attempting to block the Indians' escape. But the Indians evaded both Howard and Sturgis. On August 19, 200 warriors skirmished with troopers on the Camas Meadows, and on September 13, the Seventh Cavalry engaged the Nez Perces at the site of present-day Billings, Montana. Sturgis lost 3 men killed and had 11 wounded. The Nez Perces sought refuge among the Crows, only to discover that Crow scouts had been fighting on the side of Howard. The Nez Perces determined, therefore, to flee to Canada, to join Sitting Bull. However, they rested just 40 miles south of the Canadian border, on the northern edge of the Bear Paw Mountains. There, on September 30, with 350 to 400 men, Nelson A. Miles attacked.

The Battle of Bear Paw Mountain stretched into six snowy, frigid days, September 30–October 5. On October 5, Looking Glass was struck in the head by a stray bullet. At this, Joseph went to Miles and surrendered: "Hear me, my chiefs! I am tired; my heart is sick and sad. From where the sun now stands I will fight no more forever." With this declaration, the pursuit of the Nez Perces ended. During three months, 800 Indians had traveled more than 1,700 miles of some of the most rugged terrain on the continent. About 120 died. Despite years of petitioning the federal government for permission to return to the Wallowa Valley, Joseph and his people were consigned to the Colville Reservation, Washington, where Joseph died in 1904.

Bannock War, 1878

Buffalo Horn, an important chief among the Bannocks of Idaho, had served as an army scout during the just-concluded war with the Nez Perces. Recently Buffalo Horn had been acquiring a significant following among the Bannocks and their neighbors, the Northern Paiutes. Beginning in the mid-1870s, white incursions into Buffalo Horn's land were depleting game as well as the native camas roots, a staple food the Indians dug on Camas Prairie, about ninety miles southeast of Boise, Idaho. So important was this wild crop that the right to dig for its roots was guaranteed by solemn treaty. Lately, however, settlers' hogs had been uprooting the camas. When the Indians complained, the reservation agencies, as usual, failed to respond. This led to war on May 30, 1878, when a Bannock shot and wounded two whites. Convinced that he and his people would be punished regardless of whatever gestures of conciliation they might make, Buffalo Horn, with about two hundred warriors, including Northern Paiutes and Umatillas in addition to some Bannocks, raided southern Idaho. The foray resulted in the deaths of ten whites, and Buffalo Horn's rampage continued until June 8, when a party of civilian volunteers killed the chief in a skirmish near Silver City, southwest of Boise.

Leaderless now, Buffalo Horn's warriors rode to Steens Mountain, in

Oregon, where they found Northern Paiutes who, on June 5, had followed a militant medicine man named Oytes and a chief called Egan off the Malheur Reservation. They struck an ad hoc alliance that fielded about 450 warriors against a slightly larger number of soldiers led by General O. O. Howard. Howard dogged the Bannocks (as the mixed group was indiscriminately dubbed) relentlessly. From the end of June through the first week of July, the Indians stayed ahead of Howard, pausing only to skirmish with his troopers from time to time and to raid the luckless ranches that lay in their path. On July 8 Captain Reuben F. Bernard, leading seven troops of cavalry, discovered the Indian position on high bluffs along Birch Creek near Pilot Butte. Bernard attacked uphill, flanking the Indians. Exhausted by battle, however, Bernard's troopers were unable to give chase when the Indians bolted.

After the Battle of Birch Creek, Oytes, Egan, and their followers moved south, presumably to find refuge and allies among the Nez Perces. In response, Howard deployed his forces to block them. This prompted Oytes and Egan to turn to the north again, in the direction of the Umatilla Reservation. Captain Evan Miles arrived at the reservation on July 12, leading a substantial force of infantry, artillery, and a troop of cavalry. A battle took place on July 13, fought mostly at long range for the first six hours, until Miles ordered an advance that pushed the hostiles into the mountains to the east. On the July 15, local Umatillas took an active role in the conflict—on the side of the army. A party of Umatillas approached the Bannocks and the Paiutes on pretense of joining them. Instead, they tricked Chief Egan into coming away from his warriors, and then they killed him, presenting his scalp to Captain Miles as a trophy. After this, the Bannock-Paiute force began to disintegrate. Small groups of Northern Paiutes scattered across southeastern Oregon, and the Bannocks began to move back toward Idaho, raiding along the way. By August the Paiutes were caving in, and on August 12, Oytes surrendered. Many of the Bannocks followed a month later, fighting their last engagement in Wyoming on September 12, 1878.

Sheepeater War, 1879

The Bannock War was typical of white-Indian combat in the Far West. Battle casualties were modest—nine troopers dead, fifteen wounded, at least seventy-eight Indians slain—but long exposure to harsh elements had been physically and emotionally draining. And even after Oytes and Egan surrendered, some Bannocks took refuge among the Sheepeaters— a collective name for renegade Shoshonis and Bannocks in the Salmon River Mountains of Idaho. Either the Sheepeaters or their fugitive guests or both raided a prospectors' camp on Loon Creek, killing five Chinese miners in May 1879. In response, Howard dispatched Captain Reuben Bernard with a troop of the First Cavalry and Lieutenant Henry Catley with fifty mounted men of the Second Infantry, as well as twenty Indian scouts, to search out the murderers. The result was the Sheepeater War, waged against a mere handful of warriors, perhaps no more than thirty-five, but also waged against the inhospitable terrain of the Idaho mountains.

Catley failed to make contact with the Indians until July 29, when his command was ambushed by fifteen warriors. This small group successfully bottled up the troopers in Big Creek Canyon. They took up a position on Vinegar Hill, from which they tried to burn the troopers out. Catley, however, skillfully defended his men by setting backfires, which arrested the spread of the Indians' blazes, then abandoned all baggage and supplies so that he could steal out of the canyon with his fifty men. General Howard responded to this escape with by court-martialing Catley on a charge of "precipitate retreat before inferior numbers." His conviction was subsequently overturned by presidential order.

On August 13, 1879, Bernard's cavalry joined what had been Catley's infantry—augmented by an additional twenty-five men and now commanded by Captain Albert G. Forse—and the Indian scouts. The combined forces set out for the scene of Catley's humiliation. On August 19, Bernard's Umatilla scouts captured the contents of a Sheepeater camp— which included much that Catley had abandoned—but the warriors themselves were nowhere to be seen. On August 20 the Sheepeaters attacked the army's supply train. They were driven off, but the soldiers were too exhausted to give chase. At this, Howard called off the campaign as fruitless.

In September, Lieutenant Edward S. Farrow, who had commanded the scouts in the August campaign, set out again with the Umatillas. They captured two women and two children on September 21 and came upon an abandoned Sheepeater camp the next day. From one of the captured women they learned that the warriors were worn out and could not endure much more pursuit. Of course, neither could Farrow, but he kept up the pressure through the end of the month, when a four-day storm brought great misery to both sides. During October 1–2, fifty-one Sheepeaters (warriors as well as women and children) and a few Bannocks surrendered to Farrow. Most of the Bannocks, however, had vanished. Presumably they found refuge on the Lemhi Reservation. The Sheepeaters were confined for the winter to Fort Vancouver, Washington, and subsequently installed on the Fort Hall Reservation in Idaho.

Ute War, 1879

To the south of the Bannocks and the Northern Paiutes were the Utes of western Colorado and eastern Utah. A silver mining boom during the 1870s brought miners to the region, who persuaded the government of Colorado to invade what remained of the Ute reservation in that state and to force the removal of the Utes to Indian Territory. In the meantime, seeking to bring his Ute charges firmly under control, the Indian agent at White River, Nathan C. Meeker, attempted to convert these traditionally free-ranging people into farmers. He demanded that the reservation Utes plow up their ponies' grazing land. On September 10, 1879, a Ute medicine man known as Johnson complained to Meeker that plowing the grazing lands would starve the horses. Meeker replied: "You have too many ponies. You had better kill some of them." In response, either Johnson or a leader known as Chief Douglas threw the elderly Meeker out of his own front door. The agent urgently telegraphed military authorities for aid. Major Thomas T. "Tip" Thornburgh, commanding a mixed unit of 153 infantry and cavalrymen supplemented by an additional 25 civilians volunteers, was ordered to Meeker's relief. The news that troops had been summoned stirred the Utes to greater hostility. Realizing the gravity of the crisis he had created, Meeker asked Thornburgh to halt his column and approach the agency with only 5 soldiers for a parley. The talks were arranged, but at the last minute Thornburgh decided to move 120 cavalrymen closer to the agency as a precaution. The Utes interpreted this as a prelude to attack, and on September 25, as the Indians and the soldiers faced one another, the major's adjutant waved his hat. Presumably it was intended as a greeting, but someone—either an Indian or a soldier—took it for a signal, and a shot was fired. With this, the Battle of Milk Creek began. Thornburgh was among the first slain. The troopers retreated across Milk Creek, where they hunkered down behind their wagon train, which had been defensively circled up. By the end of the first day of battle, 11 solders lay dead and 23 were wounded; 23 Utes also were slain.

Combat stretched into a week-long siege. On October 2, two of the defenders were able to sneak through the Indian lines and summon reinforcements. Captain Francis Dodge arrived with a unit of African American troopers ("Buffalo Soldiers") but failed to break the siege—all of Dodge's ponies rapidly fell victim to Indian sharpshooters. When Colonel Wesley Merritt arrived on October 5 with a large contingent of cavalry and infantry, the Utes backed off, and the siege was lifted. Back at the agency, during the battle and the siege, Meeker and nine other agency employees were killed and the agency buildings burned. Mrs. Meeker, her daughter, and another woman and her two children were taken captive. Generals Sherman and Sheridan favored a vigorous campaign of punishment, even if it meant death for the captive women; however, Secretary of the Interior Carl Schurz, an Indian agent named Charles Adams, and an old Ute chief named Ouray managed by October 21 to negotiate the release of the captives without further bloodshed. By 1880 Chief Ouray agreed to lead the Utes to reservations in eastern Utah and southwestern Colorado.

Sioux War, 1890–1891

By the mid-1880s, with the arrest of Geronimo, the epoch of the Indian Wars had come to an end. Now almost a quarter of a million Indians were confined to reservations. Presiding over the Hunkpapa Sioux at the Standing Rock Reservation on the South Dakota–North Dakota border, Sitting Bull refused to cooperate with the agent in charge and did all he could to avoid contact with the white world. In the meantime, from out of the misery of reservation life in the late 1880s, there arose a prophet, a Paiute shaman's son named Wovoka, who preached of a new world coming, one in which only Indians dwelled and in which buffalo were again plentiful. To hasten this deliverance, Wovoka preached that all Indians must dance the Ghost Dance and, most important, must observe absolute peace. Soon many of the western reservations were alive with Ghost Dancing. Among the Teton Sioux, however, Wovoka's commandment to peace was suppressed. Short Bull and Kicking Bear, Teton apostles of the Ghost Dance religion, openly urged a militant campaign to obliterate the white man.

With or without the hostility, the Ghost Dance activity alarmed white authorities. On November 20, 1890, cavalry and infantry reinforcements arrived at the Pine Ridge and Rosebud Reservations. This motivated some three thousand Indians to gather on a plateau (dubbed the Stronghold) at the northwestern corner of the Pine Ridge Reservation. Over the protest of Standing Rock Indian agent James McLaughlin, General Nelson A. Miles decided to bring in the greatest showman the West had ever known, Buffalo Bill Cody, to persuade Sitting Bull to give himself up. Sitting Bull had been featured in Cody's Wild West Show, and Miles understood that Cody was the only white man Sitting Bull trusted; however, McLaughlin believed that the showman would attract too much attention and possibly trigger a general uprising. He kept Buffalo Bill occupied in a saloon until he could secure orders canceling Cody's mission. That accomplished, McLaughlin, on December 15, 1890, dispatched forty-three reservation policemen to arrest Sitting Bull before he could leave Standing Rock. During the arrest, a scuffle developed, and Sitting Bull was shot in the chest. Seeing that the chief had been severely wounded, reservation police sergeant Red Tomahawk decided to administer the *coup de grâce:* He shot Sitting Bull in the back of the head. The Ghost Dancers now had a martyr.

In addition to Sitting Bull, Nelson Miles had another important

Big Foot, chief of the Miniconjou Lakota Sioux, was among the slain at the Wounded Knee massacre.
Collection: Library of Congress

Ghost Dance leader to contend with. Big Foot was the central chief of the Miniconjou Sioux, who were living on the Cheyenne River. Unknown to Miles, Big Foot had recently renounced the Ghost Dance religion as futile. Miles was also unaware that Chief Red Cloud, a Pine Ridge leader friendly to the whites, had asked Big Foot to come to the reservation to use his influence to persuade the Stronghold party to surrender. Miles knew only that Big Foot was headed for the Stronghold, and he assumed that Big foot's intention was to join the other hostiles. Miles deployed troopers across the prairies and badlands to intercept all Miniconjous and, in particular, Big Foot. A squadron of the Seventh Cavalry located the chief and about 350 followers on December 28, 1890, camped near a stream called Wounded Knee. By the morning of December 29, 500 soldiers, under Colonel James W. Forsyth, surrounded Big Foot's camp. Four Hotchkiss guns—small, rapid-fire howitzers—were trained on the camp from the surrounding hills. Forsyth was to disarm the Indians and take them to the railroad so they could be removed from the "zone of military operations." In the process of disarming them, resistance broke out. Although few of the Indians were now armed, both sides opened fire, and the Indians began to flee. To contain them, the Hotchkiss guns opened up on the camp, firing at the rate of almost a round a second. In less than an hour the "Battle" of Wounded Knee was over. Big Foot and 153 other Miniconjous were known to have been killed. So many others staggered, limped, or crawled away that it is impossible to determine just how many died. Most authorities believe that 300 of the 350 who had been camped at Wounded Knee Creek lost their lives. Casualties among the Seventh Cavalry were 25 killed and 39 wounded, mostly victims of "friendly fire."

The Wounded Knee Massacre prompted "hostile" and hitherto "friendly" Sioux factions to unite in a December 30 ambush of the Seventh Cavalry near the Pine Ridge Agency. Elements of the Ninth Cavalry came to the rescue, and General Miles subsequently marshaled thirty-five hundred troops (of a total force of five thousand) around the Sioux, who had assembled fifteen miles north of the Pine Ridge Agency along White Clay Creek. Miles gradually contracted a ring of troopers around the Indians. It soon became clear even to the most resolute of the Sioux gathered at White Clay Creek that their cause was hopeless. On January 15, 1891, the Sioux formally surrendered, and the epoch of the Indian Wars ended.

CHAPTER 10

Spanish–American War and Other Imperialist Conflicts

The *United States–Mexican War, 1846–1848 (see chapter 6)* was extravagantly popular with many Americans, especially those in the South and the West, but was vehemently opposed by others, especially New Englanders, who decried the conflict as an exercise in blatant imperialism at the expense of Mexico. Except for the war with Mexico, however—and the Central American "filibustering" of an American citizen named William Walker—the United States avoided imperialist adventures until the very end of the nineteenth century. In his celebrated (and, today, largely scorned) 1893 essay "The Significance of the Frontier in American History," Frederick Jackson Turner concluded that the United States had no need to pursue empires abroad as long as vast western spaces existed to be conquered within the continent. Once the frontier was essentially settled, however, the free land divided and parceled out, the nation, Turner declared, would turn outward, to seek empire beyond the continent. Whether or not we accept Turner's thesis, the fact is the United States did launch upon an unprecedented series of imperialist wars in the Carribean, in Central America, in the Philippines, and even in China at the end of the nineteenth century and the beginning of the twentieth.

Walker's Invasion of Mexico, 1853–1854

William Walker was born on May 8, 1824, into a well-to-do Nashville, Tennessee, family. At age fourteen, Walker became one of the youngest men ever to graduate from the University of Nashville, and his parents hoped he would follow a career in the ministry, but he decided instead to become a physician and, in 1843, graduated from the University of Pennsylvania Medical School, then returned to Nashville to set up his practice. His medical career was short-lived, however. The restless young doctor soon left Nashville to enroll in the University of Edinburgh and then embarked on a tour of much of Western Europe. He subsequently returned to Nashville but was quickly off again, this time to New Orleans, where he studied law and was admitted to the Louisiana bar. In 1848, at age twenty-four, he embraced yet a *third* occupation, that of journalist, and joined the great gold-driven migration to California, where he became the editor of a San Francisco newspaper.

It was during his California days that Walker became obsessed with the idea of personally liberating the Mexican state of Sonora and establishing an independent American colony there. The charismatic and intense Walker recruited a ragtag army of forty-five men and, on the pretext of defending Mexicans from Apache raids, sailed from San Francisco on October 15, 1853, on a "filibustering" expedition, a private military action in a foreign country. He and his followers landed at La Paz, Baja California, and on November 3, 1853, summarily proclaimed the creation of a republic there, with himself as president. Next, on January 18, 1854, he announced the annexation of the Mexican state of Sonora. The response of Mexican authorities was a series of attacks on the invaders, which, within a few months, forced Walker and his followers to flee. In May 1854 Walker surrendered to U.S. authorities at the U.S.–Mexican border near San Diego. He was tried for having violated U.S. neutrality laws, but popular opinion actually approved of his filibustering, and the jury refused to convict him. Acquitted, Walker found that his appetite had been whetted for an even grander venture, an invasion of Nicaragua.

Walker's Invasion of Nicaragua, 1855–1857

During the mid-1850s, Nicaragua was ripe for revolution. Internal strife and a power struggle among several leaders had torn the country apart, and William Walker *(see Walker's Invasion of Mexico, 1853–1854)* resolved to take advantage of the situation. Late in 1854 he obtained a contract from the currently prevailing government of Nicaragua, allowing him to bring to that country approximately three hundred colonists to settle a land grant of fifty thousand acres. In return, Walker and his American colonists would be liable for military service for Nicaragua, for which they would receive monthly compensation from the Nicaraguan government. Walker legitimated his operation by subjecting the papers concerning it to review by the U.S. attorney at San Francisco and by the commander of the Pacific Division of the U.S. Army.

The "Gray-Eyed Man of Destiny," together with fifty-six or fifty-eight followers, arrived at Realejo, Nicaragua, on June 1, 1855. Walker and the others—grandiosely self-styled the "American Phalanx"—were immediately absorbed into the Nicaraguan army as a unit under Walker's direct command. The American Phalanx captured an American steamer plying the waters of Lake Nicaragua and then took the town of Granada. Walker's victories earned him popular acclaim and, incredibly enough, election as president of Nicaragua in July 1856. Even the U.S. government recognized the legitimacy of the election, at least briefly. However, Walker soon antagonized neighboring Central American states as well as U.S. business interests (especially those of shipping magnate Cornelius Vanderbilt) by interfering with schemes to build a canal across Nicaragua. In autumn 1856 a band of Costa Ricans led by Juan Rafael Mora invaded Nicaragua and captured the towns of San Juan del Sur and Rivas, as well as the road along the proposed canal route. The president of Guatemala, Rafael Carrera, also sent troops into Nicaragua and, with the help of Salvadoran volunteers and Nicaraguan conservatives, laid siege to Granada. Although Walker successfully appealed to America for volunteer reinforcements, the U.S. government prevented their departure. Walker's forces were depleted by an epidemic of cholera, and he evacuated Granada for Rivas. There he was held under siege for several weeks by the Costa Rican troops. At last, on May 1, 1857, Walker sought asylum by surrendering to U.S. Navy commander Charles Henry Davis aboard the USS *St. Mary's*.

Walker could not resist attempting to regain power in Nicaragua and returned several times before the end of the 1850s. Arrested at the end of 1857, he was deported. In 1860 he landed in Honduras rather than directly in Nicaragua, only to be arrested by British authorities, who turned him over to the Honduran army. Condemned by a court-martial, he was executed at Trujillo.

Philippine Insurrection, 1896–1898

Although the U.S. military was only peripherally involved in the 1896–1898 insurrection, the conflict created conditions of great importance in the *Spanish-American War, 1898* and the *Philippine Insurrection, 1899–1902,* both of which deeply involved the United States.

The Philippines had long languished under oppressive and corrupt Spanish colonial rule when Andres Bonifácio created the Katipunan, a secret society dedicated to the overthrow of Spain in the Philippines. When Spanish authorities discovered the existence of the Katipunan, Bonifácio decided that the only alternative to extinction of the independence movement was an immediate revolution, which he proclaimed on August 26, 1889. At first, Spanish troops quickly triumphed over the rebels, who were pushed back into the northern part of the island of Luzon. But in 1896, when colonial officials arrested, tried, and executed José Rizal, the charismatic writer who had been a founding father of the independence movement, a revolutionary martyr was born. Rebel resistance become stronger and more effective, and a full-scale insurrection began.

Within the independence movement rival factions organized themselves around Bonifácio and Emilio Aguinaldo, the mayor of Cavite Province on the island of Luzon. Ruthless and determined, Aguinaldo accused Bonifácio of treason and had him shot, thereby concentrating power with himself and focusing most of the fighting in and around Cavite. By the end of 1897, Spanish government forces had regained control of most of Cavite, but at considerable cost. The rebels and Spain concluded the Pact of Biak-na-bato, which brought a temporary end to the insurrection, and Aguinaldo, with other rebel leaders, accepted voluntary exile in Hong Kong, along with 400,000 pesos and a Spanish pledge to introduce liberal reforms into the government of the Philippines.

When the Spanish failed to introduce the promised reforms, Aguinaldo returned to the Philippines on May 19, 1898, after the U.S. Navy destroyed the Spanish fleet in Manila Bay during the *Spanish-American War, 1898.* With U.S. backing, Aguinaldo organized a Filipino army that cooperated with American troops in defeating the Spanish on the islands.

Aguinaldo declared Philippine independence from Spain on June 12, 1898, but Spain ceded the islands to the United States for $20 million as a condition of the Treaty of Paris (December 10, 1898). This became the cause of the *Philippine Insurrection, 1899–1902,* in which Aguinaldo led a revolt against U.S. rule of the islands.

Spanish-American War, 1898

From the American perspective, the *Philippine Insurrection, 1896–1898* was ancillary to a confrontation with Spain closer to home, in Cuba, off the coast of Florida. A Spanish colony, Cuba had long been rebellious when, in February 1896, Spain authorized General Valeriano Weyler to govern the island and restore order there. Among the general's first acts was to establish "reconcentration camps" for the incarceration of rebels as well as other citizens accused of supporting or even sympathizing with the rebels. Although both U.S. presidents Grover Cleveland and his successor, William McKinley, stoutly resisted U.S. intervention in Cuba, American popular sentiment, whipped up by atrocity stories published in the papers of Joseph Pulitzer and William Randolph Hearst, at last moved McKinley to order the battleship *Maine* into Havana Harbor to protect American citizens and property there.

The onset of war fever in the United States was not exclusively caused by a humanitarian concern for the suffering Cubans. By the late nineteenth century, large U.S. business concerns had made major investments in the island, especially in sugar plantations. Revolutionary unrest posed a threat to these investments; however, a successful revolution, if properly supported by the United States, could create an independent Cuban government that, beholden to the United States, was nevertheless pliant and willing to make provisions favorable to business. Alternatively, Cuba might even be annexed to the United States.

War Begins
On February 9, 1898, Hearst scored a journalistic coup by publishing a purloined private letter in which the Spanish minister to the United States

CHRONOLOGY   Principal Events of the Spanish-American War

1898

January 25: *Battleship* Maine *arrives in Havana*

February 9: *The letter of a Spanish diplomat insulting President William McKinley is published, outraging Americans*

February 15: *The* Maine *explodes, killing 266 crewmen*

March 21: *Naval Board of Inquiry concludes the* Maine *was lost to a Spanish mine*

March 26: *McKinley sends note to Spain, demanding an end to war in Cuba*

March 31: *Spain rejects U.S. demands for Cuban independence*

April 11: *McKinley asks Congress for war*

April 16: *Teller Amendment passes in U.S. Congress, forbidding U.S. annexation of Cuba*

April 19: *U.S. Congress declares Cuba independent*

April 22: *U.S. naval blockade of Cuba begins; first Spanish ship captured*

April 23: *Spain declares war*

April 25: *U.S. declares war, retroactive to April 22*

May 1: *U.S. Navy's Asiatic Squadron (Commodore Dewey) defeats the Spanish Pacific Squadron at the Battle of Manila Bay*

May 12: *U.S. Navy bombards San Juan, Puerto Rico, without warning*

May 15: *Theodore Roosevelt begins training with the Rough Riders*

May 25: *McKinley issues a call for seventy-five thousand more volunteers. The first army expedition leaves San Francisco for Manila, P.I.*

June 10: *U.S. Marines land at Guantánamo Bay in Cuba*

June 21: *Guam taken peacefully by U.S. forces*

June 22: *U.S. forces begin to land in Cuba*

June 24: *Battle of Las Guasimas*

July 1: *Battles of El Caney and San Juan Hill*

July 3: *Spanish fleet destroyed at the Battle of Santiago*

July 17: *Spanish Santiago garrison surrenders*

July 25: *U.S. Army invades Puerto Rico*

July 26: *Spanish sue for peace through the French ambassador*

August 9: *Spain accepts U.S. peace terms*

August 12: *Truce concluded*

August 13: *Manila falls to U.S. forces*

November 28: *Spain agrees to cede Philippine Islands to the United States*

December 10: *Treaty of Paris formally ends the war*

1899

February 4: *Philippine Insurrection of 1899–1902 begins*

The explosion of the U.S. battleship *Maine* in Havana Harbor propelled the United States into war with Spain. *Collection: ArtToday*

insulted President McKinley. The nation had been driven to the brink of war when, on February 15, an explosion rocked Havana Harbor. The battleship *Maine* blew up, with the loss of 266 crewmen. A naval court of inquiry concluded that the ship had struck a Spanish mine (modern analysts believe that the ship's powder magazine spontaneously exploded through no hostile action), and the Hearst and Pulitzer papers vied with one another to demonize Spain. Americans soon raised the cry of "Remember the *Maine* . . . to hell with Spain!" It was a self-conscious echo of the battle cry of Texas independence—"Remember the Alamo!"(see *chapter 6*)—and it proved highly effective. Spain tried to avert war by accelerating its withdrawal from Cuba, and President McKinley temporized throughout the early spring, but he at last yielded to popular pressure and requested Congress to authorize an invasion of Cuba. The legislators did even more, voting a resolution to recognize Cuban independence from Spain. In response, Spain declared war on the United States on April 23, 1898.

Unpreparedness

As in the *War of 1812, 1812–1814 (see chapter 4),* the bellicose aspirations of the United States were not proportionate to the nation's state of preparedness for war. While the navy had benefited from a program of expansion, which included the construction of modern battleships and the training of an excellent officer corps, the post–Civil War army was tiny, at about 26,000 officers and men, broadcast over far-flung U.S. bases. A National Guard program enrolled about 100,000 more, many of whom,

I was on watch, and when the men had been piped below I looked down the main hatches and over the side of the ship. Everything was absolutely normal. . . . I was feeling a bit glum, and in fact was so quiet that Lieutenant J. Hood came up and asked laughingly if I was asleep. I said "No, I am on watch." Scarcely had I spoken when there came a dull, sullen roar.

Would to God that I could blot out the sound and the scenes that followed. Then came a sharp explosion—some say numerous detonations. I remember only one. It seemed to me that the sound came from the port side forward. Then came a perfect rain of missiles of all descriptions, from huge pieces of cement to blocks of wood, steel railings, fragments of gratings, and all the debris that would be detachable in an explosion.

I was struck on the head by a piece of cement and knocked down, but I was not hurt, and got to my feet in a moment. Lieutenant Hood had run to the poop, and, I supposed, as I followed, he was dazed by the shock and about to jump overboard. I hailed him, he answered that he had to run to the poop to help lower the boats. When I got there, though scarce a minute could have elapsed, I had to wade in water up to my knees, and almost instantly the quarter deck was awash. On the poop I found Captain Sigsbee, as cool as if at a ball, and soon all the officers except Jenkins and Merritt joined us.

Captain Sigsbee ordered the launch and gig lowered, and the officers and men, who by this time had assembled, got the boats out, and rescued a number in the water. Captain Sigsbee ordered Lieutenant Commander Wainwright forward to see the extent of the damage and if anything could be done to rescue those forward or to extinguish the flames. . . . Lieutenant Commander Wainwright on his return reported the total and awful character of the calamity, and Captain Sigsbee gave the last sad order, "Abandon Ship," to men overwhelmed with grief indeed, but calm and apparently unexcited.

Captain Sigsbee was the last man to leave his vessel and left in his own gig.

I have no theories as to the cause of the explosion. I cannot form any. I, with others, had heard the Havana harbor was full of torpedoes [mines], but the officers whose duty it was to examine into that reported that they found no signs of any. Personally, I do not believe that the Spanish had anything to do with the disaster. Time may tell.

. . . I wish to heaven I could forget it. I have been in two wrecks and have had my share. But the reverberations of that sullen, yet resonant roar, as if the bottom of the sea was groaning in torture, will haunt me for many days, and the reflection of that pillar of flame comes to me even when I close my eyes.

—LT. JOHN J. BLANDIN'S ACCOUNT OF THE FEBRUARY 15, 1898, EXPLOSION OF THE BATTLESHIP *MAINE* however, were poorly trained. While the army was equipped with up-to-date weapons, the National Guard made do with outmoded black-powder Springfield rifles. Perhaps even more critically deficient was the army's lack of a coherent mobilization plan. No overseas deployment had ever been contemplated, and it was questionable whether National Guard units could even be employed legally beyond the nation's borders. In belated preparation for war, Congress passed the Mobilization Act on April 22, 1898, which enabled the use of National Guard units. The act initially provided for the recruitment of 125,000 volunteers, to which an additional 75,000 were soon added. A special 10,000-man force, christened "the Immunes" and consisting of persons "possessing immunity from diseases incident to tropical climates," also was authorized. The act more than doubled the authorized strength of the regular army as well, to about 65,000. By the end of the ten-week war, in August 1898, the regular army numbered 59,000 and the volunteer forces 216,000.

Initial Strategy

Amassing the required manpower was only part of the problem of prosecuting the war against Spain; indeed, enthusiastic men volunteered in ample numbers. The initial U.S. strategy, however, did not call for committing ground troops to Cuba, at least not before October and the end of the sickly rainy season, but for establishing a naval blockade of the island. This patient strategy, planners believed, would, of itself, win the war, and when the Spanish decamped, ground forces could then occupy Cuba. Against the advice of senior planners, however, and bending to the public outcry for immediate, glorious action, Secretary of War Russell M. Alger ordered regular infantry regiments to be transported to New Orleans, Tampa, and Mobile, ports from which they could be immediately dispatched to Cuba.

The disruption of the initial strategy strained logistics to the breaking point. Transportation, supply, and clothing all created tremendous problems, and inadequate sanitation and improperly prepared food, including deadly tainted canned meat, created severe crises. Corruption among contractors and red tape in the War Department were rife.

Battle of Manila Bay

Compared to the army, the navy was far better prepared for a large-scale deployment, and this fact averted disaster. Almost immediately after the war began, the United States was flooded by rumors of the approach of a Spanish fleet under Admiral Pascual Cervera y Topete, headed for the Atlantic coast. Although Rear Admiral William T. Sampson had hoped to institute his Cuban blockade with every ship in the U.S. North Atlantic Squadron, several were detached under Commodore Winfield S. Schley to stand guard against the approach of Cervera.

If the navy's Caribbean plans were thus attenuated, its war plan for the Pacific campaign, formulated as early as 1895–1897, remained intact. Anticipating a conflict with Spain, the navy had resolved to attack whatever Spanish ships were stationed in the Philippines. The object was to destroy those ships, take Manila, and blockade the Philippine ports to cut off a vital source of revenue to Spain; moreover, U.S. possession of the Philippines would put the nation in a strong negotiating position to compel Spain to agree to the liberation of Cuba. In January 1898, well before the army even began planning for war, Acting Secretary of the Navy Theodore Roosevelt sent war-preparation instructions to naval commanders, including Commodore George Dewey. His Asiatic Squadron (five cruisers and two gunboats) was ordered to assemble in Hong Kong, coal up, and prepare to sail directly to the Philippines.

The order to attack the Philippines came on April 24, and Dewey, fully prepared, made Manila Bay during the night of April 30. On May 1 he located the Spanish fleet at Cavite and launched a spectacular attack against the vessels of Admiral Patricio Montojo: four cruisers, three gunboats, and three decrepit auxiliary vessels. Although it was superior in numbers, the Spanish fleet was outgunned—and poorly managed. Dewey completely destroyed the fleet in a few hours, inflicting on the Spanish 381 casualties, killed or wounded, while suffering the loss of not a single American sailor (8 were wounded). With the Spanish ships out of the way, Dewey handily neutralized the Spanish shore batteries, took possession of Cavite, then blockaded Manila in anticipation of the arrival of land forces to occupy the city. On June 30 a total of 10,000 troops, a mix of regulars and volunteers under General Wesley Merritt, reached Manila Bay and began debarkation. Acting in concert with Aguinaldo's Filipino guerrillas and supported by Dewey's naval batteries, Merritt took Manila on August 13.

Naval Operations at Santiago de Cuba

By May 1898, General Nelson A. Miles was prepared to lead army units from Tampa against Cuba, but the whereabouts of Cervera's Spanish fleet could not be ascertained. Until this information was discovered, the attack could not be launched. U.S. naval vessels searched for Cervera, finally discovering, at the end of May, that he had slipped through the Cuban blockade and had put in at the bay of Santiago de Cuba. U.S. admiral Sampson reconnoitered and determined that the Spanish fleet—its best ships, four modern cruisers and three destroyers—had indeed attained the safety of the heavily fortified bay. Sampson decided to blockade the fleet in the harbor, which he accomplished during May–July. In a daring operation, Lieutenant Richmond P. Hobson sailed an obsolescent collier, the *Merrimac*, into the harbor mouth, then scuttled it, hoping the hulk would effectively block the narrow channel. The gallant effort failed.

Unable to silence the Spanish forts with naval bombardment alone, Sampson called for army land forces to move against the batteries. Simultaneously, Sampson landed the marines carried by his squadron of five battleships, two armored cruisers, and assorted lesser vessels. They quickly overran the Spanish defenders of Guantánamo Bay and established a base of operations there. It was the first land skirmish of the war—and the marine base at Guantánamo exists to this day, the sole bastion of U.S. sovereignty on the island.

The Army Embarks

On June 14, V Corps, consisting of three divisions, 17,000 men, mostly regular army, under Major General William R. Shafter, left Tampa after many logistical delays. The loading of transports was especially haphazard. The concept of "combat loading"—including on each vessel the men together with their necessary supplies and equipment—was largely ignored, a fact that put the troops in great jeopardy should their landing encounter substantial resistance.

It was June 20 before the transport convoy arrived near Santiago, the troops having suffered under brutal tropical heat and in overcrowded, unsanitary conditions. Admiral Sampson wanted General Shafter to land at Santiago Bay and immediately storm the fort on the eastern side of the entrance to the bay to drive the Spanish from their guns. This accomplished, Sampson could then clear the bay of mines and enter it to fight Cervera's fleet. Shafter, however, had not transported heavy artillery and therefore doubted that his troops could take the fort. He decided instead on a less direct approach. He landed at Daiquirí, east of Santiago Bay. Disembarkation began on June 22 and was not concluded until June 25, amid great confusion and the reluctance of civilian vessels chartered for the landings to make close shore approaches. Cavalry mounts were tossed overboard, left to swim ashore on their own. Many horses swam out to sea and were lost. Had the Spanish commanders responded appropriately, they might have taken advantage of the prevailing chaos to wipe out the landing force. Spain had at least two hundred thousand troops in Cuba, of whom thirty-six thousand were stationed in Santiago. Combined with about five thousand local insurgents (under General Calixto García), the U.S. forces numbered only twenty-two thousand. Fortunately for the Americans, the Spanish did nothing to resist the inept landings.

Battle of Santiago

Elements of V Corps advanced west toward the high ground of San Juan, a series of ridges east of Santiago. The topography was ideal for the defenders, who were well entrenched. On June 23 Brigadier General Henry W. Lawton led the American vanguard along the coast from Daiquirí to take and hold Siboney, which became the principal base of operations. On June 24 Brigadier General Joseph Wheeler took his dismounted cavalry units inland along the road to Santiago and captured Las Guásimas, engaging briefly the rear guard of a retreating Spanish force. V Corps units, now just five miles outside San Juan Heights, paused to await the arrival of the rest of Shafter's divisions. But time suddenly seemed of the essence; Shafter observed how rapidly the tropical conditions debilitated his troops, and he also feared the onslaught of hurricanes. In view of these dangers, the general resolved on an immediate frontal attack against San Juan Heights. Shafter assigned an infantry division under Brigadier General Jacob F. Kent to attack on the left and Wheeler's dismounted cavalry on the right. These eight thousand troops would be supported by Lawton's infantry and artillery, sixty-five hundred men, who, simultaneously with the assault on San Juan Heights, would attack and take El Caney, a well-fortified village. This would cut off supplies to Santiago, including fresh water, and would block any possible Spanish reinforcements. Once El Caney was secured, Lawton was to join in the main assault against San Juan. Finally, to deceive the enemy, Shafter detailed a freshly landed brigade to advance along the coast from Siboney. It was a diversionary feint.

The attack stepped off at dawn on July 1 and immediately began to fall apart under the merciless tropical heat and over the difficult terrain.

Shafter, felled by heat stroke, was unable to direct the battle. As troops became bottled up along the congested main trail to San Juan Heights, Spanish gunners took devastating aim on them, sighting their guns on giant tethered Army Signal Corps balloons. To compound these problems,

Lawton experienced a lengthy delay in taking El Caney, which was much more stoutly defended than had been anticipated. Nevertheless, Kent and Wheeler were able to make a vigorous assault on San Juan Heights by the middle of the day. Among the units participating were the Ninth and Tenth Cavalry—both African American regiments—and the volunteer regiment known as the Rough Riders and commanded by the dashing Lieutenant Colonel Theodore Roosevelt. These three cavalry regiments, all unmounted except for their commanding officers, seized and occupied Kettle Hill as Kent's infantry, under cover of continuous Gatling-gun fire, charged up San Juan Hill and overwhelmed the defenders, pushing them from their blockhouse and trenches. The Spanish retreated to a more strongly fortified inner line.

IN THEIR OWN *Words*

A curious incident happened as I was getting the men started forward. Always when men have been lying down under cover for some time, and are required to advance, there is a little hesitation, each looking to see whether the others are going forward. As I rode down the line, calling to the troopers to go forward, and rasping brief directions to the captains and lieutenants, I came upon a man lying behind a little bush, and I ordered him to jump up. I do not think he understood that we were making a forward move, and he looked up at me for a moment with hesitation, and I again bade him rise, jeering him and saying: "Are you afraid to stand up when I am on horseback?"

As I spoke, he suddenly fell forward on his face, a bullet having struck him and gone through him lengthwise. I suppose the bullet had been aimed at me; at any rate, I, who was on horseback in the open, was unhurt, and the man lying flat on the ground in the cover beside me was killed. There were several pairs of brothers with us; of the two Nortons one was killed; of the two McCurdys one was wounded.

—THEODORE ROOSEVELT, RECALLING THE BATTLE OF SAN JUAN HILL IN HIS *THE ROUGH RIDERS*, 1920

Despite a shaky beginning, Shafter had achieved his initial objectives, but at the higher-than-expected cost of seventeen hundred killed or wounded. Even more worrying than the heavy battle casualties was the toll taken by illness, especially now that V Corps had to tackle the best-organized and most heavily fortified line of Spanish defense. Shafter notified Secretary of War Alger that he was contemplating a strategic withdrawal, five miles up to higher ground. This would put his forces in a position both easier to supply and easier to defend, and the additional elevation, Shafter hoped, would bring a healthier environment. Alger understood, but replied that the "effect upon the country would be much better" if Shafter avoided any retreat, even a strategic one. In view of this, Shafter appealed to the navy to enter Santiago Bay at once and attack the city. Naval commanders refused, and the American forces were thus temporarily stalled.

Colonel Theodore Roosevelt, front and center among his volunteer Rough Riders. *Collection: National Archives and Records Administration*

Just as the crisis of command seemed most acute, the will of the Spanish defenders of Santiago began to buckle. Short of food, water, and ammunition, the Spaniards resolved to abandon the city, and, without land support, Cervera felt he had no choice but to make a run out of port. On July 3 he began to move out. At the time, Admiral Sampson was ashore in tactical debate with General Shafter. In Sampson's absence, Commodore Schley initiated the pursuit and, in the space of two hours, disposed of Cervera's fleet. The four cruisers, pride of the Spanish navy, were severely damaged and run aground. A destroyer also was beached, and another sunk in deeper water. Although Schley diligently set about rescuing Spanish survivors, Cervera's losses were 474 killed or wounded; 1,750 sailors were taken prisoner. American losses were 1 killed and 1 wounded. The glory of the victory was subsequently marred by Sampson's unseemly attempt to claim credit for Schley's achievement.

Shortly after the defeat of Cervera, General Shafter persuaded the Spanish officials at Santiago to surrender unconditionally. The papers were signed on July 16, and 23,500 Spanish troops gave themselves up on the following day. Had General José Toral been aware that the American troops surrounding Santiago were withering under the effects of heat and yellow fever, he surely would not have capitulated so readily.

Landing on Puerto Rico

General Nelson A. Miles, leading more than three thousand troops, sailed from Guantánamo on July 21 and, on July 25, landed at Guánica, on the southeastern coast of Puerto Rico. Here he met almost no resistance and quickly advanced to the port town of Ponce. He secured this for a base of operations, installing there ten thousand troops newly arrived from the U.S. mainland during the first week of August. From here, Miles marched four columns toward San Juan and easily brushed aside the inconsequential resistance he encountered. Many Puerto Ricans enthusiastically greeted the American troops as liberators, but the campaign was suspended on August 13 when news reached Miles that Spain had signed a peace protocol.

Fort Malate, outside Manila, Philippines, taken in action by U.S. forces on August 13, 1898. *Collection: National Archives and Records Administration*

Health Crisis

The overwhelming nature of the U.S. military victory in the Caribbean was being increasingly vitiated by the deteriorating health of Shafter's soldiers. As far more succumbed to yellow fever than to enemy bullets, a number of senior officers circulated a letter proposing evacuation of the army for sanitary and medical reasons. When the letter was made public, American officials worried that it would compromise the ongoing peace negotiations with Spain. Fortunately it did not, but the army was moved to devote unprecedented resources to its Medical Corps in a concerted effort to understand the causes of yellow fever and to develop means of effectively combating it.

Fall of Manila

While U.S. soldiers triumphed and languished in Cuba, Admiral George Dewey, during May and June, awaiting the arrival of land forces to occupy Manila, struggled to maintain cordial relations with Aguinaldo and the Filipino insurgents. It became increasingly apparent that the U.S. and Filipino agendas were far from identical. The United States wanted to annex the Philippines, while Aguinaldo wanted to achieve immediate independence. Fortunately, by the end of July, before a full-blown crisis developed, VIII Corps, about thirteen thousand volunteers and two thousand regulars under Major General Wesley Merritt, began landing near Manila. The army had learned valuable lessons from the Cuban landings, and those at

Manila were far more efficient. By the beginning of August, eleven thousand U.S. troops were arrayed to the rear of the Filipino insurgents just outside the city. Within Manila, as many as fifteen thousand Spanish troops were ready to make a defensive stand. Both Dewey and Merritt appealed to Madrid for a bloodless surrender, but the cause of Spanish honor seemed to demand at least a show of resistance. Thus, on August 13, VIII Corps attacked, supported by Dewey's naval bombardment. Poor coordination between the U.S. troops and the insurgents threatened to expand the battle beyond fighting a token resistance, for the insurgents suddenly opened up on the barely resisting Spanish with unbridled violence. American officers intervened and persuaded the insurgents to cease fire, and the Spanish garrison surrendered. On August 14 the surrender was formalized—though, in fact, Madrid had signed a general peace protocol on August 12; because Dewey had cut the submarine telegraph cable to Manila, word of the armistice had reached neither attackers nor defenders.

The cruiser *Olympia* was Commodore George Dewey's flagship at the Battle of Manila Bay. *Collection: National Archives and Records Administration*

The Treaty of Paris

Following the armistice, negotiations in Paris produced the Treaty of Paris, which was signed by the parties on December 10, 1898. Certain U.S. lawmakers, acting from their moral objections to American expansionism, had produced the Teller Amendment to the original declaration of war, which barred the outright annexation of Cuba. For this reason, U.S. negotiators at Paris did not seek to acquire the island, but instead secured Spain's grant of independence for Cuba. The Teller Amendment did not extend to other Spanish possessions, however, and President McKinley pressed his negotiators to obtain cession of Puerto Rico, Guam, and the Philippine Islands. These acts of imperialism made the treaty controversial, and the Senate fight over ratification was bitter. Those who favored the treaty argued that annexation was an expression of America's duty to serve the world as an agent of civilization. On a less philosophically pretentious level, the acquisitions in the Pacific would give the United States a crucial leg up in trade with China. In the end, the treaty was ratified by a margin of fifty-seven to twenty-seven—just two votes more than the two-thirds majority required—and Secretary of State John Hay pronounced the ten-week conflict a "splendid little war." Whatever controversy it created, the Spanish-American War firmly established the United States as a major power in the Far East and the dominant power in the Caribbean. It also triggered a four-year guerrilla insurrection against American dominion in the Philippines, which is covered next.

Philippine Insurrection, 1899–1902

After the fall of Manila in the *Spanish-American War, 1898,* the insurgents under Emilio Aguinaldo reached an informal truce with the occupying forces of the United States. In January 1899, following the conclusion of the Peace of Paris with Spain, the United States announced annexation of the Philippines, having purchased the islands from Spain for $20 million. Aguinaldo's rebels had proclaimed Philippine independence on June 12, 1898, and now they refused to accept annexation. On January 20, 1899, the Philippine Republic was proclaimed under the Malolos Constitution, with Aguinaldo as president.

Fighting began the next month. On the night of February 4, an insurgent patrol challenged an American guard post near Manila. On the eve of ratification of the Peace of Paris, the attack was most likely calculated to embarrass and overawe American forces, which had yet to be reinforced. The troops of VIII Corps were not overawed, however. Although greatly outnumbered—commanding twelve thousand U.S. soldiers against some forty thousand insurgents—Major General Elwell S. Otis nevertheless responded vigorously with several attacks that drove back the insurgents and inflicted at least three thousand casualties on the Filipinos. During February 22–24, insurgents under General Antonio Luna retaliated with a concerted attack on Manila, but U.S. forces led by General Arthur MacArthur forced them into retreat and ultimately, by March 31, pushed the insurgents back to Malolos, their capital and stronghold. After this setback, Aguinaldo took flight, disbanded the formally constituted army, and instituted a guerrilla campaign. Reinforced U.S. forces took the offensive, carrying the war into southern Luzon, the Visayan Islands, Mindanao, and Sulu. The army targeted Aguinaldo, who was captured by General Frederick Funston's Filipino Scouts on March 23, 1901.

Aguinaldo was pressured into swearing allegiance to the United States and into issuing a proclamation calling for peace. By this time, however, the guerrilla war had taken on a life independent from its original leader. For the next year, U.S. forces were subject to sporadic attack until virtually all of the Filipino military leaders had been located, rounded up, and placed under arrest. The last of these leaders concluded a treaty with U.S. authorities on May 6, 1902, and the U.S. military administration of the islands was replaced by a U.S.-controlled civil government. Its first appointed governor was William Howard Taft, who would later become the twenty-seventh president of the United States.

Boxer Rebellion, 1899–1901

In 1899, U.S. secretary of state John Hay communicated with the governments of France, Germany, Great Britain, Italy, Russia, and Japan, endorsing an "Open Door Policy" (first suggested by a British customs official, Alfred E. Hippisley) with regard to China. In sum, Hay proposed that the United States, all European nations, and Japan should have equal access to Chinese trade. The proposal met with almost universal approval among the nations of the West (only Japan balked), but China, the subject of the policy, had not been consulted on the matter. This ancient empire was currently racked by internal disturbances and was only tenuously governed by Tz'u-hsi, the dowager empress. On the verge of the dissolution of its government, China was in the throes of intense antiforeign feeling. On January 11, 1900, the dowager empress issued a proclamation approving an uprising of units of a militant secret society called the Yihe Quang, loosely translated as the "righteous harmony of fists" and called by Westerners "the Boxers." By spring, the Boxers rampaged throughout the country, committing acts of vandalism in Peking (Beijing), menacing foreigners as well as Chinese Christians, and sabotaging rail and telegraph lines.

To protect American nationals in China, two navy vessels, USS *Monocacy* and USS *Newark,* were dispatched to Taku. *Newark* joined a number of European warships off Taku Bar on May 27. Two days later, at the request of the U.S. consul in Tientsin, 49 Marines under Captain John T. Myers were landed. Additional landing parties brought the U.S. military contingent to 150. Barred by Chinese authorities from traveling to Tientsin by rail, the troops traveled by scow up the Pei-Ho River. The U.S. Marines were the first foreign troops in the city, and they were soon joined by a coalition contingent from England, France, Russia, Austria, Italy, and Japan.

Chinese pull rickshas to evacuate Catholic nuns during the Boxer Rebellion. Chinese Christians were among the chief targets of the Boxer nationalists. *Collection: ArtToday*

While U.S., Japanese, and European troops assembled in Tientsin, diplomats in Peking demanded that Chinese authorities permit the coalition forces to travel by train to the capital to reinforce the small contingent of embassy and legation guards. On May 30 that permission was granted, and on May 31, Captain Myers took 55 Marines and joined more than 300 troops from the other coalition nations on the 90-mile rail journey to the capital. Myers ordered his men to eschew baggage and to take instead 20,000 rifle rounds and 8,000 machine gun rounds.

In the meantime, Boxer riots increased in frequency and intensity. Looting and arson were common, as were assaults on Chinese Christians. On June 6 the Boxers severed the railroad between Peking and Tientsin. The coalition forces agreed that they would be commanded by Vice Admiral Sir Edward Seymour of the Royal Navy. On June 8 the Boxers cut the telegraph lines into Peking. At this point the American consul, feeling that the situation had become critical, threatened to take unilateral action to break through instantly to Peking with a larger force. Pushed to action, Seymour authorized what would come to be called the Seymour Expedition, four trains carrying 2,006 coalition troops from Tientsin to Peking. The first train left on the morning of June 10; the others followed at intervals during the rest of the day. Progress was very slow because of the sabotaged rail lines, which had to be repaired as the trains went along.

Shortly after the last of the four Seymour Expedition trains had pulled out of Tientsin on June 10, Chinese forces began shelling foreign sections of the city. A mere 1,100 foreign troops, including a small contingent of U.S. Marines, remained in Tientsin with very little available to defend themselves or the nationals of their countries: rifles, sidearms, two small artillery pieces, a dozen machine guns. Concerted effort from the Boxers and Imperial Chinese troops would have easily overwhelmed the foreign troops.

After Boxers severed rail and telegraph lines joining Tientsin to the coast, coalition commanders decided that the relief of Tientsin could be effected by taking the forts at Taku and the rail station at Tongku. Russian, German, British, Japanese, Italian, and Austrian officers issued a joint ultimatum to the commander of the forts on June 16, demanding surrender by the following day. In response to the ultimatum, the forts fired on the warships at Taku Bar. The ships returned fire for four hours, forcing the Chinese to abandon the forts. Landing parties immediately occupied them. The American vessels on the scene did not participate in the naval bombardment or the capture of the forts because the U.S. naval commanders interpreted their mandate as strictly defensive and only in direct defense of U.S. nationals. The Chinese government deemed the shelling of Taku as the commencement of war and, on June 18, ordered the Imperial Army to attack the Seymour Expedition. Troops set upon the first of the transport trains near Anting, twenty-five miles outside Peking. They also cut rail lines behind the train so it could neither return to Tientsin nor advance to Peking. Greatly outnumbered, Seymour ordered the train to be burned and the expedition to retreat, on foot, to Tientsin. The column reached Hsi-Ku Arsenal, five miles from Tientsin, on June 22.

In the meantime, imperial troops had laid siege to the international quarter at Tientsin and to the diplomatic legations at Peking. On June 17, the Chinese renewed and intensified bombardment of the foreign sections of Tientsin. Herbert Hoover, at the time a young mining engineer working for a British firm with Chinese interests, assumed direction of foreign civilians and Chinese Christians in barricading the entrances to the enclave. When the Boxers attempted to invade the quarter on June 18, they were stunned to find it heavily fortified, and they withdrew. Imperial artillery bombarded the settlement sporadically.

On June 20, U.S. Marines from the Philippines landed at Taku. They set off by rail to Tientsin and, finding the tracks too badly damaged to continue by train, they began to march, joining up with a Russian battalion along the way. The Marines and the Russians engaged Chinese forces on the morning of June 21. Outnumbered, the Marines and the Russians retired to a base at Cheng-liang Chang, where they were joined by British troops. The polyglot force resumed the advance on June 22, engaged Chinese forces several times, and arrived at Tientsin on June 24. They relieved the Seymour Expedition at Hsi-Ku Arsenal on June 25, then destroyed the arsenal to keep it out of Chinese hands.

The arrival of the Marines and other forces enabled the evacuation of Tientsin and, over the next month, operations were conducted continuously against Boxers and imperial troops in the Tientsin area. During this period the United States and the other coalition powers sent additional troops. The U.S. forces—including elements of the Ninth Infantry, the Fourteenth Infantry, the Fifth Field Artillery, and the Sixth Cavalry, together with additional Marine units—were designated the China Relief Expedition and placed under the command of army general Adna Chaffee.

On August 4, what was now an international force of more than twenty thousand men marched from Tientsin to Peking. On August 5, imperial troops attacked the Japanese left flank in the vanguard of the international column. In a six-hour battle, Japanese and British troops routed the Chinese, pushing them out of Piet Sang. A U.S. Marine contingent was attacked and even subjected to a cavalry charge, but these forays were easily beaten back, and the Marines ejected the Boxers from the Yangtsun area.

Acting on their own initiative, Russian troops advanced into Peking on August 13 and were immediately overwhelmed. The timely action of the other coalition troops saved them from being cut off. On August 14, elements of the Fourteenth Infantry and a group of marines cap-

A book illustration depicting action during the Boxer Rebellion: the fatal wounding of a Colonel Liscum. *Collection: ArtToday*

tured a section of the Tartar Wall and were able to cover British troops, who entered the Outer City to relieve the besieged legations (a Japanese and a German diplomat had been killed during the siege). On August 15, marines cleared the barricades from Chien-mien Gate and established artillery positions there. Cannon destroyed the gates of the Forbidden City. With this action—and the relief of the legations—the Boxer Rebellion dissolved. The coalition nations now drew up the Boxer Protocol, a document that imposed an exorbitant $333 million indemnity against China and that also compelled the nation to agree to the permanent stationing of U.S. and other troops in the country.

On July 3, before the United States had even committed substantial numbers of troops to the coalition, Secretary Hay, fearing that the other members of the coalition would use the Boxer Rebellion as a pretext to abrogate the Open Door Policy and carve up China among themselves, issued a "circular letter" in which he stated the policy of the United States

IN THEIR OWN *Words*

Account of Fei Ch'i-hao, a Chinese Christian, of Persecution by Boxers in Shansi, China

Late in July a proclamation of the Governor was posted in the city in which occurred the words, "Exterminate foreigners, kill devils." Native Christians must leave the church or pay the penalty with their lives. . . .

Once across the river I reached a small inn outside the wall of P'ing Yao. I had walked twenty miles that day—the longest walk I had ever taken, and I threw myself down to sleep without eating anything.

Often I awoke with a start and turned my aching body, asking myself, "Where am I? How came I here? Are my Western friends indeed killed? I must be dreaming."

But I was so tired that sleep would soon overcome me again. The sun had risen when I opened my eyes in the morning. I forced myself to rise, washed my face, and asked for a little food, but could not get it down. Sitting down I heard loud talking and laughter among the guests. The topic of conversation was the massacre of foreigners the day before! One said: "There were ten ocean men killed, three men, four women, and three little devils."

Another added, "Lij Cheng San yesterday morning came ahead with twenty soldiers and waited in the village. When the foreigners with their soldier escort arrived a gun was fired for a signal, and all the soldiers set to work at once."

Then one after another added gruesome details, how the cruel swords had slashed, how the baggage had been stolen, how the very clothing had been stripped from the poor bodies, and how they had then been flung into a wayside pit.

"Are there still foreigners in Fen Chou Fu?" I asked.

"No, they were all killed yesterday."

"Where were they killed?"

"In that village ahead—less than two miles from here," he said, pointing as he spoke. "Yesterday about this time they were all killed."

"How many were there?" I asked.

He stretched out the fingers of his two hands for an answer.

. . . My heart was leaden as I rode on the cart, with my face turned toward Fen Chou Fu. . . .

—QUOTED IN LUELLA MINER, *TWO HEROES OF CATHAY*, 1907

"to seek a solution which may bring about permanent safety and peace to China, preserve Chinese territorial and administrative entity, protect all rights guaranteed to friendly powers by treaty and international law, and safeguard for the world the principle of equal and impartial trade with all parts of the Chinese Empire." The circular letter notwithstanding, the United States did not fail to endorse the Boxer Protocol. Slated to share in the indemnity to the tune of $24 million, however, the United States subsequently agreed to reduce its share of the indemnity to $12 million, then, in 1924, forgave the unpaid balance due on that reduced amount. Although these gestures were calculated to demonstrate the good faith of the United States, the nation would repeatedly acquiesce to violations of the Open Door Policy. For example, the Taft-Katsura Memorandum of 1905, between the United States and Japan, established a foundation for a Japanese protectorate in Korea, and the United States acknowledged Japan's "special interests" in China with the Lansing-Ishii Agreement of 1917. This helped set the stage for the 1932 Japanese invasion of Manchuria, a prelude to World War II. More immediately, the Boxer Protocol proved the final undoing of the Qing (Ch'ing), or Manchu, Dynasty, which had ruled since 1644. Humiliated and weakened by the protocol, it would be overthrown in the Chinese Revolution of 1911.

Moro Wars, 1901–1913

The principal U.S. effort in the suppression of the *Philippine Insurrection, 1899-1902* was in the northern Philippines, especially on Luzon. The southern islands were largely neglected, and it was here that resistance to the U.S. presence grew early in the twentieth century. In 1899 Brigadier General John C. Bates had negotiated an agreement with the sultan of Sulu, nominal leader of the Moros, Islamic people living on Mindanao and the Sulu Archipelago, by which the sultan recognized U.S. sovereignty. In return, the Americans agreed to provide protection for the sultan's subjects, grant him sovereignty in criminal cases, respect Islamic religious customs, and even permit slavery in the area. But the sultan's control of the Moros, a people with a strong warrior tradition, was tenuous at best, and their resistance to the Americans took on the intensity of a religious war.

In November 1901 Captain John J. Pershing led two troops of the Fifteenth Cavalry and three infantry companies to Mindanao to persuade the

Moros to cooperate with the American government. With great diplomatic skill, Pershing won over those Moros living on the northern shore of Lake Lanao. Those on the southern shore, however, frequently skirmished with U.S. troops as well as with a U.S.-sanctioned Moro constabulary. Brigadier General George Davis sent twelve hundred U.S. troops to take the Moro stronghold at Pandapatan, which was neutralized at the cost of sixty Americans killed and many more wounded. At this site, the army established Camp Vicars, with Pershing in command. From this base, between June 1902 and May 1903, Pershing launched a new diplomatic campaign but failed to cajole cooperation from the Moros. Pershing then conducted a series of restrained but highly effective military expeditions, which also included diplomatic elements.

By the summer of 1903, when Pershing returned to the United States, the most acute of Moro violence had been quelled—but flare-ups were chronic, and the new military governor of the Moro province, Major General Leonard Wood, entirely lacked Pershing's understanding, skill, and tolerance in dealing with the Moro people. He was determined to beat them into unquestioning submission to U.S. authority, and he was especially zealous in his effort to eliminate slavery in the province. Wood's approach provoked a guerrilla war, fought from Moro strongholds called *cottas*. In October 1905 a major guerrilla leader, Dato Ali, was targeted by Wood, who sent Captain Frank R. McCoy with 115 men against his *cotta*. McCoy's command ambushed and killed Dato Ali on October 22. Even this victory, however, did not end the Moro resistance. At the end of 1905, a large contingent of Moros took up positions at Bud Dajo, a crater atop a 2,100-foot-high extinct volcano, which proved to be a formidable natural fortress. The existence of this stronghold became a great embarrassment to U.S. authority in the province, and on March 5, 1906, Colonel Joseph W. Duncan attacked the position in force. Bud Dajo fell on March 8, a total of 18 of Duncan's troops having died, along with some 600 Moros.

Moros at Taluk Samgay, Zamboanga Province, Mindanao, Philippines. *Collection: National Archives and Records Administration*

The reduction of Bud Dajo brought relative peace to the Moro province for the next three years, but it did nothing to salve Moro resentment against American dominion. Pershing, now a general, returned to the Philippines in 1909 and was assigned to the Mindanao region. He was distressed by attitudes there, which he considered dangerous, and, as he had done years earlier, he embarked on a campaign of building trust and positive relationships. He resolved to bring enduring peace to the Moro province by disarming the tribe. He issued a disarmament order on September 8, 1911, setting a deadline of December 1. In October, however, the Moros reacted violently and, on December 3 and 5, Pershing dispatched troops to put down an incipient rebellion. The Moros sent word that they wished to negotiate peace, but they used the ensuing armistice to begin the reoccupation of Bud Dajo on December 14. Pershing responded by surrounding the stronghold on December 22. Bud Dajo was evacuated within two days, and once again Moro resistance died down, but it did not completely end. In January 1913, following two more major skirmishes, more than five thousand Moros, including women and children, holed up on Bud Bagsak, another extinct volcano. Pershing had no desire to precipitate the slaughter of families and so attempted to persuade the Moros to evacuate. When they would not, on June 11, 1913, Pershing launched a coordinated land and amphibious assault on Bud Bagsak. Moro guerrillas had established well-defended cottas at Langusan, Pujagan, Matunkup, Puyacabao, Bunga, and Bagsak, but one by one, these fell to the assault. On June 15, Bud Bagsak was captured, and the Moro Wars quickly wound down to an end.

Moro resistance to the U.S. government greatly diminished after 1913; however, the movement throughout the Philippines for independence persisted. In 1935 the Filipino people accepted the United States' offer of sovereignty to be granted after a ten-year interim as a U.S. commonwealth, and the Republic of the Philippines was created on July 4, 1946. Since the 1970s, the Moros have agitated for autonomy within the Republic of the Philippines, even though they are now outnumbered by non-Moro Christians in the region they inhabit.

Panamanian Revolution, 1903

Philippe Bunau-Varilla was a French engineer who had been employed by the Compagnie Universelle du Canal Interocéanique, the French Panama

Canal Company, in 1884. When the French Panama canal project failed in 1889, Bunau-Varilla approached the United States with an offer to sell the right to build the canal. Bunau-Varilla was commissioned by the American government to negotiate a treaty with Colombia, of which Panama was then a province. This led to the Hay-Herrán Treaty, which U.S. Secretary of State John Hay concluded with Colombian foreign minister Tomás Herrán on January 22, 1903, providing for U.S. control of the planned Panama Canal and for U.S. acquisition of a canal zone bracketing the canal. These rights were to be gained for the bargain price of $10 million paid to Colombia and, after nine years, an annuity of $250,000. While it is true that President Theodore Roosevelt had wanted a treaty that would give the United States complete governmental control over the proposed canal zone and that the Hay-Herrán document did not fully provide this, it did offer enough to the United States to persuade the U.S. Senate to ratify it. The Colombian Senate, however, delayed ratification in the hope of increasing the price offered by the United States, and, in the end, on August 12, 1903, flatly refused to ratify the treaty—not only because of dissatisfaction with the financial terms, but also in response to a popular movement to resist "Yankee imperialism," and popular objections to relinquishing a significant measure of national sovereignty. Faced with Colombian intransigence, Bunau-Varilla now helped organize a revolt in Panama against Colombia. He cooperated with a group of railway workers, firemen, and soldiers in Colón, Panama, in an uprising on November 3–4. The rebels proclaimed Panamanian independence, and, just offshore, the U.S. Navy cruiser *Nashville* interdicted an attempt by Colombian general Rafael Reyes to land troops intended to quell the rebellion. Immediately after this action, on November 6, President Roosevelt recognized Panamanian independence and then received Bunau-Varilla as minister from the new republic. With this new minister, Secretary of State Hay concluded the Hay-Bunau-Varilla Treaty on November 18, which provided for the acquisition of a canal zone and the right to build and control a canal in exchange for the same monetary terms that had been offered Colombia.

U.S. participation in the 1903 Panamanian Revolution consisted only in the backing given Bunau-Varilla, the intervention of the *Nashville,* and the military backing that was implied by Roosevelt's summary recognition of Panamanian independence.

Nicaraguan Civil War, 1909–1912

Juan J. Estrada, Adolfo Díaz, and Emilianio Chamorro Vargas led a group of powerful and influential Nicaraguans in a revolt against President José Santos Zelaya beginning on October 10, 1909. At first localized near Bluefields, on Nicaragua's eastern coast, the rebellion slowly spread west. The American government welcomed the rebellion, since relations with the Zelaya government had long been in decline. Not only was Zelaya a brutal dictator, he was also hostile toward U.S. business interests in his country and even to U.S. diplomats in the capital, Managua. Two American citizens, Leonard Croce and Leroy Canon, volunteered for service as officers in Chamorro's revolutionary army and were captured by Zelaya's troops. Despite the warnings of his own advisers, Zelaya ordered the execution of the two Americans. Their deaths prompted U.S. Secretary of State Philander Knox to sever diplomatic relations with the Zelaya government on December 1, 1909. Simultaneously, the Navy Department was ordered to organize the Nicaraguan Expeditionary Brigade, of marines, which arrived at Cristóbal, Canal Zone, on December 12. The marines then boarded the USS *Buffalo* bound for Corinto, Nicaragua. Their arrival in Nicaragua persuaded Zelaya to resign office, on December 16, in favor of José Madriz and to flee to political asylum in Mexico. Immediately, relations with the United States improved, and the marines sailed back to Panama on March 22, 1910.

The departure of Zelaya by no means left Nicaragua peaceful, however. In the vicinity of Bluefields, where the revolt had started, fighting broke out between rebels loyal to Juan J. Estrada and forces loyal to President Madriz. Seeking to restore order, U.S. naval commander William W. Gilmer, skipper of the USS *Paducah,* riding off Bluefields, issued a proclamation to both sides forbidding fighting within the city of Bluefields. Gilmer requested a contingent of marines to enforce his proclamation. Two hundred marines under Major Smedley D. Butler arrived from the Canal Zone on May 30. The principal dispute at Bluefields was the disposition of the customs house there. Estrada's rebels had seized it and used it as a source of finance. On May 27, Madriz's army retook it, even though Estrada's forces still occupied the city. Estrada demanded that customs duties be paid to his men in the city, whereas Madriz insisted they be paid at the customs house he now controlled. U.S. authorities, feeling that

Madriz was becoming dictatorial and dangerous, ordered that customs duties be paid to Estrada. This provided the financial support he needed to continue his revolt against Madriz. While U.S. Marines maintained civil order in Bluefields—and oversaw the rebuilding of the local hospital, market, and sanitary facilities there—Estrada took Managua on August 23. He was inaugurated as president on August 30. On September 4, the marines pulled out of Bluefields and sailed back to Panama.

Yet again, however, Nicaragua was rocked by unrest. Zelaya's followers were still active, and now many in Estrada's own party became dissatisfied over the paltry shares of power and spoils they received. Some also objected to the imperialism of the United States, which received various trade considerations and monopolies. When fighting broke out in Managua, Elliott Northcott, U.S. minister to Nicaragua, persuaded Estrada to resign in favor of his vice president, Adolfo Díaz. This relieved tensions for a short time, but in 1912 General Luís Mena, who had been war minister under Estrada, took a portion of the army to Masaya and then instigated the seizure of American-owned steamships on Lake Managua. U.S. officials appealed to Díaz for assistance. He replied, in turn, with a request for U.S. military aid, and 100 sailors from the USS *Annapolis* arrived in Managua on August 4, 1912, while 353 marines, under Smedley Butler, set off from Panama for Corinto. On August 14 the marines and 80 more seamen left Corinto by train for Managua, arriving on August 15. Thus backed, George F. Weitzel, who had replaced Northcott as minister in Managua, demanded that Mena immediately return the vessels that had been appropriated. When Mena refused, more marines were called up. On September 6 the First and Second Marine Battalions of the 1st Provisional Regiment, Colonel Joseph H. Pendleton commanding, arrived in Managua to join the small force already there. Assuming command of the combined forces, Pendleton loaded three marine companies onto a train bound for Granada, to confront Mena. At La Barranca, a hill near the town of Masaya, the forces of General Benjamin Zeledon, a supporter of Mena, blocked the train. Butler set up a conference between Pendleton (along with Admiral William H. H. Southerland) and Zeledon, who, at length, agreed to allow the marines to pass. On September 19, however, within the city limits of Masaya, revolutionary troops ambushed the train, which, putting on full speed, managed to get through the city without serious harm. At San Blas, on the outskirts of Granada, Butler informed General Mena's representatives that he would attack Granada if Mena did not surrender. Ailing, Mena gave up in return for safe conduct to Panama, where he was guaranteed political asylum.

The marines had achieved control of the rail line, but still had to take Zeledon's stronghold in the Barranca-Coyatepe hills and his rebel positions in Masaya and León. On October 2, marine and Nicaraguan government troops commenced artillery bombardment of the hills, then, on October 3, stormed Zeledon's positions, readily taking them. Now the Nicaraguan troops descended on Masaya, which they ravaged and looted. Seeking to avoid Masaya's fate, León quickly surrendered to the U.S. Marines. This ended the revolt against the Díaz regime. In November 1913, most of the marines returned to Panama, leaving behind a contingent of a hundred to guard the United States legation—and to supply a modicum of muscle to bolster the U.S.-friendly, conservative Díaz government.

Villa's Raids (and the Pershing Punitive Expedition), 1916–1917

In 1913, Mexican politics was rocked by the assassination of President Francisco Madero, which left a power vacuum into which a number of candidates violently rushed. The reactionary dictator Victoriano Huerta brutally seized office, whereupon U.S. president Woodrow Wilson sent naval forces to blockade European arms shipments to the Huerta regime. By 1914, U.S. troops occupied the port of Vera Cruz, a situation that helped precipitate the collapse of the Huerta government and its replacement in 1915 by the administration of the more moderate Venustiano Carranza. Wilson favored Carranza, but Mexico's revolutionary strife was by no means at an end. Most powerful of the revolutionaries still active was the charismatic Francisco "Pancho" Villa, who worked to cultivate cordial relations with the United States in the hope of winning Wilson's support in his bid to oust Carranza as president. Wilson, however, continued to support Carranza, who scored a series of military victories over Villa. By the end of 1915, Villa had turned openly hostile to the United States, and raiders he either sanctioned or led harried the U.S.-Mexican border region.

As the pace of raids increased, Villa seems to have decided on a strategy of even more deliberate attacks on the United States. His motives for this strategy are unclear. Some historians have suggested that he merely wanted to exact personal revenge against a nation that had failed to support him. Others believe he hoped that, by provoking U.S. intervention in Mexican affairs, Carranza would appear weak and subservient to America. Still other historians believe that Villa had a grand plan to embroil Mexico in an outright war with the United States, which would inevitably destabilize and perhaps unseat the Carranza government. Whatever moved him to do so, Villa led some five hundred "Villistas" into the New Mexico town of Columbus on March 9, 1916, and fought with civilians as well as soldiers from the nearby Thirteenth Cavalry. Major Frank Tompkins led elements of the cavalry in pursuit of the raiders across the border but soon turned back. Ten U.S. civilians and fourteen U.S. soldiers had been killed in Columbus, while Villa lost at least a hundred out of his five-hundred-man raiding party.

The American public was outraged by Villa's raid on Columbus, and Major General Frederick Funston, commander of the army's Southern Department, concentrated troops along the border and formulated a plan for an expedition into Mexico. The combined National Guard and regular army troops patrolling the border eventually reached a strength of 158,000—the bulk of the active military strength of the United States in 1916. In addition to border patrols, President Wilson authorized a punitive expedition into Mexico. On March 14, 1916, Brigadier General John J. Pershing was given command of two cavalry brigades and a brigade of infantry—some 10,000 men—with orders to find, pursue, and destroy Villa's forces. The punitive expedition advanced into Mexico on March 15, initially with the consent of President Carranza, who, however, as the expedition wore on through the next eleven months, became increasingly hostile to it.

Pershing divided his forces into two columns, which marched toward Casa Grandes, a hundred miles south of Columbus. When Pershing learned that Villa had moved even farther south, he established a supply base at Colonia Dublan, then sent cavalry detachments in advance to sweep the countryside. Most of the riding was in vain. On March 29, however, a patrol of the Seventh Cavalry, a detachment of 370 men, attacked Guerrero, believed to be a Villista stronghold. Taken by surprise, the Mexicans were routed from the village, and at least 35 Villistas were killed, including Nicolas Hernández, reputedly Villa's right-hand man.

While the Seventh Cavalry had moved on Guerrero, elements of the Tenth Cavalry searched to the east without result. At Aguas Calientas, on April 1, about 150 Villistas fired on the Tenth, but were quickly driven off.

The American troopers scoured the countryside for fugitives, but aborted this operation when they were ordered, on April 10, to advance on Parral, four hundred miles south of the border.

Backing up the Seventh and Tenth Cavalry columns were several smaller "flying columns" assigned to block possible escape routes. On April 12 one of these flying columns, a squadron of the Thirteenth Cavalry, was surrounded by an angry crowd at Parral. The squadron withdrew, only to find itself under attack from "Carranzistas"—troops loyal to Venustiano Carranza. The squadron withdrew to Santa Cruz de Villegas and, on April 13, was reinforced by elements of the Tenth and Eleventh Cavalry. The situation at Parral developed into a standoff between U.S. and Mexican forces, which threatened to propel the nations to the verge of war. To avert this, Pershing ordered his troops to withdraw from Parral. Seeking to avoid further provocation, Pershing decided to use his five cavalry regiments, each to patrol a prescribed area only. While pulling back to its assigned district, the Seventh Cavalry encountered Villistas under Candelario Cervantes, and defeated them at Tomochic on April 22.

Pancho Villa remains a popular folkloric figure in many parts of Mexico, as this stenciled poster suggests. *Collection: ArtToday*

On May 5 Major Robert L. Howze led a squadron of the Eleventh Cavalry against a Villista band at Ojos Azulas.

The battles of April 22 and May 5 were the last "major" engagements of the punitive expedition—although, in minor fights during May, two of Villa's principal commanders, Julio Cárdenas and Cervantes, were killed. In the meantime, however, relations between the United States and the Carranza government deteriorated further as Mexican bands continued to raid U.S. border towns along the lower Rio Grande. A number of the raids had been led not by Villistas, but by Carranzistas. It was at this point, with the National Guard mobilized, that U.S. troop strength along the border reached six figures. On the Mexican side of the border, a sharp fight broke out in Carrizal at the end of June, when a Tenth Cavalry patrol entered the town without Carranzista permission. Outnumbered, the Tenth Cavalry patrol lost half its men killed, wounded, or captured. The bright side of this grave incident was that it shocked both governments into cooling off and coming to the negotiating table. Pershing reduced the scope of his operations, concentrating around his main base at Colonia Dublan. At length, talks with Carranza petered out, but the crisis between the two governments eased. Although Villa remained at large and even organized a new army in southern Mexico, President Wilson ordered the withdrawal of the punitive expedition. The last of the force recrossed the border on February 5, 1917.

The punitive expedition failed to capture Villa, but it was hardly the fiasco that some historians portray. As a result of the operation, Villa's army had been greatly reduced, and his most senior commanders had been killed. By the end of the campaign, raids into the United States also stopped. As for Villa's new army, it never posed a threat to the United States.

Nicaraguan Civil War, 1925–1933

A small force of U.S. Marines—about a hundred men—continuously occupied Nicaragua for thirteen years, from the end of the *Nicaraguan Civil War, 1909–1912* until 1925, when a coalition government was formed between conservative president Carlos Solórzano and liberal vice president Bautista Sacasa. On October 25, 1925, shortly after the marines left, General Emiliano Chamorro Vargas and Adolfo Díaz staged a coup that drove the liberals, including Sacasa, out of office. Soon after, Solórzano also resigned, and, in January 1926, Chamorro became president. The United States refused to recognize his elevation to office, and in the meantime, the charismatic General Augusto César Sandino led liberals in a revolt against Chamorro. In the course of the revolt, the Sandinistas seized U.S. property in Nicaragua, which prompted the United States to dispatch gunboats and marines to the country. Their presence brought about a truce, during which Chamorro stepped down as president and left Nicaragua. In October 1926 the Nicaraguan congress elected the conservative Díaz president.

At this point Sacasa returned from his exile in Mexico and, with Mexican support, set up a rival liberal government on the eastern coast of Nicaragua. This triggered a civil war between Sacasa's followers—a rebel army under General José María Moncada—and the government forces of

Díaz. At the request of the conservative Nicaraguan president, U.S. president Calvin Coolidge authorized military aid in 1927, including several warships and a contingent of two thousand marines, whose mere presence was supposed to restore order. The United States also supplied Díaz with weapons and other materiel.

U.S. intervention in the Nicaraguan Civil War incited Augusto Sandino to join the fight, leading a brilliant guerrilla campaign against the marines and other *gringo* interlopers. Sandino's avowed purpose was to expel the marines from Nicaragua, and the marines, in turn, were determined to run Sandino to ground, either capturing or killing him. In the face of this new development, Coolidge dispatched Henry L. Stimson to Nicaragua to mediate between the rival leaders Díaz and Moncada. He persuaded them to disarm and to allow U.S. supervision of the upcoming election. On November 4, 1928, Moncada, the liberal candidate, was elected—but Sandino refused to accept the U.S.-mediated result, and his guerrillas continued to clash with marines, but always eluded decisive battle. While Sandino did not succeed in ousting the marines, neither were the marines capable of ending Sandino's guerrilla activities. The United States escalated its military presence by sending light bombers over the mountain regions known to harbor Sandinista guerrillas. After the bombings, Sandino fled to Mexico, but continued to direct guerrilla activities from there. At last, in 1932, Sacasa was elected to the presidency and negotiated with Sandino. The rebel leader agreed to end the war as soon as U.S. Marines withdrew in 1933. Granted amnesty by Sacasa, Sandino returned to Nicaragua and, in 1934, was assassinated in Managua by soldiers of the Nicaraguan National Guard, which was controlled by rising dictator Anastasio Somoza Garcia. This created a liberal political martyr and an enduring symbol of resistance to oppression and to U.S. imperialism in Nicaragua. In the 1970s left-wing socialist elements calling themselves Sandinistas would clash in civil war with the ruling Somoza presidential regime, which was often supported by the United States. In 1979 Sandinista forces finally succeeded in overthrowing the Somoza regime. At first they formed a coalition government that included moderate conservatives, but in 1984, Daniel Ortega Saavedra was elected president and quickly led the Nicaraguan government to the far left, which elicited the opposition of right-wing contra guerrillas *(see Nicaraguan Civil War, 1982–1990 [chapter 15])*.

CHAPTER 11

World War I, 1914–1918

World War I began in July 1914 and ended in November 1918. The United States did not enter the war until April 6, 1917, and had not massed sufficient numbers of troops to take a major role in combat until the following year. This chapter focuses on the phase of American participation, but begins by outlining the extensive European background of the war and the long course of combat before World War I became one of America's wars.

European Alliances

Two hostile systems of alliance dominated Europe at the beginning of the twentieth century: the Triple Alliance of Germany, Austria-Hungary, and Italy, and the Triple Entente of France, Russia, and Great Britain. These broad alliances were supplemented by lesser agreements, which essentially bound the major signatories to render military aid to a number of small nations. Far from ensuring the security of Europe and the world, the alliances all but ensured that some relatively minor incident would spark a major war.

War Begins

That incident occurred on June 28, 1914. Austria-Hungary regarded neighboring Serbia as a strong political threat because its independence was a provocative example to the Balkan territories the empire held as provinces. Certain forces within Serbia (most notably a secret society of Serbian army officers called the Black Hand) worked to foment rebellion among some of these provinces, especially Bosnia-Herzegovina. The heir apparent to the Hapsburg throne, Archduke Franz Ferdinand, decided that an official visit to the Bosnian provincial capital, Sarajevo, would assert Austria-Hungary's dominance over Bosnia-Herzegovina. The Serbian

WORLD WAR I
1914–1918

CHRONOLOGY   Principal Events of World War I: U.S. Involvement

1915

May 7: *German U-boat sinks the British liner Lusitania with loss of American lives; creates a U.S.-German diplomatic crisis*

1917

January 31: *Germany proclaims unrestricted submarine warfare*

February 3: *U.S. severs diplomatic relations with Germany*

March 1: *The Zimmermann Telegram, a German proposal of an alliance with Mexico against America, is published*

April 6: *U.S. declares war on Germany*

1918

January 8: *President Woodrow Wilson declares Allied war aims in his "Fourteen Points" speech*

May 28: *American troops win their first major action, the Battle of Cantigny*

May 30–June 17: *American troops are victorious at the Battles of Château-Thierry and Belleau Wood*

July 18–August 6: *Franco-American forces push back the Marne salient during the Aisne-Marne offensive*

September 12–16: *U.S. troops clear out the St.-Mihiel salient*

September 26–November 11: *The Meuse-Argonne Offensive is the final Franco-American offensive of the war*

October 6: *In a message to President Wilson, Prince Max of Baden, Germany's new chancellor, requests an armistice*

November 11: *Armistice declared; the fighting ceases at 11:00 A.M.*

1919

May 7–June 28: *President Wilson plays a leading role in negotiating a final peace; the Treaty of Versailles is drafted and signed*

369

Black Hand responded to the planned visit by recruiting a small cadre of assassins, among whom was a student named Gavrilo Princip. On June 28 he fired a pistol at Franz Ferdinand from nearly point-blank range, killing the archduke and his wife, Duchess Sophie. Although there was no evidence of official Serbian complicity in the assassination, Count Leopold von Berchtold, Austria-Hungary's foreign minister, saw the incident as an excuse for punishing Serbia, thereby quashing Bosnian nationalism and the pan-Slavic movement. Austria-Hungary declared war on Serbia on July 29, 1914. Almost immediately, a train of alliances and treaties lurched into motion. Serbia's ally Russia commenced a general mobilization on July 30, provoking a declaration of war from Germany, which also moved preemptively against the West, beginning an invasion of France via Belgium. France, an ally of Russia, declared war. Britain, an ally of France and Belgium, also declared war. By early August, Europe was divided into two warring alliances: Britain, France, Belgium, and Russia (the Allies) versus Germany and Austria-Hungary (the Central Powers). Subsequently, Japan and Italy would side with the Allies, and Turkey as well as some lesser powers with the Central Powers.

The U.S. Position, 1914–1916

Although Austria-Hungary faltered on the Eastern Front, Germany scored a series of devastating victories against the Russians. On the Western Front, Germany made an initial spectacular advance through Belgium and deep into France, coming within the outskirts of Paris. At the end of the war's first month, however, the Germans halted, and the Western Front hardened into a line of opposing trenches stretching from the Belgian coast in the north to the Swiss border in the south. For the next four years, the war would be fought with unprecedented loss of life along this remarkably static line, which marked a bloody deadlock.

Throughout 1914–1915, President Woodrow Wilson maintained U.S. neutrality and was carried to a second term in 1916 partly on the strength of the campaign slogan "He Kept Us Out of

IN THEIR OWN
Words

I do not feel like a criminal because I put away the one who was doing evil. Austria as it is represents evil for our people and therefore should not exist. . . . The political union of the Yugoslavs was always before my eyes, and that was my basic idea. Therefore it was necessary in the first place to free the Yugoslavs . . . from Austria. This . . . moved me to carry out the assassination of the heir apparent, for I considered him as very dangerous for Yugoslavia.

—GAVRILO PRINCIP, STATEMENT AT HIS TRIAL FOR HAVING ASSASSINATED ARCHDUKE FRANZ FERDINAND AND DUCHESS SOPHIE

War." As a neutral, the United States profitably traded with all sides, but early on, public opinion as well as American business and capital began to favor the Allies over the Central Powers. U.S. financial institutions made far larger loans to England and France than to Germany and Austria-Hungary, and neutral America drifted closer to the Allied camp. The first major challenge to neutrality came on May 7, 1915, when a German U-boat torpedoed and sank the British liner *Lusitania*, with the loss of 1,198 lives, including 124 Americans. Wilson did no more than issue a stern note of diplomatic protest, and in August, a U-boat sank the liner *Arabic*, again with loss of American lives. Yet, after this, fearing U.S. entry into the war, Kaiser Wilhelm II ordered an end to unrestricted submarine warfare. This hiatus endured until January 1917, when Germany boldly announced the resumption of unrestricted submarine warfare. Shortly after the announcement, a U.S. warship, the *Housatonic*, was torpedoed and sunk, provoking President Wilson to sever diplomatic relations with Germany on February 3, 1917. On February 26 he secured from Congress authority to arm U.S.-flag merchant vessels and to take all other military measures to protect American commerce. The United States had entered a phase of "armed neutrality."

The United States Enters the War

The drift toward U.S. entry into the war accelerated in February 1917, after British intelligence authorities turned over to President Wilson a telegram that had been intercepted between Germany's foreign minister, Alfred Zimmermann, and the German ambassador to Mexico. Transmitted on January 16, 1917, the Zimmermann Telegram (as it came to be called) authorized the ambassador to propose a German-Mexican alliance to Mexican president Carranza. In return for a declaration of war against the United States, Mexico would receive Germany's support in the reconquest of its "lost territory in Texas, New Mexico, and Arizona." Carranza was also to be asked to invite Japan to adhere to the anti-American alliance. As it happened, Carranza

IN THEIR OWN *Words*

Unrestricted U-boat war would ... mean the breaking of diplomatic relations with the United States, and, if American lives are lost, would finally lead to war. ... If we take up unrestricted U-boat warfare, the attitude of all neutral Powers will be changed against us and we shall have to calculate upon establishing new fronts. Germany will in such case be looked upon as a mad dog against whom the hand of every man will be raised for the purpose of finally bringing about peace. ...

—GERMAN SECRETARY OF STATE GOTTLIEB VON JAGOW, ARGUING WITH THE ADMIRALTY IN 1914 AGAINST INSTITUTING UNRESTRICTED SUBMARINE WARFARE did not take Germany up on its offer, but the Zimmermann Telegram was sufficient to propel Wilson to ask Congress for a declaration of war against Germany on April 2, 1917. War was declared on April 6.

The Allied Situation at the Beginning of 1917

For the Allies, U.S. entry came not a moment too soon—even though the process of effective American mobilization would consume months, and American troops would not be committed to battle in any substantial numbers until well into 1918. By the start of 1917, every major Allied offensive had failed, and the Central Powers were in possession of huge tracts of Allied territory.

U.S. Mobilization

The Selective Service Act of 1917 was signed into law on May 18 of that year. Over the next two years, 23.9 million men were registered for the draft and 2.8 million were drafted. The expansion of the U.S. Army was phenomenal: From 133,000 men in 1916 it grew to 4.5 million by Armistice Day, November 11, 1918. Nevertheless, amassing, training, and transporting an army sizable enough to be effective in the Great War consumed more time than the Allies thought they could afford. Tension between the U.S. general in chief, John J. Pershing, and his Allied counterparts often ran high, as Pershing insisted on maintaining direct U.S. control of American forces (the American Expeditionary Force, or AEF) and on not committing them to battle in a piecemeal fashion, but only when sufficient unit strengths had been attained. Pershing arrived in Paris with a small staff on June 14, 1917, and a massive transport effort was organized to bring the bulk of the U.S. Army to Europe. By

IN THEIR OWN Words

We intend to begin on the first of February unrestricted submarine warfare. We shall endeavor in spite of this to keep the United States of America neutral. In the event of this not succeeding, we make Mexico a proposal of alliance on the following basis: make war together, make peace together, generous financial support and an understanding on our part that Mexico is to reconquer the lost territory in Texas, New Mexico, and Arizona. The settlement in detail is left to you. You will inform the [Mexican] President of the above most secretly as soon as the outbreak of war with the United States of America is certain and add the suggestion that he should, on his own initiative, invite Japan to immediate adherence and at the same time mediate between Japan and ourselves. Please call the President's attention to the fact that the ruthless employment of our submarines now offers the prospect of compelling England in a few months to make peace. [Signed,] ZIMMERMANN.

—THE ZIMMERMANN TELEGRAM

the end of 1917 only 175,000 U.S. troops were in Europe, even as Germany began launching a series of all-out offensives against the Western Front.

Adding to the desperation of the war-weary and depleted Allies was the onset of the Russian revolutions of 1917. The first, in March 1917, overthrew Czar Nicholas II. The second, in October 1917, brought to power the Bolshevik (Communist) regime of Vladimir I. Lenin. Almost immediately the new Soviet government concluded a "separate peace" with Germany, withdrawing from the war by an armistice of December 15, 1917. Germany was now free to concentrate virtually all of its troops on the Western Front.

The Ludendorff Offensives

Using troops freed up from the Eastern Front as a result of the "separate peace" with the Soviet Union, Germany's top commander, Erich Ludendorff, mounted a series of offensives intended to destroy the British army, which would, in turn, force the French to negotiate a favorable peace. The first, on the Somme, began on March 21, 1918, and inflicted at least 240,000 Allied casualties, although it had been equally costly to the Germans.

General John J. Pershing, commander in chief, American Expeditionary Force, photographed at AEF General Headquarters, Chaumont, France, October 19, 1918. *Collection: National Archives and Records Administration*

Undeterred by his own heavy casualties, Ludendorff mounted a second offensive, against the British at the Lys River, forming part of the Belgian-French border. By April 29, when Ludendorff broke off this offensive, British losses were 239,000. Although Germany had come close to a decisive victory, its losses were a staggering 348,300 killed or wounded.

The third German offensive, on the Aisne River, commenced on May 27 against lightly held French positions on the Chemin des Dames ridge. This was supposed to be a diversionary attack, but it was so successful that it became the major effort of the offensive. In twenty-four hours the Germans advanced twenty miles, and by May 30 they had reached the Marne, just fifty miles outside of Paris. The United States played a minor role in assisting the British on the Lys, but the first significant U.S. action of the war occurred on April 20,

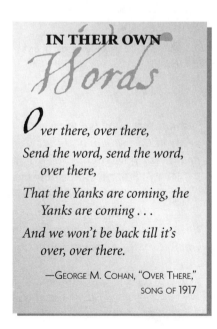

IN THEIR OWN
Words

*O*ver there, over there,

Send the word, send the word, over there,

That the Yanks are coming, the Yanks are coming . . .

And we won't be back till it's over, over there.

—GEORGE M. COHAN, "OVER THERE," SONG OF 1917

when two companies of the Twenty-sixth Division came under heavy attack near Seicheprey along the St.-Mihiel salient. About 2,800 regular German troops spearheaded by 600 elite shock troops overran the American positions. A large number of Americans were taken prisoner, and 669 others were either killed or wounded. German losses were slight. It was a deeply disappointing baptism by fire, but General Pershing rushed the U.S. Second and Third Divisions to reinforce the French along the Marne. In the meantime, Major General Robert Lee Bullard launched the first U.S. offensive of the war, at the village of Cantigny, some fifty miles northwest of the action at Chemin des Dames and about sixty miles north of Paris. Cantigny was the site of a German advance observation point and was very strongly fortified. On May 28 the U.S. First Division attacked the village and drove the Germans out. Later in the day and on the next day, the Americans successfully repulsed German counterattacks. The American victory boosted Allied morale, made up for the defeat on the Lys, and gave the U.S. troops great confidence.

The vanguard of the offensive was at Château-Thierry, on the Marne, less than fifty miles northeast of Paris. The U.S. Second and Third Divisions rushed to block the Germans from crossing the Marne at this point. The Third Division defended the Marne bridges, successfully holding them against the Germans, then counterattacking. The French Tenth Colonial Division, inspired by the performance of the Americans, joined the action, pushing the German onslaught back across the Marne at Jauglonne.

If the U.S. Army distinguished itself at Cantigny and Château-Thierry, it was the U.S. Marines who performed with extraordinary valor at Belleau Wood as the spearhead of the army's

IN THEIR OWN Words

Gee! I often think of the time when I was at home. Mama, you know I believe that one day I will come back to you and the loved ones I left behind. Wouldn't you be glad to have your soldier boy with you again? My prayer to God is that we will have peace with all the nations and we boys get back home with our dear ones.

—GEORGE W. LEE, AEF, TO HIS MOTHER IN GREENSBORO, NORTH CAROLINA, FROM FRANCE, 1917

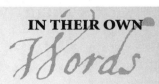
IN THEIR OWN Words

I am very happy in my work. . . . Let me tell you this, we can beat the Boche [Germans] to a frazzle if we go into this with heart and soul. . . . We can beat the Boche only by fighting, and we are better fighters and better killers than the Boche. . . . Our killing spirit must be aroused but it is rising and Lord! I hope I am in the drive when it comes—when the Americans bloody their bayonets!

—LIEUTENANT LAMBERT WOOD, AEF, LETTER TO HIS PARENTS FROM FRANCE, DECEMBER 7, 1917

Second Division. To capture Belleau Wood, the marines advanced across a wheatfield that was swept by machine gun fire. The casualties incurred on June 6, 1918, were the heaviest single-day losses in Marine Corps history (until November 1943, during *World War II, 1939–1945 [see chapter 12],* when the marines took the Japanese-held island of Tarawa). During June 9 through June 26, the marines and the army's Second Division took, lost, and retook Belleau Wood and the nearby villages of Vaux and Bouresche no fewer than half a dozen times before the Germans had been pushed out permanently.

Deserters from the increasingly demoralized German army revealed to French captors the essence of the strategy behind Ludendorff's next two projected offensives. The next assault would come at Noyon and Montdidier, just southeast of Cantigny and northwest of Château-Thierry. The French command prepared thoroughly for the assault, which came on June 9. A Franco-American counterattack checked the advance of the German Eighteenth Army by June 11, and on June 12, the Allies repulsed an attack by the German Seventh Army.

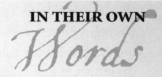

IN THEIR OWN Words

Soldiers are dreamers; when the guns begin
    They think of firelit homes, clean beds, and wives.
I see them in foul dug-outs, gnawed by rats,
    And in the ruined trenches, lashed with rain,
Dreaming of things they did with balls and bats,
    And mocked by hopeless longing to regain
Bank-holidays and picture shows, and spats,
    And going to the office in the train.

—FROM "DREAMERS" BY SIEGFRIED SASSOON, BRITISH POET AND SOLDIER

By this time more than a quarter million U.S. troops were arriving in France each month, and by June 1918, seven of the twenty-five U.S. divisions in France were in action at the front. Realizing that time was running out, an increasingly desperate Ludendorff mounted the fifth German offensive in five months. Once again his objective was the destruction of the British army in Flanders, but he decided to precede the main thrust with a preliminary offensive against the French and the Americans in the Champagne region, focusing the attack on the fortified city of Reims. Ferdinand Foch, now the supreme Allied commander, had been informed by the German deserters of the impending attack. He used his artillery to arrest the advance of German shock troops during the night of July 14–15. Thus he

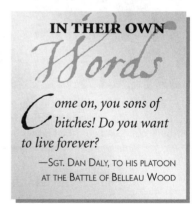

IN THEIR OWN Words

Come on, you sons of bitches! Do you want to live forever?

—SGT. DAN DALY, TO HIS PLATOON AT THE BATTLE OF BELLEAU WOOD was able to check the attack that came east of Reims. West of that city, the Germans punched through to the Marne and crossed it with fourteen divisions. Here, however, American troops became heavily engaged, and the U.S. Third Division earned the nickname "Rock of the Marne" for its determined and highly successful defense of the region west of Reims.

Second Battle of the Marne

Although Ludendorff's five offensives cost more Allied than German lives, they had nevertheless cost very many German lives—without putting Germany closer to winning the war. Worse, Germany could not replace its losses, whereas the Allies now had a vast pool of fresh American troops to draw on. On July 17, 1918, Foch concluded that Ludendorff was beginning to pull troops out of the Marne sector, which had threatened Paris, to send them north, against the British positions. In this, Foch saw an opportunity for an Allied counteroffensive, to be launched preemptively, before the Germans could commence action against the British. Although other commanders argued that any major counteroffensive should await the availability of additional American units, Foch decided that time was of the essence. He concentrated his available forces around the Marne salient, the bulge of German penetration, purposely leaving the British armies of Sir Douglas Haig exposed before the growing German concentration to the north. Foch's intention was to lure Ludendorff into further weakening the Marne sector even while Foch secretly built it up. Foch would attack here, on the Marne, after Ludendorff had withdrawn many troops but before he had concentrated enough of them in the north to overwhelm Haig. The counteroffensive stepped off at four thirty-five on the morning of July 18, 1918. The French Tenth, Sixth, and Fifth Armies, from left to right along the front, made the assault, while the French Ninth Army waited in reserve. U.S. forces also were active in the Second Battle of the Marne. The American First and Second Divisions spearheaded the main assault by French units under General Charles M. E. Mangin, and six other U.S. divisions also fought valiantly.

U.S. doughboys occupy the German crown prince's observatory after overrunning the German position at the Second Battle of the Marne, October 17, 1918.
Collection: National Archives and Records Administration

Ludendorff, taken by surprise, desperately ordered four of his reserve divisions into the Marne sector, but soon realized that withdrawal was his only realistic option. He began to move east across the Marne on the night of July 18. The Second Battle of the Marne was certainly an important Allied victory, yet, despite heavy losses, Ludendorff's army remained intact on August 6, when the counteroffensive ended.

Amiens Offensive

Sir Douglas Haig proposed an Anglo-French attack east of Amiens in northwestern France, along the Somme River to free up the rail network in the area. Accordingly, Foch placed the French First Army under Haig's direction, and Haig chose the British Fourth Army, under General Henry Rawlinson, to operate in conjunction with the French First Army. Rawlinson carried out a lightning attack along a fourteen-mile front, using artillery, infantry, and airpower, as well as virtually the entire British tank corps, 604 vehicles. The Allies rolled over the Germans, taking more than 15,000 prisoners and capturing 400 guns. Ludendorff would later characterize August 8, 1918, as the "Black Day" of the German army. Yet he did not capitulate. Instead, he reestablished a position ten miles behind what had been the nose of the German salient. On August 10, the French Third Army pushed the Germans out of Montdidier. Pausing to regroup, Haig failed to coordinate with this operation, however, and the German army was able to prepare its defenses.

The Allies resumed the offensive on August 21, when the British Third Army, on the left, and the French armies, on the right, again attacked. On August 22 the British Fourth Army came racing up the center, followed by the British First Army on the far left. The German positions crumbled, and Ludendorff withdrew not only from the Lys salient in Flanders but also from Amiens, to the south, in France. ANZAC (Australia–New Zealand Army Corps) forces struck, advancing across the Somme during August 30–31 to take the German-held village of Péronne. On September 2 a Canadian corps forced its way through the German lines near Quéant. Now the Germans fled all the way back to the Hindenburg Line. German casualties from the Amiens offensive exceeded a hundred thousand killed, wounded, or taken prisoner. Some twenty-two thousand British soldiers and twenty thousand French were killed or wounded. Ludendorff himself recommended to Kaiser Wilhelm II an end to the war.

U.S. Action against the St.-Mihiel Salient

The U.S. First Army, with the French II Colonial Corps attached to it, was assigned to the St.-Mihiel sector on August 30. Its mission was to push back this incursion of German strength, which had held since 1915. Coincidentally, on September 8, Ludendorff had ordered withdrawal from the salient, to begin on September 11. If his troops were allowed to retreat to the Hindenburg Line, the salient would be vacated, but the German army also would be saved. Pershing was determined to prevent Ludendorff from withdrawing without a fight, and, early on the morning of September 12, sixteen U.S. divisions attacked, supported by French artillery and French tanks, as well as a mixed force of American, French, Italian, and Portuguese pilots flying some six hundred planes (out of fourteen hundred deployed) under the command of U.S. military air pioneer Colonel William "Billy" Mitchell. The U.S. I and IV Corps smashed into the southern face of the salient, while the French II Colonial Corps jabbed at the salient's nose and the U.S. V Corps closed in from the west. The result was a titanic thirty-six-hour battle that forced the Germans to surrender en masse. Not only had the St.-Mihiel Salient been cleared, but also the German army had been dealt a very severe blow. The reduction of the St.-Mihiel Salient by half a million U.S. troops was the largest U.S. military operation since the *Civil War, 1861–1865 (see chapter 8).*

American engineers near the St.-Mihiel Salient. *Collection: National Archives and Records Administration*

Meuse-Argonne Offensive

Immediately after the St.-Mihiel sector had been secured, Pershing moved the entire U.S. First Army, unrested, sixty miles to the Verdun area to participate in Foch's Meuse-Argonne Offensive. The French commander's plan was for the Franco-American forces to drive forward from Verdun toward Mézières, a key German rail junction and supply depot. Simultaneously, British units would attack between Péronne and Lens, to control the rail junction at Aulnoye. These operations would gain control of German lines of supply along the Western Front. Pershing brilliantly executed the transfer of a five-hundred-thousand-man army, by night, into position for the attack that would initiate the offensive. It began at five twenty-five on the morning of September 26 against a German army group under Max von Gallwitz and another commanded by the crown prince. The German defenses were extremely well prepared and heavily fortified, and the rugged, heavily wooded terrain presented a formidable obstacle to the attackers. Although the initial advance rapidly penetrated the first two German lines, the American drive slowed along the line between Apremont and Brieulles by October 3. By October 4 it was apparent that the dense Argonne Forest offered no room for maneuver, so that Pershing's only option was to make repeated and costly frontal assaults. The Argonne operation therefore stretched through nearly the end of October before the third German line was broken.

Aerial view of the ruins of Vaux, France. The photographer was Edward Steichen, at the time on duty with the AEF. *Collection: National Archives and Records Administration*

Prelude to Armistice

During the first eleven days of November 1918, the U.S. Army, having broken out of the Argonne Forest, raced through the last German positions in the Meuse Valley. Pershing—and the other Allied commanders—were determined to exert as much pressure on the Germans as possible, even though peace seemed at hand. The U.S. First Division was about to take Sedan on November 6 when the higher command ordered a halt. The honor of conquering that city, it was decreed, must be French. On November 10 the U.S. Second Army, under Major General Robert Lee Bullard, launched an attack in its drive toward the village of Montmédy, only to break it off the next day at 11:00 A.M. sharp, the hour of Armistice.

Armistice Negotiations Commence

On September 29 Ludendorff advised Kaiser Wilhelm II to seek an immediate armistice, and the kaiser accordingly appointed as chancellor of Germany Prince Max of Baden to open negotiations—initially with President Woodrow Wilson. The president stunned Prince Max by replying that nothing short of Germany's complete and unconditional surrender would end the war. Moreover, Wilson declared that the Allies would not negotiate with what he called the present German military dictatorship. In response to this, the kaiser compelled Ludendorff's resignation on October

IN THEIR OWN Words

*G*as! Gas! Quick, boys!—
An ecstasy of fumbling,

*Fitting the clumsy helmets
just in time,*

*But someone still was yelling
out and stumbling*

*And flound'ring like a man in
fire or lime.*

*Dim through the misty panes
and thick green light,*

*As under a green sea, I saw
him drowning.*

—FROM "DULCE ET DECORUM EST" BY
WILFRED OWEN, BRITISH POET AND SOL-
DIER KILLED ON THE WESTERN FRONT,
ONE WEEK BEFORE THE ARMISTICE

The Machine Gun Battalion of the U.S. Eighteenth Infantry passes through St.-Baussant on the way to the St.-Mihiel front. *Collection: National Archives and Records Administration*

26, effective on the twenty-seventh. Yet the kaiser himself refused to abdicate in favor of one of his grandsons, and so negotiations continued to be delayed. Now a war-weary Germany began to feel the shudder of revolution, much as Russia had earlier. When, on November 7, Austria-Hungary capitulated to the Allies, Bavarian revolutionaries declared the overthrow of the German (or Hohenzollern) monarchy and the creation of the Bavarian People's Republic. In response to this, Friedrich Ebert, leader of Germany's majority Social Democratic Party, called on Prince Max to persuade the kaiser to abdicate, if only to save Germany from communism. Instead of persuading Wilhelm II to step down, Max simply announced his abdication on November 9, and General Paul von Hindenburg informed Wilhelm II that he no longer had the army's support. With this, the deposed kaiser fled to the neutral Netherlands (November 10).

In the face of these developments, the Allies opened armistice negotiations with a German delegation led by Matthias Erzberger, a civilian politician, at Rethondes, in the Forest of Compiègne, in a railway carriage that served Foch as his traveling headquarters. The armistice was set for the eleventh hour of the eleventh day of the eleventh month.

An American-manned French tank goes over the top at St. Mihiel. *Collection: National Archives and Records Administration*

Postarmistice Operations and the Treaty of Versailles

On November 17, 1918, under terms of the armistice, Allied troops began to reoccupy the parts of France and Belgium that had been held by the Germans since 1914. Allied troops, including a large U.S. contingent, occupied the German Rhineland beginning on December 9, and a peace conference—among the Allies and excluding the Central Powers—was convened at Paris on January 18, 1919.

Although twenty-seven Allied nations participated in creating the Treaty of Versailles, the four major Allied powers—Britain, France, Italy, and the United States—dominated discussions. Woodrow Wilson championed a conciliatory settlement based on the "Fourteen Points" he had enumerated before a joint session of Congress on January 8, 1918. These conditions included a guarantee of "open covenants, openly arrived at," mandating an end to the kind of secret treaties and alliances that had dragged Europe into war; a guarantee of freedom of the seas; removal of economic barriers to international trade; radical arms reduction; and modification of all colonial claims on the basis of the self-determination of peoples. Eight additional points addressed specific postwar territorial settlements, and the fourteenth point called for the establishment of a League of Nations, an international body to guarantee political independence and territorial integrity for all nations and to provide a forum for the peaceful resolution of conflict.

Opposed to Wilson's conciliatory policies, French premier Georges Clemenceau demanded vengeance as well as measures to crush Germany economically and militarily. Britain's prime minister, David Lloyd George, personally favored moderation, but he had been elected on his promise that Germany would be punished. Italy's Vittorio Orlando was primarily concerned to ensure that his nation would receive the territories it had been promised in 1915 as an inducement to join the Allied cause. In the end, the Allies produced a harshly punitive treaty that humiliated and crippled Germany and the other Central Powers. Chief provisions included German territorial cessions, German admission of guilt for the war, German disarmament, and an assessment against Germany (and other Central Powers) of ruinous monetary reparations. The Austro-Hungarian Empire was broken up, and its territory greatly reduced.

With great reluctance and in protest, Germany signed the Treaty of Versailles on June 28, 1919. Although President Wilson signed the treaty, as well as the Covenant of the League of Nations attached to it, the Republican-controlled U.S. Senate refused to ratify either document. The United States subsequently drew up brief separate peace treaties with the former Central Powers. Tragically, the punitive Treaty of Versailles contributed to the devastating political, economic, and emotional climate that promoted the rise of Adolf Hitler and Nazism and that made a *second* world war all but inevitable.

IN THEIR OWN *Words*

To me those hours seemed like a release from the painful feelings of my youth. Even today I am not ashamed to say that, overpowered by stormy enthusiasm, I fell down on my knees and thanked Heaven from an overflowing heart for granting me the good fortune of being permitted to live at this time.

—ADOLF HITLER, IN *MEIN KAMPF* (1924), RECALLING HIS REACTION TO NEWS THAT WORLD WAR I HAD STARTED

CHAPTER 12

World War II, 1939–1945

W orld War I *(see World War I, 1914–1918 [chapter 11])* had been fought, in the words of U.S. president Woodrow Wilson, as the "war to end all war," but the Treaty of Versailles, which ended that war, was aimed less at establishing a world at peace than it was at punishing Germany and keeping it a beaten nation, both economically and militarily. The treaty saddled Germany with a crippling war debt, and it limited the German army to a mere hundred thousand men, of whom only four thousand were to be officers. Heavy weapons, aircraft included, were prohibited. As for the German navy, it was limited to only fifteen thousand sailors, and the nation was barred from building any new submarines. Combined with the great worldwide depression of the 1930s, the economic hardships and the collective national humiliation wrought by the treaty pushed Germany and the Germans beyond the brink of desperation. Combine this desperate situation with the threat of Communist revolution from the nearby Soviet Union, and the conditions for renewed German aggression were at hand. All that was lacking was a leader commensurate to the desperation of the times.

That leader was Adolf Hitler.

1939

September 8: *President Franklin Roosevelt authorizes expansion of the Army and of state National Guard units*

1940

October 16: *U.S. men register in first peacetime draft*

1941

March 11: *Lend-Lease Act*

August 14: *Atlantic Charter*

October 31: *German U-boats sink U.S. destroyer* Reuben James *off Iceland*

December 7–8: *Japanese attack Pearl Harbor, Midway, Wake, Guam, Philippines, British Malaya, Hong Kong, Thailand*

December 8: *United States declares war on Japan*

December 11: *United States declares war on Germany and Italy*

December 23: *Wake Island falls to Japan*

1942

January 2: *Japanese enter Manila, occupy Cavite naval base*

March 17: *General MacArthur reaches Australia from Philippines and assumes command of Allied forces in southwestern Pacific*

April 9: *Bataan falls to Japan*

April 18: *Doolittle leads Tokyo bombing raid*

May 7–8: *U.S. Navy checks Japanese invasion fleet in Battle of Coral Sea*

May 6: *Corregidor falls to Japan*

June 3–6: *U.S. Navy defeats Japanese at Battle of Midway*

June 4–6: *Japan invades the Aleutian Islands*

July 4: *First U.S. bombing missions in Europe*

August 7: *U.S. Marines land on Guadalcanal and Tulagi*

August 19: *British-Canadian commandos and American Rangers raid Dieppe, Belgium*

November 8: *U.S. forces invade North Africa*

November 13–15: *U.S. Navy defeats Japanese off Guadalcanal*

1943

January 6: *United States raids Rabaul, major Japanese base*

February 8: *Guadalcanal falls to United States*

May 12: *German resistance ends in North Africa*

July 2–3: *Americans land on New Georgia*

July 9–10: *Allies invade Sicily*

July 25: *Mussolini is deposed*

August 17: *U.S. forces take Messina, ending the Sicily campaign*

September 3: *Allies invade southern Italy*

September 8: *Italy surrenders*

September 9: *U.S. Fifth Army invades Italy at Salerno*

November 1: *U.S. Marines invade Bougainville*

November 20: *United States invades Gilbert Islands*

November 24: *Tarawa and other Gilbert Islands fall to United States*

1944

January 22: *Allies land at Anzio*

February 12: *Allies begin attack on Cassino*

February 22: *United States captures Eniwetok in Marshall Islands*

March 7: *First U.S. troops in Burma*

March 20: *Admiralty Islands fall to United States*

April 3: *Bikini and other Marshall atolls fall to United States*

April 18: *Cassino falls to Allies*

June 4: *U.S. Fifth Army enters Rome*

June 6: *D-Day invasion at Normandy*

June 15: *U.S. Marines invade Saipan, Marianas*

June 16: *China-based B-29 raids commence against Japan*

June 19–20: *U.S. Navy wins Battle of the Philippine Sea*

June 27: *Cherbourg falls to U.S. forces*

July 21: *U.S. Marines invade Guam*

July 24: *U.S. Marines land on Tinian*

August 25: *U.S. forces enter Paris*

September 11: *U.S. First Army crosses German border*

September 15: *U.S. Marines invade Pelelieu*

October 20: *United States begins Philippine campaign*

October 23–26: *U.S. Navy defeats Japanese in Leyte Gulf*

December 16: *Battle of the Bulge begins*

1945

January 16: *Battle of the Bulge ends; last major German offensive collapses*

February 4: *U.S. forces enter Manila*

February 4–11: *Roosevelt, Churchill, and Stalin confer at Yalta*

February 15–16: *U.S. forces land on Bataan and Corregidor*

February 19: *U.S. Marines land on Iwo Jima*

March 7: *Cologne falls to U.S. forces*

March 16: *Iwo Jima falls to United States*

March 22–23: *Major Rhine crossing*

April 1: *U.S. forces land on Okinawa*

April 12: *President Roosevelt dies; Truman becomes president*

April 18: *U.S. troops cross Czech border*

May 7: *Germany surrenders*

June 21: *Okinawa falls to United States*

July 5: *Philippine liberation completed*

July 16: *Successful atomic bomb test in New Mexico*

August 6: *Atomic bomb dropped on Hiroshima*

August 9: *Atomic bomb dropped on Nagasaki*

August 14–15: *Japan accepts Allied surrender terms; ceasefire declared*

September 2: *Japan signs surrender instrument aboard USS* Missouri, *Tokyo Bay*

Adolf Hitler, Germany's dictator (right), greets Field Marshal Walther Model. *Collection: National Archives and Records Administration*

The Rise of Hitler and the Nazi Party

Seizing on the political, economic, and social unrest in postwar Germany, Hitler transformed the German Workers' Party by August 1920 into the *Nationalsozialistische Deutsche Arbeiterpartei,* commonly shortened to NSDAP or Nazi Party, and was elected president of the party in July 1921. A street-corner orator, Hitler loudly assaulted Germany's "enemies"— mainly Communists and Jews—as well as the nations that had forced upon the German people an ignominious peace. During November 8–9, 1923, he led the Munich Beer Hall Putsch, a bold but premature attempt to seize control of the Bavarian government. The abortive rebellion was put down and Hitler was arrested, tried, and convicted of treason, for which he was sentenced to five years in prison. While incarcerated, he wrote his political autobiography, *Mein Kampf (My Struggle),* in which he crystallized the political philosophy of Nazism, proclaiming eternal opposition to Jews, Communists, effete liberals, and exploitive capitalists the world over, and exulting a reborn Germany of racial purity and unstoppable national will. He wrote of a Germany that would rise again to become the dominant power in the world, a Germany that would claim and obtain *Lebensraum* (living space, a term Hitler borrowed and distorted from the work of Friedrich Ratzel [1844–1904], a German geographer and ethnographer) in central Europe and in Russia.

Hitler was released from prison after serving only nine months, and he set about strengthening his party, especially in the industrial German north. The party's greatest boon came with the worldwide economic collapse of 1929 and the depression that followed. Forging an alliance with the Nationalist Party headed by industrialist Alfred Hugenberg, the Nazis increased the number of Reichstag seats they held from 12 to 107, becoming the second-largest party in Germany. Hitler did not confine his party's activities to the Reichstag, but also developed the SA (Sturm-abteilung, or Brownshirts) into an effective paramilitary arm that quite literally beat down the opposition in the streets of Germany. Hitler ran for president of the German republic in 1932, narrowly losing to incumbent Paul Hindenberg, the aged hero of World War I. But the July elections gained the Nazis 230 Reichstag seats, 37 percent of the vote, making it the largest party represented, and Hindenberg was compelled to appoint Hitler *Reichskanzler* (Reich chancellor, or prime minister) on January 30, 1933.

From his office as chancellor, Hitler consolidated his power. When fire destroyed the Reichstag on February 27, 1933, Hitler found a pretext for legally abolishing the Communist Party and imprisoning its leaders. On March 23, 1933, he engineered passage of the Enabling Act, which granted him four years of unalloyed dictatorial powers. He began systematically dismantling all German parties, save for the NSDAP; purged Jews from all government institutions; and brought all government offices under the direct control of the party. He then purged his own ranks during the Night of the Long Knives, June 30, 1934, murdering Ernst Röhm and hundreds of other Nazis whose radicalism posed a threat to Hitler's absolute domination. Shortly after this, in August 1934, Hindenberg died, and Hitler assumed the functions of the presidency but adopted the title of Führer—supreme leader—of the Third Reich.

Germany Rearms

Yet even before Hitler's rise, the German military was finding ways to turn the Treaty of Versailles to its advantage. Under General Hans von Seeckt, the skeleton army left by Versailles became a *Führerheer*—an "army of leaders," an army of the military elite. Although it was small, it was an all-volunteer force, selective, the highly polished core around which a new, full-sized army could be quickly, efficiently, and effectively formed whenever the time was ripe. As for the treaty restrictions on military hardware,

Germany found various ways around them. One of the most ingenious was the Treaty of Rapallo with the Soviet Union (1922), which established a program of military cooperation between Germany and the USSR. The Treaty of Versailles restricted development of weapons in Germany; the Treaty of Rapallo provided facilities *in the Soviet Union* where Germany could develop advanced ground weapons and aircraft. Another agreement, the London Naval Treaty, concluded in 1935 with Britain and other nations, allowed Germany increased tonnage in warships—and gave Hitler hope that Britain and Germany might actually become allies.

Important as these treaties were to Germany, they were not absolutely necessary to that nation's rearmament. With or without treaties, Germany rearmed, secretly at first, then quite boldly, after it became increasingly apparent that the other nations of Europe, either acting on their own or through the League of Nations, lacked the will to take action in response to violations of the Treaty of Versailles. While Germany honed the *Führerheer* and rearmed, its military planners also developed a revolutionary new approach to war. It was christened *Blitzkrieg*—lightning war—and was a combination of tactics and weapons designed to move against an enemy with overwhelming force and great speed, penetrating its front-line defenses while encircling and destroying it.

Fascist Expansionism

As Germany was preparing to take the offensive, the French took other action, which all too aptly symbolized the hunkered-down, defensive attitude of non-Fascist Europe. André Maginot, France's minister of war, authorized construction of a great system of fortifications that would bear his name. Completed in 1938, the Maginot Line was a wonder of twentieth-century military engineering. It was essentially a string of fortresses connected by a network of tunnels through which troops and supplies could be transported by rail. Exposed structures were built of thick concrete designed to withstand bombardment by any artillery then known. The Maginot Line covered the entire French-German frontier, from the southern tip of Belgium down to the top of Switzerland. Out of respect for Belgian neutrality, however, it did not extend along France's border with that nation. This would prove a tragic oversight.

France's war preparations were both defensive and passive, typical of the military policies of the post–World War I European democracies. The German attitude, on the other hand, was aggressively expansionist, a pursuit of *Lebensraum*. Hitler declared it only right, natural, and inevitable that the German people should have all of the living space that the might of the German state could obtain for them. By the mid-1930s, Hitler's talk of *Lebensraum* prompted Britain, France, and even Italy to issue a joint statement of opposition to German expansion. The French also entered into a defensive alliance with the Soviets in 1935, and the Soviets concluded a similar pact with the Czechs.

But it was Italy, not Germany, that made the first overtly expansionist move by invading Ethiopia in 1935. In response, the British foreign secretary, Sir Samuel Hoare, sought to "appease" Mussolini by offering him most of Ethiopia in return for a truce that would preserve the defensive alliance against Germany. Hoare's plan not only was aborted, but it also created a scandal that caused Hoare to resign his cabinet post. Mussolini waged his war against Ethiopia, bombing and even gassing the all but defenseless nation into submission. However, the concept of appeasement had been introduced into European politics.

Having seen how Britain and France reacted to the aggression of Italy against Ethiopia, Hitler was emboldened to take the first step in his program of expansion. The Treaty of Versailles had ordered the evacuation of all German forces from the Rhineland. Now, on March 7, 1936, Hitler ordered twenty-two thousand soldiers back across the bridges of the Rhine. It was a token force—a testing of the waters—and Hitler was prepared to retreat if the French intervened. But neither France nor Britain nor Italy resisted or even protested this violation of the Treaty of Versailles. The weakness of France and Britain persuaded Mussolini to conclude a pact with Hitler. On July 11, 1936, Italy agreed that Austria should be deemed "a German state," and on November 1, Italy and Germany concluded the Rome-Berlin Axis, which was followed on November 25 by the German-Japanese Anti-Comintern Pact—an alliance ostensibly against communism but, in fact, an alliance of general military cooperation.

Appeasement Policy

In May 1937, Neville Chamberlain replaced the retiring Stanley Baldwin as prime minister of Britain. The policy Chamberlain proposed with regard to Germany was one of "active appeasement": discover what Hitler wanted and then give it to him, to conserve military resources to fight what Chamberlain saw as the more serious threats from Italy and Japan.

On March 13, 1938, Hitler invaded Austria. Unopposed by Austria or by Italy, he declared Austria a province of the German Reich. Called the *Anschluss,* the annexation of Austria put Germany in position to make its next move—into Czechoslovakia.

Chamberlain, while intent on appeasing Hitler, began by warning him to negotiate with the Czechs. When Hitler stood firm, Chamberlain caved in. He traveled to Berchtesgaden, Hitler's Bavarian mountain retreat, and baldly proposed to give Hitler all that he demanded. Stunned and delighted by his good fortune, Hitler demanded cession of the Sudetenland, the German-speaking region of Czechoslovakia. Chamberlain agreed, asking Hitler to hold off the invasion until he could persuade Paris and Prague to go along with the plan. In response, the French appealed to President Franklin D. Roosevelt, but failed to shake the United States out of its post–World War I attitude of isolationism. Most Americans—politicians and public alike—wanted no part of a new European war. Rather than stand alone against Germany, therefore, France agreed to hand the Sudetenland to Hitler.

What Chamberlain failed to grasp was that Czechoslovakia was the strategic keystone of Europe. Its geographical location was critical, and it already contained a major arms works as well as thirty army divisions. Nevertheless, Chamberlain organized the Munich Conference on September 29–30, 1938, which summarily sold out the Czechs to Germany, in return for Hitler's pledge that he make no more territorial demands in Europe. The prime minister returned to London and declared that he had returned with "peace for our time." Chamberlain and the world soon reaped the folly of "appeasing" Hitler. The ink was scarcely dry on the Munich pact before Hitler maneuvered to take all of Czechoslovakia, not just the Sudetenland. On March 16, 1939, German army units occupied Prague, and the Czech nation ceased to exist.

The Soviet-German Nonaggression Pact

As leader of world communism, Soviet premier Joseph Stalin was by definition the enemy of Adolf Hitler, who had already eclipsed Mussolini as leader of world fascism. Nevertheless, as Nazi Germany came to dominate more and more of Europe, Stalin proposed to Hitler a "Nonaggression Pact," which Hitler, eager to neutralize a potentially overwhelming enemy, signed on August 23, 1939. The pact gave Hitler free rein to invade Poland—the Soviets would even help—in return for Hitler's agreement not to interfere with Stalin's plan to invade Finland. The pact seemed to remove the one remaining check on Fascist expansion.

War Begins

As planned, Stalin aided Hitler's invasion of Poland on September 1, 1939, by attacking from the east as Hitler invaded from the west. Also as planned, Stalin invaded Finland, annexing that nation on March 12, 1940, after a short but costly war. What Stalin had failed to plan for was the magnitude of Adolf Hitler's treachery. On June 22, 1941, without warning, German armies invaded the Soviet Union.

Stalin's political purges of 1936–1938 had stripped the Red Army of most of its senior officer corps, making it easy for the German forces to roll over the Red Army in the opening weeks of the invasion. Within a short time, however, Stalin pulled himself together, took personal command of the Red Army, and mounted an increasingly effective defense.

While the war began for the Soviets on June 22, 1941, it had, for the rest of Europe, started many months before, at four-thirty on the morning of September 1, 1939, when, without a declaration of any kind, Hitler's *Luftwaffe* (air force) bombed airfields all across Poland. Simultaneously with this operation, a German battleship "visiting" the Polish port of Danzig opened fire on Polish fortifications, and the *Wehrmacht* (army) surged across the Polish frontier. The German army, superbly trained and equipped with the latest weaponry, made quick work of the valiant but hopelessly outgunned and outnumbered Polish forces, and the Polish campaign was over in little more than a month. On September 27, Warsaw fell, and the next day the town of Modlin surrendered. In a single action, 164,000 Polish soldiers became prisoners of war. By early October, the last organized Polish force, at Kock, had been crushed.

France Falls

Following the invasion of Poland, no major fighting broke out in the West. France and Britain quickly declared war on Germany but did little about it. In its first months, for them, the war become nothing more than a "Sitzkrieg," or "phony war." France and England cooperated in an attempt to mine and occupy Norwegian ports to close them to German U-boats, but the German navy and *Luftwaffe* quickly occupied Denmark and then, with the help of Norwegian turncoat Vidkun Quisling, took over Norway as well. The British would evacuate Norway on June 6, 1940. In the meantime, at the urging of Parliament, Neville Chamberlain was compelled to appoint his harshest critic, Winston Churchill, to head the War Cabinet. On May 10, 1940, as the Germans swept through Holland and the *Luftwaffe* bombed Rotterdam into oblivion, Chamberlain resigned as prime minister, and Churchill replaced him. German ground forces now advanced around the much-vaunted Maginot Line, which only extended as far north as the southern tip of Belgium, and within ten days reached Abbeville, on the French coast, just below the Strait of Dover. In the process, the Germans had cut the Allied armies in two. Belgium, in a hopeless position, surrendered on May 28, while the British Expeditionary Force, which had been dispatched to the Continent and was now in imminent danger of annihilation or capture, made a hairbreadth escape across the English Channel from the coastal town of Dunkirk. This evacuation saved Britain from immediate invasion.

French premier Reynaud wanted to continue the war, but he was outvoted and therefore resigned rather than accept an armistice. His vice premier, Marshal Henri Philippe Pétain, hero of Verdun in *World War I, 1914–1918 (chapter 11),* asked for an armistice, even as Pétain's World War I subordinate General Charles de Gaulle, in exile in London, broadcast to the French people a plea to fight on. De Gaulle's appeal was to no avail, however, and on June 22, 1940, the French signed an armistice by which the Germans occupied about two-thirds of France; the rest would be administered by Pétain as a German puppet.

U.S. Neutrality

On November 4, 1939, Franklin D. Roosevelt secured repeal of Congress's arms embargo on belligerent nations. Now, Britain and France were to be permitted to purchase war materiel from the United States on a "cash and carry" basis only. With the fall of France, America's participation in the war became more direct. Defense appropriations shot up, and most Americans, still wishing to avoid direct military involvement, nevertheless favored a policy of rendering all aid to Britain short of going to war. On December 8, 1940, Roosevelt proposed the Lend-Lease Act, which was passed into law in March 1941. This gave the president authority to aid any nation whose defense he believed vital to the United States and to accept repayment for such aid "in kind or property, or any other direct or indirect benefit which the President deems satisfactory." Soon Lend-Lease was extended beyond aid to Great Britain. In April 1941 China was included,

Two principal Allied leaders, U.S. president Franklin Delano Roosevelt (left) and British prime minister Winston Churchill. Standing directly behind Roosevelt is U.S. Army Chief of Staff Gen. George C. Marshall. *Collection: National Archives and Records Administration*

and in September, the Soviet Union. By the end of World War II more than forty nations had received Lend-Lease help, valued at a total of $49 billion.

The American public was unaware that Roosevelt was doing much more than lending money and materiel to the British. He had secretly ordered the U.S. Navy to cooperate with the British in curbing the German U-boat menace, and, in a secret conference with Churchill, he developed the Atlantic Charter, a statement of shared war aims. The charter was made public on August 14, 1941; privately, Roosevelt assured Churchill that he would "wage war but not declare it." In August and September, U.S. merchant ships were armed for self-defense.

In September 1940 Congress took a large step toward war by enacting the first peacetime draft in U.S. history. If there was a bright spot for Americans in this grim picture, it was the salutary effect war production and the draft had on the economy. The Great Depression came rapidly to an end.

Attack on Pearl Harbor: The United States Enters the War

Throughout the late 1930s and early 1940s, America nervously eyed developments in Europe, anticipating that it would soon participate in the war there. But for America, the war began not across the Atlantic, but in the Pacific.

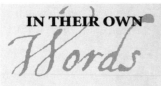

IN THEIR OWN

The Atlantic Charter, August 14, 1941

The President of the United States and the Prime Minister, Mr. Churchill, representing His Majesty's Government in the United Kingdom, have met at sea. . . .

The President and the Prime Minister . . . have considered the dangers to world civilization arising from the policies of military domination by conquest upon which the Hitlerite government of Germany and other governments associated therewith have embarked, and have made clear the stress which their countries are respectively taking for their safety in the face of these dangers.

They have agreed upon the following joint declaration. . . .

First, their countries seek no aggrandizement, territorial or other;

Second, they desire to see no territorial changes that do not accord with the freely expressed wishes of the peoples concerned;

Third, they respect the right of all peoples to choose the form of government under which they will live; and they wish to see sovereign rights and self-government restored to those who have been forcibly deprived of them;

Fourth, they will endeavor, with due respect for their existing obligations, to further the enjoyment by all States, great or small, victor or vanquished, of access, on equal terms, to the trade and to the raw materials of the world which are needed for their economic prosperity;

Fifth, they desire to bring about the fullest collaboration between all nations in the economic field with the object of securing, for all, improved labor standards, economic advancement and social security;

Sixth, after the final destruction of the Nazi tyranny, they hope to see established a peace which will afford to all nations the means of dwelling in safety within their own boundaries, and which will afford assurance that all the men in all the lands may live out their lives in freedom from fear and want;

Seventh, such a peace should enable all men to traverse the high seas and oceans without hindrance;

Eighth, they believe that all of the nations of the world, for realistic as well as spiritual reasons, must come to the abandonment of the use of force. Since no future peace can be maintained if land, sea or air armaments continue to be employed by nations which threaten, or may threaten, aggression outside of their frontiers, they believe, pending the establishment of a wider and permanent system of general security, that the disarmament of such nations is essential. They will likewise aid and encourage all other practicable measures which will lighten for peace-loving peoples the crushing burden of armaments.

FRANKLIN D. ROOSEVELT
WINSTON S. CHURCHILL

At 7:55 A.M., December 7, 1941, amid deteriorating relations between Japan and the United States, almost 200 Japanese carrier-launched high-level bombers, dive bombers, torpedo planes, and fighter aircraft attacked the U.S. Navy and Army facilities at Pearl Harbor, Hawaiian Territory. The battleships *Arizona, Oklahoma, California, Nevada,* and *West Virginia* were sunk, and three other battleships, three cruisers, three destroyers, and other vessels were severely damaged. On the ground, 180 U.S. aircraft were destroyed. Casualties totaled more than 3,400 men, including more than 2,403 killed. Japanese losses were light: 29 to 60 planes shot down, and 5 midget submarines and possibly one or two fleet submarines lost. Total deaths were fewer than 100 Japanese sailors and airmen.

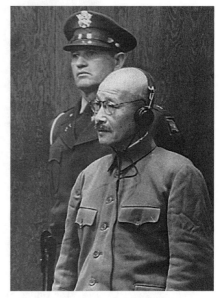

Japan's head of state was Emperor Hirohito, but the military, headed by Hideki Tojo, was the political power that propelled Japan into world war. He is shown here in 1948 on trial for war crimes. *Collection: National Archives and Records Administration*

On December 8, 1941, President Roosevelt addressed a joint session of Congress to ask for a declaration of war. Because Japan was part of the so-called Berlin–Rome–Tokyo Axis, America's declaration of war against Japan was a de facto declaration against the Atlantic powers Germany and Italy as well.

Why had Japan attacked?

Since the early 1930s, Japan had been waging war against China, openly violating the U.S. "Open Door" policy guaranteeing Chinese independence *(see Boxer Rebellion, 1899–1901 [chapter 10])*. Gradually the Roosevelt administration introduced economic sanctions against Japan in an effort to pressure it to withdraw from China. With its supply lines being choked off by the sanctions, Japan could not long continue to prosecute its war against China. Rather than withdraw from China, the militarists who controlled the Japanese government decided not only to risk war with the United States, but also to move so aggressively throughout the Pacific that America would be overwhelmed into helplessness. Although the United States had a military presence in the Pacific as well as the Atlantic, Japanese strategists counted on the war in Europe to siphon off the main strength of the U.S. military.

From a tactical point of view, the attack on Pearl Harbor was a stunning Japanese success. Strategically, however, it was a disaster, for it served to unite a nation that had been wary and passive, resistant to

The USS *Arizona* sinks under Japanese air attack at Pearl Harbor, Hawaii, December 7, 1941. The United States entered the war the next day. *Collection: National Archives and Records Administration*

entering the war in far-off Europe. Of the Pearl Harbor attack, historian Samuel Eliot Morison wrote that "one can search military history in vain for an operation more fatal to the aggressor."

Japanese Conquest, 1941

The Pearl Harbor attack was a severe blow to the U.S. Pacific Fleet, but although major battleships were sunk or disabled, the U.S. aircraft carriers were not in port and therefore escaped destruction. Nevertheless, U.S. and British holdings in the Pacific were devastated in the immediate aftermath of the Pearl Harbor attack.

Beginning on December 8, 1941, Wake Island, gallantly defended by U.S. naval personnel and marines, came under attack and held out until December 23. Guam, defended by a small garrison of marines and sailors, fell quickly on December 10. Simultaneously, in Asia, Japanese forces invaded Kowloon, Hong Kong, during December 8–10, forcing the British to withdraw to Hong Kong Island. After Major General C. M. Maltby refused a Japanese surrender demand on December 13, Hong Kong came under heavy attack during December 18–25, falling on Christmas Day. A British garrison of 12,000 was lost.

On December 8, northern Malaya was invaded by an army of 100,000 Japanese against a British force of approximately equal number. By December 31 the British forces had been pushed steadily southward and forced to fall back on Singapore.

The Philippines

Of greatest concern to the United States was the Philippines. In command there was General Douglas MacArthur, with about 130,000 men, including 22,400 U.S. regulars (among them 12,000 Philippine Scouts); 3,000 members of the Philippine Constabulary; and the Philippine Army, consisting of 107,000 men, not all of whom had been trained, organized, or even armed. MacArthur also commanded the U.S. Far East Air Force, which included 35 B-17 bombers and about 90 other combat aircraft. Most of the naval assets were being withdrawn from the islands and sent to safety in Java; however, 4 destroyers, 28 submarines, and smaller surface craft remained in the Philippines. MacArthur deployed the major portion of his ground forces north of Manila under Major General Jonathan M. Wainwright to resist an invasion via Lingayen Gulf. He planned to use the B-17s to hit Formosa (Taiwan) by way of counterattack. His principal objective was to hold out against invasion as long as possible in anticipation of a naval action that would open the way for reinforcements.

The Japanese plan of attack was to overwhelm the defenders and knock them out long before reinforcement was even possible. The attack would begin with an air assault from Formosa, which would be followed by an amphibious landing of 50,000 troops. Japanese planners discounted the ability and loyalty of the Philippine Army, so they believed that 50,000 men could take the islands within 50 days.

The attack came on December 8 and, like the attack on Pearl Harbor, came as a surprise. Japanese aircraft struck first, hitting Clark Field near Manila. More than half of the B-17s were destroyed on the ground, along with 56 fighters and other aircraft. MacArthur's planned air assault on Formosa never materialized. Next, beginning on December 10, Japanese bombers destroyed the naval base at Cavite, while Japanese troops began to land at Luzon. The Japanese established air bases in the northern Philippines, while surviving craft from the U.S. Far East Air Force were transferred to Mindanao, at the southwestern end of the Philippine archipelago. Except for submarines and a few torpedo boats, all U.S. naval craft now left for Java.

With bases already established in the north, the Japanese invaders now claimed beachheads in the south as well, at Mindanao and on the island of Jolo. The Philippine Army withdrew into the hills, and the Japanese now possessed naval bases from which they could strike at the Dutch East Indies.

On December 22 the main invasion of Luzon got under way. The poorly trained Philippine Army collapsed before the onslaught, but the U.S. and Philippine Scout units retreated in an orderly and highly effective fashion and inflicted substantial casualties on the Japanese. Just two days after the Luzon invasion began, another force landed in the south, at Limon Bay. MacArthur thus found his army within the jaws of a Japanese pincer movement and decided to save his troops by withdrawing to Bataan. Abandoning Manila, MacArthur declared it an open city on December 26, and the Japanese occupied it without resistance.

The withdrawal to Bataan was a complex and dangerous operation carried out under continual enemy attack. Although the Japanese suffered heavy losses, losses to the Americans and Filipinos also were heavy—and supplies were running to critically low levels. Nevertheless, by January 7, 1942, American and Filipino forces were ensconced in well-prepared positions across the upper Bataan Peninsula. The Japanese were stunned by the tenacious resistance they encountered, which seriously compromised the empire's timetable of conquest. By mid-February the Japanese had to call off the attacks, which were not resumed until April.

In mid-March, on President Roosevelt's orders, MacArthur left the Philippines, making a hazardous escape by PT boat through enemy lines. From Mindanao he was flown to Australia, promising the Filipinos and Americans still on the island, "I shall return." By April, however, those troops, under the command of Jonathan M. Wainwright, were starving. Following a heavy artillery attack against his position in Bataan, Major General Edward P. King Jr. surrendered U.S. and Filipino forces there on April 9. Corregidor, under Wainwright, continued to hold out until May 6. Following a five-day barrage, Wainwright surrendered unconditionally. Wainwright was forced to lead 78,000 American and Filipino POWs, many already starving and sick, on a brutal march from Bataan to a prison camp 65 miles away. About 10,000 POWs died—succumbing to starvation, disease, or the brutal whims of their Japanese captors—on this infamous "Bataan Death March."

The Japanese forced captured American defenders of Bataan, Philippines, on a "Death March" to the Cabanatuan prison camp, about May 1942. *Collection: National Archives and Records Administration*

The Death March made Americans realize just how brutal and uncompromising an enemy they faced, even as U.S. military planners struggled to formulate a strategy for blocking further Japanese advances. Gaining the Philippines gave the Japanese a formidable base of operations—as did each Pacific island claimed by the Japanese juggernaut.

Other Allied Losses

January 1942 brought British defeat on the Malay Peninsula, followed during February 8–15 by the Japanese conquest of Singapore. Thailand and Burma were invaded during January–March. With the aid of Chinese forces under the command of American general Joseph "Vinegar Joe" Stilwell, the Allies reorganized, but, under unremitting Japanese pressure, were forced to retreat from Mandalay and from Burma. China was now isolated from the other Allies. In this desperate situation, airpower became the principal means of Allied resistance. Colonel Claire Chennault deployed his "Flying Tigers"—officially, the American Volunteer Group—in China and Rangoon, Burma, to intercept Japanese bomber attacks and to defend Rangoon. The Flying Tigers and British RAF squadrons also supported Allied troops withdrawing from Burma. General Stilwell organized a continuous airlift to supply Kunming, China, after the fall of Burma. To keep Chinese forces supplied, cargo craft flew the "Hump," an exceedingly hazardous route from Indian bases to China over the eastern Himalayas. While the Chinese Army delayed Japanese advances in China, the enemy's progress was nevertheless inexorable.

Battles of the Coral Sea and Midway

In view of its success in the Pacific, against the Philippines, and in the China-Burma-India (C-B-I) theater, it is little wonder that many Japanese military planners believed their war machine unstoppable. Early in 1942 the Japanese formulated a plan to seize Tulagi, in the Solomon Islands, and Port Moresby in New Guinea while the imperial combined fleet would engage and destroy the American fleet, then capture Midway Island. This would enable Japan to establish a strong defensive chain all the way down from the Aleutian Islands through Midway, Wake, and the Marshalls and Gilberts. With these islands held, New Caledonia, the Fijis, and Samoa could be invaded. Australia would then be cut off. Most

U.S. Army Air Forces lieutenant colonel Jimmy Doolittle led a daring air raid against Tokyo flying B-25 bombers from the deck of USS *Hornet* in April 1942. *Collection: National Archives and Records Administration*

important, however, as Japanese admiral Isoroku Yamamoto saw it, was the destruction of the American fleet, in particular the aircraft carriers, which had been out of port during the attack on Pearl Harbor. To destroy these he was willing to gamble on a strategy that ultimately overextended even the great Japanese military machine. However, not everyone in the Japanese military establishment was behind Yamamoto. Indeed, the high command delayed moving on the all-out attack—until an event occurred that shocked the Japanese into immediate action.

Continually withdrawing before the juggernaut, American military planners were desperate for some counterstrike against Japan. The U.S. Army Air Force approved the plan of Lieutenant Colonel James Doolittle to take sixteen B-25s aboard the aircraft carrier *Hornet* and launch, on April 18, 1942, a surprise air raid on Tokyo. It was the closest thing to a deliberate suicide mission American military personnel ever undertook during the war, for everyone well knew that the twin-engine "Mitchell" bombers could not carry sufficient fuel to return to any American base, and even if they had had enough fuel capacity to return to the *Hornet,* the aircraft, not designed for carrier flight, would have been unable to land on the flattop. The plan was to land in China, find safe haven among Chinese resistance fighters, and somehow find a way to return home.

The daring raid went off remarkably well. Although the damage to Tokyo inflicted by a handful of medium bombers was minor, the mission's psychological effect was profound. The attack gave American morale a terrific boost (and, miraculously, most of Doolittle's bomber crews were rescued), but, even more important, it shocked the exulting Japanese, who were forced to tie up more fighter aircraft at home. Now, too, there would be no further delay in putting the Midway operation into action.

Japanese invasion forces sailed to Tulagi and Port Moresby in May 1942. Tulagi fell without opposition. The larger force, sailing to New Guinea, was intercepted on May 7 by aircraft launched from *Lexington* and *Yorktown.* The Battle of the Coral Sea began—and began well for the Americans, as the Japanese carrier *Shoho* was sunk, forcing the Japanese fleet's now undefended transports to turn back.

On May 8 the main fight began. It was entirely a duel between carrier-launched aircraft, the first sea battle in history to be fought at such great range that the opposing ships never saw one another. U.S. aircraft damaged the carrier *Shokaku,* but thirty-three out of eighty-two of the attacking planes were lost. The Japanese sank the carrier *Lexington,* a destroyer, and a tanker, losing forty-three of sixty-nine aircraft in the attack. Coral Sea was a Japanese tactical victory but a strategic defeat; although U.S. losses were heavier, the Japanese advance had been stopped for the first time in the war; Port Moresby was saved; and the Japanese fleet was driven out of the Coral Sea.

Despite the setback at the Battle of the Coral Sea, Midway remained the Japanese objective, though the Japanese would fight the battle with two fewer carriers than they had planned on having available. Yamamoto sent a diversionary force to the Aleutian Islands while Admiral Chuichi Nagumo, who had led the Pearl Harbor attack, took a four-carrier strike force followed by an invasion fleet—some eighty-eight ships in all—to Midway. His American opponent, Admiral Chester A. Nimitz, had anticipated just such an attack. Accordingly, he brought together two task forces east of Midway, designated Number 16 (under Admiral Raymond Spruance) and Number 18 (under Admiral Frank Fletcher). The task forces included the carriers *Enterprise, Hornet,* and *Yorktown* in addition to land-based aircraft on Midway itself. These Midway-based planes attacked elements of the Japanese fleet on June 3. Although the Americans enjoyed the element of surprise—the attack came some 500 miles out from Midway—it inflicted little damage, and on June 4, 108 Japanese aircraft struck Midway. The damage was severe, including the destruction of 15 of 25 U.S. Marine aircraft based there.

Despite the reverses suffered on Midway, U.S. torpedo bombers attacked the Japanese fleet. The first assault sunk no ships and resulted in the loss of 7 planes. A second assault also failed, with the loss of 8 more aircraft. A third attack, by Midway-based B-17 heavy bombers, again failed to damage or sink any of the enemy carriers. This was followed by a torpedo bomber attack launched from the U.S. carriers, in which 35 of the 41 aircraft engaged were lost—having inflicted little damage. However, this last attack opened the way for a massive make-or-break attack by 54 dive

Ground crewmen stand by an F4U, about to take off on an air raid against the principal Japanese base at Rabaul in the Pacific. *Collection: National Archives and Records Administration*

bombers from *Enterprise* and *Yorktown,* which sank 3 Japanese aircraft carriers, their planes unlaunched, in five minutes. The fourth Japanese carrier, *Hiryu,* was sunk in a separate attack later in the day—albeit not before *Hiryu's* planes had delivered a fatal blow against *Yorktown.*

Japanese forces began withdrawing on June 5, 1942. Although, on June 6, U.S. ships sank a Japanese cruiser, the American fleet was too depleted to give chase. Nevertheless, Midway was the hard-fought turning point of the Pacific war. The United States lost 307 men, 150 planes, a destroyer, and the *Yorktown,* whereas the Japanese lost 275 planes, 4 carriers, a cruiser, and about 4,800 men. From this point forward, the United States would take a relentlessly offensive posture in the Pacific.

Battle of Guadalcanal

As a result of defeat at Midway, the Japanese abandoned their plan to take New Caledonia, the Fijis, and Samoa, and focused instead on the southwestern Pacific. They would invade Port Moresby not by direct amphibious assault but overland, using troops landed at Buna-Gona, New Guinea. This meant a buildup at their naval base at Rabaul, which would be used as a staging area for the operation, along with new bases in the Solomon Islands. When the Japanese began building an airfield on Guadalcanal, more than six hundred miles southeast of Rabaul in the Solomons chain, the Americans decided to launch an offensive there and also against Tulagi, using nineteen thousand U.S. Marines in eighty-nine ships under General Alexander Vandergrift. The landings began on August 7, 1942, and took the Japanese by complete surprise on Guadalcanal. On Tulagi, however, resistance was fierce, and from Rabaul the Japanese launched a counterattack by sea. Three American and one Australian cruiser were sunk. To save the rest of his ships and transports, Admiral Richmond K. Turner had to withdraw, leaving the marines to defend themselves on Guadalcanal. What had begun as an offensive turned into one of the great defensive stands of World War II or, indeed, any war.

For the next four months, the marines resisted Japanese counterattack. At last, on the night of November 12–13, an outnumbered U.S. cruiser force under Admiral William "Bull" Halsey came to the rescue of the marines. The ships slugged it out with a superior Japanese fleet, ultimately forcing the Japanese troop convoy out into the open, where its ships fell prey to air attack. Having cut off the flow of Japanese reinforcements to Guadalcanal, the Americans landed more marines, and, by early

February 1943, the Japanese evacuated the island. As Midway had turned the tide of the sea war in the Pacific, so Guadalcanal altered the course of the land war. In the meantime, on New Guinea, combined U.S. and Australian forces defeated the Japanese attack on Port Moresby. The Australians pushed the attackers away from the port city, while U.S. and Australian troops attacked the beachhead at Buna-Gona, driving the Japanese from it as well.

Admiral William "Bull" Halsey. *Collection: National Archives and Records Administration*

The European Theater, 1942

American popular opinion enthusiastically supported the war against Japan, the evil empire that had made the treacherous "sneak attack" against Pearl Harbor. Most Americans favored concentrating on the Pacific war first before turning to the Atlantic and Europe. U.S. military planners, however, were eager to work with Britain and the Soviet Union to contain and defeat Hitler. There was intense concern that neither of these two Allies would be able to hold out indefinitely without concerted aid from a large American

U.S. troops of the 106th Infantry Regiment land at Guadalcanal. *Collection: National Archives and Records Administration*

force. Throughout 1942 the United States served both Britain and the Soviet Union as the "arsenal of democracy," rushing a continuous supply of munitions and other supplies to these nations, in the case of the Soviet Union via the hazardous "Murmansk run" along the coast of Norway and into the Arctic Ocean, or via the longer, though less dangerous, "Persian Corridor," which terminated in ports in Iran.

American military planners wanted to use England as a staging area on which to build a large force for a cross-Channel invasion. The idea was to attack German forces from the west while the Soviets resisted from the east. Ultimately the Germans would be crushed between two fronts. The British, however, were concerned that too much time would be required to build up an effective invasion force. Already, British-led attempts at invasion had failed miserably for lack of numbers, in France, Norway, and Greece. Winston Churchill and other British planners proposed delaying an assault on Hitler's "Atlantic Wall" and attempt an alternative invasion via what Churchill called the "soft underbelly of Europe." The idea was to gain victories against the Germans in North Africa, then jump off from there to Sicily, then the Italian mainland, advancing up Italy to the rest of Europe. Once much of southern Europe had been secured, another invasion might be attempted from the west. Thus the European Axis powers would be surrounded on three sides—west, south, and east.

American planners resisted the "soft underbelly" approach until the actions of the brilliant German tank commander General Erwin Rommel in North Africa forced their hand. By the autumn of 1942 Rommel, the "Desert Fox," had pushed the British back into Egypt from Tobruk, in Libya. At stake was the Suez Canal, without which Allied supplies would quickly dry up via the eastern coast of Africa. Attacking North Africa was no longer an option. It had become a necessity.

Field Marshal Bernard Law Montgomery led the British Eighth Army to a hard-fought victory against Germany's vaunted Afrika Korps at the second Battle of El Alamein during October–November 1942. On November 13 Tobruk fell to Montgomery, followed by Tripoli on January 23, 1943. Montgomery pursued Rommel's Afrika Korps across the Tunisian frontier during February.

This progress took place against the backdrop of the U.S. landings at North Africa, called Operation Torch, which began on November 8, 1942. Through a combination of military and diplomatic means, the American overall commander, General Dwight D. Eisenhower, secured bases of operation in French-occupied Morocco and Algeria by November 15. From here the Americans would launch operations eastward against Tunisia, into which Montgomery was pushing Rommel's Afrika Korps. Eisenhower's plan was to catch Rommel between the American forces and the British; however, the first engagement between U.S. troops and the Afrika Korps, at Kasserine Pass, Tunisia, during February 14–22, 1943, brought a humiliating defeat for the poorly led and poorly trained U.S. forces. Nevertheless, Rommel withdrew, leaving the American forces very much intact. Eisenhower called in Major General George S. Patton to take over command of the U.S. II Corps after Kasserine, and he quickly instilled discipline and pride in the bloodied unit. Working in concert with Montgomery, Patton forced the Afrika Korps into full retreat from its positions in Tunisia. At this point, as Patton was readied to command the invasion of Sicily, Major General Omar Bradley was put in command of U.S. forces in North Africa. The U.S. and Free French armies descended on a combined German-Italian army from the north while Montgomery's British Eighth Army came up from the south. On May 13 the Italian First Army surrendered to Montgomery, signaling the collapse of the Axis position in North Africa. In all, some 275,000 Axis troops became prisoners of war, North Africa was cleared of the enemy, and the stage was set for the Allied invasion of Europe via Sicily.

Battle of the Atlantic

Counterpointed to the war in the Pacific, Europe, and North Africa was the Battle of the Atlantic, which spanned the entire war, but was largely ended by the close of 1943. German U-boats had been taking a terrible toll on Allied surface ships, especially troop and cargo transports. In the years following World War I, German submariners had developed far more effective tactics than were used in that war. Paramount among these was the "wolf pack," in which multiple U-boats acted in concert against Allied convoys. This not only provided protection for the submarines but also ensured coordinated and more destructive attacks. During April 28–May 6, Commander Peter W. Gretton of the Royal Navy led a new kind of convoy across the North Atlantic. Up to this point convoys had been rather lightly defended and were strung out over a considerable distance to avoid giving the U-boats a massed target. Now the ships traveled in tight formation and were heavily escorted. The new tactic proved highly effective in defending even against wolf pack attack. From this time forward, German U-boats were no longer virtually invulnerable to attack, and, with increasing frequency, the hunters became the hunted. Beginning in June and extending through the end of the year, the U.S. Tenth Fleet organized a "hunter-killer" campaign directed against the U-boat menace. "Killer groups" coordinated attack by surface vessels and aircraft to locate and destroy wolf packs. Over time the campaign became highly successful, and the life span of the average German submariner grew grim and brief.

The European Air War, 1943

Although U.S. ground forces were not yet consolidating in great numbers in England, the U.S. Eighth Air Force arrived and, in coordination with the British RAF, staged round-the-clock air raids against Germany. Generally the British bombed during the night, and the Americans bombed by day. The object was to cripple German industrial capacity as well as wear down civilian morale. In fact, the air offensive proved very costly to bomber crews and ultimately inflicted insufficient damage against industrial targets to significantly impede the German war effort. As for the effect on civilian morale, the English should have known that it is quite possible for civilian populations to endure a program of intense and prolonged bombing. The British people themselves had already proven as much.

Despite its shortcomings, however, the program of round-the-clock air raids was destructive. During July 26–29, Hamburg was totally destroyed by air raids. During August 17–18, a key military installation was targeted, Peenemünde, location of development of the German V-1 "buzz bomb" (a pilotless rocket-propelled high-explosive bomb typically directed at civilian targets) and the V-2 rocket (a genuine long-range rocket weapon). The mission did not put an end to the V-1 and V-2 programs, but probably delayed them.

Other important targets in 1943 included Wilhemshaven (June 11), the oil fields of Ploesti, Romania (August 1), the ball-bearing industries at Schweinfurt (October 14), and the capital city of Berlin (November–December). Bomber crews were grateful for the introduction of new P-51 Mustang fighters at the end of the year; these high-performance aircraft had sufficient range to accompany bombers deep into enemy territory and back again, greatly reducing casualties.

Invasion of Sicily

Operation Husky, the invasion of Sicily from North Africa, commenced on the night of July 9–10, 1943. Three thousand ships and landing craft carried 14,000 vehicles, 600 tanks, 1,800 guns, and 160,000 men of the Fifteenth Army Group to a landing in Sicily. Air strikes had prepared the way for the landings, and an advance guard of paratroopers, from the British First Airborne and the U.S. Eighty-second Airborne, also participated. Although German and Italian land forces, some 350,000 strong, outnumbered the attackers, a force of 3,680 Allied aircraft achieved supremacy over the 1,400 Axis planes in the area.

The beachheads were quickly secured, and the British Eighth Army captured Syracuse on July 12, followed by Augusta on July 14. At Catania the advance was halted by Axis defenders occupying the slopes of Mount Aetna. While the British forces were stalled, Lieutenant General George Patton captured the port of Licata, then beat back a counterattack at Gela. The U.S. II Corps, under Omar Bradley, drove up the center of Sicily, taking San Stefano. Now the U.S. thrust turned east in two columns, one along the coast, the other inland. This drew off pressure from the British Eighth Army, which was thereby able to take Catania. The U.S. capture of Messina ended the thirty-eight-day battle for Sicily.

At a cost of 167,000 Axis casualties, mostly Italian, and 31,158 Allied losses (including 11,923 Americans), the Allied offensive had been brought to the threshold of the European mainland. In the wake of Sicily's fall, Italy's strongman dictator Benito Mussolini was forced out of office and replaced by Marshal Pietro Badoglio, who would seek a separate peace with the Allies. Unfortunately, however, Hitler rushed large German forces into the Italian mainland, which spoiled Allied hopes for a rapid conquest that would quickly open up the rest of Europe.

Island-Hopping in the South Pacific

With the invasion of mainland Italy, Hitler's defensive perimeter had been penetrated, however tentatively. With the Allied victories on Guadalcanal and New Guinea, the Japanese defensive perimeter also was compromised. In response, the Japanese strengthened Rabaul and the lesser positions they held in the South and Southwest Pacific. The Allies, for their part, were now fully on the offensive and focused on an "island-hopping" strategy. The idea was to reclaim key Japanese-held islands, pushing back the Japanese defensive perimeter toward the Japanese homeland itself. The first major objective was to neutralize Rabaul, the main Japanese base in the South Pacific. To achieve this, General Douglas MacArthur was given overall command of the South Pacific Area, which was now designated the Third Fleet. MacArthur directed a two-pronged offensive in the region: Admiral Halsey's fleet drove northwestward through the Solomon Islands, while General Walter Krueger led the Sixth Army through New Guinea and New Britain toward Rabaul.

The campaign in New Guinea and New Britain began when an Australian force established a forward base at Wau on January 9. At the end of June, American forces landed at Nassau Bay, New Guinea. This was followed by operations at Lae and Salamaua, New Guinea, by combined Australian and American troops, who drove the Japanese out of Salamaua by mid-September. After Finschafen was surrounded on September 22 and fell on October 2, southeastern New Guinea was sufficiently secured to use as a staging area for an assault on New Britain from October through December. By the end of the year a firm beachhead had been established on that island.

Simultaneously with the operations in New Guinea and New Britain, U.S. land and naval forces set off from Guadalcanal to take the central and northern Solomon Islands. Russell Island was the first in the chain to fall, on February 11, 1943, followed by Rendova Island on June 30. From Rendova, army, marine, and naval forces assaulted New Georgia from July 2 to August 25. Here the resistance was fierce and the jungle fighting particularly bitter. Resistance ended on August 25 only after the Japanese troops on the island had been wiped out almost to a man.

Overlapping the assault on New Georgia was an attack on Vella Lavella, which developed into another hard-fought campaign spanning August 15 to October 7. In the end, however, the central Solomons fell to the Americans—at a cost of 1,136 U.S. troops killed and 4,140 wounded. Of the 8,000 Japanese troops forming the Vella Lavella garrison, at least 2,500 died. The victory here provided a jumping-off point for an attack on Bougainville, which, with Rabaul and Choiseul, was the last Japanese bastion in the Solomons. By December, Bougainville had not only been taken, but also became a major Allied naval and air base.

Throughout the South Pacific area in 1943, land operations were closely coordinated with naval and air operations. The U.S. Seventh Fleet conducted operations aimed at securing and maintaining control of the coastal waters around New Guinea, while elements of the Third Fleet sup-

Mop-up operations on Bougainville. *Collection: National Archives and Records Administration*

ported the island-hopping operations throughout the Solomons, culminating in carrier strikes against Rabaul on November 5 and 11, which sent a major cruiser and destroyer force under Japanese Vice Admiral Takeo Kurita into retreat to Truk Island.

Air operations during this period consisted mainly of a contest for air superiority with Japanese aircraft launched from Rabaul. Air-to-air and air-to-ground encounters were frequent and heavy, but the combined Australian–American Fifth Air Force ultimately prevailed, achieving superiority by May.

Another high point in the air war in the South Pacific was the Battle of the Bismarck Sea, during March 2–4, 1943. U.S. aircraft attacked a Japanese squadron of eight destroyers escorting troop transports from Rabaul to Lae. A total of seven Japanese transports were sunk, along with four destroyers. The four destroyers that managed to escape to Rabaul were severely crippled. As a result of the battle, Japanese efforts to reinforce and supply New Guinea were sharply curtailed.

Despite attrition of Japanese air strength early in 1943, Admiral Yamamoto committed the bulk of his badly depleted air squadrons to a counterattack during April 7–12. Newly established Allied bases in New Guinea and the Solomons were targeted, but in the end, the attacks proved more costly to the Japanese than to the Allied defenders. The greatest cost of all was the death of Yamamoto himself. Acting on intercepted messages, Admiral Halsey dispatched sixteen U.S. Army Air Force fighters to intercept two Japanese bombers, one of which was known to be transporting

Admiral Yamamoto. Both bombers were shot down and, with their destruction, Japan's most important military strategist died. It was a loss from which Japan would never recover, as it could not recover from the loss of almost three thousand aircraft in the course of the Solomons campaign during 1943.

The Central Pacific Campaign, 1943

During much of 1943 the Fifth Fleet, under Vice Admiral Raymond A. Spruance, the Fifth Amphibious Force, and the V Amphibious Corps (Marines), assembled in Hawaii, the Fijis, and the New Hebrides. With seven battleships, seven heavy cruisers, three light cruisers, eight aircraft carriers, and thirty-four destroyers, the Fifth Fleet was the largest naval force the United States had ever mustered. These naval and amphibious units would coordinate a drive due west across the Pacific with the Seventh Army Air Force and elements of the Third Fleet. By the end of October the force was ready, and during November 13–20, USAAF bombers strafed Tarawa and Makin in the Gilbert Islands preparatory to an amphibious assault, which stepped off on November 20 against Makin. By the twenty-third, the island had been taken, with light losses among the ground forces, but with the sinking of the escort carrier *Liscome Bay* and all 640 hands.

From Makin, Tarawa was targeted during November 20–24. It proved to be one of the most formidable objectives of the entire war. The approach to the island was obstructed by coral reefs that grounded landing craft, making them sitting ducks for enemy fire. The island itself was honeycombed with caves and tunnels, from which the defenders exacted a heavy toll on the attackers. Although "Terrible Tarawa" was taken, the cost was staggering: 985 Marines killed and 2,193 wounded. The extent of Japanese losses is not known, save that the island was defended to the death. Of the mere 100 prisoners taken by the Marines, only 17 were Japanese combat soldiers.

As costly as the Battle of Tarawa was, it put Admiral Nimitz in position to attack the Marshalls with everything at his disposal and then to destroy the major Japanese naval base at Truk.

Action in the North Pacific, 1943

The North Pacific was something of a forgotten corner in the Pacific war. Japanese occupation forces held Attu and Kiska, the westernmost of the

Aleutian Islands, and the only part of the North American continent the Japanese succeeded in invading. In the March 26 Battle of the Komandorski Islands, Rear Admiral Charles H. McMorris's squadron of two obsolescent cruisers and four destroyers fell upon a superior Japanese force—four cruisers and four destroyers—escorting reinforcements bound for Attu. Although one of McMorris's cruisers was badly damaged, he forced the Japanese transports to divert from Attu and seriously impeded resupply of the islands. During May 11–29, U.S. ground forces cleared Attu of the Japanese invaders. A Canadian-U.S. force landed on Kiska on August 15, only to find that it had already been evacuated.

Italian Mainland, 1943

The invasion of Italy was a backdoor approach to what Hitler called "Fortress Europe" *(Festung Europa)*. Fighting in Italy, the Allies believed, also would force the Germans to withdraw some forces from the Eastern Front, thereby enabling the Soviets to push the German invaders westward. If pressure could be applied from the south and the east, then, at an appropriate time, a massive landing could be made across the English Channel and even more pressure applied from the west. The great majority of the Italian people, heartily sick of war, were ready to surrender. Mussolini was overthrown, and Marshal Pietro Badoglio concluded an armistice with the Allies on September 8. What Allied planners had not counted on, however, was just how fiercely—and skillfully—the Germans would continue to defend Italy.

On September 3, 1943, the British Eighth Army invaded Calabria, on the toe of the Italian boot. On September 9, the day after the Italian armistice was concluded, the U.S. Fifth Army under Lieutenant General Mark Clark landed at Salerno, where it was met with fiercely effective German resistance. It was not until September 18 that British and American operations could be sufficiently coordinated to enable the U.S. Fifth Army, at last, to secure the Salerno beachhead. German general Albert von Kesselring defended his positions superbly, inflicting more than 15,000 casualties on the Allies while incurring 8,000 losses to his own troops.

During September and early October, the U.S. Fifth and British Eighth Armies advanced northward, consolidating their gains in southern Italy. But progress was greatly retarded during the Volturno River Campaign (October 12–November 14), which met with staunch resistance from the Germans under Kesselring. The German commander established the "Winter Line," more familiarly called the Gustav Line, a formidable series of defenses from the Gulf of Gaeta to the Adriatic Sea. The Allied advance was stalled here and, at the end of the year, the situation stalemated in rugged, snowbound terrain five miles southeast of the Rapido River.

Despite the disappointing progress in Italy, the campaign here did wear down the German defenders and tie up forces that might otherwise have been thrown against the Soviet Union. As it was, 1943 brought a turning point on the massively bloody Eastern Front. Since the beginning of the German invasion of the USSR in 1941, the Soviets had continuously fallen back under relentless German advances. That strategic retreat continued until the long Stalingrad campaign of 1943, which ended in the loss of 300,000 Germans and the surrender of the 93,000 survivors of the German Sixth Army. The end of 1943 would see the launch of the long-hoped-for Soviet offensive against the Germans. While Allied pressure from the south was stalled, Soviet pressure was becoming overwhelming from the east. With the opening of 1944, the British and American Allies would prepare in earnest for Operation Overlord, an invasion of Europe through France.

Burmese Theater, 1944

In the war against Japan, the lion's share of Allied resources had been committed to the Pacific Campaign. The China-Burma-India (C-B-I) theater was typically given short shrift, and commanders had to make do and improvise with often woefully meager resources. Both the Allies and the Japanese planned offensives in this theater. The Allies worked to consolidate strength in India and China for an invasion of Japanese-held Burma, while the Japanese planned to invade British-held India from Burma.

At the start of 1944, the British advanced into Arakan, western Burma, and were very nearly pushed back by a Japanese counterattack during February 4–12. A British counterattack against the Japanese encircling force resulted in the envelopment of the Japanese attackers, but the entire front ground to a halt for the balance of 1944 with the onset of the monsoon season in May.

In northern Burma, the major effort was directed against the Japanese stronghold of Myitkyina, which combined American-Chinese forces under General Joseph Stilwell assaulted during May 17–18, only to be repulsed. Nevertheless, the Allied forces invested the city, even through the monsoon season, and it surrendered to Stilwell on August 3.

The campaign in northern Burma was truncated at the end of the year when Chinese troops were withdrawn to defend China against a renewed Japanese offensive. In the meantime, in central Burma, British forces successfully repelled a Japanese invasion of India, virtually destroying the Japanese Fifteenth Army by September. With this force neutral-

IN THEIR OWN *Words*

From the Tehran Conference,
November 28–December 1, 1943

We the President of the United States, the Prime Minister of Great Britain, and the Premier of the Soviet Union, have met these four days past, in this, the Capital of our Ally, Iran, and have shaped and confirmed our common policy.

We express our determination that our nations shall work together in war and in the peace that will follow.

As to war – our military staffs have joined in our round table discussions, and we have concerted our plans for the destruction of the German forces. We have reached complete agreement as to the scope and timing of the operations to be undertaken from the east, west and south.

The common understanding which we have here reached guarantees that victory will be ours.

And as to peace – we are sure that our concord will win an enduring Peace. We recognize fully the supreme responsibility resting upon us and

all the United Nations to make a peace which will command the goodwill of the overwhelming mass of the peoples of the world and banish the scourge and terror of war for many generations.

With our Diplomatic advisors we have surveyed the problems of the future. We shall seek the cooperation and active participation of all nations, large and small, whose peoples in heart and mind are dedicated, as are our own peoples, to the elimination of tyranny and slavery, oppression and intolerance. We will welcome them, as they may choose to come, into a world family of Democratic Nations.

No power on earth can prevent our destroying the German armies by land, their U Boats by sea, and their war plants from the air.

Our attack will be relentless and increasing.

Emerging from these cordial conferences we look with confidence to the day when all peoples of the world may live free lives, untouched by tyranny, and according to their varying desires and their own consciences.

We came here with hope and determination. We leave here, friends in fact, in spirit and in purpose.

ROOSEVELT, CHURCHILL and STALIN

Signed at Tehran, December 1, 1943 . . .

ized, the British advanced into central Burma, always with the object of securing the Burma Road, the great overland route of supply and communication between India and China.

China Theater, 1944

By early 1944, General Claire Chennault's Flying Tigers—now officially part of the U.S. Fourteenth Air Force—were proving extremely effective against the Japanese in China. To check Chennault, the Japanese commenced a counteroffensive in eastern China. Seven of the twelve Fourteenth Air Force airfields were captured, and the cities of Kunming and Chungking were in danger of falling. Despite continual support from the Fourteenth Air Force, Chinese resistance steadily crumbled by the late fall of 1944. At the request of China's premier, Chiang Kai-shek, General Stilwell was recalled and replaced by General Albert C. Wedemeyer, who worked more effectively with Chiang. By December, combined American and Chinese forces, with air support from Chennault, brought the Japanese advances to a halt.

America's Chinese ally Generalissimo Chiang Kai-shek listens to President Roosevelt. British prime minister Winston Churchill speaks with Madame Chiang Kai-shek, the generalissimo's influential wife. *Collection: National Archives and Records Administration*

Island-Hopping Continues in the South and Southwest Pacific

Early 1944 saw the American position in the Solomons growing ever stronger. On February 15, New Zealanders secured Green Island, and on March 20 Emirau fell. With these conquests, the Solomons and the St. Mathias group of islands were solidly in Allied hands, and Rabaul was completely cut off. West of these gains, Saidor, the Admiralties, and New Britain all fell to Allied control early in the year.

Losing ground throughout the South Pacific, the Japanese resolved to hold on to western New Guinea at all costs. During March and April, combined U.S. and Australian forces effected a complete encirclement of the Japanese position at Hollandia, New Guinea, inflicting extremely heavy casualties on the Japanese while sustaining minimal losses. From here, the islands of Wakde (May 17), Biak (May 27–June 29), Wewak and Aitape (June 28–August 5), Noemfoor (July 2–7), and Sansapor (July 30) were either neutralized or captured.

Island-Hopping in the Central Pacific

Simultaneously with operations in the South and Southwest Pacific aimed at securing New Guinea, Admiral Nimitz directed a campaign in the Central Pacific targeting the Marshall Islands. Kwajalein Island, in the Marshalls group, was invaded on January 29 by a landing force of forty-one thousand. Although Japanese resistance was, as usual, suicidal, the invaders managed to overrun the enemy while incurring relatively few losses. By February 7, Kwajalein had been cleared. The outnumbered Japanese garrison, some 8,000 strong, was almost completely annihilated: 7,870 Japanese soldiers died. In contrast, U.S. losses were 372 dead and about 1,000 wounded.

The next target was Truk, a major Japanese naval base, which was bombed during February 17–18. A large number of merchant vessels were severely damaged or sunk, and 275 of 365 Japanese aircraft on Truk were destroyed on the ground. A Japanese light cruiser and a destroyer also were sunk.

While Truk was subjected to air attack, U.S. Marine and army troops landed at Eniwetok Atoll on the island of Engebi. From here they jumped off to Eniwetok Island and Parry Island, where they were resisted—as usual—to the death.

Eniwetok next served as the rendezvous point for the large Fifth

Amphibious Force, a collection of warships and landing craft capable of delivering 127,000 men. From Eniwetok, a massive marine-army landing at Saipan was commenced on June 15.

Although little air support was available, the ground forces slowly took Saipan, successfully fending off a suicidal counterattack on July 9. The conquest of this island was one of the bloodiest campaigns of the Central Pacific war. More than 3,000 Americans were killed, and 13,160 were wounded, while Japanese losses amounted to 27,000, including many hundreds of civilians who had committed suicide by jumping off the island's cliffs, having been told by the Japanese troops that the American soldiers would torture and even cannibalize them.

Navajo Indian "code talkers"–Marine Corps troops who used the Navajo language to encrypt battlefield communications–were in the first wave of troops to land on Saipan.
Collection: National Archives and Records Administration

Battle of the Philippine Sea

The invasion of Saipan and the Marianas forced the Japanese fleet out into the open for the first time since Midway and Guadalcanal. Admiral Soemu Toyoda, who had replaced Admiral Koga—killed in a plane crash—was determined to resume the effort to destroy the American fleet. Accordingly, he ordered 9 carriers and 18 battleships and battle cruisers to attack the U.S. Navy ships supporting the Saipan landings. U.S. Admiral Spruance responded by sending the 15 fast carriers of Task Force 58, under Admiral Marc Mitscher, to intercept the Japanese fleet. The result, beginning on the morning of June 19, was the Battle of the Philippine Sea, between the Marianas and the Philippines. It was a titanic air battle between Mitscher's carrier-based planes and land- and carrier-based Japanese aircraft. After eight hours of continuous aerial combat, 330 of the 430 aircraft the Japanese committed to battle had been lost. Of 450 U.S. aircraft, only 30 were downed. Jubilant American pilots dubbed this, probably the single most decisive aerial battle of the war, the "Marianas Turkey Shoot."

During the air battle, two U.S. submarines managed to come within torpedo range of the Japanese carriers. Two carriers were sunk. By nightfall, the Japanese fleet was in full retreat with Mitscher in vigorous pursuit. On June 20 he launched 209 carrier-based planes against the Japanese ships, which were about 300 miles ahead of his fleet. The carrier *Hiyo* was sunk, along with 40 of the 75 Japanese planes sent to defend against the attack. Losses among U.S. aircraft were heavy, however, at 100, most lost not to enemy fire but in the attempt to make carrier landings at night; fortunately, many of the aviators were rescued. Despite U.S. casualties, the Battle of the Philippine Sea was devastating to the Japanese forces, which not only lost ships and planes but also most of its cadre of veteran pilots. Additionally, the U.S. Saipan landings were able to proceed unimpeded.

Closing in on the Philippines

"I shall return," General MacArthur promised when he left the Philippines at the outset of the war. The Saipan landings and the Battle of the Philippine Sea put American forces in a position to redeem that pledge.

On September 15, 1944, MacArthur made a surprise landing on the island of Morotai, south of the Philippines. Resistance was negligible. In coordination with this landing, Admiral Nimitz attacked Peleliu. There the U.S. Marines met much more formidable resistance from some ten thousand Japanese dug into coral caves and caverns, which afforded ideal defensive positions. It took a month of bitter fighting to reduce Peleliu, and then only with reinforcements from an army regiment.

Originally the plan had been to advance from Morotai and Peleliu to Mindanao and Yap, but Admiral Halsey now recommended skipping these intermediate steps and immediately launching an invasion of Leyte, at the center of the Philippine archipelago. This daring move, if successful, would split the quarter-million-man army of the Japanese there. Thus divided, the enemy could be defeated in detail: first on Leyte, then on Luzon, and finally on Mindanao. The only way for the Japanese to reestablish a continuous front across these islands would be to bring in its fleet, which would give Nimitz an opportunity to destroy it. MacArthur's return to the Philippines, therefore, began in October 1944.

During October 13–16, Admiral Halsey's Third Fleet attacked Formosa, Okinawa, and Luzon. The biggest cost to the Japanese was the loss of more than 650 aircraft as well as shore installations. Without the planes, Leyte would be all the more vulnerable. The Japanese did not inflict heavy damage on the Third Fleet—although two cruisers were severely damaged—but Japanese propaganda broadcasts announced that the Third

General Douglas MacArthur, supreme allied commander in the Pacific. *Collection: National Archives and Records Administration*

Fleet had been sunk. An exultant Halsey radioed Nimitz: "All Third Fleet ships reported by Tokyo as sunk have now been salvaged and are retiring at full speed in the direction of the enemy."

The Leyte landings commenced on October 20 and extended through October 22. MacArthur arrived a few hours after a beachhead was established. After wading ashore, he mounted a radio truck and broadcast—"People of the Philippines: I have returned! By the grace of Almighty God our forces stand again on Philippine soil—soil consecrated in the blood of our two peoples. Rally to me!"

But retaking the Philippines would not be easy. The Japanese quickly counterattacked, briefly regaining air superiority on October 24. Some forty-five thousand Japanese troops were landed on Leyte, and, in Leyte Gulf, the biggest naval battle in history got under way.

The Japanese fleet was divided into three groups. The Northern Group (Admiral Jisaburo Ozawa) was built around four carriers, the Center Force (Admiral Takeo Kurita) consisted of battleships and cruisers, and the Southern Group (Admiral Shoji Nishimura) also was a battleship and cruiser force. The plan was for the Northern Group to lure the Third Fleet away from Leyte Gulf while the Center Force came down on the American invasion fleet from the north and the Southern Force, passing up through Surigao Strait, converged on the invaders from the south. Once the invasion fleet was annihilated and the American army stranded on the Philippines, the combined Japanese forces could turn on the Third Fleet and destroy it.

At first, however, the attack went badly for the Japanese. U.S. submarines sank two Japanese cruisers, and Halsey, having now located the enemy, attacked with his carrier-based planes. The battleship *Musashi* was sunk. Kurita turned about in retreat. Believing the Center Force defeated, Halsey pursued the Northern Group—taking the Japanese bait and leaving the invasion fleet exposed. While Halsey pursued Ozawa, Admiral Jesse B. Oldendorf was left to deal with the Southern Group in what became the Battle of Surigao Strait. Oldendorf's fleet consisted of six obsolescent battleships, eight cruisers, and an assortment of destroyers and PT boats. Admiral Nishimura had two battleships, four cruisers, and eight destroyers.

The battle got under way on October 25. The American PT boats and destroyers quickly sank one of Nishimura's battleships; then, when the two main fleets closed on one another, the second Japanese battleship, *Yamashiro,* was sunk, with Nishimura on board.

During this battle, the Japanese Center force, under Kurita, turned again, slipped through San Bernardino Strait, and bore down on the still-unprotected U.S. invasion fleet. Only three modest forces of small carriers stood between Kurita and the vulnerable invasion fleet. Although severely outgunned and outnumbered, the American vessels, through bold and aggressive action, managed to drive Kurita off. Halsey, in the meantime, far to the north, was destroying Ozawa's Northern Group. All four of Ozawa's carriers were sunk, as were a cruiser and three destroyers. This was a knockout punch for the Japanese navy.

The Japanese high command tried several times to reinforce the defenders of the Philippines, but to no avail. On December 7, 1944, General Walter Krueger's troops joined the U.S. forces already landed on Leyte. The island fell to the Americans before the month was ended. From here, MacArthur launched his assault against Luzon, and thence to Bataan. Manila fell in January, and the last Japanese garrison on the islands, at Corregidor, surrendered in February 1945. Mop-up operations, especially on Mindanao, continued almost to the very end of the war. It was not until July 5, 1945, that MacArthur formally declared that the Philippines had been retaken.

Germany on the Defensive, 1944

In the European war, it was clear by the opening of 1944 that Hitler's Germany was on the defensive. The Battle of the Atlantic had at last turned in favor of the Allies, whose convoy system had made deep inroads into the U-boat menace. In desperation, Hitler launched V-1 "buzz bomb" and V-2 rocket attacks against targets in England, especially London, during the entire second half of 1944. The damage was severe, with some 20 percent of the British capital reduced to smoldering ruins; but if Hitler had hoped to sap the fighting spirit from the British, he had badly miscalculated. At home, many of his own officers had turned against him. On July 20, 1944, a cabal of high-ranking officers attempted to assassinate Hitler by detonating a bomb in his headquarters. The Führer survived the blast, and the war continued—with Hitler taking a much more personal and direct role in strategy. While Hitler's death would surely have shortened the war, his decision to take personal command was also of benefit to the Allies, for Hitler was by no means a rational, let alone brilliant, military strategist.

Italy, 1944

But the war in Europe was far from a foregone conclusion. Britain and the United States had yet to invade from the West; the ongoing strategic bombing campaign against Germany, like the German V-1 and V-2 campaign against England, was not forcing the war to a resolution; and the campaign in Italy was grindingly slow and costly.

During January, the U.S. Fifth Army and British Eighth Army advanced to the Rapido River but could progress no farther. On January 22, in the meantime, an Anglo-American force of fifty thousand landed at Anzio, virtually unopposed. Instead of driving inland, however, Major General John P. Lucas decided to wait, to consolidate his forces. This delay allowed the German commander, Kesselring, to reinforce his positions in Anzio. During February 16–29, the Germans counterattacked, forcing Lucas into retreat. He was relieved by Major General Lucian K. Truscott III. Although Truscott was a much more aggressive commander than Lucas, valuable momentum had been lost, and Anzio hardened into a costly stalemate that recalled the unproductive slaughter of *World War I, 1914–1918 (chapter 11)* trench warfare.

While the situation at Anzio languished, the Fifth Army hammered against the Gustav Line on the Rapido, with three assaults against Monte Cassino. The first two battles of Cassino (February 12 and February

15–18) resulted in Allied repulses. The Third Battle of Cassino (March 15–23, 1944), even though it was covered by massive air support, also failed to produce a breakthrough. The Anzio-Rapido-Cassino operation produced 23,860 U.S. and 9,203 British casualties during four months before a massive frontal assault during May 11–25, coordinated with Allied air force interdiction of German supply lines (Operation Strangle), finally produced a breakthrough toward Rome.

German POWs at the Anzio beachhead, below Rome, February 1944. *Collection: National Archives and Records Administration*

The drive toward Rome, however, required General Mark Clark to shift the advance of his Fifth Army. This shift spared the German Tenth Army from envelopment. Thus Rome, a political objective, was gained at the expense of a military objective. Clark entered Rome on June 4, but the German Tenth remained intact and continued to exact a heavy toll on the Allies. Nevertheless, once Rome fell, the Allied advance to the Arno River was rapid during the summer of 1944. The Fifth Army crossed the river on August 26, and although the British Eighth Army took Rimini on September 21, Clark was unable to capture Bologna during an October assault. The Italian campaign was still at issue as 1944 came to an end.

The Normandy Invasion

Allied planners at the highest levels—paramount among them President Franklin D. Roosevelt and Prime Minister Winston Churchill—decided to stage the long-anticipated cross-Channel invasion of Europe by the first week of June 1944. Plans called for the landing of a million men from southern England to France. The landing site chosen was Normandy, although a brilliant campaign of disinformation deceived the Germans into believing that the landings would come at Pas de Calais. Five Normandy beaches were targeted: The westernmost was designated Utah Beach, with Omaha Beach just to the east of it. At these two points, Lieutenant General Omar Bradley's First Army would land. Dividing this force on either side of an impassable estuary was a risky tactic; however, a landing at Utah Beach was necessary for an assault on Cherbourg, a port crit-

The view from a
landing craft as U.S.
troops land during
the D-Day invasion,
June 6, 1944.
*Collection: National
Archives and Records
Administration*

ical to logistical support of the ongoing operation. In advance of the landing, paratroopers were to be deployed to clear resistance behind the estuary so the two landings could be linked up farther inland. East of Omaha Beach were beaches designated Gold, Juno, and Sword. The British Second Army (with a Canadian corps attached), under General Sir Miles Dempsey, would land here. Overall command of the invasion, the landing phase of which was designated Operation Overlord, was given to General Dwight D. Eisenhower, supreme Allied commander; command of ground forces was given to Field Marshal Sir Bernard Law Montgomery. The initial landing force consisted of about a million men, supported by another million troops in logistical functions. Two-thirds of the invasion force was American.

What the invaders faced was Hitler's "Atlantic Wall," a network of fortifications, minefields, and underwater obstacles manned by ten Panzer (armor) divisions, fifteen infantry divisions, and thirty-three coastal-defense divisions (mostly green troops in training). The German defenders were deployed all the way from Norway in the north to the Mediterranean in the south. Geographical logic, reinforced by an Allied disinformation program, suggested that an invasion would come by way of Pas de Calais, the shortest distance between France and England. As a result, Hitler concentrated most of his troops, including the entire

Fifteenth Army, there. At Normandy, the actual site of the invasion, the smaller Seventh Army (commanded by Colonel General Friedrich Dollmann) was concentrated. Another German disadvantage was the absence of the Luftwaffe, which had been defeated by Allied air attacks, and the lack of any substantial naval defense. Essentially the Allies would be storming an enormous fortress.

Operation Overlord, the greatest amphibious operation in military history, commenced on D-Day, June 6, 1944. In the initial landings, 176,000 troops were conveyed by 4,000 ships and landing craft escorted by 600 warships. Air support was provided by 2,500 heavy bombers and 7,000 fighters. Five divisions were ashore by nightfall, and beachheads were firmly established everywhere except on Omaha Beach, where German resistance was heaviest, especially in the form of defending artillery. Here Allied casualties were very heavy, and the assault threatened to bog down. However, the initiative of individual low-level commanders pushed the advance even in this area, and during June 7–18, the Allied invasion expanded. Because Hitler had misjudged the site of the landing, concentrating his forces at Calais, German reinforcements were slow to arrive in Normandy; however, the Allied advance was greatly impeded by the topography of coastal Normandy, which was dense with *bocage,* hedgerows. British general Montgomery failed to take Caen in two attempts, on June 13 and 18, but Cherbourg fell on June 27, providing a key harbor for the ongoing invasion.

Throughout July, the beachhead expanded, and the Allies became increasingly well established. The hedgerow country continued to slow the advance, buying for the Germans time to mount a formidable defense. By

U.S. troops parade on the Champs-Élysées after participating in the liberation of Paris. The Arc de Triomphe is in the background. *Collection: National Archives and Records Administration*

German POWs are marched out of Paris after the liberation of that city. *Collection: National Archives and Records Administration*

the end of the initial phases of the invasion—the conclusion of Operation Overlord—the Allies had suffered 122,000 casualties, while the German defenders lost perhaps 114,000 men.

Beginning on July 25, Operation Overlord gave way to Operation Cobra, the breakout from the Normandy beachheads, as General Omar Bradley led the U.S. First Army against the German defenses west of St.-Lô. On August 1 the newly organized U.S. Third Army, under George S. Patton, took the Allied right and led the main breakout through Brittany by way of Avranches. This was the beginning of an incredible drive through France and ultimately into Germany itself, spearheaded by Patton and the Third Army. Patton's armor swept through Brittany, then wheeled south into the Loire, while his infantry moved to the left toward Le Mans. Behind the Third Army, the First Army pivoted left.

The Germans mounted a strong counterattack at Avranches, hoping to isolate the Third Army from the First, but the counterattack was itself counterattacked largely by British ground forces extensively supported by air cover. Nevertheless, an immediate opportunity to destroy much of the German Seventh and Fifth Panzer Divisions was lost when these units escaped through a gap in the Allied line, the Falaise-Argentan Pocket. The Allies pursued the retreating German divisions during August 20–30.

On August 25, U.S. and Free French troops liberated Paris, marking a critical milestone in the invasion, and by early autumn, German forces were now isolated in western France. The invasion effort was greatly aided by the indigenous Free French resistance movement.

On August 15, Operation Anvil-Dragoon got under way, with landings on the Côte d'Azur by the U.S. Seventh Army (including elements of Free French forces) under Lieutenant General Alexander Patch. The campaign in southern France and the Rhône Valley devastated German forces there. By the end of August there was no longer a German presence in southern France. From here, the U.S. Seventh Army advanced north to the Vosges, linking up with Patton's Third Army and other elements as part of the general drive eastward.

While American (and Free French) forces were advancing through central and southern France, the British concentrated on the north, pursuing the retreating Germans into the Low Countries. Unfortunately, this required diversion of fuel and other supplies from Bradley's army group (including Patton's Third Army), which was advancing headlong through central France. On August 30 the Third Army crossed the Meuse River, only to be halted because of a shortage of gasoline. During much of September, the Canadian First Army and the British Second Army battered away at German positions blocking Antwerp. While that city was being contested, British and Canadian forces also laid siege against Le Havre and began to take Channel ports. Of great relief to the British civilian population was the capture of several V-1 missile bases near Pas de Calais.

At Germany's Doorstep

Despite the slowdowns caused by a shortage of fuel and supplies, the Allies approached the German frontier. British field marshal Montgomery put Operation Market Garden into motion, a plan to seize intact the Rhine crossing at Arnhem and to secure the other bridges between, to ensure river crossings for the Allied drive into Germany. Market Garden depended heavily on airborne troops dropped behind German lines to prepare the way for the advance of the British Second Army. The joint Anglo-American parachute drops at Arnhem, Nijmegen, and Eindhoven met with much stiffer resistance than anticipated, and while out-and-out disaster was avoided when the British First Airborne escaped entrapment at the Battle of Arnhem (September 17–26), the German defenses remained intact. Operation Market Garden had failed in its objective; both troops and time were lost.

Montgomery nevertheless continued his effort to secure Antwerp, a port essential to continuing the Allied advance. During October–November 1944, Montgomery (with the addition of some American units) fought hard to secure the South Beveland Peninsula and Walchern Island, the two great fortresses in the Scheldt Estuary, guarding Antwerp. This was accomplished by November 8 and was followed by an extensive minesweeping operation to enable Allied convoys to use the Scheldt. The convoys began arriving at the end of November.

While Montgomery worked in the north, Bradley's army group pressed against the great German defenses of the Siegfried Line, a system of pillboxes and strong points built all along Germany's western frontier. The first breach in the line was punched through at Aachen, when the U.S. Third Army reached Metz on October 3 and the U.S. First Army captured Aachen on October 21. Throughout November the Allies conducted an all-out offensive against German forces west of the Rhine. During November 16–December 15, the Roer River–Hürtgen Forest region was heavily contested. South of this, Patton's Third Army swept through the Lorraine, while Allied forces, including the Free French, conducted operations in Alsace that resulted in the liberation of Mulhouse and Strasbourg.

Battle of the Bulge

By December 1944, the Allied advance seemed unstoppable. Hitler's armies were either collapsing or falling back. But the German leader mustered the strength to mount one last—and completely unanticipated—counteroffensive against the Allies. The German plan was to deliver a violent blow that would split the Allies, then defeat in detail the Allied forces north of the line formed by Antwerp, Brussels, and Bastogne.

The Ardennes offensive—popularly called the Battle of the Bulge—commenced on December 16. It was a massive assault by twenty German divisions coming out of fog and snow that drove a great bulge in the U.S. First Army line. Outnumbered and overwhelmed in this sector, the Allied forces scrambled to recover. Aware that Bastogne was the key to the entire Ardennes region, that to lose it would indeed allow the Germans to drive a wedge between the Allied forces, Bradley ordered the U.S. 101st Airborne to join the 10th Armored Division to hold the position. The commander of the 101st, Major General Anthony McAuliffe, set up a desperate defensive perimeter that became an Allied enclave within the German-held bulge. The situation in Bastogne became increasingly critical as bad weather prevented the use of air support for the first week of the battle. When the German commander solicited McAuliffe's surrender, the tough American commander replied with a single word: "Nuts!" In the nick of time, the weather cleared sufficiently to allow air support, and General Patton halted the advance of the Third Army in the Saar, turned his entire force ninety degrees to the north, and advanced against the German southern flank at Ardennes. This rescued the Bastogne defenders and rapidly turned the tide of the Battle of the Bulge. At the end of December, U.S. forces defeated the final German attempt to take Bastogne, and during the first half of January 1945, the Allies counterattacked in earnest. By January 16, the "bulge" had been eliminated. The cost to the Allies was 7,000 killed, 33,400 wounded, and 21,000 captured or missing. German losses were about 120,000 killed, wounded, or captured. German materiel losses were staggering: 600 tanks and assault guns destroyed, along with 6,000 other vehicles; some 1,600 German aircraft of the already badly crippled Luftwaffe also were downed.

Except for relatively minor actions in Alsace and Lorraine during January 1945, Ardennes was the last genuine German offensive of the war.

Refugees evacuate Bastogne, Belgium, which outnumbered U.S. troops held against the final German offensive of the war in the Battle of the Bulge. *Collection: National Archives and Records Administration*

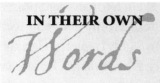
From the Fourth Inaugural Address of
Franklin D. Roosevelt, January 20, 1945

Mr. Chief Justice, Mr. Vice President, my friends, you will understand and, I believe, agree with my wish that the form of this inauguration be simple and its words brief.

We Americans of today, together with our allies, are passing through a period of supreme test. It is a test of our courage – of our resolve – of our wisdom – our essential democracy.

If we meet that test – successfully and honorably – we shall perform a service of historic importance which men and women and children will honor throughout all time.

As I stand here today, having taken the solemn oath of office in the presence of my fellow countrymen—in the presence of our God—I know that it is America's purpose that we shall not fail.

In the days and in the years that are to come we shall work for a just and honorable peace, a durable peace, as today we work and fight for total victory in war.

We can and we will achieve such a peace.

We shall strive for perfection. We shall not achieve it immediately—but we still shall strive. We may make mistakes—but they must never be mistakes which result from faint-

ness of heart or abandonment of moral principle. . . .

And so today, in this year of war, 1945, we have learned lessons – at a fearful cost – and we shall profit by them.

We have learned that we cannot live alone, at peace; that our own well-being is dependent on the well-being of other nations far away. We have learned that we must live as men, not as ostriches, nor as dogs in the manger.

We have learned to be citizens of the world, members of the human community.

We have learned the simple truth, as Emerson said, that "The only way to have a friend is to be one." We can gain no lasting peace if we approach it with suspicion and mistrust or with fear.

We can gain it only if we proceed with the understanding, the confidence, and the courage which flow from conviction.

The Almighty God has blessed our land in many ways. He has given our people stout hearts and strong arms with which to strike mighty blows for freedom and truth. He has given to our country a faith which has become the hope of all peoples in an anguished world.

So we pray to Him now for the vision to see our way clearly—to see the way that leads to a better life for ourselves and for all our fellow men—to the achievement of His will to peace on earth.

By the end of 1944, American, British, and Free French forces were poised to cross Germany's western frontier. On the Eastern Front, 1944 had seen a massive Soviet drive against the exhausted, thoroughly depleted German invaders. By December, the Russians had advanced into Poland, Romania, and the Balkans. Germany was being squeezed between the jaws of a great Allied vise.

Japan Moves Toward Collapse, 1945

As 1945 began, military and political logic, in addition to simple humanity, dictated the surrender of Japan. The empire's vast defensive perimeter in the Pacific was in collapse, and the Allies' "island-hopping" strategy was bringing American, Australian, and British forces ever closer to the Japanese homeland. But the Japanese militarists who ruled the nation were driven less by military and political logic than by a warrior code in which death was to be preferred to surrender. In defeat, Japanese resistance became, if anything, stronger than ever. And at the outset of 1945, Japan still had formidable resources on which to draw. While it is true that its Pacific perimeter was imploding and that the United States had imposed what amounted to a total naval blockade, Japan still held on to much of Burma and southern Asia, and it still controlled much of China. Strategic bombing of the Japanese mainland had done little to break the people's will to fight. Allied planners believed that nothing short of an extensive invasion of Japan itself would end the war; however, the experience of island-hopping suggested that such an invasion would be monumentally costly in Allied lives. If the Japanese held each Pacific island virtually to the last man, how much more fiercely would they defend their homeland?

Burma Operations, 1945

After years of operating on a shoestring, the China-Burma-India theater was finally getting more adequate resources. At the opening of the year, four Allied forces converged on Burma. The British XV Corps pushed through Arakan toward Akyab, while the British Fourteenth Army advanced through the dense jungle between the Chindwin and Irrawaddy Rivers. Another British force, the Northern Combat Area Command, closed in on the vital Burma Road from the west, while the Y-Force of the Chinese army advanced against the China-Burma frontier. By January 27, Chinese forces reopened the Burma Road, and land convoys began rolling into China.

By the middle of March, northern Burma was back in Allied hands, but central Burma would require further struggle. The brilliant General William Slim, commanding the British Fourteenth Army, quickly out-guessed his Japanese counterpart, General Hyotaro Kimura, who planned to lure Slim deep into central Burma, then counterattack as the Fourteenth Army attempted to cross the Irrawaddy north of Mandalay. By clever use of a decoy unit, Slim was able to effect a surprise crossing of the Irrawaddy. Slim's maneuvering culminated in the Battle of Mandalay during March 9–12, which resulted in the British capture of the city. A Japanese counterattack at Meiktila was checked, and then this town also fell to the British, marking the climax of the war in Burma. Rangoon was captured on May 2, and through the monsoon-drenched summer, General Slim pursued the remaining Japanese forces.

China and the Soviet Declaration
Early in 1945, the Japanese made extensive gains in China, especially near the border with French Indochina and, during March through May, in central China as well. However, beginning in April, the Soviet Union girded for its declaration of war against Japan. As the USSR built up its forces, the Japanese began to pull troops from coastal and central China to concentrate them in Manchuria to defend against an anticipated Soviet attack. The Soviet Union did not declare war until August 8, after the atomic bombing of Hiroshima. The Soviets began an advance into Manchuria that extended several days beyond August 14, the day of Japan's unconditional surrender.

Battle of Iwo Jima
Possession of Iwo Jima, a rocky island in the Bonin group and only eight square miles in area, was vital to the ongoing U.S. advance against the Japanese mainland. The Japanese used it as a base for fighter aircraft to intercept incoming American bombers. The Americans wanted to clear the Japanese out and then, in turn, use Iwo Jima as a forward air base. As was true of a number of other Japanese-held islands, Iwo Jima was honeycombed with hidden gun emplacements and pillboxes. It was also seeded densely with minefields.

The invasion began on February 19 when the U.S. Fifth Fleet landed Major General Harry Schmidt's V Amphibious Corps of marines on the southeastern end of the island. Fighting was extremely fierce, with the marines suffering 2,420 casualties on the first day of the assault. It was February 23 before the high ground, Mount Suribachi, was captured, the marines raising the Stars and Stripes there in an event immortalized first in a Pulitzer Prize–winning news photograph by Joseph Rosenthal, and subsequently in a sculpture group by Felix W. de Weldon. The raising came to symbolize not only the valor of the U.S. Marine Corps but also the entire American struggle and victory in World War II. The rest of the Iwo Jima battle consisted of mopping up the remaining defenders of the island, an operation that was not completed until March 24; however, B-29s began using Iwo Jima as an emergency landing strip on March 17. Total marine casualties in the battle were 6,891 killed and 18,070 wounded. Of the Japanese garrison of 22,000, only 212 lived to surrender. Before the war ended, some 2,251 B-29s used Iwo Jima to make emergency landings. It is estimated that possession of the island saved the lives of almost 25,000 U.S. airmen.

Okinawa Campaign

Beginning in March, Operation Iceberg went into action: the conquest of the Ryukyu Islands group, midway between Formosa and Kyushu, the southernmost island of Japan itself. The Ryukyus were the last stepping-stones to an invasion, and Okinawa was the major island of the group and the principal objective of Operation Iceberg.

Admiral Spruance was designated to lead the Fifth Fleet in a massive amphibious movement to land the Tenth Army, XXIV Corps, and III Marine Amphibious Corps on Okinawa. The British Royal Navy would assist. Japanese defenses were extremely formidable. The Japanese Thirty-second Army, numbering 130,000, was organized within a carefully prepared system of defenses. The civilian population of the island was nearly half a million.

During the entire second half of March, long-range bombers attacked Okinawa, but the Fifth Fleet now found itself facing a new weapon. It had made a limited debut at the Battle of Iwo Jima and was now being used extensively: the *kamikaze*. The Japanese sent pilots on one-way suicide missions to crash their explosives-laden aircraft into American ships. A few rocket planes were specially built for this purpose, but for the most part, pilots manned standard piston-engine fighter craft. At Okinawa the carriers *Franklin*, *Yorktown*, and *Wasp* were severely damaged by kamikazes, with the loss of 825 officers and men killed and 534 wounded. The initial wave of kamikazes did not deter the invasion, however, and the landings took place during April 1–4.

The toughest initial resistance on the ground came from the Machinato Line, a dense, interlocking system of defenses in the island's mountain region. At sea, in the meantime, Japanese ships and more kamikazes fiercely assaulted the amphibious force. In a massive kamikaze attack on April 7, two U.S. destroyers, two ammunition ships, a minesweeper, and a landing ship were sunk, while 24 other ships were damaged. Losses to the kamikazes were 383 aircraft and pilots. On that same day, however, American aircraft sank the great Japanese battleship *Yamato*, a terrific blow to the Imperial Navy.

In the meantime, on land, the American forces made slow but steady progress until the end of April, when a stalemate stalled the advance. Just before this, even more kamikazes—some 3,000 sorties—were launched against the amphibious force, inflicting severe casualties: 21 ships sunk, 23 damaged beyond immediate repair, and 43 permanently put out of action. Then, while the invaders were stalled on land, the Japanese counterattacked during May 3–4. The counterattack was soon crushed, and, even worse for the Japanese, the action had revealed the positions of well-hidden Japanese artillery. Targeting the artillery, the invaders were at last able to resume a full offensive during May 11–31, which culminated in June when the Japanese headquarters was overrun. The commanders on both sides perished in the great battle. U.S. general Simon Bolivar Buckner Jr. was killed by an artillery round, and Japan's Mitsuru Ushijima committed *hara-kiri* just before his headquarters was captured. Japanese casualties totaled 107,500 dead (it is believed an additional 20,000 were sealed in their defensive caves during the fighting) and American casualties were in excess of 12,000 killed and 37,000 wounded. The fall of Okinawa brought with it the loss of what remained of Japan's navy and air force.

Europe: The Air War Culminates, 1945

Despite high costs and questionable results, the Allied bomber offensive continued into the last year of the war. A serious threat to the bombers was the German introduction of the jet fighter, which could outperform even such superb American piston-engine fighters as the P-51 Mustang. However, the jets were introduced too late in the war and in too small numbers to make a truly significant impact.

During February 13–14, the RAF and U.S. Eighth Air Force conducted a massive firebombing of Dresden, creating a firestorm that killed more than a hundred thousand and leveled the great medieval city. Yet by this period of the war, the number of strategic targets in Germany was rapidly dwindling, and air operations turned increasingly to finishing off the Luftwaffe and closely supporting the ground offensive.

Victory in Italy

Even this late in the war, Allied progress in Italy remained heartbreakingly slow. Genuine breakthroughs did not occur until April, when the British Eighth Army struck the German Tenth Army southeast of Bologna. Shortly after this, the U.S. Fifth Army was able to break into the Po Valley, sending the remaining German defenders into full retreat. Bologna was now occupied, and from this point through the end of the war in Europe, the U.S. Fifth and British Eighth Armies pursued the retreating Germans far into northern Italy.

To the Rhine

On the Western Front, the Allies successfully resisted a German offensive in Alsace and Lorraine during January 1–21. In the north, the Allied advance was rapid. By early February the Colmar Pocket, a position in the Vosges held by the German Nineteenth Army, was cleared, and British and American forces went on to clear the Rhineland through March.

On March 7 a task force of the U.S. Ninth Armored Division in the vanguard of the First Army's advance found that the railroad bridge across the Rhine at Remagen had not been demolished by the enemy. The task force acted swiftly to take and hold the bridge, which greatly—and suddenly—accelerated the Allied advance across the Rhine. Much of the rest of March was consumed in enlarging and holding the Remagen bridgehead. This operation brought an end to the Rhineland campaign, at a cost of fewer than 20,000 Allied casualties. German losses were 60,000 killed or wounded and 250,000 taken prisoner.

On March 22, General Patton led the Fifth Division across the Rhine at Oppenheim in a surprise crossing that met with virtually no resistance. Within two days, multiple bridges had been thrown across the river, and the Third Army began rolling into Germany en masse. Just behind Patton was British commander Field Marshal Montgomery, who crossed his forces above the Ruhr, north of Patton's crossing. On March 24, the U.S. Ninth Army crossed at Dinslaken. The U.S. First Army broke out of

Two German mobile assault guns knocked out by Ninth Army Air Force fighter-bombers near Modrath, Germany. *Collection: National Archives and Records Administration*

Remagen on March 25 and crossed there. Additional crossings followed before the end of the month.

Germany Surrenders

Originally, Dwight D. Eisenhower, the Allied supreme commander, had targeted Berlin as an objective for U.S. and British troops. Now, in view of the rapid progress of the Third and First Armies, he sent the Twelfth Army Group east through central Germany, to advance on Leipzig instead. Berlin would be left to the Soviets, whose push westward was rapid, following the successful Soviet winter offensive. Eisenhower had opted to destroy whatever remained of the German army rather than immediately seize the key political objective Berlin represented. This decision was quite sound from a military point of view, but it was politically naive in that it gave the Soviets a firm hold on eastern Germany.

Per Eisenhower's new strategy, the Americans and the British encircled the Ruhr, entrapping there some 300,000 survivors of German Army Group B. To the north, Army Group H was being beaten into Holland and northwestern Germany. Army Group G, to the east and the south of the encircled Army Group B, continued to fight fiercely, but with little organization. From Hitler's bunker beneath the shattered streets of Berlin came a stream of orders to all German forces to "hold in place." That meant death.

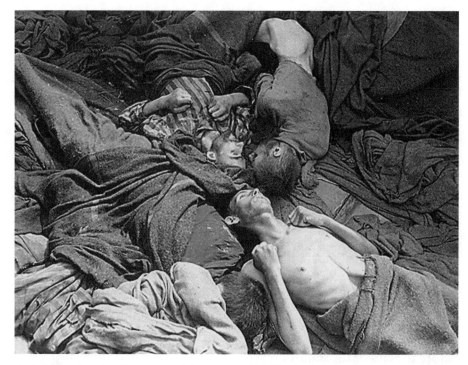

As the Allies invaded Germany and German-occupied Eastern Europe, they liberated dozens of death camps, in which the Third Reich exterminated six million Jews and approximately six million other persons Hitler's government deemed "undesirable." The image, from Dachau, is of prisoners who died en route to the camp. *Collection: National Archives and Records Administration*

British and Canadian forces defeated the last German resistance in Holland and the northwest. The U.S. Twelfth Army Group swept around far to the east, as far as Czechoslovakia, and, on April 25, made contact with the advancing Soviets at Torgau. The U.S. Sixth Army Group advanced through southern Germany and Austria, capturing, among other sites, Berchtesgaden, Hitler's celebrated mountain retreat in Bavaria. At the Brenner Pass, the U.S. Seventh Army made contact with the U.S. Fifth Army, which had completed, at long last, its struggling advance through Italy.

As the end rapidly approached, Adolf Hitler ignominiously committed suicide on April 30, having appointed Admiral Karl Doenitz as his successor. Under Doenitz, an unconditional surrender was concluded during May 7–8 and an armistice put in place on May 8–9. World War II was ended in Europe.

Japan Surrenders

The kamikaze storm that accompanied the invasion of Okinawa seemed a grim foreshadowing of what would await invaders of Japan itself. That Japan was defeated was beyond question. But when would the Japanese stop fighting?

In advance of the invasion, strategic bombing of Japan was intensified. The capture of Iwo Jima enabled fighter aircraft to escort the bombers round-trip into and out of Japan, greatly increasing the effectiveness of the air raids. All of Japan's major cities and industrial installations were hit. The most destructive raid was that against Tokyo during March 9–10, which created an incendiary firestorm that killed eighty-three thousand and wounded at least a hundred thousand more. The concept of strategic bombing was now being taken even further in Japan than in Europe. The objective was simply to destroy the nation. While fire rained from the sky, U.S. naval forces, especially submarines, tightened a blockade around Japan, sinking not only warships but also merchant vessels in an increasingly successful effort to starve the country into surrender.

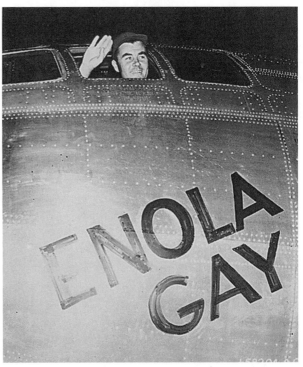

Colonel Paul W. Tibbets Jr. waves from the cockpit of his B-29, *Enola Gay* (named for his mother), before taking off on August 6, 1945, to drop an atomic bomb on Hiroshima, Japan. *Collection: National Archives and Records Administration*

From June through August, General MacArthur and Admiral Nimitz assembled an amphibious invasion force that would be even greater than the D-Day force that landed at Normandy. The two-phase invasion was slated to begin in November (Operation Olympic) and March 1946 (Operation Coronet). Then something occurred that made these plans unnecessary.

By 1938, German scientists had discovered the possibility of nuclear fission, a process whereby the tremendous energy of the force binding the constituents of the atom could be liberated. Fortunately for the world, Hitler's tyranny drove many of Germany's best thinkers out of the country, and that nation's wartime efforts to exploit fission in a weapon came to nothing. Three Hungarian-born American physicists—Leo Szilard, Eugene Wigner, and Edward Teller—appealed to a fugitive from Nazi persecution, Albert Einstein, to write a letter to President Franklin Roosevelt, warning him of Germany's nuclear weapons research. Late in 1939, Roosevelt responded by authorizing the atomic bomb development program that became known as the Manhattan Project. Under the military management of Brigadier General Leslie R. Groves and the scientific direction of J. Robert Oppenheimer, the program grew to vast proportions and employed the nation's foremost scientific minds. A prototype bomb was completed in the summer of 1945 and was successfully detonated at Alamogordo, New Mexico, on July 16, 1945. Almost immediately after

IN THEIR OWN *Words*

We have discovered the most terrible bomb in the history of the world. It may be the fire destruction prophesied in the Euphrates Valley Era, after Noah and his fabulous Ark. Anyway we "think" we have found the way to cause a disintegration of the atom. An experiment in the New Mexico desert was startling – to put it mildly. Thirteen pounds of the explosive caused the complete disintegration of a steel tower 60 feet high, created a crater 6 feet deep and 1,200 feet in diameter, knocked over a steel tower $1/2$ mile away and knocked men down 10,000 yards away. The explosion was visible for more than 200 miles and audible for 40 miles and more. This weapon is to be used against Japan between now and August 10th. I have told the Sec. of War, Mr. Stimson, to use it so that military objectives and soldiers and sailors are the target and not women and children. Even if the Japs are savages, ruthless, merciless and fanatic, we as the leader of the world for the common welfare cannot drop that terrible bomb on the old capital or the new. He and I are in accord. The target will be a purely military one and we will issue a warning statement asking the Japs to surrender and save lives. I'm sure they will not do that, but we will have given them the chance. It is certainly a good thing for the world that Hitler's crowd or Stalin's did not discover this atomic bomb. It seems to be the most terrible thing ever discovered, but it can be made the most useful. . . .

—HARRY S TRUMAN, DIARY ENTRY, JULY 25, 1945

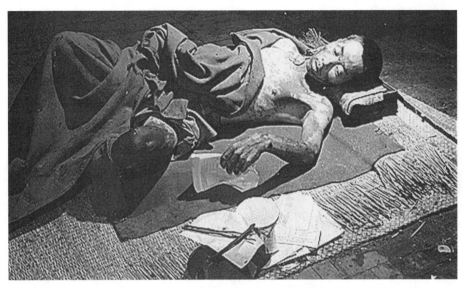

A U.S. Navy photographer recorded this victim of the atomic bomb blast in Hiroshima.
Collection: National Archives and Records Administration

this, Harry S Truman, who had become U.S. president on the death of Franklin Roosevelt (April 12, 1945), authorized the use of this new weapon against Japan.

On August 6, 1945, a lone B-29 bomber dropped "Little Boy" on Hiroshima, obliterating the city in three-fifths of a second. Three days later, "Fat Man" was dropped on Nagasaki, destroying about half the city. (The nicknames of the bombs referred to their shapes.) Some 78,000 people died instantly in Hiroshima, population about 300,000. Another 10,000 people went unaccounted for. At least 70,000 more were injured, and many subsequently died of radiation-related illnesses. Nagasaki, with a population of 250,000, instantly lost some 40,000 people; another 40,000 were wounded.

On August 10, the day after the attack on Nagasaki, Japan sued for peace on condition that Emperor Hirohito be allowed to remain as sovereign ruler. On August 11, the Allies replied that they and they alone would determine the future of Emperor Hirohito. At last, on August 14, the emperor personally accepted the Allied terms; a cease-fire was declared on August 15; and, on September 2, 1945, General MacArthur presided over the Japanese signing of the formal surrender document on the deck of the U.S. battleship *Missouri,* anchored in Tokyo Bay. World War II had ended.

The United States as Superpower

For all its complexity, World War II was a titanic contest between peoples in the service of opposing ideologies: Fascism, Nazism, and Japanese militarism on one side versus democracy uneasily allied with communism on the other. As Americans—and much of the rest of the world—saw it, the single greatest champion in this contest was the United States, which emerged from the war as one of the world's two great superpowers.

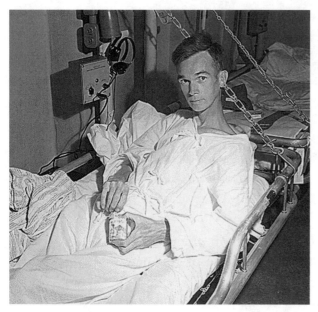

Corporal Leopold Anthony Mulikowski, one of many Allied POWs liberated after the surrender of Japan. He recuperated aboard the hospital ship *Benevolence,* having spent three years as a POW. *Collection: National Archives and Records Administration*

The other postwar superpower was the Soviet Union. With the defeat of their common enemies, the United States and the USSR now squared off against one another, democratic capitalism versus dictatorial communism. This ideological opposition threatened to produce yet a third world war, fought, perhaps, with nuclear weapons even more destructive than those deployed against Japan. At the dawn of what poet W. H. Auden called the Age of Anxiety, the postwar celebration of triumph and salvation was short-lived indeed.

CHAPTER 13

Korean War, 1950–1953

One could look to thousands of years of Korean history for the origins of the Korean War of 1950–1953. North and South had an ancient heritage of conflict, and Korea also was often subject to invasion by China or Japan. However, the more proximate causes of the war may be found in the early twentieth century and in the aftermath of *World War II, 1939–1945 (chapter 12)*.

World War II and After

By the early twentieth century, the empire of Japan was in an expansionist mode and, in 1910, annexed Korea, without creating a diplomatic ripple in the rest of the world. Then came December 7, 1941, and the Japanese attack on Pearl Harbor, Hawaii. In declaring war on Japan, the United States acknowledged, among many other things, that Japan had made Korea one of its first victims of imperialist aggression. At the 1943 Cairo Conference among China, Great Britain, and the United States, the Allies agreed to include the independence of Korea among the objectives of their joint prosecution of *World War II, 1939–1945 (chapter 12)*. However, they also anticipated a postwar period of military occupation by the Allied powers and determined that such occupation should be by a joint international commission to consist of the United States, Great Britain, China, and the Soviet Union. At the Yalta Conference in February 1945, U.S. president Franklin D. Roosevelt attempted to elicit an agreement from Soviet premier Joseph Stalin for the establishment of an international trusteeship to prepare Korea for independence following the defeat of Japan. Stalin neither objected nor approved. President Truman advanced the proposal again at the Potsdam Conference during July 27–August 2, 1945, but it was not until August 8, when the Soviets

CHRONOLOGY   Principal Events of the Korean War

1950

June 25: *North Korean troops invade South Korea*

June 27: *United Nations sanctions U.S. (and U.S.-directed coalition) action in Korea*

August 7: *United States begins counterattack from Pusan*

September 15: *General Douglas MacArthur leads Inchon landing*

October 8: *MacArthur crosses thirty-eighth parallel into North Korea*

October 25: *250,000 Chinese troops cross the Yalu River into North Korea, but retreat after two weeks*

November 24: *Final U.N. and South Korean offensive toward Yalu*

November 25: *Second Chinese attack pushes U.N. and South Korean forces back into South Korea*

December 25: *Chinese are stopped at thirty-eighth parallel*

1951

February 11: *Third Chinese attack pushes UN forces back to Han River*

February 21–April 21: *U.N. counterattack pushes Chinese back to thirty-eighth parallel*

April 11: *Truman relieves MacArthur for insubordination; Matthew Ridgway assumes U.N. command*

April 22: *Fourth Chinese attack drives Ridgway back to Seoul*

June 1: *Ridgway's "Ripper" operation pushes Chinese north of the thirty-eighth parallel*

July 10: *Panmunjon peace talks begin; war continues without major gains for either side*

1953

July 27: *Armistice signed*

declared war on Japan, that Stalin announced his full intention to abide by the Potsdam agreement to establish a trusteeship for Korea.

Following the U.S. atomic bombing of Hiroshima and Nagasaki, the Japanese suddenly surrendered on August 14, 1945, making an Allied occupation of Korea unnecessary. Nevertheless, the United States proposed that the Soviets receive Japan's surrender in Korea north of the thirty-eighth parallel while the United States accept surrender south of this line. The United States intended this partition of Korea to be a strictly temporary expedient until Korea could be restored to a full peace-time footing, but the Soviets seized on it to divide Korea and bring the northern portion into the Communist sphere. Almost immediately the Soviets began building fortifications along the thirty-eighth parallel, and although the United States and the Soviet Union agreed to create a joint commission to help the Koreans create a provisional government, the Soviets refused to move forward with this work. In September 1947, therefore, the United States requested that the United Nations intervene to bring about Korean unification. Over a Soviet objection, the United Nation decided that a unified government be established for Korea following a general election. Moreover, after the government was established, the United Nations would dispatch a security force to Korea to protect it.

Communist Resistance

Encouraged by the Soviets, the North Korean Communists barred the United Nations commission from holding elections north of the thirty-eighth parallel. South of the parallel, the elections proceeded on May 10, 1948, creating the Republic of Korea (ROK) under President Syngman Rhee. The United Nations twice affirmed that the ROK was the only lawful government of Korea. In response, the Soviets acted swiftly to establish a rival government in North Korea. On May 25, 1948, the Soviet-sponsored elections created the Supreme People's Assembly, which purported to represent all of Korea. The People's Democratic Republic of Korea (DRK) was put under the leadership of Kim Il Sung, a Soviet-trained Korean Communist. Although the United Nations recognized only the ROK, it was now the de facto government of South Korea, while the DRK was the de facto government of the North.

U.S. Military Role in South Korea: Early Phase

After setting up a North Korean government, the USSR announced that it would withdraw Red Army troops from the country by January 1, 1949. In the customary postwar rush to demobilize, the United States greeted the Soviet pledge warmly, because it wished to withdraw U.S. troops from the country as well. However, the United States had no intention of abandoning the ROK and resolved to train and equip a security force for the South and provide economic aid. In the meantime, the United States would continue to press the United Nations for the reunification of Korea.

The United States was in a delicate diplomatic situation. It wanted to arm South Korea for defense but not give the appearance that it was sponsoring South Korean aggression, which might lead to full-scale war involving the North Koreans as well as the Soviets. Accordingly, the United States proposed to train an ROK army of sixty-five thousand, a coast guard of four thousand, and a police force of thirty-five thousand. Arms would be supplied, but no tanks or artillery, which were considered offensive rather than defensive weapons. President Rhee protested that his nation needed a much larger force: a regular army of a hundred thousand men, a militia force of fifty thousand, a police force of fifty thousand, a navy of ten thousand, and an air force of three thousand. Rhee hired Claire L. Chennault, the famed U.S. major general who had commanded China's "Flying Tigers" during *World War II, 1939–1945 (chapter 12)* and now retired, to create a plan for a South Korean air force. The United States objected, but the South Koreans established an air force along with their other military assets, and the United States completed its military withdrawal from Korea on June 29, 1949, leaving behind only a five-hundred-man U.S. Korean Military Advisory Group (KMAG).

The War Begins

During *World War II, 1939–1945 (chapter 12),* many North Koreans took refuge in the USSR, where they were given military and political training and, after the war, returned to North Korea as the nucleus around which a Communist government and military force would be created. Initially, Soviet premier Josef Stalin supplied military hardware to the North Korean government of Kim Il Sung and encouraged a low-level guerrilla war with the South. In 1950 Kim persuaded Stalin to give his permission and support for a full-scale invasion, and by May 1950 KMAG detected a military buildup on the northern side of the thirty-eighth parallel. The strength of the North Korean People's Army (NKPA) was about 100,000 troops, along with a very small air force of 132 combat aircraft.

The invasion began at four o'clock on the morning of June 25, 1950, as NKPA units crossed the thirty-eighth parallel and brushed aside the inferior South Korean forces deployed along the parallel. The main invading force headed toward Seoul, the South Korean capital, about thirty-five miles below the parallel, while smaller forces moved down the center of the Korean Peninsula and along the eastern coast. Despite KMAG intelligence, the South Korean forces were completely surprised by the invasion and retreated in disorder before the advance. The NKPA took Seoul, and President Truman ordered General Douglas MacArthur, commander of

IN THEIR OWN *Words*

Cable of United Press Correspondent Jack James Announcing North Korean Invasion

URGENT PRESS UNIPRESS NEWYORK

25095 JAMES

FRAGMENTARY REPORTS EXTHIRTY EIGHT PARALLEL INDI-CATED NORTH KOREANS LAUNCHED SUNDAY MORNING ATTACKS GENERALLY ALONG ENTIRE BORDER PARA REPORTS AT ZERO NINE THIRTY LOCAL TIME INDICATED KAESONG FORTY MILES NORTHWEST SEOUL AND HEADQUARTERS OF KOREAN ARMYS FIRST DIVISION FELL NINE AYEM STOP ENEMY FORCES REPORTED THREE TO FOUR KILOMETERS SOUTH OF BORDER ON ONGJIN PENINSULA

STOP

TANKS SUPPOSED BROUGHT INTO USE CHUNCHON FIFTY MILES NORTHEAST SEOUL STOP LANDING EXSEA ALSO REPORTED FROM TWENTY SMALL BOATS BELOW KANGNUNG ON EASTERN COAST WHERE REPORTEDLY OFFCUT HIGHWAY ENDITEM NOTE SHOULD STRESS THIS STILL FRAGMENTARY AND PICTURE VAGUE SYET JAMES.

Korean women and children comb through the rubble of Seoul, the South Korean capital, November 1, 1950. *Collection: National Archives and Records Administration*

the U.S. Far East Command, to supply the ROK with equipment and ammunition because its army had abandoned much of its supplies in the retreat.

The U.S. Commitment

President Truman was caught between his objectives of helping South Korea and containing Communist aggression, on the one hand, and, on the other hand, avoiding the escalation of Korea into a major war, which might involve not only the Soviets but also the Chinese Communists, who appeared virtually certain to sustain their victory in the war against the Chinese Nationalists. Immediately, Truman ordered the U.S. Seventh Fleet to proceed toward Korea, but he subsequently decided to redeploy most of it to Taiwan, to prevent the Chinese Communists on the mainland from attacking the Chinese Nationalists' Taiwanese stronghold. Truman did direct MacArthur to use air and naval strikes against North Korean positions below the thirty-eighth parallel, then, on June 30, gave MacArthur permission to use all available U.S. forces to aid the ROK. All that was available were units of the Eighth Army as well as the Twenty-ninth

Regimental Combat Team. These units were understrength and could not be deemed fully combat-ready. The same was true of the Far East Air Force and the modest naval forces in the area.

On the diplomatic front, the Soviets signed a treaty of friendship, alliance, and mutual assistance with Communist China and announced that it would boycott all U.N. organizations and committees on which Nationalist China, which it now considered defeated and illegitimate, participated. Although the prospect of a Soviet-Chinese alliance was terrifying, the Soviet boycott meant that it was not present to veto the U.N. Security Council resolution authorizing military action against North Korea. Backed by U.N. sanctions, President Truman named Douglas MacArthur commander of U.S. and U.N. forces. On July 24 MacArthur created the U.N. Command (UNC). Various U.N. member nations would

IN THEIR OWN *Words*   **U.N. Resolution of June 27, 1950**

The Security Council,

HAVING DETERMINED that the armed attack upon the Republic of Korea by forces from North Korea constitutes a breach of the peace,

HAVING CALLED FOR an immediate cessation of hostilities, and

HAVING CALLED UPON the authorities of North Korea to withdraw forthwith their armed forces to the 38th parallel, and

HAVING NOTED from the report of the United Nations Commission for Korea that the authorities in North Korea have neither ceased hostilities nor withdrawn their armed forces to the 38th parallel and that urgent military measures are required to restore international peace and security, and

HAVING NOTED the appeal from the Republic of Korea to the United Nations for immediate and effective steps to secure peace and security,

RECOMMENDS that the Members of the United Nations furnish such assistance to the Republic of Korea as may be necessary to repel the armed attack and to restore international peace and security in the area.

participate in the Korean War, but the United States contributed by far the greatest numbers of troops and equipment.

Although backed by the United Nations, the objectives of the action were not entirely clear at the start of the war. Specifically, it was undecided whether U.N. forces would be permitted to operate north of the thirty-eighth parallel or would be constrained to remain on the defensive in the South. Furthermore, although MacArthur had supreme command of U.N. forces, he was still constrained by international political considerations, which meant that important military decisions were often delayed or attenuated by U.N. debate.

Another source of American anxiety was the postwar status of its military. Demobilization after *World War II, 1939–1945 (chapter 12)* had been swift and military budget cuts deep, resulting in a combined troop strength of 1,460,000 serving in undermanned and underequipped divisions. Budgetary constraint was not the only factor discouraging a U.S. military buildup; the Truman administration feared that augmenting the military at this time would send a bellicose signal to the Soviet Union. The prospect of a new world war was very real.

North Korean Advances

U.S. ground forces began arriving in Korea just six days after the June 25 invasion. By this time the NKPA had crossed the Han River south of Seoul and still was on the move. By July 3, Kimpo Airfield and the port of Inchon were in Communist hands. In an ideal situation, MacArthur would have waited until he could consolidate his forces and attack *en masse*. Given the speed of the Communist advance, however, it was likely that by that time, South Korea would have already surrendered. Accordingly, the U.N. commander decided to take an immediate stand with the forces now available to him. Since the North Koreans had clearly targeted the port of Pusan, MacArthur deployed "Task Force Smith" just above Pusan on July 5. At first the Americans made headway against the advancing NKPA, but they were soon outgunned and pushed into a disorganized retreat.

MacArthur deployed three more units in an effort to stem the North Korean advance, but to no avail. By July 13 the NKPA had pushed ROK and U.S. forces to Taejon, in south-central South Korea. While fighting these all but futile delaying actions, MacArthur rushed to build up forces in Japan. Two divisions were moved to South Korea on July 18 to reinforce the defenders of Taejon, but the city was lost to the NKPA on July 20.

The defeats were humiliating; however, MacArthur understood that the NKPA had a price to pay for its rapid advance: long and tenuous lines of communication and supply. Although U.S. ground troops were badly outnumbered at this point, the U.S. Air Force quickly established air superiority and began interdicting the supply lines. A naval blockade was also proving effective in cutting off NKPA supplies.

Battle of Pusan

Lieutenant General Walton H. Walker, commander of the U.S. Eighth Army, resolved to take a make-or-break stand along a line north of Pusan, the 140-mile-long "Pusan perimeter," extending in an arc from the Korea Strait to the Sea of Japan. Although Walker's forces were spread thinly along this arc, he relied on well-developed lines of communication to give him the flexibility of shifting troop strength wherever and whenever it might be needed. This tactic proved highly effective. Although the NKPA deployed against the Pusan perimeter had grown to thirteen infantry divisions and one armored division, many of the men were raw recruits. The NKPA command also made the mistake of attacking piecemeal along various points of the perimeter rather than massing a single overwhelming attack at one point. Walker's defense was not only costly to the NKPA, it also bought MacArthur the time he needed to build up forces sufficient for an offensive thrust.

Landing at Inchon

No one appreciated more than Douglas MacArthur the precarious position of the NKPA. They were far from home, their supply lines stretched to the breaking point. Attack from behind, sever the supply lines completely, and the frontmost units of the NKPA would be trapped between whatever force attacked from the north and the Eighth Army at Pusan. But how to get a sufficiently large force north of the present NKPA position? The answer was an amphibious assault, with the point of landing at Inchon.

It was a high-stakes, high-risk move. While the landing site was ideal from strategic and tactical points of view, it posed serious practical problems. Tides were extremely variable, creating terrible hazards for landing craft, and the approach to Inchon lay through a very narrow channel, yet another opportunity for disaster. Once ashore, troops would have to scale a high seawall, then fight through a well-developed, built-up area. Despite the risks, MacArthur decided to commit to it virtually everything he had, leaving nothing in reserve. If the landing came under heavy attack, there would be no reinforcements to bail it out. Indeed, such an attack would also leave the Eighth Army vulnerable, depriving it of the possibility of reinforcement.

On September 15, 1950, MacArthur rolled the dice—and everything went right. Planners had predicted the tides accurately, the ships steered safely through the perilous straits, and the troops encountered only light resistance, for no one expected a landing here. The Inchon landing was, in fact, the most brilliant military operation in the long and remarkable career of Douglas MacArthur. Within two weeks of the landing, Seoul was once again in ROK hands, and the NKPA lines were blocked. During September 16–23, General Walker's Eighth Army began to fight its way out of the Pusan perimeter, meeting very heavy resistance at first, but once the NKPA commanders realized that they were caught between the landing force and the Eighth Army, the stomach for the fight left them. The NKPA rapidly withdrew, the Eighth Army giving chase and meeting with the landing force on September 26. Although upward of thirty thousand North Korean troops probably made it back to the thirty-eighth parallel, the Inchon landing and the associated breakout from Pusan had neutralized the NKPA as a fighting force in South Korea. The integrity of South Korea had been established clear through to the thirty-eighth parallel.

Invasion of North Korea

In the afterglow of the U.N. victory in the South, planners debated whether to cross the 38th parallel and invade North Korea. There were compelling reasons to do so: At least thirty thousand NKPA troops had escaped to the North, which harbored at least another thirty thousand, making for an effective military force of sixty thousand available, at will, once again to invade the South. Moreover, defeating North Korea on its own territory would advance the cause of reunification. But there also was a compelling reason not to invade: Both Communist China and the Soviet Union had stated their intention to defend against such an invasion.

In the end, President Truman decided to take the risk. On September 27 he ordered General MacArthur to pursue the NKPA across the thirty-eighth parallel; however, Truman also issued important restrictions. The advance was to proceed only in the absence of Chinese or Soviet intervention, and once U.N. forces neared the Yalu River (the border with Manchuria) and the Tumen River (the border with the USSR), MacArthur

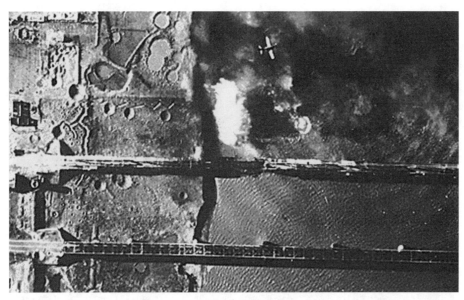

A Navy AD-3 dive bomber pulls out of a dive after dropping a two-thousand-pound bomb on the Korean side of a bridge across the Yalu River into Manchuria, November 15, 1950. *Collection: National Archives and Records Administration*

was to use South Korean troops exclusively. The American president did not relish the prospect of U.S. soldiers in direct combat with Chinese or Soviet troops.

Two ROK corps crossed the thirty-eighth parallel on October 1, and on October 9 General Walker led Eighth Army's I Corps across as well. By the nineteenth, I Corps had cleared Pyongyang, the North Korean capital, and by October 24, I Corps was just fifty miles outside of Manchuria. ROK forces were also now positioned close to the Chinese border.

When China threatened to intervene, Truman called a conference with MacArthur on Wake Island. MacArthur declared with great assurance that the Chinese talk was just that—talk. Warily, Truman authorized the advance to continue.

U.N. troops faced stiff resistance everywhere except along the coasts of the peninsula. They also faced increasingly frigid temperatures with the onset of a winter for which most of the soldiers were ill equipped. Then, on October 26, MacArthur determined that the strong resistance was being provided by Communist Chinese troops. By November it became clear that the Chinese commitment was significant, some five divisions; however, MacArthur continued to believe—and to insist—that Chinese operations were strictly defensive and that no large numbers of Chinese

Members of the Second Division, north of the Chongchon River, November 20, 1950.
Collection: National Archives and Records Administration

troops had actually crossed into North Korea. MacArthur ordered the advance to continue. On November 24, U.S. forces, part of the Seventh Division, had reached the Yalu River, North Korea's border with China.

China Intervenes

On the night of November 25, 1950, Chinese forces, in strength, hit the Eighth Army hard on its center and right. Two days later, even more powerful Chinese attacks overran units of X Corps on its left flank. By November 28, U.N. positions were caving in. It became stunningly clear that some three hundred thousand Chinese troops had entered North Korea, thirty infantry divisions in addition to artillery and cavalry units.

Walker had no choice but to withdraw U.N. troops as rapidly as possible to prevent their being enveloped by massively superior Chinese forces. Even U.N. air superiority vanished as Soviet-built Chinese MiG-15 jet fighters easily outperformed U.S. piston-driven craft. By December 15, after taking severe losses, UN forces had withdrawn all the way to the thirty-eighth parallel and were now establishing a defensive line across the breadth of the Korean Peninsula.

While these operations were under way, a massive operation to evacuate X Corps from North Korea began. In a magnificently orchestrated effort by sea and airlift, 105,000 troops, almost 100,000 Korean civilians, 17,500 vehicles, and 350,000 tons of cargo were moved south, to Pusan, out of enemy reach. In the course of the evacuation, General Walker was killed in an automobile accident, and Lieutenant General Matthew B. Ridgway was rushed from Washington to replace him as commander of the Eighth Army.

Strategic Constraints and the Relief of MacArthur

In the wake of China's intervention, Douglas MacArthur lobbied for permission to attack China, especially airfields in Manchuria. President Truman and his advisers, including Secretary of Defense George C. Marshall, wanted to avoid war with China at all costs. Not only might such a war trigger a new worldwide conflict—indeed, many U.S. planners believed that Korea was a Soviet ploy aimed specifically at starting a third world war—it would also drain U.S. military strength, compelling a great reduction of forces in Europe, which would leave the new NATO allies vulnerable to Soviet attack. Thus MacArthur was ordered to contain and limit the war, to keep U.N. forces within Korea. Should it become impossible to fight the war in this contained manner, he was to evacuate the peninsula. MacArthur countered by advocating a blockade of the Chinese mainland, and the aerial and naval bombardment of industrial targets within China. Even more provocatively, MacArthur wanted to reinforce U.N. and ROK forces with troops from Nationalist China and also use Nationalist Chinese forces to make direct diversionary attacks against the Chinese mainland.

While U.S. planners debated, Ridgway, the new commander of the beleaguered Eighth Army, concluded that his forces had been badly demoralized by the massive attacks and repeated withdrawals. The army believed itself defeated. Intelligence reports suggested that combined Chinese and North Korean forces were preparing to attack Seoul and the center of the Korean Peninsula. Ridgway believed that the only hope for holding the defensive line at the thirty-eighth parallel was to commit all reserves to the immediate reinforcement of the Eighth Army and to prepare a separate defensive position above Seoul. Despite Ridgway's preparations, a massive Chinese attack on New Year's Eve sent the Eighth Army into what was at least an orderly withdrawal toward Seoul. That capital fell on January 4, 1951. However, the Chinese did not pursue the Eighth Army south of Seoul, and within weeks, all Chinese advances had halted. Once again, overextended supply lines had stopped a Communist advance.

Ridgway believed that U.N. forces could exploit Chinese logistical shortcomings by pounding away at the stalled troops, inflicting as many casualties as possible in what would become a war of attrition. His superior, however, disagreed. MacArthur did not believe that U.N. forces could remain on the peninsula without reinforcements—and an attack on China. Again fearing that an attack on China would bring on a war of possibly global proportions, perhaps beginning with an air attack on U.S. forces in Japan, the Joint Chiefs of Staff advised MacArthur to defend his positions in Korea in a manner that inflicted as many casualties on the enemy as possible. Truman concurred.

Ridgway began a slow, methodical, and excruciating offensive—dubbed the "meatgrinder" by front-line GIs—on January 25, 1951. Meatgrinder regained Seoul by the middle of March, and by April 21, U.N. troops were back at the thirty-eighth parallel. And there they stopped, for the U.N. member nations had agreed that securing South Korea below the thirty-eighth parallel was an acceptable outcome of the war. Accordingly, MacArthur was informed that Truman would announce his willingness to commence negotiations with the Chinese and the North Koreans on the basis of current positions. Enraged and frustrated, MacArthur preempted Truman's announcement by making an

Men of the First Marine Division capture Chinese Communist troops at Hoengsong, March 2, 1951. *Collection: National Archives and Records Administration*

unauthorized announcement of his own. He declared that if the United Nations would expand the conflict to North Korea's coastal areas and interior strongholds, the Chinese would realize that they were at serious risk of suffering military defeat. Truman now felt that he had no choice but to withhold his peace initiative and await military developments. He did not want an open dispute with his top military leader.

But MacArthur forced his hand. On April 5, 1951, Representative Joseph W. Martin read into the *Congressional Record* a letter from MacArthur stating the necessity of opening up a second front against China itself, one using Nationalist Chinese troops. The general could not stomach what he saw as a war without victory in Korea, and he closed his letter by declaring that there is "no substitute for victory."

In response to this letter, and after consulting intensively with his cabinet and military leaders, including the Joint Chiefs of Staff, Truman relieved MacArthur as commander on April 11. Although the Joint Chiefs and other advisers unreservedly endorsed Truman's action, it created outrage among the public, adding to a growing disgust with the war.

A New Chinese Offensive

Matthew Ridgway, appointed to replace MacArthur as supreme commander of U.N. forces, turned over the Eighth Army to Lieutenant General James A. Van Fleet. Almost immediately, on April 22, a new massive offensive—twenty-one Chinese, nine North Korean divisions—was aimed at the U.N. forces. The first phase of this "spring offensive" petered out by April 30. It had been especially violent, costing the Eighth Army some seven thousand casualties, but it proved far more costly to the Communists, who lost ten times that number.

A Korean girl carries her little brother past a stalled U.S. M-26 tank, Haengju, June 9, 1951. *Collection: National Archives and Records Administration*

On May 14 the Communists unleashed a second phase of the spring offensive, attacking the right flank of X Corps with twenty divisions. This, however, was precisely where Van Fleet had anticipated an attack, and he had positioned ample reserves to bolster the front lines. The result was that the offensive was severely blunted, and in the space of a week, the

U.S. Marine colonel James Murray Jr. and Colonel Chang Chun San, North Korean Communist Army, initial maps showing the northern and southern boundaries of the demarcation zone during the Panmunjom cease-fire talks, October 11, 1951. *Collection: National Archives and Records Administration*

Communist forces had casualties approaching ninety thousand. Nevertheless, the Communists had hit upon a new offensive strategy, which substituted stealthy hit-and-run attacks by small units for the massive assaults they had conducted hitherto. The rest of the Korean War would consist essentially of these effective and exhausting guerrilla tactics.

For his part, Van Fleet intended to take the offensive. He advanced on May 22, 1951, and made significant headway all along the front, only to be ordered to halt and hold his position. Once again, the fear among the U.N. Allies was that sufficient provocation would bring the Soviet Union into the war. Reluctantly, Van Fleet halted, and the U.N. force set about consolidating its position mostly just north of the thirty-eighth parallel. The Communists also took time to construct strong defenses in the North as a safeguard against invasion.

Peace Negotiations
It was the Soviet ambassador to the U.N., Yakov A. Malik, who first proposed a cease-fire in Korea. The Communist negotiators did all they could to drag out the peace talks, using the initial cease-fire largely to refit their

troops and to exploit propaganda opportunities. The talks began on July 10, 1951, but it took until July 26 even to establish an agenda. The talks continued, with frequent breakdowns and impasses, for the next two years, during which grim combat continued. It was finally agreed that an armistice would require accord on a demarcation line and a demilitarized zone, impartial supervision of the truce, and arrangements for return of prisoners of war. The toughest single issue involved the disposition of POWs. U.N. negotiators wanted prisoners to decide for themselves whether they would return home; the Communists, fearful of mass defections, held out for mandatory repatriation. In an effort to break the negotiation stalemate, General Mark Clark, who succeeded Ridgway as U.N. commander in May 1952, stepped up punishing bombing raids on North Korea. At last, during April 1953, the POW issue was resolved: a compromise permitted freed prisoners to choose sides, but under supervision of a neutral commission.

After this long, bloody, and frustrating process, the only individual who remained thoroughly displeased was Syngman Rhee, the president of South Korea. Desiring nothing short of Korean unification (under his leadership) and wholly voluntary repatriation as absolute conditions for an armistice, he sabotaged the peace process by suddenly ordering the release of twenty-five thousand North Korean prisoners who wanted to

Gunners of the U.S. Fifth Air Force in Korea, September 1952. *Collection: National Archives and Records Administration*

live in the South. To regain Rhee's cooperation, the United States promised him a mutual security pact and long-term economic aid. Nevertheless, the armistice signed on July 27, 1953, did not formally include South Korea. Still, the cease-fire held, and the shooting war was over.

How many Chinese and North Korean troops were killed in the Korean War is unknown, but estimates range between 1.5 million and 2 million, in addition to at least 1 million civilians. The U.N. command lost 88,000 killed, of whom 23,300 were American. Many more were wounded. South Korean civilian casualties probably equaled those of North Korea. As of the year 2001, Korea remains divided, despite some recent gestures of reconciliation from North as well as South, and most of the world's nations look upon North Korea as an ongoing military threat not only to the stability of the region but also to the peace of the world.

The Korean War did succeed in containing communism—confining it to North Korea—but in all other respects, this costly conflict was inconclusive, except that it provided a precedent for intervention in another Asian war, this time in a divided Vietnam.

CHAPTER 14

Vietnam War, 1954–1975

T he Allied triumph in *World War II, 1939–1945 (chapter 12)* did not produce the high hopes and blithe arrogance of the victors at Versailles following *World War I, 1914–1918 (chapter 11)*. In 1918 many believed they had indeed fought and won the war to end all war. In 1945 few thought as much, for the long conflict had left much of the world dangerously unstable, and although fascism, Nazism, and Japanese imperialism had been crushed, another totalitarian ideology was poised to seize power in nations weakened by long combat. Such was the case in Southeast Asia.

Vietnam After World War II

During the nineteenth century, France had established colonial hegemony in Laos, Cambodia, and Vietnam. When France capitulated to Germany in 1940, the Japanese allowed French colonial officials nominal authority while actually assuming de facto control of these areas themselves. In 1945 with the liberation of France, the Japanese seized full control, eliminating the French police agencies and other armed authorities that had long kept in check indigenous nationalist groups that had been seeking independence. In Vietnam, the largest and most powerful of these groups was the

CHRONOLOGY   Principal Events of the Vietnam War

1954

May 7: *French defeated at Dien Bien Phu*

October 24: *President Eisenhower pledges support to the government of Ngo Dinh Diem; the Republic of Vietnam is organized the next year*

1959

July 8: *First American combat deaths: two servicemen killed*

1964

August 2 and 4: *Gulf of Tonkin Incident*

August 7: *Congress approves the Gulf of Tonkin Resolution*

1965

March 8–9: *First American combat troops (not advisers) arrive in Vietnam*

April 7: *President Johnson offers North Vietnam aid in exchange for peace; the offer is spurned*

April 17: *First major antiwar rally in Washington, D.C.*

1967

October 21–23: *Fifty thousand demonstrate against the war in Washington, D.C.*

1968

January 21: *Six-month Battle of Khe Sanh begins*

January 30: *The Tet Offensive begins*

March 16: *My Lai massacre (150 unarmed Vietnamese civilians are killed by Lieutenant William L. Calley Jr.'s platoon)*

May 10: *Paris peace talks begin*

1969

May 10–20: *Battle for Hamburger Hill*

June 8: *President Nixon announces the first troop withdrawals from South Vietnam*

November 15: *250,000 people demonstrate against the war in Washington, D.C.*

1970

April 30: *U.S. and South Vietnamese forces invade Cambodia*

May 4: *Kent State massacre*

1971

February: *South Vietnam and U.S. forces invade Laos in an attempt to sever the Ho Chi Minh Trail*

1972

December: *Christmas bombing of Hanoi*

1973

January 27: *Paris Peace Accords signed*

March 29: *Last U.S. combat troops leave Vietnam*

1974

September 16: *President Gerald Ford offers clemency to draft evaders and military deserters.*

1975

April 21: *South Vietnamese president Thieu resigns*

April 29–30: *Saigon falls; U.S. Navy evacuates U.S. personnel and South Vietnamese refugees; South Vietnamese president Duong Van Minh surrenders*

April 30: *Vietnam reunified under Communist regime*

Viet Minh, which, under the leadership of Soviet-trained Ho Chi Minh, launched a guerrilla war against the Japanese forces of occupation and soon took control of the nation's northern regions. In this, Ho Chi Minh was aided by U.S. Office of Strategic Services (OSS) military teams.

After the war in Europe had ended, Allied forces turned their attention to Vietnam (and the rest of Southeast Asia), a theater they had largely neglected during most of the war. Nationalist Chinese troops moved into the Tonkin provinces of northern Vietnam, and the British, anxious to restore France to the status of a world power to help counter the Soviet Union's rapidly expanding sphere of influence, secured southern Vietnam for the reentry of the French, who ruthlessly suppressed all agitation for independence in that region. The French began talks with Ho Chi Minh, now firmly established in the North, but these soon proved fruitless, and a state of chronic guerrilla conflict developed.

The conflict escalated during 1946, when Nationalist Chinese forces, who had occupied the North, were replaced there by the French military. It was not that Chiang Kai-shek had any love for French imperialism, but that he feared a Communist takeover in Vietnam and preferred French control of the region to that. In November, fire was exchanged between a French patrol boat and Vietnamese militia forces in Haiphong Harbor. The French retaliated by bombarding Haiphong, killing some six thousand civilians and prompting Ho Chi Minh to break off all talks, retreat with his government into the hill country of Tonkin, and conduct an all-out guerrilla war against the French.

Many in the United States strongly sympathized with Ho Chi Minh's nationalism. Like President Franklin D. Roosevelt before him, Harry S Truman was an anti-imperialist. But he also felt that an independent Vietnam would likely become a communist Vietnam. Still, Truman urged the French to reach a political solution in Vietnam and barred direct export of U.S. war materiel to French forces there—although he did vacillate to the important extent of refusing to bar arms shipments to France itself, which, of course, could transship the materiel to its troops in Vietnam.

The fall of China to communism in 1949, together with the intensification of the Cold War in Europe by the end of the decade *(see chapter 15: Cold War Conflicts since 1958),* including the forced induction of much of Eastern Europe into the Soviet camp, compelled the United States to accept French authority in Vietnam, no matter how morally distasteful. Moreover, if the newly formed North Atlantic Treaty

Organization (NATO) were to succeed as a force against communism in Europe, the full support of France was required. Its military resources drained by the fierce guerrilla warfare in Vietnam, France was hardly in a position to offer that full degree of support.

America's Earliest Involvement

Putting aside its many qualms, the U.S. government, on February 7, 1950, recognized Vietnam as constituted by the French under their puppet, the former emperor Bao Dai. Within less than two weeks, the French requested U.S. economic and military aid, threatening to abandon the nation to Ho Chi Minh if the aid were not forthcoming. Some $75 million was appropriated immediately. Shortly afterward, on June 25, 1950, Communist forces from North Korea invaded South Korea. *(See chapter 13: Korean War, 1950–1953.)* Truman responded by stepping up aid to the French in Vietnam, sending eight C-47 transports directly to Saigon.

Flown into Vietnam by American pilots, these eight aircraft were the first aviation aid the United States furnished in the region. On August 3, 1950, the first contingent of U.S. military advisers—the U.S. Military Assistance Advisory Group (MAAG)—arrived in Saigon. At this point the mission of the American advisers was primarily to supply aircraft and materiel to the French and, secondarily, to work with the French forces to improve their military capabilities. The least important aspect of the mission was to develop indigenous Vietnamese armed forces.

By 1952 the United States was financing one-third of the French military effort in Vietnam, yet it was becoming apparent that the French, although they were enjoying moderate success against the insurgents, were losing heart. At this juncture, on January 4, 1953, the first sizable contingent of USAF personnel (other than those attached to MAAG) was deployed to Vietnam. This group included a substantial complement of enlisted technicians, mainly to handle supply and the maintenance of aircraft. The contingent remained in Vietnam until August 14, 1953, when it was relieved by French forces.

Advisory Mission, 1950s

In April 1953, the Viet Minh staged a major offensive in western Tonkin, advancing into Laos and menacing Thailand. The French requested the loan of C-119 transports to airlift heavy equipment into Laos. President Dwight D. Eisenhower, wary of committing USAF crews to a combat mission, ordered military crews to fly the aircraft to Nha Trang, where nonmilitary contract pilots took them over for the flight to Cat Bi Airfield near Haiphong. General Henri Eugene Navarre, France's new commander in charge of operations in Vietnam, presented a plan to defeat the Viet Minh by luring them into open battle and reducing them to a low level of guerrilla warfare that could be contained by indigenous Vietnamese troops. Additional cargo planes were loaned to the French, and in the fall of 1953, Navarre began operations on the strategically located plain of Dien Bien Phu in northwestern Tonkin, near Laos. French paratroopers fortified an airstrip there beginning on November 20, and on December 5 the Far East Air Forces flew more C-119 transports to Cat Bi, from which civilian contract pilots or French personnel would fly them into the combat area. Ground personnel from the 483d Troop Carrier Wing, the 8081st Aerial Resupply Unit, and a provisional maintenance squadron of the Far East Air Logistics Force were stationed at Cat Bi to service the aircraft.

American military officials and the Eisenhower administration were becoming increasingly anxious, however, noting that the Viet Minh were menacing Hanoi and Haiphong—from which Navarre had withdrawn forces to bolster Dien Bien Phu—and that the Viet Minh were also massing around Dien Bien Phu. President Eisenhower authorized increased military aid—short of committing American personnel to combat—and B-26s and RB-26s were loaned to the French. However, French air units were seriously undermanned, and the fateful decision was made on January 31, 1954, to dispatch some three hundred USAF airmen to service aircraft at Tourane and at Do Son Airfield near Haiphong. This, the first substantial commitment of U.S. military personnel to the war in Vietnam, was highly classified. Addressing the American public, President Eisenhower described the forces he was committing as "some airplane mechanics . . . who would not get touched by combat."

Despite American logistical support, it became apparent daily that the French situation at Dien Bien Phu was hopeless as the defensive perimeter steadily contracted around the enclave. President Eisenhower contemplated direct U.S. military intervention, principally in the form of air support, but decided not to act in the absence of approval from the British and a demonstration of a French willingness to train and employ indigenous troops and ultimately to grant Vietnam its independence. On April 7, 1954, President Eisenhower presented to the American press a rationale for fighting communism in Vietnam. "You have a row of dominoes set up," he explained, "you knock over the first one, and what will happen to the last one is the certainty it will go over very quickly." This so-called "domino theory" would loom through the end of the decade and into the next two as a rationale for continued and ever-deepening involvement in the Vietnam War.

In 1954, however, the domino theory notwithstanding, most American military experts were not optimistic about the prospect of committing U.S. combat forces in the region, concluding that French colonialism had alienated the indigenous people and that, as a result, the South Vietnamese lacked the will to fight. Moreover, logistics in Southeast Asia were generally nightmarish, presenting support problems of overwhelming proportions. Finally, it was feared that commencing a war in Vietnam would mean beginning a war with Red China—under the worst conditions imaginable.

On May 7, 1954, Dien Bien Phu fell to the forces of Ho Chi Minh. Dien Bien Phu was followed by additional Viet Minh victories, and in July, at the conference table in Geneva, the French and the Viet Minh agreed to divide Vietnam along the seventeenth parallel and concluded an armistice.

In accordance with the terms of the armistice, the U.S. Air Force evacuated its personnel from Vietnam and assisted in the medical evacuation of wounded French troops. Ho Chi Minh felt confident that the reunification plebiscite mandated by the armistice and scheduled for July 1956 would result in a Communist victory. The United States, in the meantime, worked with French and South Vietnamese authorities to create a stable government and to build an effective South Vietnamese military. The United States also sponsored the creation of the Southeast Asia Treaty Organization (SEATO) as a shield against Communist aggression and proposed building up the MAAG staff in Saigon to accommodate its increased advisory role. However, the international commission charged with enforcing the Geneva armistice refused to approve the buildup. When 350 men were authorized as a "Temporary Equipment Recovery Mission," ostensibly assigned to inventory and remove surplus equipment, MAAG appropriated them as logistical advisers, and they became (in defiance of the international commission) the Combat Arms Training and Organization Division of MAAG. With the French now withdrawing, these men were the nucleus from which U.S. involvement in Vietnam would expand.

Expansion of the Advisory Role, 1960–1961

When South Vietnam refused to conduct the reunification plebiscite mandated by the Geneva agreement, American officials braced for an anticipated invasion from the North. It failed to materialize, and President Eisenhower decided to commit the United States to a long-term advisory role, intending to accomplish what the French had failed to achieve—the creation of an effective, indigenous South Vietnamese military. Nevertheless, North Vietnamese insurgency into the South increased during the closing years of the decade, and in September 1959 the Viet Cong (a Communist guerrilla group that succeeded and absorbed elements of the Viet Minh, Communist-oriented nationalists) commenced guerrilla warfare by ambushing two South Vietnamese army companies in the Plain of Reeds southwest of Saigon. In 1960 the United States expanded its MAAG advisory group to 685 men, including Special Forces teams assigned to train Vietnamese Rangers. Despite these efforts, relations between the South Vietnamese civil government and disaffected elements of the South Vietnamese military became strained to the point of an attempted coup against President Ngo Dinh Diem on November 11, 1960. Compounding this crisis was the situation of Vietnam's neighbor, Laos, the government of which was being challenged by military forces of the pro-Communist Pathet Lao.

When President John F. Kennedy took office in January 1961, the numbers of Viet Cong insurgents in South Vietnam had swelled to some fourteen thousand. They waged a combination guerrilla war and campaign of terror and assassination, successfully targeting thousands of civil officials, government workers, and police officers. On April 29, 1961, President Kennedy authorized an additional hundred advisers, the establishment of a combat development and test center in Vietnam, increased economic aid, and other measures. On May 11 Kennedy committed four hundred U.S. Special Forces troops to raise and train a force of irregulars in areas controlled by the Viet Cong, particularly along the border.

The first USAF unit to arrive in Vietnam on permanent-duty status were the 67 men assigned to a mobile combat reporting post, essentially a radar installation, which was secretly airlifted to Vietnam during September 26–October 3, 1961. After it was installed at Tan Son Nhut Airport on October 5, a total of 314 additional personnel were eventually assigned to the unit. These officers and airmen created the nucleus of what would become a massive and highly sophisticated tactical air control system.

Within a short time the air force also assigned photoreconnaissance personnel to the region—including flight crews, photo processing specialists, and support personnel—assigning them to a base in Don Muang, Thailand.

On October 11, 1961, President Kennedy ordered the first combat detachment to Vietnam. Officially called the 4400th Combat Crew Training Squadron, this elite force of 124 officers and 228 airmen equipped with sixteen C-47s, eight B-26s, and eight T-28s was nicknamed Jungle Jim and code-named Farm Gate. This was an "air commando" organization, and its personnel were chosen for their physical and emotional hardiness, their combat skill, and their sense of adventure. One hundred fifty-five officers and airmen were initially sent to Vietnam, but they immediately found themselves at the mercy of an ambiguous sense of mission. They were trained as a combat unit, yet were officially expected only to train Vietnamese forces. In fact, the group did train Vietnamese crews and also performed difficult and frustrating aerial reconnaissance missions. Flying actual combat strikes was another matter, and on December 26, 1961, word came from the highest level of command that the unit was to conduct combat missions only when the Vietnamese Air Force could not. Restrictions and mixed signals concerning their mission undermined the morale of Farm Gate. The situation would prove prophetic of the tenor of the entire war.

In October 1961 President Kennedy dispatched White House adviser Walt Rostow and General Maxwell Taylor to Vietnam to survey the situation there and report back to him whether the United States should continue its advisory role or commit to a direct combat mission. Taylor and Rostow recommended continuing USAF reconnaissance flights; setting up a tactical air-ground system, which included training functions; and giving Farm Gate a freer hand, but not committing substantial U.S. ground combat forces. Kennedy's approval of these recommendations on November 3, 1961, marked a shift from a purely advisory role for the United States to what was described at the time as a "limited partnership and working collaboration." The flow of aid and materiel increased dramatically, so that by June 30, 1962, there were 6,419 American soldiers and airmen in South Vietnam. Even as these forces were building, President Kennedy reported to the press and public that no U.S. combat forces were in Vietnam. However, he admitted, the "training units" there were authorized to return fire if fired upon. Yet the existence of Farm Gate had become known to the press—both in the United States and in Hanoi—and it was reported that Americans were routinely participating directly in air strikes and in operations supporting Vietnamese ground forces.

From Advisory to Combat Role, 1961–64

In the fall of 1961, the Kennedy administration authorized joint U.S.-South Vietnamese naval patrols south of the seventeenth parallel to interdict North Vietnamese maritime supply operations. Air force missions also were expanded. By March 1962, 6 officers and 6 enlisted intelligence specialists from the 6499th Support Group were aiding Vietnamese intelligence-gathering efforts. Beginning in January 1962, a total of 243 officers and airmen executed an airlift operation dubbed Mule Train, transporting large quantities of cargo and personnel into Vietnam. Army helicopters and helicopter crews of the 57th and 8th Transport Companies also participated in transporting troops of the Army of the Republic of South Vietnam (ARVN) into combat. The air force conducted Operation Ranch Hand in 1962, an early experiment in spraying chemical defoliants to reduce cover and concealment available to the Viet Cong.

On February 2, 1962, a C-123 aircraft training for this mission crashed, probably the result of ground fire or sabotage. The 3 crewmen killed were the first USAF fatalities in South Vietnam. On February 11, an SC-47 assigned to Farm Gate crashed on a propaganda-leaflet-dropping mission, killing 8 Americans (6 air force and 2 army personnel). The American press took note of this as evidence of the nation's growing combat role in the war. Indeed, by mid-August, there would be 11,412 U.S. personnel in Vietnam.

By 1962, the infusion of U.S. equipment, advisers, and military funding allowed a great expansion of the ARVN, which, at 300,000 men, now surpassed in numbers the 280,000 troops of the North Vietnam Army (NVA). Many ARVN troops had to be committed to defensive roles, protecting the industrial and transportation infrastructure of the South, which was continually targeted by North Vietnamese insurgents; nevertheless, U.S. helicopters, both army and marine, were being used increasingly to transport small ARVN units into offensive operations against the insurgents. By the beginning of 1963, ARVN numbers would approach 400,000.

By the end of 1962 and the beginning of 1963, American assistance and the buildup of ARVN forces were having an impact on the insurgents, especially on Viet Cong guerrilla units, which were seen as a bigger threat than the regular NVA. The price of this progress? At the start of 1961, some 900 U.S. military personnel were stationed in Vietnam. By the end of 1962 there were more than 11,000, a number that would rise by midyear to 16,652. As of the end of 1962 a total of 27 of these servicemen had been killed and 65 wounded. Five were prisoners of the Viet Cong. Throughout Viet Nam, the war was claiming about 2,000 lives each week.

Despite the growing U.S. presence and the progress combined U.S.-ARVN operations had made, Viet Cong attacks increased during 1963 and in the Mekong Delta, the Viet Cong escalated the war from guerrilla engagements to full-scale field operations. By the end of the year the Viet Cong were clearly gaining ground against the forces of South Vietnam.

Whereas U.S.-ARVN progress against the Viet Cong served only to stimulate and increase aggression, North Vietnamese progress against ARVN forces very quickly undermined popular support for the Diem government. The Kennedy administration's intense desire to prevent Vietnam from becoming another domino to fall to communism had, at least since 1961, caused U.S. officials to turn a blind eye to the essential unpopularity and corruption of the Diem regime. Diem's cronies had been put into high civil and military positions, and while a small number of urban South Vietnamese did prosper under Diem, the rural majority fared poorly. Moreover, the Catholic Diem became tyrannical in his support of the nation's Catholic minority and openly abused the Buddhist majority. The world was soon stunned by a series of extreme protest demonstrations: Buddhist monks doused themselves in gasoline and set themselves ablaze in the streets of Saigon. These horrific images were captured by television news crews and broadcast widely. From this point, friction between the Diem government and the United States intensified. On September 2, 1963, President Kennedy declared in a television address to the American public that the Diem government was out of touch with the Vietnamese people and that the war could be won only if it had popular support. Secretly, President Kennedy acquiesced in a CIA-backed military coup that overthrew Diem on November 1, 1963, and assassinated him the following day. A military junta set up a provisional government, which the United States recognized on November 8. Taking advantage of the confusing situation, the Viet Cong stepped up their attacks, and American forces heightened their response to them.

Gulf of Tonkin Incident, 1964

In the midst of the deteriorating situation in Vietnam, on November 22, 1963, President John F. Kennedy was assassinated, and Vice President Lyndon Johnson took office. U.S. Air Force general Curtis LeMay and the Joint Chiefs of Staff advised the new president to expand the war with quick, decisive action against North Vietnam, including the bombing of Hanoi. Secretary of Defense Robert McNamara favored a more conservative approach, confining operations principally to South Vietnam, but relaxing the rules for air engagement within South Vietnam and thereby expanding the role of air force personnel working with Vietnamese crews. A short time later, however, when Hanoi responded negatively to American peace feelers, Secretary McNamara called for the formulation of an air strike plan against North Vietnam. Devised in the summer of 1964, the plan was held in abeyance. But the situation in Vietnam took a dramatic turn on August 7, 1964, when the U.S. Senate passed the Gulf of Tonkin Resolution after the U.S. destroyer *Maddox*, conducting electronic espionage in international waters in the Gulf of Tonkin, was fired upon on two separate occasions (the second time reportedly in company with the destroyer *C. Turner Joy*) by North Vietnamese torpedo boats. The Senate resolution gave the president great latitude in expanding the war as he might see fit. (During June 1971, the *New York Times* published a series of articles on a secret government study popularly called *The Pentagon Papers*. The forty-seven-volume document, produced in 1967–1969 by Defense Department analysts, meticulously revealed how the federal government had systematically deceived the American people with regard to its policies and practices in Southeast Asia. Among many other things, the study showed how the CIA had conspired to overthrow and assassinate South Vietnam president Diem and revealed that the Tonkin Gulf Resolution was actually drafted months in advance of the attack on the destroyer *Maddox* and the attack on the *C. Turner Joy*, the events that supposedly prompted the resolution.)

During the second half of 1964, Viet Cong attacks on hamlets and outposts doubled. On November 1, 1964, Viet Cong penetrated the perimeter of the Bien Hoa air base, killing four air force personnel and wounding seventy-two in addition to destroying or damaging a number of aircraft and buildings. Although the Joint Chiefs recommended severe reprisals against North Vietnam, President Johnson, on the eve of election, bided his time. Following his victory, however, Johnson authorized a

IN THEIR OWN
Words

From the Senate Debate of the Tonkin Gulf Resolution, August 6–7, 1964

*M*R. NELSON [Gaylord Nelson, Dem., Wis.]: . . . Am I to understand that it is the sense of Congress that we are saying to the executive branch: "If it becomes necessary to prevent further aggression, we agree now, in advance, that you may land as many divisions as deemed necessary, and engage in a direct military assault on North Vietnam if it becomes the judgment of the Executive, the Commander in Chief, that this is the only way to prevent further aggression"?

MR. FULBRIGHT [J. William Fulbright, Dem., Ark]: As I stated, section I is intended to deal primarily with aggression against our forces. . . . I do not know what the limits are. I do not think this resolution can be determinative of that fact. I think it would indicate that he [the president] would take reasonable means first to prevent any further aggression, or repel further aggression against our own forces. . . .

MR. GRUENING [Ernest Gruening, Dem., Alaska]: . . . Regrettably, I find myself in disagreement with the President's Southeast Asian policy. . . . The serious events of the past few days, the attack by North Vietnamese vessels on American warships and our reprisal, strikes me as the inevitable and foreseeable concomitant and consequence of U.S. unilateral military aggressive policy in Southeast Asia. . . . We now are about to authorize the President if he sees fit to move our Armed Forces . . . not only into South Vietnam, but also into North Vietnam, Laos, Cambodia, Thailand, and of course the authorization includes all the rest of the SEATO nations. That means sending our American boys into combat in a war in which we have no business, which is not our war, into which we have been misguidedly drawn, which is steadily being escalated. This resolution is a further authorization for escalation unlimited. I am opposed to sacrificing a single American boy in this venture. We have lost far too many already. . . .

MR. MORSE [Wayne Morse, Dem., Ore.]: . . . I believe that history will record that we have made a great mistake in subverting and circumventing the Constitution of the United States. . . . I believe this resolution to be a historic mistake. I believe that within the next century, future generations will look with dismay and great disappointment upon a Congress which is now about to make such a historic mistake. . . .

program of restricted air strikes on infiltration targets in Laos (Operation Barrel Roll). When a three-hundred-pound charge exploded in the Brink Hotel, bachelor officers' quarters for U.S. advisers, killing two Americans and injuring sixty-four others in addition to forty-three Vietnamese, the Joint Chiefs again urged immediate reprisals. President Johnson again demurred. A few days later, on December 27, Viet Cong raided the hamlet of Binh Gia, then, on December 31, surrounded the U.S. Fourth Marine Battalion, which had marched to Binh Gia's relief, inflicting heavy casualties on the unit. This, combined with the Brink Hotel explosion, prompted Maxwell Taylor (now U.S. ambassador to South Vietnam, having retired from the army), who had earlier argued for restraint, to recommend immediate air action against North Vietnam.

The government that had replaced the Diem regime was unstable and, indeed, over a short period of time, would be followed by no fewer than eleven more governments, none of which proved sufficiently popular to stand alone without American support. Faced with the latest weakening Saigon government, President Johnson was undecided whether to commit U.S. forces directly against North Vietnam or to disengage at last from what might well be a losing proposition—thereby allowing the Vietnam "domino" to fall.

At the start of February 1965, Johnson sent adviser McGeorge Bundy on a fact-finding mission to Saigon. But suddenly, on February 7, all indecision came to an end when Viet Cong mortar squads and demolition teams attacked U.S. advisory forces and Camp Holloway, headquarters of the U.S. Army Fifty-second Aviation Battalion, near Pleiku, killing 9 Americans and wounding 108. The action preempted the potential results of any fact-finding mission, and Bundy, with General William Westmoreland and Ambassador Taylor, sent President Johnson a joint recommendation to strike North Vietnam. Accordingly, Operation Flaming Dart, an air strike, was launched against a major NVA barracks near Dong Hoi. An NVA counterstrike came on February 10 against a barracks at Qui Nhon, killing 23 Air Force airmen and 7 Vietnamese troops. This was followed by a U.S. reprisal the next day. These exchanges marked the unambiguous end of the U.S. advisory phase in the Vietnam War and the beginning of a long offensive escalation.

Escalation Begins, 1965

The air strikes against North Vietnam soon became known by the code name Rolling Thunder and began on March 2, 1965, continuing with a "slowly ascending" tempo until May 11, when they were suspended while the United States sought peace talks with the North Vietnamese, and resuming on May 18. Rolling Thunder operations would continue through 1968.

Corporal Atchley, squad leader, Company B, First Battalion, Ninth Marines, guards a Viet Cong prisoner on a march to a collection point, October 10, 1965. *Collection: National Archives and Records Administration*

In the meantime, President Johnson and U.S. military planners struggled to establish objectives for the war. Gone was the notion of reunifying Vietnam; instead, American war aims were restricted to keeping South Vietnam independent and to proving to the Viet Cong and the NVA that they could not win in South Vietnam. To achieve these objectives, Johnson and others in Washington wanted to wage primarily an air war to reduce the flow of North Vietnamese infiltration, to inflict heavy casualties on the North Vietnamese on an ongoing basis, and to raise the morale of the South Vietnamese. William Westmoreland, the general in charge of U.S. forces in Vietnam, argued with the Washington planners, explaining that bombing alone would have little effect on North Vietnamese intentions. Westmoreland wanted to introduce a blocking force along the major artery by which the North Vietnamese infiltrated the South. Washington opposed this; however, it did approve of the development and use of "air cavalry." The First Cavalry Division (Airmobile) was equipped with more than 400 helicopters, which were used in the campaign for the Central Highlands during late 1965 and early 1966.

In the meantime, U.S. Military Advisory Command, Vietnam (USMACV) authorized naval gunfire support on May 14, 1965, and the first major U.S. ground operation was launched on June 28. The 173rd Airborne Brigade airlifted two ARVN battalions and two battalions of the 503rd Infantry Brigade into battle in Bien Hoa Province, just twenty miles northeast of Saigon. The operation was a mixed success, but the first significant U.S. victory came during August 18–21, 1965, with Operation Starlight. More than five thousand marines attacked the Viet Cong First Regiment south of Chu Lai in Quang Ngai Province and succeeded in trapping the VC and destroying a major VC base at Van Tuong, south of Chu Lai.

As for the ongoing Central Highlands campaign, it culminated in the Battle of the Ia Drang Valley during October 23–November 20, 1965. The First Cavalry Division (Airmobile) defeated VC and NVA forces that had massed in western Pleiku Province. Both sides suffered heavy casualties, but the U.S. forces succeeded in foiling a North Vietnamese attempt to seize this region and thereby cut South Vietnam in half.

The year 1965 ended with a major U.S. air strike against a North Vietnamese industrial target, the power plant at Uongbi, fourteen miles north of Haiphong.

Escalation Continues, 1966–1967

The year 1966 began with Operation Marauder, the first foray of an American unit, the 173rd Airborne Brigade, into the Mekong Delta. During January 1–8, the brigade engaged and defeated a VC battalion and destroyed the headquarters of another battalion in the Plain of Reeds. This was followed during January 19–February 21 by Operation Van Buren, in which the 1st Brigade of the 101st Airborne Division, the 2nd Republic of Korea Marine Brigade, and the 4th ARVN Regiment secured Phu Yen Province

General William C. Westmoreland, commanding general of U.S. forces in South Vietnam, thanks perennial entertainer Bob Hope at a USO Christmas show in Vietnam, December 24, 1965. *Collection: National Archives and Records Administration*

in the central coastal region. This operation set the pattern for the "search and destroy" actions that would become typical of the war. Many of these missions were, in fact, quite successful in securing limited areas—albeit usually securing them for only a short time. North Vietnamese losses would be staggering in the course of the war, far greater than the losses incurred by U.S. forces. But the North Vietnamese were willing to absorb the losses in what became an extremely protracted war of attrition, and while the VC would yield territory to search-and-destroy missions, the Communists usually returned to that territory later. American military planners would respectfully learn that it was one thing to take territory but quite another to occupy it—and there would never be sufficient personnel to occupy and hold the territories cleared of VC and NVA.

The U.S. Army often found itself poorly equipped for fighting conditions in Vietnam, as these two M-41 tanks, mired in the mud of a monsoon, attest. *Collection: National Archives and Records Administration*

Beginning on January 24 and extending to March 6, Operation Masher–White Wing combined twenty thousand U.S., ARVN, and South Korean forces in an extensive sweep of Binh Dinh Province, on the central coast. Masher–White Wing engaged two VC and two NVA regiments, then joined forces with U.S. Marines who were moving into the northern provinces. In these provinces the marines were almost continually engaged with the enemy from March through October.

At this juncture, in April 1966, the USAF made its first B-52 deployments from bases in Guam. The giant bombers were used to attack North Vietnamese infiltration routes through Mugia Pass, near the border of North Vietnam and Laos. The use of strategic bombers in what was essentially a tactical war is typical of the problems air force planners and personnel had to solve. Officers and airmen were compelled to cope not only with the physical hardships of a tropical, poorly developed country and the physical dangers of a resolutely determined enemy, but also with the technical challenges of keeping aging aircraft in service and maintaining the latest jet equipment (as it became available) under adverse conditions.

Moreover, the air force, which took on so big a part of the Vietnam War, had been prepared to execute a global strategic mission, thermonuclear deterrence, directed principally against the Soviet Union. Equipment had been designed and personnel trained with this strategic mission in view. Now many personnel had to adapt to the demands of conventional warfare fought on an insurgency level. Daunting as this mission was, it was compounded by difficulties in training Vietnamese support personnel, a task that often fell to enlisted men ill prepared to deal with the unstable political climate of Vietnam and with cultural differences between the Vietnamese and themselves.

The Central Highlands became a hot spot again during the spring and summer of 1966 as the 25th Infantry Division, 1st Cavalry Division (Airmobile), and ARVN units moved into Pleiku Province to interdict infiltration from the North as well as through Cambodia. Simultaneously, the 101st Airborne fought vigorously in Kontum Province, and in June and July, the 1st Division, in concert with the 5th ARVN Division, was heavily engaged in Binh Long Province, seventy miles north of Saigon.

These operations from the first half of 1966 are typical of the "main force" war that was being fought in the South. The principal U.S.-ARVN strategy was to attempt to overwhelm the insurgents wherever they surfaced, and the numbers of operations multiplied to no specific strategic end other than to meet force with overwhelming force wherever and whenever possible. Among the largest of these "main force" operations was Operation Attleboro, at the end of 1966, which was conducted just north of Saigon. About 100 ARVN and U.S. troops died in this operation, while the Communists lost 1,100 or more men. Shortly after this, the U.S. Fourth Division conducted Operations Sam Houston and Francis Marion in northern South Vietnam, killing 1,900 NVA and VC in the High Plateau provinces of Pleiku and Darlac. U.S. losses included 335 dead. Clearly, the Communists were suffering much heavier losses than the ARVN and the United States, but this did not discourage them. They were seemingly willing to continue their enormous sacrifices indefinitely.

By the end of 1966, air force "Prime Beef" (BEEF: Base Engineering Emergency Force) construction teams were working miracles at Tan Son Nhut, Bien Hoa, Da Nang, Nha Trang, Pleiku, and Binh Thuy, building aircraft revetments, barracks, Quonset huts, aprons, guard towers, and adequate plumbing and electrical facilities. "Red Horse" (Rapid Engineering and Heavy Operational Repair Squadron, Engineering) engineering squadrons provided more long-range services. The idea was to decentral-ize as many operations as possible, locating many logistical organizations at the field level to make even the farthest-flung bases self-sufficient. Air force personnel found themselves engaged in a series of what amounted to massive civil engineering projects that transformed the landscape of South Vietnam into a collection of extensive bases and airfields.

On the ground, other operations during 1967 included Operation Cedar Falls, intended to clear the "Iron Triangle." The 1st and 25th Infantry Divisions, the 11th Armored Cavalry Regiment, and the 173rd Airborne Brigade participated in an operation that killed 720 VC and destroyed large quantities of rice, sufficient to supply 10,000 men for a year. U.S. deaths were fewer than 100 men. The 9th Infantry Division joined the war in 1967, at first operating east and south of Saigon, but soon wading through the swampy Mekong Delta to clear that region.

While the United States shouldered the burden of the "main force" war in 1966–1967, ARVN developed a "pacification program" intended to win the "hearts and minds" of the South Vietnamese peasantry and turn them against the Communist insurgents. Pacification included military components but also education, land reform, communications,

Medic, First Batallion, Sixteenth Infantry, First Infantry Division, watches anxiously for a medevac helicopter to evacuate his wounded comrade. The action took place during Operation Billings, June 1967. *Collection: National Archives and Records Administration*

agriculture, and other civil programs. The idea was to root out the VC infrastructure, village by village, and develop a self-defense capability within each village. By mid-1967 the pacification program came under direct U.S. supervision, and the program did produce measurable results, especially evident in increased desertion rates among South Vietnamese Communist units. A more controversial aspect of the pacification effort was the Phoenix program, which used ARVN "intelligence-action teams" to capture and/or kill South Vietnamese civilians who formed part of the VC infrastructure by supplying, sheltering, and feeding Viet Cong. Arguably, the Phoenix program violated the various international conventions of "civilized" warfare.

Controversy also surrounded the intensified U.S. bombing of North Vietnamese targets during 1966–1967. Air interdiction over the Laos panhandle targeted the Ho Chi Minh Trail, the principal supply and infiltration route into South Vietnam. In 1966, air crews estimated that they were destroying perhaps as much as 18 percent of the trucks that traveled the trail. The bombing program was intensified, but U.S. aircraft came under heavy attack from antiaircraft guns and SAMs (surface-to-air missiles). It was not just the cost of the bombing missions that made them controversial, it was also their effect on attempts to begin peace negotiations. Some believed that the bombing was essential in a war of attrition and would eventually drive the Communists to the negotiating table, while others argued that the bombing simply hardened the will of the Hanoi government. Eight times in 1967, President Johnson called a temporary halt to the bombing in an effort to facilitate talks, but repeatedly the talks failed to develop.

The American Home Front

The year 1967 was a turning point in the American popular attitude toward the war. According to polls, in 1965, President Lyndon Johnson enjoyed an 80 percent approval rating, which fell to 40 percent by the end of 1967. The reason for the precipitous decline was almost exclusively the Vietnam War. In response, Johnson waged a "media offensive," bringing General Westmoreland home to defend U.S. military achievements in the war. The numbers were indeed impressive. It was estimated that the NVA could send about 7,000 troops down the Ho Chi Minh Trail each month and that the Viet Cong could recruit, monthly, perhaps 3,500 troops within South Vietnam. In 1966, U.S. and ARVN forces claimed 8,400

Communist losses per month, whereas by the summer of 1967, they claimed 12,700—meaning that losses outpaced reinforcement. Pacification programs also seemed to be producing results. It was estimated that in 1966 a total of 800,000 to 1 million South Vietnamese villagers had been taken from Communist control. Moreover, while the insurgents had succeeded in closing 70 percent of South Vietnam's roadways and waterways in 1965, by the beginning of 1967, 60 percent were open.

And yet no end to the war was in sight. The Communists were a tenacious enemy. They knew that without U.S. aid the ARVN would be defeated, and the NVA and the VC were willing to absorb staggering losses to wear down the U.S. resolve to fight and remain in Vietnam. Despite the Johnson-Westmoreland media offensive, by the end of 1967 it was clear to many Americans that the Vietnam War was gruesomely stalemated. President Johnson continued to appear before the nation, assuring television viewers that there was "light at the end of the tunnel," but the increasing numbers of U.S. casualties created a "credibility gap" between what the administration claimed and what the public believed.

By 1967, the antiwar protest movement was in full swing. The image is from the March on the Pentagon, on October 21. *Collection: National Archives and Records Administration*

1968: The Tet Offensive

In this period of growing U.S. doubt, Hanoi staged a series of massive offensives, first along the border, with nationwide attacks beginning on January 30, 1968, Tet, a Vietnamese lunar holiday. North Vietnamese forces attacked major cities and military bases from Quang Tri and Khe Sanh near the Demilitarized Zone (DMZ), in the northern region of South Vietnam, to Quang Long, near the country's southern tip. Even the newly constructed U.S. embassy in Saigon was targeted, and airmen were called on to defend the major U.S. air base at Tan Son Nhut. Up north, near the DMZ, the marine outpost at Khe Sanh was cut off by Viet Cong

beginning on the first day of Tet, January 30, and held under heavy siege

until mid-March. During this period, in defense of Khe Sanh, B-52s and

fighter bombers flew more than 24,400 sorties, dropping 100,000 tons of

ordnance. Airlift operations to keep the isolated marines supplied were

carried out under the most hazardous conditions. Supplies were para-

chuted or simply dropped from C-123 Provider and C-130 Hercules air-

craft. Enemy antiaircraft fire was intense, and weather conditions were for

the most part poor, so that, for the first time in airlift history, crews some-

times dropped supplies in near zero-visibility conditions, relying wholly

on instruments.

The Tet Offensive was costly to U.S. and ARVN forces, but far costlier

to the NVA and the VC. Of an estimated 84,000 attackers, as many as

45,000 were killed. By any military standard, the U.S.-ARVN
defense against Tet was a triumph. Intended, certainly, to
break the fighting spirit of an
already badly demoralized South
Vietnam, Tet had the opposite
effect. In the immediate aftermath of the offensive, some
15,000 ARVN deserters voluntarily *returned* to the army,
and 240,000 South Vietnamese
young men volunteered for military service. In the United
States, however, the three-week
offensive was a devastating psychological victory for the Communists and convinced many
Americans, including politicians and policy makers, that
the war was unwinnable. With
American casualties having

A Viet Cong soldier hides in a bunker. Note the
tunnel passage into the bunker. The photograph
dates from 1968, the height of U.S. involvement
in the war. *Collection: National Archives and
Records Administration*

risen from 780 per month during 1967 to 2,000 a month in February

1968, it was hard to believe official military pronouncements that Tet was

by no means a defeat. Air force performance was even worse. The kill ratio—North Vietnamese aircraft shot down versus U.S. aircraft lost—was now even, at one to one. It was the worst performance in the history of American aerial combat.

Tet hardened public opposition to the war and sharply divided legislators, with "hawks" (war supporters) on one side, and "doves" (peace advocates) on the other. When a somewhat distorted news story broke in March, announcing that General Westmoreland was asking for 200,000 more men to be committed to the Vietnam War, a wave of outrage swept the American public. Antiwar demonstrations became increasingly frequent, bigger, and more boisterous. By the middle of March, public opinion polls revealed that 70 percent of the American people favored a phased withdrawal of U.S. forces from Vietnam, and at the end of the month, President Johnson initiated a process designed to take the United States out of the war. Although the president did not give Westmoreland anything approaching the number of troops he requested, the number of U.S. troops in Vietnam would reach a high of 536,000 by the end of 1968.

Johnson Declines to Run for Re-election

On March 31, 1968, Lyndon B. Johnson made two surprise television announcements. He declared that he would restrict bombing above the twentieth parallel, thereby opening the door to a negotiated settlement of the war, and he announced that he would not seek another term as president. He acknowledged that his advocacy of the war was not only tearing the nation apart but also would probably be an obstacle to peace negotiations.

Spurred in part by Johnson's bombing restrictions, cease-fire negotiations began in May, only to stall over Hanoi's demands for a complete bombing halt and the presence of the Viet Cong's political parent organization, the NLF (National Liberation Front), at the peace table. Johnson resisted, but in November agreed to these terms. Despite the boost this gave the sagging presidential campaign of Democrat Hubert Humphrey, Republican Richard M. Nixon emerged victorious.

Nixon's Wider War

To ensure victory in the 1968 presidential election, Richard Nixon made repeated—though vague—promises to end the war. Yet once he was elected, he did not hesitate to *expand* the war into neighboring Laos and Cambodia. He had evolved a grand strategy with his foreign policy

Words

...*Throughout this entire, long period, I have been sustained by a single principle: that what we are doing now, in Vietnam, is vital not only to the security of Southeast Asia, but it is vital to the security of every American. . . . [T]he heart of our involvement in South Vietnam—under three different presidents, three separate administrations—has always been America's own security.*

. . . Tonight I have offered the first in what I hope will be a series of mutual moves toward peace. I pray that it will not be rejected by the leaders of North Vietnam. . . .

The ultimate strength of our country and our cause will lie not in powerful weapons or infinite resources or boundless wealth, but will lie in the unity of our people. . . .

There is division in the American house now. There is divisiveness among us all tonight. And holding the trust that is mine, as President of all the people, I cannot disregard the peril to the progress of the American people and the hope and the prospect of peace for all peoples.

So I would ask all Americans, whatever their personal interests or concern, to guard against divisiveness and all its ugly consequences.

Fifty-two months and ten days ago, in a moment of tragedy and trauma, the duties of this office fell upon me. I asked then for your help and God's, that we might continue America on its course, binding up our wounds, healing our history, moving forward in new unity, to clear the American agenda and to keep the American commitment for all of our people.

United we have kept that commitment. United we have enlarged that commitment. Through all time to come, I think America will be a stronger nation, a more just society, and a land of greater opportunity and fulfillment because of what we have all done together in these years of unparalleled achievement.

Our reward will come in the life of freedom, peace, and hope that our children will enjoy through ages ahead. What we won when all of our people united just must not now be lost in suspicion, distrust, selfishness, and politics among any of our people.

Believing this as I do, I have concluded that I should not permit the presidency to become involved in the partisan divisions that are developing in this political year. With America's sons in the fields far away, with America's future under challenge right here at home, with our hopes and the world's hopes for peace in the balance every day, I do not believe that I should devote an hour or a day of my time to any personal partisan causes or to any duties other than the awesome duties of this office— the presidency of your country.

Accordingly, I shall not seek, and I will not accept, the nomination of my party for another term as your president. But let men everywhere know, however, that a strong, a confident, and a vigilant America stands ready tonight to seek an honorable peace—and stands ready tonight to defend an honored cause whatever the price, whatever the burden, whatever the sacrifice that duty may require.

Thank you for listening.

Good night and God bless all of you.

—PRESIDENT LYNDON JOHNSON'S TELEVISED ADDRESS TO THE NATION, MARCH 31, 1968 adviser, Henry Kissinger, that called for improving relations with the Soviets (through trade and an arms-limitation agreement) to disengage Moscow from Hanoi, and for normalizing relations with China. Once the USSR and China had cut the North Vietnamese loose, Nixon and Kissinger reasoned, the United States could negotiate a "peace with honor" in Vietnam. As for prosecuting the war itself, Nixon and Kissinger formulated a "two track" approach. One track consisted of ongoing U.S. military operations and military assistance, while the other track, pursued simultaneously, consisted of diplomatic initiatives emphasizing the mutual benefits of a negotiated resolution. It was a version of the classic stick-and-carrot tactic.

The problem, however, is that the two-track approach unfolded against the background of "Vietnamization" of the war, a concerted effort to train and equip ARVN forces to shoulder an ever-increasing share of combat as U.S. forces pulled out in stages. The North Vietnamese interpreted Vietnamization as evidence of the U.S. resolve to leave Vietnam. Accordingly, Communist negotiators took an aggressive and uncompromising stance in the peace talks, which ensured that the talks would be protracted and frustrating.

Vietnamization

Since the Eisenhower years, American presidents had wanted the Vietnam War to be fought and resolved by Vietnamese. Through 1963 and much of 1964, American forces operated under restrictive rules of engagement in a forlorn effort to maintain the definition of the U.S. role as "advisory" only. After the Gulf of Tonkin incident and Senate resolution late in the summer of

IN THEIR OWN *Words*

... We have adopted a plan which we have worked out in cooperation with the South Vietnamese for the complete withdrawal of all U.S. combat ground forces, and their replacement by South Vietnamese forces on an orderly scheduled timetable. ...

There are powerful personal reasons I want to end this war. This week I will have to sign eighty-three letters to mothers, fathers, wives, and loved ones of men who have given their lives for America in Vietnam. It is very little satisfaction to me that this is only one-third as many letters as I signed the first week in office. There is nothing I want more than to see the day come when I do not have to write any of those letters.

... Let us be united for peace. Let us also be united against defeat. Because let us understand: North Vietnam cannot defeat or humiliate the United States. Only Americans can do that. ...

—RICHARD M. NIXON, SPEECH ON VIETNAMIZATION,
NOVEMBER 3, 1969

1964, the advisory role, in both appearance and fact, was rapidly transformed into primary responsibility for combat operations. In January 1969, shortly after taking office, President Nixon announced as one of the primary goals of his administration an end to U.S. combat in Southeast Asia. Accordingly, Secretary of Defense Melvin R. Laird charged the Joint Chiefs of Staff with making Vietnamization of the war a top priority. In June, after meeting with South Vietnamese officials, President Nixon announced plans to withdraw U.S. forces.

All of the services, but especially the U.S. Army and U.S. Air Force, instituted rush training programs for Vietnamese ground and air forces. By the end of 1972, for example, USAF officers and airmen had trained Vietnamese personnel sufficiently to enable them to take over maintenance training for the C-130, T-28B, and other aircraft systems. At this point, with U.S. material and financial assistance, the Vietnamese Air Force had grown to forty-two thousand officers and enlisted men (with an additional ten thousand in training) equipped with two thousand aircraft of 22 types. It was now the fourth-largest air force in the world, behind Communist China, the United States, and the Soviet Union.

Members of the 501st Airborne Infantry attend to wounds after action east of Tam Ky, August 12, 1969. *Collection: National Archives and Records Administration*

Decline

In May 1969, the withdrawal of U.S. Army ground units from Vietnam began in earnest, while air support units lingered. In the meantime, the Paris peace talks, initiated in the fall of 1968 under President Johnson, circled uselessly, and the Nixon-Kissinger strategy aimed at cutting North Vietnam loose from the Soviets also collapsed when the USSR announced its recognition of the Provisional Revolutionary Government (PRG) formed by North Vietnam's National Liberation Front (NLF) in June 1969. Despite these setbacks, the Nixon administration sought to accelerate the process of Vietnamization. ARVN performance, however, proved disappointing, and now the performance of U.S. troops also deteriorated. American soldiers had little faith in Vietnamization, and as their own ranks were thinned by phased withdrawal, they came to believe that the war was a lost cause. No soldier is eager to die for a lost cause. Amid deteriorating morale, drug and alcohol abuse became epidemic among the U.S. ranks, as did a general attitude of defeatism. Whereas units in the mid-1960s engaged in bold "search and destroy" missions, troops now talked of patrols as "search and avoid" missions. For the typical soldier, the objective was no longer victory, but simply to get through the war alive.

Despite discouraging results, Vietnamization did reduce U.S. casualties, and President Nixon pressed ahead with troop withdrawals. Yet even as he pulled ground troops out of Vietnam, peace talks faltered, and Nixon sent ground forces to attack Communist supply and staging areas in Cambodia. This incursion into a neighboring country triggered angry protests in the United States, including a demonstration at Kent State University in Ohio on May 4, 1970, that resulted in the killing of four unarmed students and the wounding of nine more when inexperienced National Guardsmen, on riot-control duty, fired on them. Subsequently, a hundred thousand antiwar demonstrators marched on Washington, and Congress registered its own protest by rescinding the Gulf of Tonkin Resolution.

Soldiers carry a wounded buddy through a South Vietnamese swamp in this image from 1969. *Collection: National Archives and Records Administration*

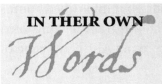
Richard Nixon's Speech on the Invasion of Cambodia, April 30, 1970

... Ten days ago, in my report to the nation on Vietnam, I announced a decision to withdraw an additional 150,000 Americans from Vietnam over the next year. I said then that I was making that decision despite our concern over increased enemy activity in Laos, Cambodia, and in South Vietnam.

At that time, I warned that if I concluded that increased enemy activity in any of these areas endangered lives of Americans remaining in Vietnam, I would not hesitate to take strong and effective measures.

Despite that warning, North Vietnam has increased its military aggression in all these areas, and particularly in Cambodia. . . .

For the past five years, as indicated on this map that you see here, North Vietnam has occupied military sanctuaries all along the Cambodian frontier with South Vietnam. Some of these extend up to twenty miles into Cambodia. . . . In cooperation with the armed forces of South Vietnam, attacks are being launched this week to clean out major enemy sanctuaries on the Cambodian-Vietnam border. A major responsibility for the ground operations is being assumed by South Vietnamese forces. . . .

Tonight, American and South Vietnamese units will attack the headquarters for the entire Communist military operation in South Vietnam. . . .

We take this action not for the purpose of expanding the war into Cambodia but for the purpose of ending the war in Vietnam and winning the just peace we all desire. . . .

The action that I have announced tonight puts the leaders of North Vietnam on notice that we will be patient in working for peace; we will be conciliatory at the conference table, but we will not be humiliated. We will not be defeated. . . .

My fellow Americans, we live in an age of anarchy, both abroad and at home. We see mindless attacks on all the great institutions which have been created by free civilizations in the last five hundred years. Even here in the United States, great universities are being systematically destroyed. . . .

If, when the chips are down, the world's most powerful nation, the United States of America, acts like a pitiful, helpless giant, the forces of totalitarianism and anarchy will threaten free nations and free institutions throughout the world.

It is not our power but our will and character that is being tested tonight. . . .

Nixon withdrew all ground forces from Cambodia, but intensified bombing raids of that country. When Communist infiltration continued unabated, the United States supplied air support for an ARVN invasion of Laos in February 1971.

Intensification of the Air War

By the end of 1971, withdrawals had reduced U.S. troop strength to 175,000 in Vietnam, somewhat calming protests at home but continuing to erode front-line morale. In March 1972, taking advantage of the reduced American ground presence, Communist forces of the National Liberation Front crossed the DMZ and seized a South Vietnamese province. This "Easter Offensive" initially routed ARVN troops until President Nixon retaliated by redoubling air attacks, mining Haiphong Harbor, and establishing a naval blockade of the North. Following the offensive and the U.S. response to it, Henry Kissinger and North Vietnamese representative Le Duc Tho finally formulated an agreement governing the withdrawal of U.S. troops, the return of POWs, and the creation of a foundation for a political settlement through establishment of a special council of reconciliation. South Vietnamese president Nguyen Van Thieu, however, rejected the peace terms because they permitted Viet Cong forces to remain in place in the South.

The fact that Nixon's negotiator, Kissinger, had been able to announce that "peace is at hand" assured the president reelection in 1972, but once in office, Nixon threw his support behind Thieu, repudiating the peace terms Kissinger had negotiated. To bring the North Vietnamese back to the negotiating table, the president then ordered eleven days of intensive "Christmas bombing" of North Vietnamese cities. This operation was carried out by B-52s out of Anderson AFB on Guam and was dubbed "Linebacker II"—though many who served on the mission referred to it as the "Eleven-Day War."

Linebacker II, conducted from December 18 to December 29, followed Linebacker I, a campaign of B-52 interdiction bombing in North Vietnam during the spring, summer, and fall of 1972. Linebacker I, in turn, had followed the sustained program of air interdiction over North Vietnam conducted from 1965 to 1968 and known as Rolling Thunder. The Linebacker II operation was far more concentrated and intensive than the earlier sustained operations. Approximately 155 giant B-52s were continuously operational for 11 days, during which the bombers flew 729 sorties against 34 targets in North Vietnam above the 20th parallel. Fifteen thousand tons of ordnance destroyed or damaged some 1,600 military structures, 500 rail targets—including 372 pieces of rolling stock—3 million gallons of fuel (perhaps one-quarter of North Vietnam's reserves), and 10 airfields, and knocked out 80 percent of electrical power production capacity.

Paris Peace Accords

Despite its high cost, Linebacker II did succeed in breaking the deadlock of mid-December. The North Vietnamese resumed negotiations on January 8, 1973, and the Paris Peace Accords were signed on January 27. The agreement reached after the bombing was not materially different from what had been concluded in October 1972, except that this time President Thieu was simply and completely ignored.

The Peace Accords did not bring an end to the fighting, and the punishment air crews delivered did not bring victory. Yet the United States was committed to withdrawing from Vietnam. On January 27, Secretary of Defense Laird announced an end to the military draft, and on March 29, the last U.S. troops departed from Vietnam, leaving behind some eighty-five hundred U.S. civilian "technicians." On June 13 a new cease-fire agreement among the United States, South Vietnam, North Vietnam, and the Viet Cong was drawn up in an effort to end cease-fire violations.

Nevertheless, from 1973 to 1975, fighting continued. The Nixon administration continued to send massive amounts of aid to the Thieu government, and both the North and the South continued freely violating the accords. To pressure the North into abiding by them, the United States resumed bombing Cambodia and menaced North Vietnam with reconnaissance overflights. But a war-weary Congress had turned against the president, whose administration was now disintegrating in the Watergate scandal. In November 1973, Congress passed the War Powers Act, which required the president to inform Congress within forty-eight hours of deployment of U.S. military forces abroad and mandated their withdrawal within sixty days if Congress did not approve. In 1974, U.S. aid to South Vietnam was reduced from $2.56 billion to $907 million, and to $700 million in 1975.

What hopes Thieu clung to for support from the Nixon administration were dashed when the U.S. president, facing impeachment, resigned in August 1974. Congress subsequently rejected President Gerald Ford's request for $300 million in "supplemental aid" to South Vietnam, and, from early 1975 on, the dispirited South suffered one military defeat after another. In January, Communist forces captured the province of Phuoc Binh, then launched a major offensive in the Central Highlands during March. South Vietnamese forces withdrew from parts of the northwest and central highlands, and on March 25, 1975, the old imperial capital of Hue fell. In April, Da Nang and Qui Nhon followed, and, after a fierce battle, the South Vietnamese gave up Kuon Loc on April 22. A day earlier, President Nguyen Van Thieu resigned and was briefly replaced by Tran Van Huong, whom the Communists found unacceptable for negotiations. Lieutenant General Duong Van Minh became South Vietnam's last president and surrendered to the forces of North Vietnam on April 30. North and South Vietnam were officially unified under a Communist regime on July 2, 1976.

Fall of Saigon

A dramatic, frenzied evacuation of Americans remaining in Vietnam followed. The spectacle of American personnel being airlifted by helicopter from the roof of the U.S. embassy in Saigon was humiliating and heartbreaking. At the cost of more than $150 billion and fifty-eight thousand Americans killed, the Vietnam War had ended in defeat for South Vietnam and (as many saw it) for the United States as well.

CHAPTER 15

Cold War Conflicts since 1958

In an 1823 address to Congress, President James Monroe issued the policy statement that became known as the Monroe Doctrine. It was a warning to European powers that the United States would act to halt any new attempts to colonize the Americas. In 1947 President Harry S Truman promulgated the Truman Doctrine, warning the Soviet Union—which supported a threatened Communist takeover of Greece and Turkey—that the United States would act to halt the spread of communism wherever in the world it threatened democracy. The Truman Doctrine had its basis in a proposal by State Department official George F. Kennan that the most effective way to combat communism was to *contain* it, confronting the Soviet Union whenever and wherever it sought to expand its ideological influence.

Containment became the policy of the Truman and subsequent administrations until the collapse of the Soviet Union in the early 1990s. And this policy was the source of the so-called Cold War, the long post–World War II period in which peace was a matter tenuous and relative, and in which chronic armed tensions between the ideologies of capitalism and communism often exploded into limited wars that involved, in greater or lesser degree, the United States.

Lebanese Civil War, 1958

Camille Chamoun, candidate of the Christian (Maronite) Party, was elected to the presidency of Lebanon in 1952 and quickly developed close ties with the West, especially the United States. In harmony with the "containment" doctrine, the United States was eager to cultivate friendly relations with nations of the Middle East, but Chamoun's policy alienated many Lebanese Muslims, about 50 percent of the population, who favored closer ties with neighboring Arab nations, many of which were hostile to the West. The alienation developed into civil unrest, which exploded, during May 9–13, 1958, in a series of violent Muslim demonstrations against Chamoun. Riots erupted in Tripoli and in the Lebanese capital, Beirut. The violence was apparently orchestrated—or at least supported—by the United Arab Republic (the union of Egypt and Syria, formed in January 1958), which also endorsed the activity of Kamal Jumblatt, a Druse chieftain who led the most militant aspects of the revolt and who had already defeated Lebanese Army forces in several encounters.

Faced with demands for his resignation, Chamoun stood fast and appealed to U.S. president Dwight D. Eisenhower for military aid. In 1957 Eisenhower had promulgated the so-called Eisenhower Doctrine, which held that the independence of the nations of the Middle East was vital to U.S. interests and to the peace of the world. As the Eisenhower administration saw it, Soviet backing of the United Arab Republic jeopardized the security of Jordan, Turkey, and Iraq as well as Lebanon—all nations friendly to the West. When Iraqi Army officers allied with the UAR overthrew Iraq's King Faisal in 1957, Egypt and the new leaders of Iraq acted to destabilize Jordan and Lebanon, arming and supporting rebels in these nations. In 1957 the Eisenhower government authorized U.S. Marines and a full army brigade to join a British regiment in Jordan to protect the government of King Hussein. At this time it was also decided to prepare for intervention in Lebanon, and three U.S. Marine battalions were made ready. The army prepared for a massive airlift if required. Thus the U.S. military was well prepared to answer Chamoun's appeal for assistance when it finally came.

On July 15, 1958, marines began amphibious landings at Khalde Beach in Lebanon. On July 16 these initial forces were joined by marines airlifted in, and on July 19, army troops arrived. U.S. troops marching into

Beirut were greeted by a mixed and subdued response. Little resistance was encountered, and some even greeted the Americans as friends. Wisely, U.S. commanders immediately defined a clear relationship with Lebanese officers. Within a short time, U.S. and Lebanese forces were integrated and working well together to patrol the explosive areas of Beirut.

On July 15, when the first contingent of marines landed, President Eisenhower called on the United Nations to intervene in Lebanon with a multinational peacekeeping force. The Soviet Union vetoed the resolution of intervention, whereupon Eisenhower dispatched Deputy Undersecretary of State Robert D. Murphy to Lebanon to mediate among the warring factions. In the meantime, the U.S. presence had enabled the establishment of a cease-fire, which, however, was tenuous at best. Sniper incidents were common, and occasionally out-and-out skirmishes developed. Despite this, U.S. forces worked with the Lebanese Army to create a twenty-mile defensive perimeter around Beirut. The principal object of this was to prevent Syrian or Syrian-backed guerrillas from attacking the capital and ousting Chamoun. The U.S. intervention bought time for Murphy to negotiate an agreement to hold a new election. Another Maronite Christian, General Faud Chehab, was elected, and after his inauguration on September 23, 1958, U.S. troops withdrew. At its peak, U.S. troop strength in Lebanon approached fourteen thousand.

Lebanese Civil War, 1975–1992

This conflict had a long history before the United States became directly involved. That background is important to understanding America's role in the war.

As mentioned in *Lebanese Civil War, 1958,* Lebanon was divided almost evenly between Christians and Muslims. The National Pact of 1943 had established the dominant political role of the Christian Phalange Party in the central government. Frequently this provision became a source of violent discord among the Muslim factions. By the 1970s, the presence of Palestinian refugees as well as the existence of bases from which the Palestine Liberation Organization (PLO) operated against Israel further destabilized the volatile Lebanese situation. In this political environment, any incident could touch off a civil war.

On April 13, 1975, gunmen killed four Phalangists during an attempt on the life of Phalange leader Pierre Jumayyil. Apparently believing that the would-be assassins were Palestinian, Phalangist forces retaliated later that day with an attack against a bus carrying Palestinians through a Christian neighborhood; some twenty-six passengers were killed. These two incidents triggered a long, extremely destructive civil war.

During the war, Lebanon became not only the scene of internal conflict, but a confused battleground for Israel, Syria, and the PLO. It was August 1982, after an agreement was finally reached for the evacuation of Syrian troops and PLO fighters from Beirut, that the United States entered the conflict. The 1982 agreement provided for the deployment of a three-nation Multinational Force (MNF) during the period of the evacuation, and by late August, U.S. Marines, as well as French and Italian units, arrived in Beirut. When the evacuation ended, these units left, the U.S. Marines departing on September 10.

During a period of relative calm, Bashir Gemayel was elected president only to be assassinated on September 14. The next day Israeli troops entered West Beirut, and over the succeeding three days, Lebanese militiamen massacred hundreds of Palestinian civilians in the Sabra and Shatila refugee camps in West Beirut. Gemayel's brother, Amine, was elected president by a unanimous vote of the parliament. He took office on September 23, 1982, and MNF forces returned to Beirut at the end of September to signal their support for the government. In February 1983 a small British contingent joined the U.S., French, and Italian MNF troops in Beirut.

President Gemayel and his government placed primary emphasis on the withdrawal of Israeli, Syrian, and Palestinian forces from Lebanon, and in late 1982, Lebanese-Israeli negotiations commenced with U.S. participation. On May 17, 1983, an agreement was concluded providing for Israeli withdrawal, but Syria declined to discuss the withdrawal of its troops. While negotiations were thus stalled, a series of terrorist attacks in 1983 and 1984 were aimed directly at American interests. On April 18, 1983, the U.S. embassy in west Beirut was bombed, with the loss of 63 lives. The U.S. and French MNF headquarters in Beirut was hit on October 23, 1983, with the loss of 298 lives, most of these U.S. Marines. Eight more U.S. nationals lost their lives in the bombing of the U.S. embassy annex in East Beirut on September 20, 1984.

Druse and Christian forces had clashed during 1982–1983, and when

President and Mrs. Reagan attend a ceremony honoring the victims of the bombing of the
U.S. embassy in Beirut, Lebanon. The photograph was taken on April 23, 1983. *Collection:
National Archives and Records Administration*

Israeli forces withdrew from the Shuf region at the beginning of September 1983, the Druse, backed by Syria, attacked the Christian Lebanese Forces (LF) militia as well as the Lebanese Army. The United States and Saudi Arabia brokered a cease-fire on September 26, 1983, which left the Druse in control of most of the Shuf region. By February 1984 the Lebanese Army had all but collapsed as many of its Muslim and Druse units defected to opposition militias. With the departure of the U.S. Marines imminent, the Gemayel government was pressured by Syria and its Muslim Lebanese allies to abandon the May 17 accord. At last, on March 5, 1984, the government announced that it was canceling its unimplemented agreement with Israel. The U.S. Marines left shortly afterward, and reconciliation talks at Lausanne, Switzerland, under Syrian auspices failed soon after. Although a new "government of national unity" under Prime Minister Rashid Karami was declared in April 1984, it made no real progress toward solving Lebanon's internal political and economic crises.

After the final departure of the MNF, the situation in Lebanon rapidly deteriorated, and the Civil War resumed. In an attempt to resolve the crisis, in January 1989 the Arab League appointed a committee on Lebanon, led by the Kuwaiti foreign minister. At the Casablanca Arab summit in May, the Arab League created a higher committee on Lebanon, composed of Saudi king Fahd, Algerian president Bendjedid, and Moroccan king Hassan. After much effort, the committee arranged for a seven-point cease-fire in September, followed by a meeting of Lebanese parliamentarians in Taif, Saudi Arabia. After a month of discussions, the deputies agreed on a charter of national reconciliation, the Taif Agreement, which divided government representation between Christians and Muslims. By spring 1992, the agreement substantially brought about an end to the Civil War.

Nicaraguan Civil War, 1978–1979

The United States had intervened in both the *Nicaraguan Civil War, 1909–1912 (see chapter 10)* and the *Nicaraguan Civil War, 1925–1933 (see chapter 10),* always supporting moderate to right-wing governments friendly to American business and financial interests. Since the end of the 1925–1933 war, the U.S. government supported and helped to bolster the economic and political dominance of the Somoza family. In 1978, domestic opposition to the Somoza dynasty and the current Nicaraguan president, Anastasio Somoza Debayle, became highly militant and well organized, concentrated chiefly in the leftist Sandinista National Liberation Front, named in honor of Augusto César Sandino, a leading figure in the 1925–1933 war, who was assassinated after the war at the behest of the father of Somoza Debayle, Anastasio Somoza García.

Even before the outbreak of the 1978–1979 war, U.S. support for the Somoza regime was weakening. In 1977 the U.S. State Department cited and criticized Somoza for human rights violations related to the brutal suppression of protest and antigovernment activity. The Catholic Church in Nicaragua accused the Somoza government of imprisoning, torturing, and murdering dissidents, including politically active Catholic clergy. But it was the murder of Pedro Joaquin Chamorro, publisher of the liberal newspaper *La Prensa,* that triggered widespread rioting and a general uprising, with calls for Somoza's immediate resignation.

Exploiting the situation, Sandinista guerrillas stormed the national palace in August 1978 and held fifteen hundred people hostage, including deputies in the lower assembly, demanding the release of fifty-nine political prisoners and their safe conduct out of Nicaragua. These terms were granted, and the prisoners as well as the hostages were freed. The revolution, however, continued to gain momentum when Sandinistas based in Costa Rica invaded on May 29, 1979. The rebels fought the U.S.-equipped and U.S.-trained Nicaraguan National Guard for the next seven weeks, steadily gaining ground against the government forces. However, the United States sent no additional aid or military forces. On July 17, 1979, Anastasio Somoza Debayle fled to the United States, which accepted its traditional ally but did not welcome him. He soon left for Paraguay, where he was assassinated in a spectacular bazooka assault at Asunción in September 1980.

After the overthrow of Somoza, the Sandinistas broadcast the commencement of a cease-fire and installed a five-member junta as the nation's provisional government. Although the United States did not take a directly active role in the war, the conflict served to intensify anti-American feeling in much of Nicaragua and prompted the Sandinista government to align itself with nations friendly to Marxism. The stage was set for a renewed civil war in which the United States would take a more central role *(see Nicaraguan Civil War, 1982–1990)*.

Honduran Guerrilla War, 1981–1990

The *Nicaraguan Civil War, 1982–1990* and the Salvadoran Civil War, 1977–1992 created large numbers of refugees, many of whom fled to Honduras. Honduran government officials correctly feared that this influx would expose Honduras to attack from leftist guerrillas operating out of El Salvador and Nicaragua. Soon, Cuban-trained guerrillas hit Honduran military and police installations and terrorized the Honduran capital of Tegucigalpa, even attacking the U.S. embassy there. The United States responded to the attacks by supplying large amounts of military hardware to Honduran government forces.

In the meantime, the anti-Sandinista Nicaraguan Democratic Force (FDN) formed within Honduras, established rebel bases there, and launched raids into Nicaragua. This provoked the Nicaraguan Sandinistas to invade Honduras to raid the FDN bases. Once again, the United States responded, providing helicopters and pilots to carry Honduran troops to the border regions to repel the invasion. The United States then sent thirty-two hundred combat troops to assist the anti-Sandinista forces, which were collectively called Contras. This, however, provoked left-wing violence within Honduras, as many objected to the American military presence in the country.

In actuality, the United States had a deeper and more extensive involvement in the Honduran war than was generally known at the time. The administration of President Ronald Reagan came into office in 1981, setting two of its top priorities as bringing about an end to the war in El Salvador and aiding the Contra guerrilla war against the Sandinistas in Nicaragua *(see Nicaraguan Civil War, 1978–1979* and *Nicaraguan Civil War, 1982–1990)*. Honduras, located between El Salvador and Nicaragua and embroiled in guerrilla warfare spawned by the conflicts of its neighbors, effectively became the base for all U.S. operations in Central America. From here, the U.S. Central Intelligence Agency (CIA) supported covert operations, including the U.S.-trained Battalion 316, a secret Honduran Army intelligence unit formed in 1982. Battalion 316 soon became notorious for committing human rights abuses. With American support, the Honduran Army suppressed the small Honduran guerrilla movement between 1980 and 1984, typically by the most brutal means available, including imprisonment and torture, in addition to outright murder.

By 1990 the Honduran war quickly wound down after the Sandinistas were defeated in the Nicaraguan elections. Revelations concerning the Reagan administration's illegal covert support of the Contras prompted the U.S. Congress to eliminate much of the American military presence in Central America at this time as well. Nevertheless, the end of the war did not bring an immediate end to the killing. Peasants seeking land reforms and threatening to seize land in default of government action were attacked and killed in 1991 after they began farming idle land. When this outrage was exposed, publicly contrite government officials pledged to end human rights abuses in Honduras and to introduce land reform there.

Nicaraguan Civil War, 1982–1990

Although the U.S. State Department had, in 1977, officially cited the Somoza government of Nicaragua for human rights violations, the U.S. government was hardly sympathetic to the leftist Sandinista regime that had defeated and replaced the Somoza government, which, after all, the

United States had supported since the end of the 1930s. That support had often been grudging and guilt-ridden—"Somoza is a son of a bitch," Franklin D. Roosevelt is reported to have said, "but he's our son of a bitch"—but, in the eyes of the Sandinistas, the United States was indeed wedded to the hated Somoza dynasty. Tensions between the new Sandinista government and the United States intensified in the 1980s when Congress delayed promised financial aid to Nicaragua. This prompted the Sandinistas, already ideologically Marxist, to turn to Cuba for aid, military advisers, and technicians. When he left office at the beginning of 1981, U.S. president Jimmy Carter suspended aid altogether on the grounds that the Sandinistas were supplying and harboring leftist guerrillas in El Salvador.

Whereas Carter's response to the Sandinistas had been hostile but largely passive, his successor, President Ronald Reagan, entered office with the explicit objective of ousting the Sandinistas. The Reagan administration applied an array of political and economic pressures against the government of Nicaragua and authorized $19 million in November 1981 to fund a Central Intelligence Agency program to train a counterrevolutionary army, mostly National Guard adherents of the Somoza regime, dubbed the Contras and referred to by President Reagan as the "Freedom Fighters." By 1986 the Contras consisted of some fifteen thousand troops trained, financed, and equipped by the United States.

The Contras were based primarily in neighboring Honduras and Costa Rica and were aided by Miskito Indians, who had fled to Honduras when the Sandinista government attempted forcibly to resettle them away from the Nicaraguan-Honduran border. In January 1982, Sandinista troops moved preemptively against the Miskitos by invading their settlements in Honduras. More than a hundred Miskitos were killed. Others eagerly joined the Contras, and still others formed their own anti-Sandinista force, the Democratic Revolutionary Alliance (ARDE).

It was not until 1983–1984 that the U.S.-supported Contras invaded Nicaragua from Honduras, targeting infrastructure in an effort to destabilize the Sandinista government. Oil storage facilities, bridges, and the like were demolished. In 1985–1986, the Sandinista army focused on the Nicaraguan Democratic Force (FDN), the largest of the Contra military groups, attacking it in Honduran territory. Although the FDN was torn by internal dissension and also was in dispute with the ARDE, it put up a stout defense, which was very costly to the Sandinistas, who were suffering from the effects of a U.S. trade embargo. At this juncture President Reagan was not content to apply economic sanctions alone. Congress had barred direct U.S. military aid to the Contras, but the Reagan administration devised a complicated means of circumventing the law.

The scheme that became known as the Iran-Contra Affair began to unravel in November 1986, when President Reagan confirmed reports that the United States had secretly sold arms to its implacable enemy Iran. The president at first denied, however, that the purpose of the sale was to obtain the release of U.S. hostages held by terrorists in perpetually war-torn Lebanon, but he later admitted an arms-for-hostages swap. Then the plot suddenly thickened. Attorney General Edwin Meese learned that a portion of the revenue raised by the arms sales had been diverted to finance—illegally—the Contras. A lengthy investigation gradually revealed that in 1985, a cabal of Israelis had approached national security adviser Robert MacFarlane with a scheme in which Iran would use its influence to free the U.S. hostages held in Lebanon in exchange for arms. Secretary of State George Shultz and Secretary of Defense Caspar Weinberger objected to the plan, but MacFarlane testified that President Reagan agreed to it. In a bizarre twist, U.S. Marine lieutenant colonel Oliver ("Ollie") North then modified the scheme in order to funnel profits from the arms sales to the Contras. Investigation and testimony implicated officials on successively higher rungs of the White House ladder—through national security advisers John Poindexter and MacFarlane, through CIA director William J. Casey (who died in May 1987), and through Secretary of Defense Caspar Weinberger. Few people believed that President Reagan had been ignorant of the scheme, and many thought that he had enthusiastically advocated it. (In the end, Ollie North was convicted on three of twelve criminal counts against him, but the convictions were subsequently set aside on appeal; Poindexter was convicted on five counts of deceiving Congress, but his convictions also were set aside; CIA administrator Clair E. George was indicted for perjury, but his trial ended in mistrial; and Caspar Weinberger was indicted on five counts of lying to Congress. All of those charged were ultimately pardoned by President Reagan's successor, George H. Bush, and while the 1994 report of special prosecutor Lawrence E. Walsh scathingly criticized both Reagan and Bush, neither was charged with criminal wrongdoing.)

Even with U.S. aid, including the covert funding from the Iran arms sales, the Contras proved unable to oust the Sandinistas. Costa Rican president Oscar Arias Sanchez brokered a peace plan that called for an end to outside aid for the Contras and instituted negotiations. A treaty was signed in August 1987, although sporadic fighting continued until free elections unseated Sandinista president Daniel Ortega Saavedra and replaced him and Sandinista legislators with an anti-Sandinista coalition in the executive and legislative branches. The new coalition quickly concluded a peace accord with all the parties involved in the civil war. Some thirty thousand persons had perished in the course of the conflict, and largely due to U.S. sanctions and embargoes, Nicaragua had been reduced to near economic ruin.

Grenada Intervention, 1983

On October 23, 1983, more than two hundred U.S. Marines were killed in their sleep when a truck loaded with twenty-five thousand pounds of TNT was driven into the headquarters of the U.S. and French contingent of the Multinational Force (MNF) stationed in Beirut, Lebanon *(see Lebanese Civil War, 1975–1992)*. This disaster brought a firestorm of criticism against American military planners and President Reagan; however, the criticism was blunted by the military action the president authorized just two days after the Beirut bombing. It was an invasion of the island nation of Grenada in the West Indies. Cuban troops had been sent to the tiny country (population 110,100) at the behest of its anti-American dictatorship, and President Reagan was determined to protect the approximately 1,000 American citizens there. As administration insiders later remarked, the president also saw the successful "liberation" of Grenada as a kind of emotional antidote to the anger and despair caused by the death of the marines in Beirut.

In 1979 a Marxist-Leninist coup led by Maurice Bishop and his New Jewel movement overthrew the government of Grenada. The United States was particularly wary when the new Communist, pro-Cuban regime devoted inordinate resources to the construction of a ninety-eight-hundred-foot airstrip, clearly for military purposes—and, it was subsequently discovered, built with the aid of Cuban military personnel. The administration of Bishop was short-lived, however. A 1983 coup killed Bishop and others, leaving Deputy Prime Minister Bernard Coard and General Hudson Austin in charge of the government. Sir Paul Scoon, Grenada's governor-general, secretly communicated with the Organization

... *Some two months ago we were shocked by the brutal massacre of 269 men, women, and children, more than 60 of them Americans, in the shooting down of a Korean airliner. Now, in these past several days, violence has erupted again, in Lebanon and Grenada.*

In Lebanon, we have some 1,600 Marines, part of a multinational force that's trying to help the people of Lebanon restore order and stability to that troubled land. . . .

This past Sunday, at twenty-two minutes after six Beirut time, with dawn just breaking, a truck, looking like a lot of other vehicles in the city, approached the airport on a busy, main road. There was nothing in its appearance to suggest it was any different than the trucks or cars that were normally seen on and around the airport. But this one was different. At the wheel was a young man on a suicide mission. The truck carried some two thousand pounds of explosives, but there was no way our Marine guards could know this. Their first warning that something was wrong came when the truck crashed through a series of barriers, including a chain-link fence and barbed-wire entanglements. The guards opened fire, but it was too late. The truck smashed through the doors of the headquarters building in which our Marines were sleeping and instantly exploded. The four-story concrete building collapsed in a pile of rubble.

More than two hundred of the sleeping men were killed in that one hideous, insane attack. Many others suffered injury and are hospitalized here or in Europe. . . .

Now, I know another part of the world is very much on our minds, a place much closer to our shores: Grenada. . . .

In 1979 trouble came to Grenada. Maurice Bishop, a protégé of Fidel Castro, staged a military coup. . . . He sought the help of Cuba in building an airport, which he claimed was for tourist trade, but which looked suspiciously suitable for military aircraft, including Soviet-built long-range bombers. . . .

There were then about a thousand of our citizens on Grenada, eight hundred of them students in St. George's University Medical School. Concerned that they'd be harmed or held as hostages, I ordered a flotilla of ships, then on its way to Lebanon with Marines, part of our regular rotation program, to circle south on a course that would put them somewhere in the vicinity of Grenada in case there should be a need to evacuate our people. . . .

Grenada, we were told, was a friendly island paradise for tourism. Well, it wasn't. It was a Soviet-Cuban colony, being readied as a major military bastion to export terror and undermine democracy. We got there just in time. . . .

—FROM PRESIDENT REAGAN'S TELEVISED ADDRESS OF OCTOBER 27, 1983, CONCERNING THE TERRORIST BOMBING OF A U.S. MARINE BARRACKS IN LEBANON AND THE U.S. INVASION OF GRENADA of Eastern Caribbean States (OECS) for aid in restoring order. It was the OECS that, in turn, asked for U.S. military intervention, to which the vigorously anti-communist Reagan administration enthusiastically agreed.

Operation Urgent Fury included a naval battle group centered on the aircraft carrier *Independence*, as well as the helicopter carrier *Guam*, two U.S. Marine amphibious units, two army Ranger battalions, a brigade of the Eighty-second Airborne Division, and special operations units. These massive forces landed on Grenada on October 25, 1983, and found themselves facing no more than 500 to 600 Grenadian regulars, 2,000 to 2,500 poorly equipped and poorly organized militiamen, and about 800 Cuban military construction personnel. The invaders seized the airport and destroyed Radio Free Grenada, a key source of government communications. The U.S. citizens were safely evacuated, and Grenada was under U.S. military control by October 28.

The invasion of Grenada was successful in that it achieved its objectives; however, it suffered from a number of problems that might have had catastrophic consequences. Intelligence was poor and poorly communicated. Coordination among the service arms—army, navy, and marines—was inadequate; shockingly, the services operated with mutually incompatible radios. Eighteen U.S. personnel died in the assault on Grenada, and 116 were wounded. Grenadan forces lost 25 dead and 59 wounded, while Cuban casualties were 45 dead and 350 wounded.

U.S. Invasion of Panama (Operation Just Cause), 1989

The 1989 invasion of Panama was unique in American military history as an act of war directed against a single person, Manuel Antonio Noriega, the president of Panama. In 1988, Noriega had been indicted by a U.S. federal grand jury for drug trafficking. Following this, the administrations of both Ronald Reagan and George H. Bush used economic and diplomatic sanctions to pressure the dictator into resigning. When these failed, the United States, in the spring of 1989, deployed additional marine units and army and air force units to U.S. installations in Panama. Noriega did not take the hint. In October 1989, a coup attempt against Noriega by members of the Panamanian Army was squelched by troops loyal to the dictator. This failure was followed by several incidents of harassment against U.S. citizens and then by Noriega's issuance of a "declaration against the United States." Shortly after this, Panamanian soldiers killed an off-duty U.S. Army officer. This precipitated, on December 19, 1989, the U.S.-sanctioned creation of an alternative government for Panama, led by President Guillermo Endara, who was sworn in by a Panamanian judge at a U.S. military base. Early the next morning, December 20, Operation Just Cause got under way.

It began when F-117 Stealth fighters bombed the Panamanian Defense Force (PDF) barracks. This was the combat debut of the new fighter, and Operation Just Cause also would serve as the maiden battle of the army Rangers' innovative light infantry and special operations forces, which had been trained specifically for operations such as this. The Rangers would be responsible for the major aspects of the operation, but among the twenty-four thousand troops who participated, navy SEALs, air force personnel, and Air National Guard units also participated.

The object of the operation was simple and well defined: to capture Noriega. Marines were assigned to guard the entrances to the Panama Canal and other U.S. defense sites in the Canal Zone. Army Rangers and other special task forces were dropped by Apache attack helicopters over key points in the Canal Zone. Troops aboard M-113 armored personnel carriers emerged from Fort Sherman and rode through the streets of Panama City, engaging whatever PDF units they encountered. The Rangers, reinforced by marines, moved toward the central Canal Zone, pausing to attack the Comandancia, headquarters of Noriega and the PDF. Simultaneously, other task forces guarded the western entrances of the Panama Canal opposite Balboa and Panama City as well as other U.S. defense sites in the Canal Zone. These forces were assigned to block the PDF from infiltrating the Canal Zone and from moving reinforcements out of Panama City. U.S. units also took and held Torrijos International Airport; the Bridge of the Americas; and Río Hato airfield, ninety miles south of Panama City. Another task force secured all U.S. military bases, and yet another was assigned to free prisoners taken by the PDF. U.S. Air Force and Air National Guard units provided continuous close-air support for the ground troops.

For the first time in its history, the Panama Canal was closed; it would reopen on December 21. Fighting continued for five days, house-to-house, as marines conducted manhunts for PDF troops as well as for

Noriega, who apparently had vanished. In the meantime, a special civil-affairs Ranger battalion was airlifted to Panama City to assist President Endara in establishing order. The civil-affairs troops also quickly created a new Panamanian police force, the Panama Public Force, to preserve civil order after U.S. troops withdrew.

By this time it was learned that Noriega had sought refuge in the Vatican embassy in Panama City. He was refused sanctuary there, but it was not until January 1990 that he was located, arrested, and transported to the United States for trial, which began in Miami in the fall of 1991. Witnesses testified that Noriega had laundered Colombian drug money in Panama and had used his country as a clearinghouse for cocaine on its way to the United States. On April 10, 1992, Noriega was convicted on eight counts of cocaine trafficking, racketeering, and money laundering. He was sentenced to forty years' imprisonment. It was the first time in history that the United States had captured, tried, convicted, and punished a head of state for criminal wrongdoing.

As for the war, it had cost the lives of 314 PDF soldiers; 124 had been wounded, and 5,313 were taken prisoner. Nineteen American soldiers were killed and 303 wounded. Civilian casualties and other "collateral damage" were significant.

Persian Gulf War, 1991

Under the dictator Saddam Hussein, Iraq had long laid claim to the small, oil-rich nation of Kuwait as a province. Suddenly, on August 2, 1990, the Iraqi Army, fourth-largest ground force in the world, invaded Kuwait pursuant to Saddam's proclamation of annexation. Within a week, Kuwait was completely under the control of Iraq. The United States, its allies, and much of the world now feared that Iraq would go on to mount an attack southward into Saudi Arabia, giving Saddam a stranglehold on much of the world's oil supply. Even if Saddam chose to press the attack no farther, his seizure of Kuwait put him in a position to threaten Saudi Arabia on an ongoing basis and thus control the flow of oil.

The United States responded to the invasion by freezing Iraqi assets in American banks and by cutting off trade with the country. The administration of President George H. Bush acted to obtain U.N. resolutions condemning the invasion and supporting military action against it. Bush and Secretary of State James Baker forged an unprecedented coalition among forty-eight nations. Of these, thirty provided military forces, with the United States making the largest contribution; eighteen other nations provided economic, humanitarian, and other noncombat assistance. Saudi Arabia and other Arab states near Iraq provided port facilities, airfields, and staging areas for the buildup of ground forces. Because the participation of Israel would likely drive a wedge between the Arab members of the coalition and the United States and other Western members, Israel agreed not to take part in any military action, except in direct self-defense.

The U.S. buildup in the Middle East began on August 7, 1990, in response to a Saudi request for military aid to defend against possible Iraqi invasion. Dubbed Operation Desert Shield, the buildup was intended to deploy sufficient forces to deter further Iraqi aggression and to defend Saudi Arabia. The first step was a naval blockade of Iraq. On August 8, U.S. Air Force fighters began to arrive at Saudi air bases. Lead elements of the U.S. Army contingent arrived on August 9. By September these forces were augmented by those of coalition members and were now at sufficient strength to deter an invasion of Saudi Arabia. By the end of October, 210,000 U.S. Army and Marine troops had been deployed, in addition to 65,000 troops from other coalition nations. Backed by these forces, the United States and the coalition countries attempted to open

President George H. Bush meets with General Colin Powell and others to discuss the situation in the Persian Gulf on January 15, 1991. *Collection: National Archives and Records Administration*

diplomatic negotiations on an Iraqi withdrawal from Kuwait. But Saddam Hussein was unresponsive, despite a series of U.N. resolutions condemning him. President Bush now prepared the American people to accept the necessity of military action against Saddam. Bush and the State Department also successfully lobbied for a U.N. resolution authorizing military force to expel Iraq from Kuwait. Secured on November 29, the resolution set a withdrawal deadline of January 15, 1991.

Mid-January also was the time at which the United States anticipated completing a second phase of the military buildup in the Middle East. As the deadline approached, 450,000 coalition troops were on the ground, ready to oppose a larger Iraqi force, some 530,000, in Kuwait. Except in troop numbers, the coalition enjoyed overwhelming advantages: more than 170 ships were now in the area, including 6 aircraft carriers and 2 battleships. Air power consisted of 2,200 combat craft.

When the deadline passed, Operation Desert Shield became Operation Desert Storm, and on the morning of January 16, a massive air campaign was unleashed against Iraq and Iraqi positions in Kuwait. This air war would continue for five weeks, during which coalition forces flew more than 88,000 missions with losses of only 22 U.S. aircraft and 9 craft from other coalition countries. The Iraqi Air Force offered almost no resistance, and antiaircraft fire and surface-to-air missiles had little effect against the coalition sorties. The Iraqis attempted to hide some of their planes in hardened revetments; others were flown into Iran. The Iraqis did make use of obsolescent Soviet-made Scud surface-to-surface missiles, which were directed against Israel and Saudi Arabia. Israel was targeted specifically in the hope that the attacks would goad it into entering the war, thereby alienating the Arab members of the coalition. Through deft diplomacy, the United States kept Israel out of the war and deployed mobile Patriot missile launchers to intercept Scud attacks. The performance of the Patriots became a subject of controversy. During the war, Defense Department analysts claimed an 80 percent success rate in intercepting Scuds in Saudi Arabia and a 50 percent rate in Israel. After the war, these claims were officially scaled back to 70 percent and 40 percent, respectively, but subsequent congressional investigations put these figures much lower, approaching 0 percent. It was probably the crudeness of the Scud system itself, not the success of attempts to intercept the missiles, that accounted for the fact that relatively few hit their intended targets. No one disputes, however, that the coalition enjoyed little success in destroying Scud launchers on the ground. Iraqi missile crews were skilled at camouflaging the mobile Scud launchers, then quickly moving the launchers to a new site. In the end, the Scud launches were the only creditable response the Iraqis offered to the coalition onslaught.

Impressively destructive as the coalition air campaign was, its main purpose was to prepare the way for the ground campaign, which was led chiefly by U.S. General H. Norman Schwarzkopf. The overwhelming air supremacy of the coalition kept Iraqi reconnaissance aircraft from discovering anything about the deployment of coalition ground troops;

IN THEIR OWN

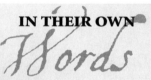

Tonight, twenty-eight nations, countries from five continents—Europe and Asia, Africa, and the Arab League—have forces in the gulf area standing shoulder-to-shoulder against Saddam Hussein. These countries had hoped the use of force could be avoided.

Regrettably, we now believe that only force will make him leave. . . .

Prior to ordering our forces into battle, I instructed our military commanders to take every necessary step to prevail as quickly as possible and with the greatest degree of protection possible for American and Allied servicemen and women. I've told the American people beforehand that this will not be another Vietnam.

And I repeat this here tonight. Our troops will have the best possible support in the entire world. And they will not be asked to fight with one hand tied behind their back. . . .

This is an historic moment. We have in this past year made great progress in ending the long era of conflict and Cold War. We have before us the opportunity to forge for ourselves and for future generations a new world order, a world where the rule of law, not the law of the jungle, governs the conduct of nations. When we are successful, and we will be, we have a real chance at this new world order, an order in which a credible United Nations can use its peacekeeping role to fulfill the promise and vision of the U.N.'s founders.

We have no argument with the people of Iraq. Indeed, for the innocents caught in this conflict, I pray for their safety. Our goal is not the conquest of Iraq. It is the liberation of Kuwait.

—FROM PRESIDENT GEORGE H. BUSH'S TELEVISED ADDRESS AT THE COMMENCEMENT OF THE PERSIAN GULF WAR, JANUARY 16, 1991 however, it was the Iraqis who made the first move on the ground, launching an attack on the Saudi town of Khafji on January 29, with three tank brigades. Although the Iraqis occupied the lightly defended town, they were pushed out the next day by a Saudi counterattack. The Battle of Khafji suggested to coalition military planners that the Iraqis were no match for U.S.-style mobile warfare.

The coalition ground offensive stepped off at 4:00 A.M. on February 24, 1991. The plan was for the army's XVIII Airborne Corps to be positioned on the coalition's left flank. This unit would move into Iraq on the far west and, striking deep within the country, cut off the Iraqi Army in Kuwait, isolating it from any support or reinforcement from the north. The French Sixth Light Armored Division covered the XVIII Airborne Corps' own left flank. The center of the ground force consisted of the U.S. VII Corps, the U.S. Second Armored Cavalry, and the British First Armored Division—celebrated as the "Desert Rats" who defeated Erwin Rommel's Afrika Korps in *World War II, 1939–1945 (chapter 12)*. The center units would move north into Iraq after the left and right flanks had been secured, then make a sharp right turn to advance into Kuwait from the west to attack Iraqi units there, including the elite Republican Guard. The right flank was also charged with breaching Iraqi lines in Kuwait. The units composing this flank were mainly U.S. Marines.

The attacks on the first day were intended, in part, to screen the main attack and to deceive the Iraqis into thinking that the principal assault would come on the coast of Kuwait. Although Iraqi defenses were well developed, relatively light resistance was offered, and many Iraqi prisoners were taken. By the second day of the ground war, French troops had secured the left flank of the coalition advance, and the U.S. forces had neatly cut off all avenues of Iraqi retreat and reinforcement. The U.S. Twenty-fourth Division ended its advance in Basra, Iraq, which sealed the remaining avenue of escape from Kuwait.

With the Iraqis in Kuwait occupied on the right, the VIII Airborne Corps made a surprise attack on the left, in the west. By nightfall of February 25, well ahead of schedule, the VIII Airborne Corps was already turning east into Kuwait. When the corps encountered units of the Republican Guard, this elite Iraqi unit fled. By February 27, however, with the Twenty-fourth Infantry having taken Basra, the Republican Guard was bottled up. The Hammurabi Division, the elite of the elite Republican Guard, attempted to engage the VIII Airborne Corps in a delaying action to allow the remainder of the Republican Guard to escape. The attempt failed, and the Hammurabi Division was wiped out.

Among the American public, haunted by memories of Vietnam, the war against Iraq had been fraught with much trepidation. In fact, the air and ground campaigns were probably the most successful military operations in modern history. This was due in large measure to overwhelming force and technology, as well as planning that was both careful and bold; but it also was due to the universal ineptitude of the Iraqi response to the coalition, and to the poor generalship of Saddam Hussein, who took personal command of much of the war. The Iraqi Air Force was essentially a no-show in the war, as were the forty-three ships of the Iraqi Navy.

A cease-fire was declared at 8:00 A.M. on February 28, shortly after Iraq capitulated on U.S. terms. The ground war had lasted just 100 hours. Operation Desert Storm had achieved its mission of liberating Kuwait, and it had done so with minimal coalition casualties: 95 killed, 368 wounded, 20 missing in action. Iraqi casualties were perhaps as many as 50,000 killed and another 50,000 wounded; 60,000 Iraqi troops were taken prisoner. Huge quantities of Iraqi military hardware were destroyed, as were communications equipment and military bases, barracks, and other facilities.

Both Iraq and the nation it had invaded, Kuwait, had suffered massive destruction of infrastructure. The environmental damage caused by Saddam's acts of destruction throughout the Kuwaiti oil fields, including raging oil fires, would take months, even years to repair. Astoundingly, however, despite overwhelming defeat, Saddam Hussein remained in power. Iraq was certainly defeated, but Saddam Hussein was not beaten.

War in Bosnia, 1992–1995

Historically, the Balkans have been torn by ethnic and nationalist violence. After *World War I, 1914–1918 (chapter 11),* the Kingdom of the Serbs, Croats, and Slovenes was formed from what had been part of the fallen Austro-Hungarian Empire and two independent states, Serbia and Montenegro. In 1929 the name of this collection of states was changed to Yugoslavia, and following *World War II, 1939–1945 (chapter 12),* the monarchy become a communist republic under the leadership of a strongman prime minister, Josip Broz Tito. As constituted after World War

II, Yugoslavia consisted of six republics: Serbia, Croatia, Bosnia and Herzegovina, Macedonia, Slovenia, and Montenegro. In addition, two provinces were attached to Yugoslavia, Kosovo and Vojvodina. Tito almost single-handedly kept Yugoslavia's jarring ethnic factions together during his long tenure as prime minister.

With the death of Tito in 1980, Yugoslavia began to fall apart. Slovenia and Croatia each declared independence, followed by Macedonia and then Bosnia and Herzegovina. During 1989-1990, in the general collapse of communism throughout Eastern Europe, Bosnia and Herzegovina, formerly part of Yugoslavia, was caught up in a tide of nationalism that swept the region. After Croatia and Slovenia quit the Yugoslav federation in 1991, Bosnia's Catholic Croats and Muslim Slavs approved referenda (February 29, 1992) calling for an independent, multinational republic as well. The Bosnian Orthodox Serbs, however, refused to secede from Yugoslavia, which was now dominated by Serbia. The result of this refusal was a civil war, which erupted in 1992 and tore apart Bosnia and Herzegovina.

Among Bosnia's three ethnic and religious groups that had been living side by side under communism, a bitter civil war now broke out. Its flames were fanned by the Serbian president, Slobodan Milosevic, who, claiming that he had a duty to protect the Serb minority in Bosnia, sent arms and other support to the Bosnian Serbs. The Bosnian federal army, dominated by Serbs, shelled Croat and Muslim quarters in the Bosnian capital city of Sarajevo. The international community responded to the growing civil war by imposing a variety of economic sanctions against Serbia in an effort to curtail its ability to supply Bosnian Serbs with weapons and other materiel. The sanctions, however, did not prevent Bosnian Serb guerrillas from carrying out brutal campaigns of "ethnic cleansing" against Muslims and Croats. Their object was to clear certain areas for the exclusive occupation of Bosnian Serbs. Attempts by the international community to send relief workers into the region were often met by gunfire. By July 1992, millions of Bosnians had become refugees. (While most of the human rights abuses were perpetrated by Bosnian Serbs with the support of Milosevic's Serbia, Croats and Muslims also carried out brutal retaliatory raids and even engaged in ethnic cleansing in the areas they controlled.)

Early in 1994, the Muslims and the Croats of Bosnia made a truce with one another and formed a confederation to oppose the Serbs. In

August the confederation agreed to a plan formulated by the United States, Russia, Britain, France, and Germany by which Bosnia would be divided 51 percent versus 49 percent, with the Serbs getting the smaller percentage. While the Muslims and Croats agreed to the plan, the Serbs kept fighting. In 1994 and 1995, Bosnian Serb forces conducted mass killings in Sarajevo, Srebenica, and other, smaller towns that the United Nations had declared safe havens for Muslim civilians.

An arms embargo imposed by the United States and the West European powers did little to stop the war. Indeed, it may have served only to deprive the Muslims and the Croats of badly needed arms, putting them at an even greater disadvantage against the Serbs. At last, beginning in April 1994, NATO, with strong U.S. participation, launched air strikes against the Serb positions. Still, the Bosnian Serbs fought on, blocking all attempts at humanitarian aid and even holding under detainment a twenty-four-thousand-man U.N. peacekeeping mission. Yet the Muslim-Croat alliance had been making military progress against the Bosnian Serbs. By September 1995, the alliance had reduced Serb-held territory in Bosnia to less than half of the country, precisely the percentage specified in the peace plan endorsed by the Muslims and the Croats. With the reduction of their territory an accomplished fact, the Bosnian Serbs finally came to the peace table. On December 14, 1995, with Muslim and Croatian leaders, Bosnian Serb leaders signed the Dayton peace accords, which had been brokered by the United States in a series of conferences held at Wright-Patterson Air Force Base outside of Dayton, Ohio. The major provision of the Dayton accords was the creation of a federalized Bosnia and Herzegovina, divided between a Bosnian-Muslim/Bosnian-Croat federation, and a Bosnian-Serb republic. In addition, the accords guaranteed that refugees would be allowed to return to their homes, that people would be permitted to move freely throughout Bosnia, and the human rights "of every Bosnian citizen" would be monitored by an independent commission and an internationally trained civilian police force. The accords also provided for the prosecution of individuals found guilty of war crimes. A "strong international force," including a contingent of U.S. troops, was provided for, to supervise the separation of military groups within Bosnia and to ensure that each side would live up to the agreements made.

Somalian Civil War, 1988–

Somalia, on the easternmost projection of the African continent, the "horn of Africa," was one of many African nations once under the colonial control of Europe and now independent but, burdened by overwhelming poverty, hardly free. In 1960, the independent Republic of Somalia was created, but after its president, Cabdirashiid Cali Sherma'arke, was assassinated in 1969, a military coup led by Major General Maxamed Siyaad Barre replaced parliamentary government with the dictatorial Supreme Revolutionary Council. The new military dictatorship allied itself with the Soviet Union and invaded the Ogaden region of Ethiopia in an attempt to annex the territory. The Soviets rapidly shifted support to Ethiopia, defeating Siyaad Barre's armies and creating chaos in already strife-torn and famine-ridden Somalia.

In the spring of 1988, the Somali "government" was dominated by feuding clans. The Somali National Movement (SNM) rose up at this time and began taking towns and military facilities in the north of the country. In these brutal campaigns, aimed at civilians, thousands were killed and many thousands more were made refugees, fleeing to neighboring Ethiopia. Even as more and more of the country fell under the control of the SNM, Mogadishu, the Somali capital, remained in the hands of Siyaad Barre. However, in March 1989, government troops belonging to the Ogadeni clan mutinied in Kismayo. That rebellion was not put down until July. In the meantime, the SNM continued to seize control of more of the country. The violence became so intense that U.N. and other aid workers were evacuated in May 1989. When the Catholic bishop of Mogadishu fell victim to an assassin's bullet on July 9, 1989, violence became universal within the capital, forcing Siyaad Barre to announce that he would hold multiparty elections. This did not satisfy the various rebel factions, which temporarily united to thwart the elections and then staged a coup against Siyaad Barre. He clung desperately to his title, if not his office, as 1990 came to a close.

Although the promise of free elections brought a brief intermission in the civil war, rival clans, led by warlords, began the war anew. Although the warring factions were numerous and the relations among them complex, the major rivals by late 1990 were General Muhammad Farrah Aydid, of the Hawiye clan and leader of the Somali National Alliance

(SNA), and Ali Mahdi Muhammad, of a different subclan of the Hawiye clan and leader of the Somali Salvation Alliance (SSA). In January 1991, Siyaad Barre was at last definitively dislodged from the presidency (he subsequently fled the country) and was immediately replaced by Ali Mahdi. In September, however, Aydid, now chairman of the United Somali Congress (USC), challenged Ali Mahdi for the presidency. The result was renewed fighting in Mogadishu and, in effect, the end of any semblance of organized government for Somalia. No single faction had sufficient support to establish unambiguous rule.

As southern Somalia disintegrated, Muhammad Ibrahim Egal led the secession, in May 1991, of northeastern Somalia, creating the breakaway Somaliland. For a brief time Egal achieved a certain amount of stability in the breakaway region, but fighting broke out in the regional capital of Hargeysa, led by factions opposed to secession. The international community also generally refused to recognize the legitimacy of Somaliland.

The anarchic civil war devastated an already desperately poor nation and people. The delicate economy of Somalia was quickly destroyed. Organized farming was disrupted, then halted by the war. Somalia's misery was compounded by a severe drought, and by the early 1990s, some 1.5 million to 2 million Somalis were starving or close to starvation.

Beginning in 1992, U.S. president George H. Bush announced the U.S.-led and U.N.-sanctioned Operation Restore Hope, to bring humanitarian aid and order to Somalia. In December 1992, the first of a contingent of twenty-eight thousand U.N. troops, including Americans, arrived to transport and distribute food and attempt to end the violence. By the end of March 1993, much food had been delivered, but U.S. and U.N. troops had not succeeded in disarming the militias of the various warlords. In June and July 1993, Aydid stepped up the violence, killing many Somalis and some of the U.N. peacekeepers. The administration of Bill Clinton, who succeeded Bush in 1993, advocated broadening the U.N. mandate to encompass concerted action against Aydid—up to and including killing him. This resulted in dissension among the nations participating in the U.N. action. In 1994, amid confusion of objectives, Aydid acted directly against U.S. forces in Somalia, and eighteen U.S. soldiers were killed. Others were taken prisoner. American television beamed grisly images of a dead American soldier being dragged through the streets of Mogadishu. With that, popular pressure to withdraw U.S. forces from

Somalia increased. No one argued against the humanitarian purpose of Operation Restore Hope, but who could win a war in which there was no order to restore—only well-meaning U.N. peacekeepers operating at cross-purposes in a nation that offered nothing more than a choice among warlords and various versions of chaos? By March 1994, most U.S. and European troops had been withdrawn from Somalia. At this time, too, Aydid and Mahdi met in Kenya to hammer out a coalition government for Somalia.

Their meeting produced nothing but additional discord, and renewed fighting flared in Mogadishu during May and December of 1994. The next March, the nineteen thousand U.N. troops (all from African member nations) withdrew from Somalia, leaving Aydid and Mahdi both claiming leadership of the country and both occupying Mogadishu while their partisans fought one another. At this point the Somali Salvation Democratic Front (SSDF) controlled the Northeast. The rest of the nation was divided among three lesser factions. Aydid was dealt a severe blow when his chief lieutenant, Osman Hassan Ali, switched his allegiance to Mahdi. In a 1996 exchange of gunfire during one of innumerable skirmishes, Aydid was severely wounded. He died on August 1, 1996, and was succeeded by Hussein Aydid, his son.

The death of the elder Aydid brought a lull in the chronic fighting, but Somalia remained fragmented, without even a semblance of central government. In 1998, factionalism within the SSDF led to formation of a new independent state in the Northeast, Puntland, which has yet to be recognized by the international community. As of 2001, a low-level civil war continues in a nation without a functioning government.

Kosovo Crisis, 1996–1999

The *War in Bosnia, 1992–1995* resulted in an uneasy peace achieved by dividing the small country into three ethnically homogenous, self-governed areas. In the meantime, Serbia and Montenegro joined to form the Federal Republic of Yugoslavia, under the leadership of Slobodan Milosevic.

Less than a year after the War in Bosnia ended, violent civil unrest erupted in the southern Yugoslav province of Kosovo as the Kosovo Liberation Army (KLA) launched guerrilla attacks on Serbian police forces.

Early in 1998, Milosevic dispatched troops to Kosovo to crush its bid for independence, and full-scale civil war was under way. NATO and the United Nations repeatedly attempted to broker a peace, but peace talks in Rambouillet, France, dissolved in March 1999, with only the KLA finally accepting the settlement. Milosevic increased his forces in Kosovo and began a campaign of military terror against the ethnic Albanian population of the region. NATO had already authorized force, and on March 23, U.S. president Bill Clinton concurred that a NATO military response was indeed called for. The next day, NATO, spearheaded by the United States, launched air strikes against Serbian Yugoslavia, hitting targets in Serbia, Montenegro, and Kosovo. In addition to bombs dropped from aircraft, U.S. Navy ships launched cruise missiles. It was the largest Allied military assault in Europe since World War II, and it was the first time NATO had ever been mobilized for actual combat.

Despite the punishment dealt Milosevic, his forces continued to drive ethnic Albanians out of Kosovo and into Macedonia, Montenegro, and Albania. Over the next ten weeks, the United States and NATO escalated the air war, flying thirty-five thousand sorties, most of them aimed against Yugoslav military targets as well as elements of infrastructure, including water, electric, and natural gas facilities. Milosevic at last backed down on June 3, 1999, declaring his acceptance of an international peace plan.

Casualties included at least five thousand Yugoslav soldiers and perhaps as many as twelve hundred civilians. NATO lost two aircraft, including one U.S. stealth fighter. The American pilots were rescued. The most serious incident was the destruction of the Chinese embassy in Belgrade, which had been mistakenly targeted. No ground assault was launched.

The Milosevic government agreed to a military withdrawal from Kosovo and committed the government to abide by the Rambouillet accords of February 23, 1999, a three-year interim agreement, largely dictated by the United States and NATO, intended to provide democratic self-government, peace, and security for everyone, including all ethnicities, living in Kosovo. The defeat of Milosevic in the Yugoslav elections of October 2000 was a hopeful sign that the peace would hold. Additional evidence of the region's resolve to avert further war was the arrest, on June 29, 2001, of Milosevic and his delivery to a war crimes tribunal convened at the Hague, Netherlands. His trial was slated to begin in 2002.

"The First War of the Twenty-first Century"

Wars end. Books end. War goes on.

By September 11, 2001, the manuscript of this book, a narrative survey of America's wars from 1493 to "the present," was complete and had been in the publisher's hands for several weeks. Until the morning of September 11, 2001, "the present" was a most opportune time to finish a book with pretensions to *comprehensive* coverage of the history of American warfare. The United States was fighting no war, and our last significant military engagement, the *Kosovo Crisis, 1996–1999,* the final entry in this book, ended in the last year of the "old" century.

At 8:45 (EDT) on the morning of September 11, 2001, a Boeing 757 passenger jetliner—later identified as American Airlines Flight 11 out of Boston—crashed into the north tower of the World Trade Center in lower Manhattan. There was an explosion and fireball, with thick black smoke pouring from the gaping black hole the aircraft had torn in the gleaming silver skin of the 110-story skyscraper. Television crews rushed to the scene, and at 9:03, as their cameras rolled, a second 757, United Airlines Flight 175, also out of Boston, hit the as yet undamaged south tower.

During the next several minutes, emergency workers, firefighters, and police officers rushed to the site. At 9:17, the Federal Aviation

Administration shut down New York-area airports; at 9:21, all bridges and tunnels in the area were locked down; at 9:30 A.M., President George W. Bush, attending an education-related function in Sarasota, Florida, announced that the nation had suffered "an apparent terrorist attack."

It was not over. At 9:40, the FAA shut down all U.S. airports—an action unprecedented in American history—and, three minutes later, American Airlines Flight 77 crashed into the Pentagon, headquarters of the U.S. military. Two minutes after this, the White House was evacuated. Back in New York, at 10:05, the south tower of the World Trade Center, which had been hit about half way up, collapsed: 110 stories of steel, concrete, glass, and humanity, gone in an instant, engulfing lower Manhattan in an evil cloud of billowing smoke and debris. Five minutes later, outside of Washington, a portion of the stricken Pentagon collapsed, and at almost exactly the same time, United Airlines Flight 93 plowed into the earth of rural Somerset County, Pennsylvania, outside of Pittsburgh. At 10:28, the north tower of the World Trade Center collapsed, ejecting another huge plume of smoke and debris, as if a volcano had suddenly come to birth in the nation's greatest metropolis.

At this point, the people of the United States could only speculate on the magnitude of lives lost. Asked later that afternoon to estimate casualties, New York mayor Rudolph Giuliani replied, "I don't think we want to speculate about that—more than any of us can bear." At this point, too, the people could do nothing but wait, watch, and brace for more attacks. The president, in the meantime, was flown from Florida, not to the White House, but to a "secure location" at Barksdale Air Force Base, Louisiana. At 1:04 P.M., he made a televised announcement from Barksdale, declaring that the military had been put on high alert worldwide and vowing that "the United States will hunt down and punish those responsible for these cowardly acts." From Barksdale, the president was flown to Offutt Air Force Base, outside of Omaha, Nebraska—a facility built to withstand thermonuclear attack. He returned to the White House shortly before 7 P.M. By that time, Building 7 of the World Trade Center, a 47-story structure, had collapsed, and the entire World Trade Center Plaza and nearby buildings were ablaze.

By this time, too, it was being reported by the media that the airplane downed in Pennsylvania had been headed for either Camp David—the presidential retreat—the White House, or the United States Capitol. It was soon revealed that all four aircraft had been hijacked by terrorists on suicide missions. Loaded with tens of thousands of pounds of volatile jet fuel, each plane was guided missile of tremendous explosive power. Some days later, the nation would learn how cell phone calls made by crew members and passengers on the doomed aircraft—calls made to airline supervisors, to 911 operators, and, most of all, to family members—gave insight into how the terrorists had operated. Handguns carried aboard a plane would almost certainly have been detected by airport security devices, so the terrorists used knives and box cutters instead. The first three aircraft hit their targets in rapid succession: the south tower of the World Trade Center, the north tower, the Pentagon. By the time the fourth plane was being taken over, passengers who called loved ones were told of the attack on the World Trade Center. A group of them decided to take action, to attempt to wrest the plane from the hijackers' control. The result was a fiery crash—in rural Pennsylvania, and not at Camp David, the White House, or the Capitol.

As early as 4 P.M. on September 11, CNN correspondent David Ensor was reporting that U.S. officials believed there were "good indications" that Osama bin Laden was involved in the attacks. A forty-four-year-old multimillionaire sponsor of terrorism, Saudi by nationality and now living in Afghanistan, bin Laden enjoyed the protection of the radical Islamic Taliban government. He had long been suspected of having masterminded the bombings of two U.S. embassies in 1998 and the attack on the U.S. guided missile destroyer *Cole,* in port at Yemen, on October 12, 2000. For at least a decade, bin Laden had led al Qaeda (Arabic: "The Base"), a center for the indoctrination, training, coordination, and financing of Muslim terrorists dedicated to carrying out what they characterized as a *jihad*—a holy war—against Israel, the West, and especially the United States.

At 8:30 in the evening of what had been a most terrible day, President Bush addressed

An estimated 10,000 to 20,000 persons were at the World Trade Center when it was attacked. Only five survivors were pulled from the rubble in the hours and days following the attack. By the end of September, the number of missing persons, presumed killed at the World Trade Center, was 6,347. Later tallies downgraded the original count, to just under 3,300 killed at the World Trade Center, the Pentagon, and in the hijacked aircraft. Hundreds of firefighters, police officers, and other emergency workers were killed when the twin towers collapsed. At the Pentagon, the death toll reached 189, including the 64 passengers and crew of Flight 77. In the Pennsylvania crash, everyone on the plane, 44 persons, died.

The attack was immediately compared to Pearl Harbor, struck by the Japanese on December 7, 1941. The death toll there was 2,403.

517

the nation, vowing that "We will make no distinction between the terrorists who committed these acts and those who harbor them."

Bush's words amounted to a declaration of war. Indeed, on September 12, the president remarked that "We have just seen the first war of the twenty-first century," but it was on September 20, in an address to a special joint session of Congress, that President Bush made the nation's war footing unmistakably clear:

> On September the 11th, enemies of freedom committed an act of war against our country. . . .
>
> Americans have many questions tonight. Americans are asking: Who attacked our country? The evidence we have gathered all points to a collection of loosely affiliated terrorist organizations known as al Qaeda. They are the same murderers indicted for bombing American embassies in Tanzania and Kenya, and responsible for bombing the USS *Cole*. Al Qaeda is to terror what the mafia is to crime. But its goal is not making money; its goal is remaking the world—and imposing its radical beliefs on people everywhere. The terrorists practice a fringe form of Islamic extremism that has been rejected by Muslim scholars and the vast majority of Muslim clerics—a fringe movement that perverts the peaceful teachings of Islam. The terrorists' directive commands them to kill Christians and Jews, to kill all Americans, and make no distinction among military and civilians, including women and children.
>
> This group and its leader—a person named Osama bin Laden—are linked to many other organizations in different countries, including the Egyptian Islamic Jihad and the Islamic Movement of Uzbekistan. There are thousands of these terrorists in more than 60 countries. They are recruited from their own nations and neighborhoods and brought to camps in places like Afghanistan, where they are trained in the tactics of terror. They are sent back to their homes or sent to hide in countries around the world to plot evil and destruction.
>
> The leadership of al Qaeda has great influence in Afghanistan and supports the Taliban regime in controlling most of that country. In Afghanistan, we see al Qaeda's vision for the world.

Having identified the enemy, the President issued an ultimatum:

And tonight, the United States of America makes the following demands on the Taliban: Deliver to United States authorities all the leaders of al Qaeda who hide in your land.

Release all foreign nationals, including American citizens, you have unjustly imprisoned. Protect foreign journalists, diplomats and aid workers in your country.

Close immediately and permanently every terrorist training camp in Afghanistan, and hand over every terrorist, and every person in their support structure, to appropriate authorities. Give the United States full access to terrorist training camps, so we can make sure they are no longer operating.

These demands are not open to negotiation or discussion. The Taliban must act, and act immediately. They will hand over the terrorists, or they will share in their fate.

In the days following September 11, U.S. military forces were deployed to strategic positions from which they could attack Afghanistan. An intense and highly successful diplomatic effort was made to secure the support—and in some cases, the direct aid—of key world nations in prosecuting what was frankly described as a *war* against terrorism. Even Islamic nations voiced their opposition to terrorism and, in varying degrees, promised their support for American action. Pakistan, which shares a border with Afghanistan and had been a supporter of the Taliban regime, agreed to permit the United States to fly over its air space and to use certain air base facilities. Even Iran, hostile to the United States since the fall of the shah and the hostage crisis of 1979–1981, agreed to allow flyovers and to accept emergency landings. Only Iraq *(see Persian Gulf War, 1991, chapter 15)* refused cooperation and pointedly withheld expressions of condolence.

With the diplomatic front secured and military resources in place, but without a formal declaration of war, the first attack against the Taliban government of Afghanistan was launched at 16:38 Greenwich Mean Time, October 7—nighttime in Afghanistan. With support from British forces, the United States attacked using B-1 bombers and the more advanced B-2 "stealth" bombers, as well as the B-52, venerable product of the 1950s. Cruise missiles were also employed. Over the next several nights, the air war continued, and after less than a week, U.S. Air Force general Richard B. Myers, newly appointed chairman of the Joint Chiefs of Staff, announced that "air supremacy" had been attained. This meant that the Afghans' major air defenses had been effectively wiped out, and American and British aircraft could operate in Afghan air space with virtual impunity. Daylight raids were added to nighttime raids, and the high-altitude bombers were replaced by lower-altitude strike aircraft, capable of targeting more specific objectives, including such "targets of opportunity" as vehicles, aircraft on the ground, and troops.

The Pentagon consistently made it clear that it was targeting military, al Qaeda terrorist camps, and Taliban-related objectives, while trying to avoid civilian "collateral damage." Indeed, simultaneously with the air raids, U.S. cargo transports dropped food packages intended for Afghan civilians. The goal of the war in Afghanistan was to destabilize and defeat the Taliban, which sheltered Osama bin Laden, al Qaeda, and other terrorist enterprises. Beyond this was the objective of capturing or killing bin Laden himself, as well as other terrorist leaders. The initial air strikes were intended to clear the way for the necessary action on the ground.

And this is where the war promised to become a far more dicey affair. It was no surprise that air supremacy was quickly achieved. Afghanistan is a desperately poor nation, with a small conventional military (estimated at 45,000 regular troops) and a minuscule air force. Most of the arms it has were either captured from the Soviets or supplied by the United States to aid Afghan *mujahedin* "freedom fighters" (as the U.S. leaders called them) in their resistance against the Soviet invasion (December 1979) and occupation. The Soviet experience was indeed sobering for any power contemplating operations in Afghanistan. The Red Army entered the country to support the regime of a puppet prime minister, Babrak Karmal, and it did so with some 100,000 troops and modern arms and equipment. Nevertheless, that army was ultimately defeated by *mujahedin* guerrillas in what many observers characterized as the Soviets' "Vietnam."

From a perspective early in the 2001 war, it seemed unlikely that the United States would follow in Soviet footsteps by sending a large conventional army into Afghanistan. On October 20, about 100 U.S. Special Forces commandos staged a first raid on the ground, destroying some Taliban facilities and obtaining Taliban documents. Presumably, many more small-force hit-and-run operations would be made in the days and weeks to come. In further contrast to the Soviet situation, the United States was fighting a government already under attack by the so-called Northern Alliance, an army of about 15,000 opponents of the Taliban regime. By supplying the Northern Alliance and operating in concert with it, the United States could well expedite the overthrow of the Taliban. Yet (again, early in what the Bush administration predicted would be a long war) American relations with the Northern Alliance were by no means clear, as the U.S. government was wary of putting into power a regime that might prove as unpalatable as the Taliban and whose presence threatened to alienate other Islamic nations, most notably Pakistan.

The question of the role of the Northern Alliance was, of course, only one of myriad unnerving uncertainties that characterized this "first war of the twenty-first century." While the bombing and commando action was taking place far away in one of the most remote places of the world, the terror had hit home and had clearly infiltrated the American homeland. FBI and other investigators rapidly exposed the suicide hijackers of the four September 11 flights as men of Middle Eastern origin who had trained in small American flight schools, who had lived in American motels and apartment complexes, who had hardened their bodies in American neighborhood gyms, who had banked at American banks, and who had withdrawn cash from local ATMs.

How many more terrorists were still in the United States, Canada, and Europe? U.S. and international law enforcement agencies made many arrests and detained more than a thousand suspected terrorists by late October 2001. But threats continued to hang over the nation. In a video-taped message recorded, apparently, in a cave in Afghanistan and broadcast to the Arab world as well as the United States, Osama bin Laden himself promised that the "storm of planes" would resume and pledged that Americans would continue to suffer as long as the United States supported Israel against the Palestinians. Even more disquietingly, our own FBI issued vague warnings of more terror attacks to come.

What form would these attacks take?

On October 4, U.S. health officials reported that a Florida man, a photo editor for a supermarket tabloid newspaper, had contracted anthrax—the first case in the United States since the 1970s. Although authorities played down a possible link between the infection and terrorism, anthrax was well known as a bioterrorist weapon, having been produced in massive quantities by the former Soviet Union and (according to U.S. and U.N. intelligence) probably still in production by Iraq. The Florida man succumbed to the disease on October 5, a second instance of exposure was discovered on October 8, and a third on October 10. On

October 12, it was announced that an employee of NBC news, personal assistant to the popular anchor Tom Brokaw, was infected with cutaneous anthrax. The source of these infections were letters laced with dry anthrax spores—the anthrax bacillus deliberately weaponized—and in the course of October, at least forty persons were found to have been exposed to anthrax. A few became ill, either with the highly treatable cutaneous form of the disease or the far more lethal inhalation anthrax. One anthrax-laced letter reached the office of Senate minority leader Tom Daschle, and on October 17, 31 members of Daschle's staff tested positive for anthrax exposure. The Capitol and several Senate and House office buildings were temporarily shut down for testing and decontamination. Tragically, however, the tainted letter (or perhaps some other piece of tainted mail) contaminated a Washington, D.C., postal facility, fatally infecting two postal employees.

On October 23, it was announced that anthrax spores had been detected in an army base facility that screens White House mail.

"I don't have anthrax," George W. Bush told a press conference later in the day. It was not a sentence the American people had ever thought to hear from a United States president. But, then, what American ever thought the nation would be engaged in a war against Afghanistan, let alone a war with that nation waged in response to unprecedented aggression against our people? Was the anthrax attack the work of Osama bin Laden and al Qaeda? Or was Saddam Hussein's Iraq responsible for it? Or was it an instance of "homegrown" terrorism? It was natural to see the hand of bin Laden in the attacks, but this was no more than a hunch or, at best, a surmise. All that was certain was that, on the cusp of the twenty-first century, America stood at the threshold of what was for it a new kind of war, "asymmetric" as military planners and theorists call it, a war in which a puny power can leverage the most modest of resources to create a disproportionate threat even against the world's only superpower.

During November, anthrax fears eased somewhat as reports of new cases dwindled and then ceased. The major headlines of this month told of the progress of combined U.S. and Northern Alliance attacks against Taliban positions in Afghanistan. By November 12, Mazar-e Sharif, vital gateway between Afghanistan and Taliban sympathizers in Pakistan, fell to the Northern Alliance after a pounding by U.S. aircraft. On November 13, the Afghan capital city of Kabul was occupied by Northern Alliance troops, and at the end of the month, Kunduz, a northern Taliban stronghold, also fell. This left Khandahar as the only major Taliban-held city, and, after a long siege, it seemed by early December about to fall.

Yet the apparent defeat of the Taliban, as President Bush repeatedly observed, would not mean an end to the war on terrorism. Osama bin-Laden and many al-Qaeda leaders were still on the loose, a new Afghan government had yet to be created, and other nations, paramountly Iraq, loomed as targets of future American assaults against the sources of international terrorism.

Sources

Acheson, Dean. *The Korean War.* New York: Norton, 1971.

Adams, Michael C. C. *The Best War Ever: America and World War II.* Baltimore: Johns Hopkins University Press, 1994.

Addington, Larry. *America's War in Vietnam: A Short Narrative History.* Bloomington: Indiana University Press, 2000.

Alexander, Bevin. *Korea: The First War We Lost.* New York: Hippocrene Books, 1986.

Ambrose, Stephen E. *Citizen Soldiers: The U.S. Army from the Normandy Beaches to the Bulge to the Surrender of Germany, June 7, 1944–May 7, 1945.* New York: Simon & Schuster, 1997.

Andrews, Charles M. *The Colonial Period of American History.* 1934–1938. Reprint, New Haven, Conn.: Yale University Press, 1964.

Andrist, Ralph K. *The Long Death: The Last Days of the Plains Indians.* New York: Macmillan/Collier, 1969.

Appleman, Roy. *Ridgway Duels for Korea.* College Station, Tex.: Texas A&M University Press, 1990.

Axelrod, Alan. *American Treaties and Alliances.* Washington, D.C.: CQ Press, 2000.

———. *Chronicle of the Indian War: From Colonial Times to Wounded Knee.* New York: Macmillan, 1993.

———. *My Brother's Face: Portraits of the Civil War.* San Francisco: Chronicle Books, 1993.

Axelrod, Alan, and Charles Phillips. *The Dictionary of Military Biography.* New York: Macmillan, 1997.

Baldwin, Hanson Weightman. *The Crucial Years, 1939–1945: The World at War.* New York: Harper & Row, 1976.

Barbeau, Arthur E. *The Unknown Soldiers: African American Troops in World War I.* 1974. Reprint, New York: Da Capo, 1996.

Becker, Elizabeth. *America's Vietnam War: A Narrative History.* New York: Clarion, 1992.

Bergerund, Eric M. *Fire in the Sky: The Air War in the South Pacific.* Boulder, Colo.: Westview Press, 1999.

Boatner, Mark M. *Civil War Dictionary,* rev. ed. New York: McKay, 1959.

———. *Encyclopedia of the American Revolution.* New York: McKay, 1966, 1974.

Boettcher, Thomas. *First Call: The Making of the Modern U.S. Military, 1945–1953.* Boston: Little, Brown, 1992.

Boritt, Gabor S. *Lincoln's Generals.* New York: Oxford University Press, 1994.

Brady, James. *The Coldest War: A Memoir of Korea.* New York: Orion Books, 1990.

Brogan, Hugh. *The Penguin History of the United States of America.* New York: Penguin, 1985.

Brogan, Patrick. *The Fighting Never Stopped: A Comprehensive Guide to World Conflict since 1945.* New York: Vintage Books, 1990.

Burg, David F., and L. Edward Purcell. *Almanac of World War I.* Lexington: University Press of Kentucky, 1998.

Buttinger, Joseph. *Vietnam: A Dragon Embattled,* 2 vols. New York: Praeger, 1967.

Catton, Bruce. *The Coming Fury.* Garden City, N.Y.: Doubleday, 1961.

———. *Glory Road.* 1952. reprint, New York: Anchor Books, 1990.

———. *Mr. Lincoln's Army.* 1951. Reprint, New York: Anchor Books, 1990.

———. *Never Call Retreat.* Garden City, N.Y.: Doubleday, 1965.

———. *A Stillness at Appomattox.* 1953. Reprint, New York: Anchor Books, 1990.

———. *Terrible Swift Sword.* Garden City, N.Y.: Doubleday, 1963.

———. *This Hallowed Ground.* Garden City, N.Y.: Doubleday, 1955.

Chambers, John Whiteclay II, et al., eds. *The Oxford Companion to American Military History.* New York: Oxford University Press, 1999.

Clark, Alan. *Aces High: The War in the Air over the Western Front, 1914–1918.* New York: Ballantine Books, 1973.

Clark, Mark. *From the Danube to the Yalu.* New York: Harper & Brothers, 1954.

Coffman, Edward M. *The War to End All Wars: The American Military Experience in World War I.* Madison: Unviersity of Wisconsin Press, 1986.

Commager, Henry Steele, and Richard B. Morris, eds. *The Spirit of 'Seventy-Six: The Story of the American Revolution as Told by Participants.* New York: Harper & Row, 1958, 1976.

Cornish, Dudley Taylor. *The Sable Arm: Black Troops in the Union Army, 1861–1865.* Lawrence: University Press of Kansas, 1987.

Davidson, General Phillip B. *Vietnam at War: The History 1946–1975.* Novato, Calif.: Presidio, 1988.

Davis, Burke. *Sherman's March.* New York: Random House, 1980.

Davis, William C. *The Commanders of the Civil War.* New York: Salamander Books, 1990.

Debo, Angie. *A History of the Indians in the United States.* Norman: University of Oklahoma Press, 1977.

Denney, Robert F. *The Civil War Years: A Day-by-Day Chronicle of the Life of a Nation.* New York: Sterling, 1992.

Duiker, William J. *Sacred War: Nationalism and Revolution in a Divided Vietnam.* New York: McGraw-Hill, 1995.

Dupuy, R. Ernest, and Trevor N. Dupuy. *The Compact History of the Civil War.* New York: Warner Books, 1993.

————. *The Harper Encyclopedia of Military History: From 3500 B.C. to the Present,* 4th ed. New York: HarperCollins, 1993.

Dupuy, Trevor N. *The Military History of World War I.* New York: Watts, 1967.

Dvorchak, Robert, et al. *Battle for Korea: The Associated Press History of the Korean Conflict.* Conshohocken, Pa.: Combined Books, 1993.

Edmonds, Anthony O. *The War in Vietnam.* Westport, Conn.: Greenwood, 1998.

Eisenhower, David. *Eisenhower at War, 1943–1945.* New York: Random House, 1986.

Esper, George, and the Associated Press. *The Eyewitness History of the Vietnam War, 1961–1975.* New York: Ballantine Books, 1983.

Fehrenbach, T. R. *The Fight for Korea: From the War of 1950 to the Pueblo Incident.* New York: Grosset & Dunlap, 1969.

Ferguson, Niall. *The Pity of War: Explaining World War I.* New York: Basic Books, 2000.

Fitzgerald, Frances. *Fire in the Lake: The Vietnamese and the Americans in Vietnam.* New York: Random House, 1972.

Foote, Shelby. *The Civil War: A Narrative,* Vol. 1, *Fort Sumter to Perryville.* 1958. Vol. 2, *Fredericksburg to Meridian.* 1963. Vol. 3, *Red River to Appomattox.* 1974. All reprint eds. New York: Vintage, 1986.

Forty, George. *At War in Korea.* London, Engl.: Allan, 1982.

Freeman, Douglas Southall. *Lee.* New York: Scribner's, 1934.

Gaddis, John Lewis. *Cold War Statesmen Confront the Bomb: Nuclear Diplomacy since 1945.* New York: Oxford University Press, 1999.

————. *We Now Know: Rethinking Cold War History.* Oxford: Clarendon Press; New York: Oxford University Press, 1997.

Gardner, Lloyd. *The Korean War.* New York: Quadrangle Books, 1972.

Giangreco, D. M. *War in Korea: 1950–1953.* Novato, Calf.: Presidio Press, 1990.

Gibson, Charles. *Spain in America.* New York: Harper & Row, 1966.

Gilbert, Martin. *The First World War: A Complete History.* New York: Holt, 1994.

Goulden, Joseph. *Korea: The Untold Story of the War.* New York: Times Books, 1982.

Gragg, Rod. *The Illustrated Confederate Reader.* 1989. Reprint, New York: Harper-Perennial, 1991.

Gray, Randal, and Christopher Argyl, eds. *Chronicle of the First World War,* 2 vols. New York: Facts on File, 1990, 1991.

Greenfield, Kent Roberts. *American Strategy in World War II: A Reconsideration.* Baltimore: Johns Hopkins University Press, 1963.

Griffiths, William R. *The Great War.* Wayne, N.J.: Avery, 1986.

Halliday, Jon, and Bruce Cumings. *Korea: The Unknown War.* New York: Pantheon, 1988.

Harrison, James. *The Endless War: Vietnam's Struggle for Independence.* New York: McGraw-Hill, 1983.

Harwell, Richard B. *The Confederate Reader: How the South Saw the War.* 1957. Reprint, New York: Dover, 1989.

Hastings, Max. *The Korean War.* New York: Simon & Schuster, 1987.

———. *Overlord: D-Day and the Battle for Normandy.* New York: Simon & Schuster, 1984.

Hearden, Patrick J. *The Tragedy of Vietnam.* New York: HarperCollins, 1991.

Herring, George C. *America's Longest War: The United States and Vietnam, 1950–1975,* 3rd ed. New York: McGraw-Hill, 1996.

Hersey, John. *Hiroshima,* new ed. New York: Knopf, 1985.

Hoehling, Adolph A. *The Great War at Sea: A History of Naval Action, 1914–1918.* London: Baker, 1965.

Hough, Richard. *The Great War at Sea, 1914–1918.* Oxford: Oxford University Press, 1983.

Ienaga, Saburo. *The Pacific War: World War II and the Japanese, 1931–1945.* New York: Pantheon, 1978.

James, Dorris Clayton. *The Years of MacArthur,* 3 vols. Boston: Houghton Mifflin, 1970–1985.

Jamieson, Neil L. *Understanding Vietnam.* Berkeley: University of California Press, 1993.

Jensen, Merrill. *The New Nation: A History of the United States during the Confederation, 1781–1789.* 1950. Reprint, Boston: Northeastern University Press, 1981.

Karabell, Zachary. *Architects of Intervention: The United States, the Third World, and the Cold War, 1946–1962.* Baton Rouge: Louisiana State University Press, 1999.

Karnow, Stanley. *Vietnam: A History.* New York: Viking, 1983.

Keegan, John. *The First World War.* New York: Knopf, 1999.

———. *The Second World War.* London: Hutchinson, 1989.

Kennedy, David M. *Over Here: The First World War and American Society.* New York: Oxford University Press, 1982.

Kennett, Lee. *The First Air War, 1914–1918.* New York: Free Press, 1991.

Kolko, Gabriel. *Anatomy of a War: Vietnam, the United States, and the Modern Historical Experience.* New York: Pantheon, 1985.

Krepinevich, Andrew F. Jr. *The Army in Vietnam.* Baltimore: Johns Hopkins University Press, 1986.

Lamar, Howard R. *The Reader's Encyclopedia of the American West.* New York: Crowell, 1977.

Leckie, Robert. *George Washington's War: The Saga of the American Revolution.* New York: HarperPerennial, 1992.

Lewis, Jon E. *The Mammoth Book of War Diaries and Letters: Life on the Battlefield in the Words of the Ordinary Soldier, 1775–1991*. New York: Carroll & Graf, 1999.

Lewy, Guenter. *America in Vietnam*. New York: Oxford University Press, 1978.

Lucas, Scott. *Freedom's War: The American Crusade against the Soviet Union*. New York: New York University Press, 1999.

MacDonald, Charles Brown. *The Mighty Endeavor: American Armed Forces in the European Theater in World War II*. New York: Oxford University Press, 1969.

MacQueen, Norrie. *The United Nations since 1945: Peacekeeping and the Cold War*. New York: Addison-Wesley Longman, 1999.

Margiotta, Franklin D., ed. *Brassey's Encyclopedia of Military History and Biography*. Washington, D.C.: Brassey's, 2000.

Matloff, Maurice. *American Military History*. Vol. 2, 1902–1996. Conshohocken, Pa.: Combine Books, 1996.

Matray, James I., ed. *Historical Dictionary of the Korean War*. New York: Greenwood Press, 1991.

McFeely, William S. *Grant: A Biography*. New York: Norton, 1981.

McPherson, James M. *Battle Cry of Freedom*. New York: Oxford University Press, 1988.

McPherson, James M., ed. *The Atlas of the Civil War*. New York: Macmillan, 1994.

Messenger, Charles. *Trench Fighting, 1914–1918*. New York: Ballantine Books, 1972.

Mitrovich, Gregory, *Undermining the Kremlin: America's Strategy to Subvert the Soviet Bloc, 1947–1956*. Ithaca, N.Y.: Cornell University Press, 2000.

Olson, James S., and Randy Roberts. *Where the Domino Fell: America and Vietnam, 1945–1990*, 2nd ed. New York: St. Martin's Press, 1996.

Phillips, Charles, and Alan Axelrod. eds. *Encyclopedia of the American West*, 4 vols. New York: Macmillan, 1996.

———. *My Brother's Face: Portraits of the Civil War*. San Francisco: Chronicle Books, 1992.

Prange, Gordon William. *At Dawn We Slept: The Untold Story of Pearl Harbor*. New York: McGraw-Hill, 1981.

Prucha, Francis P. *The Great Father: The United States Government and the American Indians*. Lincoln: University of Nebraska Press, 1984.

Purcell, L. Edward, and David F. Burg. *The World Almanac of the American Revolution*. New York: World Almanac, 1992.

Quinn, David B., ed. *North American Discovery Circa 1000–1612*. New York: Harper & Row, 1971.

Ridgway, Matthew. *The Korean War*. Garden City, N.Y.: Doubleday, 1967.

Robertson, James I. Jr. *Soldiers Blue and Gray*. Columbia: University of South Carolina Press, 1988.

Ryan, Cornelius. *The Longest Day: June 6, 1944.* New York: Simon & Schuster, 1959.

Sears, Stephen W. *Campaign.* New York: Ticknor & Fields, 1992.

Shrader, Charles Reginald, ed. *Reference Guide to United States Military History, 1945 to the Present.* New York: Facts on File, 1995.

———. *Reference Guide to United States Military History, 1865–1919.* New York: Facts on File, 1993.

Sibley, Katherine A. S. *The Cold War.* Westport, Conn.: Greenwood Press, 1998.

Sifakis, Stewart. *Who Was Who in the Civil War.* New York: Facts on File, 1988.

Smith, Page. *A New Age Begins: A People's History of the American Revolution,* 2 vols. New York: Viking Penguin, 1976.

Spector, Ronald H. *Eagle Against the Sun: The American War with Japan.* New York: Free Press, 1985.

Stokesbury, James L. *A Short History of the American Revolution.* New York: William Morrow, 1991.

Tuchman, Barbara W. *The Zimmermann Telegram.* New York: Viking, 1958.

Tucker, Spencer C., ed. *The European Powers in the First World War: An Encyclopedia.* New York: Garland, 1996.

Venzon, Anne Cipriano, ed. *The United States in the First World War: An Encyclopedia.* New York: Garland, 1995.

Washburn, Wilcomb. *The Indian in America.* New York: Harper & Row, 1975.

Watkins, Sam R. *"Co. Aytch": A Side Show of the Big Show.* New York: Macmillan, 1962.

Weigley, Russell F. *The American Way of War: A History of United States Military Strategy and Policy.* Bloomington: Indiana University Press, 1977.

Wertz, Jay, and Edwin C. Bearss. *Smithsonian's Great Battles and Battlefields of the Civil War.* New York: Morrow, 1997.

Wheeler, Richard. *Voices of the Civil War.* 1976. Reprint, New York: Meridian, 1990.

Wiley, Bell Irvin. *The Life of Billy Yank: The Common Soldier of the Union.* 1953. Reprint, Baton Rouge: Louisiana State University Press, 1978.

———. *The Life of Johnny Reb: The Common Soldier of the Confederacy.* 1943. Reprint, Baton Rouge: Louisiana State University Press, 1978.

Wilmoth, H. P. *The Great Crusade: A New Complete History of the Second World War.* New York: Free Press, 1989.

Winter, Denis. *Death's Men: Soldiers of the Great War.* New York: Penguin, 1993.

Zinn, Howard. *A People's History of the United States 1492–Present.* New York: HarperPerennial, 1995.

Index

Note: **Boldface** page numbers indicate extended discussion of topic. *Italic* page numbers indicate illustration subjects not otherwise mentioned on page.

Abercromby, James, 82, 85, 86-87
Abnaki Indians, 42, 43-44, 53-57, 59, 64-65, 67, 73, 74
Acadians, 55, 59, 66, 72, 76
Acoma Revolt (1599), **10–11**
Adams, John, 109, 113, 122, 171
Adams, John Quincy, 206
Adams, Samuel, 107, 109
Afghanistan, 519–22
African Americans, 189, 259, 332, 347. *See also* slavery
Afrika Korps, 405, 406, 505
Aguinaldo, Emilio, 338–39, 344, 349, 351, 352
Aisne-Marne offensive (1918), 369
Aix-la-Chapelle, Treaty of (1748), 67–68, 69
Alamance Creek, Battle of (1771), 102
Alamo (Texas), 208, 209–11, 341
Albany Congress (1754), 74
Aleutian Islands, 384, 400, 402, 411–12
Alger, Russel M., 343, 347, 348
Algerine War (1815), **188–89**
Algonquian-Dutch War (Kieft's War) (1639–1645), **27–30**, 34
Algonquian tribes, 16–17, 18, 28–29, 43–44, 67, 73
Ali Mahdi Muhammad, 512, 513
Allatoona Pass, Battle of (1864), 293–94
Allen, Ethan, 106, 107, 119
Alvarado, Pedro de, 8

Amelia Springs, Battle of (1865), 298
American fighting spirit, 1, 5
American-French Quasi-War (1798–1800), 2, **169–72**
American Revolution (1775–1783), **104–61**, 301
    background, 105, 107, 162–64, 168–69
    chronology, 106–7
    Indian alliances, 22, 115, 119, 134, 142–45, 164
    turning points, 140, 155
    veterans' rebellion, 162–64
Amherst, Jeffrey, 87, 90, 92, 95, 97, 98
Amiens offensive (1918), 377
Anderson, Robert, 253–54
Anderson, William ("Bloody Bill"), 260
Andros, Edmund, 41, 46, 47, 50
anthrax cases, 521–22
Antietam, Battle of (1862), 250, 268–69, 281
antiwar movements
    United States—Mexican War, 335
    Vietnam War, 460, *478*, 480, 484
    War of 1812, 183
Anzio landing (1944), 385, 421, 422
Apache and Navajo War (1860–1868), **238–41**, 260
Apaches, 9, 48–50, 68, 238
Apache War, **314–19**
appeasement policy (1930s), 389–90

Appomattox Court House (1865), 251, 299

Arab League, 493–94

Arapaho Indians, 302–7, 324

Ardennes offensive (1944–1945), 385, 427–28, 430

Arias Sanchez, Oscar, 498–99

Arista, Mariano, 217, 218, 219

Arnhem, Battle of (1944), 426–27

Arnold, Benedict, 106, 115, 118–21, 134, 138–40, 156–57

Aroostook War (1838–1839), **192**

Articles of Confederation, 162, 164

Atkinson, Henry, 200–203

Atlanta Campaign (1864), 250, 251, 287, 291–94

Atlantic, Battle of the (1939–1945), 406–7, 421

Atlantic Charter, 384, 393, 394

atomic bomb. *See* nuclear weapons

Attucks, Crispus, 109

Auden, W. H., 440

Augur, Christopher C., 233, 313

Austin, Moses, 191, 205

Austin, Stephen F., 191, 205–8

Austria, 56, 353, 354, 389, 390

Austro-Hungarian Empire, 368, 369, 370, 371, 381, 382, 508

Aydid, Muhammad Farrah, 511–12, 513

Aztec empire, 8

Babel, Jacques, 1–2

Bacon, Nathaniel, 45–48

Bacon's Rebellion (1676), **44–48**

Badoglio, Pietro, 408, 412

Baker, James, 504

Balkans, 6, 369–70, 508–10, 513–14

Ball's Bluff, Battle of (1861), 256

Baltimore, Battle of (1814), 176, 184

Banks, Nathaniel, 263, 278

Bannock Indians, 308, 330–31

Bannock War (1878), 308, **328–29**

Barbary Wars, 2, 172–74, 188–89

Barnwell, John, 60–61

Bastogne defense (1944), 427–28

Bataan Peninsula, 384, 385, 420

  Death March (1942), 398–99

Battle of . . . *See key word*

Baum, Frederick, 134, 135

Bayard, Nicholas, 51

Baylor, John Robert, 239, 260

Bear Flag Rebellion (1846), 205, **212–15**

Beaujeu, Liénard, 77, 78

Beauregard, P.G.T., 253–54, 255, 257, 290

Beaver Wars. *See* Iroquoian Beaver Wars

Bee, Barnard, 255

Beirut, 491, 492, 499, 500

Belcher, Jonathan, Jr., 93

Belgium, 370, 381, 384, 388, 392, 427–28

Belleau Wood, Battle of (1918), 369, 374–75

Bemis Heights, Battle of (1777), 106, 139–40

Bennington, Battle of (1777), 134–35, 138

Benteen, Frederick W., 321–22

Benton, Thomas Hart, 213

Berkeley, William, 15, 45, 46, 47, 48

Bermuda Hundred, Battle of (1864), 289–90

Bernard, Reuben F., 329, 330

Bien Hoa air base attack (1964), 469, 471

Big Dry Wash, Battle of (1882), 317

Big Eagle (Sioux warrior), 241, 242

bin Laden, Osama, 517, 518, 520, 522

bioterrorism, 97, 98, 100, 521–22

Birch Coulee, Battle of (1862), 243–44

Birch Creek, Battle of (1878), 329

Black Fish (Shawnee), 102–3, 144

Black Hand society, 369, 370

Black Hawk War (1832), 3, **199–204**

Black Hills, 320–25

Black Kettle (Cheyenne), 303, 309

"Black Legend," 8

Black Point, Battle of (1835), 197

Bladensburg, Battle of (1814), 176, 183–84

"Bleeding Kansas" Guerrilla War (1854–1861), **247–49**, 251

Blitzkrieg warfare, 385

Bloody Act (1771), 102

Bloody Marsh, Battle of (1742), 66

Blount, Tom, 61, 63
Blue Jacket (Shawnee), 144, 164–68
Boleck (Seminole chief), 190, 199
Bonhomme Richard (ship), 106, 151
Boone, Daniel, 144
Booth, John Wilkes, 251, 299
Bosnia-Herzegovina, 508–10, 513
Boston Charley (Modoc leader), 312
Boston Massacre (1770), 109
Boston Tea Party, 109–11
Bougainville invasion (1943), 384, 409
Bouquet, Henry, 86, 97, 98–100
Bowdoin, James, 162, 163
Bowie, Jim, 209–10
Boxer Rebellion (1899–1901), **352–57**
Bozeman Trail, 304–6, 307
Braddock, Edward, 70, 75–81, 83
Bradford, William, 42
Bradley, Omar, 406, 408, 422, 425–27
Bradstreet, John, 81–82, 87, 88
Bragg, Braxton, 276, 277, 283–87
Brandy Station, Battle of (1863), 274–75
Brandywine, Battle of (1777), 106,
    135–36
Brant, Joseph, 90, 142–43, 145–46
Breckenridge, John C., 289
Breed's Hill, Battle of (1775), 117–18
British Band, 200–204
British East India Company, 110–11
Brock, Isaac, 178, 180
Brodhead, Daniel, 143, 145, 146
Brokaw, Tom, 522
Brown, Jacob, 217, 219
Brown, John, 249, 251, 252
Buchanan, James, 253
Buckner, Simon Bolivar, 276
Buckner, Simon Bolivar, Jr., 433
Buddhist monks (Vietnam), 468
Buell, Don Carlos, 256, 276, 277
Buell, George P., 314, 315
Buena Vista, Battle of (1847), 216,
    223–24
Buffalo Bill, 310, 333
Buffalo Horn (Bannock chief), 328–29
Buffalo Soldiers, 332
Buford, Abraham, 152
Buford, John, 279–80

Bulge, Battle of the (1944–1945), 385,
    427–28, 430
Bullard, Robert Lee, 374, 380
Bull Run, 250, 254–55, 268, 273, 281
Bunau-Varilla, Philippe, 359–60
Bundy, McGeorge, 471
Bunker Hill, Battle of (1775), 116–18,
    121
Burgoyne, John, 106, 116, 132–33, 135,
    137–40
Burke, Edmund, 105
Burma, 385, 399–400, 413–15, 430–31
Burma Road, 400, 415, 430
Burnside, Ambrose E., 250, 262, 269–72,
    291
Burr, Aaron, 126
Bush, George H., 498, 501, 503–5, 506,
    512
Bush, George W., 516–19, 521, 522
Bushwhackers, 260
Bushy Run, Battle of (1763), 98–100
Bustamente, Anastasia, 207
Butler, Benjamin, 264, 287, 289–90
Butler, Smedley D., 361, 362–63

Cadwalader, John, 129, 130
Cajuns, 76
Calhoun, John C., 248
Calley, William L., Jr., 460
Calvert, Cecil, 33
Calvert, Leonard, 32–33
Cambodia, 459, 475, 480, 487
    invasion of (1970), 460, 484, 485
Camden (S.C.), Battle of (1780), 106,
    152–55
Campbell, Donald, 96–97
Canada
    French and Indian War, 70, 71, 72, 76,
        84–94
    Huron Indians, 33–34
    Iroquois-French Wars, 30–31
    King George's War, 66–67
    King William's War, 54–55
    Queen Anne's War, 57–58, 59
    surrender to British, 92
    U.S. boundary, 185, 192
    War of 1812, 3, 175, 177–80, 181

Canby, Edward R. S., 3, 239, 240, 260, 300, 312
Cannae, Battle of (216 B.C.), 155
Canonchet (Canonicus), 19, 41
Cantigny, Battle of (1918), 369, 374
Capes, Battle of the (1781), 159
Captain Jack (Modoc), 311, 312
Cárdenas, Julio, 365
Caribbean area, 36, 70, 93
    American Revolution, 141, 147–48, 150, 159
    Columbus voyages, 1, 7–8
    Grenada Intervention, 499–501
    Quasi-War with France, 171–72
    U.S. imperialism, 4, 335, 344–51
Carleton, Guy, 119, 120, 121, 123
Carleton, James Henry, 240, 261
Carr, Eugene, 309, 310, 316
Carranza, Venustiano, 363–65, 371–72
Carrington, Henry B., 304–5
Carson, Kit, 239, 240–41
Carter, Jimmy, 497
Cass, Lewis, 248
Cassino attacks (1944), 385, 421–22
Castro, José, 213, 215
Cayuga Indians, 22, 103, 142
Cayuse Indians, 231–35, 308
Cedar Creek, Battle of (1864), 296
Central America
    filibustering in, 335–37
    limited wars, 6, 494–99, 501–3
    U.S. imperialism, 4, 335, 359–63, 366–67
Central Highlands campaign (1965–1966), 472, 473, 475
Central Intelligence Agency, 468, 469, 496, 497, 498
Cerro Gordo, Battle of (1847), 216, 225–26
Cervera y Topete, Pascual, 344–45, 348
Chaffee, Adna R., 317, 318, 355
Chamberlain, Neville, 389–90, 392
Chamorro, Pedro Joaquin, 494
Chamorro Vargas, Emiliano, 361, 366
Chamoun, Camille, 490, 491
Champlain, Samuel de, 30

Chancellorsville, Battle of (1863), 250, 272–74, 287, 289
Chapultepec, Battle of (1847), 216, 227
Château-Thierry, Battle of (1918), 369, 374, 375
Chato (Apache leader), 316, 318
Chattanooga, Battle of (1863), 250, 283–85, 286
Chavez, J. Francisco, 240, 241
chemical defoliation, 467
Chennault, Claire, 399, 415, 444
Cherokee Indians, 3, 57, 63, 66, 70, 94, 165, 209
    American Revolution, 143, 144
    as Confederate allies, 259, 300
    Creek War, 187, 188
    Indian Removal Act, 193, 194–96
Cherokee Uprising (1769–1762), **94**
Cherry Valley Massacre (1778), 106, 142–43
Chew, Benjamin, 137
Cheyenne and Arapaho War (1864–1865), **302–4**
Cheyenne Indians, 244, 302–10, 312–14, 320–25
Chiang Kai-shek, 415, 461
Chickamauga, Battle of (1863), 284–85
Chickasaw Bluffs, Battle of (1862), 277–78
Chickasaw Indians, 57, 66, 193, 194
Chickasaw Resistance (1720–1724), **63–64**
China, 4, 6, 335
    Boxer Rebellion, 352–57
    Communists, 446–47, 461
    Japanese war, 395, 431
    Korean War, 442, 446, 450–55, 458
    Nixon/Kissinger policy, 482
    Vietnam War, 461, 464
    World War II, 313, 392, 399–401, 413–14, 415, 430
Chippewa, Battle of (1814), 176
Chippewas. *See* Ojibwa Indians
Chiricahua Apaches, 238, 239, 314, 316–19
Chivington, John M., 261, 302, 303
Choctaws, 57, 63–64, 93, 193, 194

Church, Benjamin, 39–43, 55, 57
Churchill, Winston, 385, 392–94, 405, 414, 422
Churubusco, Battle of (1847), 216, 227
Civil War (1861–1865), 3–4, **249–301**
  background, 246–49
  chronology, 250–51
  Confederate surrender, 299, 300
  Indian uprisings, 238–45
  military costliness, 3–4, 301
  rapid mobilization, 5
  "single bloodiest day," 269–70
  in Southwest, 238–40, 251, 261
  turning points, 250, 279, 283
  westernmost action, 261
Clark, George Rogers, 144–45, 164
Clark, Mark, 412, 422, 457
Clark, William, 130
Clay, Henry, 175, 248
Clearwater, Battle of (1877), 327
Clemenceau, Georges, 382
Cleveland, Grover, 339
Clinch, Duncan, 189–90, 198
Clinton, Bill, 512, 514
Clinton, Henry, 116, 118, 124, 139, 141, 147–49, 152, 157–59
Cochise (Apache chief), 238–40, 316
Cody, William F., 310, 333
Coercive Acts, 111
Coeur d'Alene War (Spokane War) (1858), **236–37**
Coffee, John, 187
Cohan, George M., 373
Cold Harbor, Battle of (1864), 250, 290
Cold War era, 5, 6, 489–514
  containment policy, 5, 489
  domino theory, 464, 468, 471
Cole bombing (2000), 517
Columbus, Christopher, 1, 7–8, 12
Comanches, 68, 304, 307, 309–10
  Red River War, 312–14
Common Sense (Paine), 122
communism, 5, 383, 386, 440
  Yugoslavia, 508–9
  See also China; Cold War era; Soviet Union
Compromise of 1850, 246, 248

Concord, Battle of (1775), 106, 113–15
Confederate States of America, 221, 239, 246, 253–54, 259–61
  Emancipation Proclamation, 270
  Proclamation of Amnesty and Pardon, 300
  See also Civil War
Confederate Territory of Arizona, 260, 261
conquistadors, 1, 8–11, 12
conscription. *See* draft
Constitution ("Old Ironsides"), 181
Constitution, U.S., 164
containment policy, 5, 489
Continental Congress, First, 111–12
Continental Congress, Second, 115, 116, 122, 135, 136, 141
Continental notes, 162
Contras, 367, 496, 497–99
Contrecoeur, Claude-Pierre Pécaudy de, 72, 77
Contreras, Battle of (1847), 216
Conway Cabal, 140
Coral Sea, Battle of (1942), 384, 401–2
Corinth, Battle of (1862), 277
Cornstalk (Shawnee chief), 103, 104, 143
Cornwallis, Charles, 124, 128, 130, 131, 136, 137, 152–60
Coronado, Francisco Vazquez de, 1, 9–10
Corregidor, 384, 385, 398, 420
Cortés, Hernán, 8, 9
Cowpens, Battle of (1781), 106, 154–55, 156
Crater, Battle of the (1864), 291
Craven, Charles, 63, 83, 93
Crawford, Emmet, 318–19
Crazy Horse (Sioux leader), 306, 320, 322, 323, 324
Creeks, 57, 63, 66, 94, 176, 180
  Indian Removal Act, 193, 196–97
  Seminole wars, 190–91, 196–97
Creek War (1812–1814), 3, 185, **186–88**, 193
Cresap, Michael, 102, 103
Crittenden, Thomas Leonidas, 285

Croatia, 509–10
Croce, Leonard, 361
Crockett, Davy, 187, 209, 210–11
Croghan, George, 67, 102, 103, 181
Cromwell, Oliver, 15
Crook, George, 308, 317–21, 324
Crow Indians, 320–21, 323, 327–28
Crown Point, 116, 118, 120, 121
Cuba, 8, 70, 93
    Cold War era, 497, 499, 501
    Spanish-American War, 339–48, 350
Curtis, Samuel R., 259, 260
Custer, George A., 299, 306–7, 309, 310,
    320–22
Czechoslovakia, 390, 436

Dakota Indians, 241–45
Daschle, Tom, 522
Davis, Jefferson, 221, 223–24, 259, 292,
    296, 298
Davis, Jefferson Columbus, 285
Davis, Wirt, 318, 319
Dayton peace accords (1995), 510
D-Day invasion (1944), 385, 422–25
Deane, Silas, 122, 131
Dearborn, Henry, 138, 179
Decatur, Stephen, 171, 174, 188–89
Declaration of Independence, 122–23
Declaration of Rights and Grievances,
    108
Declaratory Act (1766), 108
de Gaulle, Charles, 392
De Kalb, Baron, 153
Delaware, Washington crossing of, 106,
    128–29, 130
Delaware Indians, 23, 34, 71, 103, 104
    American Revolution, 143–44, 146
    French and Indian War, 72–75, 86, 92
    Pontiac's Rebellion, 95, 98–100
Delaware Prophet, 95
Denonville, Marquis de, 30–31
Dewey, George, 340, 344, 349, 350
Díaz, Adolfo, 361–63, 366–67
Dickerson, Susannah, 211
Diem, Ngo Dinh, 460, 468, 469
Dien Bien Phu (1954), 460, 464
Dieppe raid (1942), 384

Dieskau, baron de, 79–80, 81
Diggers (Indian tribes), 229–30
Dinwiddie, Robert, 72, 82
Dog Soldiers, 303, 307, 308, 310
domino theory, 464, 468, 471
Doniphan, Alexander, 220, 224–25
Doolittle, James, 384, 401
Douglass, Frederick, 259
draft, 372, 384, 393
    evader pardons (1974), 460
"Dreamers" (Sassoon), 375
Dred Scott decision (1857), 249, 251
Dresden, firebombing of (1945), 434
"Dulce et Decorum Est" (Owen), 380
Dull Knife (Cheyenne), 322, 324–25
Dumas, Jean-Daniel, 78–79
Dummer's War (Third Abnaki War)
    (1722–1727), 44, **64–65**
Dunkirk evacuation (1940), 392
Dunmore, Lord, 102–4
Durrell, Philip, 89–90
Dutch West India Company, 16, 24, 50

Early, Jubal, 251, 273, 280, 295, 296
Easton, Treaty of (1758), 86
Edwards, Benjamin and Hayden,
    191–92
Egan (Bannock chief), 329, 330
Einstein, Albert, 438
Eisenhower, Dwight D., 405–6, 423, 435,
    460, 462–65, 490
El Alamein, Battle of (1942), 405
El Caney, Battle of (1898), 340, 347
El Salvador, 495–96, 497
Emancipation Proclamation, 250, 270
Emathla, Charley, 197
Emerson, Ralph Waldo, 114
Emuckfau, Battle of (1814), 176, 187
Endara, Guillermo, 502
England. See Great Britain
Eniwetok Island, 416–17
Enotachopoco, Battle of (1814), 176,
    187
Erie Indians, 22, 26, 27, 98
Esopus Wars (1659–1660; 1663–1664),
    34–36
Estrada, Juan J., 361, 362

Ethiopia, 389, 511
Evans, Andrew, 309–10
Evans, John, 302, 303
Ewell, Richard S., 274, 275, 280, 289, 298
Ewing, James, 129, 130
Ezra Church, Battle of (1864), 292–93

Fair Oaks, Battle of (1862), 264–65
Fallen Timbers, Battle of (1794), 167–68
Fannin, James W., Jr., 209, 211
Farragut, David Glasgow, 250, 264
Farrow, Edward S., 330–31
fascism, 386–91, 440, 459
Ferguson, Patrick, 149, 153
Fetterman, William J., 305–6
filibustering, 335, 336–38
Finland, (1940), 391
First Abnaki War (1675–1678), **43–44,** 53
First Battle of Bull Run (1861), 254–55, 256, 261, 268, 281
First Pima Revolt (1695), **56**
First Seminole War (1817–1818), 3, **189–91,** 196
Five Forks, Battle of (1865), 251, 297
Five Nations. *See* Iroquois League
Flying Tigers, 399–400, 415, 444
Foch, Ferdinand, 376, 377, 379
Foote, Andrew, 256, 257
Forbes, John, 85, 89, 93
Ford, Gerald, 460, 487–88
Forrest, Nathan Bedford, 278, 284, 292, 295
Forsyth, George A., 308, 309, 316, 317
Fort Dearborn Massacre, 176, 178, 180
Fort Duquesne, 71–77, 83–89
Fort George, Battle of (1813), 176
Fort Jackson, Treaty of (1814), 176
Fort Mims, Battle of (1813), 176, 187
Fort Niagara, 71, 76, 79, 83, 88–90, 98, 176
Fort Pitt, 89, 90, 92, 97–100, 144
Fort Stanwix, Treaty of (1768), 102
Fort Stedman, Battle of (1865), 297
Fort Sumter, 246–47, 250, 253–54, 294–95

Fort Ticonderoga, 71, 83–87, 90, 106, 115–16, 118, 121, 132
Fourteen Points, 369, 381–82
Fox Indians, 62–63, 199–204
Fox Resistance (1712–1733), **61–63**
France, 2, 6, 53, 56, 170, 213, 352
    American Quasi-War, 2, 169–72
    American Revolution, 2, 106, 107, 122, 131–32, 140–41, 147–48, 151, 157, 159
    Maginot Line, 388–89
    Panama Canal Company, 359–60
    Seven Years' War, 2, 70, 75, 82, 93–94
    Vietnam colonialism, 459–64
    See also World War I; World War II
Franklin, Battle of (1864), 251, 295
Franklin, Benjamin, 77, 122, 131, 161
Franz Ferdinand, archduke of Austria-Hungary, 369, 370
Fraser, Simon, 132, 133, 138, 139
Fredericksburg, Battle of (1862), 250, 271, 281
Fredonian Rebellion (1826–27), **191–92,** 205
Free French, 426, 427, 430
Freeman's Farm, Battle of (1777), 106, 138–39
Free Soilers, 3, 249
Frémont, John Charles, 213–15, 256–58
French and Indian War (1754–1763), 43, **69–94,** 111, 116
    British debts from, 105, 107
    chronology, 70
    European counterpart, 2, 70, 75
    French losses, 70, 93–94, 95
    Indian alliances, 22, 31, 44, 74–75, 79, 86, 89–91, 93
    Pontiac's Rebellion, 95–100
French Revolution, 170
Frontenac, comte de, 31, 53, 55
frontier. *See* western frontier
"frontier thesis" (Turner), 4, 335
fugitive slave law, 248, 249, 251
fur trade, 12, 16, 22–31, 36, 174

Gadsden Treaty (1853), 258
Gage, Thomas, 111–13, 116, 117, 121

Gaines, Edmund, 190, 198
Gaines's Mill, Battle of (1862), 265–66
Galbraith, Thomas J., 242, 243
Gates, Horatio, 116, 138, 139, 140, 153, 154
Gemayel, Bashir and Amine, 492, 493
Genêt, Edmond, 170
Geneva agreement (1954), 464, 465
George II, king of Great Britain, 66, 69, 105
George III, king of Great Britain, 99, 100, 101, 104–5, 109–13
George, Clair E., 498
Germantown, Battle of (1777), 106
Germany, 5, 352, 354
    Hitler's rise in, 386
    Versailles Treaty effects, 382–83, 387–88
    See also Hessian mercenaries; Nazism; World War I; World War II
germ warfare, 97, 98, 100, 521–22
Geronimo, 68, 314–19, 332
Gerry, Elbridge, 171
Gettysburg, Battle of (1863), 250, 276, 279–83, 287
Ghent, Treaty of (1814), 175, 176, 184–85, 186
Ghost Dance, 332–34
Gibbon, John, 320, 321, 327
Gilbert Islands, 384, 400, 411
Gillespie, Archibald, 213, 214
Giuliani, Rudolph, 516
Gladwin, Henry, 96–97
Glorious Revolution (1688), 50, 51, 52
Gnaddenhutten Massacre, 146
gold, 9, 10, 12, 229, 320, 325, 330
Gordon, John Brown, 297, 298–99
Grant, Hiram P., 243, 244
Grant, Ulysses S., 217, 250, 251, 256–57, 259, 277–79, 286–91, 295–98, 312, 326
Grasse, comte de, 158–59, 160
Great Britain, 2, 6, 32–33, 50, 170–71, 212–13, 352–55, 385, 507
    French and Indian War, 2, 69–94
    French wars, 53, 56, 170, 175, 183
    Glorious Revolution, 50, 51, 52
    naval strength, 149–50
    Seven Years' War, 2, 70, 75, 82, 93–94
    Spanish colonial conflict, 65–66
    See also American Revolution; War of 1812; World War I; World War II
Great Swamp Fight, 40–41
Greene, Nathanael, 125, 154–56
Greenville, Treaty of (1795), 168
Grenada Intervention (1983), **499–501**
Grenville Acts, 105, 107
Groves, Leslie R., 438
Guadalcanal, Battle of (1942), 384, 403–4, 408
Guadalupe Hidalgo, Treaty of (1848), 216, 228
Guam, 340, 350, 384, 396
    invasion of (1944), 385
Guantánamo Bay, 340, 345, 348
Guilford Court House, Battle of (1781), 107, 155–56
Gulf of Tonkin Incident (1964), 460, 469, 482
Gulf of Tonkin Resolution (1964), 460, 469, 470, 482–83, 484
Gulf War. See Persian Gulf War

Haig, Sir Douglas, 376, 377
Haiphong Harbor, 461, 486
Haiti, 7, 172
Halifax, Lord, 71–72
Halleck, Henry, 256
Halsey, William ("Bull"), 403, 409, 410, 418–20
Hamburger Hill, Battle for (1969), 460
Hamilton, Alexander, 160, 168
Hampton Roads, Battle of (1862), 250, 262–63
Hancock, John, 112, 113
Hancock, Winfield Scott, 282, 289, 306–8
Hancock's Campaign (Hancock's War) (1867), **306–8**
Hand, Edward, 130, 131, 144
Hannibal, 155
Hanoi, bombing of, 460, 469, 486
Harlem Heights (N.Y.), 125–26
Harpers Ferry raid (1859), 251–52

Harrison, William Henry, 180–83
Hartford, Treaty of (1638), 22
Hartford Convention (1814), 183
Hawikuh Pueblo, conquest of (1540), 1, **9–10**
Hay, John, 351, 352, 355–56, 360
Hay-Herrán Treaty (1903), 360
Hearst, William Randolph, 339, 341
Heintzelman, H. P., 230–31
Henry, Patrick, 107
Hessian mercenaries, 2, 124, 128–39
Heth, Henry, 279, 283
High Bridge, Battle of (1865), 298–99
Hill, A. P., 265, 269, 274, 280, 298
Hindenburg, Paul von, 381, 387
Hirohito, emperor of Japan, 5–6, 439
Hiroshima, atomic bombing of (1945), 5–6, 385, 431, 439, 443
Hitler, Adolf, 382, 383, 386–87, 389, 390, 405, 408, 412, 421, 423–24, 427, 435–37
Hoare, Sir Samuel, 389
Ho Chi Minh, 461, 462, 464
Ho Chi Minh Trail, 460, 477
Holly Springs, Battle of (1862), 277–78
Honduran Guerrilla War (1981–1990), **495–96**, 497
Hong Kong, 384, 396–97
Hood, John Bell, 281–82, 292–93, 294, 295
Hooker, Joseph, 250, 264, 269, 272–76, 286, 287
Hoover, Herbert, 354
Hopi Indians, 9, 50
Horseshoe Bend, Battle of (1814), 176, 188, 193
Houston, Sam, 207, 209–12, 261
Howard, Oliver O., 273, 279–80, 292, 326–30
Howe, Richard, 123–24, 125
Howe, Robert, 147
Howe, William, 106, 116–18, 121, 123, 125–28, 131, 133, 135–38
Huerta, Victoriano, 363
Hull, William, 178, 179
Humphrey, Hubert, 480
Hunkpapa Sioux, 323, 325, 332

Huron Indians, 22–26, 30–31, 33–34, 96, 98
Hussein, Saddam, 503, 505, 508, 522
Hutchinson, Thomas, 111

Ide, William B., 214–15
imperialism, 4, 335–67, 441–42, 459, 461
impressment, 170–71, 174–75
Inchon landing (1950), 442, 449–50
Indian Removal Act (1830), 3, **193–96**, 199, 229
Indian Territory, 193, 194, 196, 199, 300, 307, 319, 324, 331
Indian Wars in the West
    early, **229–45**
    later (1866–1891), 4, **302–34**
Inkpaduta (Sioux chief), 241, 244–45
Intolerable Acts, 111, 112
Iran, 498, 505, 519
Iran-Contra Affair (1986), 498
Iraq, 490, 503–8, 519, 522
Iroquoian Beaver Wars (1638–1684), **22–27**, 30–34, 62
Iroquois-French Wars (1642–1696), **30–31**
Iroquois-Huron War (1648–1650), **33–34**
Iroquois League, 16, 17, 22–27, 30–34, 54–55, 60–63, 66, 67, 89, 95, 142–46
    British territorial treaty, 70–71, 86
    French and Indian War, 71, 73–74, 83, 86, 88, 89, 93
isolationism, 382, 390
Israel, 492, 493, 498, 505, 521
Italy
    Allied invasion of (1943), 412–13
    Allied victory (1945), 434, 436
    Ethiopian invasion by, 389
Iuka, Battle of (1862), 276–77
Iwo Jima, Battle of (1945), 385, 431–32, 437

Jackson, Andrew, 185–88, 190–91, 193, 194, 196, 202, 206, 207
Jackson, "Stonewall," 250, 255, 263–64, 267, 268, 271, 273, 274, 289

Jamestown, Va., 12–15, 46, 47
Japan
  atomic bombing of, 5–6, 385, 431, 439, 443
  Boxer Rebellion, 352–57, 395
  Korean annexation, 357, 441–42
  militarism, 5, 395, 430, 440
  occupation of Vietnam, 459, 461
  World War I, 370
  See also World World War II
Jayhawkers, 260
Jay, John, 170, 171
Jay's Treaty, 171, 174, 192
Jefferson, Thomas, 122–23, 169, 173, 174
Jenkins, Robert, 66
Jesuit missionaries, 24–25, 26, 30, 32, 65
Jesup, Thomas, 198–99
Jewish persecution, 386, 387, *436*, 438
Johnson, Andrew, 251, 299, 300
Johnson, Bushrod, 298
Johnson, Lyndon B., 460, 469, 471, 472, 477, 478, 480, 481, 483
Johnson, William, 66–67, 76, 79–81, 87, 89, 93
Johnston, Albert Sidney, 256, 257
Johnston, Joseph E., 255, 256, 261–64, 287, 291–92, 298, 299
Jones, John Paul, 106, 150–51
Joseph, Chief, 325–26
Joseph the Younger, Chief, 326, 328
Jumayyil, Pierre, 491, 492
Jumblatt, Kamal, 490

Kafji, Battle of (1991), 507
Kalb, baron de, 132
Kamiakin (Yakima chief), 233–34, 236
kamikaze suicide pilots, 432–33, 437
Kansas-Nebraska Act (1854), 248–49
Karami, Rashid, 493
Kasserine Pass, Battle of (1943), 406
Kearney, Stephen Watts, 220, 224
Kennan, George F., 489
Kennedy, John F., 465, 466–67, 469
Kent, Jacob F., 346, 347
Kent State massacre (1970), 460, 484
Kernstown, Battle of (1962), 263–64

Kesselring, Albert von, 412, 421
Keyes, Erasmus Darwin, 264
Key, Francis Scott, 176, 184
Khe Sanh, Battle of (1968), 460, 479
Kieft's War (1639–1645), **27–30**, 34
Kim Il Sung, 443, 444
Kimura, Hyotaro, 431
King George's War (1744–1748), 2, 4, **65–68**, 69
King Philip's War (1675–1676), **36–43**, 44, 46, 55
King's Mountain, Battle of (1780), 106, 153–54
King William's War (1689–1697), 2, 44, **53–55**, 56, 65
Kiowa Indians, 304, 306, 307, 309–10, 312–14
Kissinger, Henry, 482, 486
Knox, Henry, 121, 126, 130, 131, 163–65
Knox, Philander, 361
Knyphausen, Wilhelm von, 131, 136
Korea, 357, 441–42, 458
Korean War (1950–1953), 5, 6, **441–58**
  chronology, 442
Kosovo Crisis (1996–1999), **513–14**, 515
Krueger, Walter, 409, 420
Kurita, Takeo, 410, 419, 420
Kuwait, 503–8

Lafayette, marquis de, 131–32, 141, 156–58
La Glorieta Pass, Battle of (1862), 250, 260–61
Laird, Melvin R., 483, 487
La Jonquière, marquis de, 69–70, 71
Lake Champlain, Battle of (1814), 176, 184
Lake Erie, Battle of (1813), 176, 182, 183
Lake George, Battle of (1755), 79–81
Lame Deer (Sioux warrior), 323–24
Lansing-Ishii Agreement (1917), 357
Laos, 459, 465, 471, 477, 480
  invasion of (1971), 460, 486
Las Guasimas, Battle of (1898), 340
Lawton, Henry W., 319, 346, 347
League of Nations, 382, 385
Leavenworth, Jesse, 307

Lebanese Civil War (1958), **490–91**
Lebanese Civil War (1975–1992), **491–94**, 498, 499, 500
Lebensraum (Nazi policy), 386, 389
Le Duc Tho, 486
Lee, Charles, 116, 123, 127–28, 141–42
Lee, Fitzhugh, 299
Lee, Robert E., 226, 250–52, 262–76, 280, 282–83, 287–90, 296–98, 300
Leisler's Rebellion (1689–1691), **50–53**
LeMay, Curtis, 469
Lend-Lease Act (1941), 384, 392–93
Lenin, Vladimir I., 371
Leslie, Alexander, 112–13
Lewis, Andrew and Charles, 103–4
Lexington (Mass.), Battle of (1775), 106, 113–15
Lexington (Mo.), Battle of (1861), 258–59
Leyte Gulf, Battle of (1944), 385, 418–20
Lignery, François-Marie Le Marchand de, 88–89, 90
Lincoln, Abraham, 191, 200, 202, 246, 250–52, 255, 261, 263, 267, 270, 272, 274, 283, 286, 287, 294, 299
Lincoln, Benjamin, 148, 149, 154, 163, 164
Little Bighorn, 321–22
Little Sayler's Creek, Battle of (1865), 298
Little Turtle's War (1786–1795), **164–68**
Little Warrior (Red Stick Creek chief), 180, 187
Little Wolf (Cheyenne warrior), 322, 324, 325
Livingston, Robert, 122
Lloyd George, David, 382
Locke, John, 122
Logan, Benjamin, 164–65
Logstown Treaty (1752), 70–71
London Naval Treaty (1935), 388
Longfellow, Henry Wadsworth, 113
Long Island, Battle of (1776), 106, 124–25
Longstreet, James, 250, 267, 268, 271, 274, 280–82, 285, 288, 299

Looking Glass (Nez Perce chief), 326–27, 328
Lookout Mountain, Battle of (1863), 250, 286
Lord Dunmore's War (1774), **102–4**
Lost River, Battle of (1872), 311
Loudoun, earl of, 82, 83, 85
Louis XIV, king of France, 53, 56, 59
Louis XVI, king of France, 131, 140–41
Louisiana Purchase (1815), 175
Lovewell's War. *See* Dummer's War
Ludendorff, Erich, 373–74, 375, 376, 377, 378, 380–81
Lundy's Lane, Battle of (1814), 176
Lusitania, sinking of (1915), 369, 371
Luzon, 357–59, 397, 398, 420

MacArthur, Arthur, 351
MacArthur, Douglas, 384, 397, 398, 409, 418–20, 437, 439, 442, 445–55
MacFarlane, Robert, 498
Mackenzie, Ranald S., 313–14, 322
Madero, Francisco, 363
Madison, James, 175, 184
Madriz, José, 361–62
Maginot Line, 386, 388–89, 392
Mahicans, 16–17, 18, 22, 142, 176
Maine, sinking of (1898), 339–42
Malvern Hill, Battle of (1862), 266
Manassas Junction, 250, 254–55, 261, 267, 268
Manchuria, 357, 431, 450, 451, 453
Mandalay, Battle of (1945), 431
Mangas Coloradas, Chief, 239, 240
Manhattan Project, 438
Manila Bay, Battle of (1898), 340, 343–44
Mankato (Sioux warrior), 241–43
March, Peyton C., 4
March to the Sea (1864), 251, 294–95
Mariana Islands, 385, 417
Marion, Francis, 155
Mariposa War (1850–1851), **229–30**
Marne battles (1918), 373, 374–77
Marsh, John S., 241–42
Marshall, George C., 453
Marshall, John, 171

Marshall Islands, 385, 400, 411, 416

Martin, Joseph W., 455

Maryland's Religious War (1644–1654), **32–33**

Maryland's War with the Susquehan-nocks (1643–1652), **31–32**

Mason, John, 18, 20, 21

Massasoit (Wampanoag chief), 37

McAuliffe, Anthony, 427–28

McClellan, George B., 225, 250, 255–56, 261–70, 276, 287

McDowell, Irvin, 255, 263, 264

McKinley, William, 339, 340, 350

McNamara, Robert, 469

McQueen, Peter, 187, 190, 191

Meade, George G., 217, 276, 279–83, 286, 291

Mechanicsville, Battle of (1862), 265

Medicine Lodge treaties (1867, 1868), 307

Meeker, Nathan C., 331, 332

Meese, Edwin, 498

Mein Kampf (Hitler), 382, 386

Mekong Delta, 468, 473, 476

Mena, Luís, 362–63

mercantilism, 105

Merritt, Wesley, 332, 344, 349–50

Metacom. *See* Philip, King

Meuse-Argonne offensive (1918), 369, 379, 380

Mexico, 3, 8, 56, 212–13
  Apaches, 314–19
  independence (1821), 191, 205
  Texan War of Independence, 205–12
  Texas settlements, 191–92
  U.S. boundary, 228
  U.S. Punitive Expedition, 363–66
  Walker's invasion of, 336
  World War I, 369, 371–72
  See also United States—Mexican War

Miami Indians, 22, 27, 67, 71, 97, 103, 164–68, 180

Micmac Indians, 76–77, 93

Middle East, 6, 490–94, 503–8

Midway, Battle of (1942), 384, 402–3, 404

Milam, Ben, 208

Miles, Nelson A., 313, 319, 323, 324, 328, 333–34, 344–45, 348–49

Milk Creek, Battle of (1879), 331–32

Milosevic, Slobodan, 509, 513, 514

Mingo Indians, 98, 103–4, 143–45

Minh, Duong Van, 460, 488

Minnesota Santee Sioux Uprising (1962), **241–45**

Mississippi Rifles, 223–24

Missouri Compromise (1820), 246–48

Mitscher, Marc, 417–18

Mobile Bay, Battle of (1814), 176

Modoc War (1872–1873), **310–12**, 313

Mohawk-Mahican War (1624–1628), **16–17**, 22

Mohawks, 16–17, 22, 26, 27, 41, 55
  as British allies, 59, 61, 67, 74, 76, 80, 87, 90, 142, 146
  as Dutch allies, 28, 30, 36
  warrior tradition, 23

Mohegans, 18, 20

Mojave Indians, 230–31

Moncada, José María, 366–67

Monckton, Robert, 76, 77

Monitor vs. *Merrimac* (1862), 250, 262–63

Monmouth Courthouse, Battle of (1778), 106, 141–42, 152

Monocacy, Battle of (1864), 295–96

Monroe Doctrine (1823), 489

Monro, George, 84, 85

Montcalm, marquis de, 82–85, 87, 88, 91

Monterrey, Battle of (1846), 216, 220–23

Montgomery, Bernard Law, 405, 406, 424, 426–27, 434

Montgomery, Richard, 118, 119

Moore, Isaiah N., 238–39

Moravian Indians, 146

Morgan, Daniel, 106, 138–39, 154–56

Morison, Samuel Eliot, 396

Moro Wars (1901–1913), **357–59**

Muddy Creek, Battle of (1877), 324

Mule Shoe, Battle of (1864), 289

Munfordville, Battle of (1862), 276

Munich Beer Hall Putsch (1923), 386

Munich Conference (1938), 390
Muslims, 509–10, 517–20
Mussolini, Benito, 384, 389, 408, 412
Mutiny Act (1765), 107
Myers, Richard B., 519–20
My Lai massacre (1968), 460

Nagasaki, atomic bombing of (1945),
   5–6, 385, 439, 443
Naiche (Apache warrior), 316, 318
Nakaidoklini (Apache prophet), 315–16,
   317
Nanticoke Indians, 32, 43, 45
Napoleon, 172, 175, 183, 184
Narragansetts, 19, 20, 37–42
Narvaez, Panfilo, 8
Nashville, Battle of (1864), 251
Natchez Revolt (1729), **64**
Navajo Indians, 9, 68, 238–41
   World War II "code talkers," *417*
Navigation Acts, 105
Navy Department, U.S., 171, 361
Nazism, 440, 459
   Jewish persecution, 386, 387, *436*,
     438
   rise of, 382, 383, 386–87
   Soviet nonaggression pact, 390–91
Neill, James C., 209–10
Netherlands, 50, 53, 56, 392
Neutral Indians, 22, 26, 33
Neville, John, 168–69
New Georgia landing (1943), 384, 409
New Guinea, 400–403, 408–10, 416
New Market, Battle of (1864), 289
New Orleans, Battle of (1815), 176,
   185–86
New Orleans, Battle of (1862), 250, 264
New York City
   British occupation, 106, 123, 124, 127,
     141, 158
   Leisler's Rebellion, 50, 53
   World Trade Center terrorist attack
     (2001), 515–16
Nez Perces, 233, 236, 325, 329
Nez Perce War (1877), **325–28**
Niantic Indians, 18–19, 20
Nicaragua, 336, 337–38

Nicaraguan Civil War (1909–1912),
   361–63, 366, 494
Nicaraguan Civil War (1925–1933),
   366–67, 494
Nicaraguan Civil War (1978–1979),
   494–95, 496
Nicaraguan Civil War (1982–1990), 367,
   495, **496–99**
Nicholson, Francis, 50, 51, 52, 59
Nimitz, Chester A., 402, 416, 418, 419,
   437
Nipissing Indians, 22, 73
Nipmuck Indians, 38, 40, 41
Nishimura, Shoji, 419, 420
Nixon, Richard, 460, 480, 482–87
Noche Triste (June 30, 1520), 8
Non-Importation Agreement (1764),
   107
Noriega, Manuel Antonio, 501–3
Normandy Invasion (1944), 385,
   422–25
North, Oliver ("Ollie"), 498
North Africa, 2, 172–74, 173, 188–89
   World War II, 384, 405–6, 408, 505
North Atlantic Treaty Organization,
   461–62, 514
Northern Paiutes, 308, 328, 329
Norway, 391, 405
nuclear weapons, 5–6, 385, 431, 437–39,
   443, 475

Oglala Sioux, 207, 304–6, 308, 320, 323,
   325
Ohio Company, 69–70, 71
Ojibwas, 62, 74, 86, 92, 96, 98, 165
Okinawa Campaign (1945), 385,
   432–33
Old Northwest, 143–44, 164–68,
   180–81, 186
Omaha Beach, 422, 423
Oñate, Juan de, 9–10
Oneida Indians, 22, 89, 142
Onondaga Indians, 22, 26–27, 142
Opechancanough (Powhatan chief), 13,
   14–15
Open Door Policy, 352, 355–57, 395
Operation Just Cause (1989), **501–3**

Oppenheimer, J. Robert, 438
Ortega Saavedra, Daniel, 367, 499
Osceola (Seminole chief), 197–99
Ottawas, 22, 73, 74, 77, 86, 92, 103, 143–44, 164–67
  Pontiac's Rebellion, 95–100
"Over There" (song), 373
Owen, Wilfred, 380
Oytes (medicine man), 329, 330
Ozawa, Jisaburo, 419, 420

Paine, Thomas, 122
Paiute War (Pyramid Lake War) (1860), **237–38**
Pakistan, 6, 519, 520, 522
Palestine Liberation Organization, 491, 492
Palmito Ranch skirmish (1865), 251, 300
Palo Alto, Battle of (1846), 216–21
Panama, U.S. invasion of, **501–3**
Panama Canal, 359–60, 502
Panamanian Revolution (1903), **359–60**
Panmunjon peace talks (1951), 442, *456*
Paris, liberation of (1944), 385, *424*, *425*, 426
Paris, Treaty of (1763), 70, 93–94, 95, 105
Paris, Treaty of (1783), 107, 161, 164, 169–70, 174, 192
Paris, Treaty of (1898), 340, 350–51
Paris Peace Accords (1973), 460, 487–88
Paris peace talks (1968–1973), 460, 483–84, 486
Parkman, Francis, 95
Patton (film), 1
Patton, George S., 1, 5, 406, 408, 425, 426, 428–29, 434
Pavonia Massacre (1643), 28, 29
Peachtree Creek, Battle of (1864), 251, 291–92
Peach War (1655–1657), 30, **34**
Pea Ridge, Battle of (1862), 250, 259–60
Pearl Harbor attack (1941), 384, 393, 395, 402, 404, 441
  September 11 death toll vs., 517
Peninsula Campaign (1862), 262, 263–66, 276

Pentagon Papers, The (1971), 469
Pentagon terrorist attack (2001), 516, 517
Pequot War (1637), **18–22**, 30
Percy, Hugh, 114, 115, 124
Perry, Matthew C., 225
Perry, Oliver Hazard, 181, 183
Perryville, Battle of (1862), 250, 277
Pershing, John J., 357–59, 364–66, 372–74, 379
Persian Gulf War (1991), **503–8**
Pétain, Henri Philippe, 392
Petersburg, siege of (1864–1865), 250–51, 290–91, 295–98
Philadelphia
  British occupation, 106, 133, 135–36, 137, 141
  Continental Congress, 111–12, 115, 116, 135
Philip, King (Seminole), 197, 198
Philip, King (Wampanoag), 37, 38, 39–43, 44
Philip of Anjou, 56, 59
Philippine Insurrection (1896–1898), **338–39**
Philippine Insurrection (1899–1902), 338, 339, 340, **351–52**, 357
Philippines, 4, 93, 335, 340, 349–51
  Moro Wars, 357–59
  Spanish-American War, 343–44, 349–50
  World War II, 384, 385, 397–99, 418–20
Philippine Sea, Battle of the (1944), 385, 417–18
Picacho Peak, Battle of (1862), 261
Pickett, George, 251, 283, 297, 298
Pickett's Charge, 282, 283
Pillow, Gideon J., 226
Pima Indians, 56, 68
Pinckney, Charles Cotesworthy, 171
Pine Ridge Reservation, 325, 333, 334
Pinkerton, Allan J., 263
piracy, 173, 189
Pitcairn, John, 113, 114
Pitt, William, 70, 83–86, 89, 108
Plains of Abraham, 91, 119

Plattsburgh, Battle of (1814), 176
Pleasanton, Alfred, 268, 275
Pleasants, Henry, 291
Plymouth, Mass., 18–20, 37–40, 42, 54–55
Pocahontas (Matowaka), 12–13
Poindexter, John, 498
Poland, 390–91, 430
Polk, James K., 212–17, 220–23, 228, 231
Polk, Leonidas, 256
Ponce de Leon, Juan, 8
Pontiac's Rebellion (1763–1766), **95–100**
Pony Express, 237
Pope, John, 244, 245, 267, 268, 273, 304, 313
Popé's Rebellion (1680), **48–50**, 68
popular sovereignty, 248
Porter, David Dixon, 264, 266
Port Moresby, 400–404
Potawatomi Indians, 22, 74, 77, 86, 92, 98, 165, 180, 201, 202
Potsdam Conference (1945), 442–43
Powhatan War (1622–1644), **11–15**
Price, Sterling, 258–59, 276–77
Princeton, Battle of (1777), 106, 130–31
Princip, Gavrilo, 370
privateering, 170, 171
Proclamation Line (1763), 100, 101
Proctor, Henry, 180–81
Puebla, siege of (1847), 216, 228
Pueblo Indians, 1, 9–10, 48–50
Puerto Rico, 8, 340, 348–49, 350
Pulaski, Casimir, 136, 148
Pulitzer, Joseph, 339, 341
Puritans, 33, 37
Pusan, Battle of (1950), 442, 449
Putnam, Israel, 116–18, 126
Pyramid Lake War (1860), **237–38**

Qaeda, al-, 517, 518, 520, 522
Quantrill, William Clarke, 260
Quartering Act, 107–8, 111, 112, 177
Queen Anne's War (1702–1713), 2, 44, **56–59**, 64–65
Quincy, Josiah, 109
Quisling, Vidkun, 391

Raisin River Massacre (1813), 176, 187
Raleigh, Sir Walter, 12
Rall, Johann, 129–30
Rambouillet accords (1999), 514
Rapallo, Treaty of (1922), 388
Reagan, Ronald, *493*, 496–501
Red Cloud (Sioux chief), 304, 305, 307, 334
Red Fork, Battle of (1876), 322
Red River War (Kiowa War) (1874–1875), **312–14**
Regulators' Revolt (1771), **101–2**, 108–9
Reno, Marcus A., 322
Resaca de la Palma, Battle of (1846), 216, 218–19, 220
Revere, Paul, 112, 113
Revolutionary War. *See* American Revolution
Reynolds, John, 200, 279–80
Rhee, Syngman, 443, 444, 457–58
Rhineland, 389, 434–45
Ridgway, Matthew B., 442, 453–57
Riedesel, Friedrich von, 132, 133, 139
Roanoke colony, 12
Rochambeau, Jean Baptiste, 158–60
Rogers, Robert, 92–93
Rogue River War (1855–1856), **231–33**
Rolfe, John, 13
Roman Nose (Cheyenne chief), 308–9
Rommel, Erwin, 405, 406, 507
Roosevelt, Franklin D., 384, 385, 390, 392–95, 398, 414, 422, 429, 438, 439, 442, 497
Roosevelt, Theodore, 340, 344, 347, *348*, 360
Rosecrans, William S., 276–77, 283–85
Ross, Robert, 176, 183–84
Rostow, Walt, 466
Rough Riders, 340, 347
Russia, 75, 184, 352–55
World War I, 4, 368, 370, 371
See also Soviet Union
Russian revolution (1917), 373
Ryswick, Treaty of (1697), 55
Ryukyu Islands, 432–33

Sacasa, Bautista, 366–67
Sac Indians, 199–204
Sacramento, Battle of (1846), 224
Saigon, fall of (1975), 460, 488
St. Augustine, Fla., 56–57, 66
St. Clair, Arthur S., 132–33, 165–67
St. Leger, Barry, 133, 138
St.-Mihiel salient action (1918), 369, 374, 378
Saipan landing (1944), 385, 417, 418
Salerno landing (1943), 384, 412
Sampson, William T., 344, 345, 348
San Carlos Reservation, 314–19
Sand Creek Massacre, 303, 306, 309
Sandinistas, 366, 367, 494–99
Sandino, Augusto César, 366–67, 494
San Ildefonso, Treaty of (1762), 93
San Jacinto, Battle of (1836), 211
San Juan Hill, Battle of (1898), 340, 347
Santa Anna, Antonio López de, 207–12, 215–16, 221–27
Santee Sioux Indians, 241–45
Santiago, Battle of (1898), 346–48
Saratoga, Battle of (1777), 106, 138–40, 153
Sassacus (Pequot chief), 20–22
Sassoon, Siegfried, 375
Satanta (Kiowa chief), 312–14
Saudi Arabia, 494, 503–8, 517
Saunders, Charles, 89–90
Savage, James D., 229–30
Savage's Station, Battle of (1862), 266
Schaffner, Franklin, 1
Schley, Winfield S., 344, 348
Schofield, John M., 292, 295
Schurz, Carl, 280, 332
Schuyler, Philip, 116, 118–19, 134
Schwarzkopf, H. Norman, 506
Scoon, Sir Paul, 499, 501
Scott, George C., 1
Scott, Winfield, 192, 195, 196, 198, 202, 204, 220, 223–28, 254
Scud missiles, 505–6
secession, 183, 252–54, 259, 261
Second Abnaki War (1702–1712), 44, **56**
Second Pima Revolt (1751), 56, **68**

Second Seminole War (1835–1842), 3, **196–99**
Selective Service Act (1917), 372
Seminoles, 3, 189–91, 193, 196–99
Senecas, 22–24, 26, 31, 61, 103, 134, 142, 145
    French and Indian War, 71, 89, 92, 93
    Pontiac's Rebellion, 95, 98
September 11 attack (2001), **515–22**
Serbia, 369–70, 508–10, 513–14
Seven Cities of Cibola, 9
Seven Days battles (1862), 250, 265–67, 269
Seven Pines, Battle of (1862), 264–65
Seven Years' War (1764–1763), 2, 70, 75, 82, 93–94, 105
Severn, Battle of the (1654), 33
Shafter, William R., 345–49
Shawnee Indians, 67, 70, 71, 74, 92, 95, 98, 178, 180
    Kentucky raids, 143–44, 145
    Little Turtle's War, 164, 165
    Lord Dunmore's War, 102–4
Shays's Rebellion (1786–1787), 2, **162–64**
Sheehan, Timothy J., 242, 243
Sheepeater War (1879), **329–31**
Shenadoah Campaign (1862), 263–64
Sheridan, Philip, 251, 285, 288–89, 296, 297, 299, 308–10, 319–20, 332
Sheridan's Campaign (1868–1869), **308–10**
Sherman, William T.
    Civil War, 250, 251, 278, 286, 287, 291–94, 299
    Indian Wars, 306, 308, 312, 313, 316–18, 332
Shiloh, Battle of (1862), 250, 257–58
Shirley, William, 75, 76, 81, 82
Shoshoni Indians, 320–21, 330
Shultz, George, 498
Sibley, Henry Hopkins, 239, 244–45, 260, 261
Sicily, invasion of (1943), 405, 406, 408
Sickles, Daniel, 281
Siegfried Line, 427
Sigel, Franz, 287, 289

Simcoe, John G., 157, 158
Sioux Nation, 4, 204, 241–45, 303–10
Sioux War (1890–1891), **332–34**
Sioux War for the Black Hills, **320–25**
Sitting Bull (Sioux leader), 320, 321, 325, 328, 332–33
Six Nations. *See* Iroquois League
Siyaad Barre, Maxamed, 511, 512
slavery, 3, 206, 212, 246–49, 251, 301
    emancipation, 250, 270
slave trade, 185, 248
Slidell, John, 213
Sloughter, Henry, 53
smallpox, 8, 24, 53, 55, 97, 98, 100
Smith, Andrew Jackson, 231–33
Smith, Edmund Kirby, 251, 276–77, 300
Smith, Francis, 113–15
Smith, John, 12–13, 14
Smith, William Farrar ("Baldy"), 290–91
Snake Indians, 308, 328, 329
Snake War (1866–1868), **308**
Sokoki Indians, 23, 42
Solomon Islands, 400, 401, 403, 404, 408–11, 416
Solórzano, Carlos, 366
Somalian Civil War (1988–), **511–13**
Somoza family, 367, 494, 495, 497
Sons of Liberty, 107, 111, 112
Southeast Asia Treaty Organization, 464
South Mountain, Battle of (1862), 268
Soviet Union, 5, 6, 373, 383, 435
    Afghanistan invasion, 520
    Chinese Communist alliance, 447
    collapse of, 489
    defensive pacts, 388, 389–91
    Korean War, 442–44, 450, 451, 456–57
    Nixon-Kissinger policy, 482
    as superpower, 440
    Vietnam War, 461, 475, 482, 483
    war declaration on Japan (1945), 431, 442
    See also Cold War era; World War II
Spain, 65–66, 70, 169
    Philippine Insurrection, 338–39
    Seven Years' War, 75, 93–94, 105
Spanish-American War (1898), 4, 338, **339–51**

chronology, 340
Spokane Indians, 236–37
Spotsylvania, Battle of (1864), 250, 288
Spring Hill, Battle of (1864), 295
Spruance, Raymond, 402, 411, 417
Stalin, Joseph, 385, 390, 391, 414, 442–43
Stalingrad campaign (1943), 413
Stamp Act (1765), 107, 108
Standing Buffalo (Sioux), 241, 244
Stark, John, 134–35
"Star-Spangled Banner, The," 176, 184
states' rights, 248, 252–53
Steichen, Edward, *379*
Steptoe, Edward J., 236
Steuben, Friedrich von, 141, 156, 157
Stevens, Isaac, 233, *234*
Stillman's Run, 201–2
Stilwell, Joseph ("Vinegar Joe"), 399, 400, 413, 415
Stimson, Henry L., 267
Stirling, Lord, 124, 128
Stol, Joost, 51, 52
Stone, John, 18, 19
Stony Point, Battle of (1779), 106
Stuart, "Jeb," 264, 265, 267, 270, 273, 275–76, 280, 288–89
Stuyvesant, Peter, 34, 35–36
Sugar Act (1764), 107
suicide missions, 432–33, 437, 516–18, 521
Sullivan, John, 112, 120, 124, 143, 145
superpowers, 440
Susquehannock Indians, 22, 27, 31–32, 44, 46–47
Sutter's Fort, 213, 214
Swamp Fox, 158
Szilard, Leo, 438

Taft, William Howard, 352
Taft-Katsura Memorandum (1905), 357
Taif Agreement (1989), 494
Taliban, 519–22
Talladega, Battle of (1813), 176, 187
Tall Bull (Dog Soldier), 307, 310
Tallmadge, James, 247
Tarawa, Battle of (1943), 375, 385, 411

Tarleton, Banastre, 106, 149, 152–55, 157, 159–60
Taunton Agreement (1671), 38, 39
Taylor, Maxwell, 466, 471
Taylor, Zachary, 180, 198, 201, 216–21, 223–25, 227
Tea Act (1773), 110
Tecumseh, 166–67, 176, 178, 180, 183, 187, 200
Tehran Conference (1943), 414
Teller, Edward, 438
Teller Amendment (1898), 340, 350
Terrazas, Joaquin, 315, 316
terrorism, 492–93, 498–500, 515–22
Terry, Alfred, 320, 321, 325
Tet Offensive (1968), 460, 478–80
Teton Sioux, 244, 332–33
Tewa Indians, 9, 10, 49–50
Texan War of Independence (1835–1836), 3, **205–12**
Texas, 310, 313–15
  Civil War, 251, 253, 261, 300
  Fredonian Rebellion, 191–92
  U.S. annexation, 206, 212, 215–16
  U.S. settlers, 191–92, 205–8
Thames, Battle of the (1813), 176, 183
thermonuclear weapons, 6, 475
Thieu, Nguyen Van, 460, 486–88
Third Abnaki War. *See* Dummer's War
Third Seminole War (1855–1858), 3, **199**
Thirteenth Amendment, 251
Thomas, George Henry, 256, 284–86, 292, 295
Thornburgh, Thomas T. ("Tip"), 331–32
Tito, Josip Broz, 508, 509
Tobacco Indians, 22, 25, 26, 33
Tokyo bombing raids, 384, 401, 437
Tonkin Gulf. *See* Gulf of Tonkin Incident
Townshend Acts (1766), 108, 109
Trail of Tears, 196
Travis, William B., 209, 210
Treaty of . . . *See key word*
Trenton, Battle of (1776), 106, 129–30
Tres Castillos, Battle of (1880), 315, 316

Tripolitan War (1801–1805), 2, **172–74**, 188
Trist, Nicholas P., 226, 227, 228
Trois-Rivières, Battle of (1776), 120
Truman, Harry S, 385, 438, 442, 445–47, 450–55, 461, 462, 489
Truman Doctrine (1947), 489
Truscott, Lucian K., III, 421
Tupper, Tullius C., 316–17
Turner, Frederick Jackson, 4, 335
Turner, Richmond K., 403
Turner, William, 19, 42
Tuscarora Indians, 59–61, 142
Tuscarora War (1711–1712), **59–61**, 63
Twiggs, David E., 190
Twiggs, Dwight E., 225–26
Tyler, John, 212

Umatillas, 232–35, 329, 330
Uncas (Mohegan chief), 18, 20
Underhill, John, 19, 20, 21, 30
United Nations, 442–58, 491, 512, 513, 514
United States—Mexican War (1846–1848), 3, 214, **215–28**, 248, 254, 335
  background, 205–15
Ute War (1879), 331–32
Utrecht, Treaty of (1713), 56, 59, 64, 71

V-1/V-2 bombs, 407, 421, 426
Vallejo, Mariano G., 214–15
Valley Forge, 140–41
Van Buren, Martin, 192, 196
Vanderbilt, Cornelius, 337
Van Dorn, Earl, 259, 260, 277, 278
Van Fleet, James A., 455, 456
Vargas, Diego de, 49–50
Velasco, Treaty of (1836), 212, 215
Versailles, Treaty of (1918), 369, 381–82, 383, 387–88, 389, 459
Vicksburg Campaign (1862–1863), 250, 277, 278–79, 283
Victorio (Apache leader), 314, 315
Vietnam War (1954–1975), 5, 6, **459–88**
  chronology, 460
  pacification, 476–77

public opinion, 460, 477, 478, 480, 484

U.S. earliest involvement, 462

U.S. objectives, 472

Vietnamization, 482–83, 484

Villa, Francisco ("Pancho"), 363–66

Villa's Raids (and the Pershing Punitive Expedition) (1916–1917), **363–66**

Virginia Company, 12

Virginia Resolves (1765), 107

Volturno River Campaign (1943), 412–13

Wahunsonacock (Powhatan chief), 11–13

Wainwright, Jonathan M., 397, 398

Wake Island, 384, 396, 403

Walker, Walton H., 449–51, 453

Walker, William, 335, 336–38

Walker's Invasion of Mexico (1853–1854), **336**

Walker's Invasion of Nicaragua (1855–57), **337–39**

Wallace, Lew, 295

Walla Walla Indians, 232, 233, 234

Wampanoag Indians, 37–43

Ward, Artemas, 116, 117, 121

Ward, John, 238, 239

War for the Bozeman Trail (1866–1868), **304–6**, 307

War Hawks (1812), 175

War in Bosnia (1992–1995), **508–10**, 513

Warm Springs Apaches, 315, 316, 317

Warner, Seth, 132–33, 134–35

War of 1812 (1812–1814), 3, 167, **174–86**, 189, 207, 220, 254

chronology, 176

Indian involvement, 2, 3, 178, 180, 183, 185–88, 200

War of Jenkins' Ear (1739), 66

War of the Austrian Succession (1744–1748), 2, 66–68

War of the League of Augsburg (1689–1697), 2, 53, 55

War of the Spanish Succession (1702–1713), 2, 56, 59

Wars of the Indian Removal, 3, **193–204**, 302

Washington, D.C.

anti-Vietnam War protests, 460, *478*, 484

British burning of, 176, 184

Civil War, 251, 263, 295–96

slave trade ended, 248

terrorism, 516, 517, 522

Washington, George, 143, 168–71, 252

American Revolution, 106, 116–31, 135–36, 140–41, 143, 148, 152–60

French and Indian War, 70, 72–73, *75*, 77–82

Washington, John, 45

Washita, Battle of (1868), 309

Watie, Stand, 259, 300

Wayne, "Mad Anthony," 106, 136, 141, 157–58, 166–68

Weatherford, William (Red Eagle), 187, 188

Webb, Daniel, 82–85

Webster, Daniel, 248

Webster-Ashburton Treaty (1842), 185, 192

Wedemeyer, Albert C., 415

Weed, Stephen, 281–82

Weinberger, Caspar, 498

western frontier, 3, 101, 168, 170

American Revolution, 143–46, 152, 154–55

Black Hawk War, 3, 199–204

closure significance, 4, 335

early Indian Wars, 229–45

Indian removal, 193–204

Indian-settler conflict, 172, 180, 187–88, 202

Jay's Treaty, 171, 174, 192

later Indian Wars, 302–34

Little Turtle's War, 164–68

Pontiac's Rebellion, 95–100

Proclamation Line, 100, 101

Regulators' Revolt, 101–2

War of 1812, 175, 185

West Indies. *See* Caribbean area

Westmoreland, William, 471, 472, *473*, 477, 478, 480

West Point, 217, 254
Weyler, Valeriano, 339
Wheaton, Frank, 311
Wheeler, Joseph, 346
Whiskey Rebellion (1794), 2, **168–69**
White Mountain Apache, 316–19
White Plains, Battle of (1776), 126–27
Whitman Massacre, 231, 232
Wigner, Eugene, 438
Wilderness, Battle of the (1755), 70, 77–78, 79, 81
Wilderness Campaign (1864), 250, 287–88
Wilhelm II, kaiser of Germany, 371, 377, 380–81
Willcox, Orlando B., 316, 317
William of Orange (William III of England), 50–55
Williamsburg, Battle of (1862), 264
Williams Station Massacre, 237
Wilmot Proviso, 248
Wilson, Woodrow, 363, 369–71, 380–83
Wilson's Creek, Battle of (1861), 258, 259
Winchester, Battle of (1863), 275
Winchester, James, 180–81, 187
Winder, William H., 184
Winnebago Indians, 201–4
Winnebago Prophet, 200, 201
Winslow, Josiah, 37, 38, 40–41
Wolfe, James, 87, 89–90, 92
Wolf Mountain, Battle of (1876), 323
Wood, Leonard, 358
Wood Lake, Battle of (1862), 244
Wool, John Ellis, 220, 223, 235–36
Worcester v. Georgia (1832), 194
World Trade Center terrorist attack (2001), 515–17
World War I (1914–1918), 4–5, **368–72**, 383, 421, 459
  chronology, 369
World War II (1939–1945), 1, 5, 375, **382–440**
  atomic bomb use, 5–6, 385, 437–39, 443

background, 357, 382, 383–91
chronology, 384–85
consequences, 440, 441–43, 459, 461, 508
in Europe, 404–5, 408, 412–13, 421–30, 433–36
German surrender, 436
Japanese surrender, 439
in Pacific, 385, 386, 393, 395–404, 408–12, 416–20, 430–33
turning points, 403, 404, 413
World War III, 6
Wounded Knee Massacre (1890), 4, 334
Wovoka (Paiute prophet), 332–33
Wright, George H., 236, 237
Wyandot Indians, 26, 67, 71, 73, 96, 103, 104, 143–45

XYZ Affair (1798), 171

Yakima War (1855), 232, **233–36**
Yalta Conference (1945), 385, 442
Yalu offensive (1950), 442
Yamamoto, Isoroku, 401, 402, 410–11
Yamasee War (1715–1716), **63**
"Yankee Doodle" (song), 115
yellow fever, 226, 349
Yellowstone National Park, 327
Yellow Tavern, Battle of (1864), 288–89
Yihe Quang (secret society), 352
Yokut Indians, 229, 230
York, Battle of (1813), 176
Yorktown, Battle of (1862), 264
Yorktown, siege of (1781), 107, 158, 159–60
Yugoslavia, 370, 508–9, 513–14
Yuma and Mojave Uprising (1851–1852), **230–31**

Zelaya, José Santos, 361, 362
Zeledon, Benjamin, 362, 363
Zia Pueblo, 49–50
Zimmermann Telegram, 369, 371–72
Zuni Indians, 9, 48